Gilgamesh

A Reader

Gilgamesh

A Reader

Edited by
John Maier

Bolchazy-Carducci Publishers, Inc.

Art and Design
by Robert Emmet Meagher

• • •

General Editor: Laurie Haight
Contributing Editor: Gaby Huebner

Bolchazy-Carducci Publishers, Inc.
1000 Brown Street
Wauconda, Illinois 60084 USA

ISBN 0-86516-349-9 casebound
ISBN 0-86516-339-1 paperback

Library of Congress Cataloguing-in-Publication Data

Gilgamesh : a reader / edited by John Maier.
p. cm.
"... a selection of twenty-five essays ... in English that have appeared since ... 1982"--Introd.
Includes bibliographical references.
"A Gilgamesh bibliography to 1994": p.
ISBN 0-86516-339-1 (softbound : alk. paper). -- ISBN 0-86516-349-9 (hardbound : alk. paper)
1. Gilgamesh. 2. Gilgamesh--Appreciation. I. Maier, John, 1943- .
PJ3771.G6G55 1997
892'. 1--dc21 97-708
CIP

ACKNOWLEDGMENTS

"Introduction" = "Appendix" (pages 275–304) from *Gilgamesh, Translated from the Sîn-leqi-unninnī Version*, by John Gardner & John Maier (1884). Copyright © 1984 by Estate of John Gardner and John Maier. Reprinted by permission of Alfred A. Knopf, Inc.

Jeffrey H. Tigay, "Summary: The Evolution of *The Gilgamesh Epic*," from *The Evolution of the Gilgamesh Epic* (1982), reprinted with permission of The University of Pennsylvania Press.

Wilfred G. Lambert, "Gilgamesh in Literature and Art: The Second and First Millennia," from *Monsters and Demons in the Ancient and Medieval Worlds.* Ed. Ann E. Farkas, et al. (1987), reprinted with permission of Wilfred G. Lambert and Verlag Philipp von Zabern.

Benjamin Foster, "Gilgamesh: Sex, Love and the Ascent of Knowledge," from *Love & Death in the Ancient Near East.* Ed. John H. Marks and Robert M. Good (1987), reprinted with permission of Benjamin Foster.

Rivkah Harris, "Images of Women in the Gilgamesh Epic," from *Lingering Over Words.* Ed. Tzvi Abusch, et al. (1990), reprinted with permission of The Semitic Museum of Harvard University and Rivkah Harris.

Tikva Frymer-Kensky, "The Marginalization of the Goddesses," from *In the Wake of the Goddesses: Women, Culture, and the Biblical Transformation of Pagan Myth,* reprinted with the permission of The Free Press, a division of Simon & Schuster. Copyright © 1992 by The Free Press.

Tzvi Abusch, "Mourning the Death of a Friend: Some Assyriological Notes," from *The Frank Talmage Memorial Volume* I. Ed. Barry Walfish (1993), reprinted with permission of Haifa University Press.

Greg Morris, "A Babylonian in Batavia: Mesopotamian Literature and Lore in *The Sunlight Dialogues,*" from *John Gardner: Critical Perspectives.* Ed. Robert A. Morace and Kathryn VanSpanckeren (1982), reprinted with permission of Southern Illinois University Press. © 1982 by Board of Trustees, Southern Illinois University.

Walter Burkert, "'Or Also a Godly Singer,' Akkadian and Early Greek Literature," reprinted by permission of the publisher from *The Orientalizing Revolution, Near Eastern Influence on Greek Culture in the Early Archaic Age.* By Walter Burkert, Tr. Margaret E. Pinder and Walter Burkert (1992). Cambridge, Mass.: Harvard University Press. Copyright © 1992 by the President and Fellows of Harvard College. All rights reserved.

David Damrosch, "Gilgamesh and Genesis," from *The Narrative Covenant, Transformations of Genre in the Growth of Biblical Literature* (1987). Copyright © 1987 by David Damrosch. Reprinted by permission of HarperCollins Publishers, Inc.

Donald Hall, "Praise for Death," from *Old and New Poems.* Copyright © 1990 by Donald Hall. Reprinted by permission of Ticknor & Fields/Houghton Mifflin Co. All rights reserved.

Stephanie Dalley, "Gilgamesh in the Arabian Nights," from *Journal of the Royal Asiatic Society of Great Britain and Ireland* (1991). © The Royal Asiatic Society 1991. Reprinted with the permission of Cambridge University Press.

William L. Moran, "Ovid's *Blanda Voluptas* and the Humanization of Enkidu," from *Journal of Near Eastern Studies* (1991), reprinted with permission of William L. Moran and the University of Chicago Press. © 1991 by the University of Chicago. All rights reserved.

Bernard F. Batto, "The Yahwist's Primeval Myth," from *Slaying the Dragon: Mythmaking in the Biblical Tradition.* © 1992 Bernard F. Batto. Used by permission of Westminster John Knox Press.

J. Tracy Luke and Paul W. Pruyser, "The Epic of Gilgamesh," from *American Imago* (1982), reprinted with permission of The Johns Hopkins University Press.

Dorothy Hammond and Alta Jablow, "Gilgamesh and the Sundance Kid: The Myth of Male Friendship," from *The Making of Masculinities: The New Men's Studies.* Ed. Harry Brod (1987), reprinted with permission of HarperCollins Publishers Ltd.

Albert B. Lord, "Gilgamesh and Other Epics," from *Lingering Over Words*. Ed. Tzvi Abusch, et al. (1990), reprinted with permission of The Semitic Museum of Harvard University.

Eric J. Leed, "Reaching for Abroad: Departures," from *The Mind of the Traveler, From Gilgamesh to Global Tourism* (1991). Copyright © 1991 by Basic Books, Inc. Reprinted by permission of BasicBooks, a division of HarperCollins Publishers, Inc.

Robert Temple, "Introduction," from *He Who Saw Everything* (1991), reprinted with permission of Robert Temple Productions Ltd.

Carl Lindahl, "The Oral Aesthetic and the Bicameral Mind," from *Oral Tradition* (1991), reprinted with permission of Carl Lindahl.

Miles Richardson, "Point of View in Anthropological Discourse: The Ethnographer as Gilgamesh," from *Anthropological Poetics*. Ed. Ivan Brady (1991), reprinted with permission of Rowman and Littlefield, Inc.

Thomas Van Nortwick, "The Wild Man: The *Epic of Gilgamesh*," from *Somewhere I Have Never Travelled, The Second Self and the Hero's Journey in Ancient Epic* (1992). Copyright © 1992 by Thomas Van Nortwick. Used by permission of Oxford University Press, Inc.

* * *

To Helen

ki-ág-mu hé-me-en

TABLE OF CONTENTS

INFLUENCES OF GILGAMESH ON LATER LITERATURE

GILGAMESH FROM OTHER PERSPECTIVES

* * *

INTRODUCTION

THE COLLECTION

Gilgamesh: A Reader is a selection of twenty-five essays on the ancient stories of the Mesopotamian hero Gilgamesh, primarily the stories written in cuneiform Akkadian known as *Gilgamesh, The Epic of Gilgamesh* or *The Gilgamesh Epic.* The selection is limited to essays in English that have appeared since the publication of Jeffrey H. Tigay's *The Evolution of the Gilgamesh Epic* in 1982. Tigay's work synthesized a century of scholarly debate about relationships among the different versions of Gilgamesh stories, and it very quickly changed the direction of literary studies of Gilgamesh. Nine English translations of *The Epic of Gilgamesh* appeared in the one hundred years following its discovery in 1872. In the little more than a decade after Tigay's *Evolution* eight more translations have appeared. Thus Tigay's book may be said to be a watershed in *Gilgamesh* studies.

The *Reader* divides the essays into three sections. The first, PHILOLOGICAL AND LITERARY STUDIES IN ENGLISH SINCE 1982, contains eight essays written by specialists in ancient languages and literature. The second section, INFLUENCES ON LATER LITERATURE, deals with connections between *Gilgamesh* and biblical, classical, medieval, and modern literature. With the exception of the essays by Bernard F. Batto, William L. Moran, and Stephanie Dalley, the essays were written by scholars in specialties outside Mesopotamia. In the last section, GILGAMESH FROM OTHER PERSPECTIVES, the essays were written exclusively by specialists outside Mesopotamia and often outside the study of languages and literature: students of depth psychology, gender studies, myth, anthropology, oral composition—even travel literature.

It should be emphasized at the outset that all three sections are selections from a large group of *Gilgamesh* studies. While they represent the main trends in *Gilgamesh* study since 1982, they constitute only a small sampling of the work on *Gilgamesh,* and the reader is invited to read the bibliography at the end of the collection for confirmation of the painful limitations of this collection. George Smith first reported on what has come to be known as *Gilgamesh* in

1872; and, as the bibliography makes clear, there has been intense interest in the work from the start. And that interest was not in the slightest restricted to the English language. From the beginning, *Gilgamesh* study had a markedly international character to it. From German, French, and English, the interest of scholars quickly spread to authors in many other languaqes. Leon de Meyer's bibliography, which appeared in 1960, already included *translations* into French, German, English, Danish, Finnish, Georgian, Hebrew, Italian, Dutch, Russian, Swedish, and Czech. Since that time many others have appeared, from Arabic to Sibero-Eskimo. The bibliography included here, which is still far from comprehensive, will help the reader to expand beyond the limits of this small selection of essays.

Since the *Reader* largely divides essays between specialist and non-specialist studies of *Gilgamesh,* it may be useful to know what is meant here by *Gilgamesh* specialists. There are a number of scholars who have spent many years on *Gilgamesh,* but "specialists" here primarily means Assyriologists. (This collection is especially unkind to scholars like Samuel Noah Kramer, Thorkild Jacobsen, W.G. Lambert, Jeffrey H. Tigay, and Tzvi Abusch, who have written extensively on matters related to *Gilgamesh,* and scholars like Peter Jensen, F.M. Th. de Liagre Böhl, A. Falkenstein, D. O. Edzard, J.J.A. van Dijk, Cl. Wilcke, and W. von Soden, who have published mainly in languages other than English.) In some cases, the "special" field may be biblical or classical studies, but the philological and literary studies those specialists write follow the practices of Assyriology.

"Assyriologist" deserves a comment, since to the outsider to the field the term is likely to be confusing. What is otherwise known as "Ancient Near East Studies" and "Mesopotamian Studies," based on the historical periods and geo-political areas, or "Cuneiform Studies," based on the writing system developed in Mesopotamia, is known as "Assyriology" largely by accident of the archaeologist's spade. The first large collection of texts from ancient Iraq was discovered in the remains of the Assyrian capital, Nineveh. (While many texts and fragments of *Gilgamesh* have since been found in locations far removed from Nineveh, the basis of all modern *Gilgamesh* texts is still the tablets found in the library of Assurbanipal.) The writing system was deciphered by using Neo-Assyrian texts of the First Millennium B.C.E. And sign lists for cuneiform are still largely presented in Neo-Assyrian, although the signs changed form significantly from the invention of the system, about 3000 B.C.E., through the three thousand years it was employed for a variety of languages.

The "Assyrian" of the texts turned out to be, along with "Babylonian," dialects of a Semitic language known as Akkadian (so named for the capital of the first Semitic empire in Mesopotamia, established by Sargon of Akkad). At the same time, beginning late in the 18th century C.E., that scholars were identifying the structural relationships that made up an "Indo-European" family of languages, a "Semitic" family was also discovered. By the way Semitic languages like Arabic, Hebrew, and Akkadian generate, e.g., nouns, verbs, and adverbs from a triliteral root system, scholars have been able to map the relationships among ancient and modern Semitic branches of the family.

So, although the basic text for *Gilgamesh* is written in Assyrian characters from the First Millennium B.C.E. and is regularly known from the literary language in which it is written as Standard Babylonian, the language itself is known as Akkadian. Today, then, there are Assyriologists but not Babyloniologists or Akkadianologists. To confuse the matter just slightly, the earliest Gilgamesh stories are found in the Sumerian language, and there are today Sumerologists; and important texts have been found in Hittite, and Hittitologists exist today. But the common term for those scholars represented mainly in the first part of this collection is Assyriologist. While they may have specialties within the field, they have all been trained to read cuneiform texts, usually in Sumerian, and always in Akkadian. Since they know the languages and can read the texts, they are the specialists in the study of *Gilgamesh.*

(They can also be considered Orientalists, a broader term that is used in, e.g., the American Oriental Society, the professional organization that includes the Ancient Near East and other areas, notably Chinese, Japanese, and Arabic languages and literature. The term Orientalist, however, carries certain political connotations that have not been attached to Assyriologist.)

The difference, in short, between specialist and nonspecialist is between those who professionally study cuneiform texts and those who do not. The line is obscured by biblical studies, since the Hebrew Bible is an ancient Near Eastern text, Hebrew is a Semitic language, and biblical scholars make much use of other ancient Near Eastern texts. Now that classicists and comparatists of different sorts are beginning to study Akkadian, one can begin to see the dividing line wavering a bit. But by and large the distinction holds.

One of the major discoveries in this collection is the extent to which specialists and nonspecialists dealing with *Gilgamesh* have ignored one another. The first section will show that one Assyriologist will use the earlier work of Assyriologists as a basis of any new investigation, but will rarely comment on the work of outsiders. The nonspecialists, for their part, read the Assyriological work very selectively. And the astonishing—and healthy—proliferation of *Gilgamesh* translations, especially since the 1980s, shows that some are produced by Assyriologists and some are produced by translators who know no Akkadian at all.

If this collection has a purpose beyond that of presenting the insights of many gifted readers of this ancient poem, it would be to establish a common ground where Assyriologists and nonspecialists interested in *Gilgamesh* may meet.

TRANSLATING *GILGAMESH*: THREE TEXTS

The essays will introduce the story, and it should prove interesting to the reader to notice the different ways different scholars summarize the plot of *Gilgamesh.* The large episodes that make up the Standard Babylonian version or the Late Version or Canonical Edition—the one all translations are based on, even though some translations patch in sections from other texts and even other languages—are easy to sketch. Using W.G. Lambert's schema, the episodes include a Prologue, the Taming of Enkidu, Gilgamesh and the Cedar Forest, Gilgamesh and the Bull of Heaven, the Journey to the Flood Hero, the Flood, the Return, and the Conclusion. The only major question about the plot is whether the notorious Tablet XII belongs to the narrative or not. (There is no question from the First Millennium B.C.E. tablets that Tablet XII was at that time considered part of the series, or cycle of tales, that made up *Gilgamesh.*) Scholars are still divided whether, on aesthetic grounds, Tablet XII is part of a unified work or an inorganic appendage added to the late version.

The essays will also deal with relationships between the Akkadian *Gilgamesh* and earlier Sumerian Gilgamesh stories. Since the publication of Tigay's *The Evolution of the Gilgamesh Epic* in 1982, the intricate relationships among Sumerian, Akkadian, and Hittite versions have largely been settled, and close studies of the versions, especially the Old Babylonian version, have appeared. For students of literature, the settling of textual problems has meant a great gain in the literary-critical study of *Gilgamesh* in recent years. It would seem that more and more literary-critical approaches are now being tried out with the ancient poem, and more can be expected.

Since the essays themselves will introduce the narrative, this introduction will content itself with observations on three passages, and an overview of the essays in the collection.

The observations are offered largely to the reader who has no background in the decipherment and translation of cuneiform texts. The first two passages comment on the ordinary problems any translator of *Gilgamesh* faces. The third passage is presented to show how much variety there has been in translating a single stanza. Seventeen different English translations have already appeared since George Smith's translation in the 1870s. The passage selected here is part of the most sexually explicit episode in *Gilgamesh*, and since it involves religiously sanctioned intercourse between Enkidu and a woman who is both a priestess of the temple and a prostitute, the passage presents many difficulties for the modern translator and reader who no longer share the cultural assumptions about sexuality that were held in ancient Mesopotamia. George Smith, with Victorian discretion, simply left the passage untranslated. As late as 1949, Alexander Heidel retained the passage but translated it into Latin, thereby restricting the number of readers who could follow the action. Perhaps it is no small measure of the change in values in the 20th century that the sexual initiation of Enkidu has become one of the interpretive keys to the literary unity of *Gilgamesh.*

The more remote the text, the more decisions about translating it multiply. Two well-preserved passages from *Gilgamesh* illustrate procedures taken to arrive at a reasonable translation of poetry from at least as early as the Middle Babylonian Period (1600–1000 B.C.) of Akkadian literature. Both are speeches, one by the god Shamash to Enkidu (VII.iii.33–48), the second by the god Ea to Utnapishtim (XI.i.36–47). Speeches in Sumerian and Akkadian literature are usually quite formal and well-organized, as these are. Because they are designed well, the speeches shed light on the way the poet composes poetic units longer than the line or line-pair. The second, especially, raises questions about the use of figurative language in Akkadian poetry, something we have come to expect in poetry, perhaps, but a feature of ancient works difficult to translate.

GILGAMESH VII.iii.33–48

Enkidu, nearing death, has cursed the woman who has brought him from the wild to fully human life—and with it suffering and the anticipation of death. Shamash responds:

Shamash heard, opened his mouth, 33
and from afar,... from the heavens called to him:
"Why, Enkidu, do you curse the love-priestess, the woman
who would feed you with the food of the gods, 36
and would have you drink wine that is the drink of kings,
and would clothe you in a great garment,
and would give you beautiful Gilgamesh as a companion?

Listen: hasn't Gilgamesh, your beloved friend, 40
made you lie down in a great bed?
Hasn't he made you lie down in a bed of honor,
and placed you on the peaceful seat at his left hand?
The world's kings have kissed your feet.

He will make the people of Uruk weep for you, cause them to grieve you,
[will make the women], the whole city, fill up with sorrow for your sake.
And afterward he will carry the signs of grief on his own body,
putting on the skin of dogs and ranging the wilderness."

The Akkadian text of Gilgamesh VII.iii. 33–48 in transliteration:
33 ^{ilu}šamaš iš-ma-a-[ma ip-t]ì pi-i-šu
34 ul-tu ul-la-nu-um-ma... [ul-tu] šamê(e) il-ta-na-sa-aš-šu
35 am-me-ni ^{ilu}en-ki-dù ḫa-rim-[t]i ^{f}šam-ḫat ta-na-an-za-ar
36 ša u-ša-ki-lu-ka akla si-mat ilu-u-ti
37 ku-ru-un-na iš-qu-ka si-mat šarru-u-ti
38 u-lab-bi-šu-ka lu-ub-ši ra-ba-a
39 u dam-qu ^{ilu}gilgāmeš tap-pa-a u-šar-šu-ka ka-a-ša
40 [e]-nin-na-a-ma ^{ilu}gilgāmeš ib-ri ta-li-me-ka
41 [uš-na]-a-al-ka-a-ma ina ma-a-a-ali rabî(i)
42 [i-na] ma-a-a-al tak-ni-i uš-na-al-ka-ma
43 [u-ši]š-šib-ka šub-ta-ni-iḫ-ta šu-bat šu-me-li
44 [ma-al]-ka ša qaq-qa-ri u-na-aš-ša-qu šepâ^{II}-ka
45 [u-šab]-kak-ka niše^{meš} ša uruk^{ki} u-šad-ma-ma-ak-ka
46 [šam-ḫa-a-ti] niše^{meš} u-ma-al-lak-ka dul-la
47 [u šu]-u ar-ki-ka u-ša-aš-ša-a-ma-la-a pa-gar-[šu]
48 [il-tab-bi]-iš maš-ki kal-bi-im-ma i-rap-pu-ud ṣ[êri]

(Transliteration: after R. Campbell Thompson *The Epic of Gilgamesh: Text, Transliteration, and Notes* [Oxford: Clarendon Press, 1930], p.45.)

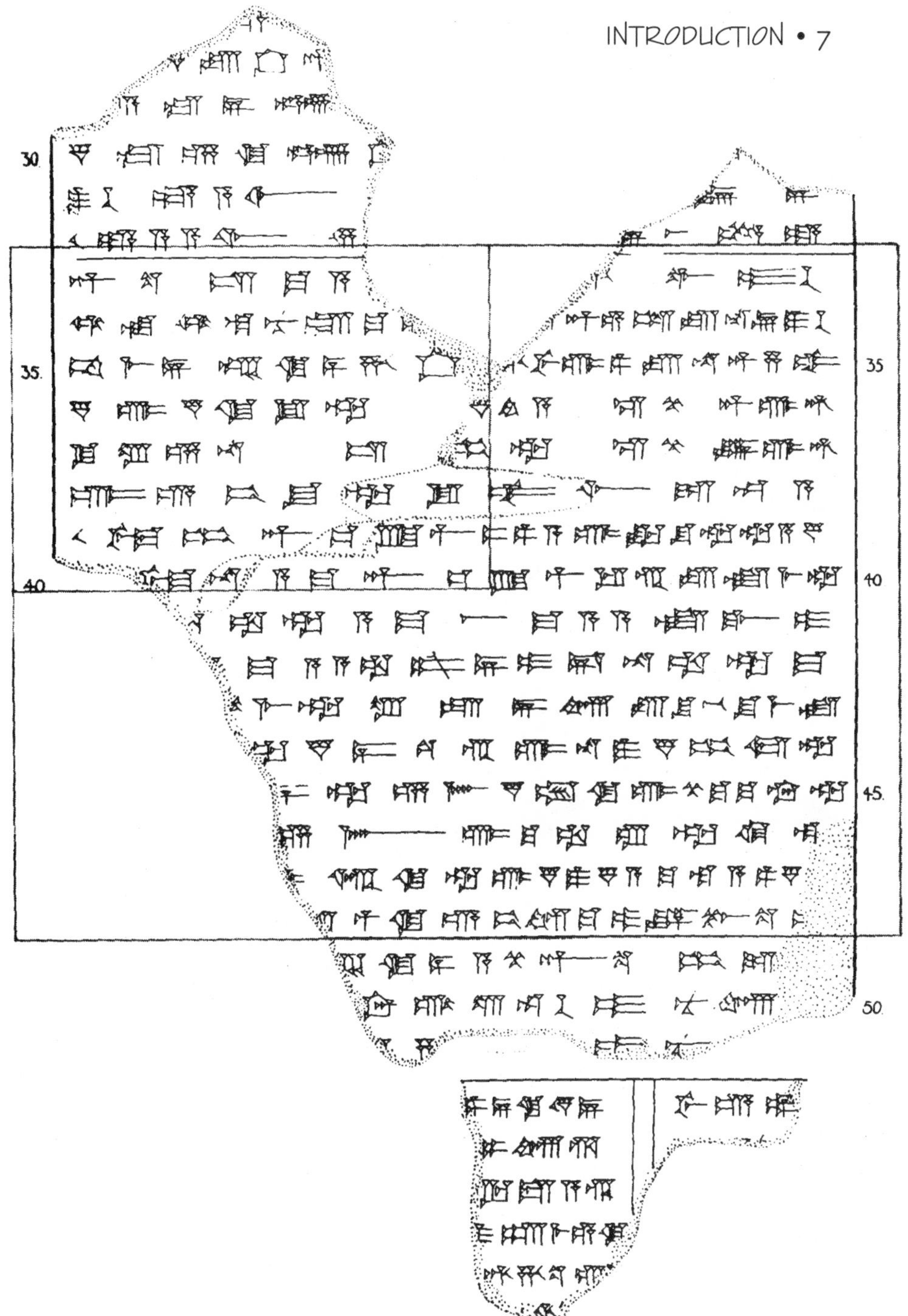

Plate 1 • Thompson's handcopy of Tablet VII.
The lines mark the two texts that provide VII.iii.33–48.

The passage does not present translators today with the maddening problems that come when large gaps in the text appear or when the vocabulary is odd or used in an unusual way. Even in the earliest translation of the lines, made by George Smith just after he discovered the tablets, the main points are clear:

> And Shamas opened his mouth
> and spake and from heaven said to him:
> ...and the female Samhat (delightful) thou shalt choose
> they shall array thee in trappings of divinity
> they shall give thee the insignia of royalty
> they shall make thee become great
> and Izdubar thou shalt call and incline him towards thee
> he Izdubar shall make friendship unto thee
> he shall cause thee to recline on a grand couch
> on a beautiful couch he shall seat thee
> he will cause thee to sit on a comfortable seat a seat on the left
> the kings of the earth shall kiss thy feet
> he shall enrich thee and the men of Uruk shall make silent
> before thee
> and he after thee shall take all...
> he shall clothe thy body in raiment and...[1]

It is worth comparing the two versions to show the kinds of materials translators used then and now. Smith already knew the passage had something to do with "divinity" and "royalty," something "great" given to Enkidu, the friendship of Gilgamesh, a bed of honor, and the "kings of the earth" kissing the feet of Enkidu. Otherwise, the passage seems a bit vague, and Smith misses a line near the end, where the passage sort of dwindles away. What he did was remarkable in the 1870s. And, though Smith did not leave his own transliteration of the passage behind, it can be shown that he read the cuneiform signs properly. How did he manage to get so close and yet translate the passage in such a different way?

Look at the handcopy of the passage made by R. Campbell Thompson (1930) for what is still the standard text of *Gilgamesh.*[2] Plate 1 is Campbell Thompson's handcopy of the end of Tablet VII, column iii. He has marked in the line numbers. (Ignore the small fragment at the bottom, marked K.10536.) The signs used by the ancient scribes are called "cuneiform" or "wedge-shaped" signs. They were impressed most often in the still-wet surface of a tablet made of clay with a reed stylus. By turning the stylus, the scribe produced small wedges horizontally [➛] or vertically [⯆], large wedges of the same type [𒀸] and [𒁹𒁹], and small and large wedges at an angle [𒌋] and [𒌋], called "Winkelhaken." Cuneiform signs are made up of combinations of the marks. Sometimes spaces in a line of text (read left to right, top to bottom) indicate separate words, but as often as not, words are not clearly separated from one another.[3] When signs are jammed together on a line, as they are in lines 34 and 39, finding the separate words can be tricky. Add to that the peculiarities of a scribe's handwriting, and it is difficult to tell where one sign begins and another ends. The clarity in which they appear in Campbell Thompson is already the result of many decisions made about just what signs have been impressed in the clay. To produce a new edition of *Gilgamesh*—as opposed to a new translation based on existing edited texts—would require a painstaking reconsideration of every sign on every line of all the fragments and duplicates that have been discovered. Note the last two signs in line 31, for example. Signs along every break can present impossible problems, and the wear and tear on the clay can lead to the rubbing away or breaking off of a small clue that might help reconstruct an entire line.[4]

Scribal handwriting is not the only problem facing the modern reader or epigrapher. The signs, which were originally pictographic but had become highly stylized in the Third Millennium,[5] changed gradually over the three thousand years they were used. To take a simple example, the first two signs in line 33 form the name of the god Shamash. The signs appear as they do in the Neo-Assyrian (1000–400 B.C.) Period, the period in which the *Gilgamesh* was recopied for the Library of Ashurbanipal. The first sign, called *dingir* (after the Sumerian word for god), is a silent determinant, indicating that the sign or signs following it form the name of a god: [𒀭]. The second sign by itself means "sun" and "sun god," Shamash: [𒌓]. In an Old Babylonian text of Gilgamesh (2000–1600 B.C.), the two signs would appear differently, the *dingir* as: [𒀭], and "sun" as: [𒌓]. Of course, the very changes that complicate the writing system give important clues to the date of a text that is unearthed.

Once the signs are recognized, they must be read, that is, interpreted. A fully pictographic text could, presumably, be read by anyone in any language, but such texts are very rare. (Consider just how universal the modern equivalents, international road signs, really are. Although the technology of automobiles and highways is very widespread, even today there are many people who would fail to grasp the meaning of the signs.) The Neo-Assyrian text of

Gilgamesh has no true pictographs. The signs are of three types: logographs, syllable-signs, and determinatives. The "sun" sign is a logograph. Reading it would depend upon the language of the text, here *shamash* in Akkadian as opposed to, say, *utu* in Sumerian—or any of the several other languages written in cuneiform (Hittite, Hurrian, Ugaritic). But the meaning would be clear even if we did not know the name in that language. The "god" sign, *dingir*, is both logographic (if pronounced, it would be *ilu* in Akkadian) and a determinative, as pointed out above, an unpronounced indicator of a god name. Most of the signs in the text are syllable-signs.

Look at line 39, "and would give you beautiful Gilgamesh as a companion." The line consists of seventeen cuneiform signs, read *u dam-qu* ^{ilu}*Gilgāmesh tap-pa-a u-šar-šu-ka ka-a-ša*. In this "transliteration" into Akkadian syllables, the words have been separated, although it is not obvious from the text where the breaks occur. The line includes the name Gilgamesh, written with four signs: [𒀭𒄑𒂆𒈦]. (Note that the *dingir* determinative, written in superscript ^{d} or ^{ilu}, does *not* mean that the whole name is a god name. As often happens with Sumerian and Akkadian names, the name is theophoric, that is, it contains the name of the god and something about the god, usually flattering to the bearer of the name, possibly for good luck. When George Smith read Enkidu as "Heabani," he was reading the signs in Akkadian, whereas we now prefer to read the signs in Sumerian, since Gilgamesh and Enkidu were originally Sumerian figures. In the name Gilgamesh, the *dingir* governs only the next sign in the complex, i.e., *GIŠ*. In the Old Babylonian Gilgamesh texts, his name is regularly shortened to just ^{ilu}*GIŠ*. Even so, it does not mean that Gilgamesh is a god because he has a theophoric name.) The reading of the hero's name is still a matter of debate after a hundred years of scholarly study. Smith called him Izdubar; now some claim he should be called Bilgamesh. What is significant is that the complex ^{d}*GIŠ-GÍN-MAŠ* can potentially be read in quite a number of different ways. "Gilgamesh" has been the conventional reading since late in the nineteenth century (A.D.), and so has been followed here.

The debate over the reading of the name Gilgamesh tells us another important fact about the cuneiform writing system. Even when the individual sign is isolated and the language of the text is known, there are still many possibilities for reading the sign. In our one line of seventeen signs, for example, the first sign, *u,* has only one pronunciation as a syllable, but we know of at least five Akkadian words the sign could stand for *(bēlu, buru, gigurû, pilšu, ubānu),* if it did not stand for the *u* meaning "and." The second sign, read *dam*, could also be read *tam*, or it could point to the Akkadian word *aššatu*, "wife." The third sign, read *qu*, could also be *kum* or *qum*, or it could stand for an Akkadian word meaning "to crush," and so forth. One sign, read here *pa* (in the word *tap-pa-a*, "companion"), has no fewer than nine possibilities as a syllable-marker *(pa, ḫad, ḫat, ḫaṭ, ḫáṣ, sàk, sìg, zák,* and *zaq)* and at least nine different possibilities as a complete word, from "scepter" to "bird." This is not to consider that the signs enter into combinations with one another in long strings that vastly multiply the power of the system.[6]

With such a bewildering array of sign values, some of which were active in one period, some in another, there is little wonder that it took years of study in the *é-dub-ba* (scribal school) for a scribe to achieve competency. Even kings took pride in knowing the mysteries of the system. Borger lists just about 600 signs in his sign list. With various logographic possibilities, many syllabic readings, and a host of combinatorial chances, one can see why only a tiny minority of the population would be literate. A simple alphabet, with twenty to forty characters, seems almost a miraculous invention after such complexity. And such did happen. The alphabet we use is a greatly simplified (and much transformed) system derived from cuneiform.[7]

The great advantage of the syllabic system is that it allows us to reconstruct the pronunciation of Akkadian with a greater fidelity than, say, biblical Hebrew, although the Hebrew texts are centuries later than the Akkadian texts. Biblical Hebrew was originally written in only consonants; only much later, after the language had changed, as languages will, was an attempt made to add vowels to the Hebrew text. The situation with cuneiform is much different. Perhaps because the cuneiform system was used in a bilingual situation at a very early date—as early as 2650 B.C. there were scribes writing Sumerian texts who had Semitic names as well as scribes who had Sumerian names[8]—the pronunciation of the signs was important. Even in the northern Syrian city of Ebla in the Third Millennium, bilingual lexical texts were concerned not only with the equivalence of words in two languages (in that case, Sumerian and Semitic Eblaite), but with the vocalization of the texts as well.[9] The literary dialect of Akkadian, called Standard Babylonian, had the following phonemes: stops /b, p, d, t, ṭ, g, k, q/, sonants /m, n, r, l/, and vowels /a, e, i, u/. There were also five spirants /z, s, ṣ, š, ḫ/. Some of the phonemes are not found in English but are common in Semitic languages. The "hard t" /ṭ/ is one; the velar palatal /q/ is another (not the /kw/ we represent by *qu* in English). The pharyngealized sibilant /ṣ/ is another "hard" phoneme. The voiceless /š/ is another sibilant, this one familiar to us as *sh,* as in Shamash. Finally, /ḫ/ is not our *h* but a tongue-based laryngeal.[10] Thanks to numerous bilingual Sumerian-Akkadian lexical texts and bilingual compositions, the ancient scribes have given us many clues to the vocalization of their texts—although there have been no native speakers of Akkadian for over two thousand years.

Akkadian is a language in the Semitic family of languages. Because it is related to living languages like Arabic and Hebrew that have been much studied, Akkadian grammar was reconstructed rather early. (By contrast, the Sumerian language, in spite of the great help from the ancient grammarians themselves, still contains mysteries that elude scholars today; it is unrelated to any known language.) Thus both phonological and grammatical features of Akkadian are known to us.[11] Dictionaries of Akkadian were begun in the mid-nineteenth century, but only recently have the vast lexical resources of the many thousands of clay tablets become available to the non-specialist, with the completion of Wolfram von Soden's *Akkadisches Handwörterbuch.* The twenty-one volume *Chicago Assyrian Dictionary* is not far behind. Based on experience gained in compiling *The Oxford English Dictionary* and the Berlin Egyptian Dictionary, the CAD has now published sixteen of the twenty-one volumes.[12]

In the line from *Gilgamesh* VII.iii mentioned above, we have an example of the assistance modern dictionaries give the translator. Line 39 reads *u damqu* *ilu**Gilgāmeš tappâ ušaršūka kâša,* which we have seen as the end of a sequence of gifts the prostitute has given Enkidu: "and would give you beautiful Gilgamesh as a companion." We learn in CAD 3(D).68–74 that much is known of the word written in two signs on the tablet, *dam-qu.* The word can be written syllabically, as it is here, or it can appear as a single sign, called SIG_5.[13] There are lexical texts from antiquity which give *damqu* as the equivalent of the Sumerian word *sig;* and bilingual texts show how Sumerian texts were translated by Akkadian scribes. The CAD is particularly generous in providing clauses and sentences from a variety of sources to show how the word is used in context. The word *damqu* can mean "good fortune" and "kindness," but these are rather unusual. Far more often the term is used as one of the relatively few adjectives in Akkadian. The CAD detects nine distinct meanings of *damqu* as an adjective and points out the distribution of each in different periods of the language. The word means "good" ("fine," "pleasant"); "beautiful" or "handsome"; "of good family"; "expert"; "of good quality"; "gracious"; "propitious"; "effective" and "canonical." The nuances are especially helpful to the translator. We follow the CAD, which cites the line, in thinking the sense here is "handsome" or "beautiful."

The peculiarities of clay tablets and the cuneiform sign system, the different values of the signs, and the range of meanings make translating Akkadian a slow and painstaking process—one that demands a word-for-word and syllable-for-syllable transliteration before any larger complexes can be addressed. Fortunately, the popularity of *Gilgamesh* among cuneiformists has meant an ample commentary on the philological features of the text. The typical Akkadian poetic line, as in our example above, helps to fix the word within the context of a clause. The poetic line, whatever metrical features it may have, usually consists of one or two clauses. Sometimes two lines are closely related couplets, the clauses of one line answering to clauses in the other. Enjambed or run-on lines occur, but infrequently. In *Gilgamesh,* enjambment appears to be the mark of a special stylistic turn. The poetic line and the heavily formulaic character of Akkadian are the reasons why a complete clause can often be reconstructed from a few signs in a highly fragmented line of text.

Reconstruction can be dangerous, though. Return to the two translations of VII.iii.33–48 above. The first four lines illustrate the problem.

> now: "Shamash heard, opened his mouth,"
> Smith: "Shamas opened his mouth"
>
> now: "and from afar,...from the heavens called to him:"
> Smith: "and spake and from heaven said to him:"
>
> now: "Why, Enkidu, do you curse the love-priestess, the woman"
> Smith: "...and the female Samhat (delightful) thou shalt choose"
>
> now: "who would feed you with the food of the gods,"
> Smith: "they shall array thee in trappings of divinity"

Why was Smith in 1876 so close and yet so far from the mark? In this case, the answer is visible from Campbell Thompson's handcopy of the text [Plate 1]. The four lines are those just below the line drawn across the text above line 33. The first three lines have a large gap right in the center of the text, and the fourth line has one sign in the middle that is broken at the top. Notice, though, that Campbell Thompson has put together two fragments, one in the upper-left corner (lines 27–40), the other right and center (lines 31–51). Notice how the broken side on the left of the larger text can be traced by the many dots in Campbell Thompson's text through broken signs. Just in the middle, a dotted line circles four signs in line 38, one sign in 39, and one sign in line 40. These are signs found on both texts. Campbell Thompson notes the variants, since the two texts sometimes disagree. The smaller text in the upper-left has the British Museum number K11659; the larger text, right and center, has another British Museum number, K3389.

The solution to the puzzle is soon clear. Smith, who discovered the K-numbered texts at Nineveh, did not join the two fragments. (Considering the many thousands of small fragments, often with only a few cuneiform signs on them, it is surprising how many Smith was able to recognize and place in his, the first, attempt at the *Gilgamesh.*) He had, in other words, only K3389 and not K11659. For the four lines in question, he tried to reconstruct the whole line from only a few signs on the right. From the first line, he could read *pi-i-šu,* "his mouth," and from that small clue he could guess the shape of the opening of a speech, a formulaic expression. From the second line, he could read that the person was called "from the heavens," and so was able to surmise that the speaker was the sun god, Shamash. The "female Samhat (delightful)" is our "love-priestess." Smith thought that the woman had a proper name, Samhat, that meant "delightful." The "female" is a silent determinative indicating that the word following, *šamḫatu,* is in a class of females; normally, it is not vocalized or translated. Smith had the verb form in the line, but guessed "choose" instead of "curse" because he did not have the larger context of Enkidu's cursing the prostitute. Indeed, he chose to place this fragment, not in Tablet VII (notoriously difficult to piece together), but in Tablet II! With what he had of the text, he concluded, quite reasonably, that the fragment was a *prediction* of what would happen to Enkidu—not a curse after the fact, when Enkidu was near death.

This is not to fault Smith. What he was attempting, with far fewer resources than we now have, is not essentially different from what is attempted today. The last of the four lines reinforces the strengths and weaknesses of the process. Again, Smith had only the end of the line to work with. He knew that the line was paired with the next line. One had something to do with the gods, the second with kings. Just what it was could not be read from the fragmented lines. So he surmised "trappings of divinity" and followed it with "insignia of royalty." With greater hindsight, we can see that he was wrong. The second fragment helps recover the true pairings, "food of the gods" and "the drink of kings." Smith did not have the verb in the line. He thought that, besides Samhat, there was yet another woman involved, and that led him to "they" as the subject; since he had thought the line involved "trappings of divinity," "they shall array thee" seemed reasonable for the first part of the line. One would like to wait until a "complete" text of *Gilgamesh* is available before translating it. One hundred years of work have not produced that complete text. In the meantime, risks have to be taken—and mistakes will be made that are likely to fill later generations with as much amusement as Smith's pioneering work occasions in us—or more, as with Leonidas Le Cenci Hamilton's 1884 *Ishtar and Izdubar.*

Recall that *Gilgamesh* VII.iii.33–48 is one of the *best*-preserved sections of the poem, that there is little controversy today about the reconstruction of the text. Even with two good fragments, the lower-left (lines 40–48) is still missing and must be reconstructed. And the gap in line 34 remains. No one has a reasonable surmise about the signs in the break. Consider what would have been the case if the few signs in lines 49–51 had not survived. We would not know what Enkidu did when he heard Shamash's advice. The episode ends with Enkidu's angry heart growing still. Enkidu, ever the very figure of rebellion, comes close here to the resignation of the lordly Gilgamesh. But for a handful of signs at the end of a column, the whole resolution would have been lost.

Translating *Gilgamesh,* then, involves careful weighing of many features peculiar to cuneiform texts, thousands of small decisions that reflect the state of the art at the moment the text is engaged. There are larger questions of translation, though, that can be illustrated in this passage.

The first thing to notice about Shamash's speech to Enkidu is that it is well designed. After the introductory formula (33–34), the speech itself falls into three clear sections (36–39, 40–44, 45–48) of roughly equal length. The second section has one more line than the other two, but it also contains the only example of enjambment in the speech (40–41) and so the sections have rather equal development. The first section tells Enkidu of the gifts the prostitute has given him. The second and third sections turn to gifts Gilgamesh has given him and will give him in future. Gilgamesh is also the last and highest of the gifts the prostitute has given Enkidu (line 39), and the two sections are thus elegantly tied together (39 and 40).

There is, of course, no attempt to capture the hesitation, wavering, fragmentary quality of ordinary discourse, the way a modern novelist might want to capture it. Instead, the speech illustrates Akkadian poetic technique beyond the single line and the line-pair.

The introductory formula itself (33–34) is worth noting. One reason why there is hesitation about reconstructing the signs in the break (line 34) is that the introduction is an unusual variation on what is usually very standardized language. As Tigay (p. 233) has pointed out, there are two distinct introductory formulas for speeches in *Gilgamesh.* "A said to him, to B" (A *ana šâšu/šâšima izzakkar[a] ana* B), and (A *pâšu īpušamma iqabbi izzakkara ana* B), "A opened his mouth to speak, saying to B." The first is typical of Old Babylonian Akkadian in *The Epic of Gilgamesh;* the second is a formula found only in late texts. The first line of our speech, *ilušamaš iš-ma-a-[ma ip-t]ì pi-i-šu,* "Shamash heard, opened his mouth," is, as we have seen, close enough to the late formula that George Smith felt he could reconstruct the line only from the last three signs. But it is not really the same, and the second line is far different—"and from afar,...from the heavens called to him." The free and unusual reworking of a traditional formula is a characteristic of Sîn-leqi-unninnī's technique.

If we consider further that there is no parallel to the episode—Enkidu's curses, Shamash's advice, the change in Enkidu, Enkidu's blessings—in the Old Babylonian *The Epic of Gilgamesh,* it would appear that this passage is one of the best to show the poet's individual technique. Even the *carpe diem* motif present in the passage, a motif so characteristic of the Old Babylonian version, is modified in line with the increasing seriousness of Sîn-leqi-unninnī's work.

Schematically, the passage looks like this:

33–34. Introductory speech formula.
35. Opening of the question that ties 36–39 together,
Why do you curse the prostitute who...?
36–39. Gifts of the prostitute: food of the gods
the drink of kings
a great garment
Gilgamesh as a companion.
40–44. What Gilgamesh has given you: to lie in a great bed
to lie in a bed of honor
to place you at his left hand
kings have kissed your feet.
45–48. What Gilgamesh will do for you:
A. He will have the city mourn your death.
B. He will mourn your death.

Even in outline, the careful building of sections is clear. The gifts are the whole life of mankind in civilized life, from those things needed to survive (prepared food and drink), to what marks Enkidu as human and not merely animal ("great garment"), to Gilgamesh himself and the trappings of power and prestige. Even the city's mourning is part of the process. Enkidu will be remembered, his death marked by the city and, returning to the personal, by Gilgamesh. In the last two lines, ironically, the expression of Gilgamesh's grief blends into the loss of self and Gilgamesh's attempt to become what Enkidu was before he was civilized, "ranging the wilderness'"*(irappud ṣ[êri])*.

What Sîn-leqi-unninnī has managed is perhaps so obvious that its importance is missed. At a moment of great change for Enkidu, just before his death when he is asked to understand what has happened to him and to accept the meaning of his life, the poet recapitulates the whole movement I have called the Apollonian movement in *Gilgamesh.* As is typical of this poet, he summarizes the action of the poem without explicitly mentioning battle; the heroic fighting of Gilgamesh and Enkidu, like the *carpe diem* motif, is made implicit and at the same time transformed in the process, subordinated to a vision of existence that includes death and understanding. The lines are beautifully lucid and make good use of hierarchical design. The speech is, of course, an *argument.* And it is an argument that the poet skillfully designed to be convincing. It convinces Enkidu, who turns his curse of the prostitute into a blessing.

That the passage develops an argument should be enough to dispel the notion that ancient myth is incompatible with reasoning, or that one is likely to find only "pre-logical" or "primitive" thought before the Greeks. Story, myth, still predominates. (Think of the different interpretations offered for Gilgamesh's return to Uruk at the end of Tablet XI. There narrative carries the entire theme of Gilgamesh's "recognition" and "resignation," without any need for the sort of explicit comment found here.)

The passage is a divine revelation. The poet emphasizes the transcendence of Shamash. Where he had inspired the men through dreams, he now speaks directly, without ambiguity—but "from afar,...from the heavens." Yet there is nothing magical about the speech. It has nothing to do with a Shamash cult. It does not serve to establish the fates. Ironically, the force behind Enkidu's curse and blessing, like Jacob's curses and blessings of his sons (Genesis 49), comes from the magical power of the word. Enkidu cannot simply change the fate of the prostitute (the entire history of prostitutes, note, not just that of the particular one who seduced him); he can only add blessings. He cannot simply cancel the curse, once uttered. Both sides stand as if Enkidu's words alone were sufficient to secure them. But Shamash's words have no such force. They are words of persuasion, not of force. And if they mollify the angry heart of Enkidu, it is because the words have convinced him.

If the outline of the passage and the themes contained in it can be captured without great difficulty by the translator, there remain a number of smaller, subtler matters that are difficult to convey in translation. In general, we do not like formal repetition in our literature today. Typically, we strive to obscure the basic orderliness of our compositions. This makes it difficult to appreciate, for example, Sumerian poetry, which seems to find as much delight in the discovery of order as we take in the discovery of chaos. Large patches of Sumerian poetry are repeated word for word, line for line. Akkadian heroic poetry, which depends for so much on Sumerian poetry, is different. Subtle variation is often preferred to straight repetition. Still, Akkadian poetry is much closer to Sumerian poetry than to modern British and American poetry.

The handling of the verbs in this passage is an example. There are a number of places where word order and the placing of words in the poetic line serve aesthetic rather than semantic purposes. The transition between sections one and two is very strongly marked. Line 39 ends the list of the prostitute's gifts by naming Gilgamesh the *tappû,* or companion, and concludes the sequence of lines 35–39 (one full sentence) with a full stop. The next sequence opens with the strong, *[e]-nin-na-a-ma,* "Now then!" or "Listen!" But instead of giving us the usual line-clause, the poet repeats the name Gilgamesh and emphasizes the companionship by not one but two appositives, *ib-ri ta-li-me-ka,* "the equal, the one with whom you are intimate," or as we have rendered it, "your beloved friend." Here the variety more than, perhaps, the precision of the terms keeps the lines separate and at the same time ties them together. The verbs and objects in the passage show a similarly elegant variation.

In the first section, the verb forms are subjunctive, after the *ša* ("who") that begins the sequence in line 36. The subjunctive forms are not simple past-tense forms; they do not merely indicate that the prostitute has fed Enkidu, given him drink, a garment, and Gilgamesh. Rather, the forms tend to define the role of the prostitute (without at the same time, casting the fate—where the poet would have used precative forms or imperatives). We had translated the sequence with the modal "would." Why curse the woman "who would feed you…,/ and would have you drink…,/ and would clothe you…,/ and would give you beautiful Gilgamesh as a companion?" At the same time we had tried to capture something of the repetition-with-variation in the word order. In line 36, for example, the Akkadian has a sequence V + Obj. + Appositive; the next line has Obj. + V + Appositive, where both appositives are in the construct form. The next two lines again vary V + Obj./ Obj. + V—but also add adjectives, one following the noun, which is the ordinary word order *(lu-ub-ši ra-ba-a),* the second fronting the noun *(dam-qu iluGilgāmeš),* "garment great" and "beautiful Gilgamesh."

Similar play can be shown in sections two and three, where causative past and future forms are employed by the poet. The point, though, is that the Akkadian manages to be correct, elegant, and beautifully clear in the passage. It is an address appropriate to Shamash, god of light. There is a kind of wisdom uttered that is the equivalent in story to the myth of the sun god battling the monster of darkness. There is skill here, but it is subordinated to a cool, dispassionate, and unambiguous rhetoric of persuasion. The trick is to translate the discourse without losing the light touch and falling into the aged heaviness of King James Version prose style.

As Benjamin Foster's article below points out, the sign Campbell Thompson read as *kal* in line 48 is now usually read *lab,* giving us not the skin of "dog," but of a "lion" *(maški labbimma).*

Foster's reading of the signs in this passage is slightly different than Campbell Thompson's in other respects. The verb form *uklat* is now preferred to *akla* in line 36. And most Assyriologists prefer the abbreviation *d* (for *dingir*) to *ilu* for the sign that indicates that what follows is the name of a god. The word *dingir,* recall, is the Sumerian word for "god" that Akkadian knew as *ilu.*

Of greater interest than the grammatical and typographical differences is the nuances of the translation. Foster's reading of Shamash's advice is very different from the one given here. He is convinced of the "absurdity" of Shamash's speech, since Foster views Shamhat and her sexual initiation of Enkidu in a very negative light, and thus sees Shamash's role, not as the bringer of light to Enkidu, but as an ironic figure, whose parallelism is "pompous" rather than convincing. Foster's translation reflects his belief "that a god should attempt to calm the rage of a man is strange enough, but the terms and language used leave little doubt as to the poet's satiric, if bitter, intent."

Since Shamash has such an important new role to play in the Standard Babylonian version of *Gilgamesh,* such a passage not only reflects a translator's view of Shamash's role but also the role of all women associated with Shamhat—and, through her, Ishtar—in the poem as a whole. The familiar hermeneutic circle is evident here: to translate a word, the context—the work as a whole—needs to be understood; but the whole can only be understood through an understanding of the smallest parts.

GILGAMESH XI.i.36–47

Gilgamesh travels to see the sage Utnapishtim in order to find life—and is given a story, the Flood. The poet seems to have anticipated the story, for Tablet I opens with Gilgamesh's most important act, his carrying back "word of the time before the Flood." In a very detailed comparison of the late version of *Gilgamesh* XI with the Old Babylonian *The Epic of Gilgamesh* on the one hand, and the versions of the Flood story known from what is called *Atra-ḫasīs* on the other, Tigay (214–240) concludes that the hero's journey to Utnapishtim was part of the Old Babylonian Gilgamesh story—but that the Flood story was not. Thus, he divides *Gilgamesh* XI into the Flood story and the non-Flood episodes. The Flood story is very close to versions of *Atra-ḫasīs,* some of which also date to the Old Babylonian Period. The poet of the late *Gilgamesh,* then, added the interest in the Flood, making it the chief discovery of the heroic quest, and used traditional materials to compose the Flood narrative. Tigay also noticed an odd stylistic variation in *Gilgamesh* XI. The non-Flood episodes show a great deal of stylistic similarity to the late version of *Gilgamesh* generally; but the Flood does not seem to have been revised to fit the late style. A number of details are not fully assimilated into a harmonious narrative. One traditional feature Sîn-leqi-unninnī retains in the telling of the Flood story is the speech of the tricky god, Ea (called by his Sumerian name, Enki, in Old Babylonian *Atra-ḫasīs* texts). Ea speaks three times in the Flood story (XI.i.19–31, 36–47, and iv.177–188) and once in Tablet XII. One of the speeches has gained great prominence in cuneiform literature: it contains the most famous use of metaphor in any Akkadian text. Because the translation of metaphor presents a number of special problems, the speech is worth looking at in some detail.

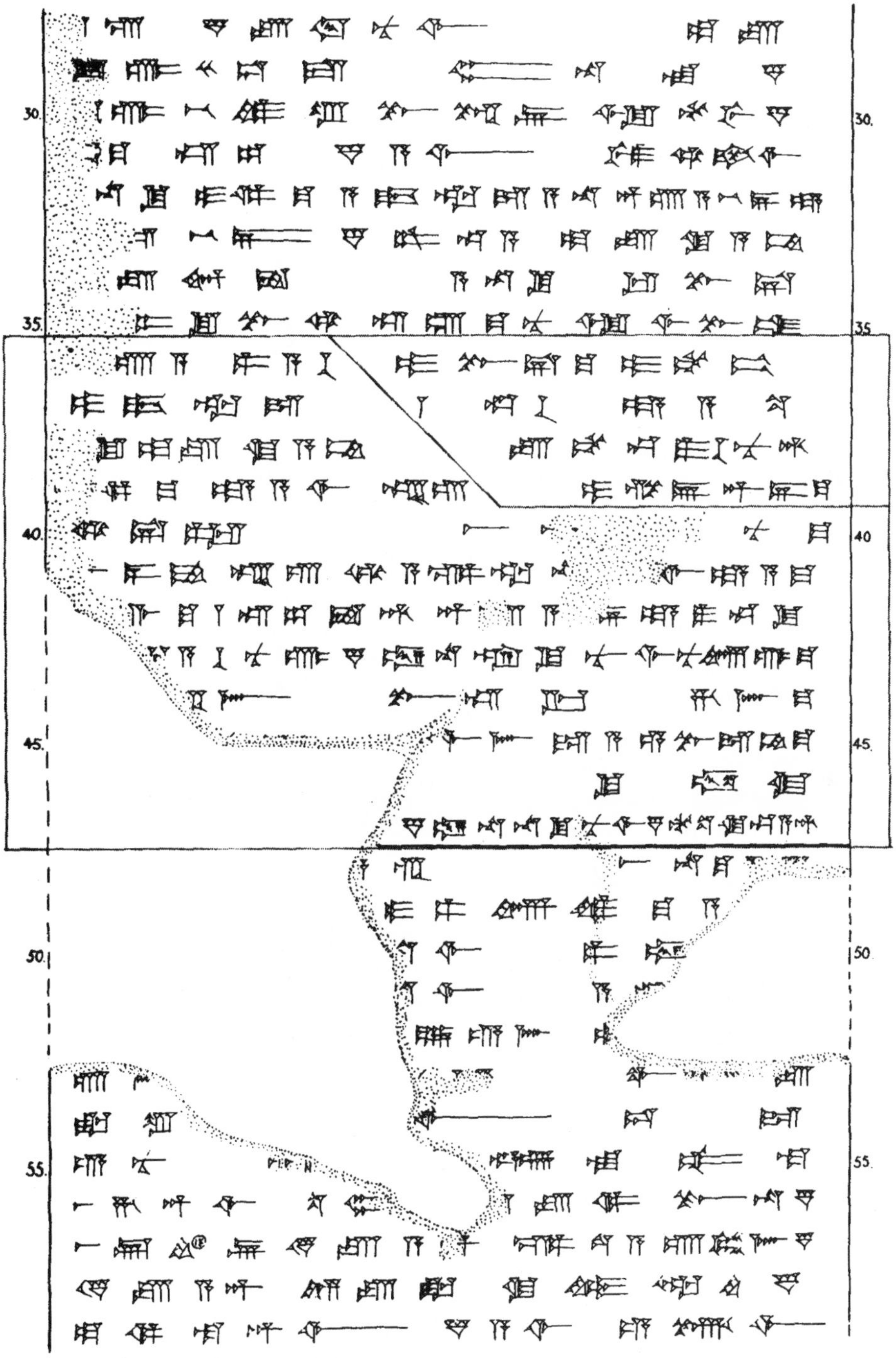

Plate 2 • Thompson's handcopy of Tablet XI.
The lines mark the two texts that provide XI.i.36–47.

Ea informs Utnapishtim (through a wall) of the Flood ordered by the god Enlil and tells Utnapishtim what to do to escape the Flood. Utnapishtim has a problem. How can he get the boat constructed without telling the citizens of the Flood? In a masterpiece of indirection, Ea tells Utnapishtim what to say to the people. He need not lie to the citizens. Rather he need only exploit the resources of language itself to trick the people into helping in the project.

"Ea shaped his mouth, saying,
saying to me, his servant,
'You, you may say this to them:
Enlil hates me—me!
I cannot live in your city
or turn my face toward the land which is Enlil's.
I will go down to the Abyss, to live with Ea, my lord.
He will make richness rain down on you—
the choicest birds, the rarest fish.
The land will have its fill of harvest riches.
At dawn bread
he will pour down on you—showers of wheat.'"

The Akkadian text of Gilgamesh XI.i. 36–47 in transliteration.

36 ^{ilu}é-a pa-a-šu i-pu-uš-ma i-qab-bi
37 i-zak-ka-ra ana ardi-šu ia-a-tu
38 lu-u at-ta ki-a-am ta-qab-ba-aš-šu-nu-ti
39 [e(?)]-di-ma ia-a-ši ^{ilu}en-lil i-zi-ir-an-ni-ma
40 ul uš-šab ina â[li-ku]-nu-ma
41 ina qaq-qar ^{ilu}en-lil ul a-šak-ka-n[a] pani-ia-a-ma
42 [ur-r]ad-ma apsî it-ti i ^{ilu}é-a [be]-li-a aš-ba-ku
43 [eli k]a-a-šu-nu u-ša-az-nak-ku-nu-ši nu-uḫ-šam-ma
44 [ḫi-iṣ-bi] iṣṣuri (?) pu-zu-ur nûni^{meš}-ma
45 [išarrakkunūš]i meš-ra-a e-bu-ra-am-ma
46 [ina šēr(i)] ku-uk-ki
47 [ina lilâtu u]-ša-az-na-na-ku-nu-ši ša-mu-tu ki-ba-a-ti

(Transliteration: after R. Campbell Thompson *The Epic of Gilgamesh: Text, Transliteration, and Notes* [Oxford: Clarendon Press, 1930], pp. 60–61.)

The final five lines are richly metaphorical. The beginning of the speech, too, is filled with wordplay. Indeed, the piece is the most conspicuous sustaining of figurative language through a complete poem in *Gilgamesh.* The figures are sustained in order to avoid the lie. The speech is not given directly, as was Shamash's in VII.iii.33–48, but within the context of Utnapishtim's first-person account of an event that took place in the past. As Utnapishtim recounts it, Ea addresses him, but avoids using the human's name—perhaps because it preserves the ruse of the reed-wall. Ea can still claim in the assembly of the gods (XI.iv.186–187) that he did not "unhide the secret of the great gods" because he did not address the sage by name. In any event, the avoidance of Utnapishtim's name brings into prominence the pronouns that refer to him. Independent personal pronouns are not needed, ordinarily, in Akkadian, because the pronominal function is included in the verb form or appears as a suffix. One consequence of the use of pronouns in the passage, which are emphatic when they are used, is a play on the name of the god, ^ilu^é-a, and the first-person pronouns *ia-a-tu* (37), *ia-a-ši* (39), and the suffix *-ia-a-ma* (41). Utnapishtim is to tell the elders: Enlil hates *ia-a-ši,* hates *-an-ni-ma.* It is a simple statement, true on one level, but it contains a kind of play that will increasingly dominate the passage. It prepares the hearer (Gilgamesh/the reader) for the language to become more intensely figurative.

The reader needs to know that the Flood will come soon to appreciate otherwise straightforward statements. Utnapishtim will indeed not be able to gaze upon the "earth" of Enlil. The three gods, Anu, Enlil, and Ea, were thought to divide the universe: Anu (heavens), Enlil (earth), and Ea (the below, the *apsû*). Utnapishtim, unable to turn his face to the land, will "go down" to the Abyss, the dwelling-place of Ea. This is true only in the sense that the earth is covered—and the *apsû* is let loose in flood upon the earth. The boat does not otherwise "go down" to the *apsû*.

The "he" of "he will make richness rain down on you" (43) is perhaps ambiguously Ea or Enlil, but the point is a minor one compared with the scandal of misdirection by which the waters below *(apsû)* and the waters above *(zanānu)* produce the great Flood. Vegetation as well as marine life is sustained by the waters below. The verb *zanānu* means both "to rain" and "pour out" and "to provide food," "to provide an institution with means of support."[14] The lines play upon Ea's traditional role, bringing waters from below and above to produce the fertile land. Compare a Sumerian Enki hymn:

> At my word the stalls are built, the sheepfolds ringed about:
> when it nears the above, a rain of plenty rains from above;
> when it nears the below, there is a carp-flood of flooding water;
> when it nears the green flood meadow,
> at my command piles of grain are piled up inside and out.[15]

Where the Sumerian is straightforward, though, *Gilgamesh* XI is devious. The result of the god's actions will be "the choicest birds" and a *puzru,* the "rarest" of fish. The waters will produce "riches" *(mašru)* and a "harvest" *(ebūru).* The elders can hardly be expected to guess what sort of baleful harvest it will be.

In fact, the people of the city are delighted. Drink is poured as if it were the water of a river (XI.ii.73). The city makes a festival like the New Year's Festival (XI.ii.74) when the boat is built. And no wonder. Through Utnapishtim Ea offers "bread" at dawn (46) and "showers of wheat" in the night (47): a pun on both *kukku,* a kind of bread or cake, and *kukkû,* "darkness" (used as a name for the netherworld); and on *kibtu,* "wheat" but also "misfortune"—both senses are exploited here. What the elders expect is bread and wheat; what they will get is darkness and misfortune.

The passage presents the usual problems of reading the cuneiform signs and putting together a text line that is broken in places. Campbell Thompson, as seen in Plate 2, used two different texts to construct lines 36–47. His D-text (S.2131) is actually a join of five small fragments; and his E-text (K.8517), of two. Even so, the lower left hand is broken away. Since the readings of the last few lines are particularly important, reconstruction of the passage is crucial. In this case, the task is eased because the last two lines are repeated in XI.ii.87, 90. That is something of a surprise, but the repetition of the key lines, "At dawn bread/ he will pour down showers of wheat" (without the suffix, "on you," note) reinforces the importance of the lines. The repetition in XI.ii.87 has been a bit of a puzzle. Many think Shamash (who is himself a surprise in the context of the Flood story) speaks the line.[16] This is not necessarily the case. In both 87 and 90, the repetition of the lines follow a reference to the "time" *(adannu)* set for the Flood to begin. The two lines, we think, have become the name of the Flood.

There is also a partial parallel to the lines in *Atra-ḫasīs.* The text is found in III.i. 15–35 of that work,[17] a speech of Enki/Ea that conflates the first two speeches of Ea in *Gilgamesh.* As in *Gilgamesh* XI.i.19–31, Ea tells the sage (through a reed-wall) to build a boat. The details of the *Gilgamesh* follow *Atra-ḫasīs* very closely, although the two accounts are not entirely the same. The sequence is the same. The *Atra-ḫasīs* account does not, however, include Utnapishtim's question about what he should say to the elders of the city. Instead of ending the speech the way it is ended in *Gilgamesh,* it concludes abruptly with two lines that recall the end of *this* speech: "I will rain down upon you/ an abundance of birds, a basket of fishes!" (34–35). There is no ambiguity in Ea's speech in *Atra-ḫasīs* about whose responsibility it will be to bring the waters, as there is in *Gilgamesh.* The lines are metaphoric, but they are not devious. So far only *Gilgamesh* has preserved this extended, tricky speech of Ea.

Most commentators consider the Flood story in *Gilgamesh* a digression.[18] If the Flood story was not part of the Old Babylonian *The Epic of Gilgamesh,* why is it given such prominence by Sîn-leqi-unninnī? If he was the first to insert the tale—and to announce it in the very beginning of Tablet I—one might guess that there is more to the story for Gilgamesh than is usually considered. This is especially intriguing if the poet took over the old materials without changing them into the style of the rest of Gilgamesh's visit to Utnapishtim. We think that the answer lies with Ea —that the clue is not so much in the story of the saving of life itself but in the saving of life through what Ea and his servant, Utnapishtim, represent: cunning. This is most obvious in Ea's third speech, where Gilgamesh is told to listen closely to Ea's words—a sure way of tipping off the audience. But the same kind of cunning dominates all three speeches—though this one is even more conspicuous than the others, as cunning has entered fully into its form and texture.

Ea's speech illustrates a problem in translating texts that draw on traditional materials. In some ways *Gilgamesh* is quite free and innovative, making new connections between old Gilgamesh stories, adding a Flood story, or, as we have seen in the previous passage (VII.iii.33–48), carefully bringing a series of tales about Enkidu to closure by an exchange in which Enkidu's life is recounted, clarified for him, and recognized by Enkidu just before his death. Like Chaucer and Shakespeare in the English tradition, Sîn-leqi-unninnī did not hesitate to use old materials in new ways. Still, comparisons of *Gilgamesh* with older versions of Gilgamesh stories and with other versions of the Flood, such as we have here, indicate great respect for the literary tradition. Unless there is a clear need to change things, the poet is content to follow the sequence, details, and even the wording of texts in the stream of tradition. The last lines of our passage, the most famous example of figurative language in the tradition, may themselves have been traditional, a saying about the Flood that had become virtually the name of the event, like the date formulas used in ancient texts to indicate a year in a king's reign. Translating figurative language is always tricky. The problem is in knowing how many contexts are involved.

Once isolated for purposes of analysis, a speech like Ea's may turn out to be organically unified or merely a string of originally unrelated sayings. Translating this passage demands that we work backward from the two lines that close the speech. Because the openings of speeches in Sumerian and Akkadian literature are usually marked explicitly by introductory formulas, the speech is usually a convenient unit for the study of compositional techniques. (The same could not be said about, say, modern fiction, where an attempt is made to capture something like naturalistic dialogue, with all its give-and-take, guided by the modern assumptions of highly individualistic characters.) This speech does appear to play with language in a certain way from the start. The reader is set up to expect increasingly clever ambiguity. The old notion, going back to Aristotle, that figures like metaphor are exchanges of names for objects, that a one-to-one correspondence holds between the "real" name of an object and the name chosen to replace it—that notion has given way to the idea that metaphor appears only in the context of, at minimum, a clause.[19] The play of metaphor in this speech extends to the last two lines and, beyond that, we suggest, to the speech as a whole.

We take the speech of Ea, then, as something more than a string of loosely related sayings. (The parallel in *Atra-ḫasīs* III.i.15–35, on the other hand, has the look of just such a string of sayings.) The context extends to the speech as a whole. But must we go further? The relevant contexts are within *Gilgamesh* and also beyond *Gilgamesh.* Ea's speech is one of three in the Flood episode. The speech occurs within a long address by Utnapishtim to Gilgamesh. Utnapishtim's "secret of the gods," the Flood story, is itself part of the narrative of Gilgamesh's visit to Utnapishtim, which consists of several episodes in *Gilgamesh* X and XI. *Gilgamesh* opens with what looks like an anticipation of the Flood story, crediting Gilgamesh's knowledge as his most important heroic achievement. And as the *Gilgamesh* advances, it becomes clear that the journey to Utnapishtim is Gilgamesh's goal after the death of Enkidu. This is all to say that it *appears* the speech is part of a larger, well-ordered composition. But, as has been seen, even the series of episodes that make up Gilgamesh's encounter with Utnapishtim show such stylistic variation that one must be very cautious with a top-down translation of even the Flood story itself.

Add to this the intertextual connections between other versions of the Gilgamesh stories, which may or may not have been available to the poet; between the Flood in *Gilgamesh* and in Sumerian and Akkadian accounts of the Flood, especially *Atra-ḫasīs;* and between

Ea's speech in *Gilgamesh* XI and a tradition of composing Ea's speeches. About this last, already more than ninety speeches of Enki/Ea have been collected in the Sumerian, Akkadian, and Hittite languages. Because Ea is the talking god, there seems to be a much greater interest in representing Ea's speech than the speech of other gods—including Shamash. The "wisdom" tradition does not show such an interest in the speech of the gods.[20] Many of Ea's speeches are part of magical rites and magical power. Even when, as is the case here, Ea speaks because someone (usually a god; only very rarely a human) has a problem of such complexity that only the god of cunning can solve it, he *only* speaks. Sumerian literature represented Enki/Ea in a variety of activities, usually involving sexual activity and the creation of strange beings. In Akkadian literature he is mainly a problem solver. When Ninurta exclaims to the Assembly of the Gods (XI.iv.174–176) that only Ea could have tricked Enlil and saved mankind from the Flood, he is just reflecting a long tradition in the Enki/Ea literature. The tradition at least leads us to anticipate that a speech by Ea is likely to display a cunning in the play of words appropriate to Ea's "character."

We feel that this cunning is the point of including the journey of Gilgamesh to Utnapishtim in *Gilgamesh* and, in particular, the point of the Flood story. It is not the confident "wisdom" of Shamash, but its complement, its underside, as it were. Utnapishtim, servant of Ea, represents the devious, ironic, often brutal truth of existence that Ea presents in his role in cuneiform literature. If Shamash convinces Enkidu on his death-bed that life in its fullness is valuable in itself, Ea and the "overly wise" Utnapishtim make the point again and again: life preserved is not life as perfect happiness or life eternal. To seek life is necessary; to seek truth, bitter but the highest good of mankind. In its very indirection, the Flood story is like the dark center of a labyrinth. Or gazing at the *nagbu,* Gilgamesh resists the existential horror as long as he can. His recognition and return to Uruk are marked, not by joy, but by the resignation in winning a tragic knowledge, a kind of dark *gnosis.*

We have, then, considered the different contexts of Ea's speech and, in spite of the difficulties, decided for translation purposes that the speech and its context in *Gilgamesh* disclose a unified narrative and a well-worked theme. Structurally, Ea's role in what I have called the Dionysian phase of *Gilgamesh* is similar to Shamash's in the Apollonian phase. It is not the drunkenness of Dionysus (which has its counterpart in the *sparagmos* of Gilgamesh), but the tragic knowledge, the mad "secret" that comes like inspiration, that has, finally, urged this notion of a Dionysian phase.

Finally, it is worth noting that Gilgamesh's long journey, which takes him in agony to Utnapishtim, is a journey into the archaic. Where Shamash is the god of light and the clarity of reason, which gives us a stable world of past, present, and future, Ea is the old father, with a very different grasp of existence. Gilgamesh does not only leave the here-and-now world of Uruk to travel through a strange space. He also travels in time. Utnapishtim has escaped human time—the only human to have done so. But he represents the past, history divided by the Flood. He lived before Gilgamesh, and his Flood story is a tale of the past. This archaic character is especially evident in the Ea literature, where his young son is, typically, the one calling upon the old father to set things straight. The gods exist in a kind of non-time, the time of origins;[21] the Flood exists in imagination, and so can be told; Gilgamesh slips out of history for the time of his journey across the waters of death. Again, like the labyrinth or the abyss, the spiral takes Gilgamesh into intimacy with a terrible truth.

Ea's speech is speech about language. Only the cunning one, the poet, can lead into the archaic and lead us back to Uruk.

GILGAMESH I.iv.16–21

A third passage illustrates a very different problem in translating *Gilgamesh.* Although tame in comparison with the sexually explicit literature common in the 20th century, the brief narrative of the sexual encounter in the wilderness between Gilgamesh's double, Enkidu, and a woman from the city (and its temple, specifically the temple of Ishtar), is arguably the most sexually explicit narrative in Akkadian literature. There is no problem with the text in this case, no breaks or gaps to fill in with educated guesses about the reading of signs. The Akkadian words are, in most cases, well-attested and their range of meaning established by a great variety of texts. The English translations of the passage differ in astonishing ways. As the translations demonstrate, the problem is not so much the Akkadian as the surprising reticence of modern English. George Smith chose not to translate the passage, and, more recently, Alexander Heidel translated it into Latin, where none but the educated could read it.

Now that the role of women in the poem has become a matter of intense critical interest, the passage holds greater importance than it had in the past.

A transliteration of the Akkadian of I.iv.16–21, which might be called Enkidu and the Woman, is:

16 ur-tam-mi míŠam-ḫat di-da-šá úr-šá ip-te-e-ma
ku-zu-ub-šá il-qí
17 ul iš-ḫu-ut il-ti-qi na-pis-su
18 lu-bu-ši-šá u-ma-ṣi-ma elī-šá iṣ-lal
19 i-pu-us-su-ma lul-la-a ši-pir sin-niš-te
20 da-du-šú iḫ-pu-pu eli ṣērī-šá
21 6 ur-ri 7 mušâti dEn-ki-dù te-bi-ma míŠam-ḫat ir-ḫi

No one questions that the woman, a *shamhatu,* whose title is now often taken as a personal name, Shamhat, meets Enkidu at a watering hole in the wilderness while he is running with the only companions he has known, the animals. In the passage, she seduces him, they make love for a week, and Enkidu finds he cannot return to the wild. It is the first step in the education, or humanization, of Enkidu, who is referred to as *lullû,* the first—and probably "primitive"—human. Benjamin Foster (see below), who considers the passage Enkidu's "first stage of knowledge, sexual awareness," has noticed a pattern that will unfold later in *Gilgamesh.* Enkidu's remarkable week-long sexual encounter—Foster thinks it is a single heroic act of intercourse—opens a contrast between sleep and wakeful arousal that will play through the narrative until Gilgamesh is given last chance for immortality, a Sleeping Test, in Tablet XI.

Foster has also noticed a certain wordplay in the passage (and what Foster himself judges as a rather "lame" translation): Shamhat's *dīdū* in line 16, her vulva, anticipates Enkidu's *dādu* in line 20, his "passionate feelings."

The translators' emphasis on the seduction has perhaps obscured the wordplay that sees in an intense life-giving vigor and luxuriance something like a union of a female principle, full of the earth and waters below and a male principle, mingling waters of the above: *kuzbu, napīšu, tēbu, reḫu,* and especially *šamḫatu* itself, as the CAD *(The Chicago Assyrian Dictionary)* makes clear. (When Shamhat removes her *dīdū,* a strip of fabric a woman wound around the hips and between the legs, she is completely naked. That she spreads her clothing on the ground and then receives Enkidu is a sign of an original human—humanizing—separation from the animals.)

Shamhat's *kuzbu,* for example, is an attribute of goddesses and gods that has a range of meanings from sexual vigor, charm, attractiveness, to abundance, luxuriant vegetation, and plentiful waters. The *napīšu* of Enkidu, taken away by the extraordinarily active Shamhat, is his "breath" (Foster considers it the "breath of life"), much like the better known *napištu,* "breath" and "wind," but also "life," "vigor," "body" and "self," "provisions for sustenance."

(Both words relate to the verb, *napāšu*, one meaning of which is "to expand," "to become abundant.") When Enkidu "rises" *(tēbima),* it is clear that he is aroused for six days and seven nights. And when he "poured himself" into Shamhat, as Stephanie Dalley translated *rēḫu*, he completes a process that is indicated by the chiastic, envelope pattern that opens and closes the passage *(urtammi Šamḫat didaša... Enkidu tēbima Šamḫat irḫi).*

The word *šamḫatu* itself, whether it is taken as a title or a proper name, would seem to pick up the resonances of the verb *šamāḫu* to which it is related. The title may be a prostitute, connected with the temple—for which see Richard A. Henshaw, *Female and Male, The Cultic Personnel* (Chapter Four)—but its appropriateness in the context is the verbal form, "to grow thickly, abundantly," and to "flourish," meanings not unrelated to extraordinary beauty.

George Smith, 1986:

7–26. Details of the actions of the female Samhat and Heabani. [not translated] (202)

Leonidas Le Cenci Hamilton, 1884:

She laughing comes again to him,—Forsooth!
Her glorious arms she opens, flees away,
While he doth follow the enticer gay.
He seizes, kisses, takes away her breath,
And she falls to the ground—perhaps in death
He thinks, and o'er her leans where she now lay;
At last she breathes, and springs, and flees away.
But he the sport enjoys, and her pursues;
But glancing back his arms she doth refuse.
And thus three days and four of nights she played;
For of Heabani's love she was afraid.
Her joyous company doth him inspire
For Sam-kha, joy, and love, and wild desire. (61–62)

R. Campbell Thompson, 1928:

The girl, displaying her bosom,
Shew'd him her comeliness, (yea) so that he of her beauty possess'd him,
Bashful she was not, (but) ravish'd the soul of him, loosing her mantle,
So that he clasp'd her, (and then) with the wiles of a woman she plied him,
Holding her unto his breast.

('Twas thus that) Enkidu dallied
Six days, (aye) seven nights, with the courtesan-girl in his
mating. (13)

William Ellery Leonard, 1934:

Then the priestess loosened her buckle,
Unveiled her delight,
For him to take his fill of her.
She hung not back, she took up his lust,
She opened her robe that he rest upon her.
She aroused in him rapture, the work of woman.
His bosom pressed against her.
Engidu forgot where he was born.
For six days and seven nights
Was Engidu given over to love with the priestess. (8)

Alexander Heidel, 1949:

Meretrix nudabat sinum suum, aperiebat gremium suum,
et is succumbuit venustati eius.
Ea non cunctabatur ei appropinquare;
Ea solvit(?) vestem suam, et is incumbebat in eam;
Ea incitabat libidinem(?) in eo, opus feminae,
(Et) is impertiebat amorem suum ei.
Sex dies et septem noctes Enkidu coibat cum meretrice. (22)

E. A. Speiser, 1958:

The lass freed her breasts, bared her bosom,
And he possessed her ripeness.
She was not bashful as she welcomed his ardor.
She laid aside her cloth and he rested upon her.
She treated him, the savage, to a woman's task,
As his love was drawn unto her.
For six days and seven nights Enkidu comes forth,
Mating with the lass. (44)

Herbert Mason, 1970:

When he awoke he saw a creature
Unlike any he had seen before
Standing near the water, its skin smooth, tan
And hairless except for its head
And between its legs.
He wanted to touch it, but then
It made sounds he had never heard,

Not like the sounds of his friends, the animals,
And he was afraid. The prostitute
Came close to him and the animals withdrew.
She took his hand and guided it
Across her breasts and between her legs
And touched him with her fingers
Gently and bent down and moistened
Him with her lips then drew him
Slowly to the ground. (18)

N. K. Sandars, 1972:

She was not ashamed to take him, she made herself naked and welcomed his eagerness; as he lay on her murmuring love she taught him the woman's art. For six days and seven nights they lay together, for Enkidu had forgotten his home in the hills. (64–5)

D. G. Bridson, 1972:

And the girl gave her bosoms and all the rest…
And what she gave, Enkidu took… Repeatedly…
For there was nothing half-hearted about that business
during seven days and nights… The girl
showed what work she had learned to make for a man,
And Enkidu went in and did it. (15)

John Gardner and John Maier, 1984:

The courtesan untied her wide belt and spread her legs,
    and he struck her wildness like a storm.
She was not shy; she took his wind away,
Her clothing she spread out, and he lay upon her.
She made him know, the man-as-he-was, what a woman is.
His body lay on her;
six days and seven nights Enkidu attacked, fucking
    the priestess. (77)

Benjamin Foster, 1987:

Šamhat unloosed her attire, opened her vulva, and he took
    her charms.
She was not bashful, she took to herself his vitality.
She stripped off her clothes and he lay upon her,
She indeed treated him, man, to woman's work.
His passionate feelings caressed her.
Six days and seven nights was Enkidu aroused and made
    love to Šamhat. (24)

Stephanie Dalley, 1989:

Shamhat loosened her undergarments, opened her legs
and he took in her attractions.
She did not pull away. She took wind of him,
Spread open her garments, and he lay upon her.
She did for him, the primitive man, as women do.
His love-making he lavished upon her.
For six days and seven nights Enkidu was aroused
and poured himself into Shamhat. (55)

Maureen Gallery Kovacs, 1989:

Shamhat unclutched her bosom, exposed her sex, and he
took in her voluptuousness.
She was not restrained, but took his energy.
She spread out her robe and he lay upon her,
she performed for the primitive the task of womankind.
His lust groaned over her;
for six days and seven nights Enkidu stayed aroused,
and had intercourse with the harlot. (9)

Robert Temple, 1991:

She had no shame for this,
Made herself naked,
Welcomed his eagerness,
Incited him to love,
Taught the woman's art.
Six days, seven nights,
That time lying together,
Enkidu had forgot his home
Had forgot the hills. (9)

Danny P. Jackson, 1992:

Shamhat let her garments loose and spread forth
her happiness which Enkidu entered as gusts of wind
enter tunnels bound for Hell.
Hot and swollen first, she jumped him fast
knocking out his rapid breath with
thrust after loving thrust.
She let him see what force a girl can have,
and he stayed within her scented bush for
seven nights, leaping, seeping, weeping, and sleeping there.
(9)

David Ferry, 1992:

And so the harlot, Shamhat, showed him her breasts,

showed him her body. The hair-bodied man
came over to her, and lay down on her, and then

she showed him the things a woman knows how to do.
For seven days Enkidu in his wonder

lay with her in pleasure (8)

Ludmila Zeman, 1992:

As night fell, Shamhat played her harp
and sang in the darkness.
Her voice cast a spell over the forest. Enkidu walked
toward the sound then stopped behind a tree.
He had never seen anything so lovely. He approached her
slowly so as not to frighten her.

Shamhat saw Enkidu and stopped singing. He looked more
like a beast than a man
but she knew he would not harm her. No one had ever
looked at her with so much tenderness.

In the days that followed, Shamhat taught him to speak
and to sing and she fell in love with him.
They explored the ways of love together and Enkidu
promised he would stay with her always. (n.p.)

The complex wordplay is only gradually coming to light, but as the different translations show, the explicitness of the Akkadian poses problems for a modern, Western language that reflects a long struggle with active sexuality. On the one hand, explicit language is still considered "dirty," and on the other, euphemisms are considered vaguely hypocritical or evasive. Yet another problem is the tendency, again quite marked in Western discourse, if Fatima Mernissi is correct (*Beyond the Veil*, 34–45), with active female sexuality.

Richard Henshaw claims that a major category of cultic officiants in Mesopotamia consists of "priests" and "priestesses" who interpret sexuality and fertility. How much actual "sacred prostitution" and how widely "sacred marriage rites" were performed in Mesopotamia is still a matter of great controversy, but it is clear that it is difficult to categorize, today, a woman who humanizes and civilizes a man—indeed, transforms the primitive Enkidu—through sexual experience. Article after article below, by specialist and non-specialist alike, return to the initiation of Enkidu by the woman. As the essays in this volume show, no single episode in *Gilgamesh* has yielded so many different interpretations, and the episode is of all episodes the closest to an interpretive key to *Gilgamesh.*

Note, to conclude, the different terms used above to translate *šamḫatu,* and contemporary concerns with gender differences in language: Joy, the girl, the priestess, *meretrix,* lass, "a creature/unlike any he had seen before," courtesan, and harlot.

❋ ❋ ❋

NOTES

1. George Smith, *The Chaldean Account of Genesis* (New York: Scribner, Armstrong and Co., 1876), pp. 197–198. A. H. Sayce made no changes in this passage when he revised Smith's *Account* in 1880. Paul Haupt, who edited the text for the first time in *Das Babylonische Nimrodepos* (Leipzig: J. E. Hinrichs'sche, 1884), presents only the right fragment (=K 3389), not the left (K 11659), p. 15, #4.
2. R. Campbell Thompson, *The Epic of Gilgamesh: Text, Transliteration, and Notes* (Oxford: Clarendon Press, 1930).
3. The overwhelming majority of the hundreds of thousands of texts already discovered are clay tablets, sometimes sun-baked, sometimes baked in ovens. Others are cut into stone or metal. Some are painted on glazed terra-cotta. A few wooden tablets covered with beeswax have been found; but whereas baked clay tablets are virtually indestructible, the wooden tablets have not survived except in very peculiar circumstances. On the tablets and the "stream of tradition" that preserved texts, see A. Leo Oppenheim, *Ancient Mesopotamia* (Chicago: University of Chicago Press, 1964), pp. 8–30.
4. Here the tendency of cuneiform documents to be written in standard forms and formulas helps greatly to reconstruct a line from just a few signs. As an example of the simple wear and tear on tablets, some twenty lines in George Smith's translation appear to show that he had more of the text in the 1870s than was available to Paul Haupt in the early 1880s; signs worn from the surface can be reconstructed from Smith's translation of the lines. (Smith left no handcopy or transliteration of his *Gilgamesh.*)
5. Sign-lists include Rykle Borger, *Akkadische Zeichenliste* (Neukirchen-Vluyn, Verlag Butzon and Bercher Kevelaer, 1971), and René Labat, *Manuel d'épigraphie akkadienne* (Paris: Imprimerie Nationale, 1963). The earliest version of these two signs would give a clue to the meaning (in any language): the eight-point star [✳] and the sun rising [◡]

(Labat, pp. 48, 174). For the origin and development of cuneiform writing from pictography to stylized signs, see Samuel Noah Kramer, *History Begins at Sumer* (Philadelphia: University of Pennsylvania Press, 1981), pp. xxiii, 381–382. For an overview of writing systems, see I. J. Gelb, *A Study of Writing* (Chicago: University of Chicago Press,1963).

6. See Borger, p. 47 (#295, *pa).* For combinations, consider the *pa* and the *dingir* signs together: read *pa-an,* it is the Akkadian *parṣu* ("divine attribute"); read *an-pa,* it could be either the god Nabû or the Akkadian complex *elât šamê,* the zenith. There are other god names beginning with *pa* but consisting of more than one element, e.g., *dḪendur-sag-gá.*

7. Walter J. Ong points out the technological differences between alphabets and scripts like cuneiform in his chapter "Writing Restructures Consciousness," in *Orality and Literacy* (New York: Methuen, 1982), pp. 78–116.

8. Robert Biggs, *Inscriptions from Tell Abu Ṣalabikh* (Chicago: University of Chicago Press, 1974), p. 12.

9. See René Labat, "L'écriture cunéiforme et la civilisation mésopotamienne," in *L'écriture et la psychologie des peuples,* with Marcel Cohen et al. (Paris: Librairie Armand Colin, 1963), pp. 73–86, with discussion, pp. 87–92. On the bilingual lexical texts discovered at Ebla, see Giovanni Pettinato, *Old Canaanite Cuneiform Texts of the Third Millennium,* tr. Matthew L. Jaffe (Malibu: Undena, 1979), pp. 10–11; also his "The Royal Archive of Tell-Mardikh-Ebla," *Biblical Archaeologist,* 39 (1976), 50. Kramer, "The First Case of Apple-Polishing," in *History Begins,* p. 11, tells of a Sumerian student who took the tablet he had prepared in the scribal school home and recited it before his father—likely a common event for a student in the schools.

10. Erica Reiner, *A Linguistic Analysis of Akkadian* (The Hague: Mouton, 1966), pp. 34–35.

11. A useful grammar is Arthur Ungnad and Lubor Matouš, *Grammatik des Akkadischen* (Munich: Verlag C. H. Beck, 1969).

12. For a history of Akkadian lexicography and the plan of the *Chicago Assyrian Dictionary,* see I. J. Gelb, "Introduction" to volume l(A), Part 1 (1964), pp. vii–xxiii.

13. The subscript 5 after the *SIG* (named from its Sumerian value) indicates it is the fifth sign discovered that can be read *sig.* By convention, the first sign discovered carries no indication *(sig);* the second is marked by an acute accent *(síg);* the third by a grave accent *(sìg).* After that, the subscript 4, 5,… x is attached. The accents, then, do *not* indicate vowel quality. On the other hand, vowel length is marked, as in *ilugilgāmeš* and *tappâ.*

14. CAD 21.41–43.

15. The transliteration and a translation of the poem from which this is taken can be found in Carlos A. Benito, *"Enki and Ninmah" and "Enki and the World Order"* (Ph.D. dissertation, University of Pennsylvania, 1969), 11. 89–93.

16. E.g., E.A. Speiser, tr., *The Epic of Gilgamesh,* in *Ancient Near Eastern Texts Relating to the Old Testament,* ed. James B. Pritchard (Princeton: Princeton University Press, 1969), p. 93; Tigay, 235.
17. W. G. Lambert and A. R. Millard, *Atra-ḫasīs* (Oxford: Clarendon Press, 1969), p. 88.
18. Tigay, 239–240, offers this as an explanation: "Perhaps the contribution of the full account [of the Flood] to *Gilgamesh* is not to be found in its meaning, but in its artistic function as a digression within the epic. With Gilgamesh having finally reached Utnapishtim, the epic's audience is anxious to know whether he will at long last learn the secret of immortality, a secret the audience, too, would no doubt like to learn. Depending on individual members of the audience, the digression may have the effect of building suspense or relaxing it. Perhaps at the beginning of the flood narrative the suspense would be heightened, but as the narrative continues, its own intrinsic interest would begin to distract attention from Gilgamesh's quest and ultimately relax the suspense over that quest. Such relaxation might help prepare the audience's mood for Utnapishtim's disappointing answer and the subdued conclusion of the epic. Like all such suggestions, this one is obviously speculative."
19. Paul Ricoeur, *The Rule of Metaphor,* tr. Robert Czerny (Toronto: University of Toronto Press, 1977), develops the point and traces the history of explanations of metaphor from Aristotle to the present. Metaphor is the subject of much investigation today, e.g., issues of *New Literary History,* 6 (1974) and *Poetics,* 4 (1975) devoted entirely to metaphor.
20. Shamash's advice is compatible, we feel, with what Giorgio Buccellati, "Wisdom and Not: the Case of Mesopotamia," *Journal of the American Oriental Society,* 101 (1981), 35–48, considers the "wisdom" tradition, Ea's with what he calls the "other" tradition.
21. This is Mircea Eliade's "mythical time" of his *The Myth of the Eternal Return* (Princeton: Princeton University Press, 1954), p. 35; elsewhere he refers to it as *illud tempus,* sacred time; see *The Sacred and the Profane,* tr. Willard R. Trask (New York: Harcourt, Brace, 1959), pp. 80–85.

❋ ❋ ❋

In the essays that follow, gaps in the selections are marked with [□].

Philological and Literary Studies in English Since 1982

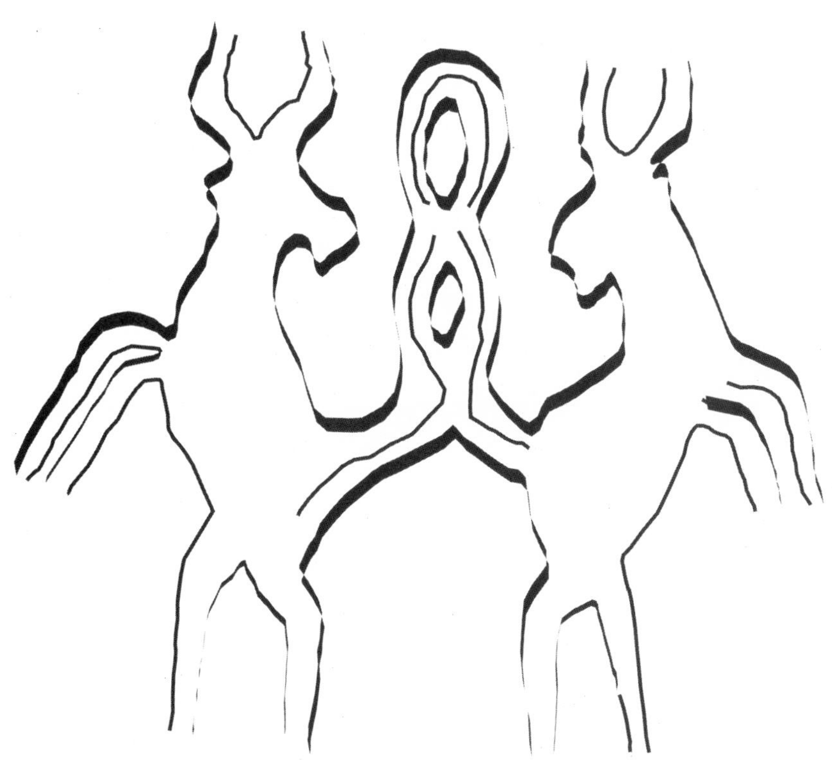

JEFFREY H. TIGAY
"Summary: The Evolution of *The Gilgamesh Epic*"

The painstaking care with which Jeffrey H. Tigay examined the evidence for the development—"evolution"—of *Gilgamesh* in its many versions quickly changed the direction of *Gilgamesh* studies. Tigay's book-length 1982 investigation of Sumerian forerunners, versions in different languages, and especially the very detailed account of *differences* between Old Babylonian and Standard Babylonian versions neatly synthesized more than one hundred years of scholarship, and his conclusions are now accepted as a matter of course. The net result has been the greater confidence with which Assyriologists have been able to turn to detailed *literary* studies of the poem.

Tigay showed the way at least seven Sumerian compositions were combined into a "unified epic on a grand scale." Some changes, e.g., the role of Shamash in the narrative, had a profound impact on the Standard Babylonian version, which was composed by the Middle Babylonian Period. Tigay emphasizes changes and borrowings in the evolution of the epic, and he traces the decreasing freedom of revision after the Old Babylonian Period.

Tigay also sketched the "afterlife" of the epic in Greek, Mandaic, and Aramaic literature—a study that has now been expanded, especially by Stephanie Dalley (see below).

It is safe to say that all English translations that have appeared since the publication of *The Evolution of the Gilgamesh Epic*—a period that has seen more translations by specialists and non-specialists than any comparable period since George Smith discovered the tablets—owe a major debt to Tigay's book, which settled many disputes about the Gilgamesh texts and rendered obsolete translations that make a patchwork of Sumerian, Hittite, Old Babylonian, and Standard Babylonian versions. Of major finds, only the discovery of an Elamite version has come since Tigay published *The Evolution of the Gilgamesh Epic.* (For the possible impact of the Elamite text, see Temple, below.) (Ed.)

We may summarize the development of *The Gilgamesh Epic* as follows.

The historical Gilgamesh was a king of Uruk during the Second Early Dynastic Period in Sumer (ca. 2700–2500). Later inscriptions credit him with building the wall of Uruk and rebuilding a shrine in Nippur. This by itself is hardly the stuff of which epics are made, and Gilgamesh's place in epic tradition is presumably due to more colorful achievements which have not come down to us in sources of a historical character. The adventures of Gilgamesh mentioned in the Sumerian stories and the Akkadian epic are so overlaid with legendary and mythical motifs that one can only speculate about their possible historical basis. They may reflect certain aspects of the magical/priestly and military roles that Gilgamesh would have played as the ruler of Uruk, and conceivably a real preoccupation of his with death. On the other hand, some elements in these stories may be anachronistic projections of later events, and some are due to folkloristic and mythological imagination.

By the twenty-fifth century, Gilgamesh was regarded as a god. It is possible that the transition from oral to written transmission of stories about Gilgamesh may have begun by about this time. The Old Sumerian texts from Abu Salabikh date from approximately this period. Although none of them is about Gilgamesh, some are forerunners (in one case, virtually identical) of other literary works which, like the Sumerian Gilgamesh texts, are known to us in Old Babylonian copies (ca. 2000–1600). It is therefore not implausible that tales of Gilgamesh had likewise been put into writing by the twenty-fifth century (a tale about Gilgamesh reportedly found among the tablets from Ebla would confirm this). This would considerably reduce the period of exclusively oral transmission, but for the present, apart from the reported Ebla text, the earliest compositions about Gilgamesh known to us are the Sumerian tales, attested in Old Babylonian copies, but currently presumed to have been composed in the Ur III Period (ca. twenty-first century), something like half a millennium after Gilgamesh's lifetime.

At least seven separate Sumerian compositions about Gilgamesh are known, four of them highly mythical in character. These four were drawn on in different ways in the course of the development of the Akkadian *Gilgamesh Epic.* The Akkadian epic was given its original shape in the Old Babylonian Period by an Akkadian author who took over, in greater or lesser degree, the plots and themes of three or four of the Sumerian tales *(Gilgamesh and the Land of the Living; Gilgamesh, Enkidu, and the Netherworld; The Death of Gilgamesh;* and possibly *Gilgamesh and the Bull of Heaven).* Either translating freely from Sumerian or working from available Akkadian paraphrases, the author combined these plots and themes into a unified epic on a grand scale. As the central idea in this epic, the author seized upon a theme which was adumbrated in three of the Sumerian tales, Gilgamesh's concern with death and his futile desire to overcome it. The author advanced this theme to a central position in the story. To this end, Enkidu's death became the pivotal event which set Gilgamesh on a feverish search for the immortal flood hero (whose story existed in Sumerian, but had nothing to do with the tales about Gilgamesh), hoping to learn how he had overcome death. The author separated the themes of Enkidu's death and Gilgamesh's grief from their original context in the Sumerian *Gilgamesh, Enkidu, and the Netherworld* and placed them after the friends' victory over Huwawa (and possibly over the Bull of Heaven). To increase the emotional impact that Enkidu's death had on Gilgamesh, and perhaps to make the depth of Gilgamesh's grief more plausible, the author seized upon one or two references to Enkidu in the Sumerian sources as Gilgamesh's friend, rather than servant, and treated him consistently as Gilgamesh's friend and equal. He even went so far as to compose accounts of Gilgamesh's oppression of Uruk, and Enkidu's creation and early life, in order to explain why Enkidu was created and how he became Gilgamesh's friend.

The Sumerian tale that the Old Babylonian author drew upon most directly was *Gilgamesh and the Land of the Living,* which became the basis of the Cedar Mountain episode in the Akkadian epic. Among the important changes introduced in the Old Babylonian version of this episode are a complete reshaping of Gilgamesh's plans for the expedition, a new understanding of the role of Shamash and of the significance of Huwawa, and a new location for the Cedar Forest. Several of these changes reflected the new geographical orientation of Mesopotamian affairs in the Old Babylonian Period and the roles of Gilgamesh, Shamash, and Huwawa in Mesopotamian religion. Another Sumerian tale which was drawn upon in the Akkadian epic was *Gilgamesh and the Bull of Heaven,* which became the basis of the Bull of Heaven episode in Tablet VI. However, it is uncertain whether this story was incorporated into the epic in the Old Babylonian Period, or not until later. The Akkadian version of this story appears to have preserved traces of the anti-Ishtar tendencies of the Sumerian original and even added to them. Drawing upon sacred-marriage literature or rituals, the Akkadian version of this episode gave an entirely new cause for the conflict between Gilgamesh and Ishtar: Gilgamesh's spurning of Ishtar's proposal of marriage.

In addition to what he borrowed from the Sumerian tales about Gilgamesh, the Old Babylonian author added a hymnic introduction, in the style of Sumerian hymns about Gilgamesh and other kings (this hymn is still reflected, possibly in expanded form, in part c of the introduction in the late version). He further unified the epic with recurrent thematic and verbal motifs. He continued the process, already begun in the Sumerian tales, of drawing upon conventional formulas and wisdom sayings. One such saying, telling Gilgamesh how to enjoy his earthly life, since only the gods are immortal, looks like the author's message to the epic's audience.

By the Middle Babylonian Period (1600–1000), the epic was known internationally, both in Akkadian and in Hittite and Hurrian translations, with a little adaptation to the interests of the translators. The Akkadian version(s) of this period, as attested by fragmentary remains and, indirectly, by the Hittite translation, retained some similarities to the wording of the Old Babylonian version, but these witnesses also indicate that the wording of the epic was moving in the direction of the late version, at times coming quite close.

Toward the end of the Middle Babylonian Period, by the last half or quarter of the second millennium, the epic had attained a form which thereafter became standard throughout Mesopotamia. Although this late version is textually related to the Old Babylonian version and although its basic form, plot, and apparently its message do not differ from those of the Old Babylonian version, the late version displays considerable divergence from the Old Babylonian. Lines are reworded in degrees varying from negligible to complete, with some lines being dropped and many more added. In some cases the reformulation modernizes the language of the epic, and in a few cases the older text has been simplified, corrupted, or misunderstood; in many other cases, the editor seems to have simply revised according to his taste. Lines and sections are revised so as to be much more similar to related lines and sections in the late version, resulting in a repetitious, pedantic, and homogenized style. Numerous thematic and verbal motifs recur throughout the epic. In addition, entire sections or episodes are restructured. Certain theological changes occur. In one section, the sun-god is given a more direct role. Hostility to Ishtar seems to have run its course, to the extent that her claim to the Inanna temple is recognized, but that hostility is still reflected atavistically in the Bull of Heaven episode. The national gods Marduk and Ashur have not been admitted to this version, presumably because they had not attained sufficient prominence by the time that this version was formulated, and later, when they had, the epic had attained its standardized form and was no longer subject to theological revision.

Three major additions, attested at least for now only in copies of the late version, but not necessarily all added at the same time by the same editor, are the prologue, the flood story, and Tablet XII. The prologue, modeled on conventional literary forms, stresses the didactic significance of the epic, underscores its message with a passage that frames the first eleven tablets, and suggests that the epic is based on an inscription written by Gilgamesh himself. The flood narrative spells out at length what Utnapishtim presumably told Gilgamesh more briefly in the Old Babylonian version; this narrative is based on a late version of *Atrahasis* and was taken into *The Gilgamesh Epic* without too much modification (although the version in *Gilgamesh* seems to have intentionally suppressed references to divine thirst and hunger). Tablet XII brings the epic's picture of Gilgamesh closer to the role of ruler of the netherworld in which he was familiar in Mesopotamian religion. This tablet is a literal translation of part of a Sumerian composition, with minimal but significant deviations from the original. The addition of Tablet XII could be connected with the interest of incantation priests, like Sîn-leqi-unninnī, in Gilgamesh as ruler of the netherworld. With the late version, the epic achieved its maximal stability in content and wording, with only a small number of relatively insignificant variants separating its manuscripts.

There is no way of determining how many stages the epic went through between the Old Babylonian version known to us and the late version. Revision could have begun as early as the Old Babylonian Period and could be reflected in some of the fragments of the Middle Babylonian Period. Those fragments may reflect two or three different intermediate stages. They do not demonstrably represent the penultimate stage on which the final editor based his work, but since these fragments are at times quite close to the wording of the late version, it is possible that the final revision which produced that version was not very extensive. A comparison of the Middle Babylonian fragments with the late version permits a rough characterization of the changes which took place between the former and the latter, although we cannot identify the editor responsible for any particular change. Where the Middle Babylonian fragments are fairly well preserved, we get the impression that the changes in the late version did not involve extensive reformulation, but were generally limited to the substitution of equivalent words. But other fragments of this period, unfortunately less well preserved, at times indicate that more extensive reformulation went into producing their later equivalents. In the late version, apart from the wording, the order of some lines was rearranged, a few lines were dropped, and lines and entire passages were added. Many additions do not give the impression of originality: They include lines synonymously parallel to those to which they are adjoined; traditional and conventional descriptions; and some material modeled upon or related to other passages in the epic and contributing to its homogenized style.

In the evolution of the epic, a pattern of decreasing freedom of revision is discernible. The greatest degree of liberty is reflected in the composition of the Old Babylonian version, the only one which constitutes a really new composition in comparison to its forerunners. This version took from the Sumerian Gilgamesh tales at most plot outlines, and sometimes no more than an idea or theme; its wording of these tales is a completely free Akkadian paraphrase. It added to the tales many motifs from other compositions, and probably much that was original. No later version of *Gilgamesh* took as much liberty with its forerunner. The Hittite and Hurrian translations adapted the epic a little to Hittite and Hurrian interests, and the Hittite abridged the narrative, but the Hittite told the same story as the Akkadian epic (the Hurrian is too poorly attested to permit us to judge). The wording of the Hittite shows affinities with both the Old Babylonian and the late version. The Middle Babylonian Akkadian fragments also reflect the same story, worded in a way which approaches the wording of the late version. The late version, although it restructured the episodes, reworded the text extensively, and added supplementary material, is textually related to its Old and Middle Babylonian forerunners and also tells the same story. This version became so widely accepted in the first millennium that scribes were no longer able or willing to modify it in any substantial way (apart from the possibly later addition of Tablet XII as an appendix which was not integrated into the epic). In content and wording, this version became practically a *textus receptus*, which, so far as we can tell, was accepted as long as the epic was known.

Where Sîn-leqi-unninnī fits in this process we cannot say. Since he probably lived in the Middle Babylonian Period, he cannot have been the author of the Old Babylonian version. The first-millennium catalogue of cuneiform literature which says that "the series *Gilgamesh* (is) according to Sîn-leqi-unninnī the ex[orcistpriest]" (ÉŠ.GÀR ^d*Gilgameš ša* pī ^Id*Sîn-leqi-unninnī* LÚ.M[AŠ.MAŠ])[1] was doubtless understood to mean that Sîn-leqi-unninnī was the author of the late version, since that was the only version known in that period. The very fact that the epic is attributed to him indicates that Sîn-leqi-unninnī must have made some important, perhaps definitive, contribution to its formulation. It is certainly possible that he was the editor of the late version, but this is not necessarily the case. It often happens that a work of literature is attributed to a figure who made a decisive contribution to its development, even though a later form of that work is the one actually in use, as is the case, for example, with *The Iliad* of Homer, the *Mishnah* of Rabbi Judah the Prince, or—to cite a modern example—*Gesenius' Hebrew Grammar.*[2] It is possible that Sîn-leqi-unninnī produced a Middle Babylonian form of *Gilgamesh* which had a substantial enough influence on the final form of the epic to associate his name with it permanently, but that the form found in the first-millennium copies was a later revision of Sîn-leqi-unninnī's text. Still, it is equally possible that he was the editor of the late version.

The Gilgamesh Epic drew heavily upon Mesopotamian literary tradition. Not only did the author of the Old Babylonian version base his epic on older Sumerian tales about Gilgamesh, but he and the editors who succeeded him made extensive use of materials and literary forms originally unrelated to Gilgamesh. The epic opens with a standard type of hymnic-epic prologue, and parts of the introduction and end of the epic are modeled on royal hymns and inscriptions, and on hymns in praise of temples and their cities. Royal hymns supplied the model for the description of the creation of Gilgamesh, while Enkidu's creation was modeled on that of mankind in creation myths. Mythical motifs about primitive man also supplied the model for the description of Enkidu's early life. The description of how Gilgamesh oppressed Uruk may have been modeled upon folklore motifs or ancient royal practices. This is not certain, but it is clear that the outline of the description is based on a stock literary pattern and that this pattern is used to account for the creation of Enkidu. Ishtar's proposal of marriage to Gilgamesh appears to be modeled on sacred-marriage texts or the sacred marriage ritual. A curse introduction and a curse in the epic seem to be modeled on passages in *Ishtar,* and Enkidu's deathbed vision of the netherworld, which certainly draws upon some conventional material, may also be indebted to that poem. The flood story is based on the account in *Atrahasis.*

Only rarely is it possible, as in the case of the flood story, to point to a particular non-Gilgamesh text as the very source from which *The Gilgamesh Epic* drew a motif or pattern. The parallels are in some cases too numerous, and in most cases insufficiently detailed to permit this.[3] The parallels permit us, at most, to identify certain circles of tradition (or customs) in which particular motifs were at home and from which they were drawn into the epic.

The present study lends a measure of vindication to the theoretical approach by which Morris Jastrow recognized the diversity of the sources, some about Gilgamesh and some not, which underlay the epic, and succeeded in identifying some of them in a general way. Of course Jastrow could hardly give a precise, detailed description of the sources, since they were not then available. Now that we have so many more texts of the epic and of its sources, we can see how extensively the late version, and even the much earlier Old Babylonian version, differ from the Sumerian sources, for example, and how much room there would be for error in trying to reconstruct those sources from the texts of the epic alone. For the literary critic, this is sobering. But the theoretical approach did not lead Jastrow so very wide of the mark in his general conception of elements the epic was composed from. Hopefully the knowledge gained about literary history in cases where the evolution of a composition can be studied empirically, coupled with a fuller knowledge of ancient history in general, will enable us to use the theoretical approach in a more sophisticated and realistic way, when we must.

What is perhaps most useful about our ability to consult the sources of a composition is the opportunity it gives us to see what was borrowed and what was changed. It is, of course, possible for a writer to borrow without modifying his source in any thoughtful way, and undoubtedly there were hacks who did just this in ancient Mesopotamia. But in the case of *The Gilgamesh Epic*, the use of traditional materials shows rather that the author and editors reflected seriously on their literary heritage and found in it new possibilities for themselves and their audiences. What they borrowed, they modified and put to use in novel ways. The epic's prologue is of a type standard in hymns and epics, but in listing the hero's virtues, it replaces the usual heroic epithets with phrases describing the wisdom Gilgamesh acquired. The hymnic description of Uruk looks like a standard temple-city hymn, but placed in the mouth of Gilgamesh, at the end of Tablet XI, it expresses the futility of his quest to overcome death and his reconciliation to immortality-by-reputation-and-achievement only. The pattern of oppression, outcry, and divine response in the sending of an agent of deliverance appears in the epic with a new and more complex twist in which the agent of deliverance distracts the oppressor and then becomes his friend. Motifs from early human history in the creation and early life of Enkidu are used to advance the epic's message by exemplifying the benefits of human life which the epic stresses in lieu of immortality. The flood story, presumably told in the first place because of its intrinsic interest, and serving in *Atrahasis* to explain the origin of infant mortality and other problems, is used in the epic to help explain why the gods' gift of immortality to Utnapishtim is not repeatable. In most cases, the traditional material has been freely recast in accordance with the writers' purposes. As a result, what were originally tales about a particular hero's life and exploits became a vehicle for exploring the problem of mortality and the way to live with the knowledge of ultimate death. Such creative use of borrowed material nicely illustrates the remarks of Wellek and Warren on the role of "commonplaces (topoi), recurrent themes and images" in literary history:

> No author felt inferior or unoriginal because he used, adapted, and modified themes inherited from tradition and sanctioned by antiquity... To work within a given tradition and adopt its devices is perfectly compatible with emotional power and artistic value. The real critical problems in this kind of study arise when we reach the stage of weighing and comparing, of showing how one artist utilizes the achievements of another artist, when we watch the transforming power.[4]

Thanks to the ample documentation available for the evolution of *The Gilgamesh Epic,* we can trace the steps by which its author and editors turned a group of commonplace tales into a powerful epic which expressed universal fears and aspirations so well that the epic lasted for well over a thousand years.

* * *

NOTES

1. Lambert, *JCS* 11:11; *JCS* 16:66 (K9717, etc., rev. 10). The meanings of the phrase *ša pī*, here translated "according to," and of related idioms consisting of a preposition followed by *pī*, are elusive. Since *pī* means literally "mouth," these idioms are sometimes used to refer to an oral source (see, e.g., Lambert, in *GSL*, p. 44), but they are often used simply to mean "according to," and this usage is sometimes found with reference to written sources (see *AHw*, pp. 873–74, *sub* 11). On the reference to "the series *Gilgamesh*," see Lambert, *JCS* 16:77 and Shaffer, "Sources," p. 3, n. 1.
2. Without entering into the Homeric question, I am assuming that Homer composed an early version of *The Iliad;* the vulgate text in use since, apparently, shortly before the Christian era, is certainly later than Homer (see Murray, chap. 12). On the *Mishnah*, see Urbach, col. 104. The work published under the English title *Gesenius' Hebrew Grammar* is a revision by A. E. Cowley of the twenty-eighth German edition, revised by E. Kautzsch (1909), of Gesenius' original work published in 1813.
3. Cf. Wellek and Warren, *Theory of Literature*, p. 258, on the pitfalls of "parallel-hunting."
4. Ibid., p. 259.

❋ ❋ ❋

Wilfred G. Lambert
"Gilgamesh in Literature and Art: The Second and First Millennia"

With the evolution of the literary Gilgamesh traced by Jeffrey H. Tigay, W. G. Lambert turns to the difficult task of identifying Gilgamesh in art.

Attempts to find Gilgamesh or episodes of *Gilgamesh* represented in Mesopotamian art have led to so many misidentifications that Lambert has to argue that the comparison of pictures and texts should be pursued, but with a great deal of skepticism. He identifies two motifs from Second and First Millennia art, mainly on cylinder seals, that can be safely related to the Gilgamesh narrative poems. The first is the episode in which Gilgamesh and Enkidu kill Huwawa/Humbaba. The second, not included here, is a scene that involves killing the Bull of Heaven.

Evidence that the scenes depict Gilgamesh episodes derives, e.g., from the presentation of two heroes, not just one, and a variation in presenting one or the other doing the actual killing of Huwawa. Lambert provides solid evidence to show that the originally benign guardian-figure, Laḫmu, came to represent Huwawa and, later, in Greece the dreaded Gorgon, slain by Perseus. The "Face of Huwawa," known from texts and depicted in clay, is the Mesopotamian prototype of Gorgon's face. Finally, Lambert notes that the popularity of Gilgamesh in literary texts is not matched by artistic representations. Although he has been able to trace the development of two motifs through two thousand years, the number of cylinder seal impressions of the two scenes is quite small. *Figures 1–9 have been re-drawn.* (Ed.)

Study of the content of ancient Mesopotamian art is severely hampered by lack of captions, which have been so helpful in the study of Greek vase painting. Some of the commonest Mesopotamian artistic motifs are unidentifiable from texts. For example, the stylized palm tree, so ubiquitous in later second- and earlier first-millennium art of Babylonia, Assyria and related areas, what moderns tend to call "the sacred tree" or (worse) "the tree of life," seems to be unknown in texts. Attempts in the other direction, that is to discover in art depictions of gods, persons and events known from literature, have been a little more successful. At least no one doubts that the figure being borne aloft by an eagle on Akkadian cylinder seals is Etana, king of Kish, whose attempted ascent to heaven is narrated in a Babylonian epic.[1] But, of course, Gilgamesh is the Sumerian king and hero better known from literature, and more appealing to Westerners because of the tragic element in the Babylonian Gilgamesh Epic. Attempts to see him in ancient art began already with George Smith, the first decipherer and translator of portions of the Epic. His attraction to the figure of Gilgamesh in the Babylonian Epic was matched by his fascination for the scenes on Akkadian cylinders showing heroes grappling with lions and sundry bovines. Accordingly he identified the nude hero with three curls on either side of his face as Gilgamesh.[2] This approach to the subject has continued, with a climax in 1979. In that year a whole book on these lines appeared: *Gilgamesh and Enkidu* (in Russian) by V.K. Afanasieva. The present writer is very skeptical. The only certain thing was pointed out by E. Porada in a paper read to the Rencontre Assyriologique Internationale in 1958: that the artistic motifs go back beyond the historical figure of Gilgamesh, so if in the Akkad period Gilgamesh is meant by the hero mentioned, this is at some point in time reinterpretation. There is no difficulty in this whatsoever, but none-the-less there are, as it seems to the present writer, two major objections. First, in Akkadian art this hero is commonly accompanied by a bovine figure doing exactly the same as the nude hero with three curls on each side of his face. This bovine has therefore been identified with Enkidu, Gilgamesh' companion on his adventures. The texts, however, make clear that Enkidu had a human frame, was in fact almost identical with Gilgamesh,[3] and there seems to be no hint of bovine connections anywhere. The attempt to identify Enkidu with the god Enkimdu is misconceived. Enkidu is an old Sumerian personal name meaning "Lord of the good place",[4] unrelated to Enkimdu apart from the initial En-. The latter is god of irrigation and arable farming, not of stock-raising. Secondly, the hero in question is plainly associated with the god Enki on many other Akkadian seals, with whom Gilgamesh has no connection, and there is good reason to identify him with the Laḫmu.[5] In contrast, there is second- and first-millennium art where it appears virtually certain that two scenes with Gilgamesh are shown, one with a demon, the other with a monster. □

Any attempted comparison of texts and pictures must of course be made with a good measure of skepticism. The ancient artists and their clients drew from their backgrounds a range of mythology and legend far greater than that to which even the best-read modern scholar can claim. Although we may feel that some ancient depiction must refer to what we happen to know from those ancient texts which have come down to us by the accidents of discovery, such a feeling must be supported by exhaustive knowledge of the comparable surviving material considered from every angle. Otherwise the subject may become ridiculous, and for many years some have refused on principle to give names to any ancient figures, since such identifications could be wrong. The rest of this paper is intended as an antidote to this attitude.

The first item for consideration is the terracotta plaque in the Berlin Museum (fig. 1).[6] A monstrous creature in the centre—a strange face and long hair, feline paws and a bird's talons for feet—is being killed by two human-looking figures, the one on the left bearded, the one on the right not. Both are holding down the monster with their feet, the bearded one also grips a paw while the beardless one holds the monster's long hair and is about to drive his sword into the creature's neck. A smaller figure, as if in the background, stands at the far left. It is proposed as a working hypothesis for the moment to interpret this scene as showing bearded Gilgamesh and beardless Enkidu killing Ḫuwawa. Three points combine to refer this to the Sumerian rather than the Babylonian version. First, the extra figure. In the Sumerian text young men of the town Uruk accompany Gilgamesh and Enkidu on the trip. The Babylonian text says nothing about any such escort and clearly implies that the two heroes were alone. Secondly, in the Sumerian text Enkidu is Gilgamesh' servant and so would look different, while the Babylonian text stresses how similar they were, identical save that Gilgamesh was a little taller. Thirdly, in the Sumerian Enkidu puts in the knife, which act Gilgamesh does in the Babylonian version. However, the differences from the written Gilgamesh stories must not be overlooked. Neither Sumerian nor Babylonian versions so far as preserved refer to the use of feet to pin down the monster.[7] Neither version details Ḫuwawa's long hair. However, these matters are not fatal objections to the identification being proposed, and will be considered further below. To judge from style, the only available criterion, this plaque is Old Babylonian in date, somewhere between c. 2000 and c. 1600 B.C.

This same scene appears later on cylinder seals. Impressions of a seal on a Nuzi tablet (fig. 2)[8] show the same two figures, though on opposite sides as compared with the clay plaque, both, as before, holding down the monster with their feet, and, as before, the younger-looking one using his sword. There is a difference in that the younger-looking one is not holding the monster's hair. The style of this seal is typical Mitanni, and even if it were an heirloom bequeathed to the person for whom it was rolled on the Nuzi tablets it could hardly be older than c. 1500 B.C. Thus it was cut after the Sumerian text had been lost. If the engraver had any literary basis either he used a Babylonian version not known to us, or he was not bothered about who actually did the killing. However, most likely the engraver depended on an artistic tradition with oral explanation. First-millennium seals are somewhat more abundant. One in Assyrian linear style (fig. 3)[9] shows the same basic scene: the two figures hold down the monster with their feet and—both this time—by the hair which hangs in two locks either side of the face, while the less important one is about to drive in his sword. In this case they are distinguished by both length of beard and by dress. The figure we take as Gilgamesh is clad in robes normally worn by gods in the art of this period. If the small figure to the right is really part of the scene, it suggests the Sumerian version, but on seals juxtaposition does not necessarily guarantee participation. Another Assyrian linear style seal of about the same date (fig. 4),[10] but lacking the bottom part and worn, while clearly in the same tradition does not allow similar specification due to its condition. The engraving on a situla of Luristan type (fig. 5),[11] no doubt dating from the earlier part of the first millennium B.C., also belongs to this tradition and is important in that the designs on such objects are generally based on Babylonian rather than Assyrian models. The only comment needed here is that the better-dressed figure, Gilgamesh as we take him, is now about to cut off the head of the fallen being, who in this case is depicted very little differently from Enkidu. This version of who struck the final blow is repeated in a fine Neo-Assyrian drilled style seal (fig. 6),[12] where, further, both Gilgamesh and Enkidu hold Ḫuwawa's hair. In this case it is very doubtful whether the extra small figure is meant as part of the scene. He is the common worshipper figure in cultic settings of this period, used as a filler here. This seal probably dates from c. 800–700 B.C. A fine, modelled style seal excavated at Assur (fig. 7)[13] needs no comment beyond the drawing of attention to the big, round face surrounded by hair. It is probably a little later than the previous one, say c. 750–650 B.C. Still another Neo-Assyrian modelled style cylinder of about the same date (fig. 8) is very similar, though there is less hair. The extra figure in this case, a worshipper, is part of a separate scene, having the spade of Marduk and the stylus of Nabû to which he directs his devotions.

To sum up, it will not be doubted that this material attests one artistic tradition, and since it all comes from areas where the continuity in cultural matters is well known for the periods involved, it is hard to suppose that there was more than one understanding of the scene during these periods and within these areas. The unusual features of the scene are, first, the active participation of two heroes in the slaying of the monster. In ancient Mesopotamia most such episodes, as with Ningirsu/Ninurta, Marduk and Tišpak, involve a single hero. Secondly, it is curious that of these two the least senior as depicted has the honor of finishing off the monster, at least in the earlier examples, but the later specimens (without there being a break in the tradition) show the more senior figure completing the victory by killing the monster. All these unusual features are explained by the assumption that the scene from the Gilgamesh Epic is depicted. The earlier artistic representations depend on the Sumerian form of the story as we know it, and the change early in the first millennium reflects a move to the Babylonian version on the part of the artists. It seems extremely unlikely to the present writer that there could have been any other narrative, written or oral, over these centuries with precisely these peculiarities, of which no trace as yet has been discovered in written remains. The differences, or rather details of the depictions which do not occur in the written Gilgamesh stories, the long hair of Ḫuwawa and the holding down of this creature with the feet of Gilgamesh and Enkidu, can be explained along with the very different versions of Ḫuwawa in the examples just presented. If the artists, starting in the Old Babylonian period, were illustrators of an oral and written story, lacking any iconographical tradition for this scene, then it is understandable that they would have improvised from originally unrelated iconographic motifs.[15] Thus the Akkadian hero with six locks, originally the Laḫmu, becomes in this tradition not Gilgamesh but Ḫuwawa.

There is indeed a variant artistic tradition which confirms this suggestion. As before, it is first attested on an Old Babylonian terracotta (figure 9)[16] of which several incomplete examples were excavated at Larsa, not allowing a full reconstruction. One complete example was found on the surface, but eroded so that the details are lost. The scene as a whole is clear: Ḫuwawa is in the middle, but his two attackers, one either side, are not so easily distinguished since the upper parts of the one on the left are preserved only on the eroded example. In dress there is no clear distinction between the two. The one on the left seems to have longer hair, reaching down to the shoulders, but it is not certain that he has a beard, though he may. Both are gripping the victim's hair and both appear to be driving swords into the victim. The one on the right has his blade clearly entering the victim's neck, but the blade of the one on the left ends at the victim's armpit, an unreal strike. Probably he is meant to be threatening only. Because of the hair and because he is taller we take the figure on the left as Gilgamesh, so that Enkidu here is actually killing Ḫuwawa. The scene is given a geographical setting. The line of cone shapes along the bottom (the complete terracotta may well have had a band of several such rows superimposed one on the other) indicates mountainous terrain, and the two trees are meant as the "cedars". A man is climbing the one tree with a rope trailing down to the ground, something not known from the written records. Perhaps the individual artist added this item as a detail of supposed local colour.

* * *

PLATES

Figure 1

Figure 2

Figure 3

Figure 4

Figure 5

Figure 6

Figure 7

Figure 8

Figure 9

NOTES

□ 1. While the identification remains plausible, the problems have never been considered. The story is first known from an Old Babylonian copy, A.T. Clay, *Babylonian Records in the Library of J. Pierpont Morgan IV* (1923) no. 2, and this is alluded to in *The Sumerian King List* (ed. T. Jacobsen, *Assyriological Studies* 11 (1939) p. 81), the earliest copies of which are no older. Thus the literary attestation is only known some 200–300 years later than the date of the seals. Also the items commonly associated on the seals with the figure being borne aloft (dogs, sheep, goats, shepherd and potter (?)) do not appear in the texts. The artistic motif of the eagle bearing up a man appears much later, apparently borrowed directly or indirectly from the Akkadian seals, on the gold bowl of Hasanlu (E. Porada, *Ancient lran, The Art of Pre-lslamic Times* (London 1965) p. 98).

2. G. Smith, *The Chaldean Account of Genesis* (London, 1876), Frontispiece, cf. plate after p. 174 and pp. 238f. with fig.

3. There is no adequate text of the epic in print, and the best translation is that of A. Schott revised by W. von Soden: *Das Gilgamesch-Epos* (Stuttgart, 1982). For the passage referred to see p. 28 line 179f.

4. The phrase ki.du$_{10}$ "good place" is well attested in Early Dynastic personal names, and the name en.ki.du$_{10}$.ga "lord of the good place" is cited from the Fara tablet VAT 12531 ii by A. Deimel, *Die Inschriften von Fara 111 (40. Wissenschaftliche Veröffentlichung der Deutschen Orient-Gesellschaft,* 1922) p. 31*. It is no argument against this etymology that the name is not construed as a genitive construction in the Sumerian epics. The grammatical elements of a personal name are not necessarily taken up in the sentence already in the later third millennium.

5. F.A.M. Wiggermann, in working on the first millennium clay figurines and related rituals, has discovered that in this material the human-looking figure with six curls is the Laḫmu ('*Exit* Talim!' *Jaarbericht van het Vooraziatisch-Egyptisch Genootschap Ex Oriente Lux* 27 (1981–82) 90–105). This fits the artificial Sumerian equivalent of the Akkadian *laḫmu* (in real Sumerian la.ḫa.ma is written) in a bilingual text of Tukulti-Ninurta I: LÚ X ŚIG.SUD ('MAN X LONG HAIR'; see the present writer in *Iraq* 38 90 obv. 11). On this basis everything hangs together. In texts there is a plurality of Laḫmus, associated with the 'sea' or 'Apsu', and forming Enki's constabulary in Sumerian myths. On Akkadian seals there is also a plurality of these heroes, who hold the 'gate post' in association with Enki/Ea (see e.g. R.M. Boehmer, *Die Entwicklung der Glyptik während der Akkad-Zeit (Untersuchungen zur Assyriologie und vorderasiatischen Archäologie,* 4, 1965), Abb. 488, 499–502). The association of Enki is confirmed by Old Babylonian terracottas showing this hero holding a jar from which streams of water flow, and the same hero holds the flowing jar to water two buffaloes on the well-known Akkad seal of Ibni-Šarrum (e. g. [P. Amiet], *Bas-Reliefs imaginaires de l'Ancien Orient* (exhibition catalogue, Hôtel de la Monnaie, Paris, June–October 1973) no. 231).

This seal raises the question that on many Akkadian seals the same hero is grappling with buffaloes, lions and similar animals, and that alongside him a 'bull-man' is doing the same. In these contexts there is no demonstrable connection with Enki/Ea, and it could be argued that in these contexts therefore the same artistic type represents an entirely different mythological figure, perhaps Gilgamesh. There is of course no law against speculation, but in view of the quantity of mythology on Akkadian seals so far totally unknown from written sources (e.g., the "winged gate" and the Bird-man before Enki/Ea), it is unwise to push a particular interpretation *faute de mieux. A priori* it is more likely that one common figure in the art of one and the same period and area represented one, and not two totally different mythological figures, and not enough is known of the Laḫmu in the Akkad period to affirm that he could not occur in contest scenes. In any case this one figure cannot be considered without taking in account related figures. We express no opinion on the identity of this figure in Early Dynastic times. The archaeological evidence is summed up by R.H. Boehmer, art. *Held, Reallexikon der Assyriologie* IV (1972–75) 294ff., but there seems to be not the least shred of written evidence from the Early Dynastic periods that is pertinent. □

6. VA 7246, see D. Opitz, *Archiv für Orientforschung* 5 (1928/9) 207ff., and (from another negative?) *Propyläen Kunstgeschichte* 14 (Berlin, 1975) pl. 186a.

7. R. Opificius, *op. cit.* 287, interprets this action otherwise "auch bei zeitgenössischen Szenen pflegt der Fürst seinem besiegten Gegner den Fuss auf den Körper zu setzen," referring to the Old Babylonian victory stele, *Revue d' Assyriologie* 7 (1910) pls. v–vi. One must, however, distinguish between placing the foot on the body of a fallen victim as a gesture of victory when the real battle is over (seen also on Old Babylonian terracottas, e.g. R. Opificius, *Das altbabylonische Terrakottarelief (Untersuchungen zur Assyriologie und vorderasiatischen Archäologie,* 2, 1961), no. 480; A. Parrot, *Iraq* 31 (1969) pl. viii a–b; and in contemporary glyptic; *idem, loc. cit.* c and *Mission archéologique de Mari* II, *Le Palais* (Paris, 1959), iii, *Documents et Monuments,* pp. 169–185) and placing the feet on arms and legs of a victim while the battle is still on. Further, later versions of the scene under discussion (see below) show the arms and legs of the attacking heroes intertwined with those of the victim, clearly having understood the older version as showing the legs of the heroes being used to restrain the victim.

8. The impressions on the tablet VAT 6039 have been published in one drawing only, first in O. Weber, *Altorientalische Siegelbilder* (Leipzig, 1920), no. 268a, reproduced by H.J. Kantor, *Journal of Near Eastern Studies* 21 (1962) 115 fig.19 B. See also E. Porada, *Annual of the American Schools of Oriental Research* 24 (1947) nos. 768–773, which show similar but less well preserved scenes.

9. E. Porada, *Corpus of Ancient Near Eastern Seals in North American Collections* I, *The Collections of the Pierpont Morgan Library* ([New York], 1948), no. 686.

10. Medelhavsmuseet, Stockholm, MM 1956-122, reproduced before by H.H. von der Osten, Medelhavsmuseet, *Bulletin* 1 (1961) 27 no. 13.

11. P. Calmeyer, *Reliefbronzen im babylonischen Stil.* Bayer. Akad. d. Wiss., phil. hist. Kl. N. F. Heft 73 (München, 1973) p. 45. P. Calmeyer, *Acta Praehistorica et Archaeologica* 1 (1970) 81ff.
12. M. Noveck, *The Mark of Ancient Man. Ancient Near Eastern Stamp Seals and Cylinder Seals. The Gorelick Collection* (Brooklyn Museum Catalogue, 1975) no. 41. Cf. P. Amiet, *Journal of the American Oriental Society* 100 (1980) 186.
13. A. Moortgat, *Vorderasiatische Rollsiegel* (Berlin, 1940) no. 608.
14. BM 89763, previously published in drawing by W.H. Ward, *The Seal Cylinders of Western Asia* (Washington, 1910), no. 644. The inscription, in Assyrian cuneiform, reads *šá*[md]*MAŠ.PAP.PAP* "Property of Ninurta-aḫa-uṣur" (or, "of Ninurta-nāṣir-aḫi"). For completeness, note the faience cylinder seal of first-millennium date from Nippur, D. E. McCown and R. C. Haines, *Nippur 1* (*Oriental Institute Publications,* 78) pl. 113 no. 13. It certainly attests the scene under discussion, but is too crudely executed to offer any light. Opificius, *Hundert Jahre Berliner Gesellschaft für Anthropologie, Ethnologie und Urgeschichte* II (Berlin, 1970) 289, cites for this same scene the Akkadian cylinder R.M. Boehmer, *Die Entwicklung* (see footnote 5), Abb. 482, where two identically clad heroes (the apparent difference in headgear seems to be due to damage alone) hold a third hero (differently attired), already down on one knee, by beard and hair. This cannot be reconciled with the Sumerian tradition of Gilgamesh and Enkidu as master and slave, and the defeated figure has no features which suggest a demon. So there is no basis for interpreting this scene as one with Gilgamesh .
15. The Berlin terracotta shows two clear and distinct influences. The lion's paws and eagle's talons derive from the Mesopotamian tradition of the *mušḫuššu,* the monster known from Old Akkadian to Late Babylonian art, most clearly depicted in enamelled bricks on the walls of Babylon as rebuilt by Nebuchadnezzar II (see the present writer in *Cahiers du Centre d'Étude du Proche-Orient Ancien* 2 (Leuven, 1985) 87ff. Sumerian literary texts specify a monster (ušumgal) as having "a lion's paws and talons of an eagle" (šu pirig.gá umbin ḫu.rí.in([mušen]).na), once as a poetic description of the god Ninurta (H. Radau, *The Babylonian Expedition of the University of Pennsylvania. Series A: Cuneiform Texts,* 29/1 (1911) 4 rev. 3ff.), once to describe the leader of seven "heroes" at Utu's disposal when Gilgamesh' journey to the cedar mountain was being planned *(Journal of Cuneiform Studies* 1 (1947) 10 37). However, the face of the monster on the terracotta seems to have been influenced, if only at second hand, by the Egyptian Bes, as has been noted for the Ḫuwawa faces of the masks. E. Porada has drawn my attention to Near Eastern examples of Bes figures: the bone plaque found "in der tiefsten Schicht der hethitischen Periode" at Alaca Höyük (H. Z. Kosay, *Ausgrabungen von Alaca Höyük* (Ankara, 1966), p. 31 and pl. xliv, A1/a 88), and the limestone statuette found in the "dépôt d'offrandes de la pro-cella du temple aux obélisques (levée XVIII)" at

Byblos (M. Dunand, *Fouilles de Byblos* II (Paris, 1950–58), p. 767 and pl. xcv, no. 15377). On Near Eastern Bes figures generally, see V. Wilson, *Levant* 7 (1975) 77–103, and for the present interest pp. 83–84 especially.

16. A. Parrot published six pieces of this plaque in *Syria* 45 (1968) 229–230, figs. 22 (bottom left and right pieces) and 23 (all four); and the complete but eroded one was published by J.-L. Huot in J.-L. Huot (ed.), *Larsa. Travaux de 1985* (Paris, 1989) p. 164, also alluding to another, unpublished piece in the Louvre AO 22563 = L.651) on p. 169. The other three pieces given by Parrot (fig. 22, upper two and middle lower) look related, being pieces of other plaques apparently showing other scenes of epic character. The lower middle fragment appears to show three tree trunks held together, but a little apart at the bases, by ropes, their upper parts (now missing) evidently meeting or crossing, while two men, one on either side, are pulling down on ropes. Is this a scene from the felling of cedars in the Epic of Gilgamesh? If so, there were at least two plaques illustrating this episode.

* * *

Benjamin Foster
"Gilgamesh: Sex, Love and the Ascent of Knowledge"

Benjamin Foster presents a very careful transliteration, translation, and commentary of many short passages in *Gilgamesh,* and in that sense the essay might usefully be compared with A. Leo Oppenheim's philological notes on selected passages. The contrast with Oppenheim, though, reflects the confidence in the text and in the development of the Gilgamesh tradition, for Foster uses the individual passages to develop what he takes is a major theme of the poem, the thematics of love.

In a volume devoted to *Love and Death in the Ancient Near East,* Foster's contribution is to see love and knowledge not only as contents of *Gilgamesh* but as part of the poetic technique of oppositions that the poet unites and dissolves, and also in the language of the poem, where distortions of speech occur. Foster's handling of narrative voices and silence, for example, allows him to go beyond the literary analysis offered by Thorkild Jacobsen. Foster's essay, in turn, opened a debate about the images and roles of the feminine in *Gilgamesh* that continues in the 1990s.

Foster argues that sex is a type of knowledge, depicted in the seduction of Enkidu by Shamhat (discussed in the Introduction), but that "continued non-productive sex" is a reversion to the animal state. Gilgamesh transcends such knowledge in a series of stages that leads him, by steps, to the highest knowledge, where the self is transcended and only accomplishments—e.g., a work of literature—remain.

Foster designates the five stages of knowledge as Knowledge of Humanity, Knowledge of Another, Beginnings of Self-Knowledge, Knowledge of the Self, and Transcendence of Knowledge beyond the Self. Of all passages he considers, Foster notes the difficulty in dealing with Enkidu's curse of the prostitute and Shamash's apparent commendation of the prostitute's role in humanizing Enkidu. (Ed.)

The Nineveh Gilgamesh epic, a complex Akkadian poem of about 3600 lines, offers a splendor of language, imagery, themes, and ideas to the modern reader.[1] Since the discovery and first interpretation of its contents in the nineteenth century, Assyriologists and other interested critics have read from this text, fragmentary though it remains, an appealing antiphony of analyses and interpretations.[2] Death, heroism, divine disposition, and friendship are but a few of the themes that have aroused the interest of the poet's readers.[3] The Nineveh poet lavished particular care on thematics of love in his poem, and it is these thematics that I will discuss in this essay. It is offered to Marvin Pope, master of the love poetry of the western Semites, as a token that their poet cousins from east of the Euphrates had eloquent thoughts too about love.

The Old Babylonian Gilgamesh epic is not so well preserved as the later version.[4] It treats some of the episodes found in the Nineveh version and preserves others that were presumably in the Nineveh version and which are now lost. The language, poetics, and thematics of the Old Babylonian poet are quite different from those of his Nineveh successor.[5] How the two poets treat the same episodes points the reader to the themes developed by each. Among other things, the Nineveh poet added certain thematics of love. He had before him a version of the Old Babylonian poem, though not necessarily the identical one that has survived to the present.[6]

By his use of thematics, the Nineveh poet portrays sex and love as types of human knowledge. The import of his thematic of sex is that sex belongs to the lowest common level of human knowledge—what everyone must know and experience to become human. Once this knowledge is attained, continued non-productive sex is no longer acquisition of knowledge or affirmation of humanity but characteristic of the street, or, at worst, reversion to the animal state. The import of his thematic on love is that love of another person is the next higher order of knowledge and makes a human into a social being. Knowledge of another leads to unity, which need not be based on sexual union. This unity is only apparent, for higher knowledge shows that it is doomed to disintegrate. Such disintegration need not be terminal for the self. The survivor has acquired the next highest human knowledge—of the self that suffering has served at last to delineate. But survival of the self is a matter of chance and following a rational course of action based on the accumulated experience of others.[7] Therefore knowledge itself is the highest knowledge and goal for man and one achieved only after all else has been discarded, even the self. When at last the self perishes, knowledge remains, but only if the self has taken responsibility for making that knowledge available to those who seek it.

This essay will show in detail how the Nineveh poet elaborated his ideas on love, and what themes and devices he chose to make his import clear. These themes are in the first place matters of content. The poet unites, for example, an independent motif of the baseness of the street with the baseness of unproductive sex. In the second place they are matters of technique, in which, for instance, the poet sets up a series of oppositions that he unites and then dissolves, all as a type for his notions on love—its attraction, false unity, and ultimate disintegration. In the third place, they are matters of language, such as artificing and distorting of speech.

This essay proposes that the emphasis on knowledge and on love and sex as intermediary stages to perfect knowledge was primarily the work of the Nineveh poet. This emphasis adds weight and density to the text rather at the expense of freshness, feeling, and spontaneity. Yet over-all, one may judge the effort as successful and appealing, for one has in the Nineveh Gilgamesh epic an interpretation of humanity worked out with a highly interesting and often moving aesthetic.

For the purposes of exposition, I have divided the relevant portions of the poem into five "episodes," each of which corresponds to a stage in Gilgamesh's ascent to knowledge.[8] These episodes may be summarized as follows.

Episode 1: Definition of Opposites (Knowledge of Humanity). Gilgamesh is king, but irresponsible as shepherd, the metaphor for kingship, and is violator of social relationships in some as yet unspecified way. His opposite is created—Enkidu, a man without humanity or society. Enkidu begins the ascent of human knowledge first through sexual awareness and second through use of his rational faculties. When Enkidu attains knowledge of his humanity, he becomes a true shepherd and emerges as a champion of human institutions, especially marriage, which, it is at last revealed, is what Gilgamesh is violating. Within this episode the poet sets up numerous secondary opposites to develop this theme.

Episode 2: Apparent Unity (Knowledge of Another). Gilgamesh and Enkidu fight in the street and become friends. This unity is apparently sanctioned by the city elders and by initiation of Enkidu into an order that consists primarily of prostitutes. This initiation reverses the unity of marriage and attraction to the opposite sex that the poet seemed to be preparing for in the first episode. He shows us thereby that opposites remain so, despite their apparent unity. Enkidu's tragedy begins with his attraction to the opposite sex, is joined by jealousy and revulsion for another of his own sex, and is now sealed by his friendship with Gilgamesh, which has no sexual basis at all. This union seems the closer for being asexual and of near equals, but hints of its falseness abound. One is the adoption or initiation of Enkidu. Others will be provided by Gilgamesh's selfishness.

Episode 3: Antithesis and Rejection (Beginnings of Self Knowledge). Gilgamesh rejects the sexual advances of Ishtar, here personification of unproductive attraction to the opposite sex. Enkidu rejects the prostitute by consigning her to her fate, the street, by a curse and reversal of a curse, both with the same effect. Ishtar descends to the street and becomes just another prostitute.

Episode 4: Disintegration of Unity (Knowledge of the Self). Enkidu dies as a consequence of a vainglorious expedition to secure Gilgamesh fame. Gilgamesh tries first to maintain his unity with Enkidu and then to separate himself from it. Each attempt fails.

Episode 5: Redefinition of Unity (Transcendence of Knowledge beyond the Self). Gilgamesh at last achieves full human knowledge, from lowest (humanity) to highest (the self). The perfection of his knowledge is attained when at last he discards his self, the death of which is inevitable, and perceives that only his accomplishments will remain. Gilgamesh refers to the city walls he had built, but the reader is to understand that his knowledge, as expressed in the text of the poem, is what really remains. □

EPISODE 1: Definition of Opposites (Knowledge of Humanity)

The Nineveh poet moves on to his second theme, seduction. He tells the story of Enkidu's entrapment by the hunter and the harlot with relish, passing lightly over the important point that it is Gilgamesh who provides the harlot (I iii 41). This turn to the story is cast somewhat in the shadow by the ponderous four-fold repetition of the seduction passage by three direct and one narrative speaker: the hunter's father, I iii 19ff.; Gilgamesh, I iii 42ff.; hunter, I iv 8ff.; narrative voice, I iv 16ff. When the actual seduction takes place, the poet conveys excitement by dropping the conventional poetic formulae introducing direct speech.[9] He describes the union of Enkidu and the harlot as follows:

Nineveh I iv 16–21 (= *GETh* Plate 5; *CT* 46 19)

16. *ur-tam-mi* ^{mí}*Šam-ḫat di-da-šá úr-šá ip-te-e-ma ku-zu-ub-šá il-qi*
17. *ul iš-ḫu-ut il-ti-qi na-pis-su*
18. *lu-bu-ši-šá ú-ma-ṣi-ma elī-šá iṣ-lal*
19. *i-pu-us-su-ma lul-la-a ši-pir sin-niš-te*
20. *da-du-šú iḫ-pu-pu eli ṣērī-šá*
21. 6 *ur-ri* 7 *mušâti* ^{d}*En-ki-dù te-bi-ma* ^{mí}*Šam-ḫat ir-ḫi*

16. Šamhat unloosed her attire, opened her vulva,
    and he took her charms.
17. She was not bashful, she took to herself his vitality.
18. She stripped off her clothes and he lay upon her,
19. She indeed treated him, man, to woman's work.
20. His passionate feelings caressed her.
21. Six days and seven nights was Enkidu aroused
    and made love to Šamhat.

Commentary:
Line 16: The poet replaces *kirimmū* of I iv 8 with *dīdū*, presumably to prepare for a play on *dādu* in line 20. This is rather lamely represented in the translation by attire/desire.
Line 17: *napīšu* "breath of life" is a significant choice of words here, for in fact, as Enkidu recognized himself (VII iii 6ff.), her seduction led to his death. A rendering "she took his breath away," while perhaps not too far from the original, has a tone that the Akkadian poet, so far as I can see, did not intend.
Line 18: The contrast of "sleep" in this line with "arousal" in line 21 is one of numerous instances in which vitality and wakefulness are contrasted in different ways with sleep and death.[10] This polarity is particularly exploited in Tablet X when the false vitality of Gilgamesh's sleeplessness is exposed by Ut-napištim.
Line 20: For *ḫapāpu* see Moran, *Biblica* 50 (1969): 31 note 3; Cooper, *Essays... Finkelstein*, 43 note 22 ("embrace"). Grayson (*Papyrus and Tablet* [Spectrum Books: 1973]: 142) has proposed "undulate."
Line 21: Despite Grayson, *ANET*, 503, I follow Diakonoff, *BiOr* 18 (1960): 62 in assuming that Šamhat is a personal name. It is difficult otherwise to account for the *status absolutus* of the noun; use of the word as a noun in the poem (I v 9 etc.) is no bar to this interpretation. In either case, the stative "aroused" makes clear that this was a single, heroic act of intercourse extending over six days and seven nights. This prepares us for its opposite: the heroic slumber of Gilgamesh in XI 199ff.

The seduction of Enkidu permits the poet to develop one of the main themes of his poem: vitality and wakefulness. As will be shown below, in the description of Enkidu's shepherdship, his wakefulness is a positive attribute, while Gilgamesh's, as seen in I ii and iv, is mere rowdyism. Both Enkidu and Gilgamesh are to lose their vitality and wakefulness: Enkidu his vitality and his life, Gilgamesh his wakefulness to sleeplessness and eventually to knowledge. At this point in the poem, the motif is introduced almost imperceptibly, as *tēbi* "aroused" and *ṣalālu* "sleep (with)," "lie down (with)" have not yet been enriched with the connotation that the poet wishes to assign them. The artistic principle at work here is evidently the same as that used in introducing the motif of violation of family in I ii; its first appearance is ambiguous and rather lost in the rush of events. This episode draws attention to Enkidu's first loss of vitality. No longer a virgin, he lacks his pristine physical strength. For this the poet has no particular regrets, as he ends on a positive note.

Enkidu has entered the first stage of knowledge, sexual awareness, and now moves to the second, represented by the ability to hear and understand language:

Nineveh I iv 28–32

28. *um-ta-aṭ-ṭu* ^{d}En-ki-[dù *u*]*l ki-i šá pa-ni la-sa-an-šú*
29. *ú šu-ú i-ši-i*[*ḫ* *r*]*a-pa-áš ḫa-si-sa*
30. *i-tu-ram-mu* [*it-t*]*a-šab ina šá-pal* ^{mí} *ḫa-rim-ti*
31. ^{mí}*ḫa-rim-tum i-na-aṭ-ṭa-la pa-ni-šú*
32. *ù x̣ x̣* [*ti*] *i-qab-bu-ú i-šem-ma-a-a uznā-šú*

28. Less was Enkidu become, he could not run
    as he had before,
29. But he gr[ew in… and] broader understanding.
30. He turned back and sat himself down
    at the harlot's feet.
31. The harlot looked into his face
32. And to [the words(?)] that she was speaking
    did his ears give hearing.

Commentary:
Lines 31ff.: Note the inventory of the rational faculties given here: sight, speech, and hearing. Enkidu's ascent to knowledge begins with hearing. Sight, hearing, and speech are developed into a more elaborate conceit in *Enuma Eliš* I 94ff:

ḫa-sa-siš la na-da-a a-ma-riš pa-áš-qa
4 IGI^{II}-*šú* 4 GEŠTUG^{II}-*šú*
šap-ti-šú ina šu-ta-bu-li ^{d}Girra *it-tan-paḫ*
ir-ti-bu-ú 4-ta-àm *ḫa-si-sa*
ù IGI^{II} *ki-ma šu-a-tu i-bar-ra-a gim-re-e*

Unheard of, hard to perceive!
Fourfold his eyesight, fourfold his hearing,
His lips in discourse a fire breaking out.
Formidable his power of fourfold hearing
And his eyesight just as much sees everything.

Line 32: Collation of the second sign in this line (K 2756^{d} = Haupt Nr. 2 p. 7) by P. Machinist "not A, probably not ḪA." According to C. B. F. Walker, the present trace is as follows: [ ]. Von Soden, *ZA* 53 (1959): 222 proposes: *ù šá!* ^{m}[^{í}*ḫa-rim*]-*ti* "and what the harlot was speaking…" □

EPISODE 3: Antithesis and Rejection
(Beginnings of Self-Knowledge)

The episode consists of two sexual rejections, one anticipatory (Gilgamesh and Ishtar), the other retrospective (Enkidu and the harlot). Both of these incidents are known only from the Nineveh version. The rejection of Ishtar is told in seventy-nine lines of text, only portions of which are quoted here. After killing Humbaba, cutting cedars, and putting the wood on the Euphrates for the journey to Nippur, Gilgamesh undresses and washes himself.

Nineveh VI 6ff.
6. *a-na du-un-qí šá* ^{d}Gilgameš *i-na it-ta-ši ru-bu-tu* ^{d}Ištar
7. *al-kam-ma* ^{d}Gilgameš *lu-ú ḫa' i-ir at-ta*
8. *in-bi-ka ia-a-ši qa-a-šu qí-šam-ma*
9. *at-ta lu-ú mu-te-ma ana-ku lu-ú áš-ša-at-ka*

6. Ishtar the princess looked covetously on the beauty of Gilgamesh.
7. "Come to me, Gilgamesh, you should be a lover,
8. Give, O give me freely of your fruits of love!
9. You should be my husband and I should be your wife."

Commentary:
Line 6: The term "princess" recurs throughout this section, and is appparently used ironically by the poet for reasons that will become clear below.
Line 7: Note omission of the formulae of speech, emphasizing the abruptness and excitement of the speaker. Note also the simple declarative statement in the second person.
Line 8: Ishtar continues in the second person ("your fruits") but gives way to an agitated first person, expressed here by the independent pronoun and the "ventive" on the one hand, and the cognate accusative (here: "freely") on the other.

I have emphasized the use of person in this passage because in this and the parallel passage (below, VI 68f.) the fluctuation of person emerges as a minor thematic of this poet.[11] Represented schematically, the distribution of persons in these three lines is as follows:

2+1	2	2
alkamma	Gilgameš	*atta*
2	1	2+1
inbīka	*iāši*	*qīšamma*
2+1	1	2
atta mūtē	*anāku*	*aššatka*

By exploiting a full range of grammatical possibilities: imperative, ventive, vocative, possessive suffixes, subjective and objective independent pronouns, the poet aptly portrays the intensity of her desire. The poet's intention is clear: Gilgamesh is first urged to be a lover, then her husband. By this device the poet undermines the legitimacy of her proposal, as not only is a woman here proposing to a man, but she is proposing intercourse before marriage.

In the following eleven lines Ishtar offers him a splendid chariot, a magnificent dwelling, abundant income, fertility and energy to his flocks, steeds, and beasts of burden. That she omits all reference to her own, personal attractions is striking, especially, so one assumes, to an audience well-versed in poetic praises of Ishtar and her loveliness. The poet prepares us, subtly still, for his ultimate revelation that Ishtar is not attractive at all, but only a harlot. This is so far only hinted at by the necessity of her bribing her lover rather than seducing him with her charms. Even the harlot was not reduced to that. Gilgamesh replies at length in a speech, coolly introduced by the conventional formulae. In the first eight lines or more he demands of her what he is to give her if he took her: food, clothing, oil—all perhaps in false humility in the face of her splendid offerings. He then abuses her ornately:

Nineveh VI 34ff.[12]
34. ^{giš}*daltu ár-ka-b*[*i-in-nu šá la ú*]*-kal-lu-ú šara u zi-i-qa*
35. *ekallu mu-nap-pi-*[*ṣa-at mārē?*] *qàr-ra-di*
36. *pi-i-ru* [*x mu*]*-ak-ki-lat ku-tùm-mi-šá*
37. *it-tu-ú mu-*[*ṭàp-pi-lat*] *na-ši-šá*
38. ^{kuš}*na-a-da mu-*[*na-ki-sa-at*] *na-ši-šá*
39. *pi-i-lu mu-*[*nap-pi-ṣa-at*] *dūr abni*
40 *ia-šu-pu-ú* [*mu-ab-bit dūri? ina?*] *māt nu-kúr-ti*
41. ^{kuš}*šēnu mu-na-*[*aš-si-kàt šēp*] *be-lí-šá*

34. "A flimsy door which does not keep out the
    wind nor blast,
35. A palace which crushes the hero['s son](?),
36. An elephant which [de]vours its own covering,
37. Pitch which d[irties] its bearer,
38. Waterskin which l[eaks on] its bearer,
39. Limestone which [undermines] a stone wall,
40. Battering ram which [destroys the wall(?)
    against(?)] an enemy land,
41. Sandal which pinches the foot of its owner..."

This passage may shock modern readers, but not perhaps always for the reasons intended by the poet. The language used here may have been familiar to its hearers in quite another context: school days, when abuse of this type, like debating, was a cultivated schoolboy art.[13] Gilgamesh is not hysterically rejecting Ishtar, but rather is talking to her as if she were a girl still in school.

The poet abandons this thematic for a moment (though it will reappear later in VI 159), and now turns to Ishtar's lovers. Her childhood sweetheart was Dumuzi, and he was left to mourning. Her next three lovers were all animals, and the next two were men whom she turned into animals: the shepherd and the orchardman. She is thus the opposite of the harlot, who made Enkidu from an animal to a human being. With stunning effect Gilgamesh mimics Ishtar's attempted seduction of the orchardman:

Nineveh VI 64ff.
64. *ta-ra-mi-ma I-šu-ul-la-nu* ^{lú}*nukarribu abī-ka*
65. *ša ka-a-a-nam-ma šu-gu-ra-a na-šak-ki*
66. *u_4-mi-šam-ma ú-nam-ma-ru pa-áš-šur-ki*
67. *i-na ta-at-ta-ši-šum-ma ta-tal-kiš-šu*
68. *I-šu-ul-la-ni-ia kiš-šu-ta-ki i ni-kul*
69. *u qāt-ka liš!-te-ṣa-am-ma lu-pu-ut ḫur-da-at-ni*
70. *I-šu-ul-la-nu i-qab-bi-ki*
71. *ia-a-ši mi-na-a ter-re-ši-in-ni*
72. *um-mi la te-pa-a a-na-ku la a-kul*
73. *ša ak-ka-lu uklāt pi-šá-a-ti u er-re-e-ti*
74. *šá ku-uṣ-ṣi el-pe-tu ku-tùm-mu-ú-*[*ia?*]
75. *at-ti taš-mi-ma an-na-a* [*qa-be-šu*]
76. *tam-ḫa-ṣi-šu a-na dal-la-li tu-ut-*[*ter-re-šu*]
77. *tu-še-ši-bi-šu-ma ina qa-bal ma-na-*[*ḫa-ti*]
78. *ul e-lu-ú mi-iḫ-ḫa ul a-rid da-l*[*u-u*]
79. *u ia-a-ši ta-ram-mìn-ni-ma ki-i ša-šu-nu*
    tu-[*ši-mìn-ni*]

64. "You even fell in love with Ishullanu,
 your father's orchardman,
65. Who always brought you offerings of date clusters—
66. Every day he made your table splendid.
67. You looked at him covetously and went up to him,
68. 'My Ishullanu, let us have a taste of your manliness!
69. So let your hand be stretched forth to me
 and—touch our vulva!'
70. Ishullanu says to you:
71. 'Me? What do you want of me?
72. Hath my mother not baked and I not eaten?
73. Shall what I eat be breads of obscenities and curses?
74. Shall [my] covering from cold be a reed?'
75. You, when you heard what [he said],
76. Struck him and tu[rned him] into a toad(?).
77. You made him live in the gard[en patch](?).
78. He can't get over a conduit or out of a bucket(?).
79. As for me, when you love me, you'll
 fate me like them." □

At this juncture [when in Tablet VII Enkidu has had great success in defeating Humbaba and the Bull of Heaven but is now inexplicably condemned by the gods to die and has cursed the temple woman for making him human] Shamash cries out abruptly from heaven that Enkidu is being unfair:

Nineveh VII iii 35ff.

35. *am-me-ni* ^{d}En-ki-dù *ḫa-rim-*[*t*]*i* ^{mí}Šam-ḫat
 ta-na-an-za-ár
36. *šá ú-šá-ki-lu-ka uklāt si-mat ìl-ú-ti*
37. *ku-ru-un-na iš-qu-ka si-mat šàr-ú-ti*
38. *ú-lab-bi-šu-ka lu-ub-ši ra-ba-a*
39. *u dam-qu* ^{d}Gilgameš *tap-pa-a ú-šar-šu-ka*
 ka-a-šá
40. [*e*]*-nin-na-a-ma* ^{d}Gilgameš *ib-ri ta-li-me-ka*
41. [*uš-na*]*-a-al-ka-a-ma ina ma-a-a-li rabi*^{i}
42. [*i-na*] *ma-a-a-al taq-ni-i uš-na-al-ka-ma*
43. [*u-š*]*e-šib-ka šub-ta ni-iḫ-ta sŭ-bat šu-me-li*
44. [*ma-al*]*-ka šá qaq-qa-ri ú-na-áš-šá-qu šēpē-ka*
45. [*ú-šab*]*-kak-ka nīše šá* Uruk^{ki} *ú-šad-ma-ma-ak-ka*
46. [*šam-ḫa-a-ti*] *nīše ú-ma-al-lak-ka dul-la*
47. [*ù šu*]-⸢*ú*⸣ *ar-ki-ka ú-ša-áš-šá-a ma-la-a*
 pa-gar-[*šú*]
48. [*il-tab-bi*]-⸢*is*⸣ *maš-ki lab-bi-im-ma*
 i-rap-pu-ud ṣē[*ri*]

35. "Why, O Enkidu, would you curse the harlot Šamhat,
36. Who fed you bread fit for divinity,
37. Gave you wine to drink, fit for a king?
38. Garbed you in a princely garment,
39. And let you get fair Gilgamesh for your very own friend?
40. Now then, Gilgamesh is your best friend, is he not?
41. Will he not lay you down in a princely sleeping place?
42. In a suitable sleeping place he will lay you down!
43. He'll make you(r cult image) sit comfortably in a seat at his left,
44. And the kings of the earth will do you homage,
45. The people in Uruk he'll make weep and cry for you!
46. [Prostitutes] and people will he fill with misery for you!
47. As for him, after you die he'll make his hair unkempt,
48. Put on a lion skin, and run through the steppe."

Commentary:
Lines 36f.: The parallelism is now ironic, as Enkidu is not a god (he has to die) and not a king (Gilgamesh is the king). Shamash is in effect saying that Enkidu had already had more than he could reasonably have expected, in that he had been almost as good as Gilgamesh, so should take his death in good part. Cf. VI 27f.
Line 39: 'very own' = *kāša*. The absurdity of this speech is emphasized by the hyperbole of lines *36* and *37,* the pompous parallelism of lines 41–42, the anticlimax of line 43, the pairing of prostitutes and people in 46 (restored from VIII iii), even using the word *šamḫatu,* the name of the person being cursed, and the final absurdity of lines 47–48 in which Gilgamesh is supposed to replace Enkidu as the hairy man of the steppe. That a god should attempt to calm the rage of a man is strange enough, but the terms and language used leave little doubt as to the poet's satiric, if bitter, intent. This is brought home by Enkidu's reply, in which he elaborately undoes his 'perpetual' curse. □

In his first adventure, the killing of Humbaba, Gilgamesh relied on his valor, and, in increasingly violent acts, seems to be gaining his goal. He approaches the scorpion man with courage, though politely. He threatens the tavern keeper, though makes no assault. He attacks Ur-Šanabi outright, and forces him to take him across the waters of death. For his final battle he is well prepared, and is astonished to find his prospective opponent languid and indifferent.

Nineveh XI 5f.
5. *gu-um-mur-ka lib-bi ana e-piš tu-qu-un-ti*
6. [ ] *a-ḫ̮i na-da-at-ta e-lu ṣe-ri-ka*

5. "My heart imagined you a maker of battle,
6. [But you do] nothing, and lie on your back."

This "no contest" disposes of Gilgamesh's valor, and Ut-napištim thereupon disposes of his great show of mourning, the trappings of his new-found independence. The village idiot, he points out, wears wretched clothes and eats bad food, but no one accords him merit for that—he is just a fool. Gilgamesh is now not only separated from his friend by death, he is separated from the new, independent self that this separation seems to have created. His lonely valor and ostentatious mourning do not make him a self that will survive. The last touch is put on this destruction by the test of whether or not he can stay awake for seven days and nights. He falls asleep at once, and thereby passes from the scene the all-night rowdy that was introduced to the reader in the first tablet. Knowledge of one's separate self is not the end of the journey.

EPISODE 5: Redefinition of Unity
(Transcendence of Knowledge beyond the Self)

The denouement is swift. Gilgamesh's last hope is that his new-found and newly lost self can be preserved by the artificial means of a magical plant of eternal rejuvenation. Because of his unwillingness to eat the plant at once, he loses it on the return journey. The final lines of the text find him speaking the poet's lines at the outset, describing the walls of Uruk, almost as if they were all that he had salvaged from his life and journey. Is this how the poet expects his reader to interpret his poem? Such an interpretation seems to find support in the parallelism of the poet's early invocation of his reader to look at the wall, and Gilgamesh's final invocation of Ur-Šanabi to do the same.[14] This interpretation, moreover, echoes a belief common enough in Mesopotamia, at least in royal ideology.

Yet the Nineveh poem is not really about royal ideology, though that was a theme useful to both poets and the Old Babylonian poet even opened with it. The Nineveh poet, by contrast, opened with an invocation of Gilgamesh's knowledge, and it is Gilgamesh's knowledge and how he acquired it that is the subject of the poem. The reader must ask, therefore, what Gilgamesh knew that set him apart from other men. Of course Gilgamesh knew from the beginning what every king knows, that if his works survive, the king's name survives. This the poet's narrative voice grants, but vitiates in a strange way. The poet transfers the words from his own narrative voice to that of his character, and reduces the poet's audience to one, another character, and a minor one at that. This reduction can be seen as a subtle denigration not only of the opening speech but of the walls themselves. Gilgamesh knew more than what he said to Ur-Šanabi, and what he knew must be what the narrative voice tells the reader in the end, the poem itself.

Mesopotamian poets were wont to refer to the circumstances of the poem's conception or composition at the end of their work.[15] The Epic of Gilgamesh is no exception, save that it employs the device at one remove—implicitly in the poet's rhetorical silence. Gilgamesh knew that knowledge was his self that transcended him, uniquely his, but, like a poem, independent of him at the moment of its fulfillment, and no longer needing his continued existence. His mortal self and the walls he built were his, but limited by immutable laws of physical existence. His inscription was more important than the walls it commemorated, for the walls without it communicated nothing beyond their existence. His knowledge was more important than the self that acquired it, but was limited to that self until he gave it independent existence, in Greek terms, "did" something with it.

Near the beginning the poet asks the reader to read well Gilgamesh's inscription, a well-known literary cachet, the metaphor for the text at hand. At the conclusion, by his final silence, the poet asks the reader to read well his poem, and know too. Therewith the poem begins over again.

❋ ❋ ❋

NOTES

1. The Akkadian text is cited from R. Campbell Thompson, *The Epic of Gilgamish* (Oxford, 1930), hereafter referred to as *GETh* or "Nineveh." For some passages reference has been made to P. Haupt, *Das Babylonische Nimrodepos* (Leipzig, 1891). I am grateful to E. Sollberger, Keeper of the Department of Western Asiatic Antiquities of the British

Museum, for the opportunity to collate a number of passages. Because of an employees' strike, I was not able to see all of the relevant British Museum tablets at the time of my visit there, so have relied upon the kindness of P. Machinist and C. B. F. Walker for further collations. Portions of col i are quoted using the Nimrud version published by D. J. Wiseman, *Iraq* 37 (1975): 157–63; for collation of that tablet, see W. G. Lambert, *RA* 73 (1979): 89. The Middle Babylonian Ur tablet was published by C. J. Gadd as *UET* VI 394 and edited by him in *Iraq* 28 (1966): 105–21 (collated). For the Assur version I have used Frankena's edition, *CRRAI* 7 (1958): 113ff. For the Sultantepe version, see O.R. Gurney, *The Sultantepe Tablets* I (London, 1957): 14 and 15, edited in *JCS* 8 (1954): 87ff. Neo-Babylonian fragments were copied by W. G. Lambert in *CT* 46. The best translation is that by A. Schott and W. von Soden, *Das Gilgamesch-Epos* (Stuttgart, 1970). The best English translation is that of E. A. Speiser in J. Pritchard, ed., *Ancient Near Eastern Texts Relating to the Old Testament* (2nd ed.; Princeton, 1969), with revisions by A. K. Grayson. I have also profited from the treatment of I. M. Diakonoff, *Epos o Gil'gameše* (Moscow / Leningrad, 1961). The most important commentaries on all or part of the poem are those of P. Jensen, *Keilschriftbibliothek* 6/I (Berlin, 1901): 421–531; A. Schott, *ZA* 42 (1934): 92–143; W. von Soden, *ZA* 53(1959): 209–33, to all of which I am indebted for many insights. My special thanks go to Karen Polinger Foster for her careful reading and comments on this essay, and to the many students who have furthered my understanding of the poem.

2. For a bibliography, see de Mayer, *CRRAI* 7 (1958): 1ff.; Matouš, *BiOr* 21 (1964): 3ff. More recent studies include Komoróczy, *Acta Antiqua Acad. Scien. Hung.* 23(1975): 41ff.; Thorkild Jacobsen, *The Treasures of Darkness* (New Haven, 1976): 193ff. For a collection of interpretive essays on the poem, see K. Oberhuber, ed., *Das Gilgamesch-Epos* (Darmstadt, 1977).

3. For summary and discussion, see Foster, review of Oberhuber, *Gilgamesch-Epos, BiOr* 36 (1979): 185–88, as well as Oberhuber's forward to his volume.

4. The Pennsylvania Tablet ("OB Pa") was copied by Langdon, *UM* 10/3, and re-edited by Jastrow and Clay in their publication of the Yale tablet, *YOS* 4/3. All passages quoted here were collated by the writer with the kind permission of A. W. Sjöberg, Curator of Tablets in the University Museum, University of Pennsylvania, and William W. Hallo, Curator of the Yale Babylonian Collection. In addition to my own collations, I have used a copy of *UM* 10/3 annotated by A. T. Clay and collations of the Yale tablet by J. J. Finkelstein. Parts of an Old Babylonian tablet corresponding to Nineveh Tablet X have been copied by Meissner, *MVAG* 7/1 (1902): 14f. and recopied by Pinches, *PSBA* 25 (1903): plates after p. 122; Millard, *Iraq* 26 (1964): 99ff. = *CT* 46 16. Other Old Babylonian material has been published by van Dijk, *TIM* IX 43, 45, 46; Bauer, *JNES* 16 (1957): 254ff. For the unity of the material,

see J. Tigay, "Was there an Integrated Gilgamesh Epic in the Old Babylonian Period?" *Essays on the Ancient Near East in Memory of Jacob Joel Finkelstein* (Memoirs of the Connecticut Academy of Sciences 19; New Haven, 1977): 215–18. Jastrow, *YOS* 4/3, 18 already noted that more than one edition of the Old Babylonian epic existed, but dated both the Meissner tablet and the Yale and Pennsylvania tablets to the Hammurabi period. For a somewhat different opinion, see W. G. Lambert, *ZDMG* Supplement 3/1, 68, who suggests, however, that a single person was responsible for his "expanded" Old Babylonian epic that included what is now Nineveh X "weil diese so viel literarische und dramatische Genialität offenbart."

5. See B. Groneberg, *Untersuchungen zum Hymnisch-epischen Dialekt der altbabylonischen literarischen Texte* (Dissertation, Münster, 1972). This built on the foundations laid by von Soden in his study of the "Hymnic-Epic Dialect" in *ZA* 40 (1931): 163ff. and *ZA* 41 (1933): 90ff.

6. For a survey of the text history of the poem, see Oberhuber, *Gilgamesch-Epos,* 1ff. I use the term "Nineveh poet" as a convenient name for the author of the text found in the Nineveh recension Tablets I to XI. Mesopotamian scholars believed that the author's name was Sin-liqi-unninni (W. G. Lambert, *JCS* 16 [1962]: 66 VI 10). When or where he lived is uncertain; one usually proposes Uruk and the latter half of the second millennium.

7. This is the import of much Mesopotamian wisdom literature, where the concept called here "chance" corresponds in varying degrees to "luck," "genius," or "divine favor."

8. These episodes do not necessarily correspond to actual episodes in the story as the poet tells it, but rather to episodes in the development of the particular themes studied here. Many other themes are interwoven with those of sex and love, each with its own dynamics of development. □

9. There are numerous instances of this device in the Nineveh poem. Compare for example XI 173ff., in which the angry Enlil speaks without a formula of speech, but Ea's conciliatory reply, 176ff., is introduced by the usual formulae. See also below, comments to III ii 10 (emotional prayer), VI 6ff. (seduction attempt), VI 84 (angry Ishtar versus father's conciliatory reply), VII iv 25 (cry for help).

10. Wakefulness: I i 11 13, 23; iv 21; v 12, 19. Sleep is first developed throughout Tablet IV as a vehicle for the numerous dreams portending the unsuccessful outcome of their expedition, then as a vehicle for the ominous dream of Enkidu, portending his death (e.g., VII ii 13 etc., as the typos for his death), later (IX i 13) as the vehicle for the dream portending Gilgamesh's last expedition, and ultimately as the typos for death itself, XI 199ff. □

11. I am indebted to Rebecca Comay for this observation.

12. The composite text is based on *GETh* and the Assur version, as edited by Frankena, *CRRAI* 7 (1958): 113ff.

13. For literature, see Foster, *JANES* 6 (1974): 80; Hirsch, *Kindlers Literaturlexikon, s. v.* “Akkadische Streitgespräche”; Wilcke, *ibid, s.v.* “Sumerische Streitgedichte.” □

14. This character seems a curious choice, but the reason may lie in a hermeneutic on his name “Servant-of-Two-Thirds” and the fabulous genealogy of Gilgamesh whereby he was one third human and two thirds divine. This proportion is treated playfully by the poet in IX ii 19ff., in which the scorpion man’s wife pedantically corrects her spouse and a paranomasia is developed on *zikaru* “man” and *zakāru* “say.”

15. E.g., *Erra* V 42ff.; Nin-me-šár-ra 136ff. (= *YNER* 3, 33); Agušaja = Foster, *Studies… Finkelstein,* 84 note 38; *Atrahasis* III viii 11ff; *Enuma Eliš* VII.158.

* * *

Rivkah Harris
"Images of Women in the Gilgamesh Epic"

Rivkah Harris very deliberately takes up the tools of contemporary literary criticism in her survey of the images and roles of women in *Gilgamesh.* Taking *Gilgamesh* as a unified whole—a "coherent text"—in light of Tigay's "evolution" of the Gilgamesh texts, Harris even finds a place for Tablet XII. Her main literary-critical device is Barbara A. Babcock's "symbolic inversion," which she sees not only in the women of the poem, but in Gilgamesh and Enkidu.

Harris sees a comic inversion, the switching of expected roles, in the ambiguous figure of Ishtar especially. But as she treats each of the women in the epic in turn, Harris notices several important tendencies. Since *Gilgamesh* was, like much of medieval poetry, written by men for a male audience, male attitudes toward women, human and divine, prevail. Women are supportive and subsidiary to men—and this may reflect the lives of real women in Mesopotamia. There is no primary role for women. Yet a number of women are depicted as wise: Ninsun, especially, but also Shamhat and Siduri. All the women are intercessors, playing intermediary roles—even possibly the Scorpion-man's wife. The two wives in the poem are, significantly, anonymous, identified only through their husbands.

Ishtar reverses the role of goddess when she is mocked by a mortal, and she behaves like a man. Gilgamesh and Enkidu, whose relationship is marked as husband and wife, includes another symbolic inversion, where the male is like a female. The pervasive interest in maternal images in the poem leads Harris, finally, to a suggestion that the paradigmatic image of the mother should be considered in other Mesopotamian myths to determine certain features of intrafamilial life in Mesopotamia. (Ed.)

Several years ago William L. Moran[1] urged Assyriologists to adopt "the more comprehensive critical strategies of contemporary literary criticism" and to adapt "to new methods" in studying Mesopotamian texts. This essay is such an attempt, tentative and programmatic, and at this juncture in no way definitive. The complex and multi-dimensional quality of the Gilgamesh Epic (hereafter referred to as GE) is too well known to require documentation. Like all classics "which frame human experience in enduring and universally meaningful forms,"[2] it cannot be encompassed in one final interpretation. The many versions of GE in ancient languages and the growing number of contemporary studies and translations attest to its enormous, abiding appeal.

Despite the many articles devoted to GE, one area—women in GE—has received no more than a passing comment or an occasional footnote. For the purposes of this paper I will treat the epic as a coherent text, bypassing the many problems of composition and evolution. Not that these are irrelevant to the topic. Elucidation of certain issues which pertain to composition and evolution might shed light on changing attitudes, if such there were, toward the roles of women in Mesopotamian society and on differences, if any, between this culture and those others whose scribes translated (and modified) GE into their native languages. Jeffrey Tigay,[3] for example, has noted the different terms used for "wife": *sinništu, ḫirītu, aššatu,* and *marḫītu,* differences in terminology which relate to the evolution of the epic. Of significance perhaps is the expanded role of Ninsun in the Late Version, in the scene preceding Gilgamesh's departure with Enkidu to do battle with Huwawa.[4]

What must be emphasized at the very outset, for it touches on all that follows, is the assumption that GE, in whatever version, was composed by men for the edification and entertainment of a presumably male audience who read or to whom the epic was read. GE is like the medieval *chanson de geste,* which was "written for a male audience, *to male taste* (my italics)."[5] Therefore what we find in the epic are essentially male attitudes toward women, human and divine. Central to GE are the concerns and activities of men, women functioning as supporting and subsidiary characters in the cast.[6] It must, moreover, be underscored that the correlation between the epic's images of women and actual women will not be "a simple unambiguous one of direct reflection or representation… images can also embody fears, fantasies and wishes."[7] The importance of women in GE relates to their relationship with Gilgamesh. Their images incorporate the anxieties, longings, fears, and wishes of men, grounded in the realities of human life.[8] These images also reflect the diversity and ambiguity that characterized the lives of real women.

Women are regarded positively only when they assist Gilgamesh (and Enkidu) in their activities, when they nurture, advise in maternal fashion. The adventures of the heroes preclude a primary role for women. Though Mesopotamians did not live in a sexually dimorphic society like that of ancient Greece, women's domain, nevertheless, did not partake of the political and military arenas which were the masculine domain.

A crucial element in the epic which I believe is linked to its images of women is the frequent use of symbolic inversion, especially status and role reversal, in the depiction of women. "Symbolic inversion may be broadly defined as any act of expressive behavior which inverts, contradicts, abrogates, or in some fashion presents an alternative to commonly held cultural codes, values and norms be they linguistic or artistic, religious or social and political." The term "derives from and conflates several existing discipline-specific uses."[9] Inversion serves more than one function in GE. I will, however, focus on "the comic principle of inversion [which] involves 'a sudden, comic switching of expected roles.'"[10] The reversal of the expected roles of certain women in GE is, in my opinion, an essential feature of GE's humor and comedy, which must have held great appeal for the ancients.

We now turn to the supporting cast in GE, to the women, who though not principal actors are, nevertheless, significant in moving the plot along.

Ninsun, the divine mother of Gilgamesh, is all that a mother should be: caring, nurturing, assisting her son in his quest, anxious though she is about it. Her name or epithet, Rimat-Ninsun, "Wild-Cow Ninsun," incorporates the ubiquitous non-erotic metaphor used to describe tender, loving mother goddesses in Mesopotamia and elsewhere.[11] The all-knowing (*mūdât kalâma*) mother is expert, as are other Mesopotamian women, human and divine, in interpreting dreams.[12] Addressed tenderly by Gilgamesh when he speaks to her, she is the only female with whom there is a loving male/female relationship in GE.[13] She laments his restless heart (*libbi lā ṣālila*) and pleads with Shamash to assist him. In a difficult passage in the Late Version (Thompson, Gilg. III iv 21), Ninsun seems to adopt Enkidu as her son, brother then to Gilgamesh. If this is so, then she, like Siduri, affirms the centrality of family and kin to human life, the importance of the private sphere to men who dominate the public sphere.

Ninsun is the only real mother, that is, biological mother, in the epic, but "motherly" also characterizes the other females, except Ishtar.

The prostitute[14] Shamhat is an intriguing woman. She and Siduri, the tavern keeper, are working women who support themselves. Shamhat belongs to a class with low repute in society. Siduri is associated with a place of low repute. And Ishtar, not incidentally, is related to both, as she is in the following hymnic passage: "when I sit at the entrance of the tavern, I am a loving prostitute" (*ina bāb aštammi ina ašābiya ḫarimtum rāʾimtum anāku*).[15]

Both prostitute and tavernkeeper belong to the extra-domestic domain; both were important in the leisure activities of Mesopotamian men.

Though the real-life Mesopotamian prostitute had a bad reputation and was seen as a threat to the stability of the family,[16] her representation in GE is quite the reverse. She is depicted, through her actions and words, as a maternal, beneficent, wise woman and not as a deceitful, lustful seductress. And significantly, like Siduri, and unlike Utnapishtim's wife, she is named, given individuality and personhood. The *ḫarimtu* is thus a prime example of role and status inversion. The lowly, marginal *ḫarimtu* is elevated to the central kin role of "mother."

The classicist Paul Friedrich[17] suggests "the connection between artful, or sophisticated, sensuousness and civilization" in understanding the role of Shamhat. But the issue is far more complex. It is the *intermediary* role of the prostitute in transforming Enkidu from one at home with nature and wild animals into a human being (*awēliš īwe*) which is crucial. What is also pertinent is the Mesopotamian view that among the *me*'s, which constitute the norms of civilized life, are included sexual intercourse and prostitution.[18] Relevant too is the fact that the prostitute in Mesopotamia, like the prostitute in ancient Israel, was a prime representative of urban life.[19] Of special value in appreciating the mediating role of the *ḫarimtu* are Sherry Ortner's comments in her seminal article "Is Female to Male as Nature is to Culture?,"[20] for she provides a frame of reference in understanding this function. Shamhat serves, as do women in other places and times, as "one of culture's crucial agencies for the conversion of nature into culture, especially with reference to the socialization of children" (p. 84). It is Shamhat who is the primary facilitator of Enkidu's socialization. What she teaches Enkidu puts "her squarely in the category of culture" (p. 79) and "on the basis of her socializing functions alone, she could not be more a representative of culture" (p. 80). Thus by profession an urban representative and by role (really a role reversed) domesticator of Enkidu, Shamhat is indeed a fitting intermediary.

Enkidu's break with his former life among wild animals is first achieved through sexual relations and is completed through learning the ways of civilized life. Shamhat's is a dual role, as a sexual creature[21] and as a maternal figure. The first is explicitly spelled out by the hunter: *epšīšumma lullâ šipir sinništi* "show him, the *lullû-man* (your) feminine wiles" (Gilg. I iv 13 and ibid. 19). The second is more implicit. Enkidu is untaught (*lā lummud*), and Shamhat teaches him the basics that every child must learn: eating, drinking,[22] dressing himself. The predominant image is that of mother, her relationship with Enkidu that of mother and child.[23] That this is to be the prostitute's function is perhaps already intimated by the hunter even before she meets Enkidu, when he says to her: *rummî kirimmīki* "release your hold" (Gilg. I iv 8); the term *kirimmu is* described in *CAD* K p. 406 as "a characteristic and functional position of a mother's arm assumed in order to hold a child safely." She later shares her clothing (*ištīnam ulabbissu*) with the naked Enkidu and clasping his hand, "guiding him like a [x],"[24] she leads him away from nature to the hut of the shepherds. No matter what simile was used here, what is certain is Enkidu's dependence on the *ḫarimtu*.

One final point should be noted, one that is, I suggest, an aspect of role reversal: Shamhat speaks in proverbial language and as a woman of wise counsel[25] (*mil[k]um ša sinništum imtaqut ana libbišu* [Gilg. P. ii 25]). She thus emulates the wise Ninsun.

Siduri, the divinized tavernkeeper,[26] is also depicted in ways which are very unlike the actual tavernkeeper. Apart from Ishtar's association with taverns (as noted above), Siduri is linked to Ishtar in a problematic way.[27] Like Shamhat, Siduri has a name and is self-employed. Her name has been interpreted as perhaps having a Hurrian origin,[28] meaning "young girl." Yet unlike Shamhat, the *ḫarimtu* who undresses, Siduri is concealed by a veil (*kutummi kuttumatma* [Gilg. X i 4]), as the modest wife of later Assyrian times would be: she is covered, as the *sābītu* in real life was surely not.[29] Here too is an example of status and role reversal. She too is represented as a supportive figure who assists Gilgamesh in his dangerous journey to find Utnapishtim, after proffering him words of advice. What she has to say deserves special attention: her discourses can be described more accurately, I think, as pragmatic and realistic than as "hedonistic" or as recommending *"carpe diem."*[30] She speaks practically, and to everyday living. And in contrast to Shamash, she stresses the goodness of food, clean clothing, washing and bathing, which all belong to woman's domain. She stresses the importance of wife and child and thus of relationship. Siduri, then, like Shamhat, voices and upholds the social norms of Mesopotamian society. She too is depicted as a wise woman, speaking in proverbial language.

The two married women in GE, Utnapishtim's wife and Scorpion-man's wife, are unnamed, anonymous creatures.[31] Their position is like that of Mesopotamian wives generally: relational, given definition as wife or daughter. Utnapishtim's wife remains entirely in the background of the flood story. She is passive, acted upon: Enlil brings her aboard the boat and has her kneel beside her husband (*uštēli uštakmis sinništi ina idiya* [Gilg. XI 191]). But she speaks and acts on behalf of Gilgamesh. Hers is an intercessary role, a not uncommon feminine and maternal role in Mesopotamian literary texts.[32] She beseeches her husband not to let Gilgamesh die when he falls asleep (Gilg. XI 208). Begrudgingly he accedes, adding the jaundiced[33] proverb: *raggat amēlūtu iraggiki* "man is wicked, he will treat you wickedly" (Gilg. XI 210). He has her bake breads to prove to Gilgamesh that he has slept for days. When Gilgamesh has failed the sleep test and prepares to return to Uruk, it is she who, mindful of society's rules of hospitality and sensitive to his enormous efforts (*illika īnaḫa išūṭa*), sees to it that he does not leave empty-handed.

Unfortunately the passage about the Scorpion-man and his wife is poorly preserved. What may be noteworthy is the specificity of her response when her husband comments: *ša illikannâši šēr ilī zumuršu* "he who has come to us is of divine flesh" (Gilg. IX ii 14). She corrects this to: "(only) two thirds of him are divine, one third is human." Whether this specificity was an aspect of real women's rhetoric cannot be ascertained without further study.[34] I would suggest that, in keeping with the pattern described above, the Scorpion-man's wife may have been instrumental in having her husband assist Gilgamesh on his way.[35]

Before turning to the most intriguing and complex of the females in GE, to Ishtar, note should be taken of the roles of the other, very minor women in GE. Aruru, the mother goddess, is told to create a replica of Gilgamesh: *eninna binî zikiršu* (Gilg. I ii 31). She follows instructions. The mediating role of the women of Uruk whose complaints against Gilgamesh are heeded by the gods should also be noted.[36] As a result the gods take action which leads to the creation of Enkidu. Finally, attention should be given to Ninsun suggesting to Shamash that Aya remind him of Gilgamesh lest he forget(?) him (Gilg. III ii 20: *Aya kallat liḫassiska*).[37]

Thus far women, divine and human, have been assisting, nurturing, caring persons. It is Ishtar alone who departs from the paradigmatic feminine role in GE. She alone does not fit the mold. And yet even she is depicted as "motherly" in the flood story related to Gilgamesh by Utnapishtim, when she cries out "like a woman giving birth" (*kīma ālitti* [Gilg. XI 116]) at the terrible destruction wrought upon mankind by the flood.[38] But her representation in the episode where she proposes to Gilgamesh and he rejects her (Gilg. VI 1–79) is ruthlessly negative. What is to be made of this?

Thorkild Jacobsen, in his sensitive analysis of Inanna/Ishtar, justly describes her as "in some respects the most intriguing of all the figures in the pantheon."[39] Although the Ishtar-Gilgamesh episode is open to various interpretations,[40] I suggest that a key to understanding it, if only in part, is the factor of inversion—the reversal of expected roles.[41] One does not expect a mortal (even one who is two thirds divine) to reject a goddess. And yet Gilgamesh does so, detailing his refusal at length with the sordid features of Ishtar's many love affairs and previous marriage. He castigates her with a series of metaphors,[42] which may provide clues to the reason for his rejection of her: she has behaved like a man in proposing marriage and in offering him gifts. She has thus assumed an active, aggressive posture, an unacceptable role for a female. In the many-faceted and paradoxical aspects of her personality, Ishtar is often depicted as warrior and hence as one who participates in the public domain of males.[43] But in GE this is rejected. Gilgamesh mocks and scoffs at her, as if she were a man. Enkidu humiliates her later in an unbelievable way (Gilg. VI 161ff.). And like a man, she retaliates.

Gilgamesh, in describing Ishtar's many affairs, is illustrating graphically the negative view toward the prostitute, as one with "countless husbands" (*ḫarimtu ša šāri mutūša*).[44] Ishtar, the prostitute par excellence in religious texts, the patroness of prostitutes, is repulsed by Gilgamesh because she has assumed an intolerable role for a female. Shamhat and Siduri are depicted positively because they act "motherly." There are then two inversions in the case of Ishtar: the status inversion—a mortal mocks a goddess; and the role (or category) inversion—a female behaves like a male.

Scholars have interpreted Ishtar's rejection as having its roots in theological, political, or historical factors. Given the assumptions of this paper, I propose a different interpretive direction, which I borrow from Wendy Doninger O'Flaherty's discussion of "Banalization and Derision of the Gods"; she writes that "the gods are often imagined to *be* men, to *be* like men in character; and here they appear not on the top but rather at the very *bottom* of the continuum, as ludicrous."[45] In the episode with Gilgamesh, Ishtar too is at the *bottom,* not on the top as one would expect a goddess to be. This is an accurate description of status inversion.

Related to the question of images of women in GE is the nature of the relationship between Gilgamesh and Enkidu. Apart from his closeness to his mother, Gilgamesh's only other intimate relationship demonstrated by kissing, embracing, and the holding of hands is with Enkidu.[46] As Thorkild Jacobsen has so aptly put it, "throughout the epic the relationship with Enkidu competes with, and replaces marriage."[47] I think that on a subliminal level, if not overtly, the composers of the epic were critical of so intense a relationship between men.[45] Anne Kilmer in her stimulating article "A Note on an Overlooked Word-Play in the Akkadian Gilgamesh," suggests that the word plays *ḫaṣṣinnu : assinnu, kiṣru : kezru,* and the sexual symbolism of *pukku* and *mekkû* point to what may well have been a homosexual relationship between Gilgamesh and Enkidu.[49] She calls attention to what I would more precisely describe as *reverse* sexual similes and metaphors: Enkidu's hair is like a woman's (I ii 36), Gilgamesh veils his dead friend like a bride (VIII ii 17), to mention a few. Several times in his early dreams, Gilgamesh makes love to Enkidu's symbols (*kīma aššate*).[50] What is noteworthy is that the relationship between them is not simply that of male and female but that of husband and wife. Theirs then was a reversal of normal societal relations, which potentially undermined the continuity and stability of the family. It is an example of category inversion—male acts like female.

In view of this, one aspect of Tablet XII needs to be underlined. Along with others,[51] I would contend that Tablet XII is an integral part of GE. Central to its theme is the importance of family, the necessity of offspring to mourn the deceased and provide the *kispu* offering.[52] And it is Enkidu, who has been treated like a woman and wife, who voices this view implicitly, if not explicitly. The non-biological immortality which Gilgamesh sought so mightily is rejected by the author(s); the importance of family and kin to a meaningful life is upheld.

Inversion then is one of the keys to understanding GE. The reversals of the norms detected in GE, of the *ḫarimtu,* of the *sābitu,* of Ishtar, of Gilgamesh and Enkidu, the inversion of the social pyramid and of expected roles and categories must have made for humor and comedy which would have had great appeal to ancient audiences. What has been said about inversions in carnival-like festivals may well be applicable to Mesopotamian society. Through inversion "a society with an acute sense of the necessity of everyday social distinctions [might experience] an apparently 'ideal' state of anarchy which it had no wish to bring permanently into being."[53]

Before concluding, we should give brief consideration to the paradigmatic image of "mother" in GE. I suspect that this is a common image in other myths and epics in Sumerian and Akkadian. For example, in the Enuma Elish, Tiamat is the mother regarded negatively: *Tiamat ālittani izirrannâši* (En. el. III 15, 73). She, like Ishtar, broke the boundary between male and female, setting up an Assembly and doing battle with Marduk, thus participating in male spheres. Damkina, on the other hand, like Ninsun, acts as a mother should: *ālittašu ušālilšu* (En. el. V 81). When Marduk is raised to kingship, her gift to him is singled out (En. el. V 81–83).

What is the significance of this mother image? One might suggest that its prevalence in GE reflects the wish for the intimacy of mother-child in infancy, for a time of deep security and ignorance of death and so, distance from the reality of human mortality.

One should also ask whether this pervasive image tells us something about intrafamilial relations in ancient Mesopotamia. Was the mother *the* significant female in a man's life even after he had grown up and married, as was and is the case in India and China?[54] Was there an "ascending scale of affection"[55] of wife, sister, and mother, with mother first in importance? Definitive responses to what must at this time remain questions require close and sensitive study of the sources of everyday life: legal and economic texts, and especially letters. Perhaps related to the issue is the parricide motif found in Mesopotamian myths such as the Enuma Elish and the Theogony of Dunnu.

The Gilgamesh Epic informs and reveals cultural stereotypes and ideals, perhaps even the irretrievable life experiences of its author(s), but what can it inform us about everyday life?

* * *

NOTES

1. In a review of W. Röllig, et al., *Altorientalische Literaturen,* in *JAOS* 100 (1980) 189–90.
2. Charles Segal, "Ancient Texts and Modern Literary Criticism," *Arethusa* I/1 (1968), p. 7. Like Moran, Segal pressed for openness to literary-critical analyses of classical texts. Since this article he and other classicists have been highly productive in this direction, especially in treating women in myth and drama.
3. *The Evolution of the Gilgamesh Epic* (Philadelphia: University of Pennsylvania, 1982), pp. 232f. The problem, of course, is whether the contractions and expansions of women's speeches really incorporate

changing attitudes or are simply literary structural changes. But I am aware that my not carefully separating the images in the different versions can create some confusion. What is sorely needed is a composite critical edition of GE.

4. Ibid., pp. 74–75. There is also more stress put on her wisdom in the Late Version. She is not only *mūdât kalâma* but also *emqet*.

5. Penny Schine Gold, *The Lady and the Virgin: Image, Attitude and Experience in Twelfth Century France* (Chicago: University of Chicago, 1985), p. 2. My thinking on images of women was greatly stimulated by Gold's study, especially by her comments in the Preface. Despite the vast differences between Mesopotamian and medieval French society, what Gold has to say about the often uncritical presuppositions of feminist historians in her field has been very helpful to me.

6. This is even true of Ishtar. Note the brevity of her proposal over against the length of Gilgamesh's refusal of her proposal.

7. Gold, op. cit. p. xviii.

8. Herein lie both the challenges and the pitfalls confronting the modern studying an ancient text. To what extent can ancient fantasies and realities be sorted out without imposing modern western views on an alien culture? A. Leo Oppenheim was acutely sensitive to this problem. See especially "Introduction: Assyriology—What and How?" in his *Ancient Mesopotamia* (Chicago: University of Chicago, 1964), pp. 7ff.

9. Barbara A. Babcock, ed., *The Reversible World: Symbolic Inversion in Art and Society* (Ithaca: Cornell University, 1978), pp. 14–15. In the introduction to this highly stimulating collection of essays, Babcock offers an excellent analysis of the various forms of inversion, their history and functions. She traces inversion back to "Greek parody of the Homeric journey to Hades" (p. 16). In my opinion, and this is at the heart of my essay, GE is a far earlier source of inversion.

10. Ian Donaldson, *The World Upside-Down: Comedy from Jonson to Fielding* (Oxford: Oxford University, 1970), p. 6. I am well aware of the need for caution in applying a literary technique common in Western literature to GE. But, as Babcock points out in her introduction (see above, n. 9) and as other essays in her book demonstrate, viewing the world as "upside down" and as topsy turvey seems to have universal comic appeal. B. R. Foster in his survey of humor in cuneiform literature in *JANES* 6 (1974), pp. 69–85, makes no specific mention of inversion. However the *aluzinnu* text discussed by Foster on pp. 74ff. (he very aptly translates *aluzinnu* as "trickster") may well belong to a genre associated with Ishtar festivities which, as I hope to show elsewhere, were very much involved with inversion. I suspect that "The Poor Man of Nippur" also fits the inversion pattern.

11. See rīmtu(m) in *AHw.*, p. 986, and Wendy Doninger O'Flaherty, *Women, Androgynes and Other Mythical Beasts* (Chicago: University of Chicago, 1980), pp. 33, 42, 91 and passim for the cow as nourishing mother and goddess in Hindu tradition.

12. A. L. Oppenheim, *Dream-book,* pp. 221f. The interpretation of dreams by mothers is often an aspect of their reassuring a troubled child.
13. This is an interesting parallel with Achilles and his mother Thetis. With both heroes, the father is very much in the background and there exists an intense relationship with another male.
14. The term *ḫarimtu* in the Enkidu episode is, in my view, a non-judgmental term for a woman who uses her sexuality to support herself. In Enkidu's curse the *ḫarimtu* becomes an object of male control and male violence. Perhaps translating it "harlot" or "whore" in the latter case might more accurately reflect the negative judgment. The feminist historian Gerda Lerner, in her highly speculative and problematic article, "The Origin of Prostitution in Ancient Mesopotamia," *Signs: Journal of Women in Culture and Society* 11 (1986), pp. 236–54, treats the *ḫarimtu*-Enkidu episode as an historical datum. She considers the *ḫarimtu* in the episode as "a temple harlot [who] is an accepted part of society." The *ḫarimtu* of the curse she views as a "commercial" harlot. She goes on to say that "the nature of this curse tells us that the *ḫarimtu* who mated with Enkidu lived an easier and better life than the harlot who has her stand at the town hall and is abused by her drunken customers" (p. 246). Lerner disregards the fact that GE is a literary work and therefore historical data must be separated from literary motifs and themes. Among other things, the curse and blessing of Enkidu reflect the ambiguous attitudes toward the prostitute and incorporate the realities of her life. Perhaps the curse of Enkidu describes the life of the poor prostitute whereas the blessing describes the prostitute with something of the status of the Greek *hetaira,* a woman of culture and artistic talents very like the *lukur* of the Ur III period. There is no evidence in GE of a "temple" prostitute over against a "commercial" prostitute. Indeed I think the existence and extent of cultic prostitution requires reconsideration and more careful study of the primary sources. It is obvious that prostitution was a social fact. The question is how, when, and where it was transformed into an organized and institutionalized phenomenon of urban life. In Sippar, as *one* text suggests, a group of prostitutes (several of them from elsewhere) lived in a group under the supervision, in some way, of the *kala-māḫu* of the Shamash temple (see my *Ancient Sippar* [Istanbul, 1975], p. 332). Yet the expected association should rather be with the Ishtar temple that existed in Sippar. It may have been a matter of administration but in no way a question of cultic function.
15. *SBH* 106: 51. See *CAD* under *aštammu* and under *ḫarimtu* for other references linking prostitution and taverns. Note that it is *aštammu* and not *bīt sābīti* which is used for tavern. For more on this last point, see below n. 26. Note that Enkidu's curse also brings prostitute and tavern together. [Cf. GÉME.KAR.AK = *za-bí-tum, ša-ma-ak-tum,* GÉME.GÀR.RA = *za-bí-tum,* in G. Pettinato, *MEE* 4, p. 340 l. 1412a,b—P.S.]

16. E.g., Lambert *BWL* 102: 73–79. R. Westbrook in *JAOS* 104 (1984), pp. 753–56, examines evidence suggesting that public authorities might intervene to restrain a husband's extra-marital liaison with a prostitute.
17. *The Meaning of Aphrodite* (Chicago: University of Chicago, 1978), p. 14.
18. G. Farber-Flügge, *Der Mythos "Inanna und Enki" unter besonderer Berücksichtigung der Liste der* me (Studia Pohl 10 [1973]), p. 56: 38f.
19. See N. K. Gottwald, *The Tribes of Yahweh: A Sociology of the Religion of Liberated Israel 1250–1050 B.C.* (Maryknoll, N.Y.: Orbis, 1979), pp. 557f., where he discusses Rahab's social position as a prostitute. Note that she may have "operated an inn," again the common association of prostitute and inn/tavern.
20. In Michelle Z. Rosaldo and Louise Lamphere, eds., *Women, Culture, and Society* (Stanford: Stanford University, 1974), pp. 67–87.
21. The masculine (pre)occupation with sexuality can be seen in the uses of *šamḫiš* and *qašdu* cited by D. O. Edzard, *Orientalia* 54 (1985) pp. 53f. the *šamḫākuma attanallak* of Gilgamesh's dream in Gilg. P. i 4 should also be added. Note, as Edzard does, that Uruk is also described as the city of *kezrēti šamḫāti u ḫarimāti* in Gilg. VI 165–166.
22. Here we find perhaps here the binary opposition of the raw and the cooked: milk of wild animals over against bread and beer which are cooked and processed. Note too that the hunter and shepherds who live in contact with the wild are also intermediary figures in GE.
23. Given the confines of this paper I will only note in passing the consummate artistry with which the author(s) delineate the subtle and significant changes in the relationship, from wordlessness to dialogue; the importance of Enkidu's looking at and listening to Shamhat, beautifully replicating a child's development which ends with leaving mother and home and entering a man's world.
24. For a discussion, with literature, of the readings suggested for the simile, see J. Renger, *RA 66* (1972), p. 90. He opts for "like a god/deity." This too would present a role reversal, the prostitute functioning as a deity and Enkidu as mere mortal! Note that when they eventually go to Uruk roles have changed, Enkidu walks "ahead and Shamhat behind him" (Gilg. P. v 8f.), in conventional(?) male-female fashion.
25. Whether there was the topos of wise woman in Mesopotamia, as Claudia V. Camp, *CBQ* 43 (1981), pp. 14ff., suggests was the case for ancient Israel, has yet to be investigated. What seems to me likely is that the proverbial language of the *ḫarimtu* (and of the *sābītu*) is an important element of inversion: from the mouths of these marginal, and I presume, uneducated, perhaps uncouth, women issue forth words of learning. See S. N. Kramer, *JAOS* 89 (1969), p. 10, for the simile "its (the bird's) mouth hurled invectives like a prostitute."

26. I opt for the translation "tavernkeeper" rather than "barmaid," for it seems more in keeping with the economic status of the *sābītu* in the OB period. Then too Siduri has the equipment of the brewer (*kannu, namzītu* in Gilg. X i 3), so she is more than a barmaid. The importance of the *sābītu* in the OB period emerges from her mention in *CH* §§108–110; Goetze, *LE* §§15 and 41, as well as in three paragraphs of the Ammiṣaduqa Edict (14–16). See *CAD* for other references. The *(bīt) aštammi* and the *bīt sābīti* were presumably not one and the same place, although there was certainly an overlap in their functions. Both provided drinks, entertainment, and a place to meet prostitutes. Although the *aštammu* probably was also an inn, providing overnight lodging to travellers, there is no such evidence for the *bīt sābīti*. Both appear to have had "bad" reputations (see *CAD* for references). For references to the literature and discussion of both and the Arzana House in Hittite sources, see H. Hoffner in *Anatolian Studies Güterbock*, pp. 113ff. An important aspect of the *aštammu* is its relationship to the cult of Ishtar. See *CAD* where ÈŠ.DAM refers to the entire temple of Ishtar. Games were "played" in Ishtar's cult, and the *aštammu* and the *bīt sābīti* were places of "games." For references see *CAD* under *mēlultu* and *mēlulu*.

27. See W. C. Lambert in *Kraus AV*, p. 208, for comments on Šidūrī as a name of Ishtar. It seems to me that for both Siduri and the *ḫarimtu* Shamhat, the association with Ishtar is significant. But what its implication is, given Ishtar's rejection alongside their acceptance in GE, bespeaks nuances that elude me at present.

28. The suggestion of E. Speiser in *ANET*, p. 89 n. 152.

29. According to *CH* §§110 a *nadītu* or *ugbabtu* who opens or enters a tavern would be punished by being burnt to death, presumably because their chastity would be called into question. It is noteworthy that this rare harsh punishment was also meted out for incest between mother and son. See *ARM* 1 28: 17f. for army deserters who come to the *bīt sābītim ana mēlulim*. There is no evidence that the *bīt sābî* was 'distinct from the *bīt sābīti*. Note too the reference cited in *CAD* under *sābû* in *bīt sābî* (*KAR* 144: 19): *limḫurki* É LÚ *sābî narāmki* "may the inn that you (Ishtar) love receive you."

30. See Tigay, op. cit, pp. 167–9, 211–12, for a discussion of her "philosophy." See also above, n. 25.

31. It is a striking contrast that men are always addressed by name in the Utnapishtim story. After all, her husband might have been addressed by his wife: *marḫīssu ana šâšuma izakkar ana ḫāʾiriša* parallel to PN *ana šašima izakkar ana marḫītišu*.

32. See the examples noted below of Aya and the women of Uruk. See also the roles of mothers in the Anzu and the Enki and Ninmah myths. This feature needs further study.

33. In GE women speaking proverbially are consoling. Note also the harsh proverbial discourse of Gilgamesh with Ishtar.

34. A close study of letters to and by women focusing on women's rhetoric in light of recent analytical methods and comparative studies in this area might yield important results. Siduri's speech might also be described as "specific" in character.
35. If this is indeed the case, it would be strong confirmation of one of the basic theses of this essay.
36. *tazzimtašina ištenemme* (Gilg. I ii 29).
37. This seems to be an echo from everyday life: the wife having to remind the busy, forgetful husband of some family matter or member.
38. It is amazing that in GE, Ishtar's name has been substituted for Mami and Nintu of the OB Atrahasis flood versions (see Tigay, op. cit., p. 224f.), given the antipathy toward her in Gilg. VI 1–79. There was no attempt to reconcile the contradiction. Though never a mother goddess in the Mesopotamian pantheon, Ishtar as the "mother" of kings is well attested. And yet the paradox is so much part of her nature. See the next note.
39. *The Treasures of Darkness* (New Haven: Yale University, 1976), p. 135. In a forthcoming article tentatively titled "The Paradox of Ishtar, Destroyer of Boundaries," I will treat the complex, paradoxical and extraordinary nature of this goddess who confuses and destroys the boundaries which differentiate the species (animals and humans), the sexes (male and female), the generations (young and old) and the social strata (high and low). Only when she attempts to break the boundary between the dead and the living is she powerless. I think that in subtle ways there are allusions to this boundlessness of Ishtar in the range of her lovers: bird, wild animal, domestic animal, and human.
40. Tzvi Abusch kindly sent me a copy of his forthcoming article on this episode (see now *History of Religions* 26 [1986], pp. 143–87). It is a comprehensive and in-depth analysis, the focus of which is very different from mine. This, once again, demonstrates the mutivalence of GE, surely the touchstone of a classic.
41. Yet even she proposes marriage and not an affair. So despite the inversion she too reinforces the social norms as do other women in GE.
42. The *nādu* "waterskin" of line 38 and the *šēnu* "shoe" of line 41, I suggest, are the masculine symbols.
43. For the bisexuality of Ishtar, see H. Hoffner in *JBL* 85 (1966), pp. 333f. n. 54. In addition to his references to *CAD*, see now also *CAD* under the lexical section of *mēlultu* for the dual nuances of this term as "play" and "battle," in connection with Inanna/Ishtar. What is an integral part of Ishtar's nature, her "manliness," is rejected in GE.
44. Lambert *BWL* 102: 72. Would the *šāra* of Gilg. VI 34 call to mind to the listener the *šāri* of the proverb?
45. *Women, Androgynes, and Other Mythical Beasts* pp. 72ff. There is I think much merit in looking to other polytheistic traditions and the scholarly work done with these to better understand Mesopotamian

attitudes to the gods. This is not to dismiss political or historical issues which I think must be considered. More questionable is the view that the "immorality" of Ishtar was rejected. See the pertinent comments of I. M. Diakonoff in *BiOr* 18 (1961), pp. 65f. Application of O'Flaherty's "banalization of the gods" deserves far more space than I devote to it here.

46. Tigay, op. cit., p. 9 n. 20, p. 274 n. for *a-ḫa-ab-bu-ub*.

47. Op. cit., p. 218*.

48. Homosexuality is banned only in the MA laws (§20) and so it may well have been a social reality. See *RLA* 4, p. 459, for a detailed discussion. However, it seems hardly to have been institutionalized as it was in classical Athens (see the study by K. Dover, *Greek Homosexuality* [New York: Vintage, 1978]). Pertinent perhaps is the proverb *ibrūtam ša ūmakkal kinātūtu ša dārâti* (Lambert, *BWL* 259: 10). Enkidu is often referred to as *ibru* by Gilgamesh and on occasion Enkidu so refers to Gilgamesh. The competition of intense friendship with kin and other ties may have been addressed in this proverb. Note the theme of failed friendship in the epics of Lugalbanda and Etana.

49. In *Kraus AV* pp. 130ff.

50. See also the simile describing the mourning Gilgamesh in Gilg. VIII ii 19: *kīma nēšti* ša *šuddat mēraniša ittanasḫur ana pānišu u arkišu* with its maternal association, and perhaps an extension of the husband/wife motif. Note too that all descriptions of physical beauty in GE are confined to Gilgamesh and Enkidu.

51. Kilmer, op. cit., pp. 130f.; B. Alster, *RA* 68 (1974), pp. 55ff.; and Abusch, op. cit., as well.

52. Incredibly, even in the netherworld unexpected mention is made of a mother, "the mother of Ninazu" in Gilg. XII 29, 47. The mention of "her breast" (*iratsa*) with its maternal association, in Gilg. XII 31, 49, should also be noted.

53. Donaldson, op. cit., p. 15.

54. Margery Wolf, "Chinese Women," in Rosaldo and Lamphere, op. cit., p. 168, notes that the Chinese mother made "full use of her husband's isolation from his children to strengthen their bond to her." For the close mother-son relationship and the importance of sons to mothers in the politics of the Indian family, see Sudhir Kakar, *The Inner World: A Psychoanalytic Study of Childhood and Society in India* (New Delhi: Oxford University, 1978), p. 57. The unusual text describing Lú-dingir-ra's message to his mother may have some bearing on the issue of the mother-son relationship in Mesopotamia. For a translation, literature on, and discussion of this text, see S. N. Kramer, "Poets and Psalmists," in D. Schmandt-Besserat, ed., *The Legacy of Sumer* (BiMes 4; Malibu, 1976), pp. 19–21.

55. This phrase is used by J. Th. Kakrides, *Homeric Researches* (Lund: Gleerup, 1949). On pp. 152ff. he discusses the ascending scale of affection in ancient Indian tales where siblings and parents rank above

spouse; in other words, brotherly love is valued more highly than conjugal or filial love. The Inanna/Dumuzi laments might also be reexamined in light of this perspective. Note the comments by S. N. Kramer in his recent review of J. Van Dijk, *LUGAL UD ME-LÁM-bi NIR-GÁL,* in *JAOS* 105 (1985), p. 137, where he differs with Van Dijk on the nature of the relationship between Ninurta and his mother. He seems to suggest incestuous overtones. Much, I think, can be learned regarding problems and methods in utilizing myths as sources for rediscovering ancient intrafamilial relations from the critical and balanced review of Philip Slater's *The Glory of Hera: Greek Mythology and the Greek Family* by Helene P. Foley in *Diacritics* 5 (1975), pp. 31–36.

* * *

Tikva Frymer-Kensky
"The Marginalization of the Goddesses"

Tikva Frymer-Kensky provides a very different context for *Gilgamesh* than earlier scholars had. She locates the unified epic of Old Babylonian times in a period of profound cultural changes. Where the Sumerian texts and sociopolitical institutions of the Third Millennium recognize the importance of goddesses and provide evidence that women occupied positions of power in the Sumerian city-states, by early in the Second Millennium the status of both had begun to change. Only the goddess Inanna/Ishtar survives the changes, and she mainly is the exception that proves the rule about women.

Frymer-Kensky provides evidence from Sumerian texts to show that goddesses that were once powerful were reduced to marginality and, where not invisible, stereotyped in texts as mother, advisor, and temptress. Even Sumerian mythological texts that ostensibly praise the goddesses depict them as losing out to their chief rival, the god Enki. With Akkadian mythological literature, especially *Atrahasis, Enuma Elish* and *Gilgamesh,* only the mother-function is preserved, and in the most extreme (but politically important) story, *Enuma Elish,* the primordial goddess Tiamat is defeated by the city god of Babylon, Marduk. In *Gilgamesh* Frymer-Kensky is most concerned with Gilgamesh's rejection of Ishtar and Ishtar's harsh attempt at retaliation, which may be part of growing anti-Ishtar feelings in the period.

With the eclipse of the goddesses and the decline of the "sacred marriage" rites—no longer state-ruled or state-centered—human and divine women tend to disappear from the Akkadian texts. Frymer-Kensky thinks the disappearance is linked to a reduced status of women. The Reforms of Uruinimgina, for example, suggest a movement from polyandry, if it ever occurred, to monogamy. Finally, Frymer-Kensky claims that the temptation to attribute the changes to ethnic change in the leadership of the region must be resisted. The development of the imperial states of Babylonia and Assyria would seem to account for changes felt in so many cultural products of Mesopotamia. (Ed.)

The Sumerian pantheon that we have been considering was never uniform or static. During the six hundred years between the time of the Abu Salabikh texts (our earliest religious documents) and the growth of Akkadian literature during the Old Babylonian period, empires came and went, wars were fought, and there were political and economic rivalries between cities. It is hard to imagine that such major changes in life would not cause a constant reordering of the pantheon. With the coming of new peoples to Mesopotamia at the beginning of the second millennium and the establishment thereafter of new city-states and—ultimately—of the Old Babylonian empire (circa 1760 B.C.E.), change continued and intensified.

These changes took place in many aspects of society: in the organization of the state, in the socioeconomic system, in the concept of the nature of kingship and political authority, and in theological conceptions of the world of gods. Among the changes in religion, one trend that becomes very clear is the ongoing eclipse and the marginalization of the goddesses. This process did not suddenly begin in the Old Babylonian period, nor should it be attributed to the influx of new peoples. On the contrary, this process seems already under way as soon as a written record becomes available. Despite the extensive roles of goddesses in Sumerian literature, one gets the impression that things are already in flux and that our documents already reflect a process of supplanting goddesses. An example of this process is the goddess Ningirim. In the earliest historical period, that of the Abu Salabikh and Fara texts, she was an important goddess, who figures prominently in the incantations as the exorcist of the gods, the goddess of magical formulae, and the mistress of purificatory water.[1] In later literature, that of the classic Sumerian period, she is still mentioned occasionally as mistress of incantations, but is a minor figure compared to Enki and his assistant Asalluhi.

Much of the diminution of the goddesses is associated with the god Enki. Enki's mother Nammu was mistress of the watery deeps, the Sumerian prototype of the later Tiamat of the Enuma Elish. However, she is rarely found in god lists or in myths or hymns, and throughout Sumerian literature, it is Enki who is acknowledged lord of the subterranean waters. Another example is the case of Ninurra, who in the third millennium was the god of pot making. She was clearly a goddess, the mother of Umma, for she is named in Early Dynastic texts as the wife of the god Shara of Umma, and is called "the mother who counsels Enki."[2] Later, Ninurra was absorbed (as a male god) into the persona of Enki/Ea.

This diminution of the goddesses continued and intensified in the Old Babylonian periods and later. There are very few stories about females in Akkadian literature, and those females who do appear are generally in ancillary roles and in the stereotypical figures of mother, advisor, and temptress. Even the major female figures of Sumerian literature have shrunk or disappeared. Gula, the goddess of healing, is still there, but often shares her role with Damu, who was probably originally her daughter,[3] but later becomes her son. Nisaba, patroness of learning, has all but disappeared. The chief figure of wisdom is Enki/Ea, while Nisaba's role as goddess of writing and patron of scribal schools was taken over by Nabu. By the later periods in Mesopotamia, only Ishtar has any real impact and persona. Other goddesses exist primarily as "consorts," mere sexual partners for male deities.

The eclipse of the goddesses can be seen dramatically by the fortunes of mother-figures. The primordial first-mothers disappear early. In the marshy south, the mother of all and the creator of humanity was Nammu, who was then eclipsed by Enki. In another strand of Mesopotamian mythology, the primordial mother was Ki, the earth. According to this theology, the gods resulted from the union of An (heaven) and Ki (earth).[4] But Ki does not appear as a major goddess in any texts. As ruler of the earth she has been supplanted by her first son, Enlil (Lord Air) who is envisioned as the ruler of all that happens on the earth. It is possible that her very name, Ki, is eclipsed by that of Enki.[5]

Ninhursag was the great and active mother-goddess in Sumerian texts. Daughter of An and Ki and sister of Enlil, she was one of the greatest gods of Sumer. Texts from the southern city of Lagash, from the time of Eannatum down to Gudea, recite as the triad of the greatest gods An, Enlil, and Ninhursag.[6] Ninhursag, too, starts to decline in later Sumerian texts. By the time of the Isin and Larsa dynasties (1900–1800 B.C.E.), the supreme divine triad has become An, Enlil, and Enki, with Ninhursag listed as fourth in rank.

Even the role of the mother-goddess in the creation of the first humans is not unchallenged in Sumerian texts. One myth, The Pickaxe, relates the story of Enlil's creation of the pickaxe, the essential agricultural tool. In this story, once Enlil had created the pickaxe, he used it to dig a hole in the earth, and laid into the hole a brick-mold that had the seed of humanity. After he did this, people sprouted up from the ground like grass.[7] In this text, Enlil is clearly the motivating power, and humans are born from the seed that he created. Earth is the womb, but it is an earth devoid of "earth-mother"; it is inanimate and without volition.

Ultimately, it is again Enki who takes over the functions of the mother-goddess. This rivalry between Enki and that of the mother is reflected in two Sumerian myths, that of Enki and Ninmah and that of Enki and Ninhursag, both of which concern birth in some fashion. According to the Myth of Enki and Ninhursag, Enki in primordial times mated with Ninhursag, the primeval mother, then with Ninnisiga, the daughter of this union; with Ninkurra, the third-generation daughter; then with Ninimma, the fourth-generation daughter; and finally with Uttu, Ninimma's daughter. This last union was a domestic arrangement. When Uttu had trouble with pregnancy, Ninhursag came and took Enki's semen out of Uttu's womb, and planted it in the ground, where it grew into plants. Enki ate the plants in order to know (and appropriate) them. However, his semen was so powerful that the plants made Enki pregnant. Since he had no womb, he became sick. Despite her anger over his eating of the plants, Ninhursag came to Enki's aid. Having placed Enki in her vulva she turned her attention to the parts of the body that were paining Enki, and gave birth to a goddess from each one. There is clearly rivalry going on between Enki and Ninhursag, but in this myth the two powers seem to have struck a balance: both Enki's semen and Ninhursag's womb are necessary for the creation of goddesses.

The Myth of Enki and Ninmah, which deals with the creation of humans, also reflects this rivalry between the mother-goddess Enki. The tale begins with a depiction of a situation that existed before the creation of humanity, when the gods were laboring to dig the rivers. When they came to complain before the dormant Enki, his mother Nammu (called "the primordial creator") urged him to arise to help the suffering gods, suggesting that he fashion a worker to do the work for the gods. Enki agreed, and, for his part, suggested that Nammu make the creature, with Ninmah her helper and the other goddesses assisting. Nammu then created humankind. This is a very difficult text to understand: there are gaps at important lines and the language is sometimes obscure. Nammu was both the originator of the idea of creating humankind and the creator. Enki has some sort of role in this creation, for Nammu does not proceed with her idea until Enki has handed her suggestion back to her. Despite the presence of Enki, it is clearly Nammu who does the actual creation of humankind.[9] But this story is only the first part of the composition, Enki and Ninmah. The myth continues with the feast that Enki then made for Nammu and Ninmah. At this feast, Enki and Ninmah began a boasting-competition, as was often the custom at banquets.[9] In this contest, Ninmah (the mother goddess who oversees the shaping of the embryo in the womb) declared that the shape of humankind—good or bad—depends solely on her. Enki, for his part, declares that he can mitigate the good or the bad. These two gods go further than mere disputation: Ninmah proceeds to create defective characters: a palsied man, a blind man, a lame man, a moron, barren woman, and a sexless creature.[10] Enki creates societal roles for these imperfect humans: the palsied man, who cannot grasp a weapon, stands at the king's head; the blind man is a musician, the lame man is a smith, the moron (who is no threat) also stands at the head of the king, the barren woman can be a weaver in the queen's household, and the sexless man is a courtier. Enki has proven his point, and Ninmah stops her act of creation. However, Enki then goes a step further, daring Ninmah to find a role for the creature that *he* could create. Enki, who has no womb, asks for a woman to whom he can entrust his semen. But without Ninmah's help, the embryo cannot develop properly, the woman aborts, and Umul is born, probably extremely immature. He cannot eat or lie down, and Ninmah says that she cannot care for him. Enki points out that he was able to find roles for Ninmah's misbegotten creatures, and Ninmah recognizes that she has been defeated. At this point, Enki is gracious and magnanimous. He points out that Umul cannot be helped precisely because he was made without the good services of Ninmah, and he declares that Umul should be a reminder that whenever people praise phallic power (which, he says, they should), they should also remember Ninmah's role. Despite this speech of Enki, Enki has clearly won his challenge, and the balance between the forces has shifted. The poet concludes with the statement that Ninmah did not equal the great lord Enki.

The subsequent accounts of the creation of humankind show the continuing rise of Enki (later called by his Akkadian name, Ea). The Atrahasis Myth was written in Akkadian during the Old Babylonian period, sometime before the main version that we have, a dated three-tablet copy made by a junior scribe during the reign of Ammisaduqa of Babylon (ca. 1500 B.C.E.). This myth is a "primeval history": it begins before the creation of humankind and ends with the re-creation after the flood. The story of the creation is very similar to that of Enki and Ninmah. The gods are laboring, digging the Tigris and Euphrates rivers. Their work is difficult, and finally they decide to strike, and menacingly surround the house of Enlil. Enlil convenes the divine council, and after the striking gods hold fast and refuse to reveal the ringleader of the revolt, Enki suggests that they create a substitute worker to relieve the gods. The council summons the mother-goddess, but she surprisingly replies,

"It is not properly mine to do these things, this work belongs to Enki."[11] Enki then conceives a plan and the time to carry it out. He gives her the clay and has the gods slaughter an (otherwise unknown) god who has rationality. Mami ("mommy"), the mother-goddess, mixes the blood with the clay and divides the result into fourteen pieces, reciting an incantation as Enki prompts her. She has fourteen birth-goddesses come to shape the clay and sits counting the nine months, after which she performs the midwifery required. After gods acclaim her as the creatrix of humanity, the text here interrupts the narrative to inform the hearers that they are to leave the birthing brick in place for a week (or nine days) and give honor to the mother-goddess whenever a baby is born. There is great praise for the mother in this account of creation, but the role of Enki is still quite considerable.

The last stage in the creation of humankind is reached by the Myth of Enuma Elish—the tale of the exaltation of Marduk written in the latter half of the second millennium, a myth that became the great state myth of Babylon. This text relates how the young god Marduk, Ea's son, became the king of all the gods, and proceeded to create the world. As the culminating benefit that this new king bestowed on the gods, he had an artful idea: to create man to be charged with the service of the gods. Ea then conceives a plan and creates humanity from the blood of a slain god:

> *...Ea, the wise, had created humankind,*
> *had imposed upon it the service of the gods—*
> *that work was beyond comprehension;*
> *as artfully planned by Marduk,*
> *Nudimmud created it.*[12]

In this composition, the clay and the mother who uses it are gone. Ea is the sole creator of humanity, and he is given a special name, Nudimmud, "the man-creator."

These versions of the creation do not replace each other. The traditions of the creation of humanity by the mother-goddess do not disappear. Popular ritual commemorates the mother at births, and later scholarly compositions make allusion to "creatures whose clay Aruru took in her fingers."[13] Her role in the bringing of fertility is remembered in the Vassal Treaties of King Esarhaddon of Assyria, which includes among the curses against whoever breaks the covenant the imprecation that Belit-ili should put an end to giving birth in his land.[14] Similarly, the combined role of Enki/Ea and the mother-goddess found in the Atrahasis myth is maintained in this myth itself, for Atrahasis endures throughout Mesopotamian history, and new versions of it are found in the library of Ashurbanipal in Assyria (circa 600 B.C.E.). All the traditions are combined in another scholarly composition, which refers to "Narru (Enlil), king of the gods, who created humankind, and majestic Zulummar (Ea), who dug out their clay, and mistress Mami, who fashioned them."[15] The traditions continue, but each successive layer is a record of an ongoing religious development, of new philosophical sensibilities that view the world in a different light.

This new sensibility that develops in the second millennium clearly sees a world of gods in which all the major figures are male. This viewpoint is encapsulated in the Enuma Elish Myth, from whose account of the creation of humanity the mother goddess is conspicuously absent. There is a mother figure in this myth: Ti'amat, the primordial mother, "she who gave birth to all." Her role in this myth is very revealing, for she represents the ancient order which Marduk must defeat in order to become king of the gods. Ti'amat is not an evil force. When her husband Apsu wanted to fight in order to stem the tide of change in the world of the gods, Ti'amat refused to join him, reacting as a protective mother: "What, should we destroy that we have built? Their ways indeed are most troublesome, but let us be patient."[16] After Apsu has been vanquished, Ti'amat tries to reestablish the old tranquil order, to avenge the death of her husband, and to bring relief to the many gods who want rest. Ti'amat forms an army and appoints a commander-in-chief, frightening the gods of the pantheon, who perceive her might and cannot do battle with her. At this point Marduk, Ea's son, steps forth from the young generation of gods. He is willing to fight her, and does not recognize her might: "what male is it who has pressed his fight against you?... Ti'amat, a woman, flies at you with weapons."[17] Marduk defeats Ti'amat in single combat, and becomes king of the gods. From her body, Marduk creates the world and organizes the cosmos as a divine state. We live in the body of the mother, but she has neither activity nor power.

Ultimately, with the establishment of the royal imperial states of Assyria and Babylonia, the Enuma Elish became a royal ritual.[18] The kings began to reenact the part of Marduk in the military and kingly role related by the Enuma Elish. They participated in the right of Marduk to rule and in the proving and bestowal of this right. Thus the late kings took part in a ritual that celebrated stability rather than fertility, order rather than union, monarchy rather than renewal. In such a ritual, women and goddesses could have no role other than as the mother to be deposed.

The royal sacred marriage did not entirely disappear. The myth with which it was associated, the tale of Dumuzi and Inanna, had a very long life. Special songs for Inanna/Ishtar and Dumuzi were still recited in the first millenium, and even the women of Jerusalem were still weeping for Tammuz (Dumuzi) in the times of Ezekiel. But this cult as a whole was no longer state-centered or run, and became a matter for private rather than public worship. A ritual of union between the gods Marduk and Nabu and their spouses was practiced in the temples after the Old Babylonian period, but it was dramatically altered. In these later sacred marriages, a king no longer played the part of the god. Indeed, no humans were involved in the conjugal union. The statues of the gods were brought to a garden (perhaps in procession), hymns were sung, and the statues were left there together overnight.[19] This ritual seems to lack the excitement and the glamour of the Sumerian sacred marriage. More importantly, by the fact that it lacks the human component, it cannot serve to bring people or kings into particular relationship with the divine. Human sexuality has lost its power to express the congress of the gods except as a vague idea; and the interchange between divine and human is completely lost.

The whole complex of divine kingship, the use of the divine titles, the object of offerings, and even the writing of hymns, all these start to disappear in the Old Babylonian period. The kings of Isin and Larsa (the Early Old Babylonian period) still claimed the special spouse-relationship with Inanna.[20] However, the time of Hammurabi was clearly the dawn of a new sensibility. Not only does Hammurabi not use the divine title "god," even though royal hymns still attribute it to him, but he counts his ancestry from early Amorites rather than from gods. After the Old Babylonian period, even royal hymns disappear.

This change in sensibility may be reflected mythologically in the Gilgamesh Epic. In this tale, written during the Old Babylonian period, Ishtar has become attracted to Gilgamesh, the mighty king of Uruk, and offers to marry him. He, however, bluntly refuses and recites an unflattering account of the fate of Ishtar's husbands. In the context of the story, Gilgamesh, who is descended from Lugalbanda and the goddess Ninsun, has rejected the world of the gods. All his actions in the rest of the epic belie his divine origins. He has fantastic adventures, but he remains the representative of every mortal man. His very quest for immortality shows his involvement in the human dilemma. Gilgamesh the king becomes the paradigm of humanity rather than the stepping-stone to the world of the gods. In the broader context of religious history, the rejection of Ishtar may be a reflection of the rejection of the entire philosophy of kingship of the Akkadian and Ur III periods. During the Old Babylonian period, the sacred marriage disappeared, and with it, all the ideas of divinity-in-kingship.

This is not to say that future Mesopotamian kings no longer had any need to differentiate themselves from the people nor to claim special status as warrant for their authority. The Gilgamesh Epic says of Gilgamesh, born of a divine mother and a god-king father, that "his body was the flesh-kin of the gods," and this kinship is also claimed by Tukulti-Ninurta, the king who marks the beginning of Assyrian power.[21] Tukulti-Ninurta is also described as the "image" *(ṣalam)* of the god Enlil, and this concept of the god's image becomes an attribute of later kings—and only of kings. It is a term of authority, and indicates that the king is god's counterpart on earth.[22] It does not indicate that the king himself belongs to the divine world. As in so many areas of religious thought, the goddesses are no longer prominent in the metaphysics of kingship. They no longer have anything to do with the king's special status, nor are they the king's pathway to the world of the divine.

There is only one goddess who escaped this eclipse: Ishtar (Inanna) not only did not disappear, but continued to grow in importance. Ishtar/Inanna was not easily eradicated. As an unencumbered woman, she could not easily be relegated to the domestic sphere. Her role as representative of sexual attraction could not be taken over by a male god in any way that would be meaningful to the males of ancient Mesopotamia. As goddess of warfare, she maintained and even increased her prominence during the warfare-laden periods of state formation and empire building. This was particularly true in Assyria, whose kings modeled themselves in many ways on the ancient Sargonic kings of Akkadian times. Ishtar, the patron deity of Agade whom Enheduanna had exalted and magnified in ancient Sumerian poetry, was revered in Assyria as "the one who smites the weapons of the enemy." Ishtar was the "manly" goddess, the exception that proved the rule about females. Ultimately, she became a "Great Goddess" to whom was attributed a wide variety of attributes and characteristics, including those of the mother-goddess.

This does not mean that Ishtar was easily loved. On the one hand, she was glorified and exalted as preeminent among gods and men. But she was, to put it mildly, intimidating and frightening. Even her very sexual attractiveness inspired fear, and men expressed their dread that such lust might lead to their doom. Alongside hymns to Ishtar's glory and preeminence, we also find negative portrayals and ultimately a demonization of her image. In the Old Babylonian Gilgamesh Epic, when Gilgamesh refuses Ishtar's propositions he is, in part, renouncing the Sumerian sacred marriage in which kings did become Ishtar's lovers and received through this union blessings and prosperity.[23] Inanna then takes revenge so wantonly destructive that it suggests that this Babylonian epic intends a conscious repudiation and vilification of Ishtar.[24] A similar negative portrayal of Ishtar is found in the Old Babylonian Agushaya Hymn, which portrays Ishtar as so indiscriminately wild and ferocious that the gods cannot control her. Anti-Ishtar feelings persist and focus either on the ferocity of her rage[25] or on the dramatic excess of her cult in Uruk.[26] Antipathy to Ishtar takes its extreme (though perhaps unconscious) form in the depiction of Lamashtu, the demon who kills newborn children. This demon, daughter of An, shares many characteristics of Ishtar, from her loose hair, to her restlessness, to her association with lions, and may very well be the fearsome side of Ishtar's character split off and demonized into a separate character, an evil doppelganger to the mighty goddess.[27]

Ishtar-bashing is not universal: the Old Babylonian period also produced the beautiful hymn "To the Goddess, Sing,"[28] which talks only about the great grace, beauty, and joy that Ishtar brings. Similarly, later hymns also concentrate on the glory, beauty, and kindness of Ishtar. It is this deep ambivalence towards the powerful sexy female that makes Ishtar such a compelling figure.

By the end of the second millennium, the religious thinkers of Mesopotamia saw the cosmos as controlled and regulated by male gods, with only Ishtar maintaining a position of power. When we see such a pattern of theological change, we must ask whether the religious imagery is leading society, or whether it is following socioeconomic development? Was the supplanting of goddesses in Sumerian religious texts an inner theological development that resulted purely from the tendency to view the world of the gods on the model of an imperial state in which women paid no real political role?[29] Or does it follow in the wake of sociological change, of the development of what might be called "patriarchy"? And if the latter is true, is the change in the world of the gods contemporary to the changes in human society, or does it lag behind it by hundreds of years? To these questions we really have no answer. The general impression that we get from Sumerian texts is that at least some women had a more prominent role than was possible in the succeeding Babylonian and Assyrian periods of Mesopotamian history. But developments within the 600-year period covered by

Sumerian literature are more difficult to detect. One slight clue might (very hesitantly) be furnished by a royal document called the "Reforms of Uruinimgina." Uruinimgina (whose name is read Urukagina in earlier scholarly literature) was a king of Lagash around 2350 B.C.E. As a nondynastic successor to the throne, he had to justify his power, and wrote a "reform" text in which he related how bad matters were before he became king and described the new reforms that he instituted in order to pursue social justice. Among them we read, "the women of the former days used to take two husbands, but the women of today (if they attempt to do this) are stoned with the stones inscribed with their evil intent." Polyandry (if it ever really existed) has been supplanted by monogamy and occasional polygyny.[30]

In early Sumer, royal women had considerable power. In early Lagash, the wives of the governors managed the large temple estates.[31] The dynasty of Kish was founded by Enmebaragesi, a contemporary of Gilgamesh, who it now appears may have been a woman;[32] later, another woman, Kubaba the tavern lady, became ruler of Kish and founded a dynasty that lasted a hundred years. We do not know how important politically the position of En priestess of Ur was, but it was high position, occupied by royal women at least from the time of Enheduanna, daughter of Sargon (circa 2300 B.C.E.), and through the time of the sister of Warad-Sin and Rim-Sin of Larsa in the second millennium.[33] The prominence of individual royal women continued throughout the third dynasty of Ur.[34] By contrast, women have very little role to play in the latter half of the second millennium; and in first millennium texts, as in those of the Assyrian period, they are practically invisible.

We do not know all the reasons for this decline. It would be tempting to attribute it to the new ideas brought in by new people with the mass immigration of the West Semites into Mesopotamia at the start of the second millennium. However, this cannot be the true origin. The city of Mari on the Euphrates in Syria around 1800 B.C.E. was a site inhabited to a great extent by West Semites. In the documents from this site, women (again, royal women) played a role in religion and politics that was not less than that played by Sumerian women of the Ur III period (2111–1950 B.C.E.).[35] The causes for the change in women's position is not ethnically based. The dramatic decline of women's visibility does not take place until well into the Old Babylonian period (circa 1600 B.C.E.), and may be function of the change from city-states to larger nation-states and the changes in the social and economic systems that this entailed.

The eclipse of the goddesses was undoubtedly part of the same process that witnessed a decline in the public role of women, with both reflective of fundamental changes in society that we cannot yet specify. The existence and power of a goddess, particularly of Ishtar, is no indication or guarantee of a high status for human women. In Assyria, where Ishtar was so prominent, women were not. The texts rarely mention any individual women, and, according to the Middle Assyrian laws, married women were to be veiled, had no rights to their husband's property (even to movable goods), and could be struck or mutilated by their husbands at will. Ishtar, the female with the fundamental attributes of manhood, does not enable women to transcend their femaleness. In her being and her cult (where she changes men into women and women into men), she provides an outlet for strong feelings about gender, but in the final analysis, she is the supporter and maintainer of the gender order. The world by the end of the second millennium was a male's world, above and below; and the ancient goddesses have all but disappeared.

* * *

NOTES

1. See M. Krebernik, *Die Beschwörungen aus Fara and Ebla,* (Hildesheim and New York: Olms Verlag, 1985), 233–263.
2. *Or.* 28 (1959): 338, lines 9–10.
3 See J. J. van Dijk, "Le motif cosmique dans la pensée sumérienne," *Acta Orientalia* 29, 196. So T. Jacobsen, *Enc Rel,* vol. 9, M, 447–469.
4. See S. N. Kramer, "Poets and Psalmists: Goddesses and Theologians," in *The Legacy of Sumer,* Denise Schmandt-Besserat, ed. (Malibu, Calif.: Undena, 1976): 3–22.
5. Enki may be read as En for "lord" and Ki for "earth": "Lord of the Earth."
6. See A. Poebel, PBS 4: 24–31. Jacobsen has suggested that the economic prominence of calving and milk in the cowherder's world might have accounted for the early prominence of Ninhursag ("Notes on Nintur," *Or.* 42), but there are many reasons to expect a mother-goddess to be prominent in early religion.
7. The text, as yet unedited, has been published (in cuneiform) in TCL 16 n. 72 and UET VI/2. For these lines, see J. J. van Dijk, *Acta Orientalia* 28. Van Dijk lists this as an example of creation "by emersio," but in fact, people did not sprout until after Enlil planted the mold.
8. Jacobsen's translation, *Harps,* 157, "[without] the sperm of a ma[le] she gave [birth] to off[spring], to the [em]bryo of mankind" certainly brings out this point. However, this is a very daring translation in the

light of all the lacunae, particularly since the word for "sperm" in Sumerian is simply *a*, which (since the rest of the line is missing) could also be a grammatical particle or a part of another noun. Nevertheless, the sense of the passage does indicate that—in the final analysis—Nammu acted alone.

9. See M. Glassner, "Mahlzeit," RIA 7 (1988): 263–264. The idea of disputations and boasting-competitions is well rooted in Sumerian culture, and a whole genre of literature, the "disputation texts," is based on the idea of dialogues that proclaim the merits of the disputing partners.

10. There is one more, the lu-a-sur-sur, who may be "incontinent" (so Jacobsen, in *Harps)* or may be "promiscuous" or "unable to hold his semen." The social role is equally obscure.

11. Atrahasis I 200–201. For text, edition, and translation, see W. Lambert and R. Millard, *The Atrahasis Epic: The Babylonian Story of the Flood* (Oxford University Press, 1969) and Stephanie Dalley, *Myths from Mesopotamia: Creation, the Flood, Gilgamesh and Others* (Oxford and New York, Oxford University Press, 1989), 1–38.

12. Enuma Elish VI 35–38. For translation, see Dalley, *Myths,* 228–277.

13. *Ludlul bel nemeqi* IV 31; cf. W. G. Lambert, BWL, 59.

14. See ANET, 538.

15. From the ancient text, "The Babylonian Theodicy," Lambert, BWL, 89 lines 276–278.

16. Enuma Elish II 45–6.

17. Enuma Elish II 110–111.

18. We do not have any information about what rituals the kings of the later half of the second millennium performed. Evidence is only available for the first millennium.

19. For this later ritual, see Bottéro, "Le Hiérogamie après l'époque 'sumérienne,'" in S. N. Kramer, *Le Mariage sacrée: à Sumer et à Babylone,* translated and adapted by Jean Bottéro (Paris: Berg International, 1983), 175–215; Eiko Matsushima, "Les Rituels du Mariage Divin dans les Documents Accadiens," *Acta Sumerologica* 10 (1988): 95–128, Eiko Matsushima, "Le Rituel Hiérogamique de Nabu," *Acta Sumerologica* 9 (1987): 131–171.

20. Note Enlilbani (A. Kapp, ZA 51 (1961): 76f.),151–158: "Inanna… brings you greatly to her holy bed and spends the night there (with you)."

21. Tukulti-Ninurta is also "poured through the channel of the womb of the gods," see P. Machinist, "Literature as Politics: The Tukulti-Ninurta Epic and the Bible," *CBQ* 38 (1976): 455–482. In line with the discussion in chapter 8, we might note the absence of the mother goddess, previously so important to kingship. It is by the decree of Nudimmud (Ea) that the king is poured through the channel of the womb, and it is not even the womb of the mother-goddess, but that of "the gods."

22. Discussion by J. Tigay, "The Image of God and the Flood: Some New Developments," in A. Shapiro and B. Cohen, eds., *Studies in Jewish Education* (1984), 169–182.
23. D. O. Edzard, WbMyth., 81–89; cf. CRRA 2 (1951): 21ff.
24. Jeffrey Tigay alludes to the fact that the Old Babylonian version of the Gilgamesh Epic refers to the Eanna as the abode of the god An, even though this temple had long been shared by Inanna-Ishtar. Tigay considers this a deliberate omission, *The Evolution of the Gilgamesh Epic* (Philadelphia: University of Pennsylvania Press, 1982), 68.
25. As in the first millennium version of the Congregational Lament Uruamirabi, Mark Cohen, *The Canonical Lamentations of Ancient Mesopotamia* (Potomac, Md.: Capital Decisions, 1988), which has an episode in which Ishtar takes harsh vengeance against a slave girl who has slept with her master.
26. The Erra Epic tablet IV 52–58.
27. For the similarities between Ištar and Lamaštu, see Wolfgang Fauth, "Ištar als Löwengöttin und die löwenköpfige Lamaštu," *WO* 12 (1981): 21–36.
28. Royal Hymn to Ištar in favor of King Ammiditana, for which, see RA 22 (1928): 170ff.
29. So T. Jacobsen, "Notes on Nintur," *Or.* 42: 294ff, who argues that the use of royal metaphors made it hard to fit a mother into the royal system.
30. See S. N. Kramer, "Poets and Psalmists: Goddesses and Theologians" in *The Legacy of Sumer*, 3–22.
31. See J. M. Asher-Grève, *Frauen in altsumerischer Zeit*, Bibliotheca Mesopotamica 18 (Malibu, Calif.: Undena, 1985).
32. So Aaron Shaffer, "Gilgamesh, the Cedar Forest and Mesopotamian History," *JAOS* 103 (1983) 310–313, who comes to this conclusion from Gilgamesh's speech to Huwawa, "I promise to bring my elder sister Enmebaragesi into the land for you as a wife."
33. Cf. Dominque Charpin, *Le clergé d'Ur au siècle d'Hammurabi (xix–xvii siècles* AV. J.C.) Geneva: Librairie Droz, 1986.
34. W. W. Hallo, "Women of Sumer," in *The Legacy of Sumer*, 23–40; P. Michalowski "Royal Women of the Ur III Period," *JCS* 31 (1979): 171–176; P. Steinkeller, "More on the Ur III Royal Wives," *Acta Sumerologica* 3 (1981): 77–92.
35. See Bernard Batto, *Studies on Women at Mari* (Baltimore: Johns Hopkins University Press, 1974).

❋ ❋ ❋

Tzvi Abusch
"Mourning the Death of a Friend: Some Assyriological Notes"

Tzvi Abusch's analysis of a brief passage in the Old Babylonian version of *Gilgamesh,* the encounter between Gilgamesh and the goddess Siduri, leads to profound implications for the Old Babylonian version as a whole—and for the evolution of the Gilgamesh narratives. Abusch's interpretation is a brief summary of two lengthy, technical articles he has published as "Gilgamesh's Request and Siduri's Denial" (Parts I and II). Appropriate to a volume remembering a scholar who was also a friend to Abusch, the article begins and ends with a recollection of Frank Talmage.

Abusch follows the line of argument he had taken in the technical studies, but in this article he expands his comparisons with later literature: the Bible (Ecclesiastes, 2 Samuel), Greek (*The Odyssey*) and Latin (Horace), and medieval Jewish poetry (Moses Ibn Ezra). The major comparison is between Siduri and Calypso.

The parallel between Gilgamesh and Siduri, on one hand, and Odysseus and Calypso on the other, helps Abusch unpack the curious sequence in what has usually been taken as a *carpe diem* theme, advice merely to "seize the day" and the "pleasures of the moment." Siduri advises Gilgamesh not to pursue a life of heedless pleasure, but to accept reality: find a wife to replace the lost Enkidu, and have children. The detailed philological and literary analysis Abusch presents in the longer essays is summarized here. Siduri's response to Gilgamesh is part of a chiastic form that includes both his speech and her response. Gilgamesh, having seen the face of the divine Siduri, proposes to remain with her—in effect, reversing the rejection of Ishtar in the Standard Babylonian version. Siduri, like Calypso, can offer a kind of immortality, but she advises him to return to normal life.

Abusch suggests that versions earlier than the Old Babylonian version may have ended with Siduri and the return of Gilgamesh to Uruk. Gilgamesh's search for Utnapishtim would not, then, have been in the design—as the newly discovered Elamite *Gilgamesh* would suggest. Ironically, Siduri's advice includes a reference that will lead Gilgamesh beyond her—to Utnapishtim.

Such a close analysis of the Akkadian text would have been most difficult without Jeffrey H. Tigay's tracing of the "evolution" of the Gilgamesh epic, which detailed the *differences* between the Old Babylonian and earlier and later versions of the story. (Ed.)

My friend, whom I love dearly,
Who with me underwent all hardships,
Enkidu whom I love dearly,
Who with me underwent all hardships,
Has gone to the fate of mankind.

With these words Gilgamesh began his lament over the death of his friend, Enkidu. In the volume dedicated to the memory of Professor Frank Ephraim Talmage, I might similarly express the love and loss that I feel when I recall the many years and the many joys and sorrows that Frank and I shared, experiences shared also by my wife and sons. We all mourned for him. On the Yom Kippur following Frank's death, I delivered a talk in his memory, on the rituals of the Day of Atonement and their similarities to rites of mourning. Here, in this memorial volume, I would offer a brief essay on the Akkadian text from which the lament cited above derives, a text that deals with grief and mourning.

This text is the justly famous encounter between Gilgamesh and the divine tavernkeeper Siduri found in an Old Babylonian version of the Epic of Gilgamesh and preserved on the Meissner Fragment.[1] Column ii of this Old Babylonian fragment begins with Gilgamesh's address to Siduri and continues with her response (= OB Gilg., Meissner, cols. ii-iii). It is to this opening exchange that I shall direct my remarks. The text has interested me for some time, and I have prepared for publication two detailed, technical studies of this text and of some of the issues that it raises. Here, I want to present in general terms some of my conclusions about the meaning of the text. The detailed argumentation in support of my interpretations and conclusions is presented in the aforementioned studies.[2] Frank saw the need to write about his field in general humanistic terms, and I hope that he would have appreciated this attempt.

Turning to the text, we may begin by characterizing the opening exchange. Gilgamesh's speech encapsulates his emotional state: past, present, and future. Beginning with a description of the death of his friend, it moves on to an expression of his present anguish, and finally to his proposal for a solution. Siduri's speech provides her response and her advice. Each speech contains three stanzas. In translation, these two speeches read:

col. ii * My friend, whom I love dearly,
1' Who with me underwent all hardships,
2' Enkidu, whom I love dearly,
3' Who with me underwent all hardships,
4' Has gone to the fate of mankind.

5' Day and night I wept over him,
6' I would not give him up for burial—
7' (saying) "My friend perhaps will rise up to me
at my cry"—
8' Seven days and seven nights
9' Until a worm dropped out at me
from his nose.

10' Since his death, I have not found life.
11' I keep roaming like a hunter
in the open country.
12' Now, alewife, that I have seen your face,
13' The death that I constantly fear may I not see.

14' The alewife spoke to him, to Gilgamesh:

col. iii 1 Gilgamesh, whither do you rove?
2 The life that you pursue you shall not find.
3 When the gods created mankind,
4 Death they appointed for mankind.
5 Life in their own hands they held.

6 You, Gilgamesh, let your stomach be full.
7 Day and night keep on being festive.
8 Daily make a festival.
9 Day and night dance and play.

10 Let your clothes be clean,
11 Let your head be washed, in water may you bathe.
12 Look down at the little one who
holds your hand,
13 Let a wife ever be festive in your lap.[3]

I

In the epic, Enkidu has died; in his grief, Gilgamesh withdraws from his life as king of the city-state Uruk and starts to wander in the wild. In his wanderings, in both the Old Babylonian version and the later Standard Babylonian version of the epic, Gilgamesh encounters Siduri, a divine alewife who dwells near the shores of the faraway ocean. In the Standard Babylonian version, Gilgamesh is seeking Utnapishtim, the Babylonian Noah who survived the flood and was granted immortality, in order to gain the secret of immortality for himself. The encounter with Siduri is simply a step along the way: she serves as one more person to hear Gilgamesh's tale, bear witness to his state, and direct him to Utnapishtim.

Gilgamesh's first speech in the Old Babylonian text has usually been understood as a description of his plight, an enunciation of his desire to attain immortality, and a request of Siduri that she direct him to Utnapishtim. Siduri's speech has been understood as a rejection of this request. The quest is futile: immortality is reserved for the gods; mankind cannot attain immortality. Hence, enjoy life. Her advice has been treated as a Babylonian 'carpe diem' comparable to Ecclesiastes 9:7–9. Thus, the Old Babylonian version of the encounter has been read as if it shared the same literary context as the later Standard Babylonian version. This in spite of the fact that the contours of the two versions of the epic are quite different, and much of what defines the character of the passage in the Old Babylonian text and renders it justly famous and powerful (e.g., Siduri's specific advice to Gilgamesh) is not present in the later Standard Babylonian version.

In an attempt to explain some discrepancies in the order of statements in the Old Babylonian version of the dialogue between Gilgamesh and Siduri, but especially in Siduri's speech, as well as some oddities of formulation, I have tried to work out the structure of the passage, the force of some of the formulations, and the overall movement and meaning of the dialogue. These studies have led me to the conclusion that the aforementioned understanding of the Old Babylonian dialogue is not wholly correct: they have suggested a different reading of the passage, a reading which I would sketch out here in partial form.

In my estimation, the Old Babylonian version belongs to a literary and cultural context different from that of the Standard Babylonian version, has a different force, and thus requires a different reading. Initially, Gilgamesh was not searching for Utnapishtim. He has wandered aimlessly, seeking but not finding his own lost sense of being alive. Agitated movement was what he needed, though perhaps he held out some hope for a respite or release from his existential/psychological pain. He was directionless until he encountered Siduri. When he meets her, he describes to her the loss of his beloved Enkidu and his inability to give up the dead Enkidu for burial and thus separate from the dead. Seeing her, he becomes aware of his wish to stop roaming and to remain with her, and states that having seen Siduri's face, he hopes never to see—that is, experience—death.

His unrealistic wish not to experience death does not mean that he believes that in finding Siduri he has found the way to Utnapishtim. Rather, it means that he wants to stay with the goddess and, thereby, attain immortality. He is proposing to the goddess. Meeting Siduri, he recognizes that he now wishes to live with a woman rather than remain in spirit with his dead male friend. But instead of choosing a normal, mortal woman, he has focused on a goddess. He wishes to live with an immortal woman because she is capable of endowing him with eternal life. In Gilgamesh's eyes, at least, Siduri is a Calypso-like character. Her house and her embrace partake of the immortal. To have sexual relations with her and to live with her is to attain the boon of eternal life and to escape death.

But in actuality, Gilgamesh has not yet completely put the dead aside; he remains obsessed with death. His continued grief for the dead is tantamount to a wish to remain with them. And in his mind, living with Siduri allows him to continue to live with the dead, for he thinks that through her he can move away from an overt state of grief without having to surrender his attachment to the dead and to re-enter the normal world. Uniting with the goddess is a fantasy that denies death and leaves unresolved the losses of life and one's own mortal destiny. To live forever with a beautiful woman, a goddess, is a pleasant male fantasy, but it is also a death wish. Siduri's is a world in which Gilgamesh can live without living and die without dying. He can thus live life through fantasy and need not let go of the dead.

In his attempt, then, to free himself from the anguish of his grief for his friend Enkidu, Gilgamesh tries to enter into a marriage with the goddess Siduri. But such a marriage cannot be, for ultimately it would bear the consequence that Gilgamesh could never again regain human life.

Not only psychologically, but also ontologically, such a union is untenable for the mortal man Gilgamesh. Siduri is a divinity, and on an ontological level, their union would be a mingling of human and god, life and death. Both death and divinity are alike in their absoluteness and eternity; both exist on a non-human—an absolute—plane. To the human being, both the dead and the immortal represent death.

Gilgamesh believes that Siduri might take him in and that he could thereby escape death. But he errs in this belief, and Siduri must disabuse him of it and send him off. Siduri wishes his welfare. The goddess recognizes both the initial impasse and the final sterility and death of the union of human and divine. A similar fate is exemplified in the *Odyssey* by the breakdown of the relationship of Calypso and Odysseus, by Odysseus's inability to live with Calypso and his recognition of the need to leave the goddess and reengage with his wife and family:

> [Calypso speaks]
>
> "So now, you gods, you resent it in me that I keep beside me
> a man, the one I saved when he clung astride of the keel board all alone,
> ....
> and I gave him my love and cherished him, and I had hopes also
> that I could make him immortal and all his days to be endless."
> ....
> ...she, the queenly nymph, when she had been given the message
> from Zeus, set out searching after great-hearted Odysseus,
> and found him sitting on the seashore, and his eyes were never
> wiped dry of tears, and the sweet lifetime was draining out of him,
> as he wept for a way home, since the nymph was no longer pleasing
> to him. By nights he would lie beside her, of necessity,
> in the hollow caverns, against his will, by one who was willing,
> but all the days he would sit upon the rocks, at the seaside,
> breaking his heart in tears and lamentation and sorrow
> as weeping tears he looked out over the barren water.
> She, bright among divinities, stood near and spoke to him:
> "Poor man, no longer mourn here beside me nor let your lifetime
> fade away, since now I will send you on, with a good will..."[4]

Recognizing the sterility that threatens a coupling of human and divine, Siduri tries to save Gilgamesh from the destruction to which their union would lead by disengaging him from her and directing him instead to a normal marriage, for only so may he free himself from death and enter into a new stage of life. She tries to disengage Gilgamesh both from death and from fantasy, from his attachment to a dead human male as well as from his hope to be attached to an immortal female.

Siduri tries to redirect Gilgamesh by means of her speech. She responds not only to his cry for Enkidu at the beginning of his speech, but also to his proposal to her at the end of his speech.

Especially to disabuse him of the idea that he, a mortal, can enjoy immortality with her, a goddess, does she present her reply as she does: the gods have designated immortality only for themselves (iii 1–5); instead, the mortal Gilgamesh should enjoy festivals to their fullest (iii 6–9) and find fulfillment, finally, with a mortal wife (iii 10–13). He cannot find a life or love that does not include death. She concludes her speech on the theme of a mortal woman not only to encourage Gilgamesh to attach himself to a living female in place of a dead male, but also to let him know that just as he cannot live forever with the dead Enkidu, so, too, he cannot live forever with an immortal female, a goddess, and must rather find fulfillment with a mortal female, a woman.

But her speech is not only an appeal for renewed human pleasure; even more it is a call for the adoption of a normal human life, for normal activities and relationships. To that purpose, she adapts what might once have been a pleasure-song of the tavern and brothel. Now, she not only highlights the woman at the end of her speech, as in the original song, but also introduces the important theme of the child immediately before mentioning the woman. Siduri is now advising sexual pleasures not with a casual partner, but rather with a familial partner, so that a child may be born who will normalize life and define its mortal and immortal dimensions. The sexual act is now also a procreative act which brings into being the posterity and future signalled by the child. Progeny implies death, and thus the woman and child also suggest mortality and are a most pronounced way for Siduri to impart to Gilgamesh the notion of his mortality and to express the hope that he accept his mortal nature. But a child is also a form of immortality, and in our passage, this is the only kind of immortality that Gilgamesh can hope for.

Our story is one in which Siduri refuses to provide a home for Gilgamesh and advises him instead to return to his own home. But Gilgamesh can neither accept her advice nor think of another realistic solution. Instead, he focuses on the idea of immortality and the thought of Utnapishtim. Thus, instead of heeding her advice, he perceives in Siduri's speech the possibility of attaining immortality, for he has heard of Utnapishtim (or rather Utana'ishtim as he is called in the Old Babylonian text) and knows that, contrary to Siduri's contention, a human being actually once attained immortality. And the appropriateness of seeking out Utnapishtim in the present context is promoted by the obvious connection and play between *ul ūta balāṭam,* "I did not find life" in ii 10', and *Ūta-na ʾ i-štim*/Utnapishtim.

In its evolution, the epic will eventually take as its focus the journey to Utnapishtim and the quest for immortality, and the Gilgamesh-Siduri encounter will change into a meeting which serves primarily to highlight Gilgamesh's plight and further his progress toward Utnapishtim. These developments have surely taken place in the later Standard Babylonian version. But even our Old Babylonian text represents a stage in the development of the epic. For already in the Old Babylonian recension before us, Utnapishtim seems to have become part of the story. Thus, while our Old Babylonian text still emphasizes the original idea of Gilgamesh as an aimless wanderer, that Old Babylonian piece already represents a step in the transition from the earlier perspective to the later idea that set Utnapishtim as a goal.

The Old Babylonian fragment preserves neither the original nor the latest form of the encounter. A form of the story earlier than that preserved on the Old Babylonian fragment may well have ended with Siduri sending Gilgamesh back to Uruk in the care of a boatman, perhaps Urshanabi, who here serves as a form of Hermes. Thus, this earlier account would have proceeded from the Gilgamesh-Siduri dialogue (and perhaps some version of the encounter with Urshanabi) to SB Tablet XI 239, where originally it would have been Siduri, and not Utnapishtim, who advised the boatman to wash Gilgamesh and return him to Uruk (XI 239–246). Utnapishtim was not originally part of the tale.

Actually, even the form of the story in which Siduri sends Gilgamesh back to Uruk may not have been the earliest form of the episode. Gilgamesh's original mistake regarding what he could expect from Siduri suggests an interesting possibility and allows for some further historical speculation. Surely, Gilgamesh did not construct out of whole cloth the possibility that he might be able to stay with Siduri. Rather, he made this mistake because he saw in her a form of goddess like the later Calypso and Circe. And if Gilgamesh's expectations were not wholly farfetched, and Siduri did, in fact, share at least some of the characteristics of Calypso and Circe and of their stories, then it seems quite possible that in an earlier tradition, Siduri acceded to Gilgamesh's proposal and allowed him to stay with her.

Actually, Calypso and Circe are examples of a goddess who invites the travelling or returning hero to dwell with her. This tradition is known in the ancient Near East and even appears in the Standard Babylonian version of the Gilgamesh Epic in the form of Ishtar's proposal to Gilgamesh in SB Tablet VI. And if, as we think, Siduri is indeed like Calypso and Circe, she too may have once proffered an invitation to Gilgamesh. Thus, we may speculate further and suggest that in another—probably earlier—form of the story, Siduri was the initiator and herself proposed that Gilgamesh stay with her. Indeed, we need not rely on Greek or even Canaanite analogues (e.g., "Anat and Aqhat"), for on the Mesopotamian side, Siduri's invitation would have been like Ishtar's proposal to Gilgamesh and Ereshkigal's to Nergal in "Nergal and Ereshkigal."

In any case, the theme of the wandering hero and the goddess did not originate with Gilgamesh. Presumably, the original story and perhaps even its several earliest forms involved a different traveller or wanderer. Only later would the theme be taken over and developed by the Gilgamesh tradition, and Gilgamesh made into the hero of the story.

II

There are several other interesting observations to be made regarding the text. Here, I would address the meaning of the advice contained in Siduri's second stanza.

> You, Gilgamesh, let your stomach be full.
> Day and night keep on being festive.
> Daily make a festival.
> Day and night dance and play.

Earlier we observed that Siduri's advice to Gilgamesh that "Let a wife ever be festive in your lap" is not simply a call to sensual pleasure, but also a call to family life, responsibility, and progeny, and that the progeny represents the mortality and immortality of the progenitors. Similarly, the second stanza of Siduri's speech is not merely a call to merriment and is thus different in attitude from the forms of 'carpe diem' found, for example, in Horace, *Odes*, Book 1:11, Ecclesiastes 9:7–9a, or Isaiah 22:13b, "'Let us eat and drink, for tomorrow we die."' Her advice is not a simple call for pleasure, but rather a response to Gilgamesh's earlier statement:

> Day and night I wept over him,
> I would not give him up for burial—
> (saying) "My friend perhaps will rise up to me at my cry!"—
> Seven days and seven nights
> Until a worm dropped out at me from his nose.

Gilgamesh has failed to come to terms with reality and free himself for life. He has been unable to observe correctly the several funeral and mortuary rites of his society. Consequently, he has neither given the dead their due nor separated from his dead friend. Actually, he has distorted the rites, for he is governed by the delusion that his friend might rise up from the bier upon hearing his lament. Thus, he does not bury his friend immediately after death, but holds back his body from burial; he mourns before—rather than after—burial, and continues to mourn indefinitely. The purposes of mourning rites have not been achieved.

In response, the alewife tries to pry him loose from the burial place and bring him back to everyday life. She advises that he enjoy and celebrate life through the vehicle of the feast (note the centrality of forms from *ḫadû,* 'to rejoice' in the two central lines). The feast represents the affirmation of life through joy as well as the affirmation of the goodness or pleasure of life. But it is more. The banquet and this type of advice are often attested in mortuary contexts. Banquets are festive occasions for the living, but they may also be associated with the dead: the eternal daily (and festival) banquet of the dead, a banquet concretized and punctualized in such occasions as the funeral and the periodic offerings in which the living participate. In the context of a response to Gilgamesh's uncontrollable grief and futile desire to live forever with Enkidu and remain with the dead, the evocation of the banquet seems to be also an ironic reuse of a scene resonant with netherworld associations. Siduri recalls—mimics—the rites for the dead. She advises Gilgamesh to utilize a rite which is associated with both death and life—but to use it for life—and thereby to come to terms with death as well as with life. By using a *topos* with both netherworld and mundane associations, Siduri is able to acknowledge Gilgamesh's struggle, his struggle with grief, his clinging to death and mourning, his confused identification of death and life, and to help him disentangle life from death. Thus her advice to enjoy life now effectively serves to redirect his energies away from the dead and back to this world. And the reuse and redirection are made easier by the fact that banquets of the dead and their songs not only sometimes involve the living, but were originally also modelled on banquets of the living. She refocuses the scene away from its mortuary dimensions and transfers it back to the mundane enjoyment of the pleasures of the world.

The second stanza of Gilgamesh's speech represents a description of the failure of mortuary rites. The corresponding second stanza in Siduri's speech represents an attempt to free a human being from attachment, even identification with the dead and to redirect him to enjoyment with the living.

Just as Siduri directed Gilgamesh back to normalcy by transforming a physical, perhaps even a sexual involvement with a dead man or a living goddess into a familial/sexual relationship with a woman, so she changes the banquet of the dead into a feast of this world, a feast in which the living participate and by which they reaffirm their lives. Perhaps she is telling him to have a festive meal every day—not just on the occasion of a death.

Siduri has attempted to transform a grief which had taken the form of clinging to the dead, refusal and paralysis, failure to disengage and attach anew—even an active wish to live with the dead. In its place, Siduri urges Gilgamesh to celebrate life through its everyday, yet joyful activities.

• • • •

The Gilgamesh who comes to Siduri might originally have seconded David's lament over Jonathan in 2 Samuel 1:25–27:

> How have the mighty fallen
> In the thick of battle—
> Jonathan, slain on your heights!
> I grieve for you,
> My brother Jonathan,
> You were most dear to me.
> Your love was wonderful to me
> More than the love of women.
> How have the mighty fallen,
> The weapons of war perished![5]

Siduri's response is intended to draw the mourner away from the desert of grief back to the city of life. Some of the confusion in interpretation of her advice results from the fact that her words would sound equally natural an age and a world away, where a more hedonistic version of the 'carpe diem' theme occurs in the Hebrew poetry of the Spanish Golden Age, a period and tradition that Frank loved:

> Immerse your heart in pleasure and in joy,
> And by the bank a bottle drink of wine,
> Enjoy the swallow's chirp and viol's whine.
> Laugh, dance, and stamp your feet upon the floor!
> Get drunk, and knock at dawn on some girl's door.

This is the joy of life, so take your due.
You too deserve a portion of the Ram
Of Consecration, like your people's chiefs.
To suck the juice of lips do not be shy,
But take what's rightly yours—the breast and thigh!
(Moses Ibn Ezra[6])

We visited Frank's resting place on Har ha-Menuḥot in the mountains of Judah. We wept over his death and our loss. But the location of his grave compelled us to see more. Around us rose the mountains of Judah and the city of Jerusalem that he treasured. By his grave, we could see and again feel the joys of the life and of the world that Frank so loved. May his memory be a blessing.

❋ ❋ ❋

NOTES

My work on this Gilgamesh text has benefitted greatly from discussions with several friends. I am particularly grateful to Stephen A. Geller and Kathryn Kravitz, as well as Mordechai Cogan and William L. Moran, for their valuable suggestions.

1. The Meissner fragment was published by Bruno Meissner. *Ein altbabylonisches Fragment des Gilgamosepos,* Mitteilungen der Vorderasiatischen Gesellschaft 7/1(Berlin, 1902). More recently, it has been joined to a fragment in the British Museum; see A. R. Millard. "Gilgamesh X: A New Fragment," *Iraq* 26(1964): 99–105. For translations of both the Old Babylonian text and the later Standard Babylonian version of the epic, see, e.g., E. A. Speiser and A. K. Grayson in *Ancient Near Eastern Texts Relating to the Old Testament,* ed. J.B. Pritchard, 3d ed. (Princeton, NJ, 1969), 72–99, 503–7, and Stephanie Dalley, *Myths from Mesopotamia: Creation, The Flood, Gilgamesh and Others* (Oxford and New York, 1989), 39–153. For studies of the epic, cf. e.g., Thorkild Jacobsen, *Treasures of Darkness: A History of Mesopotamian Religion* (New Haven, 1976), 195–219; J. H. Tigay, *The Evolution of the Gilgamesh Epic* (Philadelphia, 1982); Tzvi Abusch, "lshtar's Proposal and Gilgamesh's Refusal: An Interpretation of The Gilgamesh Epic, Tablet 6, Lines 1–79," *History of Religions* 26(1986): 143–87.

2. The two more technical studies are "Gilgamesh's Request and Siduri's Denial. Part I: The Meaning of the Dialogue and its Implications for the History of the Epic" (Festschrift Hallo), and "Part II: An Analysis and Interpretation of an Old Babylonian Fragment about Mourning and Celebration" (Festschrift Muffs [*Journal of the Ancient Near Eastern Society* 22]).

3. Following the end of the third stanza of Siduri's speech, there are an additional three lines that are largely broken. These lines might read:

> This alone is the conce[rn of man/woman.]
> [Gilgamesh, whither do you rove?]
> Let him who is aliv[e enjoy life].

The first of these lines and perhaps the two that follow seem to be a final summation of Siduri's message.

4. Homer, *Odyssey* 5.129–131, 135–136, 149–161 (trans. Richmond Lattimore [New York, 1975] 91–92).

5. *Tanakh* (Philadelphia, 1985), 471.

6. R. P. Scheindlin, *Wine, Women, and Death: Medieval Hebrew Poems on the Good Life* (Philadelphia, 1986), 91.

* * *

Sara Mandell
"Liminality, Altered States, and the *Gilgamesh Epic*"

Drawing on certain folklore motifs, Sara Mandell follows the transformation of Enkidu and Gilgamesh in the Standard Babylonian version of *Gilgamesh* from liminal characters to ones who are finally civilized and humanized in the process. The key figures in Enkidu's transformation are the Harlot Woman, Hunter Man, and especially Hunter Man's Father. From Joseph Campbell Mandell takes the suggestion that Enkidu is the Alpha Beast. As the Master of Animals, Enkidu must be altered by the only *persona* in the epic that is not himself altered in the process, the shaman who is the Hunter Man's Father. It is his wisdom that begins the transformation of Enkidu. The process of humanization is not complete with the seduction by the Harlot Woman. The instruction he receives from her, the Single Combat with Gilgamesh, the companionship that takes them to a Never-Never-Land to kill Humbaba all ritually change him, but he remains liminal until he is subject to death for killing the Bull of Heaven. Only then is Enkidu fully human.

Gilgamesh, too, is liminal, two-thirds god and one-third man. Although he is king of the city, he is not fully civilized, even when he and Enkidu meet and form a rudimentary society. When Enkidu dies, as the Substitute King, so that Gilgamesh can continue living, Gilgamesh is able to complete the transformation to a fully human and civilized being. (Ed.)

It is characteristic of certain types of myths and folk-tales, in which there is Single Combat between reasonably paired entities, for one combatant to take the place of the other for what is usually a fixed period of time, or for both to join together in some common adventure.[1] There is generally some change in status associated with this,[2] and the events may even be related to the interaction between the inherently sacred world and the, albeit sacralized, mundane one. For example, some hero or unusual figure from a sacred or liminal place, be it the Netherworld, Never-Never-Land, or some garden paradise, may exchange places with a hero or unusual figure from this world. But it might also happen that there is no such exchange of places. Rather the hero from this world, be he alone or joined with his former combatant, often makes a journey into some liminal or even sacred locale that is frequently depicted as a type of Never-Never-Land.

This type of interchange occurs, but with a variant that is also characteristic of folklore—particularly that in which there are doubles or twins,—in the composite reconstruction of the Standard Babylonian *Gilgamesh Epic.* The hero, Gilgamesh, and anti-hero,[3] Enkidu, each of whom is an image of Anu, and therefore a double of the other, engage in Single Combat. But instead of changing places, this interaction results in their becoming companions and going off into Never-Never-Land, in this case the Cedar Forest, to kill Humbaba. So they join together to enter an objectified liminality, to confront and do battle with the sanctified object of the hunt. And ultimately they are forced to accept what appears to be an unequal liability for their joint conduct.

In the extant (and I iterate composite) text of the Standard Babylonian *Gilgamesh Epic* that we have arrived at by "filling in" missing portions with what we believe to be the corresponding part in other Gilgamesh texts, the traditional folklorist displacement of one *persona* by the other, who is to all intents and purposes his double,[4] is itself displaced in accordance with the variant I have just noted. But there is yet another mutation of the paradigm. Gilgamesh and Enkidu do exchange something: Enkidu dies in Gilgamesh's place. Although their joint combat against Humbaba is appended to the justification for this, the decree is not given until they slaughter the Bull of Heaven *that had been sent because of Gilgamesh's hubris vis à vis Ishtar* if the Old Babylonian text does properly reflect what had later been incorporated into the unified Standard Babylonian epic. The bard makes note of this when he depicts Enkidu's anger at his impending death. Enkidu clearly does not willingly accept this sole liability, whereby he has to die and enter the Netherworld and Gilgamesh does not.

Somewhere in the development of the Gilgamesh traditions, there was a bard who must have had another agenda, which itself may have been related to the explication of some ritual paradigm related to humanization and civilization as well as initiation into young manhood. He superimposed this model on the archetypal exchange of place paradigm, treating it as a question of liability unjustly adjudicated. But the long-standing tradition whereby Gilgamesh became a judge in the Netherworld hints at the possibility that at one time there had been a myth in which Gilgamesh had been compensated either for having been sent to the Netherworld unwillingly or for having gone there willingly rather than trying to escape death.

The Standard Babylonian *Gilgamesh Epic* is a work of literature, not a set of myths that are vital to some set of rituals, however. Nevertheless we can still demarcate elements of the subtending myths and rites that are not totally obfuscated. Consequently, we can interpret the epic as literature at the same time as we can pay attention to its ritology.

From both the literary and the ritual studies viewpoint then, it is notable that Enkidu is specifically created to put Gilgamesh's depredations in Uruk to an end. At first, he is neither fully humanized nor civilized.[5] Although he is feral enough to be accepted by the wild beasts, he has the appearance of some type of primal man. And he does have the potential to become both humanized and civilized.[6]

A pivotal role in Enkidu's metamorphoses into a civilized character is played by Harlot Woman, whose literary depiction is ingenious. The bard portrays her as an ambiguous, flat *persona.* Not only does she lack a well defined identity, but she actually lacks any personality. And her very lack of a definable character, particularly notable insofar as she is merely a vehicle to fulfill what has been ordered and what has been ordained,[7] itself defines her as "No-One." She is named "The Giver of Joy" by virtue of, and because of her clearly sexual function in the narrative. This double naming creates a conundrum, however: when Harlot Woman, *functionally* defined as the Giver of Joy, seduces Enkidu, she is no longer nameless or faceless; so she is no longer No-One and yet she has never stopped being No-One.

Hunter Man, whom the bard of the literary work has trivialized, really plays a pivotal role in the ritual process. He is responsible for starting the action whereby Harlot Woman, that is No-One, seduces Enkidu so as to bring about his "Alteration of State." Like Harlot Woman, Hunter Man is also depicted as a flat *persona,* without identity. And being defined and named only by his function as hunter, his lack of oneness itself defines him as No-One. Hunter Man does not require specificity. His role in the plot of the Standard Babylonian *Gilgamesh* is merely to seek help from his father, whose *persona* is incontestably shamanic.

As Shaman, Hunter Man's Father, defined only by his relationship to Hunter Man, has knowledge of the killing of the animals, and particularly of the killing of the Master of the Animals. The latter, however, is the consummate and representative exemplar, the Platonic Idea or Form, of the primary hunted beast whose death is completed by a revivification in an eternal round of death and regeneration. And so it is particularly important that Hunter Man's Father, that is the Shaman with special Knowledge/Wisdom, is the only *persona* in the entire Gilgamesh tradition as we have it that does not suffer any Alteration of State. And it is no accident then that it is Hunter Man's Father that resolves the problem of what to do about Enkidu. It is his idea to ensnare Enkidu by having him seduced, and to ask Gilgamesh to send Harlot Woman with Hunter Man to accomplish this.

This suggests that there may have existed some tradition, long since forgotten by the time in which the Gilgamesh traditions were incorporated into their literary format, in which Enkidu was the Master of Animals, and Hunter Man's Father was the Shaman who made everything "work." That is, Enkidu was what Joseph Campbell has repeatedly called the "Alpha Beast," whose slaughter would ultimately be followed by regeneration and a renewed life for all beasts of his kind, within his herd that itself represents the totality of the species; and this would be effected by the very Shaman responsible for the slaughter itself.

Because it is of no importance to the narrative, we ourselves like the implied reader[8] do not know or are we expected to care whether the literary character, Hunter Man's Father, is aware that the ultimate goal is the ensnaring of Gilgamesh himself; and it was for this that Enkidu had been created.[9] Also, like the implied reader, we are not expected to wonder who Harlot Maid really is, whence she comes, or what she thinks or feels. These are not of relevance to this epic's plot.

What does matter is that Harlot Maid does what her role demands and what Hunter Man's Father had ordained: she seduces Enkidu. By leading him to Uruk, she goes beyond the implied reader's expectations, although not beyond those of the real reader, precisely because this is not specifically set forth by Hunter Man' s Father. And, moreover, neither Hunter Man nor his father had said anything about humanization or civilization. Rather, they were both concerned with Hunter Man's ability to continue hunting.

Thus it should not be surprising that Harlot Woman's seduction of the primitive Enkidu neither *fully* humanizes him because he is not yet subject to death, nor civilizes him insofar as he has not yet learned to live in the human domain together with other men. He is, however, said to become human by virtue of the seduction. But the literary presentation of the narrative itself makes it clear that this is not totally effected. Rather the beginning of the seduction separates him from his former *Sitz im Leben,* whereas the seduction itself begins the period of instruction that is demanded by the underlying rituals. So it is precisely at this point that he has changed form, thereby signifying that the humanization by de-beastizing process had begun.

He has, then, undergone a metamorphosis that will ultimately make him human when he becomes subject to death. But until that happens, Enkidu is liminal. [10] Most importantly, however, by virtue of his new found appearance, this liminal character becomes fit to descend to Uruk so as to engage Gilgamesh in "Single," that is "Heroic Combat." By taking Gilgamesh on in Single Combat, he learns his role as an hero as well as the human man he will become, if only for a brief moment.

Enkidu is not the only *persona* in the Standard Babylonian epic to undergo some type of metamorphosis or to experience liminality. Just as Enkidu is liminal, Gilgamesh himself is also liminal, being neither humanized nor civilized when the narrative begins. And more importantly, Gilgamesh, who had been created in the image of Anu, was two-thirds divine and only one-third, that is marginally, human. Although King of Uruk, he was oppressing the population, and acting in an un-kinglike manner. Most interestingly, however, his actions epitomize the status of one who is about to become something, thus stressing his liminality. Since he is already king, we may presume that his actions suggest that he is about to become either humanized or civilized or both.

A change in Gilgamesh's *persona* seems to have been wrought after he and Enkidu engage in Single Combat. Once this encounter has been brought to completion, the two work in concert—that is, they form the rudiments of a society. But their joint venture does not take them back into the civilized world, thus showing them to be uncivilized even though they now form the base of a society. Rather it takes them into the realm of an extended liminality: Never-Never-Land. That is, they enter the Cedar forest so as to hunt and kill Humbaba. But it is this killing, their "first blood" that would make them eligible for marriage in an archetypal initiation ritual. And it is because this ritual does subtend the text that the Ishtar pericope must follow the Humbaba one, on which it is consequent.

Despite their joint venture, Gilgamesh and Enkidu are not deliminalized and, therefore, humanized simultaneously. The process of humanization is completed for and only for Enkidu not after he and Gilgamesh had succeeded in their hunt for and slaughter of Humbaba, but more importantly only after they had slaughtered the Bull of Heaven. The death that one of them, that is Enkidu, must suffer is what finally defines him as a mortal human being.

It is precisely Enkidu's death, which leads Gilgamesh to suspect that he too *could* die, that causes him to go on a quest to seek an escape from death. But while on this quest, he remains liminal; and so he cannot yet be aggregated into society at Uruk as the now manly king, engaged in a man's and a king's pursuits, and sexuality within marriage as befits someone in the Hunter Warrior class. And he cannot yet do this because he will still be liminal until he has lost all chance of immortality: that is, until he has lost what could have made his two-thirds godliness prevail over his one-third humanness.

But even though the predicated differential between the two as exemplified by the necessity for Enkidu to die, and Gilgamesh's quest to escape that fate is basic to the received epic, it need not have been a late literary development. Rather, as I noted at the beginning of this essay, it may and actually must be an archetype that subtends the entire Standard Babylonian literary presentation of the *Gilgamesh Epic.* In some earlier tradition or even in the subtending archetype(s), Enkidu most likely merely displaces Gilgamesh.

But even in the Standard Babylonian epic, Enkidu takes on the role of the Substitute King,[11] who must die not only for their slaughter of Humbaba, but perhaps more importantly for their joint killing of the Bull of Heaven. So it is meaningful that the Bull of Heaven had been sent by Anu to avenge Gilgamesh's rejection of Ishtar, which is not so much a fertility rite as the desired result of entrance into the Hunter-Warrior class.

Because of this, the narrative has to develop in such a way that Enkidu must die. From a ritual studies perspective, he must die *vis à vis* his former status. But from a purely literary perspective, Enkidu must die so that Gilgamesh the King, who has the potential to escape death until he loses the plant of life, may continue to live. And perhaps the need for Gilgamesh to continue living may be the basis of those earlier traditions in which it is Enkidu who does not want to spare Humbaba.[12]

But Enkidu's death serves an added purpose in the epic as well as in some of its subtending rituals. It is Enkidu's displacement of Gilgamesh in death, as well as in becoming subject to death, that really defines Enkidu as human, and therefore a good Substitute King. Hence, Enkidu may have been civilized as represented by his working in concert with Gilgamesh even before he had become humanized.

In the Standard Babylonian narrative as well as that of earlier "fragments," Gilgamesh, a city dweller known for his Wisdom, is not depicted as either humanized or civilized. Hence he is the counterpart of Enkidu. But he is also his opposite. Whereas Enkidu is innocent of sexuality until seduced by Harlot Woman, Gilgamesh is epitomized by his sexuality until he and Enkidu engage in Single Combat. And Gilgamesh categorically expresses his sexuality in a bestial, albeit not feral, uncivilized manner. He is not yet totally humanized, possibly because part of him is divine and his death is not yet inevitable.

If there had ever been a time in which Gilgamesh had been civilized, he may be viewed as becoming re-civilized once he and Enkidu have succeeded in their joint venture of killing Humbaba. But since there is no suggestion in the extant texts that he had ever been civilized, we must presume that he became civilized after Enkidu's death.

Not until the Standard Babylonian epic's end, however, is Gilgamesh depicted as losing his immortality, although the possibility of his losing it is raised when one of the two must die for the killing of Humbaba,[13] and for the slaughter of the Bull of Heaven,[14] thereby becoming human. However, since Gilgamesh is the seducer rather than the seduced, his sexuality in Uruk does not initiate the change. The implications, if valid, regarding his relationship with Enkidu, however, may be part of this paradigm. Clearly, then, both Gilgamesh and Enkidu experience civilization through sexuality, and humanization by becoming subject to death. And, in any case, in the Standard Babylonian version, the respective cycles in which they do so overlap.

* * *

NOTES

1. This scenario may even be considered a type scene. And it is found with many variants in heroic literature from diverse cultures.
2. This type of substitution may be related to the "Substitute King" paradigm, but it may also be related to the more pressing problem of twins, doubles, etc.
3. An anti-hero must not be construed as a villain unless the narrative demands it. The anti-hero in this epic is the secondary heroic *persona* that is "played against" the primary heroic *persona.*

4. Although each is a "likeness"—this is not the place to discuss the problematics of this translation of *zikru*—of Anu, we are not told that they are proportionally divine and human in correspondence with one another.
5. See Jeffrey H. Tigay *The Evolution of the Gilgamesh Epic* (Philadelphia: University of Pennsylvania, 1982) 202. We must remember that civilization and humanization are not the same although they sometimes may be concomitant. In any case, Tzvi Abusch ("Ishtar's Proposal and Gilgamesh's Refusal: An Interpretation of the *Gilgamesh Epic*, Tablet 6, Lines 1–79" *History of Religions* 26 [1986] 181) sees Gilgamesh as being re-humanized when Enkidu dies, therefore implying that he had become dehumanized.
6. See J. H. Tigay *The Evolution of the Gilgamesh Epic* 202; Erica Reiner "City Bread and Bread Baked in Ashes" *Languages and Areas: Studies Presented to George V. Bobrinskoy* (Chicago: University of Chicago, 1967) 118.
7. Harlot Woman has acted on the orders of Gilgamesh no matter who instigated or initiated the process.
8. I use the basic conventions of New Criticism wherever it is pertinent. That New Criticism is no longer the newest method of analysis, having been supplemented but not supplanted by more recently developed forms of criticism, does not affect my choice of nomenclature. So I differentiate between the implied reader, an unnamed character to whom the narrative is directed, and the real reader, who is not a character in the narrative. I do not however reject that the real reader may, and perhaps must affect the narrative, in accord with the rubric of various categories of Reader Response Criticism. This is beyond the scope of this essay, and I shall pursue it elsewhere.
9. Our Gilgamesh traditions are literary. So the ritual paradigms that subtend them must not be construed as absolutely determinative of all people and events in the received texts.
10. And he has not, as John Maier points out in agreement with Ricoeur, suffered a "Fall" ("*Gilgamesh*: Anonymous Tradition and Authorial Value" *Neohelicon* 14 [1988] 86–87). See also Paul Ricoeur *The Symbolism of Evil* (Boston: Beacon, 1967) 187.
11. The use of a Substitute King was not unknown in Mesopotamia. See, for example, Jean Bottéro "The Substitute King and His Fate" *Mesopotamia: Writing, Reasoning, and the Gods* (Chicago: University of Chicago, 1992) 138–155.
12. J. Maier "*Gilgamesh*: Tradition and Value" 89.
13. This supports Jastrow's thesis that the traditions centering about Enkidu, Hunter Man and Harlot Woman were once independent of those centering about Gilgamesh. See Morris Jastrow "Adam and Eve in Babylonian Literature" *ASJL* 15 (1899) 193–214. Moreover, it suggests that the redactor(s) first responsible for integrating the traditions

centered around them into whatever version they first were conjoined with those centering around Gilgamesh did not substantially alter them in the process. Logically, after all, it should have been the hero, Gilgamesh, alone, who is created, humanized/civilized, goes on adventures in which he ultimately seeks to find immortality.

14. Meaningfully, the Bull of Heaven episode seems to be late. It is not found in the extant fragments of the OB text. See J.H. Tigay *The Evolution of the Gilgamesh Epic* 48.

❋ ❋ ❋

Raymond J. Clark
"Origins: New Light on Eschatology in Gilgamesh's Mortuary Journey"

Although Raymond J. Clark's essay does not make extensive references to Homer's *Odyssey*, the epic tradition so important to an understanding of Western literature is central to his argument that Gilgamesh, in journeying to see Utnapishtim, is engaged in a Mortuary Journey. The standard version of *Gilgamesh* is much older than the *Odyssey*, and looks forward to the later journeys to the Land of the Dead in Homer, Vergil, and Dante. The place to which Gilgamesh travels is more akin, though, to Homer's Elysian Plain than it is to Odysseus's kingdom of Hades.

Clark's main argument is that the Babylonian bard transforms earlier Sumerian literature, especially in the way Gilgamesh travels, not to the underworld, where Enkidu dreamed he was headed and to which (in Tablet XII) he does descend, but to a special Afterworld, a Land of the Departed where only special persons—only two, Utnapishtim and his wife—live. Both Enkidu's descent to the underworld and Gilgamesh's journey to the Land of the Departed are variants of Inanna's Descent to the Netherworld. Where Enkidu is unsuccessful in following the goddess and is trapped forever in the world of the dead, Gilgamesh is successful in the journey and in his return to Uruk, although he does not find the immortality he seeks. Inventing a new type of Afterworld, the Babylonian bard of *Gilgamesh* prepared the way for two versions of the Land of the Departed in the epic tradition. (Ed.)

In the notes to his new rendition of *The Epic of Gilgamesh* D.P. Jackson remarks: "When investigating Dante… teachers often exploit what students already know about Vergil or Christianity. When students deal first with Vergil, they can rely on whatever is already known about Homeric precedents that form the *Aeneid*. In the case of Gilgamesh this cannot be done, as no earlier models or allusions exist."[1]

It is perfectly true that no earlier precise models exist for the Epic as a whole. But in fact the Epic is indebted to earlier sources in exactly the same sense that Dante is indebted to Vergil, and Vergil to Homer, and so forth. That is to say, each is a new creation arising out of and transforming what is old. Accordingly this chapter will consider the origin of the Babylonian (i.e., Semitic) epic—especially that part of it which pertains to Gilgamesh's journey to Utnapishtim—with the particular objective of showing how for this journey, which is the climax of the epic, the Babylonian bard made use of earlier Sumerian literature for his own eschatological purpose. Mortality and eschatology are not the only underlying themes of the epic, but I dwell on them as being germane to this particular investigation of the Babylonian bard's poetic art.[2]

My claim that the Babylonian bard had an eschatological purpose also presupposes that Gilgamesh, king of Uruk, journeyed to a Land of the Dead in the way that Homer's Odysseus or Vergil's Aeneas or Dante himself did, the latter having described his own descent in his *Divine Comedy.* But did Gilgamesh in fact make such a journey? That he did so I have already advocated in a work tracing the descents to the underworld of many mortal heroes throughout the Near East and Graeco-Roman worlds in the two millennia before Christ.[3] The argument rests upon the premise that in Tablet XI of the *Epic of Gilgamesh* the Babylonian survivor of the flood, Utnapishtim, dwells in what can be regarded as a Land of the Dead, or, as we may also call it—since he enjoys everlasting life there—an Afterworld. Gilgamesh's journey to Utnapishtim's abode in Tablets IX–X to consult the hero of the flood about the secret of everlasting life is therefore conceived within the context of the epic as a Journey of the Dead made by a living man in the flesh.

Since this interpretation is trying to change the way readers currently understand the epic, some review of my argument in greater detail is necessary in order to dispel a widespread resistance to the idea that the epic is, or rather contains, a mortuary myth. While many modern scholars have been ready to accept similarities between the Gilgamesh story and Homer's *Odyssey,* they stop short of saying that Gilgamesh actually journeys to an Abode of the Departed. Even Webster, though struck by the fact that "Utnapishtim supplies the information that Gilgamesh needs, just as Teiresias supplies the information that Odysseus needs,"[4] refrained from attributing such a journey to Gilgamesh. Sandars, who translated the epic in the widely read Penguin edition, gave what is the conventional view when she wrote in her introduction: "this is not an underworld journey."[5] And Graf similarly rejected the notion that Gilgamesh made a mortuary journey.[6] He thus reinstated the conventional position which I am trying to dislodge. His criticism is especially valuable insofar as it focuses, as no previous argument has done, upon a problem faced by the epic-maker in placing

Utnapishtim within the epic. The response which this critic's argument elicits will be the starting point in my examination of the eschatological purpose of the Babylonian bard.

Graf based his objection to regarding the dwelling-place of Utnapishtim as a Land of the Dead on the fact that it was clearly separated in the epic from the Netherworld of which Enkidu dreams in Tablet VII, and about which he returns to speak as a ghost in the so-called "inorganic appendage" to the epic in Tablet XII.[7] He thinks that the mortuary interpretation of Gilgamesh's journey introduces a discrepancy that actually violates the twelve-tablet version of the epic, that is to say its most complete text.[8]

The objection is worth examining closely, because what is at stake is a fundamental piece of evidence illuminating both the nature of Gilgamesh's journey and a central part of the epic-maker's meaning. The epic speaks for itself, of course, without the need to refer to its sources. But since it is a composite work, the unique eschatological purpose of Gilgamesh's Journey may be further established by seeking to identify the sources of its themes with the objective of gleaning what the epic-maker may have intended by his re-use of them. For great poets often combine earlier poems or folkloric reminiscences and so forth, and redistribute their elements, for their own new purposes. With this perspective and with Graf's objections held in mind it will be shown, I hope, not only how Utnapishtim's dwelling place was transformed from its Sumerian prototype into a Land of the Departed, but why it was appropriate that this Afterworld was separate in the epic from the Netherworld with which Enkidu was associated.

The first six Tablets tell how Gilgamesh gained a friend in the man Enkidu, who had lost his pristine innocence in what is virtually the Fall-of-Man theme, and how they journeyed together to a distant cedar forest and its mountain, which reaches to heaven, and killed the dragon-like guardian Humbaba. For this forest-episode the Babylonian bard made extensive use of one of five known tales belonging to the older Sumerian Gilgamesh-cycle.[9] It is clear from the Sumerian poem known as *Gilgamesh and the Land of the Living*,[10] sometimes called *Gilgamesh and Huwawa* after the monster's Sumerian name, that Gilgamesh makes his journey to the cedar forest in part to escape the common lot of mankind: "I have looked over the wall," he says before setting out, "and I see bodies floating on the river, and that will be my lot also (vss. 25–27)."[11] The Babylonian epic keeps the same motivation, but shifts Gilgamesh's lament so as to reflect on the numbered days of mankind as compared with the everlasting life of the gods.[12] The journey to the cedar forest in both the Sumerian poem (vss. 5–7) and the epic (III.iv.25) will enable Gilgamesh to set up for himself "a name that endures"—possibly by erecting an inscribed monument. The idea of creating an enduring name is underscored by whatever editor added the first 26 lines of the prologue. In it Gilgamesh is said to have engraved a record of "all his toil" upon an inscription (I.i.8)—presumably the one that told also of his exploit in the cedar forest—and to have placed it (so that it was removable and could be read aloud from) in the foundation of the walls of Uruk, which Gilgamesh built for future generations to remember him by (I.i.9–26). The building of magnificent works recalling the builder's identity and the performance of heroic deeds recorded on inscriptions are two separate ways of perpetuating one's name—a conventional device, widespread in the Near East,[13] for attaining an indirect sort of immortality. The idea that a person's name could save him from the oblivion of death was one of the reasons why "calling the name" of deceased ancestors was so important in the ritual of Mesopotamian cults of the dead.[14]

Victory over Humbaba in the cedar forest brings the radiant Gilgamesh an offer of marriage from the Babylonian goddess of love Ishtar—which he promptly rejects. He recounts that he has no desire to share the fate suffered by a list of her former lovers beginning with Tammuz, all of whom she turned into animals.[15] Spurned and anxious for vengeance, Ishtar persuades the sky god Anu to send down against Uruk the Bull of Heaven—which Gilgamesh and Enkidu kill also. This, their second joint adventure, is inspired by a second Sumerian poem called *Gilgamesh and the Bull of Heaven.*[16]

The sequel in Tablet VII does not derive from this Sumerian poem. Enkidu falls sick and has two dreams. In the first he sees the gods in council decree his own death for the killings of Humbaba and the Bull. In the second—the dream to which Graf referred[17]—he sees all the horrors that lie in store for mortals in the House of Darkness. What Enkidu describes in his second dream, while he lay sick, could not have given the Mesopotamian House of Darkness worse publicity. No wonder Gilgamesh fell into despair upon his friend's death twelve days later. Grief-stricken and enraged, Gilgamesh buries his friend and makes the long journey to Utnapishtim "the Faraway" in Tablets IX–X. He undertook this journey for the same reason as he journeyed to the cedar forest: from a desire to avoid the common lot of mankind. But in this journey Gilgamesh is no longer satisfied with the conventional methods of transcending death by reputation. He seeks immortality directly.

It is now appropriate, with this context in mind, to consider the grounds for thinking that Gilgamesh's Journey to Utnapishtim's abode was conceived of as a journey made by a living man to a World of the Departed.

After wandering far in the wilderness Gilgamesh came to the twin-peaked Mashu mountain, whose peaks reach up to heaven and down beneath the Underworld. Its entrance-gate is guarded by the Scorpion-man and his wife, "wardens of Shamash, both at his rising and setting."[18] This is the mythical mountain of the sun, where the sun goes when he is not visible on earth, the place of both sunset and sunrise frequently depicted on early Babylonian seals.[19] Darkness and prayers to the moon-god Sin[20] suggest that Gilgamesh was journeying westward to the place of sunset. Since Gilgamesh is two-thirds divine but one third mortal, he is at first not permitted to pass through the gate. He is told by the Scorpion-man and his wife that no mortal has ever gone this way before.[21] When he prevails upon them to let him through, he passes into the subterranean tunnel of the mountain beyond the confines of this world and thereby experiences a descent of sorts which no mortal before him has had. After journeying through the dark tunnel, which "follows the sun's road to his rising,"[22] Gilgamesh emerges into the bright, jewelled garden of the sun, where Shamash the Babylonian sun-god walks in early morning. Shamash repeats the warning already given by the guardians of the gate that Gilgamesh will not find the immortality he seeks,[23] but Gilgamesh, declaring that "one who indeed is dead may behold yet the radiance of the sun" (X. Old Babylonian version i.16), continues his journey until he meets the barmaid Siduri, who lives at the edge of the garden by the sea. She too attempts to dissuade the wandering Gilgamesh from proceeding further, but since he is determined to continue she directs him to the place where Urshanabi daily ferries Shamash over the Ocean in a boat. Urshanabi is discouraging in turn and at first refuses to take Gilgamesh on board. When he erupts in anger and smashes a vital part of the boat, Urshanabi relents—on condition that Gilgamesh first cut down three hundred (or in the Assyrian version one hundred and twenty) punting-poles. Again, Urshanabi tells Gilgamesh that no mortal has made this journey either before.[24]

Once on the far shore, Gilgamesh learns from Utnapishtim that his own immortality was acquired as a gift of the gods after he survived the flood in an ark. The story of the flood-hero Utnapishtim which lies behind this episode derives from the Sumerian poem called *The Deluge*.[25] But unlike the other Sumerian poems already mentioned from which the epic-maker borrowed, the Sumerian flood-story has nothing to do with Gilgamesh and did not belong to the older Sumerian cycle of Gilgamesh poems.

The extent of the Babylonian bard's innovation in relation to Gilgamesh's journey to Utnapishtim has not hitherto been fully appreciated, though some parts have been acknowledged to be new. In the first place the whole theme featuring Gilgamesh in quest of the flood-hero to seek immortality from the one man who suceeded in obtaining it, must be an invention of the Babylonian epic-maker, since Gilgamesh had no connection with Utnapishtim in earlier literature.[26] The Babylonian bard also changed the third person of the Sumerian flood-story to the first-person, so as to make Utnapishtim the narrator of his own experiences to Gilgamesh.[27] Enkidu's death as the motivation for Gilgamesh making the journey is also a new element and was, in fact, born of a multiple invention. For quite apart from its role in motivating Gilgamesh's newly invented quest, the story itself of the death and burial of Enkidu has no Sumerian prototype and is therefore, as Kramer observed, "in all likelihood of Babylonian rather than Sumerian origin."[28] Kirk tried to make a case for thinking that the link in the epic between Enkidu's death and the slaying of the Bull of Heaven was the result of a "minor adjustment," since his death could have been determined by the gods in revenge for the slaying of Huwawa.[29] But Enkidu's punishment by death for helping Gilgamesh kill both Humbaba and the Bull is not told in connection with either monster in the extant portions of the Sumerian poems about them. Moreover, in other Sumerian poetry Enkidu did not even "die" in the normal sense of the word at all—a fact that will bring us now to consider the epic's "finale" in Tablet XII.

Tablet XII is regarded as an "inorganic appendage" to the epic because (among other contradictions) it depicts Enkidu as still alive at the end and is not fully integrated into the epic. It tells how Enkidu volunteers to retrieve from the Netherworld Gilgamesh's mysterious *pukku* and *mikku*—perhaps his drum and drumstick or some playthings—which have fallen into it. Enkidu descends alive into the Netherworld, where he gets "caught," rather like the Greek hero Theseus in his descent.[30] His ghost then returns through a hole in the ground to tell Gilgamesh what he has seen in the Land of the Shades. This event, which depicts Enkidu's "death" differently from the main body of the epic, is virtually an Akkadian translation, with some variations of detail, of the second half of yet another Sumerian poem known as *Gilgamesh, Enkidu and the Netherworld.* [31]

Yet, despite these differences, one cannot help wondering whether the Sumerian poem inspired the Babylonian poet to create not only the story of Enkidu's death and burial, as the motivation for Gilgamesh's journey, but also Enkidu's dream of the horrors awaiting him in the Mesopotamian House of Darkness. The dream, for which no Sumerian prototype exists, is in any case practically a doublet of what Enkidu's ghost reports from the land of the dead in the Sumerian poem, and may be a variation on it.[32]

As for the actual stages of the journey, it has been well observed that the theme of Gilgamesh's journey through the Mashu mountain has no Sumerian prototype.[33] Commentators have passed in silence over the fact that Gilgamesh's ocean-crossing has no known earlier counterpart either. The standard view is to comment, as Kirk does, to the effect that the garden of jewels, where Shamash walks, and the waters of death and so forth are fantastic elements of fairy tale or folklore origin "which add greatly to the richness of the narrative but little to its central subject."[34] So far as I know, the question of how the introduction of the ocean-crossing may have transformed the traditional setting of the flood-hero's distant abode has not caught the attention of scholars, though the imagery would surely not have escaped the notice of the ancients.

Commentators have been content to note that the intervention of the ocean-crossing between the garden of the sun "eastwards in Eden" and the dwelling-place of Utnapishtim poses a problem, but have been satisfied if they show that the Babylonian and Sumerian accounts can be harmonized. Thus Sandars names Utnapishtim's dwelling-place "Dilmun" and gives its location as being—curiously enough in light of Siduri's warnings at n.39 below—"in the garden of the sun" and also "at the place of the sun's transit, eastward of the mountain."[35] By these means Utnapishtim's abode is harmonized with that mentioned in the Sumerian poem *The Deluge* at verse 261, where Utnapishtim's Sumerian counterpart, Ziusudra, was immortalized after the flood in Dilmun, "where the sun rises."[36]

But the fact is that the epic-maker both left Utnapishtim's abode unnamed and introduced a new dimension into its location. What, *pace* Sandars, is incontrovertible, is that the eastern setting of Utnapishtim's unnamed abode is confirmed in the Old Babylonian version of the prologue to the epic, which declares that Gilgamesh is a "[cros]ser of the ocean, the vast sea, to where the sun rises (I.i.38)."[37] And Gilgamesh has already passed through the Mashu mountain along the road of the sun eastward to the bright jewelled garden of the sun, where "the dawn breaks."[38] But Siduri then tells Gilgamesh quite unambiguously that Utnapishtim's shore is separated from the garden by both the ocean and the waters of death.[39] In other words, the epic-maker, by inserting the Ocean crossing, in his episodic manner makes Gilgamesh go along the road of the sun beyond the Mashu mountain a second time, and this time the poet is influenced by a purely Semitic belief—not, therefore, found among the Sumerians—that the sun travels at night from the west to the east by crossing the Ocean and its underworld waters. In short, the Babylonian bard has added a new dimension to the flood-hero's eastern abode by suggesting that it can be reached by travelling—albeit with some duplication over the sun's journeys—beyond the sunset mountain which marks the world's western horizon.

Gilgamesh's journey westwards and the identification of his subsequent journey with the journey of the sun beyond the mountain was doubtless helped by the fact that in Mesopotamian literature the Sun-god was associated with the Underworld and was actively involved, in cults of the dead, with deceased ancestors.[40] Moreover in Ugaritic literature we read of such idioms as "to reach the sunset" or "to enter the host of the sun," both signifying death.[41] The same distinction is observed later in Greek eschatological belief: the dead are thought to live either below the surface of the earth or across Ocean beyond the horizon.[42] The mortuary significance of the ocean crossing is further emphasized by Gilgamesh's need subsequently to cross over the waters of death, which Siduri says lie between the sea and Utnapishtim's abode.[43] It is a three days journey to reach these waters, which the poet thus conflates with the ocean, and then Gilgamesh must take each of the poles he has cut down for a single thrust, so that his hand may not touch the fatal waters.[44] In sum, the mortuary imagery of the waters of death, over which Gilgamesh must cross, perhaps borrowed also from the Sumerian river of death,[45] serves to emphasize that Gilgamesh is journeying to a veritable Land of the Departed.

To Gilgamesh's journey to the realm of the dead we may compare the descent-myth of the Sumerian goddess Inanna. It may have been a direct, or indirect model, in addition to Enkidu's descent to be mentioned again immediately below. Moreover, the descent by Inanna's Babylonian counterpart Ishtar has a parallel structure. Both goddesses descended alive into the Netherworld, got "caught" there for three days, were set free on the condition that they send below a substitute to replace themselves, and sent below as victims their respective husband-lovers Dumuzi and Tammuz.[46] Gilgamesh, we remember, cites Ishtar's ill-treatment of Tammuz as his reason for rejecting the goddess' invitation to marry her.[47] Enkidu's descent into the Netherworld appears to be the case of a mortal who followed in divine footsteps. But he, being mortal, was less successful than either of these goddesses, so that, when "caught" in the world below, he, unlike his divine counterparts, stayed there for ever, save for a brief respite, to speak as a ghost to Gilgamesh, in the necromantic seance.

From all of the foregoing it will be seen that (i) Enkidu's descent is a Sumerian mortuary myth that is older than *The Epic of Gilgamesh,* and that (ii) Gilgamesh's journey to Utnapishtim is practically a variant of it. Perhaps, to expand on what has already been said above, *Gilgamesh, Enkidu and the Netherworld,* which itself resembles a divine descent-pattern, gave the Babylonian epic-maker the idea for creating not only the episodes of Enkidu's death, dream, and burial, as the motivation for Gilgamesh's quest of immortality, but also the story itself of Gilgamesh's own mortuary journey. The story was made possible by transforming the traditional flood-story's immortal hero into a person to be consulted by the mortal Gilgamesh desiring to obtain immortality. But instead of descending alive into the Netherworld, Gilgamesh visits Utnapishtim's Blessed Abode separated from this world by the such boundaries as the mountain at the western horizon, the ocean, and the waters of death.

To return to the objections raised by Graf: it is perfectly true that this Afterworld inhabited by Utnapishtim is not the dismal Netherworld in which Enkidu resides. But it would have been pointless to make Gilgamesh descend thither. Gilgamesh knows already from Enkidu's dream that the secret of immortal life was not to be had from the realm below. So Gilgamesh avoids this Netherworld and sets out for what can only be conceived as an alternative Land of the Departed, reserved for those special inhabitants—so far restricted to the two survivors of the flood Utnapishtim and his wife—who have escaped the dreary lot awaiting mankind in the usual Mesopotamian Land of the Dead. It was, as I believe, the brilliant conception of the Babylonian bard that he at least contemplated for mortals a new type of Afterworld distinguishable from that visited by Enkidu—achieved at a stroke by relocating Dilmun beyond the Mashu mountain and beyond the Ocean and the Waters of Death marking the boundaries of this world. This Afterworld was not an abode for the ordinary dead comparable to the Kingdom of Hades visited by Odysseus, but was more akin to Homer's Elysian Plain located at the world's end, whither a few highly favoured mortals were "translated" from this world and continue to live for ever.[48] Perhaps Utnapishtim's Afterworld would have received other mortals departing this life if only they could first acquire immortality. Unfortunately Gilgamesh failed to obtain it, though he came close to succeeding. He learnt from Utnapishtim where a magic plant of youth was to be found, at the bottom of the sea, and he even acquired it. But when he put it down to bathe on his way home to Uruk, a snake came and snatched it for itself. And so Gilgamesh lost to a snake the immortality which might have been man's.

There is, finally, no substance to Graf's claim that the Babylonian twelve-tablet text of the epic is violated by the notion that Utnapishtim's abode was conceived within the epic as an Afterworld. Tigay has pointed out at length that the epic is thematically framed by a number of motifs and phrases which echo through it. He cites a particularly pertinent instance. The hymnic description of Uruk at the end of tablet XI, where Gilgamesh urges the boatman Urshanabi, after their return to Uruk, to examine the walls for their strength, recalls the prologue celebrating Gilgamesh's achievement in building these walls. The repetition of the prologue in Gilgamesh's mouth at this point expresses the futility of his intervening quest to overcome death in other than the conventional manner of setting up a name for himself. Gilgamesh here realizes that the most he can hope for is the conventional, indirect immortality, through the perpetuation of his name as the royal builder. Similarly we can add that Enkidu's dream-vision of the horrors in the Mesopotamian House of Darkness and Enkidu's ghostly report of its horrors at the end in the twelfth tablet enclose Gilgamesh's journey to Utnapishtim's blessed Afterworld in a kind of ring composition. Gilgamesh, unlike Enkidu, does at least return successfully from this Land of the Departed—in this he resembles the goddesses Inanna and Ishtar—though he does not succeed in the purpose for which he went. What Gilgamesh learns from the lips of his dead friend Enkidu in Tablet XII serves to remind all mankind, even the royal Gilgamesh himself, of the inevitable fate awaiting all mortals in the Mesopotamian world beyond this world.

* * *

NOTES

1. D.P. Jackson, *The Epic of Gilgamesh* (Wauconda, IL: Bolchazy-Carducci Publ., 1992), XXXIV—henceforth abbreviated as *EG*. The method of referring to the epic by tablet, column, and verse in this and other translations is explained in n.12 below.

2. That the author whom I call the Babylonian "bard" or "epic-maker" borrowed and modified his Mesopotamian heritage has most recently been investigated on a major scale by J.H. Tigay, *The Evolution of the Gilgamesh Epic* (Philadelphia 1982), which, however, does not cover

the subject of my own enquiry. Evolution of the epic from its earliest, i.e., Old Babylonian, version (c. 2000–1600 BC) to its "late" (also called "standard") version found primarily in the library of the Assyrian king Ashurbanipal (668–627 BC) in Nineveh, will concern us only insofar as variants are germane to the theme under discussion. Tigay, who may be consulted for all such details, summarizes (p. 246) thus: "The late version, although it restructured the episodes, reworded the text extensively, and added supplementary material, is textually related to its Old and Middle Babylonian forerunners and also tells the same story." Generally, changes made subsequent to the Old Babylonian version are designed to emphasize the themes already implicit in the original, and sometimes later versions must be used to reconstruct lost portions of the Old Babylonian version.

3. R.J. Clark. *Catabasis: Vergil and the Wisdom-Tradition* (Amsterdam 1979). Part of my first chapter examined whether there was a basis for W.F. Jackson Knight's remark in his *Cumaean Gates* (Oxford 1936), 18: "the Epic of Gilgamish may be the earliest mortuary myth in the world," which was an intuitive insight rather than an argued position.

4. T.B.L. Webster, *From Mycenae to Homer* (London: Methuen, 1958 and 1964), 83, with reference to Homer, *Odyssey* XI.

5. N.K. Sandars, *The Epic of Gilgamesh* (Harmondsworth 1960; latest revd. ed. 1972), 38.

6. F. Graf, with reference to my book (above n.3), *Gnomon* 35 (1981), 545–548.

7. *Ibid.* 545f.: "das befriedigt nicht recht, trennt doch die babylonische Zwölftafelversion, unser vollständigster Text, den Aufenthaltsort des Utnapistim deutlich von der Unterwelt, von der Enkidu träumt (Taf. VI) und aus der sein Geist berichtet (Tafel XII, freilich eine unorganische Appendix)." Reasons why Tablet XII is regarded as an "inorganic appendage" are given below. Graf's reference to Tablet VI is a slip for VII.

8. The argument will be taken up later. It may be noted here that Sandars, *op.cit.* (above n.5), 118f., omits the twelfth tablet and substitutes as her own ending the Sumerian poem *The Death of Gilgamesh*—on which see further n.26 below. Tablet XII is translated in Jackson, *EG*, 87–92.

9. Of these five Sumerian poems one has already been mentioned in n.8 above and three will be mentioned at various places below. For what has already been inferred concerning the use of these in the epic see S.N. Kramer, "The Epic of Gilgamesh and its Sumerian Sources," *J.A.O.S.* 64(1944), 7–23, 83, with additions in *J.C.S.* 1(1947), 3–46, and his *History Begins at Sumer* (Philadelphia 1981), 181–198, originally published as *From the Tablets of Sumer* (1956); L. Matouš, "Les Rapports entre la version sumérienne et la version akkadienne de l'épopée de Gilgameš" in P. Garelli (ed.), *Gilgameš et sa légende* (Paris 1960), 83–94; and Tigay, *op.cit.* (above n.2), 23ff. and *passim.*

10. The translation by S.N. Kramer in J.B. Pritchard (ed.), *Ancient Near Eastern Texts* (Princeton 1969), 47–50— henceforth abbreviated as *ANET*—lacks much of the ending supplied in Kramer's earlier publication entitled *The Sumerians* (Chicago 1963), 190–197.
11. Stephanie Page rightly explains the river-imagery as referring to the river on which the dead are carried down by boat to the place of burial, reported in G.S. Kirk, *Myth: Its Meaning and Function in Ancient and Other Cultures* (Cambridge 1971), 141. The walls will then be the walls of Uruk—Gilgamesh's city on the Euphrates—which Gilgamesh built according to the prologue in Tablet I. Kirk, *op.cit.* 142, adds his own view that the river-detail is suppressed in the epic in order to postpone Gilgamesh's understanding of death until Enkidu dies. But the epic—see the sentence in the text immediately below—merely omits the river-imagery and not the fact of man's mortality. Sandars, *op.cit.* (above n.5), 72, incorporates the detail of the river-imagery from the Sumerian poem into her version of the epic, it being her (misleading) acknowledged practice (p. 51) to employ Sumerian sources in her translation of the epic.
12. See tablet III (Old Babylonian version) col.iv. verses 6–7 in *ANET.* 79. Pages 72–99 of this translation by E.A. Speiser, with supplements on pp. 503–507 by A.K. Grayson, contain the Old Babylonian and subsequent versions (n.2 above). Further supplements are collected by Tigay, *op.cit.* (above n.2), *passim.* Speiser's arrangement by tablet, column, and verse in *ANET* is adapted from R. Campbell Thompson's edition of the late version in *The Epic of Gilgamish* (Oxford 1930). Jackson numbers verses continuously throughout each tablet, as distinct from each column, and hence gives the above *ANET* citation (in *EG.* p. 21) as tablet III, col.iv. verses 57–59. In the interests of providing a continuous story Jackson's and Sandars' translations conflate different versions; the latter provides no references to tablets etc.
13. Evidence is assembled by Tigay, *op.cit.* (above n.2), ch. 7, who here also argues that these 26 verses of the prologue, fully translated by himself pp. 141f. and Jackson, *EG.* 2f. [but not by Campbell Thompson, Speiser, or Sandars], belong to the "late" version, on which see n.2 above.
14. T.J. Lewis, *Cults of the Dead in Ancient Israel and Ugarit* (Harvard Semitic Monographs 39, Georgia 1989), 53, 119, 169, 173.
15. Tablet VI. 46ff.
16. Though not extant in the sporadic tablets of the Old Babylonian version, this episode almost certainly belonged to it. The Sumerian original, itself only partially preserved, was last edited by P.M. Witzel, *Analecta Orientalia* 6 (1933), 45–88.
17. See n.7 above.
18. Campbell Thompson's translation (above n.12), 42 (IX.ii.9), is to the point. Cf. *ANET.* 88 and Jackson, *EG.* 56 (IX.ii.30).
19. Henri Frankfort, *Cylinder Seals* (London 1939), 67–69, and *Stratified Cylinder Seals From the Diyala Region* (Chicago 1955), 40ff., correctly

explains such scenes as representing the chthonic aspect of the sun's boat between sunset and sunrise. The analogy to Gilgamesh's journey of the sun's journey depicted on cylinder seals contradicts what T.H. Gaster, "Semitic mythology" in Funk and Wagnall's *Standard Dictionary of Folklore, Mythology and Legend,* ed. M. Leach (NY 1949–1950), II. 989, calls the conventional interpretation of Gilgamesh's "progressive journey of the sun through the constellations of the zodiac," for which there is no evidence. It is worth adding that the Mashu mountain is not to be thought of in strictly geographical terms. Nor does the common identification of the cedar forest with Lebanon and Anti-Lebanon belong to the original strata of material—it only has meaning for dwellers in, e.g., Syria, where the location just mentioned is found in Hittite translations.

20. Jackson, *EG.* 55 (IX.i.14–20) = *ANET.* 88 (IX.i.8–10).

21. Jackson, *EG.* 56f. (IX. iii.64ff.) = *ANET.* 88 (IX. iii.9–13).

22. Sandars' translation (above n.5), 99, corresponds to IX.iv.89f. in Jackson, *EG.* 57 and IX.iv.45 in *ANET.* 89. Speiser here translates "along the road of the sun" and argues (n.152) that Gilgamesh travels through the mountain from east to west, as though along the sun's daytime road. But this view is contradicted by the Old Babylonian version of the prologue quoted in the text at n.37 below.

23. Gilgamesh's encounter with Shamash in the jewelled garden is preserved in fragmentary state in the Old Babylonian version (X.i. in *ANET.* 89). Jackson, *EG.* 59, follows the late (see n.2 above) version, which omits the encounter.

24. Tablet X (Assyrian version) ii.22–27 in *ANET.* 91 = X.ii. 76ff. in Jackson, *EG.* 63.

25. Edited by M. Civil in *Atra-Ḫasis: The Babylonian Story of the Flood* ed. W.G. Lambert and A.R. Millard (Oxford 1969), 138–145 and 167–172. It should perhaps be explained that the Old Babylonian version of the epic is dependent structurally upon the flood-story, but is shorter than the late version since it does not make Utnapishtim narrate the actual story of the flood. Utnapishtim's account in the late version is related more closely to *Atra-Ḫasis,* an independent Akkadian poem on the flood, than to the Sumerian original.

26. This argument contributes to T. Jacobsen's claim in his *The Treasures of Darkness. A History of Mesopotamian Religion* (New Haven 1976), 214, that there is no known Sumerian prototype for Gilgamesh's quest for immortality either, though the Sumerian poem *The Death of Gilgamesh* (see n.8 above), which glorifies Gilgamesh as one who had been granted kingship but not eternal life, may have given the Babylonian bard the idea to create such a quest.

27. Observed by Kramer, *History Begins* (above n.9), 190.

28. *Ibid.* 193.

29. Kirk. *op.cit.* (above n.11), 141.

30. The earliest scene depicting this version of Theseus' descent appears on a Peloponnesian shield-band dated c. 600 BC, reproduced in, e.g., K. Schefold, *Myth and Legend in Early Greek Art* (London 1966), 69 fig.24. Pausanias 10.29.9 refers to a similar scene depicted at Delphi by the mid-fifth century artist Polygnotus and to a literary description by the slightly earlier epic poet Panyassis. In some versions Theseus was rescued by Heracles, e.g., Euripides, *Herc.Fur.* 1170.
31. Edited, in two versions, by A. Shaffer, *Sumerian Sources of Tablet XII of the Epic of Gilgamesh* (Pennsylvania PhD. 1963); translated by Kramer, *The Sumerians* (above n.10), 197–205. On Gilgamesh's *pukku* and *mikku* see Tigay, *op.cit.* (above n.2), 5, 190f., who (27) with others (138 n.41) assigns tablet XII to the late version of the epic. For a translation of this, the Akkadian, version see n.8 above.
32. There are, to be sure, differences between the two detailed by Tigay, *op.cit.* (above n.2), 105f. In the dream Enkidu mentions people in the netherworld who had enjoyed privileged positions on earth; in the Sumerian poem and the twelfth tablet of the epic Enkidu's ghost mentions their family situation and mode of death. The dream could be an adaptation suited to Gilgamesh's royal status. According to A.L. Oppenheim, "The Interpretation of Dreams in the Ancient Near East," *Trans. Amer. Philosophical Soc.* 46(1956), 213f., Enkidu's dream is the model for the Akkadian poem *Vision of the Netherworld* (*ANET.* 109f.). Tigay, *op.cit.* 174, objects that both may draw on conventional material. Perhaps they did, but the Sumerian poem is not, thereby, ruled out as the inspiration suggesting the idea for Enkidu's dream.
33. Observed by S.N. Kramer, *J.A.O.S.* 64(1944), 18 n.82. I should add here that similarities between (i) this event and (ii) Gilgamesh's earlier journey to the cedar mountain (in turn derived, as we have seen, from the Sumerian *Gilgamesh and the Land of the Living*) suggest that the journey to the cedar forest nevertheless helped create part of the episode of the Mashu mountain. This helps explain why the Babylonian bard suppressed in the epic the sun god's association with the cedar-mountain, which is prominent in the Sumerian version—he wished to emphasize the sun's association more especially with the Mashu mountain visited by Gilgamesh later in the epic.
34. Kirk, *op.cit.* (above n.11), 145.
35. Sandars, *op.cit.* (above n. 5), 97 and 105 respectively. I have already referred in n.11 above to this translator's misleading practice of incorporating Sumerian sources within the epic. Dilmun is likewise mentioned at the beginning of Tablet IX in Jackson's version, *EG.* 55.
36. Before Ziusudra was placed there, only the gods lived in Dilmun and it had a paradisiacal character; see the Sumerian *Enki and Ninhursag* (*ANET.* 37–41).
37. Without explanation Tigay, *op.cit.* (above n.2), 152 and 158, regards this verse as a commentary on Gilgamesh's journey to the cedar-forest and mistakenly thinks that the prologue first alludes to Gilgamesh's journey to Utnapishtim only in the following verse.

38. Cf. tablet IX.v.45 in *ANET.* 89 with n.22 above. Jackson's translation (see n.23 above) obscures Gilgamesh's location at this point.
39. See refs. in n.43 below.
40. Much of this literature—especially new finds in Ugaritic—has been reviewed by Lewis, *op.cit.* (above n. 14), 37–46. Cf. also the Hittite tale of "Kessi the Huntsman" in which Kessi is told, "this is the door of the sunset, and beyond it lies the realm of the dead. No mortal who passes through it can ever come back" (trans. T.H. Gaster, *The Oldest Stories in the World* [1952 repr. Boston 1958 and 1971] 148f.). Observe, too, that it is the Sumerian sun-god, Utu, who opens the hole for Enkidu's ghost to come forth to converse with Gilgamesh in *Gilgamesh, Enkidu and the Netherworld.*
41. Lewis, *ib.* 37.
42. Instances are assembled by, e.g., E.B. Tylor, *Primitive Culture* (rept. New York 1958), ch.13, M.C. Stokes, "Hesiodic and Milesian Cosmologies," *Phronesis* 7(1962), 19–21; and W. Wagenvoort, "The Journey of the Souls of the Dead to the Isles of the Blessed," *Mnemosyne* 24(1971), 113 ff.
43. Tablet X (Assyrian version) ii. 25 and 27, iii.50, iv.1ff. and X (Old Babylonian) iv.8 in *ANET.* 91f. and 507 = X.iii.112, 165, and 184 in Jackson, *EG.* 65–67.
44. Campbell Thompson, *op.cit.* (above n.12), 85, suspected that this intent lay behind the use of the poles long before it was confirmed by the publication, in 1964, of the Old Babylonian fragment cited in the previous note. Jackson, *EG.* 69, translates as though Gilgamesh were rowing rather than punting, and re-using each oar rather than thrusting once with each pole.
45. An infernal river had to be crossed by the dead and by a boatman who ferried them across in the Sumerian myth *Enlil and Ninlil.* Lugalbanda also crossed it in another Sumerian myth. See for the respective myths Kramer, *The Sumerians* (above n.10), 133, 145ff., and *History Begins* (above n.9), 231.
46. For the Sumerian descent see S.N. Kramer, "*Inanna's Descent to the Nether World* Continued and Revised," *J.C.S.* 5(1951), 1–17, which incorporates new information from a Yale tablet not included in the later (1969) edition of *ANET.* 52–57. For the Babylonian counterpart see E.A. Speiser, "Descent of Iṣhtar to the Nether World," *ANET.* 106–109. Kramer reviews the discovery of later tablets in his "Sumerian Literature and the British Museum," *Proceedings of the American Philosophical Society* 124(1980), 299–310.
47. See at n.15 above.
48. Homer, *Odyssey* 4.561–569.

❋ ❋ ❋

II Influences of Gilgamesh on Later Literature

Greg Morris

"A Babylonian in Batavia: Mesopotamian Literature and Lore in *The Sunlight Dialogues*"

Since its rediscovery in 1872, *Gilgamesh* has inspired literature and other arts, from Hans Henny Jahn, who wrote the score for Gilgamesh lyrics into a strange and brilliant novel, to Bohuslav Martinu's oratorio, "The Epic of Gilgamesh," and Anselm Kiefer's painted photographs of Enkidu. Not all that much has been written about the intertextual relationships between the ancient poem and modern art. One exception is Greg Morris's 1982 article on novelist John Gardner's use of *Gilgamesh*, "A Babylonian in Batavia: Mesopotamian Literature and Lore in *The Sunlight Dialogues*." Gardner was fond of using a "collage technique" in his fiction, and he made massive use of A. Leo Oppenheim's *Ancient Mesopotamia* in *The Sunlight Dialogues,* set in Batavia, New York, a novel that pitted the sheriff, Fred Clumly, against a mad philosopher, Taggert Hodge. The four "dialogues" of the title are all filled with Mesopotamian lore gleaned from Oppenheim. Dialogue 3 is the one most directly concerned with *Gilgamesh.* Morris is useful in pointing out the Mesopotamian connections and in suggesting how Gardner thought a conflict between Babylonian and Hebraic thought still reverberates in even very ordinary circumstances of modern life. (Ed.)

It is a fact that John Gardner is an inveterate borrower. In nearly all of his fiction, he has transposed or transcribed material from other authors—be they historians, philosophers, or artists like himself. For instance, in *The Wreckage of Agathon* Gardner leans heavily upon Plutarch and his *Lives,* while in *The King's Indian*—specifically in the novella of the same title—Gardner lifts entire passages from Poe's *Arthur Gordon Pym,* as well as quotations and misquotations from Melville.[1] His liberal use of others' scholarship in his own The *Life and Times of Chaucer* stirred a furor in both the academic and popular press, and most recently, a small controversy has arisen over Gardner's "appropriation" of material from another man's work for his latest novel, *Freddy's Book.*[2]

To defend or attack this tendency in Gardner is not my purpose. Instead, I wish to examine the extent and aim of his borrowings in *The Sunlight Dialogues,* to discuss the reasoning behind his use of certain creative and historical writings, and to suggest the range of one of his most ambitious works.

The broad sweep of Mesopotamian history and lore and cultural tradition is central to The *Sunlight Dialogues;* it is the dominant influence upon the book's thematics, providing primary and background support for Gardner's grand structure. To supply himself with the needed historical data, Gardner resorted to one main scholarly source: A. Leo Oppenheim's *Ancient Mesopotamia: Portrait of a Dead Civilization,* published in 1964 by the University of Chicago Press. How Gardner came upon this book is uncertain; just as unclear is the process by which he went about incorporating the Babylonian material into his novel, whether it was originally planned as a part of the book, or whether his reading in Oppenheim came after or during the composition of the novel and had to be worked into the mass of writing already completed. What can be demonstrated, however, is the degree to which Gardner borrowed from Oppenheim, and how Gardner went beyond mere appropriation and plunder, and on to what he has called a "collage technique," which he has defined (in self-defense) as the art of:

> bringing disparate materials together in new ways, transforming the whole into a seamless fabric, a vision, a story.... Collage technique... has nothing to do with plagiarism. In every phrase, every nuance, it acknowledges its dependency. To the ignorant but good-hearted reader it gives a rich and surprising prose style—an interesting story filled with curious odds and ends that make a scene more vivid, a passing idea more resonant. To a knowledgeable, sophisticated reader it can give an effect of dazzling texture and astonishing intellectual compression.[3]

Whether one agrees or disagrees with Gardner's position, whether or not one thinks Gardner consistent with his own moral aestheticism, it must be admitted that Gardner is faithful in his own practice in *The Sunlight Dialogues,* where he does so amazingly weave fiction and fact, history and art, into a vast "seamless fabric, a vision." It is this that makes the novel his most compelling and most challenging work to date.

There are two ways in which Gardner makes *direct* use of Oppenheim's *Ancient Mesopotamia:* in the titling of his chapters, and in Taggert Hodge's lectures in each of the four dialogues. The origins of Gardner's chapter titles can be located in several places in Oppenheim. In *Ancient Mesopotamia,* Oppenheim includes a large number of plates depicting, for the most part, Assyrian palace reliefs. Gardner adopts the titles of several of these photographs as chapter titles: "Winged Figure Carrying Sacrificial Animal" (Chapter XX); "Workmen in a Quarry" (Chapter XIX); "Lion Emerging From Cage" (Chapter III); and "Hunting Wild Asses" (Chapter V).

Gardner also takes five other chapter titles from *Ancient Mesopotamia.* Chapter II of *The Sunlight Dialogues* is entitled "When the Exorcist Shall Go to the House of the Patient...." This comes from the introit to a collection of omens, *Enuma ana bit marsi dsipu illiku,* meaning "[If] the exorcist is going to the house of a patient..." (Oppenheim, p. 223). Gardner changes the title a bit, adopting the formulaic "When the" opening used in a number of other introits. The title of Chapter IV, "Mama," refers to the Babylonian mother goddess, whom Gardner (as shall be shown later) links with Millie Hodge; in fact, the epigraph to Chapter IV is quoted directly from Oppenheim: "The story seems to begin with the creation of mankind by the goddess Mama" (Oppenheim, p. 266). The title of Chapter IX, "Like a robber, I shall proceed according to my will," has its roots in one of the many Naram-Sin legends (Oppenheim, p. 227), and is also later reused in Chapter XI ("The Dialogue of Houses"), when Taggert illustrates his argument with a story taken from Oppenheim. "*Nah ist—und schwer zu fassen der Gott*" is the title to Chapter XIII of *The Sunlight Dialogues;* the quotation, which comes originally from Hölderlin, is also used by Oppenheim as a chapter title to Chapter IV of his own book. Finally, the title of Gardner's Chapter XXIII, "*E silentio,*" appears in Oppenheim's discussion of *The Epic of Gilgamesh* (Oppenheim, p. 258).

Further, in each of the four dialogues in *The Sunlight Dialogues,* Gardner borrows, often word-for-word, from material in *Ancient Mesopotamia.* For the sake of brevity and simplicity, I have listed below a summation of Gardner's gleanings from Oppenheim, stating the page numbers of each book and a general indication of which passages in *The Sunlight Dialogues* are derived from *Ancient Mesopotamia.* To discover the actual extent to which Gardner borrowed from Oppenheim, one need merely compare the corresponding sections from each book:

I. "The Dialogue on Wood and Stone"

The Sunlight Dialogues[4]	*Ancient Mesopotamia*
pp. 315–16 (the gods)	p. 184; pp. 194–95
p. 317 ("acid wit of their derision")	p. 185
p. 317 (feeding of the gods)	pp. 188–89

II. "The Dialogue of Houses"

The Sunlight Dialogues	*Ancient Mesopotamia*
pp. 419–20 (*šimtu* and *ištaru*)	pp. 201–2; p. 204
p. 420 (Naram-Sin legend)	p. 227

III. "The Dialogue of the Dead"

The Sunlight Dialogues	*Ancient Mesopotamia*
p. 532 (The Gilgamesh Epic)	p. 257

IV. "The Dialogue of Towers"

The Sunlight Dialogues	*Ancient Mesopotamia*
p. 630 (The walls of Babylon)	pp. 327–28
pp. 630–31 (The tower of Babylon and Bel)	p. 328

□

Gardner's achievement rests, in part, on the ways he employs certain ideas drawn from that oldest of Babylonian literary works, *The Epic of Gilgamesh.* Mortality, for example, an obsession for Babylonia and Gardner, renders human relations like friendship and kingship overwhelmingly important because there is nothing beyond them, no substitute heaven where dead lovers reunite and the worthy meek inherit the world. This world is all there is. One of the main conflicts in *The Sunlight Dialogues* focuses upon man's desire for immortaliy in an inexorably mortal world. Fred Clumly pursues, among other things, a wish for remembrance, yet as we learn in the "Prologue," he has been effortlessly forgotten: "In Batavia, opinion was divided, in fact, over whether he'd gone away somewhere or died" (p. 3). Clumly learns, as Gilgamesh learns, that "When the gods created man they allotted to him death, but life they retained in their own keeping."[5] Man is destined to perish; all that ever remains is a memory, a story, a legend. This fatalism breeds the sort of "profound pessimism" that characterizes Mesopotamian and, Gardner would add, contemporary existence. But mortality is not futility. We are wrong, Gardner suggests, in our denial of the value of human action. We begin to enjoy a living death: heroes and demigods begin to disappear for want of interest and belief, men slide into existentialism, death becomes a distressed relief, life becomes immoral.

What also emerges from *The Sunlight Dialogues* is a tragic friendship akin to that of Gilgamesh and Enkidu in the *Epic.* Clumly and Taggert Hodge (like their ancient counterparts) first encounter each other in struggle, but come to embrace each other as near brothers ("'I want you to know, I feel friendly toward you, Fred'" [p. 634]). Like Enkidu, too, Taggert is a cosmic scapegoat, sacrificed to the demands of order and the discipline of the gods, and the tragedy of his death drives Clumly to heroic understanding and epiphany, and to a realization of his mortal predicament. So, like Gilgamesh, Clumly descends into the underworld, becomes "Chief Investigator of the Dead."

Death, in fact, becomes the symbol for all that is wrong in this "house of dust." It represents the awful separation of man from his gods, the quizzical wonder of man at the insane dualism of the world. It is "the relationship of the individual to the deity" (Oppenheim, p. 198), with its strange and absolute finality, and its frequent inexplicability, that most occupies the human mind (Mesopotamian or modern). It is the eternal perplexity concerning the gods' whimsicalness and man's propensity for death—the entire content of the Mesopotamian psychology, in short—that Gardner found so intriguingly presented in *The Epic of Gilgamesh* and then amplified and explained in Oppenheim's *Ancient Mesopotamia.* By the time he had finished with these two works, it was natural that Gardner figure it all somehow into his novel and make it an inextricable part of his modern imaginative world. He had to bring Babylon to Batavia. □

Taggert takes up this subject once more in the third confrontation, when the Sunlight Man and Clumly meet, with morbid appropriateness, in a funeral crypt for "The Dialogue of the Dead." The Sunlight Man introduces the Gilgamesh epic, explicating it as a tale of man's foolish longing for immortality. Gilgamesh (and modern man) misunderstand death, and battle vainly against the consuming paradox of man's corruptibility. The Babylonians, Taggert says, understood: "In Babylon...personal immortality is a mad goal. Death is a reality. Any struggle whatever for personal fulfillment is wrong-headed" (p. 532). Man cannot deny his physicality, nor can he deny the ultimate end of that physicality. Man is a victim of Time and Space: his years run out and his body perishes. As Oppenheim explains, death is simply a part of one's *šimtu:*

> In certain religious contexts… the establishing of the *šimtu* refers typically to the specific act through which each man is allotted—evidently at birth, although this is nowhere stated explicitly—an individual and definite share of fortune and misfortune. This share determines the entire direction and temper of his life. Consequently, the length of his days and the nature and sequence of the events that are allotted to the individual are thought of as being determined by an act of an unnamed power that has established his *šimtu*. It is in the nature of the *šimtu*, the individual's "share" that its realization is a necessity, not a possibility… *Šimtu* thus unites in one term the two dimensions of human existence: personality as an endowment and death as a fulfilment, in a way which the translations "fate" or "destiny" fail to render adequately. (Oppenheim, p. 202)

There is nothing beyond death but the void and the black nether world. Life is invested with value by the actions carried out in life; there is no concern with sickness and with the distressing collapse of the body.

Taggert asks his own question, the logical question—"'Why act at all then?'"—and answers it without hesitation, "'Because action is life'" (p. 533). The Babylonians never denied the worth of action, never declared life meaningless, never descended to nihilism. On the contrary, they held tenaciously to the idea that if one fails to act, one loses the freedom and the ability to act, thus losing the very essence of freedom itself. Taggert follows again with the "right" question, and supplies the response:

> Once one's said it, that one must act, one must ask oneself, shall I act within the cultural order I do not believe in but with which I am engaged by ties of love or anyway ties of fellow-feeling, or shall I act within the cosmic order I *do* believe in, at least in principle, an order indifferent to man? And then again, shall I act by standing indecisive between the two orders—not striking out for the cosmic order because of my human commitment, not striking out for the cultural order because

> of my divine commitment? Which shall I renounce, my body—of which ethical intellect is a function—or my soul? (p. 533)

Again, it is a question of allegiance and value. Melville would have asked, "Does one keep time by chronologicals or horologicals?" but the problem is the same.

Speculation becomes actual choice when, at the end of their dialogue, Taggert peers into the near future and tells Clumly of what will be in the final meeting between the two men. There will be the gun and the choice: do you act for humanity and kill the wizard, or do you "blink" and act for the universe? Clumly insists upon more of a "choice," a greater variety of alternatives, because he is a humanist. He also senses the flaw in Taggert's reasoning, though he cannot finger it: there is no real distinction between humanity and the universe, humanity *is* the universe. □

Taggert's death and the destruction of the towers of Stony Hill Farm mirror and effectively complete the emotional destruction of the Hodge home and family by Millie Jewel Hodge, a woman with a mind of honed steel and a heart "painstakingly fashioned of ice" (p. 181). She is almost always detestable, even when for that one odd flash, the Sunlight Man is attracted to her (a flare up of a buried passion, and an echo of Gilgamesh's rejection of Ištar in the *Epic*).[6] Her character is clear; she is, in fact, quite honest about it: "She was a bitch. She made no bones about it.... Bitchiness was her strength and beauty and hope of salvation" (p. 180). Millie tortures and taunts her exhusband, Will Hodge, Sr., who is trapped, like the lion in the palace reliefs, in the "cage of his limitations" (p. 126). Millie breeds into one son, Luke, a physical and emotional anguish that, like his Uncle Taggert, stamps him as someone linked to the gods through a vicious *šimtu*: ("Finally, he knew, he was the one who'd been marked. His luck" [p. 637]). She gives to her other son, Will, Jr. (by a persistent ignorance of him) a single-mindedness that drives a wedge between him and his own family, and a mottled sort of self-reliance that swings between fear and hearty confidence ("He drove with authority and grace, head back, jaw thrown forward: an Assyrian king" [p. 331]). Millie is the moral opposite of Esther Clumly, Fred's long-suffering, blind wife, who exists to be a saint and an emblem of patience and understanding (she went "about the house with her lips moving as though she were some kind of old-fashioned priestess forever at her prayers, or insane" [p. 8]).

In short, Millie Hodge plainly represents the Babylonian goddess, Ištar, the "most notoriously faithless of all the gods."[7] She is Mama, creator of mankind (recall the epigraph to Chapter IV of *The Sunlight Dialogues,* the epigraph taken from Oppenheim), origin of life, yet she rejects a part of that role:

> [She had been] forced into the shabby role for which she had not the faintest desire and from which she drew, she devoutly believed, no satisfaction (she knew what satisfaction was, knew where she would prefer to be)—the role of God or archetypal mother or stone at the center of the universe—because by senseless accident she had borne sons. *I exist. No one else. You will not find me sitting around on my can like some widow, or whining for the love of my children.* (p. 181)

Millie keeps for herself the portion of her spirit that turns her into the bitch goddess, and she repudiates the loving, sympathetic, humane aspect that would bring her into the general regard of mankind. As Ištar, she is distanced and feared by man, unapproachable and nearly unloveable.

Millie is not the only character who might be linked in some way to the Mesopotamian pantheon. Several of the major personalities in *The Sunlight Dialogues* possess qualities and quirks that tie them to specific gods and goddesses of Babylonian religious tradition.[8] It is doubtful, however, that Gardner intended any clear, one-to-one connection between god and character. There are far too many cases where the distinctions blur, where one god might serve several characters. Instead, Gardner merely suggests the connection; using the knowledge of these gods to enrich his texture and meaning, he thus adds to the multi-layered pleasure of the novel.

That, in fact, is the entire point of Gardner's borrowing. Certainly it enlarges the book (both physically and philosophically), and turns it more grave, but it also serves to delight the reader as phrases and images ricochet from within the unconscious. The connections gradually become clear and significant; the universe of the novel and universe of man's existence finally merge, their meanings drawn together by Gardner's weaving of thought and history and imagination. In his view we are emotionally and intellectually still either Babylonian or Hebraic; somewhere in between lies the proper ethical and political stance most appropriate for the twentieth century. It is up to the reader to find the truest mix of anarchy and conservatism, foresight and immediacy, devotion to culture *and* to destiny.

* * *

NOTES

1. These borrowings will be documented in a forthcoming dissertation by the author.
2. In a review of *Freddy's Book* for the *Chicago Tribune* (16 March 1980), William Logan criticized Gardner for his free and unacknowledged use of a book on Swedish history, *The Early Vasas,* by Michael Roberts. Logan saw in Gardner's extensive use of Roberts' work a contradiction with Gardner's own highly publicized literary ethic. Gardner responded to Logan's charges in a letter to the *Tribune* book section (13 April 1980); it is in this letter that Gardner set forth his argument for a "collage technique."
3. John Gardner, *Chicago Tribune Book World,* 13 April 1980, Section 7, p. 10. □
4. John Gardner *The Sunlight Dialogues* (New York: Knopf, 1972). All page references are to this edition. □
5. N. K. Sandars, *The Epic of Gilgamesh,* rev. ed. (Middlesex: Penguin, 1972), p. 102. All page references are to this edition.
6. One of the more interesting exchanges in *The Epic of Gilgamesh* comes when Gilgamesh responds to Ištar's luxurious offer of marriage. The Goddess offers him a variety of pleasures and riches, all of which Gilgamesh rejects after a catalogue of Ištar's faithlessness: "As for making you my wife—that I will not. How would it go with me? Your lovers have found you like a brazier which smolders in the cold, a backdoor which keeps out neither squall of wind nor storm, a castle which crushes the garrison, pitch that blackens the bearer, a water-skin that chafes the carrier, a stone which falls from the parapet, a battering-ram turned back from the enemy, a sandal that trips the wearer. Which of your lovers did you ever love for ever?" (Sandars, p. 86). If anyone approaches the fickleness and duplicity of the goddess Ištar in *The Sunlight Dialogues,* it surely is Millie Hodge—though admittedly even she has her sympathies and her "humanities."
7. Sandars, *The Epic of Gilgamesh,* p. 42.
8. To illustrate these connections I have listed below a collection of several of the novel's characters with passages from Oppenheim's *Ancient Mesopotamia* and N. K. Sandars's edition of *The Epic of Gilgamesh* describing the particular gods and goddesses which resemble those characters from Gardner:

Millie Hodge: *Ištar*—Ištar ... alone stands out because of the dichotomy of her nature associated with the planet Venus... and with divine qualities extremely difficult to characterize. This complex embraces the function of Ištar as a battle-loving, armed goddess, who gives victory to the king she loves, at the same time it links her as driving force, protectress, and personification of sexual power in all its aspects. (Oppenheim, p. 197)

Will Hodge Sr: *Ea*—He appears as a benign being, peace-maker, but not always a reliable friend, for, like so many exponents of primitive wisdom, he enjoyed tricks and subterfuges and on occasion was not devoid of malice.... His origins are obscure, but he is sometimes called the son of Anu, "Begotten in his own image... of broad understanding and mighty strength." (Sandars, p. 26.)

Arthur Hodge Sr: *Anu*—Old gods were such once-powerful deities as Anu the Sumerian sky god, and a Sumerianized substrate god Enlil... both of whom seem to have become more and more removed from the world of man and more misanthropic in character in the course of history. (Oppenheim, pp. 194–95)

Judge Sam White: *Enlil*—Anu was a father of gods, not so much Zeus as Uranus, but neither is he any more the active creator of gods. This supreme position was gradually usurped by Enlil, and in our poem it is Enlil who pronounces destinies in sign of authority. (Sandars, pp. 23–24)

Taggert Hodge: *Šamaš*—Šamaš had a unique position. Not only was he the sun god but the judge of heaven and earth, and in this capacity he was concerned with the protection of the poor and the wronged and gave oracles intended to guide and protect mankind. (Oppenheim, pp. 195–96)
The sun is still 'shams' in Arabic, and in those days Shamash was the omniscient all-seeing one, the great judge to whom anxious mortals could make their appeal against injustice; and know that they were heard.... Most of the gods had both a benign and a dangerous aspect, even Shamash could be terrible.... (Sandars, p. 25)

Kathleen Paxton: *Aya*—The dawn, the bride of the Sun God *Shamash*. (Sandars, p. 120)

❋ ❋ ❋

John Maier
"Charles Olson and the Poetic Uses of Mesopotamian Scholarship," with an Appendix, "Musical Settings for Cuneiform Literature: A Discography" by J.M. Sasson

When George Smith published the first translation of *Gilgamesh* in *The Chaldean Account of Genesis,* he could take for granted that his readers would want to know about connections between Mesopotamia and the Bible. Smith could also expect the educated reader to know something of the Greek and Latin classics. As the essays in this section show, the precise relationships between *Gilgamesh* and the two streams of Western civilization, Judeo-Christian and Greco-Roman, are still of great interest to scholars. Modernist authors like T.S. Eliot, Ezra Pound, and James Joyce are conspicuous in their advocacy of the Great Tradition.

One strain of Postmodern art is, in opposition to Modernism, to challenge the Great Tradition. The newly discovered ancient literature of Mesopotamia could be valued because it was pre-biblical and pre-Homeric. John Gardner's novel, *The Sunlight Dialogues,* is an example of fiction that has been influenced by that opposition, as Greg Morris showed in the previous essay. Charles Olson, influential poet and teacher, has been even more thorough and more explicit in his uses of Mesopotamian thought. Maier's essay, written for a volume that recognized the many contributions of Sumerologist Samuel Noah Kramer, discusses the implications of a new "primitive-abstract" poetics that would replace the Great Tradition's "Classical-representational" poetics. Olson's "transpositions" of *Gilgamesh* provide the best evidence of the Postmodern shift in post-WWII American poetry. They also indicate the poet's interest in the controversial Tablet XII, often considered an inorganic appendage to *Gilgamesh.*

Sasson added a valuable list of audio recordings that show Mesopotamian influence (though not Mesopotamian music itself) on 20th-century composers. Just as *Gilgamesh* is the most prominent literary work influencing 20th-century literature, it is a major influence on experimental, nontraditional music. And Bohuslav Martinu, like Olson, "invests the 12th tablet with more legitimacy" than does Assyriology, as Sasson observes.

> Once, as best I can recall, we were discussing heroes, and I tried to get him to discuss the concept of hero, from the individual-as-hero of the Greeks through the society-oriented hero of the Romans, mentioning several well-known scholars, but he refused even to consider it. "You're too much influenced by Greek and Latin already; too much of our literature and concepts are traced there already. Go beyond that, to the Sumerians, and before. Break the hold time has on you; get outside it."

The curious reminiscence belongs to O.J. Ford, who was recalling an exchange with his teacher, the American poet Charles Olson (1910–1970).[1] Olson came to poetry rather late in his life. His impact as a poet on American poetry was felt after World War II. He was a poet and a teacher of poets, an intellectual who distrusted intellect, a man driven to read deeply the scholarship on the Ancient Near East who yet rejected ordinary scholarship. Nothing is more characteristic of Charles Olson than his rejection of the Western tradition in favor of Hittite, Akkadian, and especially Sumerian literature. Olson's poetry and his writings about poetry are filled with his attempt to get back to the "origins," and that attempt meant at least a rejection of the Judeo-Christian and Greco-Roman ways of looking at the world. Not since Gustave Courbet grew an Assyrian beard has any Western artist attempted such a sweeping rejection of the roots of Western civilization and identified with the Ancient Near East "beyond" Homer and "beyond" the Bible. For him the Sumerians were crucial to the attempt. Sumer was at the "center," at the point of "origin." Although he was not and did not consider himself a scholar, Charles Olson was guided in his attempts by Ancient Near Eastern scholarship, most notably by the work of Samuel Noah Kramer. The two men never met, but they corresponded briefly. This essay traces the influence of Sumerian scholarship on Charles Olson, an influence that is in large measure the impact of Samuel Noah Kramer.

As a student in American Studies under the direction of F.O. Matthiessen, Olson produced an important critical study of Herman Melville, *Call Me Ishmael* (1947). Less than a decade later he was applying for a Fulbright lectureship, hoping that a program in Baghdad would open up. He wrote in 1951 that,

> I have found it increasingly important to push my studies of American civilization back to origin points on this continent and this, in turn, has involved me increasingly in questions and in the development of methods to investigate the origins of civilization generally.... My desire is to go to IRAQ to steep myself, on the ground, in all aspects of SUMERIAN civilization (its apparent origins in the surrounding plateaus of the central valley, the valley-city sites themselves, and the works of them, especially the architecture and the people's cuneiform texts.... The point of a year of such work at the sites and in collections is a double one: (1), to lock up translations from the clay tablets, conspicuously the poems and myths (these translations and transpositions have been in progress for four years); and (2), to fasten—by the live sense that only the actual ground gives—the text of a book, one half of which is SUMER.[2]

To prepare himself for such a task, Olson had begun to collect books and articles on Ancient Near Eastern history, archaeology, myth, and literature, and he continued to do so until his death.[3] His prose and poetry reflect this drive to Sumer.[4] *The Special View of History*, a series of lectures given at Black Mountain College, where Olson was rector,[5] takes off from a saying of Heraclitus, "Man is estranged from that with which he is most familiar," and leads Olson to this principle.

> I am persuaded that at this point of the 20th century it might be possible for man to cease to be estranged, as Heraclitus said he was in 500 B.C., from that with which he is most familiar. At least I take Heraclitus' dictum as the epigraph of this book. For all this I know increased my impression that man lost something just about 500 B.C. and only got it back just about 1905 A.D.[6]

Olson was one of many who grappled with the idea of a "prerational" or "prelogical" or "mythic" thought, still available in Homer and especially Hesiod and the Pre-Socratic philosophers, but covered over by the Classical Period.[7] The distinction between *logos* and *muthos* directed Olson to the "orality" of literature.[8] Again, Olson was but one of many to turn to "oral literature," but what is more surprising is his belief that his period in the 20th Century offers the possibility of overcoming the "estrangement" that has dominated our thinking since the Classical Period. He proclaimed a "new localism, a polis to replace the one which was lost in various stages all over the world from 490 B.C. on."[9] The "falsest estrangement of all," which he called "contemplation," was brought in with logic and classification in the 5th Century B.C.[10] Since it was myth that was displaced, and "all myth is projective, and thus has to be seen in its root or etymology,"[11] only a return to myth would overcome the grasp of the rational. Olson was one of those who call themselves "post-modern" thinkers, and "post-modern" man aims at recovering "the Pleistocene"[12] and thus overcoming the split between *logos* and *muthos.*

Between the estrangement brought about by Greek philosophy and the Pleistocene lay Sumer. In the Sumerians Olson found a "will to cohere" that was lost through the expansion of thought westward and the exhaustion of Mesopotamian thought.[13] Post-modern, post-humanist, and "post-historic" man is engaged in the process of recovering mythic thought. Olson felt he was a moving force in the movement, and he challenged traditional ways of writing, arguing, persuading, and expressing himself poetically through the use of unusual prose styles, poetic devices, and even in his style of teaching.

Sumer even appears in an Olson attack on American education.

> What I am kicking around is this notion:
> that KNOWLEDGE either goes for the CENTER
> or it's inevitably a State Whore—which American
> and Western education generally is, has been, since
> its beginning. (I am flatly talking Socrates as the
> progenitor, his methodology still the RULE:
> "I'll stick my logic up, and classify, boy, classify you
> right out of existence.")[14]

The "center" turns out to be Sumer. One may be jolted by the combination of Olson's three scholars:

> Which brings us home. To Porada, & S.N. Kramer's
> translations of the city poems, add one L.A. Waddell.
> What Waddell gives me is the chronology: that,
> from 3378 B.C. (date man's 1st city, name and face
> of creator also known) in unbroken series first at

> Uruk, then from the seaport Lagash out into colonies in the Indus Valley and, circa 2500, the Nile, until date 1200 B.C. or thereabouts, civilization had ONE CENTER, Sumer, in all directions... that a city was a coherence which, for the first time since the ice, gave man the chance to join knowledge to culture and, with this weapon, shape dignities of economics and value sufficient to make daily life itself a dignity and a sufficiency.[15]

Whatever one may think of this as history (or as geography!), it is this schema that drives Olson's idea of "the Sumer thrust."[16] The "will to cohere" leads Olson to meditate on Sargon of Agade, "GUDA, King of the port Lagash" and the subtle tale of Gilgamesh, who "was sent the rude fellow Enkidu to correct him because he, even Gilgamesh, had become a burden in his lust, to his city's people."[17] The conclusion to this rather misty (or mystified) historical excursus, though, makes a telling point:

> it is an incredibly accurate myth of what happens to the best of men when they lose touch with the primordial & phallic energies & methodologies which, said this predecessor people of ours, make it possible for man, that participant thing, to take up, straight, nature's, live nature's force.[18]

No wonder Olson once lamented that "The trouble is, it is very difficult to be both a poet and, an historian."[19] History tends to become swallowed up in myth when Olson deals with Mesopotamia. On the other hand, it is postmodern (and "post-historic") man that most excites him, and Olson's most singular and most important formulation of things Mesopotamian is, not surprisingly, a very brief allusion in a letter about the project for poetry. The "Letter to Elaine Feinstein" (1959) is usually paired with "Projective Verse" as Olson's most impressive statement on the contemporary project of poetry.[20] In the "Letter" Olson sounds a by now familiar note:

> I am talking from a new "double axis": the replacement of the Classical-representational by the *primitive-abstract* ((if this all sounds bloody German, excuse the weather, it's from the east today, and wet)). I mean of course not at all primitive in that stupid use of it as opposed to civilized. One means it now as "primary," as

> how one finds anything, pick it up as one does
> new—fresh/first. Thus one is equal across history
> forward and back, and it's all levy, as present is,
> but sd that way, one states... a different space-time.
> Content, in other words, is also shifted—at least
> from humanism, as we've had it since the Indo-
> Europeans got their fid in there (circum 1500 B.C.)
> ((Note: I'm for 'em on the muse level, and agin 'em
> on the content or "Psyche" side.))[21]

This sets up the mother/father, Tiamat/Zeus contrast in Olson's notion of the "image":

> Image, therefore, is vector. It carries the trinity
> via the double to the single form which one
> makes oneself able, if so, to issue from the "content"
> (multiplicity: originally, and repetitively,
> chaos— Tiamat: wot the HindoEuropeans
> knocked out by giving the Old Man (Juice himself)
> all the lightening. The Double, then, (the "home"/
> heartland of the post-Mesopotamians AND the
> post-Hindo Ees: At the moment is comes out the
> Muse ("world").
>
> ---
>
> The Psyche (the "life")[22]

What does this shift from "Classical-representation" to "primitive-abstract" mean for Olson's own poetry? He wrote to Robert Creeley in July of 1952 that:

> and i take it, a Sumer poem or Maya glyph is more
> pertinent to our purposes than anything else,
> because each of these people and their workers
> had forms which unfolded directly from content
> (sd content itself a disposition toward reality which
> understood man as only force in field of force
> containing multiple other expressions[23]

To that end, Olson worked on what he called "transpositions"[24] of ancient poems. Two such "transpositions" that derive ultimately from "Gilgamesh, Enkidu and the Nether World" were produced by Olson, the first, "La Chute," appearing in 1951,[25] and the second, "La Chute (II)," appearing posthumously in 1973.

"La Chute" is a re-working of the opening lines of the Twelfth Tablet of *The Epic of Gilgamesh,* which Olson knew from E.A. Speiser's translation in *ANET*. Olson's version expands what is basically two lines in the original:

> "Lo, [who will bring up] the *Dr*[*um*
> from the nether world]?
> [Who will bring up] the *Drumstick*
> [from the nether world]?"[26]

The *pukku* and *mekkû*, whose nature are still being debated today, Olson takes as "drum" and "lute."

La Chute

my drum, hollowed out thru the thin slit,
carved from the cedar wood, the base I took
when the tree was felled

o my lute, wrought from the tree's crown

my drum, whose lustiness
was not to be resisted

          my lute,
from whose pulsations
not one could turn away

                    They
are where the dead are, my drum fell
where the dead are, who
will bring it up, my lute
who will bring it up where it fell
   in the face of them
where they are, where my lute
   and drum have fallen?

Conspicuous, of course, is the violation of the Akkadian poetic line; Olson's version in its broken typography and white spaces adds emphases where the Akkadian (in translation) does not. The first three lines, which are bundled together (and should be read aloud together), were suggested, not by the Twelfth Tablet itself, but by Speiser's introductory comment, which sets the Sumerian background of the piece. By setting this apart from the single line 4, which in a sense completes it, a powerful emphasis is placed on the working of the wood to produce the drum and lute. The drum is "hollowed out" and "carved," while the lute is "wrought." Olson preserves the noteworthy feature of Sumero-Akkadian poetry in the repetition of the simple sequence: drum/lute, drum/lute. First the working of the drum and lute: the "lustiness" of the drum in "not to be resisted" and the "pulsations" of the lute are so tempting that "not one could turn away." This elemental force of the musical instruments owes its power to the source in nature from which it is taken and transformed.

Very likely, Olson saw in the seductive force of drum and lute not merely a connection with the Sumerian story, which binds the tree to the fascinating Inanna, at whose request Gilgamesh and Enkidu fell the tree; but also to the opening of Tablet One of *The Epic of Gilgamesh*, where, according to one interpretation, Gilgamesh tyrannized the citizens by the drum that "aroused his companions" and caused the people to cry out for relief.[27] The drum is power and is also heavily erotic ("lustiness"), the drum of battle and the summons to the first-night privileges of the lord. The "pulsations" of the lute further emphasize the powerful sway and erotic fascination of "my lute." Gilgamesh speaks here in such a way to underscore the power in his hands to use the (sacred) instrument; the others could not resist.

The felling of the tree, also by the hands of Gilgamesh, is picked up in the last five lines, another bundle, where the fallen drum is assimilated to the fallen dead. If the earlier part of the poem tied the drum to Gilgamesh's earlier arrogance, the final part of the poem is a touching lament that spreads death over all. Olson's diction in the poem (except for the archaic "wrought" and "lustiness" and rather stilted "pulsations") is simple, clean. The elemental fact of death is everywhere glimpsed in the "life" and "death" of the drum itself. Olson picks up a chunk of Akkadian poetry, and his "transposition" of it does not contain a hint of consolation that the lamented "death" will somehow be overcome.

"La Chute (II)" exists in two versions, one published in *Alcheringa*, and an earlier draft in the Olson Archives.[28] It picks up where "La Chute" left off, in the sense that it contains Gilgamesh's advice to Enkidu on the way to enter the land of the dead. While Olson had worked with the Akkadian in *ANET*, "La Chute (II)" shows evidence of reworking in the light of Kramer's translation of the same passage in *Sumerian Mythology*.[29] (That Olson knew the passage in *The Epic of Gilgamesh*, Tablet XII, was itself a translation of a Sumerian original, is clear from his markings in Kramer's *From the Tablets of Sumer*, p. 222, which Olson possessed from January, 1957.)

La Chute (II)

If you would go down to the dead
to retrieve my drum and lute
a word for you, take my word
I offer you directions

Do not wear a clean garment
they below will dirty you
they will mark you
as if you were a stranger

Nor rub yourself with oil
the finest oil from the cruse.
The smell of it will provoke them
they will walk round and round
alongside you

Carry no stick. At least
do not raise it,
or the shades of men will tremble,
will hover before you

Pick up nothing to throw, no matter the urging.
They against whom you hurl it will crowd you,
will fly thick on you.

Go barefoot. Make no sound.
And when you meet the wife you loved
do not kiss her
nor strike the wife you hated.
Likewise your sons. Give the beloved one no kiss,
do not spit on his brother

Behave, lest the outcry shall seize you
seize you for what you have done
for her who, there, lies naked
the mother
whose body in that place is uncovered
whose breasts lie open to you and the judges

in that place
where my drum and lute are

Olson's poem does not, at first glance, seem to offer much of a departure from either Akkadian or Sumerian original. The sequence of clothes, oil, throw-stick, sandals, kissing and striking wives and sons in the instructions Gilgamesh gives Enkidu is retained. (Olson nowhere indicates the source, however, and does not make it evident at all that the speaker is Gilgamesh or the listener is Enkidu.) The grouping of lines is not as striking as in "La Chute"; indeed, it mainly follows Kramer's stanzaic translation (Speiser's is not sectioned into stanzas). Olson has taken pains to remove the trappings of traditional rhetoric thought appropriate to "epic" poetry (or derived from Biblical translations of the Renaissance). Consider Olson's ll.21–26, with its direct and colloquial English, against either Speiser's:

> Sandals to thy feet thou shalt not fasten,
> A sound against the nether world
>   thou shalt not make,
> Thy wife whom thou lovest
>   thou shalt not kiss,
> Thy wife whom thou hatest
>   thou shalt not strike,
> Thy son whom thou lovest
>   thou shalt not kiss,
> Thy son whom thou hatest
>   thou shalt not strike!

or Kramer's:

> Do not put sandals on thy feet,
> In the nether world make no cry;
> Kiss not thy beloved wife,
> Kiss not thy beloved son,
> Strike not thy hated wife,
> Strike not thy hated son.[31]

Gone in Olson are the "thy's" and "thou shalt not's" and the correct but ponderous "whom thou lovest's" of Speiser's (and to a lesser degree, Kramer's) versions. "Go barefoot" and "Make no sound" are direct and forceful. On the other hand the "sound" which is "in" or "against" the nether world is largely, though not entirely dropped by Olson's colloquial rendering. Olson retains something of the rigid symmetry of the original—but only a hint. And "do not spit on his brother" for the "Strike not thy hated son" may simply miss the mark of the original. In general, though, Olson's is a looser but more vigorous "transposition" of the scholarly treatments.

In two respects, though, Olson has modified the original in striking ways. He has introduced the "drum and lute" where the originals do not specify them at all. That Olson introduces them at the beginning and then again at the end shows that he saw the descent into the nether world as a shamanic journey, and that he thought the poetic closure gave the piece a unity it may not originally have had. Even more striking is his treatment of the goddess, Ereshkigal. He avoids the specification, "mother of the god Ninazu," and thus reduces the goddess to elemental "mother." There is some question why Ereshkigal should be described the way the Sumerian and Akkadian originals portray her, but Olson's interpretation makes it clear that *he* thinks the mother lying naked, her body uncovered, her breasts exposed to "you and the judges" is an image of erotic seduction—more like Inanna than her sister. Finally, Olson downplays the "outcry" of the nether world, with all its magical properties, and plays up instead an ambiguity in the original. Is Enkidu really to be seized "for what you have done/for her"? The statement, never clarified, suggests a descent to the mother/mistress, a life/death goddess because of an action for/against her. The possibilities open up in the Olson version, and no attempt is made to reduce the ambiguities in his "transposition."

Whatever else Olson was doing in his "transpositions" of Sumerian poetry, he was listening for the utterance of man at the "origin," listening for a word of the earliest known poets and myth-makers, a word not yet split into *logos* and *muthos*. The transpositions are likely to strike the scholar and the critic as a little too close to the scholarly translations to be independent compositions, a little less flamboyant than the usual Olson offering. The perception is true, but the judgment is false to Olson's careful listening. Olson's poetry is for the most part highly idiosyncratic—not, indeed, an unusual case among contemporary poets. For Olson, though, the "subjectivism" of Western poetry from the Greeks to at least the beginning of the 20th Century was a major problem, and he proposed instead, "objectism."

> Objectism is the getting rid of the lyrical interference
> of the individual as ego, of the "subject" and his soul,
> that peculiar presumption by which western man
> has interposed himself between what he is as a creature
> of nature (with certain instructions to carry out) and
> those other creations of nature which we may, with no
> derogation, call objects.[32]

The very fidelity with which Olson keeps close to the Sumerian is evidence of his listening closely, his avoidance of "the lyrical interference of the individual as ego."

Charles Olson' s reputation depends, for the most part, on his essay, "Projective Verse," and his long poem, *The Maximus Poems.* Sumerian and Akkadian allusions are many and important to these works, but they are not, of course, the only ancient and non-Western concerns in his works. Olson had a deep interest in Mayan culture, for example, and the Mayan materials were more accessible to him than Sumero-Akkadian materials. Because he does not speak of these matters with immediate reference to his personal life and to the political issues of the day, it is difficult to say how much personal and political causes help sustain the ancient, mythic images in his writing. Olson declined a political occupation after World War II. Certainly he believed that America in the post-war era had certain connections with a very ancient Sumerian civilization. Beyond the overcoming of the Greek "estrangement" by going beyond the Judeo-Christian and the Greco-Roman traditions, though, very specific causes are difficult to discern. It may come as a surprise, though, that the prototype of Maximus, the poet-hero of Olson's complex "long" poem, was Olson's "Bigmans." And the early "Bigmans" is a transposition of what Olson knew of that most sturdy of Sumero-Akkadian heroes, Gilgamesh.[33]

APPENDIX

Musical Settings for Cuneiform Literature: A Discography.
J.M. Sasson

Dr. Maier's paper has focused on the effect that a recovered cuneiform literature had on a specific modern poet. To be sure other poets (e.g., A.R. Ammons, "Gilgamesh Was Very Lascivious," "Sumerian," etc.) and novelists (e.g., R. Lehrman, *Call Me Ishtar*) participated in this reshaping of ancient materials into contemporary visions. But it may not be amiss, in this context, to briefly append a listing of musical works, *available on disks,* wherein nineteenth- and twentieth-century composers imaginatively distilled the contents of Mesopotamian myths and epics and presented them either as extended compositions which fused works to music or as shorter, purely instrumental, pieces. This brief survey is but a sampling, and it does not interpret or assess the various attempts. Additionally, I have avoided speculating on the contexts which quickened musical interest in ancient literature. I have, however, included one or two bibliographical citations for those who would like to pursue the topic further. Compositions which depended on classical or biblical formulations regarding Assyria and Babylon (e.g., Handel's *Belshazzar* etc....) are not included. The discography is American; but European equivalent is available. I would like here to thank Dr. Maier for permitting me to usurp a bit of space for this enterprise.

ISHTAR

Vincent D'Indy (1851–1931). D'Indy visited the British museum in 1887 and was struck by Assyriological monuments that were then displayed: "Quel bel art et quel flagrant délit de vie et de vérité dans ces tableaux d'une civilisation qui valait bien la nôtre!...J'éprouve une impression bien plus grande et plus réellement artistique devant l'art assyien du VIIIe siècle avant J.-C. que devant celui de Périclès..." He composed *Ishtar, variations symphoniques, Op. 42* nine years later. This very complex series of variations purports to duplicate Ishtar's progressive stripping of clothings and ornaments as she reaches her sister's inner sanctum. D'Indy's work, about fifteen minutes in length, reverses the usual approach to thematic variations, and actually presents the melody in its fullest form only when Ishtar is totally naked and defenseless (a musical technique which was later much favored by Sibelius).

Recording: EMI C. 069-14043. Orchestre Philharmonique des Pays de la Loire; Pierre Dervaux, cond.

Bibliography: L. Vallas, *Vincent D'Indy, II: La Maturité; la vieillesse (1886–1931)*. 1950. 235–41. [Quotation is from 238, n. l.]

Bohuslav Martinu. (1890–1954). The Czech composer wrote *Istar* (H. 130) in Prague during 1918–21 and added "The Dance of Priestesses" while in Paris in 1923. The ballet, in three acts and five scenes, was inspired by the Sumerian accounts regarding Dumuzi and Inanna, freely expanded to include materials drawn from Ishtar's *Descent*, from *Gilgamesh's* 6th tablet, and from Julius Zeyer's mystical imagination. The first act told of Tammuz's capture by Irkalla, the evil (sic) goddess of the Underworld; the second of Ishtar's arrival before her sister and her recovery of her dead lover. The last act finds Ishtar and Tammuz emerging into a world which progressively warms up and regains happiness. The gods, in their joy, eternalize the pair and they ascend to the highest heaven. The score, about two hours in duration, is for a very large orchestra, but Martinu, then strongly under French musical influence, often achieves impressionistic settings. The added 'Dance of Priestesses' includes a woman's chorus that is reminiscent of Ravel's *Daphnis and Chloe.*

Recording: (Selections) Supraphon 1 10 1634. Brno State Philharmonic Orchestra; Jirí Waldhans, cond.

N.B. Orchestral suites based on *Istar* (arranged by B. Bartoš) are sometimes individually recorded.

Bibliography: H. Halbreich, *Bohuslav Martinu.* 1968. 324–6. B. Large, *Martinu.* 1975. 26–7.

GILGAMESH

Bohuslav Martinu. In 1954 Martinu was in Nice. By the end of the year, upon finishing a cantata about Christ's passion, *Mount of Three Lights*, he immediately turned to composing the Oratorio, *The Epic of Gilgamesh* (H. 351) and used Campbell Thompson's translation. With a German libretto by A. H. Eichmann, *Gilgamesh* lasts about an hour and is scored for largish orchestra, chorus, soloists, narrator, and speaker. Part I, derived from Tablet 1 and 2, introduces Gilgamesh, a lonely king for whose benefits the gods produce Enkidu. After his own *éducation sentimentale*, Enkidu challenges and befriends Gilgamesh. Part II focuses on Gilgamesh's reaction to Enkidu's death (Tables 7, 8, 10) and on his awareness of human mortality. Part III, loosely based on tablet 12, contains Gilgamesh's 'invocation,' his meeting with Enkidu's ghost, and his multiple inquiries which are met by detached responses. The oratorio ends with Gilgamesh never quite learning anything beyond what he already knew; a rather startling philosophical development from Martinu's previous involvement with Near Eastern literature (see above). It is worth noting, perhaps, that Martinu's imagination invests the 12th tablet with more legitimacy than does the Assyriologist's.

Recording: Supraphon 1 12 1808. (Sung in Czech). Czech Philharmonic Chorus; Prague Symphony Orchestra, Jirí Belohlávek, cond.

Bibliography: Halbreich ibid., 279–82; Large, ibid., 110–1. See also the informative remarks added to the recording.

Augustyn Bloch (1929– Grudziadz, Poland). Written in 1968, the ballet-pantomine *Gilgamesz* has been recorded only in its concert version, and that is what I report on. The piece, about twenty-five minutes long, is inspired by the Akkadian epic. The author contends that its sections rejoice over happiness, exult over power, and lament over death. A chorus punctuates the orchestral music with quasi-Gregorian chants. The score, however, is often striking since it eschews violins, oboes and horns, in favor of saxophones and percussion.

Recording: Musa SX 1208. Warsaw National Philharmonic Orchestra and Choir, Andrzej Markowski, cond.

Bibliography. *The New Grove Dictionary of Music and Musicians,* (s.v.)

Per Nørgård (1932–, Gentofte, Denmark). *Gilgamesh, Opera in Six Days and Seven Nights* was composed in 1971–72. As of this writing, the release of this opera had just been announced, and I have not had access to it. Nørgård's interest in Mesopotamian culture goes back at least to 1966 when his oratorio, *Babel* (for clown, rock singer, cabaret singer, chorus and small orchestra) was produced.

Recording: Denmark-DMA 025-6. Members of the Swedish Radio Orchestra, Tamas Veto, cond.

Bibliography: *The New Grove Dictionary...*, s.v. [The Swedish journal, *Nutida musik* 17 (1973–4), 5ff. has devoted a whole issue to *Gilgamesh*].

THE SEVEN (EVIL) GODS

Sergei Prokofiev (1891–1953). Having just completed his *Classical Symphony,* Prokofiev decided to compose "something cosmic" to parallel the momentous events of the summer of 1917: "The revolutionary events that were shaking Russia penetrated my subconscious and clamored for expression. I did not know how to do this, and my mind, paradoxically, turned to ancient themes. The fact that thoughts and emotions of those remote times had survived for many thousands of years staggered my imagination."

Once more (cf., *Songs,* Op. 9, 23), Prokofiev turned to the poetry of the "Decadent Symbolist" K.D. Bal'mont (1867–1943), and chose the last's resetting of a "Chaldean Invocation engraved in ancient Assyro-Babylonian cuneiform on the walls of an Akkadian temple"

("In the deep abyss/Their number is seven;/In the Azure sky,/Seven, they are seven..." From *Voices of Antiquity*. 1908.) Prokofiev shortened the poem, harped on the number seven, and added a quatrain which was certainly meant to comment on contemporary events, although it is still a matter of debate whether Prokofiev sought thusly to exorcize the Russian Revolution or the German advances toward Petrograd.

The score is for a piece that, pointedly enough, lasts seven minutes. It has a highly expressionistic series of thunderous *tutti* alternating with deafening silences. Shrill piccolos, shrieking choruses, beating drums, and bleating woodwinds evoke slaughter and plead laments. Greeted as an example of bourgeois decadence, it was not performed in Russia until the late '60s.

Recording: Quintessence PMC 7196. Moscow Radio Symphony Orchestra, Gennady Rozhdestvensky, cond.

Bibliography: I.V. Nestyev, *Prokofiev*. 1960. 149–54. [Quotation from 151, note.] On Bal'mont, E. Lo Gatto, *Histoire de la littérâture Russe*, 1965. 629–32.

ENUMA ELISH
Vladimir Ussachevsky (1911– Manchuria; US citizen). Ussachevsky works in two areas of music, choral, where he is influenced by Russian liturgical music, and electronic, where he displays a predeliction for transforming pre-existing material. In 1959 he took part in the founding of "Columbia-Princeton Electronic Music Center." *Creation-Prologue*, composed in 1960–61, is an eight-minute piece recorded at a concert where other compositions, each remarkably different in texture and invention, found first presentation. I quote from the record's jacket:

> The work begins in Akkadian, the language of Babylon, implying the chaotic state but giving no description of it. The composer says: "I felt a need of interpolating some such description from another ancient source, and thus the opening lines of [Ovid's] *Metamorphoses*, rendered in Latin, are inserted, or musically speaking superimposed on *Enuma Elish*. I sought to exploit the contrast between the archaic quality of Akkadian and the sound of classical Latin...the antiphonal manner of the performance assists in sharpening this contrast."

> The composition is written for four full choruses and may be performed in various combinations of live performers and pre-recorded chorus, or simply as an entirely recorded work from two or four tape tracks. Antiphonal treatment of the material is frequently employed, and in several instances a dense dissonant texture is achieved by the use of multi-choral polyphony.

Recording: Columbia MS 6566. [I know of this recording thanks to A. Hurowitz and, especially, to Sh. Paul.] An apparently more elaborate version of this composition is listed in the *International Electronic Music discography*, 1979, under the composer's name as *Three Scenes from the Creation* (CRI, SD 297, a record not available to me).

Bibliography: *The New Grove Dictionary....* s.v.; E. Schwartz, *Electronic Music: A Listener's Guide*, 1973, 55ff.

❋ ❋ ❋

NOTES

1. O.J. Ford, "Regaining the Primordial (Charles Olson as Teacher)," *Athanor*, 1 (1971), 52. Material for this essay was gathered in part under a grant from The Research Foundation of State University of New York. George Butterick, Curator of the Olson Archives, University of Connecticut, has been very helpful in my research, as have been Douglas Calhoun, editor of *Athanor*, and my research assistant, Parvin Ghassemi.
2. *Alcheringa* 5 (1973), 11–12. He had applied for Turkey and Iran, but was allowed to switch his application when a program in Iraq did indeed open up; but the disposition of the application is not known.
3. George Butterick has been publishing lists of Olson's reading in *Olson*, the journal of the Olson Archives. Many of the books and articles gathered by Olson and now in the Olson Archives have been annotated by Olson. These notes and extensive files have not as yet been published. While Olson was rector of Black Mountain, he invited scholars like Robert Braidwood to speak about the Ancient Near East. He corresponded with Samuel Noah Kramer about the possiblity of convening a seminar in "Pre-Homeric Literature," and Kramer was quite receptive to the idea. Kramer in turn suggested that Olson contact Cyrus Gordon and Hans Güterbock, and they, too, were interested in the seminar. But the school folded before the meeting could take place.

Olson had hoped to run the seminar in 1955–1956. When, in 1959, a symposium was held in Mexico City that eventually became *Mythologies of the Ancient World*, 1961, Black Mountain was only a memory; but Olson would use *Mythologies*, a book that comes as close to his idea of the seminar as anything produced, in his classes at other schools. It was a suggestion of Kramer that led Olson to purchase *Ancient Near Eastern Texts*, the second edition of which is heavily annoted by Olson. See Kramer's letters in the Olson Archives for 5/24/52, 1/23/57, and 11/18/59. According to George Butterick, Olson's Ancient Near Eastern materials amounted to well over one hundred books and articles, from *BASOR* (1941–1947) and the *American Journal of Archeaology* (1942, 1943, 1948) through works by Alexander Heidel, N.K. Sandars, W.G. Albright, Cyrus Gordon, Hand Güterbock and others. The most heavily annoted are the second edition of *ANET* and three of Kramer's works: *From the Tablets of Sumer* (1956), *Sumerian Mythology* (revised edition, 1961), and *Mythologies of the Ancient World* (1961). Two works by L.A. Waddell, *The Aryan Origin of the Alphabet* (1927) and *The Indo-Sumerian Seals Deciphered* (1925) are in the Olson Archives and made an impact on Olson, but the copies are not marked. Olson was clearly offended by Waddell's racist views. In "Mayan Letters" (1953), in *Selected Writings* (ed. Robert Creeley), 1966, 97–98, he wrote to Creeley:

> until we have completely cleaned ourselves of the biases of westernism, of greekism, until we have squared away at historical time in such a manner that we are able to see Sumer as a point from which all "races" (speaking of them culturally, not, biologically) egressed, we do not have permission to weigh the scale one way or another (for example, Jakeman, leaves, so far as I have read him, the invention of maize to the Mongoloids, as well as the arts of ceramics, weaving, and baskets! And, *contra* (contra all these prejudiced Nordics, among whom I include Hooton, who has sd, from skull-measurements, that it is true, there were Caucasians here), there remains China, ancient and modern China. Until the lads can verify that the Chinese, as well as the people of India, came off from the Tigris-Euphrates complex, they better lie low with their jumps to conclude that only the Caucasian type was the civilizing type of man). ((As you know, this whole modern intellectual demarche, has, at its roots, a negative impulse, deeper, even, than the anti-Asia colonialism of Europe: at root, the search is, to unload, to disburden themselves, of Judaism, of Semitism.))

4. Allusions are quite frequent in his work, from an Uruk tablet in "logography," *Additional Prose* (ed. George Butterick), 1974, 26. He acknowledges his debt to I.J. Gelb in that essay. In *Causal Mythology*, 1969, 13, he refers to Enki, seeing in the Sumerian god a similarity to Prometheus, and he expresses his admiration for the Gilgamesh stories. In *Letters for Origin*, 1950–1956 (ed. Albert Glover), 1970, 57, he observed that the ancients exactly reversed our modern metaphors (e.g., the phallus), an observation which led to a discussion of Sumer. He wrote to Creeley about the Sumerian logogram, *a*, *Selected Writings*, 96. In his poetry, too, he refers often to Sumerian and Akkadian motifs: to Inanna and the world-tree in "for my friend," for example, *Archaeologist of Morning*, 1970, n.p.; to Mesopotamian ziggurats in *Maximus, The Maximus Poems, Volume Three*, ed. Charles Boer and George F. Butterick (NY: Grossman, 1975), pp. 77, 84, 119; to Tiamat in an unpublished poem "she is the sea...," in *Olson* 9 (1978), 19: to the plant given Gilgamesh by Utnapishtim in one work, *Olson* 9 (1978), 20; to the *kishkanu* tree in "The four quarters," to Inanna before Ereshkigal in "like two spiders," and to Humbaba in "Dog-town the Dog Bitch," *Olson* 9 (1978), 38, 39, 46. See also in the same issue, "A Norm for my love in her NOMOS, or...." In "Watered Rock..." he alludes, by way of "Bigmans," to Gilgamesh, *Olson* 9 (1978), 37.
5. *The Special View of History* (ed. Ann Charters), 1970, 1. For Olson at Black Mountain, see Martin Duberman, *Black Mountain, an Experiment in Community*, 1972, 368–385, and Sherman Paul, *Olson's Push*, 1978, 67–114.
6. *The Special View of History*, 15.
7. Surprisingly, he did not seem to know Thorkild Jacobsen's work in *The Intellectual Adventure of Ancient Man* (now *Before Philosophy*), 1946.
8. *The Special View*, 20.
9. *The Special View*, 25.
10. *The Special View*, 25.
11. *The Special View*, 30.
12. *The Special View*, 37.
13. *The Special View*, 51; *Additional Prose*, 26–32, 40. See also "Notes for the Proposition: Man is Prospective," *boundary 2* 2 (1973/1974), 1–6.
14. "The Gate and the Center," in *Human Universe and Other Essays* (ed. Donald Allen), 1967, 17–23.
15. "The Gate and the Center," 19.
16. "The Gate and the Center," 20.
17. "The Gate and the Center," 22–3.
18. "The Gate and the Center," 23.
19. "Mayan Letters," 130.
20. "Letter to Elaine Feinstein," in *Selected Writings*, 27–30.
21. "Letter to Elaine Feinstein," 28.
22. "Letter to Elaine Feinstein," 29.
23. "Mayan Letters," 113.

24. See *Alcheringa* 5 (1973), 5–11, for a sampling of Olson's "transpositions." Following upon Kramer's attempts to *Sumerian Mythology*, pp. 39–41 and again in pp. 73–75, to find a more or less consistent structure in the very heterogeneous Sumerian "myths of origin" and to describe that structure in a "rational" and then a "theological" way, Olson tried his hand at a Sumerian "creation myth" that linked the various elements together. The result is a poem, first called "FABLE OF CREATION" and revised to "a sumer fable." The poem was not published in Olson's lifetime. In *Alcheringa* 5, 5, the orignal typed copy and Olson's handwritten revisions of the text have been reproduced.

25. Reprinted in *Archaeologist of Morning*, n.p.

26. *ANET*, 97.

27. See *ANET*, 73–4. Olson had marked his copy of the second edition concerning the *pukku* and *mekkû* in *The Epic of Gilgamesh*.

28. *Alcheringa* 5 (1973), 7–8. The draft is in the folder 1260–2 of the Olson Archives. There are over twenty variations between the drafts, almost all of them in the accidentals of capitalization and punctuation. Of the more meaningful changes, the lines about striking and embracing the sons at first contained the injunction, "do not embrace the beloved son," and "the hated" for the hated son, instead of the phrase, "his brother," that replaced it. The breasts of the mother were at first merely "bared," and they were bared "to the dead" instead of lying open to "the judges." The final line of the poem has been improved greatly by removing the "have fallen" (for the drum and lute), and adding instead the stark "are."

29. *Sumerian Mythology*, 35.

30. *ANET*, 97.

31. *Sumerian Mythology*, 35.

32. "Projective Verse," *Selected Writings*, 24.

33. The Olson Archives files 566–79, "Bigmans," contain "Bigmans" I, II, and III. "Bigmans" (I) is an invocation, not directly from *The Epic of Gilgamesh*. Another "Bigmans" (on the verso of the typed sheet, "Bigmans II") is a transposition of the opening of the Akkadian epic. "Bigmans III"—otherwise known as "III The Brother"—is a transposition in different versions of Gilgamesh on the hunter and Enkidu, as the harlot is picked to seduce the wild man. The piece was left unfinished and is, in any case, pretty poor stuff. Olson's partly handwritten, partly typed notes to "Bigmans III" are more interesting. The manuscript is signed and dated August 24, 1950. As is usual with Olson's prose, the notes are difficult and digressive, but they make a point of the "single" and the "double" involved in the complex relationships of Gilgamesh, Enkidu, and the harlot.

❋ ❋ ❋

Walter Burkert
"'Or Also a Godly Singer' Akkadian and Early Greek Literature"

A scholar of the classics who has attempted to find an historical context for very precise connections between specific literary texts and early Greek literature—an attempt that goes beyond just "individual motifs" but tries to account for "more complex structures" in the influence of Akkadian on, especially, Homer, is Walter Burkert. Chapter 3 (of three) in his *The Orientalizing Revolution: Near Eastern Influence on Greek Culture in the Early Archaic Age* (1984, 1992) is an extended treatment of little-noted influences of *Atrahasis, Enuma Elish, Erra,* and *Gilgamesh* on Greek texts. Most of his observations depend on an expert knowledge of the Greek texts, because the influences of Akkadian are best seen in those passages and structures that are anomalies. *Gilgamesh* examples include Ishtar's complaint to Anu and Antum after her rejection by Gilgamesh; Burkert notes the similarity to an odd passage in Homer where Aphrodite complains to Zeus and Dione about her treatment by the hero Diomedes. Where the Ishtar passage is "firmly anchored" in Gilgamesh, it is not similarly anchored to the *Iliad.* Burkert suggests a ritual background to both passages, by the way: the "hunters' taboo," "sexual restraint that ensures a successful hunt" (in the case of *Gilgamesh,* the Bull).

Other examples Burkert provides are the prayer and offering of Ninsun to Shamash and its parallel in Penelope's prayer to Athena in *The Odyssey;* the complicated narrative technique of the flood story in Tablet XI compared with Odysseus's first-person stories of his adventures; and a larger concern, "a certain ethos of mortality of human beings" in *Gilgamesh* and the *Iliad.* Even the herb of rejuvenation provides a parallel, with Burkert noting, as others usually do not, that real snakes do not usually feed on herbs (or drugs, as in the Greek parallel).

Burkert is convinced that by the 8th Century B.C.E., military advances, settlements, imports of goods and craft skills, images, the appearance of seers and purification priests, and the appearance of the alphabet in Greece argue for a far more extensive influence of post-Bronze Age Akkadian on the "Greek miracle" than has been accepted by classicists in the past. (Ed.)

Since the rediscovery of the Akkadian epics and of *Gilgamesh* in particular, there has been no shortage of associations between motifs in these and in the Homeric epics, especially the *Odyssey*.[1] These motifs can be highlighted and used to surprise, but hardly to prove anything: Approximately the same motifs and themes will be found everywhere. Instead of individual motifs, therefore, we must focus on more complex structures, where sheer coincidence is less likely: a system of deities and a basic cosmological idea, the narrative structure of a whole scene, decrees of the gods about mankind, or a very special configuration of attack and defense. Once the historical link, the fact of transmission, has been established, then further connections, including linguistic borrowings, become more likely, even if those alone do not suffice to carry the burden of proof. □

Complaint in Heaven: Ishtar and Aphrodite

The "apparatus of the gods" which accompanies the sequence of events narrated in the *Iliad* and, in a modified form, in the *Odyssey* has more than once been called a "late" element in the tradition of Greek heroic epic.[2] There has also been an awareness of oriental parallels with precisely these scenes involving the gods.[3] It is true that the double stage of divine and human actions, which is handled so masterfully by the composer of the *Iliad*, is not found in this extensive form in the Mesopotamian epics. Still, *Atrahasis* and *Gilgamesh* repeatedly introduce the gods interacting with the deeds and sufferings of men; and kings are made to win their heroic battles in direct contact with their protective gods.

In *Gilgamesh* in particular, there is a famous meeting between deity and man: When Gilgamesh has killed Humbaba and cleansed himself of the grime of battle, Ishtar "raised an eye at the beauty of Gilgamesh": "Do but grant me of your fruit!" she says, and she offers fabulous goods for him. But Gilgamesh scornfully rejects her, reciting the catalogue of all her partners whom she once "has loved" only to destroy or to transform subsequently. "If you would love me, you would [treat me] like them." Whereupon

> Ishtar, when hearing this,
> Ishtar was enraged and [went up] to heaven.
> [Forth went Ishtar before Anu, her father;
> before Antum, her mother [her tears were flowing]:
> ["Oh my father! Gilgamesh has heaped insults upon me!
> Gilgamesh has recounted my insults,
> my insults and my curses."

Anu opened his mouth to speak,
he said to glorious Ishtar:
"Surely you have provoked [the King of Uruk],
and (thus) Gilgamesh recounted your insults,
your insults and your curses."[4]

Compare this with a scene from the *Iliad*:[5] Trying to protect Aeneas, Aphrodite has been wounded by Diomedes; her blood is flowing. "But she, beside herself, went away, she felt horrible pain." With the help of Iris and Ares she reaches Olympus. "But she, glorious Aphrodite, fell into the lap of Dione, her mother; but she took her daughter in her arms, stroked her with her hand, spoke the word and said: "Who has done such things to you, dear child?" Aphrodite replies: "Wounded has me the son of Tydeus, high-minded Diomedes." Mother sets out to comfort her with mythical examples; Athena her sister, less sympathtic, makes a scornful comment; but Zeus the father smiles: "He called golden Aphrodite and said to her: 'My child, not for you are the works of war! But you should pursue the tender offices of marriage…'" In other words: It's partly your own fault.

The two scenes parallel each other in structure, narrative form, and ethos to an astonishing degree.[6] A goddess, injured by a human, goes up to heaven to complain to her father and mother, and she earns a mild rebuke from her father.

Of course this may be called a universal scenario from the realm of children's stories. The scene repeats itself with variations in the battle of the gods later in the *Iliad*.[7] Artemis, after being beaten by Hera, climbs weeping onto the knees of father Zeus. He pulls her to him and asks, laughing: "Who did this to you?" And she replies: "Your wife beat me." The scene from the Diomedes book is simpler in that both parents appear as a refuge, the stepmother being left out, with the father taking the stance of slightly distant superiority. This corresponds exactly to the *Gilgamesh* scene.

But what is more: The persons involved in both scenes are, in fact, identical, the sky god and his wife, and their common daughter the goddess of love. Aphrodite is in general the equivalent of Ishtar; she has offered herself to a mortal man, Anchises the father of Aeneas, and Anchises suffered some strange fate as a result of his contact with the goddess—another case of what Gilgamesh is blaming on Ishtar. It is possible that the name Aphrodite itself is a Greek form of western Semitic Ashtorith, who in turn is identical with Ishtar.[8] And by force of an even more special parallelism, Aphrodite has a mother who apparently lives in Olympus as Zeus's wife, Dione; Hera seems to be forgotten for a moment. Dione at Olympus makes her appearance in the context of the Diomedes scene, and only there. The contrast with Hesiod's account of Aphrodite's birth from the sea, after Uranos had been castrated, has been found disconcerting since antiquity. Dione is attested in the cult of Dodona; scholars have also referred to the Mycenaean goddess Diwija.[9] In any event, the mother of Aphrodite is given here a name which is crystal clear in Greek, being just the feminine form of *Zeus*. Such a system of naming is unique in the Homeric family of gods, where couples enjoy complicated private names. But it is this very detail which has its counterpart in the Akkadian text: Antu mother of Ishtar is the usual, obviously feminine form of *Anu*, Heaven. This divine couple, Mr. and Mrs. Heaven, is firmly established in the worship and mythology of Mesopotamia. Homer proves to be dependent on Gilgamesh even at the linguistic level, forming the name Dione as a calque on Antu when recasting an impressive scene among the gods. This may be seen as a counterpart to the relation Tethys/Tawtu, though rather at the level of narrative structure and divine characters than of cosmic mythology.

A few observations may be added about Diomedes in relation to the Aphrodite scene. Diomedes belongs to Argos, as the catalogue of ships has it; it is at Argos that we find a ritual corresponding to the Iliadic narrative, the shield of Diomedes carried in a procession with the image of Pallas Athena on a chariot.[10] But Diomedes also belongs to Salamis on Cyprus; it is said that there was human sacrifice for Diomedes and Agraulos, performed in the sanctuary of which Athena had her share, in the month of Aphrodisios; the victim was killed with a spear and burnt.[11] Thus we find Diomedes, Athena, and Aphrodite in strange company combined with spear-killing; some have found the Cypriote holocaust reminiscent of Semitic practice.[12] At any rate an aspect of the Diomedes legend, which seems somehow to tie in with the Aphrodite scene in Homer, points to that island where Hellas and the Semitic East enjoyed their closest contact and where precisely in the Homeric period the Assyrian kings commemorated their power in inscriptions.[13] In this perspective the connection between the Homeric and the Akkadian epic hardly appears astonishing any more.

Still, among all the similarities it is important to keep sight of the differences. Ishtar's meeting with Gilgamesh is firmly anchored in the structure of the *Gilgamesh* epic; it constitutes the narrative link from the Humbaba theme to the next heroic deed, the vanquishing of the bull of heaven. Glorious Ishtar, in her revenge, has the bull of heaven make his attack, thus giving Gilgamesh and Enkidu the opportunity to overcome the bull and thus establish sacrifice. The ritual background is clear even in details. Gilgamesh's rejection of Ishtar corresponds to the hunters' taboo: It is sexual restraint that ensures a successful hunt. Hence the denial of love causes the bull to appear.[14] Also the transformations of Ishtar's lovers as reported in Gilgamesh's catalogue have their special meaning and function, being basically myths about the installment of culture: In this way the horse was bridled.[15] What has remained in Homer is the narrative thread of a genre scene, all the more carefully presented because it is, on the whole, functionless. It has its own charm and aesthetic merit in the framework of the *Iliad*, but it does not carry the same weight either in the narrative or in terms of ritual background as in the Akkadian epic. The manner in which Akkadian demons have been turned into fantastic monsters, more amusing than frightening—Lamashtu transformed into the Gorgon—has its counterpart on the level of epic poetry about the gods.

The influence of *Gilgamesh* may also be detected in a scene from the *Odyssey*. The *Odyssey* once describes a form of prayer which historians of religion have found confusing: When Penelope learns about the risky journey undertaken by Telemachos and the suitors' plot to kill him, she first bursts into tears and laments. Then, calming down, she washes and dresses in clean clothes, goes to the upper story with her maids, taking barley in a basket, and prays to Athena for the safe return of Telemachos; she ends with an inarticulate and shrieking cry.[16] Both the basket with barley and the cry (*ololyge*) have their proper place in blood sacrifice; their use in this scene is unparalleled elsewhere. So scholars either spoke of an "abbreviation of sacrifice" or of an otherwise unknown ritual of bloodless offering or of an invention of the poet, if not incompetence of the "redactor."[17] But look at *Gilgamesh*: When Gilgamesh together with Enkidu is leaving his city to fight Humbaba, his mother "Ninsun enters her chamber, she takes a…[special herb], she puts on a garment as befits her body, she puts on an ornament as befits her breast… she sprinkles water from a bowl on earth and dust. She went up the stairs, mounted the upper storey, she climbed the roof, to Shamash [the sun god] she offered incense, she brought the offering and raised her hands before Shamash"; thus she prays, full of distress and sorrow, for a safe return of her son.[18] The situation, mother praying for an adventurous son, is not a special one. Yet in its details the scene from the *Odyssey* comes close to being a translation of *Gilgamesh*; in fact it is closer to the *Gilgamesh* text than to the comparable scene of Achilles' prayer in the *Iliad*.[19] Whereas the ritual is odd in the *Odyssey*, none of these oddities is found in the passage of *Gilgamesh*: Burning incense on the roof is a well-known Semitic practice,[20] and it is especially appropriate when turning to the sun god. Ceremonial prayer in the women's upper story is otherwise unheard-of in Greece. It seems the poet knew that burning incense was out of place in the heroic world, so he took as a subsititute the female part in normal sacrifice, that is, throwing of barley (*oulochytai*) and *ololyge*. Even the use of religious ritual as an effective motif in epic narrative has its antecedent in the oriental tradition. □

Common Style and Stance in Oriental and Greek Epic

Ever since the mythological texts from Hattusa and Ugarit have attracted the attention of classicists, parallels from Hesiod and Homer in motifs and narrative techniques have been collected, occasionally also touching on Mesopotamian materials. Recently, Luigia Achillea Stella has presented an extensive catalogue of correspondences.[21] She pleads decisively for the Bronze Age cultural bridge. But comparisons by themselves do not provide specific indicators for either an earlier or a later borrowing, indeed for any borrowing at all in contrast to the chances of parallel development. In any case, uncertainties about the date of "influence" should not distract us from acknowledging how extensive these correspondences are.

In a sense, of course, Greek epic is a very self-sufficient flowering. The formulaic system, which Milman Parry discovered and explained in terms of its necessary function within an oral tradition, is tied to the Greek language.[22] From this point of view Homer has become the model example of an oral tradition.[23] By contrast, the eastern epic, at least in Mesopotamia, is based in a fixed tradition of writing and schools of scribes spanning more than two millennia. Within this tradition tablets are copied and recopied again and again, and sometimes also translated within the cuneiform systems.

One should expect therefore to encounter quite different principles of style in the East and in the West. Yet anyone who cares to consider both sides will be struck by the similarities. The most important of these have been indicated long ago; a partial listing follows.

In both cases "epic" means narrative poetry which employs, in form, a long verse which repeats itself indefinitely, without strophic division. As to content, the tale is about gods and great men from the past, often interacting. Main characteristics of style are the standard epithets, the formulaic verses, the repetition of verses, the typical scenes.

Epithets have always appeared to be a special characteristic of Homeric style. We are familiar with "cloud-gathering Zeus," "Odysseus of many counsels," "Odysseus of many sufferings." But in Akkadian epic, too, the chief characters have characteristic epithets. The chief god, Enlil, often appears as "the hero Enlil,"[24] the hero of the flood is "Utnapishtim the far-away,"[25] and the dangerous Seven in the Erra are "champions without peer."[26] Similarly the Ugaritic epics have fixed formulas such as Baal "the rider of clouds," "the Virgin Anat," and "Danel the Rephaite."[27] What sounds even more Homeric is the designation of a combatant as "knowledgeable in battle."[28] It is less clear why the "mistress of the gods" is "good in shouting,"[29] but it was also unclear even to Greeks why Kalypso as well as Kirke should be "a frightful goddess using speech," *deine theos audeessa.* Be that as it may, an epic poet cannot do without epithets: The earth is "the broad earth,"[30] and a god of heavens can be called "father of gods and men."[31] The epithets are decorative insofar as they are neither essential to the actual context of the current situation nor modeled specifically for it. Among other things, they are extremely helpful to fill out a half-verse.

In formulaic verse what is most striking is the complicated introduction of direct speech. The lavish use of direct speech, the representation of whole scenes in the form of dialogue is, indeed, a peculiarity of the genre. In Akkadian, the introductory formula is, in literal translation: "He set his mouth and spoke to...he said [the word]."[32] The simple meaning of *speak* is expressed in three synonyms—just as the well-known Homeric formula "he raised his voice and spoke the winged words." It is perhaps even more remarkable that characters in *Gilgamesh*, reflecting on a new situation, "speak to their own heart." "Consulting with her heart she spoke, indeed she took counsel with herself"—direct speech follows.[33] In a similar way Homeric heroes speak to their own "great-hearted *thymos*" or to their "heart." When Gilgamesh is travelling, the new day is always introduced with the same formula: "Barely a shimmer of the morning dawned,"[34] reminiscent of Homer's famous line "But when early-born rosy-fingered Eos appeared." It is natural for a narrative to move on from day to day, but to employ stereotyped formulas for sunrise and sunset, pause and action is a specific technique used in Gilgamesh as in Homer.

Among the repetitions which cover a whole sequence of verses a striking feature is the exact verbal correspondence between command and performance, reporting and repetition of the report. The Mesopotamian scribes, weary of wedges, occasionally used a "repeat" sign, which the Homeric scribes did not permit themselves.

Among typical scenes the assembly of the gods is prominent. Akkadian has a fixed expression for it, *puḫur ilāni*; the designation is the same in Ugaritic, and the respective scene is also fully elaborated in the Hittite *Song of Ullikummi*.[35] That in the assembly of the gods it is often decided to send out a messenger is natural and still worth noting.

Similes are a popular device in the Akkadian epic as in related poetry; details need not be given here.[36] What seems more remarkable is that in *Gilgamesh*, the longest and highest-ranking text, more complicated forms of narrative technique are being tried out, as is the case especially in the *Odyssey*. In the eleventh tablet of *Gilgamesh* a distant but particularly gripping piece of action, the great flood, is incorporated through direct speech by the main participant, Utnapishtim the far-away. The dual action at the beginning of the epic which has to bring together Enkidu and Gilgamesh is set out in such a way that the narrative first follows Enkidu's adventures and his transformation to civilization and then recounts Gilgamesh's preparations for the meeting through direct speech which the prostitute addresses to Enkidu (I v 23–vi 24). Thus even the narrative technique of the poet of the *Odyssey*, who incorporates most of Odysseus' adventures in a first-person speech by Odysseus himself to the Phaeacians and devises a double plot to bring Odysseus and Telemachos together, is not totally isolated. The similarity between the openings of *Gilgamesh* and the *Odyssey* has struck readers too: Attention is called to the hero who wandered wide and saw many things while his name is intentionally withheld.[37]

Foreshadowing the *Iliad*, as it were, *Gilgamesh* in particular exhibits a certain ethos of the mortality of human beings. The main theme of the poem is, in its own words, the "fates of humanity" (*šimatu awilūtim*), which means death, in contrast to the life of the gods, which only Utnapishtim succeeded in winning for himself. Before his fight with Humbaba, Gilgamesh draws the heroic consequence: "The gods, with Shamash [the sun god] they sit forever; as for mankind, numbered are their days… But you here, you fear death?… I will go ahead of you… If I myself were to fall, let me still set up my name."[38] Thus, precisely because man is denied eternity, all that remains for him is to win fame through risking death, fame which survives beyond death; imperishable glory (*kleos aphthiton*), in contrast to mortal men, these are the concepts set out in the *Iliad* in Greek. "Yes, dear friend! If, having escaped from this war, we were to live forever ageless, immortal, even I would not fight among the front ranks... But now, as the demons of death stand before us anyhow... Let us go! whether we bring glory to another man or someone gives glory to us"—this is Homer.[39] This insight into the limits of the human condition does not, however, lead to caution in relation to the gods. Far from it, aggressive outbursts may occur. Enkidu throws the hind leg of the bull of heaven to Ishtar and shouts: "If I caught you, like this I would do to you."[40] Indeed I would take revenge if I only had the power," cries Achilles to Apollo, who has deceived him.[41]

But man is weak and changeable. "Of such a kind is the insight of mortal men, as the day which the father of gods and men brings on" states one of the most famous passages of the *Odyssey*.[42] Practically identical is a sentence about mortals from the Akkadian composition *I Will Praise the Lord of Wisdom*: "Their insight changes like day and night. When starving, they become corpses; when replete, they vie with their gods."[43]

Closer comparisons could also be made of actual battle scenes. One notable example is the Egyptian poem about Ramses II in the battle of Qadesh. The hero finds himself alone amidst the enemies, he prays to his father the god, the god hears him, whereupon the hero attacks and kills all the enemies.[44] Another suggestive text is incorporated in the *Annals of Sennacherib* and refers to the battle of Halule in 691 B.C.; it tells how the king takes up his armor, mounts his chariot, and with the assistance of god knocks down the enemies; so finally "my prancing steeds, harnessed for my riding, plunged into the streams of blood as into a river; the wheels of my chariot, which brings down the wicked and the evil, were bespattered with blood and filth"[45]—note the standard epithets; and just like Ramses the Egyptian, the Assyrian king, too, is represented fighting from his Bronze Age chariot. We are irresistibly reminded of the *Iliad*: "Thus under greathearted Achilles his one-hoofed horses stepped on corpses and shields together; with blood the whole axle was bespattered, and the rails around the seat, which the drops from the hoofs of the horses were hitting..." Considering the date of the Assyrian text, one might even toy with the idea that some Greek singer had arrived in Assyria together with the mercenaries, and that he composed this song on the battle of Halule which so much pleased the king that it was incorporated in the official annals, where it forms a strange contrast to the standard dreary and dull list of battle and plundering.[46] But more systematic research into this genre would be due. The "Song of Deborah and Barak" should not be forgotten in this context; it has, among other stirring events, a remarkable "battle at the river."[47]

Some further connections in detail between East and West, though striking, have remained a mystery. This applies to the "Word of Tree and Stone" as it appears in Ugarit, in Jeremiah, and in Homer and Hesiod; it seems to be connected with a myth about the origin of man in the Old Testament and in the *Odyssey*, but is used as a less lucid saying in Ugarit as in the *Iliad* and in Hesiod.[48]

Less surprising is that the blessing of the land under the rule of a good king is established in Mesopotamia, but it also appears in Homer and Hesiod: The earth brings forth her crops, the trees their fruit, the animals thrive, and "People thrive under him" the good king; compare Ashurbanipal on himself in his own account: "Since the gods… benignly made me take my seat on the throne of my father, my begetter, Adad released his torrents of rain, Ea opened his springs, the ears of the crops grew five ells high… the fruits of the field flourished… the trees brought their fruits to an abundant growth, the cattle bred successfully. During my reign there was abundance, during my years good things overflowed."[49]

Enough of parallels. Style is hardly separable from content. For stylistic elements, direct dependence is hard to prove: Each language has its own laws and its own life. In Homer we cannot ascertain the presence of "younger," additional elements against the older epic tradition in the characteristics discussed so far, in contrast to the mythological concepts found in the context of the "Deception of Zeus," the opening of the *Cypria*, or the *Seven against Thebes*. For the style of battle scenes we definitely reach the Bronze Age with Ramses' account. Still, considering the fact that we are dealing with spatially and chronologically linked spheres of civilization anyhow, to insist on completely separate developments and purely coincidental parallels is begging the question. One has to reckon with multiple contracts, to be set against both the general human background and common tendencies of historical-social developments. What was in fact a heritage of the Bronze Age could also be revitalized by new incentives. It is probably symptomatic that besides the traditional Greek loan-word for lion, *leon*, another word of clearly Semitic-Palestinian pedigree, *lis*, has been adopted in some Homeric similes.[50] In any event, the eastern evidence offers such closely related material that it should not be overlooked in the interpretation of Homer. This finding must set certain limits to assessments of purely "Indo-European" heroic tradition.

The establishment of the first Greek library—the *Iliad* written down on twenty-four(?) leather scrolls—and of the great library of Ashurbanipal at Nineveh, who ruled from 668 to 627, may well have taken place at about the same time. Even this may not be totally coincidental. The Semitic East still held the cultural lead until that date. □

❋ ❋ ❋

NOTES

1. "The Gilgamesh Epic… may well be called the Odyssey of the Babylonians"; A. Heidel, *The Gilgamesh Epic and Old Testament Parallels* (1949[2])1. A catalog of parallels in Auffahrt (1991) 136–139; see also Gresseth (1975); Wilson (1986); Burkert (1991). Jensen (1902), (1912/13), (1924) and Ungnad (1923) called attention esp. to Kalypso and Siduri the ale wife, Alkinoos, and Utnapishtim. Utnapishtim's ferryman quits his service after the transport of Gilgamesh (XI 234–236), just as the transport of Odysseus is the last ever done by the Phaeacians (*Od.* 13.125–187). See also G. Crane, "Circe and the Near East," in *Calypso. Backgrounds and Conventions of the Odyssey* (1988) 61–85. Fries (1910) reached an extreme position; more solid is Wirth (1921). Most specific is Enkidu coming up from the dead to meet his friend (*Gilgamesh* XII), just as Patroklos' soul meets Achilles (*Il.* 23.65–107): "The comparison...is, indeed, almost irrestible"; G.S. Kirk, *Myth* (1970) 108; cf. idem, *The Nature of Greek Myths* (1974) 260 f.; see also Chapter 2, "Spirits of the Dead and Black Magic," at note 4. There are also connections with *Od.* II, the *Nekyia*; cf. C.F. Lehmann-Haupt, *RE* XI 433; G. Germain, *Genèse de l'Odyssée* (1954) 342–346; Dirlmeier (1955) 30–35; "A fairly possible model": G.S. Kirk, *The Songs of Homer* (1962) 107. For the beginning of the *Odyssey* and of *Gilgamesh* see Chapter 3, "Common Style and Stance in Oriental and Greek Epic," at note 17. □
2. See, e.g., P. Von der Mühll, *Kritisches Hypomnema zur Ilias* (1952), who assigns practically all the divine scenes to his "Bearbeiter B"; cf. 96 f. on *Il.* 5.353–431.
3. Esp. L.A. Stella, *Il poema di Ulisse* (1955) 188–205; Stella (1978) 73–123.
4. *Gilgamesh* VI I–91; *ANET* 83 f., modified according to von Soden.
5. *Il.* 5.330–431.

6. This was noticed by Gresseth (1975) 14, who also compares the threat of Ishtar to release the dead from the underworld, if Anu does not grant her wish (*Gilgamesh* VI 96–100), with the reverse threat of Helios in the *Odyssey* to go down to the underworld, if Zeus does not grant his wish (12.382 f.). See also Burkert in *Eranos Jahrbuch* (1982) 335–367.
7. *Il.* 21.505–513.
8. Cf. Burkert (1985) 152–156; for Anchises and Aphrodite see L.H. Lentz, *Der Homerische Aphroditehymnus und die Aristie des Aineias in der Ilias* (1975), esp. 104–107, 144–152. Helck (1979) 243–249 holds that practically the whole Homeric pantheon reproduces North Syrian/ Late Hittite gods.
9. Dione is mentioned Hes. *Theog.* 17 in a catalogue which is close to Homer (cf. West [1968] 156) and is *Theog.* 353 among the daughters of Oceanus; for Dodona, see Strab. 7 p. 392, who says that Dione has been secondarily introduced there; cf. Escher, *RE V* 878–880. G. Murray, *Five Stages of Greek Religion* (1925) 77, argued that Dione had preceded Hera as Zeus's wife; this is refuted by Linear B, where Hera is the wife of Zeus. For *Diwija* see M. Gérard-Rousseau, *Les mentions religieuses dans les tablettes mycéniennes* (1968) 67–70. The suffix –ώνη remained productive in the Greek language, so that female names could always be formed with it; cf. Danae Akrisione, *Il.* 14.319; Helena Argeione, Hes. fr. 23a20.
10. Callim. *Hymn.* 5, esp. 5.35 with schol.; see Burkert, *Zeitschrift für Religions- und Geistesgeschichte* 22 (1970) 36 1f.; see also the Catalogue of Ships, *Il.* 2.559–568; Ø. Andersen, "Die Diomedesgestalt in der Ilias," *Symb. Oslo.* suppl. 25 (1978). Note that Diomedes is immortal (*Thebais* fr. 5 Davies).
11. Porph. *Abst.* 2.54 f.; this section is not taken from Theophrastus, but no further details can be made out; neither "King Diphilos of Cyprus" nor "Seleukos the theologian" mentioned in the text is known elsewhere. Cf. *RE* I A 1835 s.v. *Salamis.*
12. F. Schwenn, *Die Menschenopfer bei den Griechen und Römern* (1915) 71 f. argues against this thesis.
13. See Chapter I "Historical Background," at note 19; and below, "The Overpopulated Earth," note 12.
14. See Burkert (1983a) 60 f.
15. *Gilgamesh* VI 53–57; see above, "From *Atrahasis* to the 'Deception of Zeus,'" note 18.
16. *Od.* 4.759–767.
17. A kind of vegetable offering: L. Deubner, *Kleine Schriften zur klassischen Altertumskunde* (1982) 625; cf. Schol. 761 and Eust. Invented by the poet: S. West in A. Heubeck, S. West, and J.B. Hainsworth, *A Commentary on Homer's Odyssey* I (1988) 240; "ohne jede Analogie" according to K. Meuli, *Ausgewählte Schriften* II (1975) 994 n.1.
18. *Gilgamesh* III ii 1–21; *ANET* 81; Dalley (1989) 65; supplemented according to von Soden (1982) 38.

19. *Il.* 16.220–253.
20. Cf. Jeremiah 44:17–19 and the Greek Adonia; cf. also the Ugaritic epic of Keret ii 73–80, *ANET* 143. □
21. Stella (1978) 362–391, with the cautionary statement that direct influence should be excluded: "esclusa naturalmente ogni eventualità di influssi diretti su Omero" (368). Comparisons of Homer with Babylon began with Jensen and Fries and were carried on by Wirth (1921) and Ungnad (1923); for the more recent developments see esp. Bowra (1952), Dirlmeier (1955), Gordon (1955), Walcot (1966), Gresseth (1975), Helck (1979) 249–251. See also Burkert (1991).
22. See M. Parry, *The Making of Homeric Verse* (1971).
23. The bibliography has become abundant. Suffice it to mention R. Finnegan, *Oral Poetry. Its Nature, Significance, and Social Context* (1977); J.M. Foley, *Oral-Formulaic Theory and Research. An Introduction and Annotated Bibliography* (1985).
24. *quradu Enlil* in *Atrahasis* I.8 = *Gilgamesh* XI 16. See for this and the following also Bowra (1952) 241.
25. *Utnapištim ruqu* in *Gilgamesh* X–XI passim.
26. *qarrad 'la šanan* in *Erra* passim.
27. *rkb ʿrpt* in *Baal* passim, *btlt ʿnt* in *Baal* and *Aqhat* passim, *dnl rpe* in *Aqhat* passim.
28. *mûdu tuquntu* in *Gilgamesh* IV vi 30.
29. *tabat rigma* in *Gilgamesh* XI 117.
30. *erṣetim rapaštim* in *Gilgamesh* VIII iii–iv 43, 46, 47, p. 49. Thompson; cf. εὐρεῖα χθών. As to "black earth" (γαῖα μέλαινα), Öttinger (1989/90) argues for Hurrite-Hittite provenience.
31. Sumerian prayer to the moon god in *SAHG* 223 = Castellino (1977) 336 line 16. In Hittite Ullikummi is called "father of the gods"; *ANET* 121 f., as El is *ab adm*, father of men, in Ugarit.
32. *pašu ippuš-ma iquabbî, ana…(amatam) izakkar* with slight variations; see F. Sonnek, "Die Einführung der direkten Rede in den epischen Texten," *ZA* 46 (1940) 225–235; the formula occurs also in fables, e.g., Lambert (1960) 178.7.
33. *Gilgamesh* X i II f.; cf. X iv, 12–14; *Etana* II 99; J.V. Kinnier Wilson, *The Legend of Etana* (1985) 98; in Hittite: J. Siegelova, *Appu-Märchen und Hedammu-Mythus* (1971) 48 f.; in the Old Testament, too, people "speak to their heart": Gen. 27:41 f., I Samuel 1:12 f.; cf. Stella (1978) 365; D.O. Edzard, "Selbstgespräch und Monolog in der akkadischen Literatur," in *Lingering over Words: Studies in Ancient Near Eastern Literature in Honor of W.L. Moran*, ed. T. Abusch, J. Huehnergard, and P. Steinkeller (1990) 149–162.
34. *mimmu šeri ina namari* in *Gilgamesh* XI 48 = 96; cf. Ungnad (1923) 30.
35. *ANET* 124: the weather god sends Tashmeshu as Zeus sends Hermes in *Od.* 5. An important assembly of the gods also takes place in *Gilgamesh* VII 1 3 ff., where the gods decide about the death of Enkidu. The entrance of victorious Ninurta into this assembly, who threatens

to rouse panic but is appeased by his mother, in the Sumerian poem *ANGIM* 71 ff. (Bottéro and Kramer [1989] 381 f.), has a marked resemblance to *Hom. Hymn Apoll.* 3–13 (I owe this observation to C. Penglase). For Ugarit, see E.T. Mullen, *The Assembly of the Gods: The Divine Council in Canaanite and Early Hebrew Literature* (1980).
36. See Bowra (1952) 266 f., who includes materials from *Gilgamesh.*
37. See Wirth (1921) 112 f.; A.B. Lord in A.J.B. Wace and F.H. Stubbings, *A Companion to Homer* (1967) 198.
38. *Gilgamesh* III iv 141–148 (in the reconstruction of von Soden), p. 27 Thompson; *ANET* 79; Dalley (1989) 145. *šimatu awilutim* in the Babylonian version X ii 4 p. 53 Thompson. Cf. Gresseth (1975) 14; T. Bauer, *JNES* 16 (1957) 260, who also refers to the expression "to set one's name for people of later times" (*šakin šumim ina niši uhhurati*) in school texts; on Greek-Indo-European ἄφθιτον κλέος see R. Schmitt, *Dichtung und Dichtersprache in indogermanischer Zeit* (1967) 61–69.
39. *Il.* 12.322–328, imitated by Stesichorus S 11 Page-Davies.
40. *Gilgamesh* VI 162 f., *ANET* 85. Bowra (1952) 63 translates "member" of the bull, which might be misleading. For *imittu*, hind leg, see *AHw* 377.
41. *Il.* 22.20.
42. *Od.* 18.136 f., taken up by Archilochos 131–132 West, then by Heraclitus B 17.
43. *Ludlul bel nemeqi* II 43–45; Lambert (1960) 40 f. translates the text *ki pitê u katami*, "like opening and shutting the legs," which may be the original sense, but the commentary on the passage from the library of Assurbanipal (Lambert 40; cf. 291) paraphrases "day and night"; hence *ANET* 435; so this was the way the passage was understood at the time of Archilochos.
44. See M. Lichtheim, *Ancient Egyptian Literature* II (1976) 57–72 on the various versions, the documents—inscriptions and a papyrus text—and the earlier editions.
45. D. Luckenbill, *The Annals of Sennacherib* (1924) 43–47; transcription in Borger (1979) I 83–85; translation in Luckenbill (1926/27) II §§ 252–254. *Il.* 20.498–501.
46. For mercenaries see Chapter I, "Oriental Products in Greece," at notes 63–68. Cf. the conclusions drawn from the bowl of Praeneste (Figure 7), Chapter 3, "The Overpopulated Earth," at note 15 (which also has the chariot for the prince).
47. Judges 4.
48. For Ugarit see H. Gese, *Die Religionen Altsyriens* (1970) 54; Dirlmeier (1955) 25 f.; Jeremiah 2:27; *Il.* 22.126; *Od.* 19.163; Hes. *Theog.* 35.
49. *Od.* 19.107–114: ἀρετῶσι δὲ λαοὶ ὑπ' αὐτοῦ (114); Hes. *Erga* 225–247; Assurbanipal in Streck (1916) II 6 f.; cf. Walcot (1966) 92 f.; Jeffery (1976) 39; West (1978b) 213.
50. See above, Chapter 1, "Loan-Words," note 30. □

❋ ❋ ❋

David Damrosch
"Gilgamesh and Genesis"

David Damrosch is a comparatist who provides "an extended close reading" of *Gilgamesh* in his 1987 work, *The Narrative Covenant: Transformations of Genre in the Growth of Biblical Literature.* While one aim is to appreciate the "beauty" of the *Gilgamesh* poem, Damrosch has a larger purpose in discussing *Gilgamesh:* he wants to reunite literary and historical analyses of ancient texts, to apply "structural and genre analysis to the historical problem of the development of biblical narrative." The chapter in which he considers *Gilgamesh* is, then, not surprisingly, devoted to *Gilgamesh* and Genesis 1–11.

Damrosch's attempt at a new kind of genre study would have been impossible, in the case of *Gilgamesh,* without Jeffrey Tigay's *Evolution of the Gilgamesh Epic.* From Tigay he learned of three major additions to earlier Gilgamesh materials in the late version, and he takes up each one in turn to demonstrate that they have been integrated fully into the larger poem: "Enkidu and the World of Nature," "The Rejection of Ishtar," and "The Flood and the End of the Age of Myth." His analyses are extensive and subtle. They depend on the existence in Mesopotamia of a "creation-flood epic." From that perspective Damrosch can appreciate the transformation of the genre. As one example of his analysis, he eventually ties in the opening of *Gilgamesh* to the three narrative sections he had analyzed, and finds in the opening what he calls "artifactualism," which provides three images unifying the poem: stela, walls, and clothing. (Ed.)

The *Gilgamesh Epic* is the longest and most beautiful of the Mesopotamian epics to have come down to us, and it provides the fullest example of the treatment of historical concerns within the epic tradition. The full richness of this text has rarely been appreciated, as biblical scholars have usually examined it only cursorily as a source for surface parallels to the Flood story. To be genuinely effective, however, a comparison must treat the Mesopotamian text as fully as its biblical counterpart. The first half of this chapter will accordingly develop an extended close reading of the *Gilgamesh Epic*, as only in this way can one properly appreciate both the text's beauty and its relevance to the Bible.

The comparison needs to be developed not only with similar care in both cases, but also with similar methods: like Genesis, the *Gilgamesh Epic* can best be understood through an examination of its historical development.[1] The epic's intricate compositional history has been slighted in accounts that focus on the theme of mortality, which has often been treated as the mark of the Old Babylonian version of the epic, but this theme gradually loses its dominance as the epic develops over the course of the second millennium. The epic's eventual standard form, produced around 1250, interweaves a whole series of themes in a synoptic exploration of the limits and meaning of culture. It is this final form of the epic that is closest in time and in theme to Genesis. Consequently, a close examination of the development of the epic can tell us much about the Bible's debt to the old epic tradition as well as its differences from it. □

In respect of genre, both the *Gilgamesh Epic* and Genesis 1–11 can best be understood in relation to an ancient literary form: the epic story of primordial times, from the creation of human beings to the Flood. Both the *Gilgamesh Epic* and Genesis 1–11 owe much to this genre and also distance themselves from it in its classic forms, through a process of adaptation, suppression, and outright polemic. The creation-flood narrative was a major and long-established genre; surviving examples are found both in Sumerian and in Akkadian. A given epic may range over the whole of this period, with a focus on the Flood, as in the case of the *Atrahasis Epic* and the Sumerian "Flood Story,"[2] or it may concern itself only with primordial history up until the creation of humanity, as in the case of *Enuma elish*. These texts remain closely linked, however, and it could be said that the flood stories represent a historicizing extension into human history of primordial conflicts depicted among the gods in *Enuma elish*.[3] We do not have enough evidence to say whether an older, purely heavenly tradition developed human-history analogues in Sumerian times late in the third millennium, or whether the two variant traditions coexisted from much earlier.[4] In either case, as Claus Westermann says, "the creation and the flood are the themes which occur most often in the stories of primeval times... creation and flood complement each other" (*Genesis 1–11*, 5).

Four fundamental story elements appear in the creation-flood epics: the creation of the world, the creation of human beings, the cataclysm of the Flood, and the establishment of the post-Flood human order, symbolized in the *Atrahasis Epic* by the re-establishment of ritual and in *Enuma elish* by the building of a temple for Marduk in Babylon. All these elements are taken up into Genesis 1–11, though with major thematic alterations, as will be seen below. If Genesis 1–11 develops away from this ancient paradigm, the *Gilgamesh Epic* develops *toward* it. In the process, the text loses its former exclusive emphasis on the problem of death and becomes a wider meditation on the limits from the problem of mortality to the theme of knowledge in Genesis 1–11.

The earliest Gilgamesh stories, in Sumerian, described the heroic adventures of Gilgamesh, who was sometimes accompanied by his servant Enkidu. These unconnected stories were refocused in the Old Babylonian period into an exploration of the problem of mortality. Enkidu is elevated from Gilgamesh's servant to his best friend, enabling the author to unify the epic around the tragedy of Enkidu's early death. As Tigay says, "The epic is not a study of friendship per se. The motif of friendship serves as a device whereby Enkidu's death can be made to shock Gilgamesh into an obsessive quest for immortality" (28). As alternative to the immortality Gilgamesh fails to achieve, the Old Babylonian version suggests a *carpe diem* policy, expressed in a speech by a barmaid. She tells him to eat well, make every day into a feast day, have good clothing, and enjoy his wife and children.[5]

The late version of the epic, though usually viewed as having the same theme, in fact redirects it altogether. The barmaid's hedonistic speech is displaced and de-emphasized, a prologue and epilogue with a broader wisdom perspective are added, and a series of striking additions to the body of the epic expand the scope of the work. Three of these are particularly noteworthy: an extended description of the creation and early life of Enkidu; a marriage proposal from Ishtar to Gilgamesh; and a long account of the Flood, retold by its hero Utnapishtim, whom Gilgamesh visits in search of immortality.

These scenes have usually been viewed as inorganic accretions; even Tigay, who gives a spirited defense of the importance of the increased emphasis on Enkidu, merely notes the new material on Ishtar without attempting to account for it; of the longest addition, the flood story, he suggests only that it serves as a delaying device to heighten our suspenseful interest in knowing how things will work out after the interruption.[6] All three of these additions, however, take on coherent meaning and unified purpose if they are seen in relation to the creation-flood epics; for the consistent effect of these additions is to assimilate the *Gilgamesh Epic* toward this genre.

The remarkable thing about this assimilative process is its occurrence at the very time that the poetic epic tradition reaches its furthest degree of historicizing aspects of the sort noted above in the *Atrahasis Epic* and the *Erra Epic*. These tendencies were developed much further in the late version, but not, as one might have expected, through a simple abandonment of the mythic tradition. Rather, the late version takes up the mythic epic tradition in its fullest form, the creation-flood epic, not in order to demythologize but in order to carry through a far-reaching process of self-definition vis-à-vis the mythic tradition. In this way the late version explores the nature and limits of human culture and history through an explicit process of separation from divine culture and divine ways of acting, as represented in the older creation-flood epics.

This process is of direct value in assessing the relation of Genesis 1–11 to its polytheistic past, as a related effort at separation and self-definition can also be observed there. The similarity here between Genesis and the late version of the *Gilgamesh Epic* is neither a chance occurrence nor necessarily a sign of direct dependence of one tradition on another, but is a natural feature, perhaps almost an inevitable feature, of the self-definition of historical epic as it separates itself from the trans-historical patterns of myth. In this respect, indeed, the *Gilgamesh Epic* has as much in common with the *Iliad* as with Genesis; some of these parallels will be noted below. The *Gilgamesh Epic*, like the opening section of Genesis, is very much a transitional form, and this may indeed be an aspect of its compelling power, as it gains in richness, almost producing an effect of parallax, from the coexistence of elements that had formerly been separated and had now been mixed but not yet collapsed into each other.

Enkidu and the World of Nature

The first major narrative expansion in the late version, the early story of Enkidu, introduces the theme of the definition and meaning of culture. In this instance the epic defines culture against precultural life. Enkidu has become more than just a friend, his Old Babylonian role; now, he begins life as an image of the primitive human being, and his early adventures suggest the forces distinguishing primitive life from "civilization," as exemplified by the city life of Uruk.

At the start of the epic, Gilgamesh is terrorizing his own city-state, oppressing his people in various ways.[7] The nobles pray to the gods, who decide to create Enkidu as a companion for Gilgamesh, to contend with Gilgamesh and quiet him down. Enkidu could simply have been placed at the gate of Uruk, but instead the author uses the episode as an opportunity to meditate on the origins of human culture. Enkidu is created in the form of a primordial man, covered with shaggy hair "like a woman" (I, ii, 36), looking like Nisaba, the goddess of grain. He roams naked across the steppe in the company of the animals, eating grass and drinking at watering holes. In his primitive union with the animals, Enkidu is actually hostile to human culture: he tears up the traps that the shepherds have set for the animals that prey on their sheep. Enkidu has perhaps been made more fully in Gilgamesh's image than the gods had planned: as Gilgamesh disturbs civil order in Uruk, Enkidu disturbs the pastoral order in the countryside.

The shepherds develop a plan, which Gilgamesh ratifies, to separate Enkidu from the animals: they send a temple prostitute to him. He sleeps with her for six days and seven nights. At the end of this time, his powers are diminished, and he cannot run as well as before; still worse, the animals are not afraid of him. If we suspect a hint of a parallel to Eve's seduction of Adam and the loss of Eden, the parallel becomes direct when the harlot speaks to the "fallen" Enkidu: "You are [wi]se, Enkidu, you have become like a god!" (I, iv, 34).[8] Enkidu's sexual knowledge has brought him godlike wisdom and separated him from the state of nature. In this respect the parallel is very close to the Eden story, though with a direct development of the sexual aspect that is only indirectly present in Genesis. The scene in the *Gilgamesh Epic* differs markedly in its effects, however, as society can counter the loss of nature with equal or greater compensations. Seeing Enkidu's new wisdom, the harlot suggests that he should abandon his limited rustic life for the wider scope and greater pleasures of the city:

> "Why with the wild creatures do you roam over the steppe?
> Come, let me lead you [to] ramparted Uruk,
> To the holy temple, abode of Anu and Ishtar,
> Where lives Gilgamesh, accomplished in strength,
> And like a wild bull lords it over the folk."
> As she speaks to him, her words find favor;
> His heart enlightened, he yearns for a friend.
> (I, iv, 35–41)

Thus, though deprived of his animal friends, Enkidu will find in the city a bull-like man for a new companion.

A temple prostitute is a somewhat unusual bearer of wisdom for Near Eastern literature; certainly in the Bible, when Tamar disguises herself in that fashion in order to bring her father-in-law, Judah, to acknowledge his duty, the success of her ruse depends on Judah's not looking for instruction from that corner (Genesis 38). The epic does not altogether endorse the harlot's hedonistic view of the values of the city, in fact, but goes on to show such views as limited (on this, more below). At the same time, the harlot's perspective is perfectly valid, so far as it goes, and suits her limited understanding of the drama she is involved in: presumably she knows that her job is to divert Enkidu from terrorizing the countryside, but presumably only the gods know that her advice serves their larger plan of restoring Gilgamesh to proper behavior.

This dynamic knowledge and concealment is comparable to the problematics of understanding that Meir Sternberg has shown to be at work in various biblical narratives, such as the story of the wooing of Rebekah (*Poetics of Biblical Narrative*, 131–52). It also shows that the Babylonians, at least in their epics, displayed a more complex sense of causality than a simple native faith that one prays to the gods, who give clear and immediate aid. The shepherds, terrified and bewildered by Enkidu, devise a stratagem to neutralize him, with no way of knowing that the gods themselves have created this evil as a way of responding to the prayers of Gilgamesh's oppressed subjects. Indeed, the shepherds' stratagem figures as an essential link in the gods' plot. This complex and ironic view of divine aid in times of crisis is very like the sorts of analysis that will be applied to contemporary history by the biblical historians, and if Near Eastern chronicle rarely (if ever) approached this degree of subtlety, it was because the genres of prose chronicle had an ideological stake in minimizing both divine complexity and human ignorance. When Shalmaneser goes to war, Nergal gives him weapons and Shamash strengthens his arm. Thutmose can take his wretched enemies by surprise but would never be shown to be caught unawares himself. Here, though, even Gilgamesh himself does not know the real story behind the appearance of Enkidu. He cannot know of the gods' purpose in creating Enkidu; further, there is not even any indication that either he or the shepherds anticipate that Enkidu will be brought to the city, a development that is presented purely as the harlot's own initiative. Such a degree of ignorance on the part of a king, and such a degree of dominance by unforeseen contingency, would be unthinkable in the prose chronicles, whereas the Gilgamesh Epic goes out of its way to emphasize these points;

the only function of the scene in which the shepherds ask Gilgamesh to approve of their plan for quieting Enkidu down is to show Gilgamesh unwittingly setting the stage for his own reformation.

Unknown in the prose chronicles, such a scene has no direct equivalent in the older mythic epic tradition either. The Sumerian and Old Babylonian mythic epics were fully alive to paradoxical behavior on the part of the gods, but they focused on timeless patterns and showed relatively little interest in working through issues of divine behavior in response to specific crises in human historical experience. It was left for the confluence of poetic epic and prose history to produce such a scene as this, in which the interaction of different social groups and the very tangible political problem of an irresponsible ruler—the story's hero—are viewed from the perspective of the mysterious complexities of myth.

A corollary to the historicizing of the poetic epic is the beginning of divine withdrawal from direct action in the story, a process clearly visible in the Bible as well. The gods are perfectly able to talk directly, and even to engage in sexual relations, with extraordinary figures like Gilgamesh, but their preference is for indirect dealings. Thus, they create Enkidu rather than intervening in person; later, when Ishtar wishes to harm Gilgamesh, she sends down the Bull of Heaven, an intermediary figure presented almost as a kind of robot. Indirect action is matched by new emphasis on indirect communication: the epic contains numerous dreams, for which the human recipients must seek interpretations. Even though the gods can talk directly to Gilgamesh, they more often communicate even with him in this indirect fashion, a manner clearly resembling people's historical experience of communication with the gods.

The new emphasis on history within the epic tradition has a further corollary in a new interest in the idea of nature. In part, a highlighted nature begins to replace the presence of the withdrawing gods, and in part nature assumes a new authority as the locus of the hidden divine presence. Thus Gilgamesh will provide a substitute for the world of nature Enkidu has lost: in place of his former animal friends, the harlot tells him, he will have a new and better friend in Gilgamesh, who "like a wild bull lords over the folk." Thus the godlike Gilgamesh is also the animal-like Gilgamesh, and as a wild bull he will meet his greatest opponent in the Bull of Heaven sent down by Ishtar. The relation of civilization to the animal world is thus bivalent; it is essentially metaphoric, but the metaphor can move in either direction, and even, as in the example just given, in both directions at once. It can be said that Mesopotamian thought (like much "mythic" thought) sees the world not as a great chain of being but as a great circle. Humanity stands between the gods and the animal world of the divine, metaphorically representing the literal truths of the unseen world of the gods.

Interestingly, Enkidu's transition from the state of nature to life in the city is not direct, but requires an intermediate stage among the pastoralists. The harlot dresses Enkidu, dividing her clothing with him, and leads him to a community of shepherds: "Holding on to his hand,/She leads him like a child" (II, ii, 31–32). The next section (II, iii) describes how, like a baby, Enkidu must learn from the shepherds how to eat solid food, to wear clothing, and to take part in adult activities. Perhaps this is the earliest extant case of the trope, still common in recent times, of viewing primitive culture as childlike.

In opening with this movement away from the childlike state of nature, the epic gives an initial statement of the value of culture. The harlot, urging Enkidu to go to Uruk, praises the city in terms close to the barmaid's *carpe diem* philosophy in the Old Babylonian version. The harlot describes Uruk as a place

> Where people are re[splend]ent in festal attire,
> (Where) each day is made a holiday,
> Where [...] lads...,
> And la[ss]es [..] . of figure.
> Their ripeness [...] full of perfume.
> (I, v, 7–11)

She then praises Gilgamesh's beauty ("He is radiant with manhood, vigor he has./With ripeness gorgeous is the whole of his body," I, v, 16–17) and describes him as even stronger than Enkidu. A fitting friend—or a fitting husband; there are sexual undertones running through the relationship of Gilgamesh and Enkidu. In addition to hearing the praise of clothing, festivity, and erotically charged friendship, Enkidu learns from the shepherds the pleasures of strong drink and of demonstrating his prowess through capturing wolves and lions—a direct contrast to his previous tearing up of traps (II, iii, 10–36).

Implicit in the comparison of primitive life to babyhood is the suggestion that civilized life involves a loss of an unconscious, direct relation to the natural/divine world, but also brings about the gain of an adult, conscious, deliberate relative to the gods. Enkidu now combs (or perhaps sheds) his hair and no longer looks like the goddess of grain, but he can now worship the gods and serve them in ways animals cannot. The very first thing the harlot mentions, in fact, as awaiting Enkidu in Uruk is "the holy temple, abode of Anu and Ishtar" (I, iv, 37). The essential duty of humanity, the reason for which humankind was created, is to serve the gods, supplying them with ritual sacrifices, as we know from *Enuma elish* and the *Atrahasis Epic.* In going to the city, then, Enkidu loses his unconscious similarity to the gods but gains human consciousness of his duty to the gods that animals lack. In service to the gods and to Gilgamesh, he can fulfill his humanity; he becomes wise and godlike, in a change that has both similarities and differences with the Genesis story (on which more below).

Enkidu goes to Uruk, where everyone is struck by his likeness to Gilgamesh:

> The people were gathered,
> Saying about him:
> "He is like Gilgamesh in build!"
> . . . .
> The nobles rejoiced:
> "A hero has appeared
> For the man of proper mien!
> For Gilgamesh, who is like a god,
> His equal has come forth."
> (II, v, 13–15, 23–27)

If Adam is created in God's image, Enkidu is the image of Gilgamesh, who is himself like a god, *kima ilim*, the same phrase used by the harlot to describe Enkidu after she sleeps with him. Barring Gilgamesh's way as he sallies out on one of his nocturnal expeditions, Enkidu wrestles with him.[9] For the first time, Gilgamesh has met his match, and they become fast friends. Enkidu turns Gilgamesh's thoughts toward legitimate exploits of valor, and they make an expedition to a distant mountain, slaying the monster Humbaba and cutting down his precious grove of cedar trees. The scene shows a close interweaving of mythic and historical elements. On the one hand, Humbaba is "a terror to mortals" (III, iv, 2), a divinely created guardian monster, full of elemental strength and mythic resonance; on the other hand, expeditions to cut down cedar trees in distant hill country were a common heroic (or heroic-economic) activity of Mesopotamian kings, described in several chronicles.[10]

In recounting this episode, the late version closely follows the plot of the old Sumerian version of this story, the adventure tale known as "Gilgamesh and the Land of the Living" (*ANET*, 47–50).

The thematic development of the story emphasizes heroic action as a means of gaining fame, which in turn eases the oppressiveness of the prospect of death. The story opens with Gilgamesh explaining to the sun god Utu his reasons for wishing to undertake the expedition:

> O Utu, a word I would speak to you, give your ear to my word,
> [I would have it reach you], give ear to it.
> In my city man dies, oppressed is the heart,
> Man perishes, heavy is the heart.
> I [peered over] the wall,
> I saw the dead bodies… [floating on] the river;
> As for me, I too will be served thus; truly it is so.
> The tallest man cannot reach to heaven,
> The broadest man cannot [cover] the earth.
> Not [(yet) have brick and stamp] brought forth [the fated end];
> I would enter the "land," I would set up my name,
> In its places where the names have been raised up,
>   I would raise up my name,
> In its places where the names have not been raised up,
>   I would raise up the names of the gods.
> (lines 21–33)

Utu allows Gilgamesh to proceed, and he goes off, swearing an oath by his divine mother, Ninsun, and his mortal father, Lugalbanda, not to return without having fought Huwawa (the Sumerian version of "Humbaba"). The body of the tale describes Gilgamesh's fearless heroism and his successful struggle against the monster.

The late version carries on the themes of the fear of death and the virtue of heroism, but fills out these themes within its new preoccupation with the problems of knowledge and of the nature of human culture.[11] In place of Gilgamesh's passing reference to his parents in his oath, the late version gives an entire scene in which Gilgamesh and Enkidu go to Ninsun to ask her to pray to Shamash (the Akkadian name of the sun god) on their behalf. She does so, and her request for Shamash's protection begins with a personal reflection:

> Why, having given me Gilgamesh for a son,
> With a restless heart did you endow him?
> And now you have moved him to go
> On a far journey, to the place of Humbaba,
> To face an uncertain battle,
> To travel an uncertain road!
> (III, ii, 10–15, Assyrian version)

Here the restlessness of mortals faced with the prospect of death is movingly presented through the sorrow of Gilgamesh's immortal mother. The scene is notably close to the scene early in the *Iliad* in which Achilles asks his divine mother, Thetis, to intercede with Zeus for aid in the battle against the Trojans. Thetis's reply to Achilles begins in terms not unlike the beginning of Ninsun's speech to Shamash:

> Thetis answered him then, her tears falling:
> "Oh, my own child; unhappy in childbirth,
> why did I raise you?
> Could you but stay by your ships,
> without tears or sorrow,
> since the span of your life will be brief, of no length."
> (1.413–16)

The Homeric epic goes on to develop the scene much further than the Gilgamesh epic of five hundred years earlier, but the Akkadian epic already presents in an early form a characteristic aspect of the confluence of myth and history: an assessment of human culture from a viewpoint outside that culture. □

* * *

NOTES

1. See Jeffrey Tigay for a discussion of ways in which the evolution of the text of *Gilgamesh* can provide analogies to the evolution of the biblical texts (*Empirical Models*, 21–52).

2. "The Sumerian Flood Story," M. Civil, ed., in Lambert and Millard, *Atra-Ḫasīs*, 138–45, 167–72. Though the text is incomplete, missing its beginning and large sections thereafter, the extant portions describe the initial pre-deluge building of cities and establishment of agriculture, as well as the Flood.

3. Notably, the cause of conflict is the same in each case. In the *Atrahasis Epic*, it is the noisiness of the humans that determines Enlil to destroy them, and in the creation epic, the tumultuous younger gods disturb the rest of the first-generation gods, leading Apsu, the primordial sky god, to exclaim to Tiamat, the sea goddess:

> Their ways are verily loathsome unto me.
> By day I find no relief, nor repose by night.
> I will destroy, I will wreck their ways,
> That quiet may be restored. Let us have rest!
> (*ANET*, 61, lines 37–40)

The beleaguered younger gods, led by Marduk, finally defeat and subdue Tiamat, who figures as their chief opponent, though the hostilities have been initiated by Apsu. As Tiamat is the primordial ocean, this struggle itself is a heavenly version of the human effort to survive the waters of the Flood.

4. The creation epic *Enuma elish*, at least as we now have it, actually appears to be of later date (1600–1200) than the *Atrahasis Epic* (2000-1600) and is Sumerian antecedent. It is thought to have been composed at this late date as a celebration and justification of the new prominence then being given to Marduk. It may have been created purely through a retrojection of Flood motifs into prehuman primordial history, or both strands of tradition may go far back in time, with some variants dealing with the time of creation and other variants setting similar conflicts and themes at the time of the Flood.

5. For the barmaid's speech, see Tigay, *Evolution of the Gilgamesh Epic*, 50. This form of *carpe diem* wisdom was not uncommon in the Near East; particularly good parallels survive from Egyptian, in the genre known as "Harper's Songs"; see Miriam Lichtheim, *Ancient Egyptian Literature*, I, 193–97, and II, 115–16.

6. Unable to see the flood as having any direct connection to the epic, Tigay thus tries to make a narrative virtue of its very irrelevance. Tigay himself is aware that this interpretation is somewhat forced, noting that it is "obviously speculative" (*Evolution*, 240). It is difficult to see suspense as a primary consideration in the text, which begins by giving away its plot. Further, the subsequent "denouement" of the loss of the root of immorality is briefly told, not developed as a dramatic climax; the flood narrative gets much more space. Any retarding effect it may have must be a secondary consequence and not the motivating force for the story's insertion.

7. Gilgamesh's oppression seems likely to include some or all of: forced labor, heterosexual or homosexual rape, and sporting contests in which he as victor would enslave his opponents or their women.

8. The parallel to Genesis may be a little overstated in this translation, as the phrase "you are wise" is a reconstruction. It is, however, a plausible one, followed as well in the German translation of Schott and von Soden, and if true would make a nice folk etymology for "Enkidu" in the word "wise," *enqata;* see further below on the quasi-renaming of Adam as "subtle" at a similar point in the Genesis story. Even apart from the conjectural "you are wise," however, the parallel to Genesis is quite clear enough in the second phrase, "you have become like a god," a phrase repeated when the scene is recapitulated on the next tablet: "As I look at you, Enkidu, you have become like a god" (II, ii, 11).

9. A further parallel to Genesis might be seen in the fact that Enkidu gains acceptance by wrestling with Gilgamesh, just as Israel does in the person of Jacob, renamed "Israel" (He who wrestles with God) after his match with God in the form of the angel (Genesis 32).

10. For example, Tiglath-Pileser I records that Anu and Adad commanded him to journey to Lebanon in c. 1100 to cut cedar beams for their temple (*ANET*, 275). Another ruler, a Mesopotamian king named Yahdun-Lin, describes the journey to the Cedar Mountain as one of the greatest feats of his bold career (*ANET*, 556).

11. The issue of knowledge was first introduced in the Old Babylonian version, in a speech of warning by the elders of Uruk: "You are still young, Gilgamesh, your heart has carried you away./You do not know what you are attempting to achieve" (III, v, 10–11). Knowledge is an issue here, though not yet a problem, for Gilgamesh (foolhardy though he may be) proves to have no difficulty in overcoming Humbaba; it is the elders who are mistaken in believing that Gilgamesh is taking on more than he can handle. □

* * *

Donald Hall
"Praise for Death"

"Praise for Death," which appeared first in *The Gettysburg Review*, was quickly reprinted in *The Best American Poetry 1990*. The poem catalogues death, waste, loss and change in such variety that no single emotion emerges to dominate the meditations for long. From the death of a family friend and of a family cat to the covering over of agricultural land by developers, from a Henry Adams remembering his wife's suicide to the account of a horrible murder witnessed by a wife and young son, the poem snakes through periods of grief and despair and anger. The variety in this catalogue recalls, at times, Enkidu's in Tablet XII.

The "smothered alluvial soil" connects the asphalt of roadways and malls to, perhaps, the most ancient of Hall's references, the "Between-the-Rivers" land the Greeks called Mesopotamia. The story of Gilgamesh frames the poem. In Stanza #5 the King of Uruk is called "dole's aboriginal singer," and in the final three stanzas, Gilgamesh finds his voice. The stanzas are like the Standard Babylonian version, but are not a translation. Lamenting the death of his "blood-brother" Enkidu, Gilgamesh speaks of his wanderings, sleepless, violent, and despairing. In Stanza #37 it is Gilgamesh who articulates the poem's terror that what has happened to Enkidu will happen to Gilgamesh the poet.

Traditionally in the West, elegies end, not with the praise of death, but with consolation in the face of the inevitable. By ending this poem in the voice of Gilgamesh, Hall takes a different turn. When he can no longer deny the reality of death—when "On the ninth day worms crawled from the skin of his neck"—Gilgamesh decides to seek out Utnapishtim, "who alone of all men after the flood lives without dying." Readers of *Gilgamesh* know how that search will end. (Ed.)

1

Let us praise death that turns pink cheeks to ashes,
that reduces father from son and daughter, that sets tears
in the tall widow's eye. Let us praise death that gathers
us loose-limbed and weeping by the grave's edge in the flat
yard near the sea that continues. Let us praise death

2

that fastens my body to yours and renders skin
against skin sometimes intolerably sweet, as October
sweetens the flesh of a McIntosh apple. Let us praise
death that prints snapshots, fixing an afternoon forty
years ago on a shady lane. While we stand holding

3

each other, let us praise death as a dog praises
its master, bowing, paying obeisance, rolling over;
let us praise death as a spaniel praises a pitbull.
What remained of her at the end, compared to my friend
eight months before, was the orange peel to the orange:

4

as if the shard of fruit—once pungent and moist, now smeared
with coffeegrounds—pulsed, opened an eye, and screamed
without stopping. As we enter the passage of agony,
imagining darkness prepared underground, we recollect
Jesus who drank from the cup: "Why have you forsaken me?"

5

Praising death we sing parts with Between-the-Rivers,
with the King of Uruk, dole's aboriginal singer.
The Victorian with his imperial figleaf praises death
like the Inca, or like the first emperor of Qin
who models a deathless army in terra cotta. Let us

6

praise rictus and the involuntary release of excrement
as the *poilu* does, and Attila, and the Vestal Virgin.
We remember the terrified face behind the plexiglass mask
as Hadrian remembers Antinous. Are you rich, young,
lucky, and handsome? Are you old and unknown?

7

Are you Mesopotamian, suburbanite, Cossack, Parisian?
We praise death so much, we endow our children with it.
At seventy-eight, Henry Adams spent the summer of 1916
discussing with Brooks "the total failure of the universe,
most especially *our* country." From London he heard

8

that Harry James was dead, who "belonged to my wife's set,"
he wrote Elizabeth Cameron, "and you know how I cling
to my wife's set." Thirty years before, he discovered Clover,
still warm, her lips damp with potassium cyanide.
"All day today," he wrote, "I have been living in the '70s."

9

By the river abandoned factories tilt like gravestones,
Mills collapse behind broken windows over soil broken
to build them, where millhands wore their lives out
standing in fractured noisy stench among endless belts
and hoses steaming waste to the fish-killing river.

10

Commerce dies, and commerce raises itself elsewhere.
If we read the Boston *Globe* on a Monday, we find fixed
to the business section the part-index: *Deaths, Comics.*
The old father's dignity, as he daily and hourly rehearses
the lines of his pain, stiffens him into a tableau vivant.

11

All day he studies the script of no-desire, scrupulous
never to want what he cannot have. He controls speech,
he controls desire, and a young man's intense blue eyes
look from his face as he asks his grandniece to purchase,
at the medical supply store, rubber pants and disposable pads.

12

Let us praise death that raises itself to such power
that nothing but death exists: not breakfast nor the Long
Island Expressway, not cigarettes nor beaches at Maui,
not the Tigers nor sunrise except under the aspect
of death. Let us praise death that recedes: One day

13

we realize, an hour after waking, that for a whole hour
we have forgotten the dead, so recently gone underground,
whom we swore we would mourn from the moment we opened
our eyes. All night in sleep I watch as the sinewy, angry
body careers and hurtles in harmless air, hovering

14

like a hang glider over the western slope of Kearsarge,
fired from the Porsche that explodes, rips open, settles,
and burns while the body still twists in the air, arms
akimbo, Exxon cap departing frail skull, ponytail out
straight, until it ends against granite. Let us praise

15

death that bursts skull, lungs, spleen, liver, and heart.
Let us praise death for the piano player who quit high school
in 1921 and played *le jazz hot* through France and Italy;
who recorded with *Lud Gluskin et son Jazz* four hundred
sides of a barrellhouse left hand; who jammed with Bix

16

at Walled Lake in 1930; who tinkled foxtrots for Goldkette
and Weems, suitcase depression nights of Wilkes-Barre
and Akron; who settled down to play clubs, give lessons,
run the musician's Local, and when he died left
a thousand books behind, with the markers still in them.

17

Let us praise the death of dirt. The builder tells us
that the most effective way to preserve topsoil
is to pave it over. Peterson's farm in Hamden raised
corn, beans, and tomatoes for sale at New Haven's markets.
For a hundred years they ripened in Adams Avenue's

18

countryside among the slow cattle of dairy farms.
Now slopes extrude hairy antennae; earth conceals itself
under parking lots and the slimy, collapsing sheds
of STOP&SHOP, BROOKS, BOB'S, CALDOR, AND CRAZY EDDIES.
The empire rots turning brown. Junkyards of commerce

19

slide into tar over dirt impervious to erosion, sun, wind,
and the breaking tips of green-leafed, infrangible corn.
Beside his right eye and low on his neck shiny patches of skin
blaze the removed cancer. The fifty-year-old poet and I
drink seltzer together in the Grasshopper Tavern; he rants

20

like Thersites denouncing his Greeks. Probably it won't
kill him, but toadstool up each year: "*I want*" —he looks
longingly; desire remakes his face—"*I want so much to die.*"
Let us never forget to praise the deaths of animals:
The young red tomcat—long-haired, his tail like a fox's,

21

with bird feathers of fur upstarting between his toes,
who emitted a brief squeak of astonishment, like the sound
squeezed from a rubber doll, when he jumped to the floor
from a high bookcase; who rattled a doorknob trying to open
a door for himself; who, if we then opened the same door,

22

declined our absurd, well-meaning suggestion that he use it;
who bounced and never walked; who moused assiduously
and lacking mice ripped out carpet pads for swatting;
who spent most waking hours birdwatching from the pantry
window; who sprawled upside down in our arms, splaying

23

long legs stiffly out, great ruffled tail dangling—
abruptly wasted and died of liver failure: We buried him
this morning by the barn, in the cat's graveyard
under blue asters, tamping dirt down over a last red ear.
Downstairs her nieces gather weeping among soft chairs

24

while neighbors bring casseroles and silence;
in the bedroom the widower opens the closet door
where her dresses hang, and finds one hanger swaying.
At Blackwater Farm beside Route 4 the vale bellies
wide from the river, four hundred acres of black dirt

25

over glacial sand, where Jack and his uncles spread
a century of cow manure. They milked their cattle
morning and night, feeding them grain, silage, and hay
while the renewable sisters drank at the river's edge,
chewed cuds, bore yearly calves, bounced and mooed

26

to praise each other's calving, and produced a frothing
blue-white Atlantic of Holstein milk. Yesterday the roads
went in, great yellow earthmachines dozing through loam
to sand, as Jack's boy Richard raises fifty Colonial Capes
with two-car garages and driveways, RIVERVIEW MEADOW FARMS

27

over smothered alluvial soil. "Death tends to occur,"
as the Professor actually said, "at the end of life."
When I heard that his daughter coming home from her job
found Clarence cold in his bed, I remembered the veiny
cheeks and laconic stories: For one moment I mourned him.

28

Then I felt my lungs inflate themselves deeply, painfully:
I imagined my own body beneath the disordered quilt.
For the first time in a year I felt myself collapse
under the desire to smoke. Like you, I want to die:
We praise death when we smoke, and when we stop smoking.

29

After the farmer fired him, the drunk farmhand returned
at nightfall and beat him to death with a tire iron
while his wife and six-year-old son stood watching.
As his father's body flopped in the wet sand, as blood
coiled out of ears, the boy—who had observed

30

hens without heads, stuck pigs, and a paralyzed mule
twitching in a stall—cried, "Die! Please die. Please."
Let us praise St. Nihil's Church of the Suburban Consensus;
at St. Nihil's we keep the coffin closed for the funeral;
when we take communion at St. Nihil's, the Euphemism melts

31

in our mouths; *pass, pass away, sleep, decease, expire.*
Quickly by shocking fire that blackens and vanishes,
turning insides out, or slowly by fires of rust and rot,
the old houses die, the barns and outbuildings die.
Let us praise death that removes nails carpenters hammered

32

during the battle of Shiloh; that solves the beam-shape
an adze gave an oak tree; that collapses finally
the settler's roof into his root cellar, where timber sawn
two centuries ago rots among weeds and saplings. Let us
praise death for the house erected by skill and oxen.

33

Let us praise death in old age. Wagging our tails,
bowing, whimpering, let us praise sudden crib-death
and death in battle: Dressed in blue the rifleman charges
the granite wall. Let us praise airplane crashes.
We buried thirty-year-old Stephen the photographer

34

in Michigan's November rain. His bony widow Sarah, pale
in her loose black dress, leaned forward impulsively
as the coffin, suspended from a yellow crane, swayed
over the hole. When she touched the shiny damp maple
of the box, it swung slightly away from her

35

as it continued downward, Stephen's mother Joan
knelt first to scrape wet dirt onto the coffin lid;
then his father Peter lifted handfuls and let them drop,
then his sister Sarah, then his widow Sarah. Under
scraggly graveyard trees, five young gravediggers stood

36

smoking together, men tattooed and unshaven, wearing
baseball caps, shifting from foot to foot, saying
nothing, trying never to watch in Michigan's November rain.
"Bitterly, bitterly I weep for my blood-brother Enkidu.
Should I *praise* master death that commanded my friend?

37

"I wander hunting in the forest weeping salt tears;
in my anger I slaughter the deer. Bitterly I cry:
'Nowhere can I lay my head down to rest or to sleep!
Despair sucks my liver out! Desolation eats bitter meat
from my thigh! What happened to my brother will happen to me.'

38

"I stood by his body eight days. I implored him to throw
death over, to rise and pull his gold breastplate on.
On the ninth day worms crawled from the skin of his neck.
Now, therefore, I climb to the sun's garden, to Utnapishtim
who alone of all men after the flood lives without dying."

* * *

Stephanie Dalley
"Gilgamesh in the Arabian Nights"

Stephanie Dalley is an Assyriologist translator of *Gilgamesh* and other Mesopotamian narratives, who has been able to trace the influence of *Gilgamesh* not only beyond ancient Mesopotamia but into medieval literature. Her main interest in the essay is the complex tale found in the *1001 Nights,* or the Arabian Nights, "The Tale of Buluqiya." (Since the name Gilgamesh should probably be read Bilgamesh, Buluqiya may itself point to the hero of *Gilgamesh.*)

The remarkable persistence of *Gilgamesh* through not only the Dead Sea scrolls and a tradition of Manichaean storytelling but into the Arabian Nights illustrates the tenacity of important stories and motifs in very different ages and cultures. Dalley's careful examination of the evidence for Gilgamesh and Enkidu in "The Tale of Buluqiya" is matched by her meticulous care in comparing and contrasting Akkadian and much later Arabic stories. In *Gilgamesh* and "The Tale of Buluqiya," a king/hero travels with a faithful companion on a journey that takes him to cosmic regions, where, after the loss of his companion, the hero encounters a sage-like human who has been changed into an immortal. A plant of rejuvenation is offered to the hero as an alternative to immortality, but the plant is lost. Buluqiya is a "typical apocalyptic hero" like Enoch, Solomon, Daniel, or Noah; and Dalley points out how the name Gilgamesh appears in the *Book of Enoch.* In addition to her handling of textual and historical evidence for the persistence of Gilgamesh in later times, Dalley makes the point that, until recently, the West has resisted the idea that the Semitic East has had much influence on Indo-European thought and literature. (Ed.)

It is difficult to lose a good story. Many of the best folk tales transcend the boundaries of language and nationality, and the Gilgamesh Epic, attested in Hurrian, Hittite, Elamite and Akkadian cuneiform, is no exception. The latest Akkadian tablets to be inscribed with the story come from the site of Uruk of the late Babylonian period, some time after the fall of Babylon in 539 B.C. and perhaps as late as the Seleucid period,[1] after the reign of Alexander the Great. The story had been popular for some two thousand years. Despite this popularity in so many countries and for such a very long period of time, the story of Gilgamesh was supposed to have died more or less with the death of cuneiform writing, although some residual themes were recognized in various versions of the Alexander Romance.[2]

J. Tigay, in his book *The Evolution of the Gilgamesh Epic*, expressed surprise that so little evidence had survived for the continuing development of the Epic after the late Babylonian period; and from the slight references which he found to Gilgamesh after that time he was forced to suppose that the story might not have survived the death of the cuneiform system of writing, even though the names of the main characters had been found among fragments of the Dead Sea scrolls.[3] Although he collected evidence which showed a continually evolving oral tradition in early antiquity during the late third and second millennia B.C., such as might have indicated that the story was not simply dependent on the written tradition of cuneiform texts, no evidence seemed to be available to show that such an evolution continued into later times.[4] That Islamic scholars had identified the great sage of Islamic lore, al-Khidr "The Green Man" as Atra-hasis, the Babylonian Noah, was ignored by Tigay and indeed by Assyriologists in general.[5] E. Littmann referred to motifs from the *Epic of Gilgamesh* in the journeys of Buluqiya in the Arabian Nights, transmitted through Jewish literature, but his insight passed unnoticed by cuneiformists.[6]

Certainly other tales from antiquity survived the downfall of ancient Mesopotamian civilization. The Flood story not only had an important part to play in the Hebrew book of Genesis and was translated into Greek in the Septuagint; it had also been recognized, somewhat altered, in the Greek myth of Deucalion, of which a particular version local to Hierapolis in Syria is narrated by Lucian of Samosata in the second century A.D. He tells how the flood waters disappeared down a rift in the bedrock which underlay the great temple of the Syrian Goddess there.[7] Other Flood stories were current in Phrygia in the Roman period, again with local color added: the biggest hill in the vicinity was named Mt. Ararat.[8] From indisputable evidence in stories about Gilgamesh, the principle has been established that a single story may exist in different versions with different geographical locations. This means that details of place, however specific they may be, cannot be used to pinpoint the country where the story was first composed, and are not significant in making connections between stories.

Ever since the Arabian Nights were first translated into English, two folk-tales from the Odyssey: the tale of Polyphemus the man-eating giant who lived in a cave, and the story of Circe the enchantress who could turn men into beasts by tempting them with magic food, have been recognized as recurring, in altered form, in the third and fourth voyages of Sindbad the Sailor, stories which found a new location in Basra during medieval Islamic times.[9] The Middle Egyptian *Tale of the Shipwrecked Sailor*, composed at least as early as the Middle Bronze Age and presumably set in the East Mediterranean, is a clear forerunner of a voyage of Sindbad the Sailor, particularly the seventh, transposed to a location further in the East.[10]

A story theme that bridges the gap between ancient Greek and Akkadian has long been recognized: in the Odyssey of Homer the episode of Odysseus and Calypso bears some strong resemblances to the episode of Gilgamesh and the ale-wife Siduri: the sorrowing hero is befriended by a goddess who dispenses food and drink, and has to cut down timber before sailing on to the next location, where he meets a man of immortal status, Alkinoos in Greek, Ut-napishtim in Akkadian.[11]

Two echoes from Akkadian literature have already been recognized in Arabian Nights stories. The ancient custom of putting a substitute king upon the throne when a particular eclipse presaged the king's death, the substitute being eventually put to death in the king's stead, may be attested in the story of Abu-l-Hasan, or *The Sleeper Awakes.*[12] A satirical, humorous story told at the expense of authority, known as *The Poor Man of Nippur* in Akkadian, has been recognized as one given by Richard Burton in his supplemental stories under the title, *The History of the First Larrikin*;[13] it is the tale of how a poor man, ill-treated by the Mayor of Nippur, by a series of tricks which play on the mayor's obsequious treatment of wealthy people, extracts fitting revenge for his humiliation.

The Tale of Buluqiya is known in at least three rather different versions in Arabic, and some of the changes that have taken place in it can be traced to various sources. To trace the transition of a story across the gap of so many centuries and cultures, and to prove that resemblances are not mere coincidence, presents difficulties of method, for there are very few objective criteria. Other difficulties arise for historical reasons: there has long been a certain traditional resistance among many western Europeans to any close links between Semitic and Indo-European material, a prejudice that dates at least from the Renaissance. In addition, cuneiform Akkadian literature has generally been studied by people trained in the Classics and the Old Testament, with the result that Islamic links in particular are scarcely recognized. Three strands of method: overall story line, phonetic transmission or else translation of personal names,[14] and certain close similarity in points of detail, can each be used to show that the story of Buluqiya is a descendant of the *Epic of Gilgamesh.* □

The story of Buluqiya in Arabic

The Arabic story of Buluqiya as preserved in collections of the 1001 Nights is set in the kingdom of the Banu Israil. It is known in at least two, very different versions, the first from unknown sources used by Mardrus for his translation into French and translated from French into English by Mathers,[15] and the second the Bulaq manuscripts of Calcutta used by Sir Richard Burton for his translation into English.[16]

Mardrus was a cosmopolitan and well-traveled physician, whose attractive and popular translations have been criticized severely by scholars of Arabic. Not only is his translation inaccurate, but also he adapted certain episodes to appeal to a western, European audience, and reinterpreted nuances of social custom that he did not understand. This has been demonstrated for stories taken from the Calcutta edition of the Arabic text used also by Burton, and his claim to have used other sources has been doubted because it has never been substantiated.[17] The claim may be impossible to prove, for some manuscripts of the Nights were destroyed by puritanical Muslims who thought the stories gave a bad impression of Islam,[18] and others may have been destroyed by time, accident and neglect.

In the case of this particular story, however, there are certain episodes in which Mardrus's translation alone finds parallels in the *Gilgamesh Epic* which were not known when he published his translations, and it seems impossible that he could have invented them by accident. Moreover, neither mistranslation nor fashionable elaboration explain why Mardrus's version diverges from Burton and Tha'labi in, for instance, setting the story in a time when Greek was spoken, or in describing Buluqiya and 'Affan traversing the Seven Seas together before the main heroic episode, in contrast to Burton and Tha'labi who describe his traversing the Seven Seas alone after the main heroic episode in which 'Affan dies. There is no alternative open to the present writer (who is, in any case, not an Arabist) to using Mardrus's version (in its English translation by Mathers) with a strong warning that Mardrus may, in this story as in others, have translated unreliably and may have omitted, shortened or elaborated passages according to his own taste and imagination.

In Mardrus's version the basic story is of the hero Buluqiya, who becomes king of the Sons of Israel at the death of his father, and finds in the palace a gold box in an ebony casket on a white marble column containing parchment written in Greek. The text gives instructions how to obtain the magic ring of Solomon which bestows power over all living things, and immortality. His advisers recommend him to set out with the wise man 'Affan. The two men travel through the desert to the subterranean kingdom of Queen Yamlika, who gives them magic juice from a plant. This enables them to walk across the Seven Seas to Solomon's tomb. They reject her advice to give up their plan and to be content with another plant which gives eternal youth to those who eat it. After marvelous journeys across the Seven Seas, Buluqiya and 'Affan arrive at the Isle of the Seven Seas with apple trees which are guarded by an enormous giant who does not allow them to eat the fruit. On the island they find the tomb of Solomon in a cave and find the corpse wearing the ring lying in great splendor. Their courage nearly fails, but then 'Affan plucks up courage and approaches the body, leaving Buluqiya to pronounce conjurations. But Buluqiya in the moment of stress says the words backwards, whereupon a drop of liquid diamond falls upon 'Affan and reduces him and the precious plant juice to a handful of dust. Buluqiya runs out of the cave and wanders around alone and despairing. An army of demonic creatures gallops aggressively up and spirits him off over a fabulous distance to the kingdom of King Sakhr, king of the demon world, which lies behind the cosmic mountain Qaf. Sakhr entertains him with a feast, and then tells him the story of the world's origins. For the first time the narrative becomes Islamic: Allah created the world for the coming of Muhammad the Prophet and for the punishment of infidels. Sakhr himself will never grow old and die, for he has drunk from the Fountain of Life which is guarded by the sage al-Khidhr. When Sakhr has finished explaining, he has Buluqiya spirited straight back to his own kingdom.

In Burton's version Buluqiya is king of the sons of Israel, but he lives in Cairo. At his father's death he finds a secret book concealed in a gold box in an ebony casket resting on a white marble column, which tells not of the Ring of Solomon, but of the coming of Muhammad, so he plans to set out on his travels in order to foregather with the Prophet. His mother tries unsuccessfully to dissuade him. At this stage, still alone, for 'Affan has not entered the story, he sets out by boat for Syria, but becomes stranded and abandoned on an island, for the ship sets sail while he sleeps. He meets giant serpents who praise Allah and Muhammad and tell him about plans for heaven and hell. Buluqiya is inspired, finds another ship and lands on a second island where he meets the Queen of the Serpents who also knows that Muhammad will come. He goes on to Jerusalem, and there he meets 'Affan who knows about Solomon's ring and about the magic juice of the plant that enables men to walk over the sea, which the Queen of the Serpents can find for them. When they have the ring they will be able to drink from the Water of Life in the Main of Murks (not the Fountain of Life) and so remain alive to see the coming of Muhammad. They set off together back to the second island, capture the Queen of Serpents in a cage, make her show them the magic plant, prepare the juice and then release the Queen. She tries to dissuade them, saying that the ring is not for them, and they would have done better to take another plant which would enable them to live until the First Blast. They leave in a penitent spirit and she goes back to Mount Qaf. Then Buluqiya and 'Affan travel across the Seven Seas with the help of the magic juice and find the tomb of Solomon guarded by a terrible serpent. In spite of conjurations uttered by both heroes, when 'Affan tries to take the ring he is blasted to ashes by the serpent's fiery breath. Buluqiya faints, and is rescued by the angel Gabriel. Gabriel advises him that he cannot obtain the ring nor drink from the Fountain of Life. Buluqiya travels on alone and repentant, still using the magic juice, back over the Seven Seas and has an adventure on each one. Finally he arrives on an island with apple trees guarded by a giant, who will not let him eat the fruit, and says it belongs to King Sakhr. When Buluqiya has told his story, the giant allows him to eat and then to travel on. He meets an army of King Sakhr's mounted warriors, who take him to see Sakhr beyond Mount Qaf. Sakhr gives him a feast and tells him about the world's origins, and about the seven hells, but does not continue with information about other features of the cosmos, as happened in Mardrus's version. Instead, he sends Buluqiya on a tour to regions beyond the everyday world, to meet other immortal beings from whom he hears how Mount Qaf encircles the earth, and about the sea of eternity, and the Day of Judgement. These cosmic travels with introductions to angels at the highest level are absent from Mardrus's version, and form a significant and detailed part of Burton's version.

Certain particular features in this story are quite different from those of Mardrus's version. Cairo, Syria and Jerusalem "The Holy City" are all named, whereas Mardrus's version named no placenames. Burton's version names four angels: Gabriel, Israfil,

Michael and Azrail, whereas Mardrus's version had no angels at all. Al-Khidhr is briefly mentioned as guardian of the Fountain of Life in Mardrus's version, but plays no part at all in Burton's story. Buluqiya does not return home at the end of Burton's version.

A third version of the story of Buluqiya comes not from any collection of Arabian Nights, but from the writings of Tha'labi who died in A.D. 1036 in the composition called *'Ara'is al-majalis.*[19] This version gives an early date to the composition; moreover, it attributes it to a Jewish companion of Muhammad, Abdallah ibn Salam. This evidence, if reliable, would indicate from an Arabic source that the story is pre-Islamic. Buluqiya's father is named as Ushiya (Josiah) king of Israel, but living in Egypt. At his death Buluqiya finds writings in an iron box which tell of Muhammad's coming. He obtains consent from his mother to travel to Syria to find out more. On his way he meets serpents who confirm the coming of Muhammad; they are guarded by Tamlikha, a small yellow serpent, who sends her greetings to Muhammad should Buluqiya ever meet him. Buluqiya arrives in Jerusalem, meets 'Affan and they set off together. They catch Tamlikha in a cage, and come across a tree which voluntarily tells them it contains magic juice with which they can travel the Seven Seas. They cut it down, take the juice and let Tamlikha free. With the help of the juice they cross two seas and come to the cave where a body lies on a golden throne guarded by a serpent. 'Affan recognizes it as Solomon's, and knows the ring's significance; he wants to take it in order to stay alive until Muhammad's coming. Buluqiya reminds him that nobody might have as much power as Solomon until the Day of Resurrection, but 'Affan dismisses his objection and goes to take the ring. The serpent warns him off and breathes at him, but Buluqiya pronounces Allah's name and averts harm. Gabriel descends and distracts Buluqiya, so that the serpent's fiery breath succeeds in incinerating 'Affan. After a brief conversation Gabriel departs, and Buluqiya resumes his quest, still using the magic juice. He crosses six seas without elaboration. On the seventh he reaches an island where he is menaced by warriors, but when he says the name of Allah they are respectful and introduce him to their king Sakhr, who tells him how jinns were created. Buluqiya leaves and in a tour of the cosmos meets a series of pious angels. Eventually he meets al-Khidhr, who arranges for him to be transported home to mother on the back of a white bird.

This version has no giant guarding trees, no jewel garden, no offer of a plant of rejuvenation as a second-best offer, and no Fountain of Life or Water of Life. Buluqiya does not feast with the demon king Sakhr; the secret document is found in an iron casket locked with an iron key, not a gold box in an ebony casket; the angels named are: Gabriel, Yuhayil, Michael, Hazqiyael and Israfil; the sad youth mourning at the tomb is an integral part of the story, not the following, separate, story. Notable also is the fact that Buluqiya recites the Torah; the coming of the prophet Muhammad is to be appended to the Torah, and Hell, which is full of serpents and scorpions, is not described as a place for Jews and Christians. The story is fully committed to the coming of Muhammad from the beginning, and several episodes that are comparable to episodes in the *Epic of Gilgamesh* are omitted.

The Akkadian and Arabic Stories Compared

The Akkadian and Arabic stories can be compared in outline for similarities as follows. A king leaves his country and travels far abroad with one faithful companion, searching for immortality. As a result of bravery in a heroic but sacrilegious feat, the faithful companion dies, leaving the king to travel on alone, and to visit cosmic regions peopled by immortal individuals. A plant that confers rejuvenation is unsuccessfully proffered as an alternative to immortality. The hero finds that he cannot attain immortality, although he meets a sage-like figure who has made the transition from mortal to immortal.

The two personal names Buluqiya and al-Khidhr can be connected with extreme antiquity. Buluqiya is not an Arabic name, nor is it a name for a king of Israel, even though Tha'labi's version calls him son of Josiah. The name can be explained as a hypocoristic of Gilgamesh's name in a pronunciation attested both in Sumerian and in Hurrian: Bilgamesh.[20] In the element *bilga* the third consonant exhibits a standard change, from G to unvoiced K, the Akkadian hypocoristic ending *-ya* is added, and the second element *mesh* is omitted. The name Gilgamesh is presumed to be Sumerian, although it does not conform to any clear type of name in that language. The affix *-ya* is typical of Akkadian names, and it corresponds very closely to the Sumerian hypocoristic affix *-mu*.[21] The ending *-ya* is, however, capable of an alternative interpretation; as a short, theophoric element standing for Yahweh. This analysis would give credence to the secondary use of the name for a supposedly Israelite king, even though no such king is named in the Bible.[22] If this is the correct explanation of the name, it would imply that the pronunciation Bilgamesh continued alongside Gilgamesh during the first millennium B.C. Vowel changes in abbreviated Akkadian names are regularly found, such as Šūzubu from Mušēzib-Marduk.[23] This analysis of Buluqiya as a form of Gilgamesh goes hand in hand with the choice of Mesopotamia's most famous hero for showing that the coming of Muhammad was preordained. Pseudo-prophecies such as this are always put into the mouths of famous men of old, to give them the stamp of authority.[24]

Although some Islamic scholars have accepted that al-Khidhr is a re-interpretation of Atra-hasis as the epithet of the ark-builder who survived the Flood in the epics of *Atra-hasis* and *Gilgamesh*, as already mentioned, the evidence should not be used in connection with the story of Buluqiya without some reassessment of its validity.[25]

The Babylonian epithet Atra-hasis is applied not only to the survivor of the Flood, Ut-napishtim, but also to the entirely different sage Adapa-Oannes: both are semi-divine figures of Mesopotamian mythology who begin life as mortals but then achieve some kind of immortality. The connection with the Ugaritic demi-god *kṯr-w-ḫss* is a distant one, yet there are points of contact. In the first place, the epithet *hasīs* has been used for yet another sage-like character. In the second place Philo of Byblos describes the god as Chousor who was the first to sail in boats, an attribute that may be compared with the boat-building and sailing of Ut-napishtim, and with the profession of Adapa the fisherman. Most of all, Philo emphasizes that Chousor was a mortal who was deified because of his notable achievements, and this description puts *kṯr-w-ḫss* into the same category as Ut-napishim and Adapa.[26] The first two consonants of the word *ktr* have certainly not been transferred directly into Ugaritic from Akkadian; *atra* appears to mean "extra" from the root *wtr* whereas *ktr* would be cognate with Akkadian kāšir, either *kāšir* or *kašīr* "renewer or renewed,"[27] a meaning which is earlier and preferable to the widely quoted "successful." In Arabic *khadhir* means "green," for which an Akkadian cognate word is *haṣartu*. The similarity between the three elements *atra*, *kṯr* and *khadhir* is therefore superficial, and could only be explained as transmission by invoking a re-interpretation each time that altered the consonants slightly. Attributes of *kṯr-w-ḫss* as builder and metalworker have emerged from Ugaritic myths; from Philo's information we know of his sea-going, which is a major attribute also of al-Khidhr, and of his original mortality and eventual deification.

The main way in which al-Khidhr can be identified as Ut-napishtim is through an episode in the Alexander Romance. It has been accepted[28] that Alexander is identified there in part with

Gilgamesh: he is searching for immortality, he travels through a Land of Darkness, he crosses Mt MSS (Syriac version, taken as a phonetic rendering of Akkadian Mašum through Greek Masios),[29] and he fails to find and drink from the Fountain or Water of Life, whereas his guide al-Khidhr succeeds in doing so. Thus the connections are: al-Khidhr begins as a mortal and ends as god; Alexander meets him at a specific stage on his travels, and the overarching theme of that section of the Romance consists of a quest for immortality.[30]

Individual episodes and minor themes can also be compared. The episode of obtaining Solomon's ring has replaced the slaying of Humbaba as the heroic centerpiece, although a large vestige of Humbaba is still recognizable in the giant who guards the apple trees; in the Mardrus version he is still in the vicinity of the main heroic episode, whereas in the Burton version he has shifted to a later episode, is named Sharakhiya, and lives in the kingdom of King Sakhr. The replacement of the main heroic episode is undoubtedly the main reason why Buluqiya has so long remained unrecognized as Gilgamesh.

A brief episode found in Mardrus's version but not in Burton offers a very close and specific comparison with the Akkadian version. After the heroes set out on their adventures, 'Affan drew a magic circle around Buluqiya. Yamlika is speaking:

> Followed by the learned 'Affan he (Buluqiya) left the city and journeyed into the desert. Only when they had gone some way did Affan say to him: "Here is the propitious place for those conjurations which will show us our way." They halted; Affan drew a magic circle about him in the sand, and, after performing certain rituals, brought to light the spot which was the entrance, on that side, to my subterranean kingdom.

This curious incident can be compared with one in *Gilgamesh* tablet IV, where the heroes have traveled 50 leagues into the desert on their way to find Humbaba:

"Gilgamesh went up on to the mountain / And made his flour-offering to [ ], (saying), / 'O mountain, bring me a dream, a favorable one.' / Enkidu arranged it for him, for Gilgamesh. A dust-devil passed by, and fixed [ ]. / He made him lie down inside the circle."

The comparison shows, I think, that Mardrus cannot have invented his version from his own imagination. This part of the Gilgamesh epic was not yet known when he published his translations.

A less specific comparison of incidents can be made with the Jewel Garden and the Cosmic Mountain, both quite common in other Arabian Nights stories. It occurs in the Mardrus version when the hero wanders afar after the tragic death of his friend, and reaches the dwelling of King Sakhr behind Mount Qaf, the cosmic mountain of Islamic tradition.

"He found this to be a magnificent plain, seamed with canals having gold and silver beds. The floor of it was covered with musk and saffron and it was shaded with artificial trees whose leaves were emeralds and their fruit rubies."

In the ninth tablet of *Gilgamesh* the hero wanders afar after the tragic death of his friend, and travels along a tunnel through the inaccessible cosmic mountain Mashum, emerging into a garden where:

"Carnelian bore fruit,/Hanging in clusters, lovely to look at,/ Lapis lazuli bore foliage,/Bore fruit, and was delightful to view."

The obvious difference is that carnelian and lapis lazuli are replaced by rubies and emeralds, which were unknown to the ancient Mesopotamians. The two stories describe the two most precious gemstones of each culture, transferring the terms rather than translating them, although these themes could perhaps be regarded as part of the Arab story-teller's repertory rather than indicating direct connections between the Akkadian Gilgamesh and the Arabic Buluqiya stories.

Another episode is that which concerns the juice of the magic plants. Buluqiya and 'Affan have to obtain from Yamlika the juice from a magic plant which, when rubbed upon the soles of the feet, enables men to walk over the sea. In *Gilgamesh* IV, vi in a broken context, Gilgamesh says to Enkidu:

"My friend, experienced in conflict, who has... battle, You have rubbed yourself with plants so you need not fear death."

The comparison shows that magic juice is used in both Gilgamesh and Buluqiya, but probably with different purposes.

In the *Epic of Gilgamesh* the wife of Ut-napishtim offers the hero a chance to obtain the plant of rejuvenation. He accepts the offer but loses the plant. In Burton's version Yamlika offers, as an alternative to the plant with magic juice, another plant which will allow the heroes to live until the First Blast, but they refuse it. In Mardrus's version Yamlika offers a plant which bestows eternal youth, but they reject her advice to find it. In this respect too, Mardrus's version is close to the *Epic of Gilgamesh.*

In Mardrus's version, Sakhr has drunk the Water of Life and become immortal, and the Water of Life is guarded by al-Khidhr. In the *Epic of Gilgamesh* Ut-napishtim has become immortal and lives at the Mouth of the Rivers. Both episodes introduce the hero who hopes for immortality to the man who has become immortal; the latter explains to the hero that his hopes are vain, despite his efforts in the main heroic episode and his solitary travels.

The hidden document that causes Buluqiya to set off on his travels may be an expansion and reinterpretation of the reference in the prologue to *Gilgamesh* in which the audience is invited to take a lapis lazuli tablet out of its locked box and read its secrets.[31]

A series of interviews with non-mortal individuals, each time introduced by a formulaic, repetitious dialogue, is common to *Gilgamesh* IX and X, as well as to the two Arabic stories; both follow the death of the hero's friend. The perfunctory end to the main Gilgamesh epic, tablet XI, has often been remarked upon as unsatisfactory. The hero's homecoming is expressed in three lines:

"At 20 leagues they ate a ration. At 30 leagues they stopped for the night. They reached Uruk the Sheepfold."

In Mardrus's version Buluqiya takes his leave of King Sakhr, and "mounting astride the shoulders of a very strong Jinni, was carried in a flash of time through space and set down gently upon earth he knew, near the frontier of his own country." The ending in Burton's version is less satisfactory; the story just fades into the tale of Janshah.

There are, of course, many very important differences between the Akkadian and the Arabic stories. Most striking, perhaps, is that the theme of a quest for immortality, to win fame and to escape death in the *Epic of Gilgamesh*, is reused as a means by which the famous hero of extreme antiquity can survive to witness the coming of Muhammad. In this way the story becomes a pseudo-prophecy for the prophet's coming. Other major differences are: the Arabic story has no dreams, no gods and goddesses, 'Affan is a wise sage, not a wild man with savage origins, and the heroes do not actually kill anyone or anything. The story of the Flood, which is thought to have been included in the *Epic of Gilgamesh* only at a late stage, does not feature in the Arabic story. The quest for immortality begins at a later stage in the *Epic of Gilgamesh* than in the tale of Buluqiya. From a literary point of view, the Buluqiya story lacks the development of character and the tensions which make the *Gilgamesh Epic* an appealing work to the modern reader. Buluqiya is, by contrast with Gilgamesh, a static character who serves only to connect together a long series of disparate episodes and introduce the audience to various demons and angels. He is also totally devoid of the sexual interest which is so strong a feature in the early part of the *Gilgamesh Epic.*

In the Akkadian epic, the Water of Life does not occur. The hero hopes first to obtain fame through noble deeds and bravery, then to find out from Ut-napishtim how to become immortal, and then to use the plant of rejuvenation. Yet in the Arabic tale of Buluqiya, as in legends about Alexander the Great, the hero hopes to obtain immortality by drinking the Water of Life, sometimes to be found at a fountain. An Akkadian myth known as *Ishtar's Descent to the Underworld*, which shares its opening passage with lines in the *Epic of Gilgamesh*, does, however, mention the Water of Life: it is to be found in a waterskin in the Underworld where its use will revive the corpse of a goddess. The parallel is not a close one, for in the Akkadian myth the water has the power to bring a dead goddess back to life, whereas in the Arabic story it can give a living mortal immortality. In Akkadian, the concept is closely linked to the funerary custom of pouring cold water in regulation libations to satisfy the ghosts of the dead. The other epic in which the Water of Life is attested is the Story of Adapa, the first sage, whose epithet *atra-hasis* was discussed above. In that story the sage refuses the water of life when he is offered it in heaven, for he believes that it is the Water of Death. Since the end of the story is not yet extant, we do not know whether Adapa was allowed a second chance and became immortal, although it appears to be true that all antediluvian sages were regarded as immortal.

Differences between the Akkadian *Gilgamesh Epic* and the tale of Buluqiya are so great that comparison of the two has largely to be made on the basis of individual, separate episodes and motifs. Changes can be seen to occur according to rules which Tigay has formulated:32 changes of geographical location, changes of order in episodes, reinterpretation of themes, and selective use of relevant material. Such selection is facilitated by the nature of such stories, in which episodes are strung together and seldom have any compelling connection. The same rules can be applied to the differences between the three Arabic versions.

Buluqiya as a Typical Apocalyptic Hero

These are characteristics of much apocalyptic writing: the hero lacks the emotions and appetites of mortals for whom we might feel sympathy. In the Akkadian epic Enkidu drinks huge quantities of beer; Gilgamesh is lustful and headstrong; but he is also filled with fears and doubts, and when he is exhausted, he cannot stay awake even though he earnestly intends to do so. He cares about his clothes until he becomes depressed at his friend's death. Buluqiya, on the other hand, suffers from none of the frailties and vanities of real people. He might as well be any great hero from early antiquity as portrayed in the writing of late antiquity: Enoch, Solomon, Daniel or Noah. His visionary journeys to the remotest corners of the cosmos, his interviews with the angels, might have happened to anyone with no change in the manner of their description. His character does not alter or develop as a result of his experiences. The angels who are named by Tha'labi and in Burton's versions can be found in many apocalyptic works as well as in the Aramaic magical texts inscribed on incantation bowls. Only Mardrus's story attempts to make up for the lack of human interest: Yamlika peels a banana for Hasib and eats a fig herself during an interlude in the main narrative; we are told that Buluqiya was so fond of crystallized fruits and all sweet things, that he stayed on the island where the trees bore sweets for eleven days in order to indulge his craving, and only left when he got a bellyache; on an island of terrible monsters he cannot sleep for fear; Sakhr the demon king offers the information that each jinn eats ten camels, twenty sheep, and drinks forty cauldron-sized ladles full of soup each day.

Not only in matters of human character does the Buluqiya story show signs of influence from apocalyptic literature; in numerous details of cosmology, in the central motif of divine revelation, and in referring to the coming of a new world leader and to an impending Day of Judgement or Day of Resurrection all three Arabic versions bear strong traces of Judaic apocalyptic literature, particularly of the *Book of Enoch*. In that work, best known in its Ethiopic version, the hero like Burton's Buluqiya tours the farthest recesses of the universe, hears about the Day of Judgement and has a series of interviews with different angels.

Gilgamesh and the Book of Giants

These comparisons with the *Book of Enoch* are of a general nature, and relate mainly to the second part of Burton's version, which elaborates at length the travels of the hero. They rest upon general grounds of similar story elements, apart from the names of angels, who are by nature ubiquitous, and such narrative elements were common to many other stories of late antiquity. Is it possible to make some specific comparisons?

The Ethiopic *Book of Enoch* (I Enoch) is a collection of several works, of which the second, Ch. 37–71, is known as the Similitudes or the Parables. At Qumran many fragments of the *Book of Enoch* in Aramaic have been found, but the Similitudes section is not represented among them. On the other hand, a work known as the *Book of the Giants* is indeed attested at Qumran, and for a variety of reasons most scholars have agreed that the people of Qumran possessed a *Book of Enoch* in which the second section consisted of the *Book of the Giants*, later to be replaced by the Similitudes.[33] The only grounds for dispute lay in whether the *Book of the Giants* was a separate book originally or an extension of the first section of Enoch, which is generally known as the *Book of Watchers*.[34] J.T. Milik, in his edition of the fragments, found the name of Gilgamesh twice in the *Book of the Giants*, with only one letter missing in one of the occurrences, together with a version of Humbaba's name.[35] He also thought the name of the Babylonian cosmic mountain Mashum was roughly translated into Aramaic as Daddu'el. Discovery of Humbaba's name at Qumran was supported from a fragment in Middle Persian from the oasis of Turfan in Central Asia, published by W.B. Henning in 1943–6, which he recognized as being a part of a Manichaean *Book of the Giants*, a work which, along with other parts of the Book of Enoch, likewise represented in the Turfan fragments, had a formative influence on Mani, the founder of the heretical Manichaean sect who was brought up in Babylonia.[36] In fact, the *Book of the Giants* became a part of the canon of Mani's faith, and perhaps for this reason it was eventually excluded from the Jewish *Book of Enoch*. Henning's Middle Persian fragments included the name Hobabiš, which is very close indeed to Milik's HWBBŠ.[37] Since the name of Gilgamesh in some form is not preserved in the Middle Persian fragments, Henning did not equate the name with Humbaba, but Milik, who found the name of Gilgamesh in the Aramaic fragments, made the connection.[38]

Why Gilgamesh and Humbaba should feature as giants in the Qumran fragments may be suggested partly from the (again) fragmentary Anatolian version of the Gilgamesh epic as unearthed in Hittite cuneiform at Bogazköy. This version dates from the mid-second millennium B.C. In it, Gilgamesh is specifically described as a giant, 11 cubits (about 5 m) tall. Humbaba is also a giant, for in the late version of Tablet V in Akkadian, Humbaba says that he would not even satisfy his stomach by eating Enkidu. A Middle Bronze Age terracotta shows a Gilgamesh-type hero standing upon the head of Humbaba, and the head is represented as gigantic.[39] In Mardrus's story Humbaba can easily be identified as the giant who guards trees.

Gilgamesh and Enoch

Since Gilgamesh and Humbaba are found in one part of the Qumran *Book of Enoch*, it needs to be asked whether any traces can still be detected in the remaining part of the composition, and whether any clues survive in the tale of Buluqiya.

First, George the Synkellos gives the name of the fourth dearch, who is Kokabiel in I Enoch 6:7, as Khobabiel.[40] The variant is easily explained as a corruption, commonly made between B and KH in Hebrew or Aramaic, but it also resemble Khobabiš with the ending changed from *-iš* to *-el*. Second, in I Enoch 8 the order of dearchs is altered, and Kokabiel, previously the fourth dearch, is there next to Baraqiel, previously the ninth dearch. Baraqiel is given as Balqiel by George the Synkellos, again explicable as a corruption, a shift L–R being very common, but also remarkably close to Buluqiya. In the Persian *Book of the Giants* from Turfan, Virogdad who is found together with Hobabiš is, according to Henning's suggestion, a rough translation of Baraqiel.[41] In other words, the ninth dearch definitely has a close connection with Humbaba in the *Book of the Giants.* These observations might imply that the Qumran version of Enoch incorporated two traditions: the one found in the *Book of Watchers,* in which Gilgamesh and Humbaba had already been assimilated into Jewish tradition as dearchs, and parts of another found in the *Book of the Giants* in which they still bore the older, Babylonian forms of their names. However, since both Baraqiel and Gilgamesh are found in the Qumran *Book of the Giants* according to the fragments published by J.T. Milik, and since also no inscribed incantation bowls from Mesopotamia have Khobabiel and Baraqiel as a pair, there is no evidence that these resemblances in names are more than coincidental, even though conditions for syncretism by similarity of name appear to be favorable.

Gilgamesh and Humbaba, in any case, were giants in a part of the early *Book of Enoch,* although the story in its present fragmentary form bears little resemblance to the Babylonian *Epic of Gilgamesh.* What has happened to Babylonian Enkidu, the wild man who was created by the gods to become the counsellor and equal of Gilgamesh? His part is taken in the Arabian Nights by ʿAffan, wise man of Jerusalem, who bears no trace of wild origins, but whose role parallels that of Enkidu in that he travels with Buluqiya to the main heroic episode, draws the magic circle, and dies as a result of brave endeavor. Enoch himself shares certain aspects of character with Enkidu as well as a superficial similarity in name (Hebrew Hanoch, Arabic Ukhnukh): both come to save mankind from lustful abuse, and Enkidu's dream vision of entering the Underworld is comparable to Enoch's vision in I Enoch 14. Such a comparison does not exclude the associations of Enoch with Enmeduranki king of Sippar where the solar deity was pre-eminent, and with Oannes, which have been argued by many scholars,[42] but would simply be another addition to the already eclectic nature of Enoch. It may be pertinent to point out that, in the standard *Epic of Gilgamesh*, the sun god Shamash plays a key role as protector only as long as Enkidu is present in the story; Shamash is the divine guardian of Gilgamesh alongside Enkidu the mortal guardian. Enoch's character as a diviner[43] may be compared with the performance of a dream inducing ritual by drawing a magic circle by Enkidu and by ʿAffan. If aspects of Enoch are derived from the character of Enkidu, they would still remain only a small part of the whole; further evidence to test the suggestion may come forward if it becomes possible to reconstruct the complete story of the *Book of the Giants.*

In all three versions of the tale of Buluqiya, King Sakhr describes to Buluqiya the seven regions of hell in which different categories of sinners will be punished, and the monsters who were created to guard and torture them. In Burton and Mardrus, closely comparable passages name the different stages and the types of sinners for which they are reserved. The versions of Burton and Thaʿlabi contain further cosmological information: the serpents whom the hero first meets, after setting out on his travels, explain briefly to him why hell is both hot and cold, and why it was created: to punish sinners. The latter two versions also append to the main story a tour of heavenly regions in which Buluqiya meets various angels who, in response to his questions, each tell him their duties and describe their region. Such descriptions of the regions of heaven and hell, most particularly when given in the form of a tour with question-and-answer dialogue, belong to Judaic and Christian traditions that were also used in Islamic literature, best known in the Isra' and Miʿraj of Muhammad.[44] They have been traced back to the *Book of Watchers* in I Enoch.[45] Given the dreams of hell found in the Gilgamesh Epic, the repetitious dialogue with superhuman beings when the hero tours regions beyond the Cosmic Mountain, and the question-and-answer dialogue revealing how different ranks of men fare in the Underworld in tablet XII, there is evidently a case to be made for certain strands of continuity in this genre of literature between ancient Babylonia and Islam, in which I Enoch played an intermediate role. □

* * *

NOTES

1. E. von Weiher, *Spätbabylonische Texte aus Uruk*, iii (Berlin, 1988).
2. This paper has grown out of a lecture delivered to the Royal Asiatic Society in December 1989. It is part of an extensive study that includes investigation of themes from the Odyssey, the Alexander Romance and from tales of Sindbad the Sailor, as well as the Jewish background to the tale of Buluqiya. Many colleagues have read and criticized various drafts, and their generous help has led to many improvements.
3. Tigay rightly called attention to S.N. Kramer, *JAOS* 64, 1944, p. 8 n. 2, who thought the work of P. Jensen, *Das Gilgamesch-Epos in der Weltliteratur*, had been much too harshly condemned.
4. J. Tigay, *Empirical Models for Biblical Criticism* (Philadelphia, 1985) pp. 39–46.
5. See Wensinck, *Encyclopedia of Islam* s.v. "Al-Khadhir"; H.T. Norris, *Cambridge History of Arabic Literature* i, ch. 19, p. 375. It is not mentioned in the *Reallexikon der Assyriologie.*
6. E. Littmann, "Alf Layla wa-Layla," *Encyclopedia of Islam*, 2nd ed., i (Leiden, 1979).
7. H.W. Attridge and R. Oden, *De Dea Syria* (Chico, Calif. 1976).
8. See E. Schürer, *The History of the Jewish people in the Age of Jesus Christ*, iii/I (Edinburgh, revised ed. 1986).
9. A detailed account of connections between Greek literature and themes in the Arabian Nights is given by G.E. von Grunebaum, *Medieval Islam* (Chicago, 2nd ed. 1953), ch. 9.
10. M. Lichtheim, *Ancient Egyptian Literature*, i. (Berkeley, 1973), pp. 211–15, gives an up-to-date translation in English. I am grateful to Friedhelm Hoffmann for pointing this out to me.
11. A. Ungnad, *Gilgamesch-Epos und Odyssee*, Kulturfragen 4/5 (Breslau, 1923), p. 31.
12. See S. Parpola, "Letters from Assyrian scholars" 2, *AOAT* 5/2, pp. xxii ff, although the echo is very faint.
13. O.R. Gurney, *Anatolian Studies* 6, 1957, pp. 145ff.
14. For translation of names in ancient Mesopotamia, a clear example is Esarhaddon's queen Naqi'a "pure" (Aramaic), also known as Zakûtu "pure" (Akkadian).
15. J.C. Mardrus, *The Book of the Thousand Nights and One Night*, translated by P. Mathers, (London, 1947) from translations published in French in 1899–1904.
16. R.F. Burton, *A Plain and Literal Translation of the Arabian Nights' Entertainment*, iv, 1897, pp. 251–74.
17. E. Littmann, *op. cit.* p. 360; M.I. Gerhardt, *The Art of Storytelling, A Literary Study of the 1001 Nights* (Leiden, 1963), pp. 93–104. However, N. Elisséeff, *Thèmes et motifs des mille et une nuits, Essai de Classification* (Beyrouth, 1949), p. 62, does not entirely dismiss the claim.
18. R. Khawam, *Les Mille et une Nuits*, i (Paris 1986), pp. 19–24.

19. I am most grateful to Professor A.F.L. Beeston for translating the story from majlis 28 for me; his translation will be given verbatim in the final version of this study.
20. See A. Falkenstein, in E. Ebeling and B. Meissner et al., *Reallexikon der Assyriologie*, s.v. Gilgameš.
21. See H. Limet, *L'anthroponymie sumérienne* (Paris, 1968), p. 98.
22. The suggestion that the name is a form of Hilqi-Yau, Josiah's High Priest (J. Horovitz, *ZDMG* 55, 1901, p. 522 n. 2) involves an unparalleled shift from H to B. The names of Josiah's sons are known: Johanan, Jehoiakim, (also called Eliakim), Zedekiah, and Shallum who became king under the throne name Jehoahaz.
23. Alternatively one might seek for phonological changes among other languages, particularly Persian or Arabic.
24. See R. Borger, "Gott Marduk und Gott-König Sulgi als Propheten," *Bibliotheca orientalis* 28, 1971, pp. 23–23.
25. I. Friedländer's extensive study, *Die Chadhirlegende und der Alexanderroman* (Berlin and Leipzig, 1913) is summarized in *Encyclopaedia of Islam*, 2nd ed., 1978, s.v. al-Khadhir by A.J. Wensinck, and E. Littmann *loc. cit.* also accepts the Babylonian prototypes for the Water of Life and for Khidhr. Ugaritic material has become available gradually since the 1930s, and may be examined for possible connections since the second element of the demi-god name *kṯr-w-ḫss* resembles Akkadian *ḫasīs* and the first resembles Arabic Khid̲hr/K̲hadhir.
26. In taking this statement at face value, one implicitly rejects the interpretation that it can be attributed to Hellenistic euhemerism.
27. "Renew" seems to be the earliest attested meaning of the word; in later periods "successful" develops from it; see von Soden, *Akkadisches Handwörterbuch* s.v. kašāru. The *Chicago Assyrian Dictionary's* division of the verb into three separate roots is not well founded, and is rightly ignored by von Soden, *op. cit., Nachträge.*
28. E.g. S.K. Eddy, *The King is Dead* (Nebraska, 1961), p. 112. For the original study see B. Meissner, *Alexander und Gilgamos* (Leipzig, 1894).
29. See E.A. Wallis Budge, *The History of Alexander the Great, being the Syriac version of the Pseudo-Callisthenes*, (Cambridge, 1889) p. 168.
30. Themes that connect versions of the Alexander Romance with the tale of Buluqiya, yet which have no connection with the *Gilgamesh Epic* will be discussed in our forthcoming study.
31. That prologue has been known only since 1975: D.J. Wiseman "A Gilgamesh Epic fragment from Nimrud," *Iraq* 37, 1975, pp. 157–63.
32. *Empirical Models*, pp. 29–52.
33. E.g. G. Vermes, *The Dead Sea Scrolls* (London, 1977), p. 210.
34. M. Blac, T*he Book of Enoch*, pp. 9–10.
35. J.T. Milik, T*he Books of Enoch. Aramaic fragments of Qumran*, pp. 311 and 313, $_4$QEnGiants^b and $_4$QEnGiants^c.
36. W.B. Henning, "Ein manichäisches Henochbuch," *SPAW* 1934, pp. 1–11; "The Book of the Giants," *BSOAS* XI, 1943, pp. 52–74.

37. The wide variety of spellings for Humbaba in Akkadian are given in the *Reallexikon der Assyiologie* by C. Wilcke, s.v. Huwawa.
38. In one instance, the name is complete; in the other, Milik restored the first letter G. The final sibilant is different in the two occurrences; for a possible parallel cf. two different sibilants in the Aramaic spelling of Sennacherib's name; see K. Tallqvist, *Assyrian Personal Names* (Helsingfors, 1914), p. 196.
39. R. Opificius, *Das altbabylonische Terrakottarelief* (Berlin, 1961), no. 485: redrawn as Abb. I in *Reallexikon der Assyriolgie*, iii, p. 374.
40. A.A. Mosshammer, *Georgius Syncellus, Ecloga Chronographica* (Leipzig, 1984), pp. 11f.
41. "Soghdische Miszellen," *BSOAS* VIII, 1935–7, p. 583; *ZDMG* 90, 1936, p. 4.
42. R. Borger, "Die Beschwörungsserie bīt mēseri und die Himmelfahrt Henochs," *JNES* 33, 1974.
43. J.C. VanderKam, *Enoch and the Growth of an Apocalyptic tradition.* CBQ Monograph Series 16, 1984, pp. 116f.
44. See M. Asin Palacios, *La Escatologia musulmana en la Divina Comedia* (Madrid, 1919) with the important criticisms of T. Silverstein, "Dante and the Legend of the Mi'raj," *Journal of Near Eastern Studies* 11, 1952, pp. 89–110, 187–97.
45. M. Himmelfarb, *Tours of Hell. An Apocalyptic Form in Jewish and Christian Literature* (Philadelphia, 1983), esp. p. 67 and p. 169.

❋ ❋ ❋

William L. Moran
"Ovid's *Blanda Voluptas* and the Humanization of Enkidu"*

William L. Moran, already commended (Harris, above) for urging Assyriologists to use contemporary literary-critical principles in interpretation of Mesopotamian literature, calls attention to parallels between ancient Near Eastern literature and the writings of classical authors. The parallels are particularly inviting since classicists like Walter Burkert are increasingly interested in the influence of the ancient Near East on the classical world. Moran's essay points to the education of Enkidu and its later parallel in Ovid.

Moran speculates that a Babylonian audience—particularly an audience of men in the *aštammu* pub where prostitutes gathered—would appreciate the humor in Enkidu's humanization through sexuality. The humanization of Enkidu is part of an older tradition in Mesopotamia dealing with the nature of primitive humankind. Moran points out, further, that Enkidu's acceptance of Gilgamesh as king was necessary to complete the process, since kingship was needed for the full humanization of the human condition.

Drawing upon the History of Ideas, Moran locates the story of Enkidu in the long tradition of antiprimitivism, which saw human origins in an ugly and savage, animal and pre-human state. Ovid's *Ars amatoria* was certainly influenced by that tradition, which he could have learned through Lucretius and Cicero. The transforming power of soft and gentle love in Ovid is the closest parallel in classical antiquity to Enkidu's union with the harlot, a union that sets him on a path to the city and to Gilgamesh. (Ed.)

Thorkild Jacobsen, optimo magistro et
fideli amico, octogesimum septimum
annum suae aetatis prospere degenti,
gratulor gratoque animo opusculum offero

The Enkidu whom we first meet in the "Gilgamesh Epic" is a Mesopotamian Perceval, a "fole in the filde" who "in the wilde wodde went, With the bestes to play."[1] He is a strange figure, and much has been written about him and his subsequent humanization.[2] It now appears that he was modeled on other and earlier traditions about the life of primitive man.[3] Thus, at least in broad outline, the Enkidu story is the human story.

Parallels for the various features of this child of nature have been sought not only in Mesopotamian and other Near Eastern sources, but also in the vast materials of folklore and anthropology. Yet, broad as the sweep of the search for parallels has been, one source, and a rich one, the classical tradition, seems to have been largely overlooked. There, in fact, one discovers a picture of man's earliest days that is remarkably similar to the life of Enkidu and his probable Mesopotamian prototypes. It seems worthwhile, then, especially in view of the ever increasing evidence for the influence of the Near East on the classical world,[4] to call attention, however briefly, to the writings of classical authors.

These writers present us with two radically opposed views of man's earliest days. Lovejoy and Boas called them primitivism and anti-primitivism,[5] which coexisted in tension and a dialectic of mutual influence.[6] According to primitivism, in both its "hard" and "soft" versions, the beginning was the best of times. In those days, it is said, man's life was either one of complete ease and constant enjoyment, or, if hard, pristinely simple, uncomplicated, free of the clutter of culture — *beatus ille qui procul negotiis.*[7] According to anti-primitivism, in the beginning life was not only hard, it was ugly and savage, a prehuman, animal existence—*thēriōdēs bios (diaita), ferus victus (fera vita).*[8] Man lived in the open, in caves or on mountains, scattered and lacking all social bonds. He ate earth, progressing to grass, plants, roots, and nuts. He went naked or clad only in animal skins. He was without law, a murderer, a cannibal. Only with the discovery or revelation of agriculture and viticulture, fire and metal and tools, navigation and speech (with eloquence), did the truly human life gradually emerge.

Among these various forms of primitivism it is of course the last variety, anti-primitivism, that is so strikingly reminiscent of the early Enkidu and Mesopotamian primitive man. Indeed, in view of the other Near Eastern influences, it is hard to believe that the anti-primitivism of classical sources does not derive, ultimately, through a long and complicated process of transmission, its general inspiration and even some of its specific lore from Near Eastern sources. The classical tradition also suggests how rich the Near Eastern traditions, written and oral, must once have been.

Within this tradition I should like to call attention to one passage in particular. It is the description by Ovid, in the *Ars amatoria* 2.467–80, of primitive man and his humanization. To show the power of love, Ovid recounts the story of cosmic and human origins:

prima fuit rerum confusa sine ordine moles
unaque erat facies sidera, terra, fretum;
mox caelum impositum terris, humus aequore cincta est,
inque suas partes cessit inane chaos;
silva feras, volucres aer accepit habendas;
in liquida, pisces, delituistis aqua.
tum genus humanum solis erravit in agris
idque merae vires et rude corpus erat;
silva domus fuerat, cibus herba, cubilia frondes,
iamque diu nulli cognitus alter erat.
blanda truces animos fertur mollisse voluptas:
constiterant uno femina virque loco.
quid facerent, ipsi nullo didicere magistro;
arte Venus nulla dulce peregit opus.

At first there was a mass, unordered, undefined,
A single sight the stars and land and sea.
Soon sky was over earth, the ground by the
ocean girded,
And to its place did empty void recede.
The woods received wild beasts to keep,
the air the birds,
And you, O fish, did hide in flowing waters.
Then did the human race wander in lonely fields
Was but sheer strength and body without grace.
The woods had been their home, the grass
their food, and leaves their beds.
And long was each to each unknown.
Gentle love (they say) softened savage hearts:
A man and a woman, in one place, had paused.
What to do they learned by themselves.
There was no teacher.
Venus performed her sweet task.
There was no art.[9]

What is most striking in this bit of light-hearted anti-primitivism is the role Ovid assigns to sexual love. While but brute strength and graceless bodies,[10] a man and a woman meet, and their union changes their spirits. In context, the long pause between *blanda* and *voluptas* makes the latter seem like a proclamation.[11] Persuasive, soft, and gentle—*blanda* is all of these—love transforms. To quote Hermann Fraenkel: "This amounts to proposing that it was love that gave man a feeling soul in addition to his body, and that it was sexual love which taught him to know and understand and love his fellow-beings, so that he would build up society."[12]

To the reader of the "Gilgamesh Epic," however, what makes Ovid's thought truly extraordinary is the parallel it provides—the closest by far that I know of—for the transformation of Enkidu by his union with the harlot. Fraenkel's statement differs little from what Morris Jastrow wrote about Enkidu many years ago, "...through intercourse with a woman he awakens to the sense of human dignity."[13]

But the striking likeness granted, what are we to make of it? Though Ovid claims, in typically neoterist fashion,[14] to be citing a tradition (*fertur*), it does not follow that he merely reflects the thought of his source. Certainly in no other classical author do we find sexual intercourse intervening so decisively in the humanization of man, and nothing could be more Ovidian than the claims here made for love.[15] There are thus no grounds for postulating a lost Alexandrian Enkidu known to Ovid and his model for the power of love.

However, Ovid does depend on a tradition, and the nature of the tradition and Ovid's dependence on it suggests, I think, a line of speculation on the development of the Enkidu story. One expression of the tradition that Ovid certainly knew was *De rerum natura* 5.1011–27.[16] There, as Lucretius traces the long history of early man, he tells how, after man acquired huts and hides and fire, woman was joined to man in marriage.[17] Next were children, and "then did mankind begin to grow soft. For fire made their shivering bodies less able to endure the cold under the open sky, and Venus sapped their strength, and children by their caresses easily broke the fierce spirit of their parents. And then neighbors began eagerly to unite in friendly agreement with one another neither to do nor to suffer violence."[18]

Obviously this is a much more complex and more serious view of human development. Sexuality is present, but it is only part of the story, though an important one, and it is seen only in the context of marriage. There it diminishes man's powers—again compare Enkidu and his diminished speed—and produces children, who charm their parents into gentleness. Families are then neighbors, and this leads to the very human institution of pacts for peaceful relations. And so the story goes on. All these Lucretian solemnities, with mock didacticism, Ovid transforms—frivolously, says Cole[19]—into a light and amusing (*nullo magistro, nulla arte*) simplicity.

Lucretius had his predecessors. For them sexual love is universal, shared by gods, men, and animals.[20] It is all-powerful, taming, and subjecting, and none can escape it.[21] It bears, therefore, *in nuce*, all of society and the origins of social transformation. The sexual act is, as Cole remarks,[22] a purely natural and universal form of *koinōnia*. Cicero sums it up quite well:

> *itaque primos congressus copulationesque... fieri propter voluptatem: cum autem usus progrediens familiaritatem effecerit, tum amorem efflorescere tantum ut, etiamsi nulla sit utilitas ex amicitia, tamen ipsi amici propter se ipsos amentur.*
>
> therefore the first comings together and copulations... are inspired by sexual love; when, however, constant dealings with one another have created a sense of intimacy, then love blossoms to the point that, even though nothing useful can come from friendship, still the friends themselves are loved for themselves.[23]

Now, Ovid must have known all this, but his silence about marriage and children and friendship rejects it and in effect mocks it. For the others, the story only begins with *voluptas*; for Ovid, it ends there. Nothing else matters.

All this urges us to think about the Enkidu story again and to speculate a bit. It is certainly possible and, in fact, in the light of the classical tradition, it seems even likely that in some Mesopotamian myth or myths on the development of primitive man, under the guidance of the gods sexuality and marriage played a part not unlike what we have seen in Ovid's predecessors. Now, if Enkidu were modeled on some such tradition, obviously some adaptions would be necessary. A married Enkidu would not do. Marriage would distract from the narrative line, raise ungermane questions, and detract from the future bond with Gilgamesh. And so—we speculate—Enkidu's story was given a new twist, one worthy indeed of Ovid himself: not a wife for Enkidu, but a harlot. This is a transformation that we may suspect would have been as recognizable and as humorous to a cultivated Babylonian audience as Ovid's was to his sophisticated Roman readers. It would, too, be quite in the spirit of the description that follows of Enkidu's gawking at the bread, his mighty thirst, his beery gladness.

It is this spirit, however, that suggests another line of speculation. Perhaps the adaptations we postulate were made, not for the figure of Enkidu in the epic, but earlier, before their application to him, in the tradition on primitive man. If we look for a setting for such a tale, the *aštammu*, pub and gathering place of harlots and the bibulous, seems the most likely. There we can imagine the telling of tales, among them that of primitive man and his humanization, and we also can readily imagine that it would not go unchanged but would be adapted to the audience and reflect their interests and mood. In such a telling, to the ribald amusement and satisfaction of all, harlotry and insobriety would be recognized as quite civilizing and their contribution to man's evolution duly acknowledged. And—final step in our speculation—it was this *aštammu*-version that the epic bard, inspired by the *musa iocosa* and anticipating the principle *ludicra seriis miscere*, borrowed, bowdlerized, and attached to Enkidu.[24]

All speculation aside, certainly a reference to *Ars amatoria* 2.467–80 belongs in everyone's marginalia to *Gilgamesh* Tablet I.

The humanization of Enkidu begins with a week of love-making. It ends, it is generally held, when he has been introduced to bread, beer, clothing, and toilet. I would suggest one more step. It occurs when he reaches Uruk and, at the end of their first and decisive encounter, he addresses Gilgamesh (P vi 27-33):

> *kīma ištēn-ma ummaka ulidka*
> It was as one unique your mother bore you
> *rīmtum ša supūri Ninsuna*
> —Wild-cow of the Pen, Ninsuna.
> *ullu eli mutī rēška*
> Placed high, high over men, are you.
> *šarrūtam ša nišī išīmkum Ellil*
> The kingship of the people Ellil decreed for you.

The importance of kingship in the Mesopotamian scheme of things needs no discussion here. In brief, kingship is the final and perfect ordering principle of human existence, and in its absence the human story is incomplete. This is implied by the Sumerian King List,[25] is clear from the introduction to the myth of Etana, and now has a new and striking illustration in *VS* 24 92:32'–33'.[26] Ea addressed Belet-ili and says: *at-ti-ma tab-ni-ma* LÚ.U$_{18}$.LU-*a a-me-lu*/ *pi-it-qi-ma* LUGAL *ma-li-ku a-me-lu*, "It was you who created primal-man, so Fashion too a king, counsellor–man." As in Etana, what kingship means is counsel, guidance in both war and peace. It is the institution without which there is no human fulfillment.[27]

It would seem, therefore, that Enkidu's acknowledgment and acceptance of the kingship of Gilgamesh is not irrelevant to his humanization, especially in a narrative that has been so deeply concerned with this process. I submit, then, that until Enkidu comes into the city and begins life under a king, he is still not wholly removed from his original condition of *lullú-amēlu*. Only in Gilgamesh does he find counsel and, in counsel, full humanity.

❋ ❋ ❋

NOTES

* I wish to thank Charles Rowan Beye of City University of New York and Wendell Clausen of Harvard University for generously giving of their time to read the first draft of this essay and of their knowledge to make it less the work of an amateur. They indicated omissions in the bibliography and offered criticisms that were instructive and encouraging, a gratifying *nihil obstat.* Of course the shortcomings of the essay and any errors that may have crept into the revised version are my responsibility. Thanks, too, to I. Tzvi Abusch, who made some helpful comments from the Babylonian camp.

1. Cited from John Speirs, *Medieval English Poetry: The Non-Chaucerian Tradition* (London, 1971), p. 123.

2. For a recent survey, see Jeffrey H. Tigay, *The Evolution of the Gilgamesh Epic* (Philadelphia, 1982), pp. 196–213.

3. Ibid., pp. 202–3; G. Komoróczy, "Berosos and the Mesopotamian Literature," *Acta Antiqua* 21 (1973): 140–42; J. Bauer, "Leben in der Urzeit Mesopotamiens." *AfO* Beiheft 19 (1982): 377–83. The Mesopotamian traditions on primitive man Berossos sums up very briefly: "they lived without laws just as wild animals" (Stanley Mayer Burstein, *The* Babyloniaca *of Berossos*, SANE 1/5 [Malibu, 1978], pp. 155, translating *zēn d' autous ataktōs hōsper ta thēria*; see also n. 8 below).

4. See, for example, Walter Burkert, *Die orientalisierende Epoche in der griechischen Religion und Literatur*, Sitzungsberichte der Heidelberger Akademie der Wissenschaften, phil-hist. Kl. (Heidelberg, 1984), p. 1; M.L. West, "Near Eastern Material in Hellenistic and Roman Literature," *Harvard Studies in Classical Philology* 73 (1969): 112–34, and his commentaries in *Hesiod, Theogony* (Oxford, 1966), pp. 28–30 (the Succession Myth) and *Works and Days* (Oxford, 1978), especially pp. 174–77 (the metallic ages). Thorkild Jacobsen, "The Eridu Genesis," *JBL* 100 (1981): 521, points in Sumerian literature to a most striking parallel to the life of Hesiod's Silver Age Man. See, too, idem, *The Harab Myth*, SANE 2/3 (Malibu, 1984) and his discussion of the western

parallels. Also much debated is Near Eastern influence on Homer, especially by the Gilgamesh tradition: T.B.L. Webster, *From Mycenae to Homer* (London, 1964); Michael N. Nagler, *Spontaneity and Tradition: A Study in the Oral Art of Homer* (Berkeley, Los Angeles, and London, 1974); Gerald K. Gresseth, "*The Gilgamesh Epic* and Homer," *Classical Journal* 70 (1974–75): 1–18; John R. Wilson, "*The Gilgamesh Epic* and the *Iliad*." *Echos du monde classique: Classical Views* 30 n.s. 5 (1986): 25–41; Gregory Crane, *Calypso: Background and Conventions of the Odyssey* (Frankfurt am Main, 1988). For the diffusion and curious distortion of the legend of Gilgamesh, note his presence at Qumran as a giant called *glgmys* or *[g]lgmyš* (J.T. Milik, with the collaboration of Matthew Black, *The Book of Enoch: Aramaic Fragments of Qumran Cave 4* [Oxford, 1976], p. 313). Humbaba probably lies behind another giant called *ḥwbbš* which corresponds to Middle Persian *ḥwb' byš* (ibid, p. 311).

5. A.O. Lovejoy and B. Boas, *Primitivism and Related Ideas in Antiquity* (Baltimore, 1935). The distinction between "hard" and "soft" is also theirs. (It might be noted that Erwin Panofsky, in his famous essay, "*Et in Arcadia ego:* Poussin and the Elegiac Tradition," in *Meaning in the Visual Arts* [Garden City, 1955], p. 297, does not reflect accurately their distinctions. He calls "hard" primitivism what they call anti-primitivism.) Thomas Cole, *Democritus and the Sources of Greek Anthropology*, Philological Monographs, American Philological Association, no. 25 (Cleveland, 1967), p. 1, whose work Beye and Clausen called to my attention, sees the basic distinction as between "the myth of the Golden Age and the myth of human progress—Hesiodic fantasy and Ionian science." In Homer and the epic tradition, according to Cole, glorification of a vanished age of heroic power and splendor belongs to the former. After the Ionians, if in a cyclical view of history earlier civilizations were considered more elaborate and splendid, they are "always separated from the present world by some sort of cataclysm; men are thereby reduced to the level of bare subsistence and must proceed by gradual stages to the modicum of civilization they now enjoy" (ibid., p. 2).

6. In addition to Cole, see Bodo Gatz, *Weltalter, goldene Zeit und sinnverwandte Vorstellungen*, Spudasmata, vol. 16 (Hildesheim, 1967). The *conspectus locorum*, pp. 228 ff., is invaluable: note especially the references under *ferus priscorum temporum status.*

7. Lovejoy and Boas also call this "cultural primitivism," which is inspired by nostalgia for the simplicity of the good old days.

8. Cf. the language of Berossos (n. 3 above), whose use of *ataktōs* anticipated Diodorus (*ataktōi kai thēriōdei biōi*, cited by Cole. *Democritus*, p. 28, n. 4) and Sextus (*hot ataktos ēn anthrōpōn bios*, ibid., p. 189, n. 31).

9. The text is that of E.J. Kenney, *P. Ovidi Nasonis Amores. Medicamina faciei femineae. Ars amatoria, Remedia Amoris.* Oxford Classical Texts (Oxford, 1961).

10. In context, *rude (corpus)* must refer to crudeness, lack of refinement; *artis adhuc expers et rude volgus erat* (Fast: 2.292). Elsewhere (*Epistulae* 4.23; *Metamorphoses* 9.27; *Tristia* 3.3) Ovid speaks of the *rude pectus* in connection with love, and there *rude* means "unerfahren, unteilhaftig" (Franz Bömer, *P. Ovidius Naso, Metamorphoses,* Books 8–9 [Heidelberg, 1977], p. 493, on 9.720. A diligent reader of Ovid might sense a certain ambiguity about *rude corpus.*
11. Ovid found it in *De rerum natura* 4.1085: *blandaque refrenat morsus admixta voluptas.*
12. *Ovid: A Poet between Two Worlds,* Sather Lectures (Berkeley, 1943), p. 67. Fraenkel also points to *Fasti* 4.107–14 where Ovid makes love the prime mover of civilization. Clausen notes the effective juxtaposition of the virtual antonyms *blanda* and *truces.*
13. Morris Jastrow and Albert T. Clay, *An Old Babylonian Version of the Gilgamesh Epic, on the Basis of Recently Discovered Texts,* YSOR 4/3 (New Haven, 1920), p. 20. See also Samuel Noah Kramer, "The Gilgamesh Epic and Its Sumerian Sources: A Study in Literary Evolution." *JAOS* 64 (1944): 9, n.5.
14. According to E. Norden, *P. Vergilius Maro, Aeneis Buch VI*[3] (Leipzig and Berlin, 1934), p. 123, commenting on *ut fama est* in 4.14, this and similar expressions were used in four ways: (1) to cite as true but without criticism: (2) to emphasize, by repeated use, that one's tale is traditional: (3) occasionally to indicate that the tradition is not certain, or must be rejected or reinterpreted in rational terms: (4) to indicate one's own doubts about the tradition. Ovid reflects the second use. (I owe this reference to Clausen.) C.J. Fordyce, *Catullus* (Oxford, 1961), p. 276, cites as illustrative of the scholar-poet Callimachus: "I sing of nothing unattested" (*amartyron ouden aeidō*): "the story is not mine but others'" (*mythos d' ouk emos all' heterōn*).
15. Of course Ovid was not alone in exalting love. "The elegiac poets in the time of Augustus are alien to the 'res publica', indifferent to marriage, the family, procreation. They declare the primacy of love and the individual" (Ronald Syme, *History in Ovid* [Oxford, 1979] p. 200). Ovid was, however, unique, to his lasting woe and tribulation, in arousing the wrath of Augustus that, ailing and at the age of fifty, he was sent into remote exile, never to return, and his *Ars* banished with him. Augustus may have been a prude, but the problem he faced was real. Marriage and procreation were the ancient world's only answer to extremely high mortality rates; see Peter Brown, *The Body and Society: Men, Women and Sexual Renunciation in Early Christianity* (New York, 1988), p. 2.
16. See Fraenkel, *Ovid,* p. 203, n. 30. This is the common opinion and it is shared by Beye and Clausen. Note especially *blanda voluptas* (see n. 1 above), and cf. *De rerum natura* 5.1014, *tum genus humanum primum mollescere coepit,* and *Ars amatoria* 2.473, *tum genus humanum (solis erravit in agris),* 477 (*blanda truces animos fertur) mollisse (voluptas).* Markus Weber, *Die mythologische Erzählung in Ovids*

Liebeskunst: Verankerung, Struktur and Funktion, Studien zur klassischen Philologie vol. 6 (Frankfurt am Main and Bern, 1983), p. 200, n. 30, calls our passage a "Parodie auf die epikureische voluptas-Lehre." Peter Green, *Ovid: The Erotic Poems* (London, 1982), p. 376, questions the relevance of Lucretius only to admit that Ovid may allude to him with "his tongue, as so often, in his cheek."

17. This latter detail seems certain even though the text may be corrupt.

18. The translation is that of Lovejoy and Boas, *Primitivism*, pp. 228–29.

19. Cole, *Democritus*, p. 7.

20. See the Homeric "Hymn to Aphrodite," lines 1 ff. In their commentary, T.W. Allen, W.R. Halliday, E.E. Sikes, *The Homeric Hymns* (Oxford, 1936), p. 352 (reference from Beye), compare Theognis 1526–29. Sophocles fr. 941, Euripides *Hippolytus* 447, 1269; Lucretius 1.1. See also Hesiod, *Theogony* 121; *Antigone* 788–89; *Iliad* 14.199. Explaining the very early position that Love occupies in Hesiod's outline of origins, Jasper Griffin, *The Oxford History of the Classical World*, ed. J. Boardman et al. (Oxford and New York, 1986), p. 89, writes that "Love has no children of his own, but he is the principle of procreation which is to create the world."

21. For Sophocles, Eros is "unconquerable" (*anikate machan,* Antigone 785) and, for both gods and men, "inescapable" (*phyximos oudeis*, ibid., 788); Aphrodite is "invincible" (*amachos*, ibid., 800). In the epic tradition a verb used of Aphrodite or Love (*philotēs*) is *damazō* and congeners (*Iliad* 14.199, 316, 353; *Hymn to Aphrodite* 3, also Theognis 1388), which are also used of taming animals.

22. Cole, *Democritus*, p. 144, where Cole comments on the role of sex in the ethnology of Herodotus and the more general theory of Polybius.

23. *De finibus* 1, §69, cited by Cole, *Democritus*, p. 84, n. 12. Cf. also *De officiis*, 1§54:

> *nam cum sit hoc natura commune animantium, ut habeant libidinem procreandi, prima societas in ipso coniugio est, proxima in liberis, deinde una domus, communia omnia. Id autem est principium urbis et quasi seminarium rei publicae.*
>
> Again, since it is by nature common to animals that they have an urge to procreate, the first society is in marriage, the next in children, then one house, all things in common. And in fact this is the beginning of the city and the nursery as it were of the state.

For the translation of *nam*, see Andrew W. Dyck, "On the Composition and Sources of *Cicero De officiis* 1.50–58," *California Studies in Classical Antiquity* 12 (1979): 82, n. 6. Dyck discusses the apparent inconsistencies of Cicero's thought and their possible source.

24. I am aware of course that the identification of the comic and humorous across cultural boundaries is a very parlous enterprise, but the erotic, nudity, and food—all central elements of the Enkidu story—are common comic motifs, which tend to be universal: see E.R. Curtius, "Comic Elements in the Epic" and "Kitchen Humor and Other *Ridicula*," *European Literature and the Latin Middle Ages*, trans. Willard R. Trask (New York, 1953), pp. 429–31 and 431–35.

25. Among the pre-Etana, pre-kingship rulers, the name of the second, Kullassina-bel, "All of them (the people) are lord"(?), and the animal names of others, are perhaps meant to suggest a period of anarchy and savagery—*ho ataktos bios.* What Etana brings is order and organization (mu-un-gi-na, Jacobsen, *The Sumerian King List*, AS II [Chicago, 1939], p. 80:18; gi-na = *kunnu*).

26. For an edition of the text, see W.R. Mayer, "Ein Mythos von der Erschaffung des Menschen und des Königs." *Orientalia* n.s. 56 (1987): 55–68.

27. The conception of the ideal king or hero as one uniting in himself prudence and power, brains and brawn, has a long history in the West. Awareness of the polarity in Mesopotamia makes one question that in the West the phenomenon must be seen as a survival of prehistoric Indo-European religion as reconstructed by Georges Dumézil; so Curtius, *European Literature*, pp. 171–72. In any case, the ideal is in the epic tradition down to Virgil, declining to the status of topos in Late Antiquity and the Middle Ages and surviving into the Renaissance in the formulas "arms and studies," "pen and sword" (ibid., pp. 177–79; see also Thomas Greene, *The Descent from Heaven: A Study in Epic Continuity* [New Haven, 1963], p. 364). Note, too, in Hellenistic historiography the pairs used to describe the best rulers: "prudence and manliness" (*phronēsis, andreia*: Moses); "strength and intelligence" (*ischys, synesis*: first kings); "beauty and might" (*kallos, rōmē*: Dionysus in India); "manliness and intelligence" (*andreia, synesis:* Zeus in Crete, thereby gaining the kingship); add "manliness and judgment" *(virtus, consilium*: first kings): for the loci, see Cole, *Democritus*, p. 94, n. 23, who adds a number of references to authors who associate early kingship with the reign of law.

* * *

Bernard F. Batto
"The Yahwist's Primeval Myth"

Bernard F. Batto reinterprets Genesis 1–11, from Creation through the Flood, by concentrating on the way the Yahwist narrator made creative use of earlier Mesopotamian myths, especially *Atrahasis* and *Gilgamesh.* Identifying a Yahwist source of the Pentateuch is not new with Batto, but it enables Batto to identify certain features in Genesis as deriving from Mesopotamia. (He has a companion chapter that interprets the later Priestly source of the Pentateuch.) What is most striking about Batto's interpretation is that it challenges the mainstream Christian tradition of a "fall" of humankind in Adam and Eve. Instead, Batto thinks the Yahwist presents a created universe that is anything but perfect at the outset, and a deity that reconsiders humankind after initial plans for the creature had failed. Rather than a "fall" Batto sees a "continuously improved creation."

Mesopotamian myth provided the Israelites with the symbols of chaos (dragonlike flood and land beasts symbolizing the barren desert), with gods that are clothed, with trees of life, and with a wisdom tradition. Adapting these to a monotheistic setting, where, e.g., a mother-goddess is an unacceptable concept and the goddess functions are translated into human terms with Eve, the Yahwist portrays a deity "innocently mistaken" in his handling of Adam and Eve. Following *Atrahasis,* the Yahwist saw the Garden of Eden as a paradise, not for humans but for God. Humans were formed to relieve God of having to work in the garden. Yahweh, in this interpretation, failed to foresee the rebellion of the creatures that had been formed. As they attempt to become like gods, wearing clothing and possessing wisdom, humans have an uncertain relationship to animals and the divine, a status that is only resolved by the Flood, the story that is closest to its Mesopotamian analogues.

In *Gilgamesh* Batto is particularly interested in the formation of Enkidu and the humanization of Enkidu through intercourse with Shamhat. The search for immortality and the failure to achieve it is a conspicuous reworking of Gilgamesh's search for and loss of the plant (a version of the Tree of Life). The association of Gilgamesh and wisdom, a divine characteristic, Batto thinks, stands behind the Yahwist's second tree, the Tree of the Knowledge of Good and Evil. Key elements of the Yahwist's vision derive, then, from Mesopotamian myth. (Ed.)

It is appropriate to begin consideration of mythopoeic speculation in biblical tradition with a study of the Yahwist's Primeval Myth. "The Yahwist" is, of course, part of the so-called Documentary Hypothesis, which is currently under attack from a number of quarters. Nonetheless, this theory remains in its broad outline the best and most widely accepted explanation of the development of the Pentateuch, the first five books of the Bible. To be sure, numerous aspects of the theory as originally formulated in the classical statement by Julius Wellhausen toward the end of the nineteenth century must be revised in light of more recent research. But as an explanation for the many doublets and apparently contradictory narratives in the Pentateuch, the Documentary Hypothesis remains unsurpassed. Even many of the theory's critics either continue to hold to many of its tenets or else invent substitutes that end up looking very much like the hypothesis they purport to replace. Accordingly, in this chapter I will assume the validity of the Documentary Hypothesis, mindful of the fact that it is a heuristic device for understanding the complex process by which the Pentateuch as we now know it came into existence.

Nevertheless, the Documentary Hypothesis fails to account fully for the literary unity of the Pentateuch. In its classical formulation the Documentary Hypothesis posits that the Pentateuch is composed of four originally disparate sources—or, more accurately, literary strands—identified as the Yahwist, the Elohist, the Deuteronomist, and the Priestly Writer (abbreviated as J, E, D, and P, respectively).[1] These literary strands are thought to vary widely in date, from perhaps the tenth century to approximately the fifth century B.C.E., and to have been assembled only gradually by a succession of redactors, or editors, during the course of some five or six centuries to form a single "Torah." Recent studies, however, have emphasized that the Pentateuch exhibits a greater thematic and literary coherence than previously allowed. This is evident from the presence of such literary conventions as chiasmus, parallel episodes aligned in matching sequence, repetition of themes, linkage of units together through catchwords and phrases, and a host of others besides, which cut across the boundaries of the individual sources as set forth by the Documentary Hypothesis.[2]

Rather than scrap the whole Documentary Hypothesis as some have suggested, it seems more in keeping with the literary data of the Pentateuch to modify the Documentary Hypothesis along the lines suggested by Frank Cross.[3] Cross maintains the basic four pentateuchal traditions, but posits that the early epic traditions (J and E) were subsequently reworked by P, who added his own editorial structure and priestly materials to form a Tetrateuch (viz., Genesis through Numbers[4]). (Following Martin Noth, Cross separates out Deuteronomy, which originally was linked to the books of Joshua through 2 Kings, forming a Deuteronomistic History.) P never existed as a separate source, even though individual portions may have existed in an earlier form. Rather, P's method was to incorporate his[5] own priestly views and materials into an already existing epic tradition, in such a way as to preserve as much of older "Israelite epic" as possible.

My approach will be primarily diachronic. This is not to deny the validity of a synchronic approach. But for my purposes it is necessary to chronicle the various stages of development that a text has undergone. A demonstration of *the process* of mythopoeic speculation in the Bible depends upon being able to glimpse how biblical texts changed shape during their complex history of composition. Accordingly, in this chapter I will consider the earliest (J) form of the Israelite primeval myth. In the next chapter I will discuss how the myth was radically transformed by a later (P) redaction of the Torah. □

• • • •

The thesis I am expounding here stands, of course, in direct opposition to the opinion commonly encountered in commentaries on this passage, namely, that the garden was a place of sublime happiness for "our first parents" prior to their "fall." In that interpretation the garden is assumed to be a symbol of the deity's utter unselfishness and "grace." That is, God created humankind to share his own condition of eternal bliss and immortality, which by definition excluded any form of pain and suffering. If my thesis is correct, this was not the Yahwist's intention at all.

As I said, in the Yahwist's account the original intention of the Creator in fashioning humankind is the cultivation of the ground and improvement of the deity's garden. Very shortly, however, the author will introduce the seeds of premonition that humankind will not live up to its vocation. Rather than furthering creation, humankind will bring a curse upon the ground (3:17). Ultimately, the ground will even cry out in protest from the human violence to which it will be subjected, as when it is forced to drink Abel's spilled blood (4:10–14). Not until the time of Noah and the flood would the ground derive any real benefit from human activity (5:29; 9:20).[6]

A second indication of the tentativeness of the inceptive phases of creation is in the formation of humankind. The original divine blueprint for humankind proved less than adequate. The original human (*hā-ʾādām*) was a solitary being, undistinguished as to gender. Realizing that "it is not good for the human to be alone" (2:18), Yahweh molded additional creatures—the various animals—from clay.[7] Yahweh reasoned that, since these animals were made of the same substance, the human would naturally consort with them. However, the error soon became obvious. Humankind, although similar to animals in many ways, was clearly distinct. But just what constituted humankind's essential character remained yet to be defined.

The dependency of the Yahwist upon stock ancient Near Eastern creation motifs is once again evident.[8] The *Gilgamesh* epic describes the creation of Enkidu similarly. At first Enkidu was not fully human. Indeed, he is not called a human but rather a *lullû-amēlu,* which should be translated as "primeval human," or even "prototype human."[9] At this stage Enkidu is only incipiently human; he is portrayed as having more in common with animals than with humans. He wears no clothes but is instead covered with hair like an animal. He consorts with the beasts, roaming over the steppe as one of them. He eats and drinks as they do. In order to realize his human potential, he must abandon animal companionship for human companionship. His sexual intercourse with the harlot Shamhat is a metaphor for his humanization (*awēliš iwē*) "he become human" (Old Babylonian *Gilg.* II.iii.25, cf. 27). Through Shamhat Enkidu learns of his need for a female companion of his own kind. The harlot is more than a sexual partner, however; she is also a kind of midwife or mother who gives birth to Enkidu the human and educates him. "Holding on to his hand, she leads him like a child" (II.ii.31–32) to civilization and into full humanity. Previously Enkidu had sucked the milk of the wild beasts. Now through the harlot's coaxing, he learns to eat and drink in a human manner (II.iii.1–25). Finally, she clothes him like herself and his transformation is complete.

The human in Genesis 2–3 is portrayed similarly. When Yahweh discovers that the animals are not suitable companions for the human, he redoes his creation of humankind by dividing it into a male and a female: "man" and "woman." The usual translation of *ṣelāʿ* as "rib" obscures the Yahwist's meaning here. The semantic range of the Hebrew vocable includes "side" as well as "rib."[10] The image here is that of reworking "one of his sides," that is, of reshaping the whole into two complementary halves.[11] With this redefinition of humankind, creation has been advanced tremendously, according to the Yahwist. The tiller of the garden now has a "helpmate [*'ēzer*] corresponding to himself." The complementarity of the sexes is immediately confirmed in the institution of marriage, which is presented as the natural conclusion of the creation of man and woman.[12] With these advances the distinction between humans and animals is clear; humankind is a species unto itself and subject to an entirely different order.

But what of the relationship of humankind to the deity? If humankind shared with the animals a common origin from clay, it also shared divine life with the Creator. Yahweh had breathed his own breath of life into the original humanoid clay figure to make it into a living being. How much of the divine prerogative could the humans exercise without threatening Yahweh's sovereignty as Creator?

At the end of Genesis 2 the humans are described as being naked (*'ărûmmîm,* 2:25). This is normally interpreted as a symbol of innocence and sinlessness. Clothes were superfluous until concupiscence perverted the relationship between the male and the female of the species so as to require refuge one from the other, and until sin introduced an imbalance in nature so as to necessitate protection against a hostile environment. In the Yahwist's mind, however, the transition from nakedness to clothed seems to function as another metaphor for humankind assuming its proper place above the animals but below the divine.

In Mesopotamia the ancient bards had long since used the nakedness of the first humans to symbolize that these primitives, without benefit of the divinely bestowed gifts of civilization, were little better than animals. I have already mentioned how in the *Gilgamesh* epic the *lullû* Enkidu originally roamed naked among the animals. Still earlier the Sumerian myth "Ewe and Wheat" (or Lahar and Ashnan) described the original, uncivilized condition of primitive humankind in these words:

> Shakan (god of flocks) had not (yet) come out on dry land;
> Humankind of those distant days
> Knew not about dressing in cloth
> Ate grass with their mouth like sheep,
> Drank water from the water-hole (like animals).[13]

Another Sumerian text (*Ur Excavation texts,* 6.61.i.7'–10'), perhaps a variant of the Sumerian flood story, contains a very similar description of humankind before they learned how to cultivate the earth (i.e., became civilized):

Humankind of those distant days,
Since Shakan had not (yet) come out on dry land,
Did not know how to dress in cloth;
Humankind walked about naked.[14]

In Mesopotamian tradition the humans' donning of clothes was accomplished with the good graces of the gods. Clothes were one of the gifts of civilization, along with knowledge of irrigation agriculture and the building of cities, which the gods bestowed upon humankind for their advancement. Whereas it was the nature of animals to go about without clothes, gods wore clothing. Along with the horned cap, the flounced garment was the principal symbol of divinity in Mesopotamian iconography. Accordingly, clothes were an effective metaphor of the dignity of humanity, beings closer in nature to the gods than to animals.[15]

Once again the genius of the Yahwist is apparent in the way he manipulated this motif to his own purposes in Genesis 2–3. Traditionally the notice in Genesis 2:25, that the primeval humans were originally naked but felt no shame, has been linked with the verses that precede and regarded as a comment on male-female relationships. Thematically, however, this verse is linked to the succeeding verses and should thus be regarded as the introduction to the human couple's relationship with the deity. As in Mesopotamian tradition, in the Yahwist's story the original nudity of primeval humankind symbolizes the lack of a clear demarcation between humans and animals at this stage in creation. The motif is thus of a piece with the Creator's assumptions earlier in thinking that "the human" could find a suitable companion among the animals.

Although these humans at first were not ashamed of their original condition (Gen. 2:25), the serpent's words stirred their imagination to aspire for a higher dignity, "to become like gods" (3:5). Their eating of the wisdom tree opened their eyes to their nakedness. That is, they recognized that they were closer to animalhood than to the divinity to which they aspired. The act of making clothes for themselves must be seen, therefore, as an act of defiance of their creator and a grasping at divinity.

The crudity of their attempt at clothing—making garments of leaves—reveals the futility in their ambition. Ashamed of their nakedness but unable to make proper clothes for themselves, they hide from the deity whose status they aspired to. For his part the deity, in recognition that these humans had indeed proven to be more godlike than animallike, eventually clothes them, apparently like himself (3:21, cf. 3:22). But the author implies that this investiture is of a compromise. The garments are made of skin rather than cloth, apparently as a reminder that humankind shares the attributes of both deity and animals.

The "problem" of this dual nature of humankind is woven into the very fabric of the Yahwist's primeval myth. On the one hand, the human body is said to have been molded from the same substance (clay) as the animals; on the other hand humans are animated by the Creator's own divine life principle (2:7). Once again the Yahwist appears to have been guided by the themes borrowed from prior myths, *Atrahasis* especially. In that story also, as I have shown in the preceding chapter, the relationship of humankind to the gods was ambivalent and needed further definition. Created out of clay moistened with the divine blood of the slain rebel god, humankind contained an earthly substance animated by a divine life principle.[16] The task of *Atrahasis* was the working out of the proper role of humankind as subordinate to the gods but yet having their own proper function within the order of being. But considerable patience was required as the gods only gradually through a process of trial and error arrived at a workable "solution." The Yahwist adopted this basic cultural model but consciously modified it to accommodate the requirements of his Yahwistic beliefs.

The ambivalent status of the original human prototypes—at home with neither the animals nor the gods—is suggested also by their presence in the deity's garden.[17] Despite the common assertion that Yahweh created the garden for the benefit of the humans, the narrative suggests otherwise. The garden is presented as the deity's personal preserve where he grew the two divine trees, the tree of life and the tree of knowledge of good and evil.[18] The latter tree is unknown from elsewhere. But the tree of life is a traditional motif in ancient Near Eastern literature and iconography.[19] In iconographic exegesis, the fact the "Adam and Eve" had access to the tree means that they were destined to have eternal life, until their sin subverted God's plan. The Yahwist very likely intended another meaning, however. That the protohuman couple had access to the source of immortality suggests that humankind's status was not yet entirely defined, that the human experiment was still in the developmental stage.

Parallels can be found in both the *Adapa* myth[20] and the *Gilgamesh* myth; in both stories a human progenitor failed to gain immortality. In the one case, Adapa failed to eat "the bread of life" and drink "the water of life" offered him by the king of the gods. Adapa refused at the advice of Ea, the god of wisdom, who claimed that the food and drink were "the bread of death" and "the water of death." Since Adapa is depicted as a special creation of Ea, and since it is unlikely that the god of wisdom would not have known the true nature of the food and drink, one may conclude that Ea deliberately steered Adapa away from immortality, lest humans acquire a prerogative that belongs rightly only to the gods. In the other case, Gilgamesh strove valiantly to gain immortality, with near success. In the end, however, Gilgamesh lost "the plant of life" when the serpent smelled its goodness and stole it away while Gilgamesh was relaxing. In both stories, as in the Yahwist's tale, immortality is found to be inappropriate to humankind and is forever "lost."

The Yahwist posited a second divine tree in the garden, namely, the tree of knowledge of good and evil, whose fruit is highly desirable for its power to make one wise (3:6). The motif of a wisdom tree is not elsewhere attested; it seems to have germinated in and grown from the fertile imagination of the Yahwist. But it was inspired by thematic precedents.

Wisdom, according to ancient Near Eastern psychology, was a trait the progenitors of the human race were supposed to possess. Atrahasis's own name proclaimed that he was the "exceedingly wise" one. Adapa is called "the sage from Eridu." The hero Gilgamesh was also said to have possessed godlike wisdom: "of him Shamash is fond; Anu, Enlil, and Ea have broadened his wisdom" (*Gilg.* I.v.21–22). Indeed, the opening lines of the epic are nothing short of an encomium of Gilgamesh who "was granted all wisdom" (I.i.4). Perhaps most suggestive of all in this context is the transformation of the *lullû* Enkidu that followed his intercourse with the harlot Shamhat. Although he lost something of his closeness with the animals, he is said to have gained wisdom through a broadening of his understanding (I.iv.29), even to have become "like a god."[21]

Wisdom, though shared in by humans, was apparently considered first and foremost a divine characteristic. In Mesopotamia wisdom was especially associated with the god Ea (Enki), who was credited with creating humankind. So it is particularly noteworthy that Adapa and Atrahasis, archetypal humans, are both devotees of Ea and both noted for their wisdom. The imparting of wisdom by the creator to the first humans therefore must have been something of a standard motif. And as noted in the preceding chapter, when the flood story was added to *Gilgamesh,* making it also a quasi-primeval myth like *Atrahasis,* the editor found it appropriate to transform the hero Gilgamesh into a primeval, antediluvian sage as well.[22]

The genius of the Yahwist was that he thought to turn inside out the motif of primeval human wisdom so as to emphasize a distinction between deity and humankind. In his primeval story humankind was forbidden to eat any fruit of the tree of knowledge of good and evil. The exact meaning of the phrase "knowledge of good and evil" is disputed. But the context favors a meaning of universal knowledge or wisdom.[23] The phrase "good and evil" is thus a merism expressing both poles of possible knowledge, and includes everything in between. An equivalent English expression would be, she knows everything from A to Z. Now obviously, omniscience is a divine prerogative; it is particularly characteristic of the Creator. The forbidden fruit of the tree of knowledge of good and evil, then, is the author's symbol for an initial but unsuccessful attempt by the deity to establish a clear demarcation between Creator and creature by declaring wisdom off limits to humankind.[24]

The serpent, the wiliest of the creatures, sized up the situation very quickly. The serpent recognized the prohibition for what it was, a ploy on the part of the Creator to preserve his own turf. In Christian tradition the serpent has been maligned as a figure of Satan, who duped an innocent couple through a blatant lie. But that is hardly the figure the Yahwist intended. In his telling, the serpent spoke the truth. The woman and her husband did not die, as Yahweh God has said, "on the day you eat of it" (2:17). Rather, as the serpent correctly surmised, wisdom is highly to be desired, since its possession makes one "like gods, knowing good and evil" (3:5).

The serpent was said to be "shrewder than all the beasts of the field" (3:1). As has long been recognized, there is a pun intended between the shrewdness (*ʿārûm*) of the serpent and the nakedness (*ʿărûmmîm*) of the human couple in the preceding verse. But the pun extends beyond mere assonance. I have already noted that nakedness is a symbol of the lack of demarcation between the animals and humankind. Neither the primeval human couple nor this serpent is content to be mere animal. It is likely that the Yahwist derived the character of the serpent in part from Gilgamesh, as J's serpent bears some semblance to the serpent that had a part in depriving the semidivine Gilgamesh of the plant of life. In any case, the serpent of Genesis 3 is more a mythic character than an ordinary animal, as is evident from its ability to talk and to walk upright. (The serpent began to "walk on its belly" only after it was cursed in 3:14.) Indeed, given the later presence of cherubim to guard the divine tree of life (3:24), one wonders whether the serpent here is not to be connected with the awesome seraphim who stand in the presence of Yahweh (Isa. 6:1–7), which in turn are to be identified with the divine winged uraeus or cobra well known in Egyptian art as the protector of the deity, and thus a semidivine figure in its own right.[25] The serpent's principal distinction, however, was its possession of wisdom. Notice the intentional blurring of a demarcation between creator and creature in this scene. The perceptiveness of the serpent came from the fact that it, too, possessed divine wisdom. Just so, it perceived an affinity between itself as *ʿārûm* and primeval humankind as *ărûmmîm*. This would account for its urging of humankind to eat from the wisdom tree, as a kind of "divine right." (Put in psychological terms, the serpent is a projection of humankind's own illegitimate aspiration to be divine.) In any case, *ʿārûm* and *ărûmmîm* turn out to be connected. By the end of this story both will have to undergo further delimitation so that the divine prerogatives of the Creator and the limitations of creaturehood are properly defined. □

* * *

NOTES

1. For a recent, revised statement of the Documentary Hypothesis, see Richard Elliott Freidman, *Who Wrote the Bible?* (New York: Summit Books, 1987).
2. See, for example, Isaac M. Kikawada and Arthur Quinn, *Before Abraham Was* (Nashville: Abingdon Press, 1985); Robert Alter, *The Art of Biblical Narrative* (New York: Basic Books, 1981); Michael Fishbane, *Text and Texture* (New York: Scholcken Books, 1979); K.R.R. Gros Louis in several articles on Genesis 1–11 in the two volumes by K.R.R. Gros Louis, et al., *Literary Interpretations of Biblical Narratives* (Nashville: Abingdon Press, 1974, 1982); J.P. Fokkelman, *Narrative Art in Genesis* (Amsterdam: van Gorcum, 1975); Jack M. Sasson, "The 'Tower of Babel' as a Clue to the Redactional Structuring of the Primeval History [Gen. 1–11:9]," in *The Bible World: Essays in Honor of Cyrus H. Gordon*, ed. G. Rendsburg, et al. (New York: KTAV Publishing House, 1980), 211–219; Gary A. Rendsburg, *The Redaction of Genesis* (Winona Lake, Ind.: Eisenbrauns, 1986).
3. Frank M. Cross, *Canaanite Myth and Hebrew Epic* (Cambridge, Mass.: Harvard University Press, 1973), 293–325.
4. This composition originally would have ended with an account of the death of Moses, which was subsequently removed and spliced together with Deuteronomy 34, when at a still later date Deuteronomy was joined to the Priestly work to form the present Pentateuch.

5. The masculine pronoun is used here on the assumption that biblical authors were men. Presumably in ancient Israel, as in the ancient Near East generally, the scribal profession rested mostly in male hands. Nevertheless, there is nothing to preclude the possibility of the Yahwist having been a woman; see Friedman, *Who Wrote the Bible?* 85–86. However, Harold Bloom (*The Book of J* [New York: Grove Weidenfeld, 1990]) exceeds the meager biblical evidence in pinpointing J as a royal woman in the court of Rehoboam, son of Solomon. In contrast, P likely was a man (or a group of men), if the common assumption is correct that P was transmitted by *priestly* tradents. □

6. For a good treatment of the importance of the theme of "the ground" (*hā-ʾădāmâ*) in the Yahwist's primeval story, see Patrick D. Miller, Jr., Genesis 1–11: *Studies in Structure and Theme,* JSOTSup 8 (Sheffield: University of Sheffield, 1978), 37–42.

7. *Atrahasis* does not preserve a motif of animals being created from clay, but it was implied if not made explicit since the flood would have wiped out animalkind as well as humankind, had not the flood hero saved a remnant of both species (III.ii.32–38; text W, lines 9–10; note also Atrahasis's charge to *na-pí-iš -ta bu-ul-li-iṭ,* "save life," in III.i.24). The poem of Erra, which is dependent upon *Atrahasis* for the motif of humankind being almost destroyed because of its cries of rebellion that disturbed the deity, likewise parallels the threat of annihilation for both humankind and animalkind (Erra I.41–45); and a bit further: "Let men be frightened and may their noise subside; / May the herds (animalkind) shake and turn into clay again" (Erra I.74–75; cf. IV.150). Erra supposes that humankind and animalkind are drawn from the same matter and guilty of the same crime (I.77); see L. Cagni, *The Poem of Erra,* Sources from the Ancient Near East, 1/3 (Malibu, Calif.: Undena, 1977), 29, n.19.

8. The resemblances between Genesis 3 and *Gilgamesh* have long been recognized. The first "human" couple lost their chance at immortality because the serpent "tempted" them; Gilgamesh lost his chance at immortality because a snake deprived him of the plant of life. The first couple, originally naked, are clothed by Yahweh; Enkidu, originally adorned only with hair like an animal, is clothed by the harlot. In both stories an original state was "lost" but divine wisdom was acquired in the process.

9. The term *lullû* is attested only in contexts referring to primordial humankind. Speiser (*ANET,* 38, n. 86) translates it as "savage"; but *AHw's* "Ursprünglicher Mensch" is closer to the texual evidence. See J. Tigay, *The Evolution of the Gilgamesh Epic* (Philadelphia: University of Pennsylvania Press, 1982), 202.

10. *HALAT* III.965. The interpretation of *ṣelāʿ* as "side" is attested already in early Judaism (*Mishnah Rabbah,* Gen. 8.1, 17.6). The traditional interpretation of *ṣelāʿ* as a bone ("rib") derives in large measure from the joyous exclamation of the human in 2:23,

This one, this time, is bone from my bone
and flesh from my flesh!
This one shall be called "woman"
because from "man" this one was taken.

The function of this poetic couplet, however, is to emphasize the consubstantiality of the male and the female of the human species and the mutuality of their relationship; it is not intended to define the material derivation of the female of the species. Also to be discounted is the frequently repeated theory of S.N. Kramer (*Enki and Ninhursag: A Sumerian 'Paradise' Myth*, BASOR Supplementary Studies 1 (New Haven, Conn.: American Schools of Oriental Research, 1945], 8–9) that the Genesis topos derives originally from a Sumerian pun involving cuneiform TI, which ambiguously signifies both "life" and "rib"; repeated by J.B. Pritchard, "Man's Predicament in Eden," *RR* 13 (1948/1949), 15; T. Gaster, *Myth, Legend, and Custom in the Old Testament* (New York: Harper & Row, 1969), 21–23; Westermann, *Genesis* 1–11, 230. This theory is based upon the Sumerian myth of "Enki and Ninhursag" (*ANET*, 37–41). In the concluding portion of Ninhursag saves Enki, who unwittingly has impregnated himself with his own semen but as a male is unable to give birth; Ninhursag places Enki in her vulva and vicariously gives birth to the eight deities with which Enki is pregnant. The eight children are named for the various parts of Enki's body in which they developed: tooth, mouth, arm, etc. The goddess born from the rib is named Nin-ti. The pun with TI, "rib," is clear but derives solely from a similarity in sound, as it is unlikely that the corresponding syllable (TI) in that name Nin-ti is the word for life. (See T. Jacobsen, *The Harps That Once...: Sumerian Poetry in Translation* [New Haven, Conn.: Yale University Press, 1987], 203, n. 26.) Moreover, the myth makes no connection with "life." Whatever the correct interpretation of this myth, it has nothing to do with the creation of the female of the human species. Instead the myth seemingly speaks about the Mesopotamian concern for the generative power of water and irrigation within what would otherwise be a barren steppe; see T. Jacobsen, *The Treasures of Darkness: A History of Mesopotamian Religion* (New Haven, Conn.: Yale University Press, 1976), 112–113; G.S. Kirk, *Myth: Its Meaning and Functions in Ancient and Other Cultures* (Berkeley/Los Angeles: University of California Press, 1970), 91–99. In a different direction, Hans Goedicke's ("Adam's Rib," in *Biblical and Related Studies Presented to Samuel Iwry*, ed. Ann Kort and Scott Morschauwer [Winona Lake, Ind.: Eisenbrauns, 1985], 73–76) ingenious speculation that the Genesis tradition about Eve being created from Adam's rib may derive from a confusion *in Egyptian* of the two homophones *imw* "rib" and *imw* "clay," is unconvincing because there is no corroborating evidence that the Genesis account is in any way dependent upon Egyptian tradition, much less upon an obscure *and erroneous* conflation of homophones in that tradition.

11. The question of whether "the human" originally was androgynous (bisexual) (so W. Doniger O'Flaherty and Mircea Eliade in *The Encyclopedia of Religion,* s.v. "Androgynes") or sexually undifferentiated (so P. Trible, *God and the Rhetoric of Sexuality* [Philadelphia: Fortress Press, 1978], 141, n. 17) need not be settled here. A bisexual interpretation is attested already in *Mishnah Rabbah* (Genesis) 8.1.
12. To my knowledge, no one has remarked upon the fact that in *Atrahasis* at the corresponding position in the myth the institution of marriage is established, which provides additional confirmation to my thesis that the Yahwist's primeval myth is patterned on *Atrahasis.* The relevant passage in *Atrahasis* occurs in a damaged section and must be restored from several fragments (texts E, S, and R, as designated by Lambert and Millard, the latter misplaced by the editors). Improving upon the restorations by C. Wilcke ("Familiengründung im Alten Babylonien," in *Geschlechtsreife und Legitimation zur Zeugung.* Veröffentlichungen des Instituts für Historische Anthropologie e. V., 3, ed. E. W. Muller [Freiburg/München: Alber, 1985], 295–298), I read: "(When) a young woman develops breasts on] her chest, / a beard [appea]rs [o]n the cheek on a young man, / [in gar]dens and in the streets / [let them choo]se one another the wife and her husband" (I.271–276). I treated this passage and its biblical analog in "The Institution of Marriage in Genesis 2 and in Atrahasis," a paper read at the Catholic Biblical Association meeting, Los Angeles, Aug. 10–13, 1991.
13. Published by E. Chiera, *Sumerian Religious Texts* (Upland, Penn.: Crozier Theological Seminary, 1924), no. 25, obv. i. 3–6 (= lines 18–22 of Chiera's translation, 29); also trans. S. N. Kramer, *From the Tablets of Sumer: Twenty-five Firsts in Man's Recorded History* (Indian Hills, Colo.: Falcon's Wing, 1956), 145. The text has been studied most recently by B. Alster and H. Vanstiphout, "Lahar and Ashnan: Presentation and Analysis of a Sumerian Disputation." *Acta Sumerologica* 9 (1987), 1–43. The translation given here is based upon T. Jacobsen, "The Eridu Genesis," *JBL* 100 (1981), 513–529, esp. 517, n. 7.
14. Translation based upon the restorations proposed by Jacobsen. "Eridu Genesis," 17, n. 6. See also B. Alster, "Dilmun, Bahrain and the Alleged Paradise in Sumerian Myth and Literature," in *Dilmun: New Studies in the Archaeology and Early History of Bahrain,* ed. Daniel T. Potts, BBVO 2 (Berlin: Dietrich Reimer, 1983), 39–74, esp. pp. 56–57.
15. Robert A. Oden, Jr. ("Grace or Status? Yahweh's Clothing of the First Humans," in *The Bible Without Theology: The Theological Tradition and Alternatives to It* [New York: Harper & Row, 1987], 92–105) is thus wrong in arguing that nudity is a symbol of (near) divinity. His thesis is correct, however, to the extent that in Mesopotamian and Israelite myth the investiture of primeval humans with clothes does signify their full humanization.
16. One is reminded of the biblical injunction against eating flesh containing blood, "because the life is the blood" (Deut. 12:23; similarly Gen. 9:4).

17. In Ezek. 28:13, in a passage containing many thematic and verbal similarities to Genesis 2–3, Eden is identified as "the garden of God." Although not found in Genesis, this Ezekielian phrase is an authentic commentary on the Yahwist's intended meaning. See chapter 3. Also in Isa. 51:3, Eden and "the garden of Yahweh" are given as parallel terms.
18. I prescind from the debate as to whether the narrative originally spoke of only one tree or whether there were originally two parallel narratives in Genesis 2–3. □ In my reading of the text, the two trees have been consciously woven into a unified narrative.
19. On the concept of the "sacred tree" in Mesopotamian literature and iconography, see H. York, "Heiliger Baum," in *Reallexikon der Assyriologie* 4 (Berlin/New York: Walter de Gruyter, 1972–1975), 269–282, and the literature cited there.
20. See *ANET*3, 101–103.
21. The well-known reconstruction of the first part of this line as "Thou are [wi]se, Enkidu, art become like a god!" (so Speiser, *ANET* 75) must now be given up. Maureen Gallery Kovacs (*The Epic of Gilgamesh* [Stanford, Calif.: Stanford University Press, 1989], 9) notes that "a recently published Akkadian fragment from Anatolia confirms the restoration 'beautiful' instead of 'wise.'" Accordingly, any dependence of Gen. 3:5, 22 upon Gilgamesh is much less than is frequently assumed by commentators.
22. Noah is the biblical counterpart of Ziusudra/Atrahasis/Utnapishtim, the Mesopotamian pious survivor of the flood from whom the earth was repopulated. This apparently is the source of the tradition that grouped Noah with Job and Dan'el in Ezek. 14:14, 20. Job, of course is well known as a righteous man in the wisdom tradition. Dan'el in Ezek. 28:3 is depicted as a wise man of legendary fame. In Genesis wisdom is not ascribed to Noah, but the Ezekiel passage suggests that wisdom was indeed characteristic of Noah, like his Mesopotamian counterpart Ziusudra/Atrahasis/Utnapishtim.
23. There are three leading theories about the meaning of the phrase "to know good and evil": (1) sexual maturity, that is, the period from puberty until senility when one is able to enjoy sex; (2) moral independence, that is, the ability to determine for oneself what is right and wrong, which implies the possibility of going against divinely imposed standards of morality; and (3) universal knowledge, the meaning favored here. Each of these theories claims biblical grounding by appeal to different passages; indeed, they are not necessarily mutually exclusive. The author, as we argue, was almost certainly familiar with *Gilgamesh* and its story of Enkidu acquiring his humanity through sexual intercourse. Likewise, Genesis 3 suggests that moral independence is part of becoming fully human.
24. The correctness of this interpretation is confirmed by Ezekiel 28, where the hubris of Tyre is depicted as an illegitimate aspiration to divine wisdom. The allusions to the Yahwist's creation myth are patent and can serve as a commentary in helping to understand the Yahwist's meaning. See chapter 3.

25. See Karen Raldoph Joines, "Winged Serpents in Isaiah's Inaugural Vision," *JBL* 86 (1967), 410–415; and Othmar Keel, *Jahwe-Visionen und Siegelkunst,* Stuttgarter Bibelstudien 84/85 (Stuttgart: Verlag Katholisches Bibelwerk, 1977), 46–124. The serpent is here termed *nāḥāš* rather than a *śārāp;* however, the two terms are joined in the "fiery serpents" (*hannĕḥāšîm haśśĕrāpîm*) with which God punished the Israelites in the desert (Num. 21:6, 8; cf. Deut. 8:15). The terms *nāḥāš* and *śārāp* are used interchangeably throughout Num. 21:6–9; cf. 2 Kings 18:4. A flying or winged serpent (*śārāp mĕ-ʿôpēp*) is mentioned in Isa. 14:29 and 30:6. Finally, for a possible linking of cherub with serpent in the garden of god (Eden) in Ezekiel 28, see chapter 3, pp. 95–96. □

* * *

Marianthe Colakis
"Gilgamesh and Philip Roth's Gil Gamesh"

Marianthe Colakis compares the ancient hero to the anti-hero, Gil Gamesh, of Philip Roth's 1975 *The Great American Novel.* In Roth's novel Colakis finds "more allusions to mythical heroes and less heroism" than in any other piece of modern literature. Gil Gamesh is the star pitcher for the Ruppert Mundys baseball team during the early years of the Cold War. Like Gilgamesh, Gil is an arrogant overachiever and the angry son of a "half-crazy" father. They boast of being the only Babylonians in America.

He has a kind of Enkidu-like companion in the umpire, Mike "the Mouth" Masterson. When the unbeatable Gil Gamesh hits Masterson with a fastball to Masterson's throat, the umpire is in effect killed, in that he is mute for life. Gil runs off, and later tells of his wanderings through the U.S., when he becomes a Stalinist and a Communist spy, then returns, "reconciled to life's limitations," names names of Communists in baseball, and is finally executed in the U.S.S.R. as a double agent. Never a sympathetic character, Gil Gamesh is the antithesis of a noble hero.

This dark comic novel includes an Ishtar-like figure, the powerful manager of a team, Angela Whittling Trust, who takes as lovers all the great baseball stars. A man-destroyer, she offers herself to Gil Gamesh, and in a switch from the ancient story, he yields to her. Colakis sees in Roth's novel the disillusionment in America caused by Vietnam and Watergate. (Ed.)

It is difficult to imagine a novel with more allusions to mythical heroes and less heroism than Philip Roth's *The Great American Novel.* The title is ironic, since the loose plot revolves around the misadventures of the fictional last-placed Ruppert Mundys in the Patriot League, an imaginary low-ranked league. By focusing on losers rather than champions, Roth uses baseball as a basis for creating a "counter-myth" to America's "benign national myth of itself."[1] At the same time, he also spoofs the mythological framework used seriously by modern novelists, who may also take baseball very seriously (Bernard Malamud in *The Natural*).[2] At every possible point, the author appears determined to undercut the heroic stature of gods and heroes from various civilizations by giving their names to hideously unheroic characters. For example, Rama, the Hindu demigod, becomes Mike "the Ghost" Rama. Mike Rama's chief trait is his obliviousness to the outfield wall, into which he repeatedly crashes and injures himself.[3]

Yet the mythical names are not always chosen simply for comic incongruity and contrast. There are genuine parallels as well as differences between the heroes of old and their modern counterparts: Roth simultaneously satirizes and follows heroic myth. This paper looks at the most illustrative example, the comparison between the legendary king of Uruk, Gilgamesh, and Roth's pitcher Gil Gamesh.

Gil Gamesh occupies a unique position in the novel. The first chapter following the prologue chronicles his heroic rise, his downfall, and his subsequent exile. The final chapter tells what happened on his return from his wanderings. His story, which names the novel, fits the pattern of miraculous deeds, downfall/descent, and return that characterizes the prototypical hero myth.[4] His name is also unique. While the other men's names pair a common American name with a mythic god/hero's (i.e., Bud Parusha) or suggest a composite mythical character (i.e., Roland Agni—the French hero plus the Lamb of God, *Agnus Dei*), Gil Gamesh shares an almost identical name with his legendary counterpart. Therefore, we can expect him to resemble Gilgamesh more closely than the other characters resemble their namesakes.[5]

As is typical of the hero, Gilgamesh and Gil Gamesh have an unusual parentage that alienates them from others in society. Gilgamesh's mother is a goddess named Ninsun; his father is Lugalbanda, who according to one interpretation was a *Lil-la*, translated as "imbecile" or "half-crazy." Therefore, "From his paternal, human side, Gilgamesh is here shown to have a dark, imperfect heritage, which would not be meaningless in view of his not infrequent emotional outbreaks."[6] Gil Gamesh has a similar dark heritage from his father (we learn nothing about his mother). He is described as the "enraged son of a crazed father" (256). This proud and angry father informs his son that they are the only Babylonians in America. The national origin of the ancient hero becomes for the modern one an occasion for his first demonstration of power. Young Gil hones his pitching skills by throwing rocks at his tormentors who call him a "lousy little Babylonian bastard" (254).

That is all we learn about the heroes' backgrounds; we come upon them in the full glory of their strength. Gilgamesh and Gil Gamesh are very similar in their matchless abilities. As Roth's narrator, A. Word "Smitty" Smith describes his rookie pitcher (55):[7]

> Gamesh, throwing six consecutive shutouts
> in his first six starts, was an immediate sensation,
> and with his "I can beat anybody" motto,
> captured the country's heart as no ballplayer
> since the Babe began swatting them out of the
> ballpark in 1920... The tall, slim, dark-haired
> left-hander was just what the doctor had
> ordered for a nation bewildered and frightened
> by a ruinous Depression—here was a kid who
> just would not lose, and he made no bones
> about it either.

The description of the prowess of Gil Gamesh resembles the formulaic attributes of the warrior-king Gilgamesh as he is depicted in the first tablet of the Gilgamesh Epic (hence GE):[8]

> overpowering kings, famous, powerfully built—
> hero, child of the city Uruk, a butting bull.
> He takes the forefront, as a leader should...
> Is there a king like him anywhere?
> Who like Gilgamesh can boast, "I am the King!"?

The language in GE is "a string of descriptive phrases and epithets" which "combine to portray the ideal warrior-king in a very traditional way."[9] Comparable to this formulaic language are the clichés that Roth uses—"captured the country's heart," "just what the doctor had ordered," "a kid who simply would not lose and made no bones about it"—to create a picture of the ideal American folk-hero athlete.

However, both heroes are problematic as well as remarkable. Both Gilgamesh and Gil Gamesh are arrogant and spoiled creatures who abuse their power. Gilgamesh "runs wild with the young lords of Uruk through the holy places" and "oppresses the weak" (Tablet I, Column ii).[10] Gil Gamesh

> would glare defiantly at the man striding
> up to the plate (some of them stars when
> he was still in his cradle) and announce out
> loud his own personal opinion of the fellow's
> abilities: "You couldn't lick a stamp"...
> He knew a hundred ways to humiliate the
> opposition, such as late in the game
> deliberately walking the other pitcher, then
> setting the ball down on the ground to wave
> him from first on to second. (56)

In both cases, higher authorities must intervene to keep the heroes' powers in check. The gods create Enkidu to be a match for Gilgamesh, "that Uruk may have peace" (Tablet I, column ii, 32). General Oakhart, the President of the Patriot League, calls upon Mike "the Mouth" Masterson, the world's toughest and fairest umpire, to force Gil Gamesh to observe the rules.[11] The heroes shortly thereafter face the most strenuous opposition they have ever encountered. As Gilgamesh approaches a bride's house, Enkidu bars the way, and the two fight violently (Tablet II, column ii). Masterson calls a pitch of Gil Gamesh a ball, and orders Gamesh off the field when he protests (59–61). The stance of Enkidu "plant[ing] his feet" at the bride-house gate resembles that of Masterson "jaw raised, arms folded, and legs astride home plate...very like the Colossus of Rhodes." After he encounters Enkidu, we hear no more about Gilgamesh's tyranny; General Oakhart congratulates Mike for "civiliz[ing] the boy" (70). As a result of encountering their equals, the heroes, far from being diminished, continue to add to their glories. Gilgamesh and Enkidu kill the monster Humbaba; Gil Gamesh and Masterson have the greatest year of their careers. Only nature can stop Gil Gamesh's winning streak—when a game is called on account of rain. This foreshadows his later downfall, when he learns there are situations he cannot control, and is similar to Gilgamesh's confrontation of nature's immutable laws.

The heroes have contrasting reactions to their opponents. Gilgamesh acknowledges Enkidu's worth and the two become the best of friends, while Masterson remains Gamesh's bitter enemy. Yet Enkidu and Masterson play a similar role in forcing Gilgamesh and Gil Gamesh to confront their limitations. Gilgamesh and Enkidu slay the Bull of Heaven, but the gods demand Enkidu's life as a price. When Enkidu dies, Gilgamesh feels the reality of his own mortality for the first time (Tablet IX, Column i, 3–5):

> Me! Will I too not die like Enkidu?
> Sorrow has come into my belly.
> I fear death; I roam over the hills.

He then departs from his kingdom and begins his dark wanderings. Gil Gamesh, whose cry had been "I'm an immortal, whether you like it or not" (67), likewise learns he is not an immortal through the fate of Masterson. When Gamesh's fastball strikes Masterson in the throat, the umpire is at first believed killed. In fact, he has been rendered mute for life—and what is a mute "Mouth" if not dead? As a result, Gamesh is forced to leave town abruptly. For the first time, he learns that he is subject to laws.

One detail about the secondary heroes is worth noting. Both Enkidu and Masterson yield to pent-up resentment while they are *in extremis.* Enkidu curses the Stalker who first spotted him and the temple prostitute Shamhat who introduced him to culture and indirectly to Gilgamesh. Masterson expresses rage at the years of abuse he endured and concludes “STUFF OUR LEAGUE!” and “STUFF BASEBALL!” (78).

While the saga of Gil Gamesh is suspended in the novel at this point, his presence remains. Mysterious spectators who turn up in the stands at various points are rumored to be he. His role as tester of limits is taken over by others. A continual motif in the novel is the conflict between the letter and the spirit of the rules of baseball. Characters such as “Spit” Baal (originator of the messy pitch that bears his name), Isaac Ellis (inventor of Wheaties that bestow superhuman abilities), and the African converts to baseball (who insist upon unnecessary sliding) occasion spirited debates on the ethics of the game.

Gil Gamesh in person next turns up in a flashback—the story told by Angela Whittling Trust, manager of the champion Tri-City Tycoons, about her affairs with great baseball players. Mrs. Trust deserves some attention, since she has her analogue in Gilgamesh’s story. Greater in age and prestige than her lovers, Mrs. Trust resembles the love-goddess Ishtar, who takes her inferiors as her consorts. Both have five named lovers, not counting their husbands. Ishtar has a bird, a lion, a stallion, a shepherd, and Ishullanu, her father’s gardener, in addition to her husband Tammuz. Mrs. Trust has Ty Cobb, Babe Ruth, Jolly Cholly Tuminikar, Luke Gofannon, and Gil Gamesh. Ishtar and Mrs. Trust are the most complex and formidable female characters in GE and in *The Great American Novel.* Ishtar departs from the paradigmatic female role in being neither a mother-figure like Ninusn, a whore like Shamhat, or a wife, like the unnamed spouses of Utnapishtim or Scorpion-man. Mrs. Trust is likewise unique in the novel. She is neither a mother, a “groupie,” nor a wife, although she combines elements of all these.[12] These powerful females may nurture men, but their characters are also associated with destruction and death. Gilgamesh upbraids Ishtar in a series of general insults, and then catalogues her former lovers whom she destroyed (Tablet VI, columns i and ii). Her Sumerian counterpart, Inanna, descends to the Great Below and returns to the upper world only when she sentences her husband, Dumuzi, to death in her place.[13] Mrs. Trust likewise has her underworldly, man-destroying aspect. A man is of no use to her once his abilities are gone (she rejects Tuminikar for this reason). She resides in an underground bunker where she keeps the baseball bats of her greatest players along the wall (241–245). It is obvious from the following exchange that the bats are symbolic of penises (245):

> "Look at the length of that thing!"
> "Thirty-eight inches."
> Agni whistled. "That's a lot a'bat, ain't it?"
> "He was a lot of man."

Gilgamesh attacks Ishtar for being unreliable, like (among other things) a palace that crushes its defenders or a well whose lid collapses. Angela Whittling Trust is a name that hints at a similar undependability. Her first name suggests near-divinity, but her last two imply a breakdown (whittling away) of trust.

While Gilgamesh in GE rejects Ishtar, Gil Gamesh does become one of Mrs. Trust's lovers. Yet the contrast is not as glaring when we consider that in other myths, Gilgamesh is a consort of the goddess and on friendly terms with her. In the Sumerian story of "The Huluppu Tree" (a version of which is narrated in the controversial twelfth tablet of GE), Gilgamesh and Inanna are joined together in a mutual exchange of benefits. The position of Gil Gamesh in the sequence of Mrs. Trust's lovers is also noteworthy. He is the fifth; Gilgamesh was the fifth king of Uruk, ruled by Ishtar, and kings received their power through sacred marriage with the goddess.[14] While there is no hint that Gil Gamesh or the others are champions *because* they make love to Mrs. Trust, her choices of only the greatest players give her affairs the quality of sacred marriages. Gil Gamesh is also her last lover; after him, her husband dies, and she becomes a "responsible human being" (239). Elsewhere in GE, Ishtar also displays a more responsible side. During the Great Flood, she cries out with remorse at allowing this evil to come upon her people (Tablet XI, column iii, 116–23).

After the death of Enkidu, Gilgamesh wanders to the ends of the earth in search of immortality, and paradoxically endures a kind of death to obtain it. His wandering in the dark (Tablet IX, column 5) is like a voyage through the Underworld. The once-fearless hero is now afraid for his life (Tablet IX, Column i, 9–12):

> Lions I see, and I am terrified.
> I lift my head to pray to the moon god Sin:
> For…a dream I go to the gods in prayer:
> ' … preserve me!'

Gil Gamesh tells of a similarly lonely and furtive existence during his wanderings "beneath forty-watt bulbs in rooming houses in each of the forty-eight states…" (339). Although it is difficult to tell how much of the story he relates is true, there is no doubt that he does undergo "death" and return.

The heroes return from their exiles when they discover a purpose outside themselves. While he fails to obtain immortality, Gilgamesh learns from the wise man Utnapishtim that he can gather a youth-restoring plant. For the first time, Gilgamesh considers how his great deeds may benefit others as well as himself: "I will carry [the plant] to Uruk-of-the-Sheepfold; I will give it to the elders to eat; they will divide the plant among them … I too will eat it, and I will return to what I was in my youth" (Tablet XI, Column vi, 280–82). While we are never told Gilgamesh's age, we receive indications of profound changes in him. While he was a brash and irresponsible young man at the outset (adolescent in character, if not in chronological age), he speaks here like an elderly sage.

Gil Gamesh undergoes equally radical changes. He ends up seduced by Communism as a spy in the Soviet Union, which was for years demonized as a kind of "hell" in American popular mythology. Instead of absorbing the wisdom of a benign patriarch, he becomes indoctrinated with Stalinism. But he returns to America seemingly ready to stop thinking only of himself (328):

> God knows, I wasn't a Russian. Nor was I ever
> a Babylonian, really, in anything other than
> name. Least of all was I a member of mankind.
> No, it wasn't for humanity, or the working
> class, that my heart ever bled, but only for *me*,
> Number 19. Or so I thought, until I looked
> out my window one night last October…
> And I thought… The Cardinals, the Tycoons,
> and the Yanks are playing in the World Series,
> even as I sit here! *Who's pitching? What's
> the score?*

Convinced of Gamesh's contribution at becoming a Communist, General Oakhart (at Mrs. Trust's urging) allows him to become manager of the Ruppert Mundys.

The returns of Gilgamesh and Gil Gamesh to their respective homelands are worth comparing. Both had previously been concerned only with their own heroic glory, even to the detriment of others. Now that they have become reconciled to life's limitations, there is a new emphasis upon their functioning as authority figures, as upholders of the social order. GE ends with Gilgamesh proudly showing the walls of Uruk to Urshanabi, the boatman of Utnapishtim. Gilgamesh abandons his hopes of personal immortality but gains appreciation of what it means to be a king.[15]

Gil Gamesh's authority is more problematic. He leads his team to intermittent victories by indoctrinating them with hatred for their opponents, the spectators, and all America. He also "names names" of Communists in baseball and is hailed as a great patriot. Now that he is observing the rules instead of testing their limits, his tactics are paradoxically both subversive (he is still a Communist spy) and all-American. This drive for victory at all costs, the philosophy of "Nice guys finish last," is definitely American. It was also a part of Gilgamesh's society, but he managed to transcend it.[16]

Both Gilgamesh and Gil Gamesh lose heroic stature at the end. Philosophical resignation is not a quality commonly associated with heroes, and some scholars have expressed uneasiness or a sense of letdown at the ending of GE (if we assume that it does end at Tablet XI).[17] Although he accepts his mortality, Gilgamesh is never fully restored to human society. When he shows off his city walls to Urshanabi, he is viewing them from the outside. The detached coldness he here shows provides vivid contrast with his earlier passionate outbursts. We know nothing more about his fate except that he becomes a judge in the Underworld after his death. As for Gil Gamesh, he ends up even more of an outsider. Even though he is honored as an American hero, he is executed in the Soviet Union as a double agent. It is fitting that he, like Gilgamesh, ends his career "in the Underworld."

The heroic myth, like all great stories, is amenable to many treatments. What in one context can be the basis for folktale or religious revelation can become in another the occasion for tragedy or even black comedy. The latter is the result when there is no set of societal values that causes the hero's actions to be seen as meaningful. The ending of GE may not be exactly what we expect of a hero's story. But the poem as a whole unquestionably contains a vision that sees personal achievement as valuable, even if the consolation for the finality of death is slight. When the same story is told by an author steeped in Vietnam/Watergate cynicism, we would be surprised if any hopeful possibility were realised. Fortunately, Gil Gamesh never becomes a three-dimensional character about whose fate the reader cares, or Roth's nihilism could become overwhelming. The twentieth-century Gilgamesh remains a darkly cartoonish composite of heroic motifs.

❋ ❋ ❋

NOTES

1. "On *The Great American Novel*" in *Reading Myself and Others* (New York: Farrar, Straus, and Giroux, 1975), 89–90. Other general discussions on the book's mythic nature chronicle its indebtedness to American tall tales, particularly those of the Southwest. Bernard F. Rodgers Jr. notes that "often the heroes of the Southwestern tales were mysterious strangers shrouded in an aura of myth and legend" (*Philip Roth*, Twayne Publishers, Inc., 1978, 112). See also Walter Blair and Hamlin Hill's "The Great American Novel" in *Critical Essays on Philip Roth*, ed. Sanford Pinsker (Boston" G.K. Hall and Co., 1982), 217–28.

2. Despite the obvious differences in tone between Roth's and other contemporary baseball novels, it is noteworthy that all focus on loss, disaster and death rather than victory and joy. This observation is made by Thomas W. Edwards in his review of *The Great American Novel* (*New York Times Book Review*, May 6, 1973. 27). For a detailed discussion on baseball and American myth-making in fiction and journalism, see Ben Siegel, "The Myths of Summer: Philip Roth's *The Great American Novel*" (*Contemporary Literature* 17.2, Spring 1976, 171–90). Danny Jackson, who has recently done a translation of the Gilgamesh Epic, pointed out to me that another baseball novel, Mark Harris's *Bang the Drum Slowly*, contains a Gilgamesh theme. Its hero, Henry Wiggen, confronts grief for the first time through the mortal illness and death of his teammate Bruce Pearson, much as Gilgamesh does through the loss of Enkidu.

3. A complete survey of the parallels and comic differences between Roth's fictional characters and those of myth and real-life baseball is Frank R. Ardolino's "The Americanization of the Gods: Onomastics, Myth, and History in Roth's *The Great American Novel*," *Arete* 3.1 (Fall 1985), 37–60. Ardolino is particularly thorough on the subject of significant names.

4. Joseph Campbell, in *The Hero with a Thousand Faces* (Cleveland: Meridian Books, 1956) and Lord Raglan in *The Hero* (London: Watts and Co., 1936) are the best-known authors who list the motifs that recur in hero myths worldwide. These aspects are also discussed in David Adams Leeming's *Mythology: The Voyage of the Hero* (J.B. Lippincott Co., 1973), who provides an anthology of literary excerpts according to theme.

5. Ardolino acknowledges the importance of Gil Gamesh in stating that he "bestrides the novel like a colossus and his rise and fall epitomizes Roth's method of deflating the gods through their translation into the American baseball and political scenes." (56) Yet he does not, except in very general terms, discuss the parallels between the legendary kind and the baseball player.

6. Rivkah Schaerf Kluger, *The Archetypal Significance of Gilgamesh* (Switzerland: Daimon Verlag, 1991), 24.

7. Philip Roth, *The Great American Novel* (New York: Farrar, Straus, and Giroux, 1973). All further references are to this edition. An examination of the relationship between Roth and Smitty, the novel's narrator, is beyond the scope of this paper. In discussing language or narrative, I refer throughout to Roth rather than Smitty, since these refer to a literary creation that belongs to the author rather than his fictional storyteller.
8. *Gilgamesh, Translated from the Sin-leqi-unninni version* by John Gardner and John Maier (New York: Vintage Books, 1985). All quotes are taken from this translation unless otherwise indicated.
9. Gardner and Maier, 63.
10. The exact nature of Gilgamesh's oppression of his people is disputed. Presumably it has something to do with his using of citizens for forced labor and his abuse of sexual rights to the women. However, there is an interesting allusion in the older Sumerian epic "Gilgamesh, Enkidu, and the Netherworld" to his oppression of the young men of Uruk through some sort of athletic contest played with a *pukku* and a *mekku*. These have been interpreted as (among other things) a wooden ball and a mallet. What the game was is unknown; Jacob Klein suggests polo ("A New Look at the 'Oppression of Uruk' Episode in the Gilamesh Epic," unpublished manuscript). Yet the connection with baseball is irresistible. It is not known whether Roth was aware of this particular aspect of Gilgamesh, but the resemblance is too close to leave unmentioned.
11. Although I see Masterson primarily as an Enkidu-figure, he also possesses some characteristics of the sage Utnapishtim in GE, who ultimately convinces Gilgamesh of the futility in seeking immortality. There are also analogies with the characters of Achilles and Agamemnon as they are conceived in the *Iliad*. Masterson shares the loss of a child with Agamemnon. Agamemnon sacrificed his daughter Iphigenia so that the Greek fleet could sail to Troy. Masterson's daughter Mary Jane was kidnapped and murdered when her father refused to be blackmailed. Both men value their public duty over their children, and suffer a grievous fate as a result.
12. On the range of female roles in GE, see Rivkah Harris, "Images of Women in the Gilgamesh Epic," in *Lingering Over Words: Studies in Ancient Near Eastern Literature in Honor of William L. Moran*, ed. Tzvi Abusch, John Huehnergard, and Piotr Steinkiller (Atlanta, GA: Scholars Press, 1990), 219–30. A discussion of the women in Roth's book is Janis P. Stout's "The Misogyny of Roth's *The Great American Novel*" (*Ball State University Forum* 27.1 [Winter 1986], 72–75.
13. For this and other myths about the goddess, see *Inanna: Queen of Heaven and Earth* by Diane Wolkstein and Samuel Noah Kramer (New York: Harper and Row, 1983).
14. The origin and development of this custom is discussed in Samuel Noah Kramer's *The Sacred Marriage Rite* (Bloomington: Indiana University Press, 1969), particularly in chapters 3 and 4.

15. The contrast between the settled ruler (who must often sacrifice for the benefit of others) and the independent hero (who seeks personal glory) is discussed in W.T.H. Jackson's *The Hero and the King: An Epic Theme* (New York: Columbia University Press, 1982). Gilgamesh is both hero and king since his story was written before epic conventions became fixed.

16. Samuel Noah Kramer speaks of the Sumerians' "one very special psychological drive which motivated much of their behavior and deeply colored their way of life—the ambitious, competitive, aggressive and seemingly far from ethical drive for pre-eminence and prestige, for victory and success" in *The Sumerians: Their History, Culture, and Character* (University of Chicago Press, 1963), 264. He notes the similarity to modern American culture (268).

17. Hope Nash Wolff, in "Gilgamesh, Enkidu, and the Heroic Life," points out that Gilgamesh "suffers no tragic or glorious end, but returns quietly home, defeated in his demand for a better life." She calls the ending of GE "unique and peculiar." (*Journal of the American Oriental Society* 89.2, 1969, 392) Thorkild Jacobsen, in "The Gilgamesh Epic: Tragic and Romantic Vision," concurs: "One can hardly avoid a feeling that by 'growing up' Gilgamesh somehow 'grew down,' lost stature. True, in finally facing reality Gilgamesh...became normal, and sensible. But in so doing he lost of course what had made him heroic, and for a work of literature it is not good to lose its hero to the commonplace." (In *Lingering Over Words*, 231–49.)

* * *

Gilgamesh from Other Perspectives

J. Tracy Luke and Paul W. Pruyser
"The Epic of Gilgamesh"

In 1982, J. Tracy Luke and Paul W. Pruyser wrote the most extensive Freudian analysis of the poem yet, one that finds a narcissistic-phallic crisis and an oedipal conflict, latency, and a maturing process in Gilgamesh. They note that Freud himself had commented in passing that Gilgamesh and Enkidu were "twins," and Enkidu is something like Gilgamesh's "afterbirth."

Luke and Pruyser, convinced that *Gilgamesh* was enacted as a liturgical drama in "the religious cult," see in the poem both the liturgical drama and a "developmental process," using Erik H. Erikson's stages of human growth. *Gilgamesh* derives its narrative from developmental history, but its "temporal form" from the worship of Ishtar.

The stages of Gilgamesh's development open with "The Narcissistic-Phallic Crisis," as the hero, a "child-king" and "rampaging stud" claims everyone for his lust. The ambivalence with the harlot humanizing Enkidu, separating him from his "idyllic animal innocence," is treated in the stage, "Elaboration of the Oedipal Crisis." (Shamhat is the "mother-lover" who "incestuously weakens Enkidu.") Later stages include the "Onset of the Latency Interlude" and "Reaching Toward Identity and Intimacy," when Gilgamesh and Enkidu fight, embrace, and then decide upon the adventure that takes them away from the city.

Since depth psychology makes much use of dreams, perhaps Luke and Pruyser are the most impressive in reading latent meaning in the dreams recounted in the poem, where the characters themselves, e.g., Ninsun, read only the manifest content in the dream.

When later a "matured" Gilgamesh refuses Ishtar, the Bull—an imago of the father—is sacrificed, and the sacrifice of Enkidu comes immediately after it. The quest of Gilgamesh is considered "A Crisis-Precipitated Regression." Gilgamesh matures, though, and leaves Utnapishtim "an old, wise and humble ruler." In the latest stage, the adult Gilgamesh is now prepared for the sacred marriage with Ishtar. In pursuing this line of argument, Luke and Pruyser connect *Gilgamesh* with *The Descent of Ishtar.* (Ed.)

The ancient Mesopotamian Epic of Gilgamesh, recovered by archaeologists more than a century ago, has been carefully reconstructed, and widely studied from the historio-comparative–literary point of view. Freud and Jung once exchanged brief comments on the epic in their correspondence, and Joseph Campbell focused on its archetypal concerns.[1] However, the Gilgamesh Epic has been relatively neglected in psychoanalytic studies of ancient narratives. Like some other epics, this one covers a sizeable time span in the hero's life course and can thus be approached as a developmental history. Moreover, the epic was in all likelihood enacted as a liturgical drama in the religious cult, and can therefore be approached as a pedagogy; we should imagine a fascinated audience making temporary identifications with the epic's *dramatis personae.*

Sigmund Freud was fascinated with ancient mythology.[2] Clinical observation led him to associate dream symbolism with mythic images, and neurotic symptoms with ideation or characterization in ancient stories. The classic illustration of this process in Freud's research is of course his discovery of the Oedipus complex, which he described through the imagery of Sophocles' tragedy. Central and fundamental to psychoanalysis as this discovery remains, the oedipal theme does not exhaust Freud's use of mythology. Of equal importance to Freud was the way in which myths confirm the theory of phylogenetic inheritance.[3] This was a profound observation in an age that was all too eager to disassociate modern rational man from "primitives." Freud maintained that our psychic inheritance was far more pervasive and influential than his contemporaries conceded, and he was wise enough not to pretend that we could disavow that heritage, nor to absolutize it by fixating its themes and images into archetypes residing as templates in a collective unconscious, as Jung did.

Freud repeatedly encouraged his psychoanalytic colleagues to interpret mythology, and considered such studies essential in the ideal psychoanalytic education. With characteristic modesty, he understated his own contributions to modern myth studies.

We will seek to extend Freud's focus by a consideration of the therapeutic potential of mythology. Bennet Simon's recent study deals with therapeutic qualities in ancient Greek epic poetry, drama, and philosophy, and we build upon his work by noting that some of these qualities appear in the ancient Epic of Gilgamesh.[4] While rather specific in this intent, our study shares with a much broader literature the view that ancient stories are highly potent, creative, life facilitating and value setting expressions of human experience and longing. Harry Slochower in his *Mythopoesis* examines this outlook in detail while offering a psychoanalytic appraisal of mythic themes in literature from the Old Testament story of Job to the writings of Thomas Mann. He emphasizes the remarkable tenacity of mythic themes through the process of mythopoesis, the essential contribution of myth to human self understanding, and the precarious situation of mythopoesis in the flux of contemporary life.[5]

Known in considerable detail since the late nineteenth century, the Gilgamesh Epic consists of eleven sections (tablets), each with three hundred or fewer lines of narrative poetry. The story's central figure, Gilgamesh, was an early Sumerian king whose historicity is now certain. He had become legendary long before the full development of this epic poem, ca. 2000 B.C. Discovered fragments indicate that this epic was popular throughout the Ancient Near East from the beginning of the second millennium B.C. until at least the mid-sixth century B.C. References to the document in this study will follow the reconstruction and translation by E.A. Speiser, in James B. Pritchard, ed., *Ancient Near Eastern Texts Relating to the Old Testament* (Princeton, 1955) [hereafter abbreviated *ANET*], and "The Epic of Gilgamesh: Notes and Additions," by A.K. Grayson, in James B. Pritchard, ed., *The Ancient Near East: Supplementary Texts and Pictures Relating to the Old Testament* (Princeton, 1969).

The Epic of Gilgamesh is a highly formalized and ritualized story about a heroic king whose arrogant behavior initially results in a social crisis in Uruk, the city where he reigns. The gods intervene by creating his double from a savage who is humanized in the hope of thereby constraining Gilgamesh. However, Enkidu, the double, and Gilgamesh become fast friends. They set out on a great adventure and are highly successful; but their exploits also bring them into conflict with the gods, who retaliate and punish them by inflicting a fatal disease on Enkidu. His death precipitates a further crisis for Gilgamesh. Now, fearing death, he embarks on a search for immortality, ignoring the advice that his quest is folly and that there are other alternatives. With the aid of Urshanabi, a boatman, he crosses the mysterious ocean to the dwelling place of Utnapishtim, the Mesopotamian flood hero and the only mortal to have ever been granted immortality. He too must disappoint Gilgamesh, but sends him home with a magic prickly plant of 'eternal youth' which Gilgamesh loses to a serpent trickster. The tale ends with Gilgamesh returning to Uruk, now pointing out its grandeur to his new friend Urshanabi. The original crises appear to have ended and Gilgamesh is ready to resume his kingly responsibilities.

From this sketch, we sense that the narrative involves a developmental process and is a liturgical drama. As we examine the story in detail, we will use Erikson's developmental stages of human growth as a general guide,[6] asking what specific life stages are suggested by the story; what the intent may be of the crises described; what regressions or progressions occur; and what is the meaning of the apparent growth and conflict resolution. We will watch the rise and fall of critical emotions and events, the roles of *dramatis personae* and ritual acts.

In all likelihood, the epic also served as story line in the Mesopotamian New Year's festival which centered in the cult of the goddess Ishtar. Thus, a double reading is indicated. On the one hand, the epic is a narrative about one man's developmental history, with which any reader can identify. On the other hand, the story is the temporal frame for a lengthy ritual whose object is the worship of Ishtar. Supported by a chorus and punctuated by priestly acts, the epic was ritually enacted in front of a crowd which was to attain personal guidance for life and achieve healing from its participation in the liturgy. □

Reaching Toward Identity and Intimacy

The journey of Gilgamesh and Enkidu to the Cedar Mountains is marked by close companionship, some role confusion regarding who will lead and who will follow, and moments of fear and isolation, mixed with acts of mutual reassurance. The heroes have left their mother(s) behind, exhibit considerable bravery and willingness to take risks. Idealistically, they believe that their assault on the Huwawa monster will bring an end to evil. We watch them struggle with growth from latency to adolescence and young adulthood, and when, with the aid of the Sun god Shamash, they succeed in slaying the evil monster, it would appear that their journey will meet with total success. Yet, beneath the surface, serious difficulties remain. As Gilgamesh chops down the cedar forest to reach the monster, and as we learn that the monster guards the sacred mountain abode of Ishtar, he finds himself enmeshed in vestiges of an earlier crisis: this time, Gilgamesh has succeeded in smashing the door to her chamber. But Enkidu, who once prevented him from penetrating her abode, is now on his side. The ominous danger of incest looms again, hidden in what passes as a noble deed.

After slaying the monster, Gilgamesh washes himself and puts on his royal attire. We have not yet mentioned the earlier account of ritual washing, cutting of the hair, and reattiring of Enkidu at the time of his domestication. Such washings are familiar elements of blood guiltiness, expiration, and purification in ancient Babylonian myths and rites and we will see their reappearance at later turning points in this cultic drama.

As soon as Gilgamesh has purified himself and put on his royal robes and crown, the goddess Ishtar appears as a seductress, proposing marriage to him. She also offers material gifts of unimaginable splendor. Her offer seems irresistible. But now, Gilgamesh has indeed matured; entirely on his own, he refuses her offer. Unfortunately, his new self is so frail that the refusal is clumsy. In fact, Gilgamesh's terror of Ishtar shows through as he rages at her, calling her an untrustworthy whore, and reciting her many infidelities with other lovers. Nowhere else in this story are the heady dangers of incest and total union with the gods so vividly and explicitly portrayed. Gilgamesh's fierce handling of his powerful emotions triggers Ishtar's rage. She becomes a mean divine child and manipulates her father Anu, forcing him to send down the Bull of Heaven to retaliate for her injured vanity. In the ancient Near East, the symbol of divine male power, this Bull of Heaven is always the image of the father, out to slay the wayward sons, only to run the risk of being slain by them. In what appears to be another ritual dance, the two heroes engage in combat with the cosmic bull, and when Enkidu (not the irate Gilgamesh) drives his sword into the neck of the bull, the dance becomes a sacrifice: the successful slaying of the father must be followed by an expiatory act. The awesomeness of these events is verbalized by two choruses. The women of Ishtar begin a wail of mourning, while the men of the city admire the kill, divide it as booty and trophy, and set in motion a heroic banquet for the victors.[7] Gilgamesh and Enkidu now enter the great gate at Uruk. The wailing women have disappeared, and in their place, erotic lyre maidens raise a festive chant. It would appear that the heroes have come of age through their daring adventure.

Caught up in this celebration, we might fail to notice that Ishtar has disappeared. How totally out of character for the great Queen of Heaven to leave us with neither a blessing nor an admonition! Rejected and defeated, she just seems to slip away, leaving the drama as the heroes did earlier. Where has she gone? Perhaps we have discovered here the cultic context for another Akkadian story known as "The Descent of Ishtar to the Nether World." Just as Gilgamesh passed through a narcissistic rage, so did the Queen of Heaven. Momentarily, in the drama, Gilgamesh will begin a final regressive-progressive journey, from which he will return to kingship in Uruk.

Apparently, Ishtar must make a parallel journey in order to prepare for her return to eventually meet the king at her sacred temple bed, where their intercourse will generate the New Year. The epic drama has now reached a critical turning point. The phallic arrogance of our child-king and the castrating envy of the daughter of heaven are now left behind and a new motif is introduced: that all men are mortal. □

Progression, Generativity, and Maturity

Hidden within emotional crisis are seeds of new insight and growth. This promising vision, rediscovered in our century, was apparently held in antiquity. All historic religious claims of "redemption," however they state the problem, its origin, or the desired outcome, ascribe to this view. In our epic drama, Gilgamesh will now receive this profound insight from Utnapishtim. The power and intent of the conclusion of this epic are easy to overlook because Gilgamesh does not get what he came seeking, which introduces an unmitigated disappointment. More significantly however, a snake-trickster episode in this final scene draws the modern reader's attention to a more familiar paradise-lost story in which a snake and a woman wanting to be helpful to a man (Utnapishtim's wife urges him to give Gilgamesh a departure gift) result in their despair, their expulsion from a garden of immortality, and a pronouncement of the inevitability of death.

Utnapishtim helps the sleep-confused Gilgamesh arise and calls Urshanabi the boatman in order to instruct him:

> Take him, Urshanabi, and bring him to the
>   washingplace.
> Let him wash off his grime in water
>   clean as snow,
> Let him cast off his skins, let the sea carry
>   (them) away,
> That the fairness of his body may be seen.
> Let him renew the band round his head,
> Let him put on a cloak to clothe his nakedness,
> That he may arrive in his city,
> That he may achieve his journey.[8]

Urshanabi carries out these instructions. A ritual bathing of the king and preparation for his reinvestiture are clearly the cultic prescriptions. The casting off of the lion's skin and allowing himself to be seen as he really is are tell-tale symbols of the regeneration and renewal that the liturgy is intended to produce. Gilgamesh is no longer a young, narcissistic aggressor, but an old, wise and humble ruler.

Just when Gilgamesh and Urshanabi are ready to set off to sea for their return to the ordinary world, the wife of Utnapishtim, perhaps failing to understand what has transpired, urges her husband to give Gilgamesh a prickly plant whose possession bestows eternal youth. It lives at the water's bottom. All Gilgamesh must do is to tie rocks to his feet and dive for the plant, risking the pain of grasping it. Perhaps Utnapishtim's wife is a final female enticer, disguised to be sure, but not completely lacking in power to lure Gilgamesh even if for only a moment. At any rate, Gilgamesh dives for the plant, obtains it, heads for home with Urshanabi, seeming now to have obtained everything he wished for and more.

Having landed near Uruk, Gilgamesh sees a cool well and decides to bathe once more. We will be tempted to see him as obsessive, but this time, he has something to be obsessed about! He must make a risky choice between following the instructions of Utnapishtim or preserving the magic of the immortal's wife. While Gilgamesh is washing, a snake steals the plant and carries it off, eating it as he goes. Lest we imagine that the plant had no magical power, the snake promptly sheds its skin, thereby hinting to Gilgamesh that it now has the immortality (or eternal youth) which the hero had wanted.

Gilgamesh experiences brief remorse and weeps; weeping and sadness overtook his earlier raging and ambitiousness. Then he arises and the mythic drama comes suddenly to a close. We are back where we began at ramparted Uruk, and this time we walk in procession behind Gilgamesh and Urshanabi. Our old king is remarkably different from the brazen youth he had been. He looks zestful and refreshed, though older. He holds Urshanabi gently with one hand and points with the other to features of the city. 'Look at the terraces, the foundations, and the brickwork. This is Uruk. I am responsible for these buildings. Look at the orchards and fields around the city, how lush they are. Observe the gaiety of the people. And here is the Eanna, the temple of Ishtar. I built and care for her house, because she is my protectress.'

Mature and adult, Gilgamesh is now the guide of the boatman who once guided him. He takes pride in his city and his accomplishments, but knows that he needs the city and its people as much as they need him. As Gilgamesh approaches the temple of

Ishtar, we note that he no longer has his sacred axe, and his mother is nowhere in evidence. He does not need weapons or her advice any more. And of one thing we can be sure: this time he will not need to smash his way into the temple of Ishtar. As he comes to her now, she will welcome him to her chamber, having herself returned from an underworld journey in preparation for this moment of the king's rearrival.

And so our ritual drama concludes. Its setting is not in doubt. Here is the story that must be told, the experience that must be lived, over and over again in preparation for the *hieros gamos*, the sacred marriage of king and goddess, the latter represented by a priestess. We have discovered through our psychoanalytic approach to the epic how both the trials of Gilgamesh and the story of Ishtar's descent to the Nether World were part of the religious life and thought of the ancient Babylonians and Assyrians. The potency, danger, and awesomeness of sexuality are apparent throughout this drama. We sense that in this setting, sacred intercourse was not a decadent, magical, orgiastic rite that sought to ease the pain of living through periodic overstimulation and legitimated promiscuity. Only with the maturity achieved by arduous reinterpretation of the erotic past and the absorption of eros by *thanatos* are the participants made ready for the union of the *hieros gamos*. The New Year's ceremony was not merely concerned with the fertility of fields and the viability of government. The epic—and the cult around it—reach specifically toward individual maturation and familial relations.

The Gilgamesh epic is not merely about death and rebirth; it is notably a liturgical drama in which youthful erotic preoccupations become overtaken by thoughts of death, first leading to fierce narcissistic protest, and then to acceptance in sober resignation that still leaves room for living-on with periodic renewal. Nature has its cycles, but human beings have to make do with a limited time span whose end is foredoomed. What counts is the quality of their trek through life, the experiences that men garner and what they learn from each leg of their journey, each turning point they encounter, each fork they find in the road, each crisis they meet. Though men will not live forever, they should love and work as long as they can, taking pride in their city and their institutions.

❋ ❋ ❋

NOTES

1. Sigmund Freud and C.G. Jung, *The Freud/Jung Letters*, William McGuire, ed., Ralph Manheim and R.F.C. Hull, trans. (Bollingen Series, XCIV) Princeton, 1974, pp. 445–446, and 448–449. Jung hints at linking Utnapishtim, the Gilgamesh epic flood hero with gnomic utterances (later in his own work Jung would associate Utnapishtim with Longfellow's Hiawatha and the Wandering Jew (p. 445, n. 2). S. Freud (pp. 448–449) referred to the brothers, Gilgamesh and Eabani (=Enkidu), correctly sensing that the story intends for them to be twins and thus from a common mother. He does not elaborate his suggestion that Enkidu is Gilgamesh's "afterbirth" (p. 449), nor do we. Joseph Campbell's interpretation is in his *The Hero with a Thousand Faces* (New York, 1949), pp. 185–188. Elsewhere in psychoanalytic literature Theodor Reik, *Myth and Guilt: The Crime and Punishment of Mankind* (New York, 1957), pp. 67–68, briefly describes the Gilgamesh epic and accurately senses its connection with Genesis.
2. For the collected references on myth and mythology, see conveniently, Angela Richards, compiler, "Indexes and Bibliographies," in Sigmund Freud, *St. Ed.*, 24 (London, 1974), pp. 325–326.
3. Sigmund Freud, "An Infantile Neurosis and Other Works," *St. Ed.*, 17 pp. 119–122, 203–204, 261–262; "Introductory Lectures on Psycho-Analysis (Part III)," *St. Ed.*, 16, p. 371.
4. Bennett Simon: *Mind and Madness in Ancient Greece: The Classical Roots of Modern Psychiatry* (Ithaca and London, 1978), pp. 78–88.
5. Harry Slochower: *Mythopoesis: Mythic Patterns in the Literary Classics* (Detroit, 1970), pp. 12–46. Slochower recognizes a similarity between the Gilgamesh Epic and Western mythopoesis and identifies the epic as "the first major story which explicitly sounds the motif of unrest in the hero's quest," see pp. 336–338, and notes 21–25.
6. Erik H. Erikson: *Childhood and Society*, second edition (New York, 1963), pp. 247–274. □
7. We will want to note carefully how the sacrificial killing of the Bull of Heaven, the father imago, is followed almost immediately in the story by the compensatory sacrificial death of Enkidu. Readers will not miss the remarkable way in which this early story supports Freud's thinking in "Totem and Taboo," *St. Ed.*, 13. Perhaps no story from antiquity declares as unequivocally as this epic, Freud's perception that the attempts at resolution through sacrificial rites were always inadequate. □
8. *ANET*, p. 96; XI, 238–244.

* * *

Dorothy Hammond and Alta Jablow

"Gilgamesh and the Sundance Kid: The Myth of Male Friendship"

The intense attachment of Gilgamesh and Enkidu has not escaped recent debates on the nature of homosexuality and gender differences generally. David M. Halperin, in "Heroes and their Pals," considered *Gilgamesh* in a study of friendship, as it is represented in ancient, especially Greek texts. Halperin argues that Homer's depiction of Achilles and Patroclus should be seen as an extension of an older narrative pattern seen in *Gilgamesh* rather than as the Greeks themselves later viewed the friendship: as a sexual relationship. Dorothy Hammond and Alta Jablow, in "Gilgamesh and the Sundance Kid: The Myth of Male Friendship," deconstruct the culturally prestigious myth of male bonding from an anthropological perspective. Warfare is the setting of important stories that depicted friendship as a voluntary bond outside kin groups (where responsibilities toward kin were largely unrelated to emotional satisfaction). Hammond and Jablow focus on the gods' selection of a friend for Gilgamesh rather than a wife and family. "Gilgamesh and Enkidu first met as Gilgamesh was about to be married, but Enkidu barred access to the bride's house," in their interpretation. In the many stories of male bonding from the ancient world to the present, Hammond and Jablow find *Gilgamesh* fitting the pattern in all but one important respect: the "divine creation of a special friend" (247). Quite unlike most interpreters of *Gilgamesh,* who are content to point out patterns in the narrative, Hammond and Jablow find it important to point out the persistence of the ideology underlying friendship myths even in our time, when such myths are counterproductive, especially for women. (Ed.)

Until recently, anthropological studies of society, like those of all the social sciences, have been almost exclusively male oriented. Contemporary studies of women's roles have shown that this orientation yielded only a partial, and hence distorted, view of society. Generalizations about the institutions and culture of any society from the prefeminist perspective not only ignored the roles of women but undoubtedly skewed the descriptions of men's roles as well. It has become imperative to rethink the public roles of men, formerly so stressed in ethnographies. In the public sphere, men must cooperate to achieve their personal and institutional goals. Their cooperation has been attributed not only to its practical necessity but as fulfillment of a need perceived as intrinsic to males. That it is in the nature of men to bond with one another has become a truism that shaped the thinking of anthropologists as separate in generation as Schurtz and Tiger.[1] Tiger goes so far as to attribute the dominance of men in the public sphere directly to their unique capacities for bonding.[2]

That men bond to form friendships is an ideal that derives less from the work of scholars than from an overriding cultural assumption. This cultural article of faith is expressed in an elaborate stereotype of men and a related stereotype of friendship as the special proclivity and province of men. The stereotype idealizes men's capacities for loyalty, devotion, and self-sacrifice. It further implies men's potential for commitment to larger causes and their readiness to fight for them. The image totally excludes women and the domestic sphere. Men are most manly when they are fighting side by side in a world without women.

A contrary, and indeed, pejorative stereotype exists about women. They are presumed to be unable to form loyal friendships. As young, unmarried women, they are rivals for men's attentions; as married women, they are committed to their families and absorbed in the daily round of domestic life.

The stereotype of male friendship has been made familiar through repetition in a large body of literary materials from modern Western cultures and their antecedents. No such narratives exist about women. Only under the stimulus of the feminist movement have women's friendships been discussed or even acknowledged.

The image of male friendship closely parallels that of romantic love. Both idealize a dyadic relationship and set expectations of undying loyalty, devotion, and intense emotional gratification. Twelfth-century narratives established the theme of romantic love, which has predominated in most fiction up to the present. The theme is not merely a literary convention; romantic love became a social convention, as the only desirable basis for sexual relations between men and women, and as the prime motive for marriage. Lacking institutionalization, friendship is more private, less open to scrutiny than courtship and marriage. There are no rituals to describe and no statistics to report.

Our concern in this paper is with the content and persistence of the stereotype of male friendship and its relation to the realities of modern life. A review of anthropological studies of friendship in modern Western societies, which we include here, presents a picture so at variance with the literary and popular stereotypes that its viability seems even more remarkable. It constitutes, in essence, a myth of male friendship. Admittedly, we are stretching the definition of *myth* to include a wide variety of literature—a necessity for literate societies. All the pertinent literature buttresses and reflects the popular stereotype to create a coherent myth.

The Malinowskian axiom that myth is a charter for institutions is not applicable to friendship, since it is hardly a concrete institution in Western society. Nevertheless, Malinowski's theoretical position also encompasses the idea that myth serves as a charter for values, and this is the relevant factor in the persistent stereotype of friendship.[3]

We therefore hypothesize that the myth persists because it provides an ideology that enhances the idea of friendship between men. The myth is so pervasive that we cannot cover all the pertinent literature. We analyze the content of the relevant major epics, ancient legends and stories, and a sampling of contemporary materials.

ANTHROPOLOGICAL APPROACHES

The study of friendship in Western societies challenges the concepts of anthropology because they have been shaped by the institutionalized forms of friendship in the non-Western societies: blood brotherhood, trade friends, and bond friends. These relationships all entail clearly defined rights and obligations that have jural sanction and ritual validation. They are, as well, fully integrated into the overall social structure. For anthropologists, the difficulties of studying Western friendship are inherent in its very nature. Friendship in Western society, for the most part, lacks formal structure; it is based on individual volition and mutual affection, and is interstitial in the social structure. Friends establish their own terms for the relationship in which there are no obligations except those freely embraced, no rights except those freely given. Nadel recognizes the unstructured quality of Western friendships as having "general coordination of behavior whose precise aim content is mostly indeterminate, in other words, friends will act as such, assisting and showing their regard for one another on almost any occasion, no activity being excluded or specifically referred to in the relationship formula."[4] Elsewhere, Nadel states that "friend" can be described only as a "quasi-role."[5] The fluidity of the concept can encompass relationships in which roles are not socially defined, and in which expectations are set by the participants rather than by the formal structure of society. So amorphous a relationship, however important to the individual participants and the society, tends to escape the anthropological mesh.

Anthropologists have attempted in various ways to deal with what is for them refractory material. Brain affirms the affective nature of friendship. He contrasts friendships in the Western worlds with the highly structured friendships in the Cameroons and concludes that, lacking the support of formal organization, Western friendship can be only a fragile relationship. He calls for legal and ritual institutionalization to buttress a relationship that, otherwise, would seem to be floating in social midair.[6]

Eisenstadt and Pitt-Rivers also stress sentiment as the essential core of the relationship. Eisenstadt, however, views the private dyad of friendship as potentially oppositional to the values of the total society.[7] Pitt-Rivers, in contrast, indicates that the practical realities of Andalusian life are antagonistic to the maintenance of the *simpatia* required of the relationship.[8] While recognizing the ideal of affect, both authors predicate an inevitable tension between society and friendship.

Certain studies of friendship in small, closed communities in Newfoundland and Ireland, minimize the issue of sentiment.[9] They fail to confront the lack of institutional forms inherent in the relationship by asserting that friendship is an institution "with a force and vitality of its own."[10] Their analyses set out institutional parameters in which friendship serves as the basis for recruitment of fishing crews or drinking partners, settlement patterns or political and economic alliances. They are, perforce, focussed on the transactions between and among friends, rather than with the nature of the relationship itself.

Other anthropologists have dealt with modern friendship in purely theoretical terms, creating conceptual structures where there is no social structure. Du Bois, Cohen, and Wolf have developed typologies of friendship based on a scale from "affective" to "instrumental" or "expedient," rephrasings of the Aristotelian distinction between "good" and "useful" friends.[11] Du Bois includes several more parameters: intimacy and mutability. Cohen distinguishes four levels of friendship ranging from inalienable to expedient, linking each to a particular kind of community:

inalienable to maximally solidary; close to solidary–fissile; casual to nonnucleated; and expedient to individuated. Wolf reverts to the Aristotelian twofold category: the expressive or emotional friendship and the instrumental. Like Cohen, he links the expressive kind to solidary social units and the instrumental to individuated societies.

However neat these linkages seem, the actual correlations are suspect because the institutionalized friendships of solidary societies, expressive or not, are often highly instrumental. For instance, in Melanesian societies where trade is conducted through friends, they are far more concerned with the unimpeded exchange of trade goods than with sentiment. Close, affective friendships are not lacking in contemporary Western individuated societies. Commerce is impersonal and contractual; friendship is a relationship of "mutual liking...mutual service...mutual confidence."[12]

Although the typologies recognize a continuum between the polarities of affective and instrumental friendship, the poles are seen as distinct types. Both are, however, components of any friendship. Aristotle was right to add to his typology that even perfect friendship retains some element of the useful and that the moral imperative of sentiment colors even the highly expedient friendship.

THE LITERATURE

The large body of literary materials about friendship in the Western world includes novels, films, songs, and even opera, along with myth and legend. Despite the variety in form and content, all reiterate similar themes concerning friendship. A persistent literary tradition has developed from pre-Babylonian times, appearing among ancient Semites, pagan Greeks, medieval Christians, and the modern secular West. The tradition always dramatizes the devotion between male friends, usually a dyad, forged in an agnostic setting.

The earliest recorded version of the myth is in the Gilgamesh epic, but it was unknown to the modern West until the cuneiform tablets from the royal library in Ninevah were excavated and decoded in the late nineteenth century. This was the literary version of Akkadian myths and legends of a much earlier period. Similarly, the story of David and Jonathan, as we know it from the Bible, and the story of Achilles and Patroclus in the Iliad, had much earlier oral antecedents. Although the myth thus exhibits long historical continuity, the classical Greek narratives were probably the model for all later narratives.

All the variants of the myth, over more than 3000 years, retain the essential core despite drastic changes in culture and society. With the exception of imperial Rome, earlier societies share characteristics that contrast with modern industrial society. Early Sumer, ancient Greece, and medieval Europe were all small-scale polities engaged in endemic warfare; they were socially stratified with a small, literate upper class at the apex. In all of them, membership in the extended kin determined rank and wealth. A man without kin had, at best, little place in society and, at worst, small chance of survival. What then, would be the place of an ideal friendship in such a society? The kin group was undoubtedly supportive, but membership in it entailed obligations and constraints that could be very onerous. Aries points out that the extended kin line was the primary unit of loyalty but functioned "without regard to the emotions engendered by cohabitation and intimacy."[13] Friendship, in contrast, provided a volitional alternative source of support without the restrictions of kinship and may well have given more emotional gratification than the obligatory amity of kin.

In such societies, marriages were arranged with an eye to considerations of property and useful alliance; emotional attachment between spouses was not essential. All the more reason to value the affection of a chosen friend. Women's roles, even in the upper classes, were confined to the household, but there the women were in control. A man's place in his home was honorific but involved little participation. A man who limited himself to home and hearth was considered less than a man.

The public domain was the province of men where their participation made men's relationships with one another politically significant. A friend was also an ally. In the Greek city-states, every citizen (citizenship was limited to men of the upper stratum) was expected to be a warrior. Warfare was the quintessential form of political action. War not only separated men from their families but thrust them into dependent and sometimes long-lasting relationships. Warfare is the prime setting for the drama of male friendship.

With hindsight, the narratives of friendship seem to be political propaganda for abrogating familial ties in favor of male solidarity. In them friendship was idealized, war glorified, and the warrior the ideal man.

The conventions of the myth express an ideology upholding the moral worth of friendship and the social premium placed on it. The myth is retained in form and content even in societies such as

Rome and the modern West, which are mass societies, where the soldier replaces the warrior, bureaucracy dominates political and economic life, and loyalty to the state supersedes loyalty to kin. The myth could not be impervious to such radical change if it did not evoke a positive emotional response. Changed contexts, however, base that response on different values and needs.

The literary epic of Gilgamesh, dating from approximately 1600 B.C., combines what were probably separate narratives, from earlier oral traditions. The episode of Gilgamesh and Enkidu in the early part of the epic contains the basic themes of ideal friendship between two men. The gods, having determined that Gilgamesh, king of Uruk, suffered from loneliness, pitied him and created Enkidu to be his friend, one "who can measure up to him and give him companionship."[14] The gods, interestingly enough, chose to provide a friend rather than a wife and family to assuage loneliness. Enkidu, an artifact of the gods, was a total isolate. Without kin or community, he could be absolutely committed to his friend and concomitantly became the instrument that prevented Gilgamesh's marriage. Gilgamesh and Enkidu first met as Gilgamesh was about to be married, but Enkidu barred access to the bride's house. They engaged in a hand-to-hand fight in which Enkidu defeated Gilgamesh and then said, "'Gilgamesh, you have proved full well that you are the child of a goddess and that heaven itself has set you on your throne. I shall no longer oppose you. Let us be friends.' And raising him to his feet, he embraced him."[15] Gilgamesh's heart was won, and forgetting about the marriage, he embraced Enkidu as his true friend. Together they went on to have many heroic adventures. Their final exploit so seriously offended the gods that they caused Enkidu's death, leaving Gilgamesh inconsolable.

Enkidu, whom I love dearly
Whoever went through all hazards with me,
The fate of man has overtaken him.
All day and night have I wept for him,
And would not have him buried.
. . .
Since he is gone I can no longer comfort find.
Keep roaming like a hunter in the plains.[16]

This story is exceptional only in the divine creation of a special friend; otherwise, it conforms to all the narratives of heroic friendship that follow. All make high drama of the relationship, endowing it with glamour and beauty. The friends are heroes:

aristocratic, young, brave, and beautiful. In their free and wholehearted response to one another, they openly declare their affection and admiration. They engage in many adventures and battles, sharing danger, loyal to the death. Throughout life, they remain devoted and generous to each other. □

Despite variations in theme, and the great differences in religion and culture, the narratives through medieval times project and validate the earlier ideals of friendship. The stories belong to a tradition that was about and for aristocrats. The major change in modern versions of the myth is the loss of the aristocratic tradition. The class structure of the modern Western world, along with much else, has been revolutionized, but the ideals of friendship have not undergone radical change. They persist in modern popular literature and films that depict situations of danger and isolation. The modern protagonists, often heroes in spite of themselves, are usually of the lower class: common soldiers, seamen, prospectors, cowboys, criminals, and policemen. Their dangerous occupations provide the arena for the drama of friendship.

Warfare, the typical context for earlier tales of friendship, gave purpose to the lives of the earlier heroes. They welcomed it for the opportunity to gain personal honor and fame, unlike the modern conscript for whom warfare is a hell to be endured. His goal is to survive and return to civilian life. Sharing the danger, hardships, and boredom with a special friend enables a modern soldier to retain his sanity and identity in the dehumanizing bureaucracy of the army. □

MYTH AND REALITY

The narratives of male friendship define the role of friend not only in terms of expectations and attitudes but also in terms of status and code of behavior. Friends are described as male peers cooperating in a hazardous venture, whether it is robbing a bank or slaying monsters. They support each other throughout a life of adventure and danger, in which they exhibit great courage and fortitude. Mundane affairs such as marriage, making a living, or having a family, which make up the lives of other men, do not concern them. The emotional bonds between them are stronger than any other, even ties to wives, children, or kinsmen. Their prime attachment is to each other, expressed in open affection and lifelong loyalty. If they do not die together, the death of one strikes to the heart of the other.

Much of this definition of the role lacks relevance to modern times. Heroic action, mutual self-sacrifice, and loyalty to the death are anomalous in a bureaucratized world. Aubert and Arner found that "the social structure of the Norwegian Merchant Marine includes a near taboo on personal friendships."[17] The ship is a tightly integrated bureaucratic institution in which work roles predominate and status in the structure precludes the formation of close dyads. Similarly, bureaucracy, along with its promotion of competitiveness, inhibits the formation of friendships in the appropriately agonistic settings described in the training of the first astronauts[18] and the designing of a new microcomputer.[19]

The agonistic drama of the mythic tradition of friendship is likewise incongruous in modern society. The men engaged in dangerous occupations rarely dramatize their jobs. Most men work within corporate structures whose goals are mainly financial, and success is achieved through individual competition rather than dyadic or group bonding. Men's lives are constrained by the institutional framework of society, and the routines of daily life hardly provide an area for the heroic exploits of devoted friends. Agon gives way to anxiety.

The open avowals of devotion or physical expressions of affection prevalent in the early literature are considered embarrassing behavior for men in this society.[20] Emotional restraint is the general rule among male friends: "...love between men that is neither romantic nor sexual is terribly hard for most men to acknowledge to one another."[21] The behavior patterns in the literature do not serve as a model for men in modern society.

The value of male solidarity and the definition of manliness implicit in the myth have lost much of their force for modern society. The myth contains the message that a man should hold himself aloof from the world of women. His loyalties should be to other men: friends, political leaders, and his fellows in the group. Overinvolvement with a wife, children, or kin inhibits a man's wholehearted participation in the male world. In modern society, the dichotomy between the worlds of men and women is no longer so clearly drawn. Men are not considered unmanly for their participation in the domestic sphere, and women are active outside it. Marriage and the creation of a nuclear family are now volitional. Unlike earlier societies, in which marriages were arranged, men and women seek fulfillment of their emotional needs in the family. It is here that the most intense relationships exist, and friendship plays a secondary role.

Solidarity among men is peripheral to the major concerns of the individual man and interstitial in the functioning of society. Political life in Athens involved the active participation of every citizen; it is now reduced to the yearly visit to the voting booth. Work may require that men cooperate, but it does not require solidarity or loyalty. On every level of economic and political life, bureaucracy sets the terms for cooperation, and those terms exclude emotional affect. In the myth, friends are partners whose whole lives are inextricably intertwined. In modern society, work and friendship belong to distinct compartments. The place of friends is limited to leisure activities.

The myth has always expressed the fulfillment of a wish. In the past, the wish may have been release from the obligations imposed by the lineage, desire for the emotional warmth to be found neither in lineage nor family, and the hunger for fame and glory. Now the wish may involve escape from the hothouse intensity of the nuclear family and its disappointments, the dull routines of work, or the frustrations of living in a mass society. The fantasy of an ideal friendship is a response to whatever specific discontents a particular society induces.

The myth persists, not because it instructs the specifics of conduct, but because it still promotes and legitimizes a code of values. The ideology of friendship—affection, loyalty, and trust—has never gone out of style. The affirmation of these values elicits a positive response, perhaps even more now than in the past. Urbanization and bureaucratization, social and geographical mobility, all may foster instrumental and expedient relationships, but they surely induce a sense of individual isolation. All forms of permanent affiliation, even the bonds of kinship, are attenuated. The human need for enduring, emotionally satisfying relationships often remains unfulfilled. The hunger for affiliation is certainly one of the major factors accounting for the viability of the myth of friendship. The search for a "best friend" begins in the playground, often at the urging of adults, who believe that having friends is a necessary socializing experience. And Ramsøy points out that, throughout life, to lack friends is a source of shame.[22] Even without the formal social organization to define relationships and instruct them, people often make enduring and gratifying friendships.[23] Both old and contemporary versions of the myth offer the image and promise of true friendship.

The myth conveys other messages as well. Shifting focus away from the affective core of bonding, we perceive an all-too-familiar image of men: the traditional stereotype, in which men are dominant, independent of women but sexually exploitative of them, and their manliness is expressed through violence. The myth especially exaggerates male aggressiveness and the value placed on combat. The heroes are always fighters and the settings always agonistic.

In the narratives, the behavior of the heroes is often socially irresponsible, so centered are they on each other, ego and alter ego. Wives, children, kin, society at large, and even the gods are disregarded. Ordinary life is tame and dull compared to the high-pitched quality of their adventurous careers. The image is thus implausibly youthful, and, literally, the heroes die young, obviating any need to come to terms with maturity. Such an image is wholly antithetical to the realities of society where men must meet the responsibilities of ongoing life. No matter how preposterously distorting, the myth is legitimized in the beautiful name of friendship.

CONCLUSION

In sociology and anthropology, studies of friendship are based on the assertion that it is an institution and, as such, open to investigation. The institutional aspects of friendship are its recurrence and its social importance. But contemporary Western friendship lacks other defining characteristics of an institution: regularity and consistency of behavior, clear-cut definition of roles, and jural or ceremonial status. The patterns of behavior in friendship vary from one set of friends to another. Mutual habituation defines its unique roles and creates its own structures, its own rituals and styles of communication. In the face of such discrepancy, social scientists tend to retreat by qualifying the term; Ramsøy calls friendship a "vague institution," and Paine describes it as an "institutionalized non-institution."[24] It is, at best, a quasi-institution, as friend is a quasi-role.

We must first loosen the nexus between institution and role to comprehend fully the nature of friendship in Western society. The process of self-definition of the role is the point at issue. Other prevalent dyadic relationships exhibit the same lack of institutionalization. Couples of the same or opposite sex form households without marriage, without models for behavior or even standard terminology for the relationships. These pairs must also make their own rules and set their own terms. In our rapidly changing society, roles, even in as formal an institution as marriage, are subject to individual definition. Women in the business and professional world have just begun to reject the male model for their conduct and dress to redefine their roles. Despite the fluidity of roles and their definitions, ideology remains intact. Professional women still are achievement oriented and ascribe to the competitive ethos. Sex or marital partners retain the belief in love and stability of the relationship. Friendships are still maintained on the basis of loyalty, trust, and mutuality. Ideology thus seems to be the stable element in "quasi-institutions."

We therefore chose to focus on the ideologically stable core of friendship between men. To this purpose, we turned to the literary sources to trace the historical development of what we have chosen to call the myth of friendship, finding its first and full-blown formulation in the earliest recorded epic of Gilgamesh. The essential content of the myth remained notably unchanging throughout the vagaries of different times and different cultures. It has persisted, despite its present incongruity, as a charter for the values of male friendship.

❋ ❋ ❋

NOTES

1. H. Schurtz, *Altersklasse und Männerbunde* (Berlin, 1902); and L. Tiger, *Men in Groups* (New York: Random House, 1969).
2. Tiger, *Men in Groups*, pp. 132–155.
3. B. Malinowski, "The Psychological Function of Myth," in *Magic, Science and Religion* (Garden City, N.Y.: Doubleday, 1954).
4. S.F. Nadel, *The Foundations of Social Anthropology* (London: Cohen and West, 1951), p. 91.
5. S.F. Nadel, *The Theory of Social Structure* (London: Cohen and West, 1957), p. 28.
6. R. Brain, *Friends and Lovers* (New York: Basic Books, 1976).
7. S.N. Eisenstadt and L. Roniger, *Patrons, Clients and Friends: Interpersonal Relations and the Structure of Trust in Society* (Cambridge, England: Cambridge University Press, 1984), pp. 282–283.
8. J.A. Pitt-Rivers, *The People of the Sierra* (New York: Criterion, 1954), pp. 137–160.
9. R. Schwartz, "The Crowd: Friendship Groups in a Newfoundland Outpost," in *The Compact: Selected Dimensions of Friendship*, ed. E. Leyton, Newfoundland Social and Economic Papers No. 3 (Toronto: University of Toronto Press, 1974); E. Leyton, "Irish Friends and 'Friends': Friendship, Kinship, and Class in Aughnaboy," in Leyton, ed., *Compact.*
10. Leyton, "Irish Friends," p. 104.

11. C. Dubois, "The Gratuitous Act: An Introduction to the Comparative Study of Friendship Patterns," in Leyton, ed., *Compact*; Y.A. Cohen, "Patterns of Friendship," in *Social Structure and Personality*, ed. Y.A. Cohen (New York: Holt, Rinehart and Winston, 1961); and E. Wolf, "Kinship, Friendship and Patron–Client Relationships in Complex Societies," in *The Social Anthropology of Complex Societies*, ed. M. Banton (London: Tavistock, 1966), pp. 3–27.
12. Pitt-Rivers, *People of Sierra*, p. 139.
13. P. Aries, *Centuries of Childhood* (New York: Vintage, 1965), p. 356.
14. T. Jacobsen, *The Treasures of Darkness* (New Haven: Yale University Press, 1976), p. 196.
15. T.H. Gaster, *The Oldest Stories in the World* (Boston: Beacon, 1952), p. 55.
16. Jacobsen, *Treasures of Darkness*, pp. 203–204. □
17. Quoted in O. Ramsøy, "Friendship," in *International Encyclopedia of the Social Sciences*, 1968, 6:14.
18. T. Wolfe, *The Right Stuff* (New York: Farrar, Straus and Giroux, 1979).
19. T. Kidder, *The Soul of a New Machine* (Boston: Atlantic-Little, Brown, 1981).
20. R.R. Bell, *Worlds of Friendship* (Beverly Hills: Sage, 1981), pp. 77–84.
21. E.G. McWalter, "Hitting the Road," *New York Times Magazine*, May 27, 1984, p. 46.
22. Ramsøy, "Friendship," p. 14.
23. Bell, *Worlds of Friendship*; and M.B. Parlee *et al.*, "The Friendship Bond," *Psychology Today* 13, no 4 (1979):42–54, 113.
24. Ramsøy, "Friendship," p. 13; and R. Paine, "In Search of Friendship: An Exploratory Analysis in 'Middle-Class' Culture," *Man*, December 1969, p. 514.

⁕ ⁕ ⁕

Albert B. Lord
"Gilgamesh and Other Epics"

Albert Lord published "Gilgamesh and Other Epics" in a volume designed mainly for ancient Near Eastern scholars, *Lingering over Words* (1990). In the article he examines a certain "mythical pattern" in *Gilgamesh*, Homer, and *Beowulf*. The pattern involves a sequence of five figures and narrative moves: a male monster, often a cannibal (in *Gilgamesh*, Humbaba); a female figure that threatens death (Ishtar bringing down the Bull of Heaven); the death of the hero's companion (Enkidu, who has invaded the sacred precinct); the hero's journey to the world of the dead, a journey that involves the discovery of the time of his death; and finally, the return to the real world. In *Gilgamesh*, the last is seen in Gilgamesh's return to Uruk, which closes the movement.

Lord provides a comparison between Gilgamesh and Odysseus, then one between Gilgamesh and Beowulf. The major change in the pattern, between *Gilgamesh* and *The Odyssey* on one hand, and *Beowulf* on the other, is Christianity. Lord then provides a next step in the process: the hero gains immortality. This he sees in the medieval *Song of Roland*.

The essay is surprising more for what it does not consider than for what it does: the theory of oral composition for which Lord and Milman Parry are best known. Carl Lindahl, below, takes up the theory, which had been considered by Assyriologists at least as early as Jack M. Sasson's 1972 article, "Some Literary Motifs in the Composition of the Gilgamesh Epic." (Ed.)

The *Epic of Gilgamesh* has proven an invaluable aid in understanding epics from the eastern Mediterranean. It allows one to observe several patterns of narrative, which I believe to be mythic, at a very early date. Its evidence tells us that they existed and were known in a variety of versions in the Ancient Near East in that period, and they may have spread to other regions with the movements of peoples.

One of those patterns, later forms of which I have been fascinated to note in Homer and in at least one medieval epic, namely, *Beowulf*, consists of the following items in sequence: 1) a male monster who is cannibalistic, 2) a female figure who also threatens a kind of death, 3) the death of a companion to the hero, 4) the hero's journey to the land of the dead and the discovery of the time of his own death, and 5) return to the real world.[1]

The form of the pattern in *Gilgamesh* is as follows:

1) Although Humbaba's cannibalism is not specified, it can possibly be inferred; at any rate, he is a real threat to the lives of Gilgamesh and Enkidu. We do not have a very detailed description of Humbaba in the *Epic of Gilgamesh.* It is limited mainly to such lines as:[2]

> Humbaba—his roaring is like that of a flood-storm,
> his mouth is fire, his breath is death!
> At sixty double-hours he can hear the wild cows of his forest;
> who is it who would go down to his forest?

Attention is focused on his mouth and on what emanates from it, but he seems also to have acute hearing. From the texts in Heidel's translation we know little of the type of creature that possesses these characteristics, except that he walks, since he leaves a path wherever he goes. Heidel calls him an "ogre"; that fits our purposes very well.

It is worthy of note that Gilgamesh is almost overcome in his struggle with Humbaba, to the point that he calls upon Shamash for help. Shamash saves him and decides the outcome by sending[3]

> The great wind, the north wind, the south wind,
> the whirlwind,
> The storm wind, the chill wind,
> the tempestuous wind,
> The hot wind; eight winds arose against him
> And beat against the eyes of Huwawa.

In short, Gilgamesh needed divine assistance in this adventure.

In *Gilgamesh* the cedar and the cedar forest provided a significant background for the monster Humbaba, who was its guardian. The forest is huge, and Humbaba appears to be located at its center; it holds a mountain of cedar, which Gilgamesh wishes to climb.[4]

> To a distance of ten thousand double-hours
> the forest extends in each direction.
> To preserve the cedar, Enlil has appointed him
> (Humbaba) as a terror to mortals.
> And on him who goes down to the forest
> weakness takes hold.

In answer to Enkidu's description of Humbaba, Gilgamesh says:[5]

> "The mountain of cedar I will climb."

The whole setting of the monster Humbaba is holy and he is to guard its holiness. When Enkidu and Gilgamesh come to the forest,[6]

> They stood still and looked at the forest.
> They beheld the height of the cedar.
> They beheld the entrance to the forest.
> Where Humbaba was wont to talk there
> was a path;
> Straight were the tracks and good was the passage.
> They beheld the mountain of cedar, the dwelling-
> place of the gods, the throne-dais of Irnini.
> The cedar uplifted its fullness before
> the mountain;
> Fair was its shade and full of delight.

Gilgamesh and Enkidu violate that holiness, albeit at the behest of a rival god.

2) Marriage with Ishtar would also bring death, or its equivalent in a drastically changed "lifestyle," for Gilgamesh. It is unnecessary to quote in full the long passage of his insulting address to the goddess; a few lines will serve our purpose here:[7]

> "For Tammuz, thy youthful husband,
> Thou hast decreed wailing year after year.
> The variegated roller thou didst love,
> Yet thou didst smite him and break his wing.
> Now he stands in the groves, crying *'Kappi!'*
> Thou didst love the lion, perfect in strength,
> But thou didst dig for him seven
> and yet seven pits...
> You didst love the shepherd of the herd...
> Yet thou didst smite him and turn him into a wolf."

2a) Ishtar is no monster, whatever the results of submission to her may be. But associated with her is an animal that just might qualify, the Bull of Heaven. And he is let loose on mankind at the request of Ishtar to her father Anu. This monster is slain and Ishtar is defied.

3) The death, of course, is that of Enkidu, and it serves as the central and pivotal element of the pattern. Up to this point in the epic nothing has been said about Enkidu's being mortal, although we know that he was made by a god but is not divine, even in part. His death is caused by invading the sacred precincts of the gods, as in the case of the Cedar Forest, or by insulting or offending them, as was the fault of both Gilgamesh and Enkidu in their treatment of Ishtar and the Bull of Heaven.

4) Gilgamesh's journey to the land of the "far-away" and his discovery of his own mortality form this entry in the pattern.

5) Gilgamesh's return to Uruk and the reality of its walls, the accomplishment of the mortal Gilgamesh, closes the pattern. The opening of the epic stressed the wisdom of Gilgamesh and described its walls. The poem ends with a recall of those words:[8]

> "Urshanabi, climb up on the wall of Uruk
> (and) walk about;
> Inspect the foundation terrace and examine
> the brickwork, if its brickwork be not
> of burnt bricks,
> And (if) the seven wise men did not
> lay its foundation!"

The pattern is tightly knit. A god (Enlil) is angered, and a goddess (Ishtar) is angered; as a result the council of the gods decides that the hero's mortal companion must die. This death raises the question of his own possible mortality in the mind of the partly mortal Gilgamesh, and he travels to consult with a mortal (Utnapishtim), who had been spared from death by the gods, in order to learn whether he too must die. Having learned the truth of his own destiny, Gilgamesh returns to the land of the living to live out the full life of a mortal. It was necessary to recapitulate the story's essence here in order that we may have it in our minds as we turn to Homer's *Odyssey.*

• • • •

The two heroes are renowned for their wisdom and for their journeying, but Gilgamesh is two-thirds god and one-third man, whereas Odysseus is fully man. While most of the parallel elements are clear in the wanderings of Odysseus, even if they are sometimes confused by being duplicated, the central and pivotal element, the death of the companion, exists only vestigially there. (The death of Achilleus's companion, Patroklos, in the *Iliad* belongs in a different pattern, that of Absence-Devastation-Return, and I shall suggest later that it may be that the two patterns are mingled, or interlocked, in *Beowulf.*)

1) Polyphemos is an easy counterpart for Humbaba and his blinding by Odysseus and his men anger Poseidon, even as Humbaba's death incurred the anger of Enlil. It is worth noting that even as Polyphemos was blinded by Odysseus so also Humbaba was blinded by the eight winds, which rendered him motionless and enabled the heroes to cut off his head. The element of blinding is shared by both epic narratives.[9] The Laestrigonians constitute a duplication of the threat of cannibalistic death, but no god seems to be angered, and the episode is not a full multiform of the encounter with the Cyclopes.

Homer described Polyphemos in Book 9 of the *Odyssey:*[10]

> "Inside
> there lodged a monster of a man,
> who now was herding
> the flocks at a distance away, alone,
> for he did not range with
> others, but stayed away by himself;
> his mind was lawless,
> and in truth he was a monstrous wonder
> made to behold, not
> like a man, an eater of bread,
> but more like a wooded
> peak of the high mountains seen
> standing away from the others."

Odysseus commented on the monster's deep voice after he had heard him speak:[11]

> "So he spoke, and the inward heart in us
> was broken
> in terror of the deep voice and for seeing him
> so monstrous."

Polyphemos's habitat is more human-like than Humbaba's and it has not the air of being in any way sacred:[12]

> "But when we had arrived at the place,
> which was nearby, there
> at the edge of the land we saw the cave
> close to the water,

high, and overgrown with laurels,
and in it were stabled
great flocks, sheep and goats alike,
and there was
built around it with a high wall
of grubbed-out boulders
and tall pines and oaks with lofty foliage."

This cave might justifiably give us pause, for caves have easy access to the underworld—and one is reminded that all of the wanderings of Odysseus are in another world, or perhaps a series of other worlds, from that in which ordinary mortals dwell. It is "sacred" in Eliade's sense of the term. In every episode of the story Odysseus and his men penetrated that sacred world, even as Gilgamesh and Enkidu invaded the sacred world of the Cedar Forest.

2) Circe is an oft-cited parallel to Ishtar. Odysseus' "marriage" to her was rendered harmless through the gift of Hermes, but she transformed his men into animals. Odysseus is also saved from becoming a permanent mate of Kalypso, often considered a duplication of Circe, again by Hermes, who was sent by Zeus to order the hero's release from Ogygia. Odysseus is an "unwilling" captive of both these ladies, whose purposes to keep him in the other world are thwarted by the hero with divine help. Unlike Ishtar, Circe and Kalypso do not rebel at being flouted by the hero but accept the intervention by Hermes and Zeus. There appears to be no equivalent of the episode of the Bull of Heaven in the *Odyssey* narrative here. To this extent these episodes may belong somewhat vestigially in our pattern.

3) Elpenor is a vestige of Enkidu and in the pattern his death represents that of the companion; he was the youngest of Odysseus' men. His death occurs just before the journey to the Land of the Dead, but it does to motivate that voyage, although it provides motivation for the return to Circe's island, namely, to give him burial. Other companions have been killed and will yet be killed up to the final shipwreck, but only Elpenor's death is placed strategically in the pattern.

4) Odysseus' journey to Hades could well be considered a vestige of the journey to discover one's mortality, because his learning of the time of his death is not exactly the same as finding out that one is mortal. Odysseus knows that he will die some day. He is not the son of a god, nor in any way partly divine. But the question of his death comes up in the course of his consultation with Teiresias.[13]

> "…you must take up your well-shaped oar
> and go on a journey
> until you come where there are men living
> who know nothing
> of the sea, and who eat food that is not mixed
> with salt, who never have known ships…
> When, as you walk, some other wayfarer
> happens to meet you,
> and says you carry a winnow-fan
> on your bright shoulder,
> then you must plant your well-shaped oar
> in the ground, and render
> ceremonious sacrifice to the lord Poseidon,
> one ram and one bull, and a mounter of sows,
> a boar pig,
> and make your way home again and
> render holy hecatombs
> to the immortal gods who hold the wide heaven, all
> of them in order. Death will come to you
> from the sea, in
> some altogether unwarlike way,
> and it will end you
> in the ebbing time of a sleek old age…"

It is not inappropriate to observe that there is a similar journey of discovery made by Menelaos, in which he consults the Old Man of the Sea about sailing instructions and is also told of his destiny, namely that, as husband of Helen, the daughter of Zeus, he will be translated to the Elysian Fields.

The pattern begins to lose its strength with its application to a mortal hero with mortal companions. Mortals may, and in the case of Odysseus and his companions they do, offend the gods, but their mortality is not a punishment for those offenses. They do not lose an immortality that was never theirs. Yet death was their reward; none of Odysseus' companions survived the wanderings, "fools, who devoured the kine of the immortal Sun, whereby he took away the day of their return."[14] In that large other world that encompasses all of the wanderings all the companions die. Odysseus himself almost perishes in the shipwreck from which he is saved by another female figure, Ino, just as Gilgamesh would have slept eternally, had not Utnapishtim's wife awakened him. In both cases, the hero himself almost dies in the other world.

One should also point out that the journeying between worlds ceases to provide any more round trips.
Urshanabi, the boatman, has brought back his last mortal from the world of the dead. The ship of the Phaiakians was turned to stone, fulfilling an old prophecy.

5) Odysseus alone returned home to the stability of mortal life, the norm represented by the three generations of the family in the last scene of the song. In *Gilgamesh* the return was to mortal accomplishment; immortality in the works of man's hands. In the *Odyssey* immortality is assured in the survival of the generations of man.

There are, then, many parallel elements in the narrative pattern in question as manifested in *Gilgamesh* and in the *Odyssey*, although with the change from a partly divine to a fully mortal hero, some elements are present only vestigially.

• • • •

With *Beowulf* we make a long journey forward in time, from approximately 800 B.C. to approximately 800 A.D. Strangely enough, the first few elements of the pattern have survived best, are most clearly represented, although they too have undergone a sea-change.

1) Grendel, the male monster in the Anglo-Saxon poem, is a grotesque equivalent to Humbaba, or perhaps better, a degenerate form of Polyphemos. He is described, together with his mother, as follows:[15]

I have heard it said by subjects of mine
who live in the country, counsellors in this hall,
that they have seen such a pair
of huge wayfarers haunting the moors,
otherworldly ones; and one of them,
so far as they might make it out
was in woman's shape; but the shape of a man,
though twisted, trod also the tracks of exile
save that he was more huge than
    any human being.
The country people have called him from of old
by the name of Grendel; they know of
    no father for him,
nor whether there have been such beings before
among the monster race.

One of Grendel's distinguishing features in addition to his size are his eyes. As the monster enters the hall Heorot where Beowulf is waiting, the poet notes:[16]

Hastening on,
The foe then stepped onto the unstained floor,
angrily advanced; out of his eyes stood
an unlovely light like that of fire.

One is reminded not only of the eye of the Cyclops but even more especially of the fact that many winds blinded the eyes of Humbaba. There is something special about the eye, or eyes, of our male monsters, some uncanny power. In the cases of Humbaba and Polyphemos it seems to have been necessary to eliminate that power.

Humbaba was sacred to Enlil, the storm-god, and Polyphemos as a child of Poseidon was of partly divine origin, but Grendel had no illustrious or divine protector; he was a descendant of Cain, the fratricidal son of Adam. Whereas the killing of Humbaba was an act of sacrilege for which Enkidu paid with his life, and the blinding of Polyphemos caused Poseidon relentlessly to pursue Odysseus, the killing of Grendel was a meritorious act of destroying evil in the world. In the person of Beowulf the good triumphed in the pre-Christian world of the poem. Beowulf did not offend the Lord in killing Grendel. The sacrilege that led to the death of the companion in the other epics is absent in the Grendel episode in *Beowulf.*

Humbaba dwelt in the sacred Cedar Forest, Polyphemos in a pastoral setting—with his sheep, Grendel inhabited a noisome mere, with vile reptilian creatures as neighbors. The poet described the wild country in which Grendel and his mother lived:[17]

Mysterious is the region
they live in—of wolf-fells, wind-picked moors
and treacherous fen-paths; a torrent of water
pours down dark cliffs and plunges into the earth,
an underground flood. It is not far from here,
in terms of miles, that the Mere lies,
overcast with dark, crag-rooted trees
that hang in groves hoary with frost.
An uncanny sight may be seen at night there
—the fire in the water! The wit of living men
is not enough to know its bottom.

The hart that roams the heath,
    when hounds have pressed him
long and hard, may hide in the forest
his antlered head; but the hart will die there
sooner than swim and save his life;
he will sell it on the brink there,
    for it is not a safe place.
And the wind can stir up wicked storms there,
whipping the swirling waters up
till they climb the clouds and clog the air,
making the skies weep.

2) That was Grendel. How about the female monster? Except for sex, Grendel's mother provides no parallel to Ishtar or Circe. In all other respects she is a duplication of her son. These elements of the pattern are there in the literal sense, a male monster and a female monster overcome by the hero. What was said about Grendel can be said about his mother as well, but no more can be added. The second element has, to all intents and purposes, been lost; it has been replaced by a duplication of the first element. All that remains is the sex of the second creature, but that sex seems to play no role in the incident. The pattern is there superficially still—though I think not coincidentally—but the meaning in it has changed from sacrilege to the triumph of good over evil. The sexual element is vestigial. It argues for the strength of the pattern that it is there at all. The hag is found in Scandinavian analogues, of course, so the Germanic tradition in the person of the *Beowulf* poet did not need to invent her. He needed only to continue to keep her in place.

Yet it is a mistake to dismiss this episode so summarily. In his fight with Grendel's mother in the other world of death, the Mere, Beowulf was almost killed. He was saved by the miraculous appearance of the ancient sword with which he killed the hag. We have noted the "almost deaths" of both Gilgamesh in the home of Utnapishtim, when the latter's wife awoke him from the sleep of death, and of Odysseus after Poseidon caused the shipwreck of his raft, from which he was saved by Ino. An "almost death" should probably be a part of the pattern that we are considering. It is a concentrated symbol of the basic concept of the epic, that the hero dies and returns to life.

Odysseus' "almost death" does not occur during his visit to the Land of the Dead in Book Eleven, but closer to his return to Ithaca, just before his landing at Phaiakia, his last stop before home. It is tempting to see a possible duplication of this "almost death" in his sleep aboard the ship of the Phaiakians as they bring him home to Ithaca, back to living reality. Perhaps so, but there seems to be a threat of never awakening. He is on his way home and nobody, not even Poseidon, is pursuing him any longer.

3) The death of a substitute is present in *Beowulf*; it is even duplicated. But it is not in its proper place in the pattern. It should come after the second act of sacrilege, but the killing of Grendel and of his mother are not sacrilegious but meritorious. The first death in the Grendel episode is clearly that of a substitute; Beowulf watches while Grendel eats his companion Hondscio alive. Immediately afterwards the hero takes on Grendel. Why not before? The incongruity of Hondscio's death and the fact that it is out of its rightful place in the pattern, I believe, mark it as a vestige of the death of a substitute.

There is another death of a companion in *Beowulf*, that of Ascere, who is killed by Grendel's mother. He was not Beowulf's companion but Hrothgar's, if you will, his counsellor. His death does motivate a journey, that to the Mere to seek out the hag.

4) The journey too is duplicated in *Beowulf*. After the first death there is a journey to the Mere following the spoor of the luckless Grendel. This journey is repeated after the second death, but this time it leads to entrance into a real land of death, the Mere itself. But there is no Utnapishtim there to answer the hero's question of his own mortality, if he had any; nor even a Teiresias to advise him when he would die. Death itself awaited him in the person of Grendel's mother; as I have said, he almost succumbed. He was saved by a miracle. The journey is a vestige of the journeys in the mythic pattern.

The journey to the Mere is within the framework of a larger journey, that from Sweden to Denmark and return, even as Odysseus' journey to the Land of the Dead occurs within the parameters of his wanderings. Our mythic pattern is to be seen as interwoven into another pattern, that of a trip to the other world and a return from it, a pattern of death and resurrection.

5) Beowulf returns from the Mere to Hrothgar's court and then back to Sweden, where eventually he becomes king. His return home completes the pattern. All three heroes go back to their kingdoms to reign successfully for the rest of their lives. Only in *Beowulf* is the hero's death actually related in the epic itself.

The great change that had come about in the mythic pattern between the ancient *Gilgamesh* and *Odyssey* on the one hand and the medieval *Beowulf* on the other was caused by the advent of Christianity and its gradual absorption into the epic tradition.

The ancient non-biblical pattern, like the biblical one in Genesis, was meant to explain the mortality of man and its inevitability. But blameless Beowulf, champion of the good, slayer of evil monsters, must also die. It is in a final battle with evil that his own destiny is fulfilled. It took a truly Christian epic such as *The Song of Roland* to move to the next step, to the immortality of the soul; for Gabriel came down to receive the soul of Roland, killed in fighting the enemies of Christianity.[18]

> God sent to him His Angel Cherubine,
> And great St. Michael of Peril-by-the-Tide;
> St. Gabriel too was with them at his side;
> The County's soul they bear to Paradise.

Beowulf comes close.

❋ ❋ ❋

NOTES

1. I have written separately about this pattern in widely distanced articles, one of which was published in Italy and the other in California. I have taken this opportunity to put them together here in a paper dedicated to Professor William L. Moran, whose lectures on the *Epic of Gilgamesh* graced Humanities 9 for a number of years. His presentation of *Gilgamesh* will be remembered by students, as it is by myself, as one of the great highlights of that course.
2. Alexander Heidel, *The Gilgamesh Epic and Old Testament Parallels*, Phoenix Books, University of Chicago Press, 1963, pp. 35–36, Tablet III, lines 3–4 of the Assyrian version.
3. Ibid., p. 48–49, lines 14–17, from a Hittite fragment.
4. Ibid., p. 35, Tablet III, column iii, line 107, and p. 36, lines 5–6, from the Assyrian version.
5. Ibid., p. 35, Tablet III, column iii, line 118.
6. Ibid., p. 45, Tablet V, column i, lines 1–8.
7. Ibid., p. 51, Tablet VI, lines 46–52, 58, and 61.
8. Ibid., page 93, Tablet XI, lines 303–305.
9. For further on this see Mary Louise Lord, "Near Eastern Myths and the Classical Relatives," in *The Teaching of Classical Mythology*, Sand Hill Press, 1981, p. 10, who cites A. Heidel, Theodor Gaster, and Joseph Fontenrose.

10. Lines 186–192, translated by Richmond Lattimore, Harper Colophon Books, 1965.
11. Ibid., Book 9, lines 256–257.
12. Ibid., Book 9, lines 181–186.
13. Ibid., Book 11, lines 121–124, 127–136.
14. George Herbert Palmer translation.
15. *Beowulf, a Verse Translation*, trans. Michael Alexander, Penguin Books, 1973, lines 1345–1357.
16. Ibid., lines 724–727.
17. Ibid., lines 1357b–1376a.
18. Lines 2393–2396, translated by Dorothy L. Sayers, Penguin Books, 1957.

* * *

Eric J. Leed
"Reaching for Abroad: Departures"

Works on *Gilgamesh* by nonspecialists since the end of World War II suggest certain persistent interests in the West that have led many to consider *Gilgamesh* as particularly important to the Western tradition. Eric J. Leed discusses "Gilgamesh: The Search for Fame" in a book on the history of travel, subtitled *From Gilgamesh to Global Tourism* (1991). Leed distinguishes between heroic travel—voluntary, to set up a name—and unheroic travel, which is forced, often penitential, and involves suffering.

Although Gilgamesh travels initially to gain fame, he is depicted as ambivalent, and Leed suggests that any departure involves "separation anxiety," protest, grief, and then detachment, as it does with Gilgamesh. Travel, in the words of Leed, "excorporates" Gilgamesh and "incorporates" what he calls the "traveling-body." Leed considers the Mesopotamian hero one of the first to leave home, and his travel was divinely ordained by Shamash. Ninsun's questions to Shamash indicate that the question still remained why humans undertake departures.

Leed's counter to Gilgamesh in the ancient world is the story of Adam and Eve, certainly a forced, non-heroic journey. (Ed.)

FOR A HISTORY OF TRAVEL

What gives value to travel is fear. It is the fact that, at a certain moment, we are so far from our own country...we are seized by a vague fear, and the instinctive desire to go back to the protection of old habits. This is the most obvious benefit of travel. At that moment we are feverish but also porous, so that the slightest touch makes us quiver to the depths of our being... This is why we should not say that we travel for pleasure. There is no pleasure in travelling, and I look upon it as an occasion for spiritual testing... Pleasure takes us away from ourselves in the same way that distraction, as in Pascal's use of the word, takes us away from God. Travel, which is like a greater and graver science, brings us back to ourselves.

—Albert Camus, 1963

Travel is a common, frequent, everyday occurrence in our present. In fact, it is a source of our commonality, as in 1987 over forty million Americans traveled abroad, and many more at home. Comprising less than 5 percent of the world's population, U. S. citizens accounted for over 25 percent of the world spending for domestic and international travel—estimated at $2.3 million. If one counts all the California trips and journeys seasonally made, north and south, it is not merely a metaphor to say America is on the move and connected through mobilities. Travel, in the form of tourism, is becoming increasingly pervasive in our world. By the turn of the millennium, it will be the most important sector of world trade, surpassing oil, and is currently the second largest retail industry in the United States. The impression of the commonality of travel is intensified when one includes in the ranks of travelers those who obviously belong but do not appear in the tourism statistics—business travelers, nomads, commuters, itinerant laborers, refugees, members of the armed services, diplomatic personnel, temporary and permanent immigrants. Indeed, in the first half of the twentieth century, military tourism was a common form of popular mobility and the only form of mass travel the masses could afford. A 1958 survey by the University of Michigan found that one adult American out of five had been overseas at some time in their lives, two out of three with the armed services.[1]

The term *mass tourism* conveys the scale of modern tourist business, the mass production of journeys, the infinite replication of trips to the point that even a formerly extraordinary voyage—to Machu Picchu, say, or to the Forbidden City or to Tashkent—has become something rather ordinary, a kind of norm rather than an escape from the norm. The sheer number of travelers crowding the terminals, roads, holy and sacred grounds, merchandising marts and markets alerts us to the fact that we are a society of travelers. In this society the journey is the ordinary way members link their lives and consume a world of meanings and places.

Though living in an era of mass tourism, the average American tourist is by no means representative of the masses of Americans. A survey of Americans traveling abroad in 1986 found that the average overseas tourist had an annual income of $55,519, was a member of the professional, managerial, or technical class (61 percent of overseas travelers), male (57 percent), forty-four years old, most likely to come from New York or California (46 percent), traveling for pleasure on a holiday (57 percent), was a repeat rather than a first-time traveler (91 percent), booked through a travel agency, traveled economy class

(74 percent), and most likely going to one country (68 percent) in Western Europe or to the United Kingdom (60 percent).[2] Indeed, "travel for pleasure" remains as it was through the ages, a mark of success and status, while travel under compulsion of some necessity or in service of need is a mark of commonality and a common fate.

If one broadens the definition of travel to encompass all passage across significant boundaries that separate differing persons, kinds of social relations, activities, then it becomes obvious that travel is much more than common. It is an activity that weaves the fabric of contemporary lives. Very few of us eat, sleep, work, and play in the same place—this would be a definition of confinement and unfreedom. Normally our lives are segmented into places of work, play, privacy, to be joined through territorial passage along the corridors and passageways, road and rail networks of modern metropolitan areas—those extended "cities" that differ so markedly from ancient cities, like the city of Nejef in Iraq where the twentieth-century adventurer and travel writer Freya Stark once found herself:

> To sit there among the pressed houses, so crowded within the security of their wall that there was scarcely room in front of the mosque for the little stone-flagged square, was to realize what for several thousand years of our history has constituted the feeling of safety, the close-packed enclosure of small cities crammed within walls. Outside are the wilderness, or the neighboring unfriendly cities, or the raiding deserts; inside the intimacy where strangers or dissenters are watched with fear or anger.[3]

There, in the ancient city, citizens and insiders confront the outside as a world of strangers held at bay with rampart and wall; here, in modern metropolitan corridors, the vast majority of human relations are relations between strangers, who are served by a variety of roads, markets, communicational networks, pathways that constitute our cities. The contrast is sufficiently powerful to draw millions of tourists out of our modernity back into those ancient cities of Mesopotamia, Egypt, ancient Europe, to experience the difference between contained lives and lives lived openly and in passage.

The commonality and familiarity of travel may also be seen in the fact that travel is the most common source of metaphors used to explicate transformations and transitions of all sorts. We draw upon the experience of human mobility to define the meaning of death (as a "passing") and the structure of life (as a "journey" or pilgrimage); to articulate changes of social and existential conditions in rites of initiation (of "passage"). In their now-classic works the anthropologists Arnold van Gennep, Victor Turner, and Mircea Eliade have found rites and symbols of passage everywhere and in all periods of human history.[4] If the essence of a metaphor or a symbol is the use of the familiar to grasp the less familiar or ineffable,[5] then the universality of symbols and rites of passage testifies to the sheer normality of the experience of travel.

Travel is as familiar as the experience of the body, the wind, the earth, and this is why at all times and in all places it is a source of reference, a ground of symbols and metaphors, a resource of signification. The anthropologist and historian of religions Mircea Eliade laments the absence of genuine rituals of initiation in modern life and suggests that "modern man has lost all sense of traditional initiation."[6] But perhaps it is only that the reality of passage has replaced the ritual, and the most important transitions we experience are written into our journeys, which make of our lives a procession and spectacle more engrossing and transforming than any ritual could possibly be.

But the point is made: travel is, in contemporary civility, normal and a source of norms. Usually, contemporary lives are connected, segmented, sequenced through journeys—small ordinary journeys of a few miles or larger, extraordinary trips of hundreds and thousands of miles. Contemporary society, as many have noted, is a "mobile" society, but even more than that, it is a society of travelers. We may find in the history of travel the origins, the evolution, the manners, the forms of knowledge characteristic of our present, of this society of travelers. Contemporary life is perhaps unprecedented in the scale, quantity, and global organization of modern journeys, and yet it is clear that travel is not a new human experience. Mobility is the first, prehistorical human condition; sessility (attachment or fixation to one place), a later, historical condition. At the dawn of history, humans were migratory animals. Recorded history—the history of civilization—is a story of mobilities, migrations, settlements, of the adaption of human groups to place and their integration into topography, the creation of "homes." In order to understand our present, we must understand how mobility has operated historically, in the past as a force of change, transforming personalities, social landscapes, human topographies, creating a global civilization.

Travel has not yet been claimed as a field of history, nor is it clear that it need be, that an understanding of the way in which mobility transforms individuals, social relations, cultures would add significantly to our understanding of the past and the present. A case has to be made for the centrality of travel as an activity creative of a human condition, in the past as in the present—as I aim to do in this introduction. □

REACHING FOR ABROAD: DEPARTURES

The last belch from America had expired on the outer edge of the Venice lagoon, and moving through the still, sun-heavy Adriatic, I was now definitely gone. It was a refreshing feeling, like a return to very early youth; there was a sense of morning, and even of innocence about it. That was what travel did for me, but only in the furthest reaches of abroad.

—John Knowles, 1964

It is no small contradiction to human nature to leave one's home.

—Father Navarette, 1704

In every parting there is a latent germ of madness.

—Goethe, 1788

The departure charters the journey, establishing its motives and first meanings. The departure also establishes the initial identity of the traveler. Ceremonious and public departures begin the heroic journeys of kings and would-be kings, while forced, surreptitious, or routine departures initiate the journeys and identities of captives, exiles, fugitives, and professional travelers. The four departures I will discuss in this chapter—of Gilgamesh, Adam and Eve, Yawain, and Alexander Kinglake—suggest the motives activating all who have undertaken and suffered departures.

These specific departures also suggest a historical shift in the perception and definition of the meaningful journey and the heroic traveler. In the Middle Ages, certain features of ancient heroic and nonheroic journeys are combined to produce a new, ennobling species of journey which is both an exile and a search for fame.

This redefinition is implicit in modern adventure-travels, such as those undertaken by Alexander Kinglake and generalized in modern tourism as an escape from civility and modernity.

Different ages and cultures may value the significant departure differently—as a beginning of selfhood, or a loss of self; as the beginning of freedom, or alienation—but the essence for departure does not change. Always, everywhere, it separates the individual from a defining social and cultural matrix. The subjective character of the events also remains remarkably consistent through the ages. In the earliest Western travel literature can be found the protest, despair, and detachment that John Bowlby (the authority on attachment and loss) describes as "separation anxiety." It is against these objective and subjective continuities of departure that a history may be seen, a history that is at once collective and personal.

JOURNEYS—HEROIC AND NONHEROIC

I have not established my name stamped on bricks as my destiny decreed; therefore I will go to the country where the cedar is felled. I will set up my name in the place where the names of the famous men are written, and where no man's name is written yet I will raise a monument to the gods.

—Gilgamesh, c. 1900 B.C.

The heroic journey is designed to extend an identity across space and through time, to display power and status. Initially, a public and ceremonious departure establishes the identity of the leave-taker and affirms those relations in which this identity is rooted. The departure not only "excorporates" a member from a social body, it also "incorporates" and inaugurates the mobile body, whether an individual or a group. The heroic journey is a means of becoming known in the world, of garnering recognitions, and extending power. Fame, the extension of social being across space and time, is the chief characterizing motive of heroic travel: the mythical travels of Osiris, Dionysus, and Heracles; the legendary travels of Odysseus, Jason, Theseus, and Gilgamesh; the historical travels of Alexander and Caesar. The armed expedition was not only a way for an aspiring male to become known in the ancient world, but also a means of extending the boundaries of civility and of the world. Pliny assumed that the armed expedition was the chief means of gaining a knowledge of the world and this was why the sources of the Nile remained mysterious in his own day, having been "explored by unarmed investigators, without the wars that have discovered all other countries."[7] Heroic departures also characteristically assume a return, at least in their ancient form: they are round trips, rather than exiles or migrations. The circular form of the heroic journey is implicit in its purpose—the geographical and temporal extension of identity. A journey undertaken to fix a persona in the sites of his deeds, in literature, in monuments, in human memory, assumes an observing public without whom there can be no fame. Passing strangers or the eye of the god may fulfill this function, but most often the role of the observing "third person" is filled by a place such as the one to which Gilgamesh returns to engrave on a stone the whole story of his journey.

In addition to asserting the identity of the traveler and establishing the purpose of the journey as a means of acquiring recognition, the heroic journey is voluntarily undertaken rather than forced. The willingness of Gilgamesh to depart is, of course, ambivalent, occurring as a result of a revelation by the god of inevitability of death, the final departure and separation. But Gilgamesh does have a choice, as is clearly not the case in the nonheroic departures of exiles and fugitives. This element of choice becomes increasingly significant in the medieval heroic journey, and is essential to the conception of the journey as a means of asserting a "second," nonbiological nature.

The heroic journey in its ancient form is invariably a circuit, a form taken by modern tourism and adventure travels. But despite its prominence in the travel literature, this is not the only form of human mobility. The ritual tour, whether a pilgrimage, voyage, or parade, is clearly uncharacteristic of the vast majority of human travels which are undertaken by nomads, exiles, refugees, captives, colonists, or fugitives. The nonheroic journey is a forced departure: the traveler is not moved by his own motives but propelled by necessity, chance, disaster, crime, or the violation of some norm. The forced departure initiates a journey that is suffering or penance rather than a campaign or a voyage. Often one-way or endless journeys, they muddle rather than define the persona of the traveler.

GILGAMESH: THE SEARCH FOR FAME

The earliest departure detailed in Western travel literature, that of Gilgamesh, a king of Uruk, upon his campaign against Lebanon c. 2500 B.C., is divinely ordained. It is initiated by Gilgamesh's god Shamash, who revealed through a dream of Enkidu, Gilgamesh's follower, that the king's fate is to be death, not eternal life. Enkidu, originally a wildman of the hills who has been captured by trappers, conquered by Gilgamesh, and transformed into a follower and a servant, now eats the king's bread and drinks his wine. He has his own motives for a departure. His strength has been sapped on his civilizing journey, which brought him from the peripheral site of his bestial freedom to the densely ordered urban core, and he is bored: "I am weak, my arms have lost their strength, the cry of sorrow sticks in my throat, I am oppressed by idleness."[8] Gilgamesh's motives are different and characteristic of the heroic journey: he desires fame, and the journey is a means to this end.

The desire for fame, for extensions of the self in space and time, is a prominent motive of male, heroic travel and prestige trade.[9] Here this motive is generated by the presentiment of finality, of the terminability of human life, of death. Gilgamesh's journey is a circumvention of the god's incomprehensible decree denying immortality to mere men: the proximity of death supplies the chief motive for his departure, and for many departures of kings and would-be kings after him. The circumvention of death, too, is at the root of travel literature, those stories of journeys that seek to fix and perpetuate something as transient and impermanent as human action and mobility. The ideas of death and departure have long been linked historically. In Gilgamesh's test, the order of their occurrence is meant to suggest a causality: the idea of death awakens the idea of departure.

A variety of motives, however, conspire in this most ancient of recorded departures. Enkidu would regain his energy and freedom, scouting his childhood haunts and beyond. Gilgamesh would fix his image more permanently in the "bricks" and claim the briefer immortality granted by human memory; moreover, he would achieve this in spite of, even *through*, his death: "Then if I fall I leave behind me a name that endures; men will say of me, 'Gilgamesh has fallen in fight with ferocious Humbaba' [the guardian of the forest]. Long after the child has been born in my house they will say it and remember."[10] Gilgamesh's departure reveals the most ancient motives for a heroic journey: kings and would-be kings seek to circumvent death by achieving the extension of self we call fame; servants like Enkidu seek liberty; the king's subjects, relief from the oppressions of the state.

This departure contains the essence of all historical and observable departures. First of all, it separates an individual from a fixed social matrix—in this case, Uruk, Gilgamesh's home—and from that nest of relations that define identity. This detachment of the individual from the social matrix is an event that constructs one as an autonomous and self-contained social entity. Of course, the degree and intensity of the departure vary with the strength and meaningfulness of the bonds that stretch or break in parting and with the usualness of partings. A departure from a "home," a space that conforms to the body and all its needs, evokes with great intensity those emotions characteristic of all partings: protest, grief, despair, mourning. Gilgamesh first mourns for himself, or for an image of himself as unaccommodated man wandering through an insecure world, and protests before his god: "The tears ran down his face and he said, 'Alas, it is a long journey that I must take to the Land of Humbaba. If this enterprise is not to be accomplished, why did you move me, Shamash, with the restless desire to perform it!'"[11] Gilgamesh's "sacrifice of tears" moves the god to provide him with numerous well-armed followers (a band of brothers), the aid of the winds, and good counsel about routes and objectives. The tears of the mother at this separation move the god to further assurances and provisions for the journey.

The subjective nature of the events of parting might be found in the sequence of emotions at Gilgamesh's departure—protest, despair, and detachment. This sequence, which psychoanalysts have termed "separation anxiety," occurs with an infant's loss of attachment to significant others. John Bowlby observed this sequence of affect in toddlers left by their mothers in a nursery: "At first he *protests* vigorously and tries by all means available to him to recover his mother. Later still he seems to *despair* of recovering her and is vigilant for her return. Later he seems to lose interest in his mother and to become emotionally *detached* from her" (italics in the original).[12] This sequence is typical of many historical departures. Detachment, the last phase of separation anxiety, is a persisting condition of repression, the result of many separations, a defense against the painful emotions of parting. As a "character trait" of the seasoned traveler, it may be called "objectivity," "distance," or "disinterestedness." The modern celebration of departures—the routine, unemotional departures that are the norm in a society of travelers—is a product of a history that resembles what Bowlby found in children who, in parting, gave no sign of protest or despair. "The only children . . . who appear undisturbed have been those who have never had any future to whom they can become attached, or who have experienced repeated and prolonged separations and have already become more or less permanently detached."[13] The emotional sequence inherent in separation anxiety may thus indicate repeated change, a loss whereby one gains detachment and separability.

One cannot read about ancient partings without feeling pity at the sorrow expressed. The event of parting and separation is a species of human suffering. This leads us to wonder about the strength of the motives causing the voluntary undertaking of an act that "is no small contradiction to human nature." Why do men, in great numbers and at great expense, undertake departures at all?

The answer to this question may be found in the emotional sequence just described. Each separation from place must be understood in terms both of the specific history of the individual and the specific breaks, ruptures, and severances that have made up that person's past. Because every departure, no matter how routine and unexceptional, is part of a history of separations, each may echo the primal departures from the mother and from other significant figures. Such associations are evident in a poem Olearius—court mathematician, librarian, and counselor to the Duke of Holstein—introduced into his travel journal upon his departure from his hometown for Russia in 1636:

> *Oh Germany! You draw away your sheltering hands.*
> *As you see me lured off to foreign lands.*
> *Now mother, good night, I shall not wet with tears*
> *The lap where happily I lay these many years.*
> *Of myself I leave with you indeed the better part.*[14]

Olearius's departure, like so many others, introduces a division within the self, a self-reflective, often self-pitying contrast between an accommodated and an unaccommodated identity—as in Gilgamesh's weeping for himself as traveler. The departure of Olearius, like that of Gilgamesh and many heroic travelers, is voluntary, but the journey may awaken memories of those involuntary earlier separations and become the repetition of a history, the artful elaboration and celebration of a fate begun with the first departure—birth—and terminated with death. Habitual travelers may celebrate and require their departures, as neurotics may celebrate and require their symptoms, to ameliorate deep-seated conflicts. Departure is always a break, both an ending and a beginning: it evokes a past and projects a future. In this we may find the "latent germ of madness" inherent in every parting.

Finally, Gilgamesh's departure both "excorporates" him from those relations that make him an identifiable person, and "incorporates" the traveling body, the transportable social organism that will serve as his armor against a dangerous and uncertain world. Just how the departure creates a separable and transportable social body within which Gilgamesh retains his social being is illustrated by the act of Ninsun, who ritually incorporates into her womb Gilgamesh's chief servant, Enkidu, making his servant also his brother. Gilgamesh departs in company, surrounded by those armed men who will be his chief support and instruments for the display and extension of his identity across space and through time. □

* * *

NOTES

1. John B. Lansing et al., *The Travel Market, 1958, 1959–60, 1961–62* (Lansing, Mich.: University of Michigan, Survey Research Center Reprint, 1963).
2. Donald E. Lundberg, *The Tourist Business* (New York: Van Nostrand Reinhold, 1990).
3. Freya Stark, *The Journey's Echo* (New York: Ecco Press, 1963), p. 19.
4. See Arnold van Gennep, *The Rites of Passage* (Chicago: University of Chicago Press, 1972); Victor Turner, "Betwixt and Between: The Liminal Period in Rites of Passage," in *Betwixt and Between*, ed. Louise Mahdi, Stephen Foster, and Meredith Little (La Salle, Ill.: Open Court, 1987); and Mircea Eliade, *The Rites and Symbols of Initiation* (New York: Harper Torchbooks, 1965).
5. This is Frederik Barth's definition of metaphor in *Ritual and Knowledge Among the Baktaman of New Guinea* (New Haven: Yale University Press, 1975), p. 204.
6. Eliade, *Rites and Symbols*, p. 134. □
7. Pliny, *Natural History*, vol. 2, trans. H. Ruckhum (Cambridge: Harvard University Press, 1947), p. 257.
8. N.K. Sandars, trans., *The Epic of Gilgamesh* (New York: Penguin Books, 1975), p. 70; see pp. 70–71 for epigraph quote.
9. See Nancy Munn, *The Fame of Gawa* (New York: Cambridge University Press, 1986).
10. Sandars, *Gilgamesh*, p. 71.
11. Ibid., p. 72.
12. John Bowlby, *Attachment and Loss*, vol. 2 (New York: Basic Books, 1976), p. 26
13. Ibid., p. 16.
14. *The Travels of Olearius in Seventeenth Century Russia*, ed. and trans. Samuel Baron (Stanford, Calif.: Stanford University Press, 1967), p. 82.

* * *

ROBERT TEMPLE
"Introduction" to *He Who Saw Everything*

Robert Temple's introduction to his translation of *Gilgamesh* is particularly useful in that it is recent enough to incorporate the news of the Elamite version of *Gilgamesh* reported by I.M. Diakonoff and N.B Jankowska in 1990. Temple is not the first to maintain that the speeches in *Gilgamesh*, with their formulaic openings (as stage cues?), could indicate that it was a sacred drama, and the Elamite story of Gilgamesh and Siduri would seem to support that theory, since it contains not only speeches but a chorus. Temple cites Theodor Gaster on Hittite and Canaanite "liturgical dramas" as well as Egyptian texts and, of course, Greek drama.

Temple is also interested in the influence of *Gilgamesh* on Greek myth and on modern writers like Rainer Maria Rilke. He himself used a number of translations (by Campbell Thompson, Kramer, Heidel, Speiser, Grayson, Bridson, and Sandars) in making his own.

Temple thinks Gilgamesh is an "astro-poem" that includes the precession of the equinoxes. The poem contains much other esoteric meaning as well.

The Royal National Theatre in London performed a stage production of Temple's translation, with a cast of eighteen. He commented on the extraordinary response of the participants: "It was generally agreed that the production was a success. It was favourably reviewed in the leading London newspapers. The material was cut down so that the performance lasted two hours and fifteen minutes continuously with no interval. Many aspects of the Epic were revealed only through staging, rehearsal, and performance, which had never occurred to me before. The production was preceded by unusually lengthy rehearsals lasting four and a half months at the Royal National Theatre Studio, in which more than 35 actors took part. The actors became so absorbed in the material that they began spending their spare time in the British Library doing research, and they bought lots of books about ancient Babylonia and Assyria. I took an active part in the rehearsal process for the entire period. We realised as we went along that the trance elements of the Epic were far more prominent than we had imagined simply from the written word. I therefore helped the actors learn about limb rigidity and other aspects of trance, but eventually it was realised that I needed to hypnotise many members of the cast, which I did. One actor, particularly susceptible to hypnosis, went on a very vivid 'shamanic journey', roaming the steppes in the manner of Gilgamesh. He discovered that he had as his companion a lioness who gazed lovingly into his eyes as they ran across a savannah together. All of the actors and actresses involved in this strange project agreed that their deep immersion in such extremely archaic material had significantly affected them psychologically, and all agreed that the result was a positive enrichment. They all spoke of being 'humbled' by the material. For the entire four and a half months, no one ever said a cross word to anyone else, and it was agreed that none of the participants had ever known such a happy professional experience lacking in personality clashes. Many of them attributed this to the material. A peculiar enchantment seems to have emanated from the archaic material, which worked powerfully upon the psyches of all involved, and many said it was the most amazing experience of their lives. In some strange way, immersing ourselves so deeply in aspects of thought and experience which were so many thousands of years old seemed to speak to a buried, elemental level of our psyches, and it was the enactment and performance which brought this alive, like turning on an electric fire which had been inert for millennia. The staging of the Epic at the National Theatre was the conclusive demonstration of the fundamentally dramatic nature of the Gilgamesh material, as at every performance (all were sold out), the audience were as if mesmerised, sitting silently and intently absorbed for the entire performance as if they were worshippers at some ancient religious ceremony. It was a true sacred drama which took place." (Ed.)

The Fascination of the *Epic*

The Epic of Gilgamesh is alive and wriggling. You might as well try and catch hold of an eel in the water as imagine you can get hold of the *Epic*. Over the years I have often kidded myself that I could guess what the missing fragments of the *Epic* contain. But as the archaeologists discover more fragments in their excavations, what they find is always a surprise. You can never second-guess the *Epic*. Its images are astonishing and unexpected. It will always leap at you in the dark and put a bag over your head just when you thought you could sit down and have a nice cup of tea and relax.

Those who come across *The Epic of Gilgamesh* often become deeply intrigued, or even obsessed, by it. An example of this occurred with the poet Rainer Maria Rilke. In 1980 William L. Moran published the first account of Rilke's infatuation with the *Epic* in the *Journal of Cuneiform Studies* (see Bibliography for this and other works mentioned in the introduction). I have translated Rilke's enthusiastic outbursts and given them below. Rilke's exalted excitement is contagious:

> Gilgamesh *is an immensity! I know it from the edition of the original and rate it the highest possible. From time to time I recount it to various people—the whole thing—and every time I have the most astonished listeners. The abridgement of Burckhardt is not entirely successful, I feel—it falls short of the vastness and the significance of the* Epic: *I* tell *it better. And it* suits *me.*
> Letter to Katharina Kippenberg, 11 December 1916

In another letter of about the same time to Helene von Nostitz (of which Moran gives no date), Rilke wrote:

> *Have you seen the volume in the Insel Library which contains a kind of résumé of an ancient Assyrian poem, the* Gilgamesh? *I have used the accurate scholarly translation (of Ungnad) and have come to love this truly gigantic mass and form of a fragmentary work, which belongs to the very greatest, which can bring the exchanged word to any Age. I would most dearly love to relate it to you—the little Insel volume, so elegant it might be put together and embezzled from the true power of a 5,000-year-old poem. In the fragments (which I must take in hand and render in a first-rate translation) we find a truly immense happening and standing-forth and fearing, and for me personally the large gaps in the text somehow operate constructively, in that they act to keep the magnificently massive fracture-surfaces separated. Here is the* Epic *of death-dread, arisen from that which is immemorial amongst men, by which above all the splitting apart of death and life is rendered definite and momentous. I am certain, also, that your husband would have the liveliest pleasure in perusing its pages. For weeks now I have lived almost wholly within this influence.*

As more and more literary readers encounter the Gilgamesh material in a form which can speak to them, the impact of this ancient work should become increasingly significant. Now that the region of present-day Iraq (setting for much of the *Epic* and home of the cultures which gave birth to it) can be unknown to no one, following the terrible conflicts of the region and the United Nations war against a local dictator whose many follies included an attempt to reconstruct ancient Babylon out of bricks each one of which bore his own name stamped on it (an attempt all too similar, I fear, to the megalomaniac feats of many an ancient Babylonian king), Gilgamesh may seem more relevant than ever. □

The *Epic* as Theater

The *Epic* was more than a work of literature, however; it was also a drama. Indeed, we now have the archaeological proof of this. But before this evidence was published, I myself had become convinced of it. So much of the *Epic* consists of speeches, for instance. Throughout, the formula recurs: 'So-and-so opened his mouth,/ Said to so-and-so.' Sometimes I have rendered it that way; more often I have rendered it: 'So-and-so said to him,/Said to so-and-so.' This quaint turn of phrase seemed to me to be like a stage cue. We do not know if masks were worn, but if so, the narrator saying that the character opened his mouth to speak would be useful, as the mouths of masks are in a fixed position. Working as closely as I did with the material in attempting to get it into English, I could not escape the irresistible, intuitive feeling that I was dealing with the script of a sacred drama. To perform the whole thing would be quite a lengthy undertaking. Perhaps the reason why the earliest form of the material seems to have been in separate installments is that each one was of a convenient length to be performed on a separate ceremonial occasion without taking up the whole proceedings. I have no doubt that other surviving pieces of literature of the period, in which Gilgamesh does not appear, were also performed.

Proof has now emerged that this material was staged. In the issue of a German Assyriological journal for the first half of 1990 an article by two Russian archaeologists, I.M. Diakonoff and N.B. Jankowska, reports some excavations of theirs in Armenia. Their article bore the title 'An Elamite Gilgamesh Text for Argistihenele, Urartu' (Urartu was the ancient name of Armenia), which I considered somewhat puzzling, in that Elamite was an obscure language from Elam, hundreds of miles from Armenia, in what is today south-western Iran. What could the connection be?

The archaeologists surmise is that an Elamite princess traveled to Urartu (Armenia) to marry the king of that country. And for her marriage ceremony she took with her an entourage who performed part or all of *The Epic of Gilgamesh* in her own language.

Delving further, one also finds that the Elamites seem to have been related (if only linguistically) to the Indus Valley Civilization that existed before the Aryan invasion of India (circa 1200 B.C.) and which is known to have been a major trading partner with the ancient Sumerians (who originated the Gilgamesh *Epic*). However they came to be, the Gilgamesh fragments seem to be the only literary texts known to survive in Elamite, a language otherwise known only from administrative documents and formal inscriptions. Diakonoff and Jankowska were therefore only able to guess at much of the meaning and indeed, after the first eighteen lines of their translation, they left the rest in Elamite, contenting themselves with a few footnotes, and saying that most of the words were now clear. Rendering this material for inclusion at the appropriate place in this translation was therefore like piecing together the most fiendish jigsaw-puzzle imaginable.

The Elamite material is in the form of a script, and most of what is spoken is uttered by the Chorus, called *Pap*, which in Elamite means 'All'. No one knows exactly who 'All' consisted of on stage. The archaeologists speculate that 'All' may have represented the original fifty companions who accompanied Gilgamesh on his adventures in the earliest, Sumerian, version of the *Epic*. They were equivalent to the fifty companions who later accompanied Jason on his voyage—the Argonauts. It is doubtful if fifty men actually stood on stage; a smaller number would have represented them.

On the other hand, the Chorus may simply have been a chorus in the Greek sense—an anonymous group who did not figure in the action at all. At the very end of Tablet VI, lines 184 and 185 of the Assyrian text preserve a choral response by a chorus of lyre-maids to a rhetorical question uttered by Gilgamesh in lines 182 and 183. This indicates that performances were accompanied by lyre music, that the musicians chanted responses probably accompanied by music, and that the 'standard' Assyrian text is probably an epic narration adapted from a dramatic version used for performance by actors and musicians.

Diakonoff and Jankowska mention people who had earlier speculated that the *Epic* was performed (something which was unknown to me):

> The text confirms de Liagre Boehl's old suggestion that the epics were performed antiphonally... in the epics, the introductory text preceding the further verse parts couched in the first person was pronounced separately:

> in a rhythmically different way or simply in prose. The obvious fact that the Ancient Oriental written literature was influenced by the oral tradition can be supported by postulating a stage of development characterized by antiphonal or choral recitation of the epic texts during a sacral-dramatization of the plot. Such dramatization presupposed a stage-director, as pointed out for the Greek theater by A.I. Jankowski... The stage-director being, at the same time, the protagonist actor, the play, if staged in another country, would still necessarily be performed in this actor's language, like Euripides's *Bacchae* in Artavasdes II's Armenia, or the Gilgamesh 'play' in Urartian Argistihenele, at a very considerable distance from the country of origin.

It is good that they remind us that the *Bacchae* of Euripides was performed in Armenia in Greek at a later date. We now see that the performance of the *Epic* and the performance of the *Bacchae* form a continuous tradition, most evidences of which have vanished. The Greek dramas are known to have been performed all over Asia under the Greek kingdoms left behind after the conquests of Alexander.

The fragments excavated are of rather a late date, being only from the eighth century B.C., but they do not draw upon the Assyrian Gilgamesh texts. They represent instead an extremely archaic version of the material, more than a thousand years older:

> Chronologically our new Elamite version is slightly older than the founding of Ashurbānapli's library, but both typologically and as a ritualistic text it is very archaic. The name of the protagonist, Gilgamesh, is spelled in the Old Babylonian way... The Elamite spelling points to contacts with the Old Babylonian version of the Gilgamesh tale as opposed to later versions.

We thus have evidence of the dramatized form of the *Epic* apparently traced back to about 1800 B.C. But in all probability it went back to Sumerian times as well, say about 2500 B.C. In fact, it is highly likely that the dramatized *Epic of Gilgamesh* was being staged two thousand years before Aeschylus, although at that early date it was probably not in its full form and consisted instead of separate episodes performed individually.

Anyone who finds the idea of Gilgamesh on stage in the ancient Near East wholly surprising has not seen Theodor Gaster's book *Thespis: Ritual, Myth and Drama in the Ancient Near East*, published first in 1950. Gaster showed that there were Hittite and Canaanite 'liturgical dramas or the spoken accompaniments of ritual acts'. He discussed also 'the Egyptian "dramatic" texts from Edfu and from the Ramesseum, and the so-called "Memphite Creation Play" inscribed on the celebrated "Shabaka Stone"'. Gaster gives a fascinating background to what we have now discovered about the Gilgamesh material, though it is curious that he nowhere recognizes the dramatic nature of *The Epic of Gilgamesh*, and indeed only mentions it once in passing.

Students of Greek drama will also be familiar with the religious origins of drama. A.E. Haigh commences his book *The Attic Theater* with these remarks:

> The Attic drama, like most ancient forms of art and poetry, was originally the offspring of religious enthusiasm. It was developed out of the songs and dances in honor of Dionysus, the god of wine and vegetation... Dramatic representations at Athens were confined, from first to last, to the great festivals of Dionysus. They were regarded as a religious ceremonial, as an act of homage to the god. They never became, as with us, an ordinary amusement of everyday life.

And, similarly, we may be sure that the *Epic* retained through its long history a sacred status, with the underlying theme of its hero's quest for eternal life. □

Other Hidden Meanings

The underlying symbolism of the *Epic* is a complicated subject, and this is not the place to try and explain it in detail. An example of its complexity is the geodetic scheme that comprises the sacred mountain peaks connected with the ark. The ark mentioned in the Bible is said to have come to rest after the Flood on Mount Ararat. The Greeks had a Noah as well, whose name was Deucalion. His ark is said to have come to rest either on Mount Tomaros or Mount

Parnassos. It is no coincidence that Mount Tomaros and Mount Ararat are on precisely the same line of latitude. Nor is it a coincidence that Mount Parnassos is precisely one degree south of them. As for the ark in *The Epic of Gilgamesh*, it is said to have come to rest on 'Mount Nisir'. This seems to have been a mountain in the Zagros range on the same line of latitude as Babylon. These geodetic points all form part of a larger pattern.

The Epic of Gilgamesh teams with intriguing mysteries. It is largely written in a kind of code language whereby it has the semblance of a secular saga while permitting the priests and sages to conceal its deeper meanings by means of puns, *double-entendres*, and symbolism. To give a brief example, the *Epic* says that Gilgamesh is 'two-thirds god, one-third man'. Nobody ever seems to have noticed before that no one can be two-thirds anything or one-third anything else. The scholars may have forgotten that parents come in pairs. I have never met anybody who was two-thirds English and one-third Italian. Have you?

So what were they getting at? Clearly this is a symbolic statement, for which there are various possible explanations. To take one: Gilgamesh is associated with the planet Mercury, and Mercury was watched with fanatical attention by the Babylonians. They knew that Mercury as it goes along the sky does not move through the whole zodiacal band. In fact, it only moves through two-thirds of it (eight degrees of the twelve-degrees width of the band). If you consider Mercury as a god, then the planet's path in the zodiac is 'non-god'. Is this what the formulaic expression 'Gilgamesh is two-thirds god' is trying to say? Maybe it is, or maybe it isn't. But we can be sure that some such esoteric tradition is behind it, and knowing the Babylonians, it is likely to have something to do with astronomy.

One other oddity which I should mention is the strange recurrence throughout the *Epic* of the period of 'six days and seven nights'. Not only is this the length of time of the storm of the Great Flood, but in both Tablets I and II it is on two occasions the length of time for which Enkidu copulated with the harlot; in Tablet X it is the length of time Gilgamesh says he wept over his dead friend before giving him up for burial; and in Tablet XI it is the most important period of all. For in that tablet it is the length of time which Ziusudra says that Gilgamesh should try and stay awake without sleeping if he wishes to achieve immortal life. Instead, Gilgamesh sleeps for that same length of time. It is clear that this period of time has some ritual or special significance; but what?

Here a strange experience of my own should be mentioned. For I once stayed awake without sleeping for that precise length of time—a feat which Gilgamesh sadly could not equal. And the reason I say it was a strange experience was because it had the most peculiar psychological effect on me, so that I believe there may have been a literal truth behind the suggestion of Ziusudra that Gilgamesh try and keep awake for that length of time. I presume that actual experiments by ancient priests may have shown them that if this feat could be accomplished, a very important psychological experience could occur, one similar to my own. Briefly, the effect it had on me was to convince me of the independent existence of the soul apart from the body—which amounts to 'achieving eternal life', in the sense that one *experiences its reality*. It is difficult to describe or explain, but after I had transcended the incredible bodily exhaustion, I seemed to reach a plateau that was beyond the body altogether. I enjoyed 'perpetual wakefulness', which is what I believe it must be like to be dead. (Hence the people who kill themselves seeking oblivion are making the most terrible mistake!) Far from being a state of 'sleep', I believe that death is *waking*. I delighted in being freed from the need to sleep, of being awake by day and by night. I wrote, I read, I walked about London; I was making use of my full twenty-four hours in every day and loving it. Subjectively I became quite unable to remember what the state of sleep was or even to comprehend the idea of it. I would walk at three or four in the morning and see all the windows of all the houses black, and I would say to myself: 'There are bodies lying in those rooms, motionless, on beds. *What are they doing?*' I could no longer remember. The concept of 'sleep' had become meaningless to me. I cannot stress enough that subjectively sleep no longer existed, that the only form of existence of which I could conceive was one where I would be awake for ever. I had no out-of-the-body experience or anything obvious like that. I had no hallucinations of any kind. Everything was perfectly normal in every way. Except for one thing: waking was eternal; no cessation of waking was possible.

I believe that that subjective experience was one which ancient priests must have gone through as part of their ascetic rituals, and one which I stumbled on by chance. (Though my motive was simply to test my tolerance, see how long I could stay awake).

When strange Akkadian or Sumerian words occur in the translation in italics and untranslated, that is generally because nobody knows what they mean. There are also some names of gods, winds, demons, and so forth, which are unusual and for which we have no further information. And when the meaning of a name or word is hotly in dispute and I have no particular view, I tend just to leave it, sometimes commenting in a note. Serious readers are urged to look at the notes at the end of each tablet, as they sometimes convey important background information. Most of my corrections to the more usual translations are due not to innovations as much as to a more conservative and literal approach, by adherence to which many of the hidden meanings become evident. Attempts to gloss over awkward meanings in the interests of clarity have in the past generally been misguided, and have resulted in the obscuring of much of importance. My general approach has been always to take the ancient authors literally at their word—no matter how bizarre that might be—and thus to reveal the concealed meanings which cannot be elucidated by glossing over either in editing or translating. We should trust our ancient authors more, for it is only by listening closely, closely, that the whispers may be heard.

To return to the translation, I would only stress one main point in offering advice to readers: remember that in the ancient cultures which produced *The Epic of Gilgamesh* there was no such thing as a purely entertaining work of literature or drama. Everything had religious connotations. Our desacralised world did not yet exist. There were gods on every street corner. The *Epic* was not written just for fun or amusement. The Sumerians, Babylonians, Assyrians, Hittites, Hurrians, and Elamites would all be horrified if they knew that we even thought such a thing for an instant. When reading the translation which follows, step into the skin of someone from ancient times and try and see it as he or she saw it. Be a Babylonian for a day. □

* * *

CARL LINDAHL
"The Oral Aesthetic and the Bicameral Mind"

The journal that was developed around the study of orality and literacy, *Oral Tradition*, has already shown some interest in *Gilgamesh*. In a position paper that was published in 1991, "The Oral Aesthetic and the Bicameral Mind," Carl Lindahl took up the claim made by Julian Jaynes in *The Origin of Consciousness in the Breakdown of the Bicameral Mind* (1976) that the author of *Gilgamesh* in the era of the bicameral mind was not yet conscious of consciousness. Lindahl uses a passage from *Gilgamesh* as an example of "archaic aural literature" but also more recent examples of oral art, i.e., oral performance, 19th-century English ballads, African-American blues, to demonstrate that an "oral aesthetic" prefers the concrete "oral image" to abstract language.

Lindahl offers four psychological reasons for the preference. There is no need to posit a not-yet-functioning corpus collosum to account for the description of Gilgamesh's emotions in terms of external action. The problem all oral performance faces is to "overcome the passivity of the audience," not that the poet or audience is incapable of introspection. (Ed.)

Ancient epic presents worn faces, but seldom shows the minds they hide. In the world's oldest story, emotions surface visually, unaided by revelations of the characters' thoughts: "tears streamed" on the face of Gilgamesh as he mourned his best friend. The hero wept "six days and seven nights" until his face, "weathered by cold and heat," became "like that of a man who has gone on a long journey" (Gardner and Maier, 1984:166, 168, 210, 212). Ancient epic depicts gigantic actions without naming their causes and motivations. "Like a lioness whose whelps are lost," grieving Gilgamesh "paces back and forth"; "he tears off… and throws down his fine clothes like things unclean" (*ibid.*:187–88). In *The Iliad*, written down a thousand years after *Gilgamesh*, grieving Achilleus groans like "some great bearded lion when some man… has stolen his cub" and dirties his clothes, scattering "black ashes over his immortal tunic" (Lattimore 1951:18.23–25, 318–23).

Throughout the first millennium of surviving literature, epic explained love, death, strength, and suffering as the products of monstrous gods—present sometimes as voices, sometimes in the full vision of their godhead. Such descriptions and images lead Julian Jaynes—in his book, *The Origin of Consciousness in the Breakdown of the Bicameral Mind* (1976)—to posit that the ancients could describe their own bodies, but could not examine the content of their own minds; that they performed actions without knowing their motivations; that, because of the dual nature of their thought processes, they habitually hallucinated the voices and forms of the gods that directed their actions. Such poems as *Gilgamesh* and *The Iliad* are therefore the *literal* records of what ancient people experienced—accounts little altered by fiction, faulty memory, theology, imagination, or artistry.

Jaynes presents epic imagery as the major surviving evidence of the era of the bicameral mind, when the "hallucinatory area" in the right lobe of the brain—corresponding to Wernicke's area in the left—generated poetry and visions, producing an archaic and incomplete form of consciousness. As Wernicke's area now generates speech, the hallucinatory area generated inner voices. Signals from the hallucinatory area seemed to come from outside the body; thus they were interpreted in life and in literature as voices and visions of divine beings that controlled human fate. Actions were portrayed without motivations and heroes' minds were not inspected because people were not yet conscious of their own consciousness. Only when Wernicke's area and the left cerebral hemisphere began to exercise the greater power and the hallucinatory area became more or less vestigial did the process of introspective consciousness begin.

Yet there is another sort of evidence that cannot be ignored. The same sort of imagery cited by Jaynes as proof of preconscious thought is found universally in archaic *aural* literature—whenever recorded—as well as in most recently recorded *oral* art, wherever practiced in the world. The "incomplete" perceptual record of *Gilgamesh* and *The Iliad* can be simply explained as part of an oral aesthetic, an aesthetic rooted in the fact that all oral poets share certain imperatives: they must always *perform* their work, and in so doing engage constantly the imagination of their audiences.

Roger D. Abrahams proposes a list of three imagistic universals in oral art: 1) overstatement and understatement, 2) concrete and specific language, and 3) translation of idea and emotion into action and symbol.[1] All three generate such imagery as is found in

Gilgamesh and *The Iliad.* Consider two stanzas, one from a nineteenth-century English ballad, one from a recent Afro-American blues. In the ballad, a mourning man lets his plan of action express the nature of his grief:

> I'll do as much for my sweetheart
> As any young man may;
> I'll sit and mourn all on her grave
> For a twelvemonth and a day.[2]

In this floating blues stanza, a man dramatizes his wife's greed:

> She takes all my money,
> throws it against the wall;
> She gives me what sticks
> and keeps what falls.[3]

Both passages employ understatement and overstatement, but in a very specific way, overstating action to the point of near-parody but leaving no room for explanation or emotion. Moreover, both images are concrete expressions of ideas that could as easily have been rendered abstractly. Thus, both images fulfill Abrahams' final criterion, which could be called the master trope of oral art: the translation of idea and emotion into action and symbol. This is the most concise way of expressing how all three rules produce their effects.

Another way of saying the same thing is that oral poetry tends to be *unglossed*: listeners are presented a striking picture, but each must individually caption it, and draw personal conclusions concerning the ideas and emotions implicit in the poem. There is evidence that oral artists not only avoid, but *disdain* the glossing of their images. Bluesmen and blues fans have commented on the lack of artistry in the blues imitations of the Rolling Stones:

> The Stones don't understand how you sing
> the blues. They don't understand that when
> you sing about drugs, you really mean sex, and
> when you sing about sex, you really mean drugs.
> They mix things up and mess up their songs.
> They don't have any self-control.[4]

So the oral image, exaggerated as it may seem, is in reality subject to the strictest control: in its presentation of emotion and in the metaphorical encoding of its message—a message that is meant to stop short of the direct expression of the thoughts and feelings that gave rise to the song.

Perhaps the most important explanation for the prevalence of the unglossed oral image lies in the needs of the audience, the ultimate determinant of what songs are sung again and again. Worldwide accounts attest that the audience exerts life-and-death control over a traditional song. In various contexts, unimpressed listeners will shout down a performer, or fall asleep, or simply walk away. In some traditions the inattentiveness of one listener will end the performance for all.[5]

The oral artist's objective, then, is to overcome the passivity of the audience, to ensure their complicity and support in creating a successful performance. Artist and audience increase their opportunities for mutual engagement by creating a certain aesthetic system, a metaphorical language that ensures that something important will remain unsaid, requiring further interpretation. More than merely leaving room for listeners to "fill in a blank," unglossed imagery allows a significant range of response. As Andrew Welsh has noted (1978: 76), "the more precise the poetic Image, the less we can limit with prose definitions the meanings and emotions involved in it."

Whenever researchers have taken the time to know oral artists, it has been shown that the same people who perform concrete, externalized songs—translating idea and emotion into action and symbol—are more than capable of introspection, that they are acutely conscious of the workings of their own minds, and that they can explain very articulately what is going on in their heads and hearts. But it is simply not their aesthetic choice or rhetorical strategy to make such explanations within their performances.

This point is made dramatically in Betsy Whyte's recording of the ballad "Young Johnstone" (Child 88). This Scottish singer presents the song in a restrained, almost ethereal voice, despite the fact that it describes a murderous central character. In the progress of this song, Johnstone—whose "first instinct," states Francis J. Child (1882–98: II, 288), "is as duly to stab as a bulldog's is to bite"—kills his sister's lover, then his own lover, and finally himself. Johnstone's actions, like those of Achilleus and Gilgamesh, are concrete and exaggerated. Betsy Whyte's characters do not look into themselves, and as she sings—almost matter-of-factly—she leaves no impression that she wishes to examine their minds. Yet as soon as she stops singing she adds her own interpretation in emphatic, emotional tones:

> I've forgotten the last wee bit, but—I know the
> end. They were supposed to be lying together
> on the floor, [solemnly] dead. But—it was
> [emphatically] *true.* It was really a true—ballad.
> Well—usually when they said they were true
> in these old times they *were* true. He was *jealous*
> o her, you see, he was this *type*, you would have tae
> understand the Johnstons to ken that type...[6]

Betsy Whyte has obviously lived with this song. In her mind, there is no doubt of its meaning, and hers is not a meaning that most outsiders, including Child, would be likely to infer. Her personal and emotion-filled reading demonstrates beyond doubt that she is fully capable of supplying feelings and motivations for the ballad characters. But, again, not one hint of this interpretation emerges in her sung presentation. Betsy Whyte has chosen to separate what she considers to be a great song from her deeply personal experience of it.

In suppressing her own vision of Johnstone, Betsy Whyte is filling a great communicative need. Recent psychological experiments, though far from settled on a single interpretation, point toward, if not yet inevitably to, the following conclusions. First, an oral image is much more likely than a visual image to spur an audience to create mental images. Second, listeners will respond more quickly and dramatically to concrete than to abstract language. Third, listeners will also remember concrete images longer than abstract ones. Finally, the images that listeners remember longest and most vividly are voluntary—that is, images that emerge from one's own imagination rather than in response to the specific instructions of a speaker. Taken together, these findings suggest that sharp but sparse and open-ended oral images will create the strongest and longest-remembered response of any form of poetic communication.[7]

To bolster his claim that the ancients could not read their own minds, Julian Jaynes can offer no more powerful evidence than concrete poetic imagery—the same kind of unglossed pictures favored by today's aural artists. Yet contemporary singers possess great powers of introspection; they simply recognize that the strength of their art lies in avoiding interpretation. In explaining how she performs such dramatic ballads as "Mary Hamilton" (Child 185), Almeda Riddle (West 1986) insists on distance: "Get behind the song. If you get behind it, they'll see it. If you get in front of it, they'll just see you and get disgusted." The listener's greatest power is the power to be suggested to. Only by thus empowering the audience does the oral artist maintain the right to perform.

Addendum

Few poems owe more to the oral esthetic of concrete imagery than does *Gilgamesh.* It is true that the latest and fullest version of the epic contains passages that open up the hero's mind and heart and allow readers' access to a subjective soul. Sîn-leqi-unninni gives us a man who baldly admits, "I am terrified" [IX, 1, 9], who publically parades his darkest fears. But, even at his most emotional, the hero juxtaposes his confessions with revelations in the form of concrete images that will linger long in readers' minds:

> Six days and seven nights I wept over him
> Until a worm fell out of his nose.
> Then I was afraid.
> [X, iii, 23–25][8]

His fears may be the first sign that Gilgamesh is not as godlike as he had seemed, but rather human. As the poem nears its end, the godliness of Gilgamesh grows more remote and he grows more human and more sympathetic. Like Achilles in another, later great epic, Gilgamesh can become heroic only by surrendering his godhead and *unlearning his divinity.*

In the last three great scenes of the eleventh tablet, at the climactic moments of the action, the poet must convert Gilgamesh from a god to a man. At these crucial junctures of the story, Sîn-leqi-unninni commits himself fully to an oral esthetic of unglossed images illustrating how the semidivine hero learns his limits. Any satisfactory reading of the eleventh tablet requires us to translate idea and emotion into action and symbol.

Having begun his story as an outsized monster, Gilgamesh has learned a form of humanity only through his companionship with Enkidu, a figure outwardly as monstrous as—and even more inhuman than—himself. Then, driven to a more human despair by Enkidu's death, Gilgamesh only slowly gives up his fight to join the gods in inhuman immortality. Utnapishtim the remote has told him, "From the beginning there is no permanence" [X,vi, 32]. But this is a lesson that Gilgamesh must learn firsthand, a lesson which the poet conveys through three series of powerful oral images.

First, there is the hero's test of sleeplessness: if he can remain awake for seven days he will live forever. Sleep, of course, immediately creeps like a mist over Gilgamesh: the poet is now saying, far more effectively than Utnapishtim has, that "the sleeping and the dead, how like brothers they are" [XI, vi, 33]. Against his will, Gilgamesh surrenders his consciousness and his immortality in the same instant.

For every day of Gilgamesh's portentous seven-day sleep, Utnapishtim's wife bakes a loaf of bread. The collected loaves symbolize both the futility and the waste bound up in Gilgamesh's journey:

> [Utnapishtim speaks:]
> Come on, Gilgamesh. Count your wafers.
> I'll show you how many days you've slept.
> Your first one is dried out,
> the second is leathery, the third moist, the fourth turned white,
> the fifth has gray on it, the sixth is rotten,
> the seventh—suddenly as you were touched, you came alive.
> [XI, v, 223–28]

This baking lesson is as vividly clear as it is impossible to translate exactly: while Gilgamesh lay dreaming his dream of immortality, the real concern of his life, his daily bread, lay rotting in the world his fantasies had abandoned.

Something of this lesson, unspoken except through images, has stayed with the hero, because in his second, final, and failed attempt at immortality, he has shifted the focus of the quest from the lonely uniqueness of godhead to Uruk, his proper home. He captures the flower of immortality and calls it "The-Old-Man-Will-Be-Made-Young"[XI, vi, 281]: his goal is to go home and share it with his subjects. Any immortality he can gain from it will be centered in and spent on the human world.

Then, in another unforgettable imagistic moment, a snake seizes the flower as Gilgamesh is bathing and immediately sheds its skin. Once more, unsaid is the obvious: that a snake may shed its skin and live on, but a human being cannot. The speed with which the snake takes the flower, like the speed with which Gilgamesh fell asleep at the onset of his first immortality test, only underlines the futility of fighting against the divine limits set on human life.

In surrendering the flower without eating it, Gilgamesh has finally unlearned his divinity and once more committed himself to his kingship—a mortal kingship. In the final image of the eleventh tablet, Gilgamesh brings Urshanabi back to Uruk. Like Enkidu, the ferryman Urshanabi has surrendered a superhuman role to help Gilgamesh. By steering a living man to the land of the dead, Urshanabi has broken divine law and is now in exile. Gilgamesh takes him back to Uruk and in words that nearly duplicate lines from the opening passages of the poem, says:

> Go up, Urshanabi, onto the walls of Uruk.
> Inspect the base, view the brickwork.
> Is not the very core made of oven-fired brick?
> Did not the seven sages lay down its foundation?
> [XI, vi, 304–307; compare I, i, 17–19]

On the surface, nothing has changed. The great difference, however, is that now it is Gilgamesh and not the poem's narrator who proclaims the magnificence of the wall. A quest for eternal life that ends with a celebration of a man-made wall could seem an utter, ironic failure. But in this simple, if glowing, description of a great civic work, Gilgamesh for the first time measures his identity in terms of the acts that a human being, rather than some god, can accomplish. The unglossed image of the wall is the poet's signal that his hero has finally unlearned divinity and committed himself firmly to the majesty possible within the limits of mortality.

Thus, at the end of the eleventh tablet, the poet's symbols affirm what he had said at the very beginning: Gilgamesh is the man who built the wall of Uruk and brought back a story of the days before the flood. We are left with just a story and a wall, perhaps mere substitutes for immortality, but impressive substitutes. So far, they have lived as long as anything of their human kind: a story filled with concrete images and a wall of burnt bricks, have tellingly and remarkably survived for more than 4000 years.

* * *

NOTES

1. Abrahams and Foss 1968:7–11. Abrahams confines himself principally to the study of British-American oral poetry, but I have applied his analysis to the poems of the thirteen cultures represented in Finnegan 1978. Although there is considerable variation from culture to culture (e.g., Yoruba and Hopi artists almost invariably translate emotion into action and symbol, while Eskimo poets tend to express emotion more directly), all thirteen cultures translated idea and emotion into action and symbol with notably greater frequency than the literary poets (Wordsworth, Shelley, Whitman, and Longfellow) I examined for purposes of comparison.
2. Stanza 2 of "The Unquiet Grave" (Child 78) in a version recorded in Friedman 1956:32–34. For a brief discussion of the power of this ballad to express indirectly the mixed and otherwise unspeakable emotions of mourners, see Lindahl 1986.

3. Tampa Red is among the many blues musicians who have performed this floating stanza.
4. Paraphrase of personal communications made to me by blues fan Arthur Kempton and musician Earl Strayhorn during an interview in April 1969 in Cambridge, Massachusetts. Among the blues artists I have consulted, concrete, uncoded imagery is regarded as a major option, but not as an imperative—while some artists express emotion directly in their lyrics, others prefer indirection.
5. Among the best records of audiences forcefully editing tellers and singers of tales are Lord 1960: esp. 14–17 and Dégh 1969: 49–53, 71–119. See also Abrahams 1972.
6. Betsy Whyte's version of "Young Johnstone," as well as her comments on the song, are recorded in "The Muckle Songs: Classic Scots Ballads," Tangent TNGM/D, Scottish Tradition 5, recorded through the auspices of the School of Scottish Studies, Edinburgh. An accompanying booklet provides a transcription of Betsy Whyte's remarks. Emphasis is found in the original transcription; I have slightly altered the punctuation of that version.
7. These four conclusions are supported by the following articles: Begg et. al. 1978; Dickel and Slak 1983; Doll 1983; Jamieson and Schimpf 1980. See also Morris and Hampson 1983: 240–99.
8. All quotations and line references in this addendum are from John Gardner and John Maier, trans. and ed., *Gilgamesh: Translated from the Sîn-leqi-unninnī Version* (New York: Random House, 1984).

❋ ❋ ❋

Miles Richardson
"Point of View in Anthropological Discourse: The Ethnographer as Gilgamesh"

For Miles Richardson, in *Anthropological Poetics,* it is not so much Gilgamesh's departure as it is the experience and the return, especially the return that drove Gilgamesh to record his story on stone. Richardson used "Gilgamesh the Inscriber" to develop a theory of participant observations, with the anthropologist as storyteller, or in Richardson's terms, "The Ethnographer as Gilgamesh."

Against both the literary-critical movement known as New Criticism, which saw literary works as autonomous works of art, and structuralism, Richardson claims that narrative and behavior have in common the construction of "narrative selves." In *Gilgamesh,* it is Gilgamesh the place-builder and secret-bringer that most interests Richardson. "To be human is to be in story… to speak… to act… to observe… to inscribe… and to tell a story." (Ed.)

In the search to comprehend what it is to be human, anthropology pursues a multiparadigmatic strategy. For some the secret of being human lies in our biological makeup; for others the secret resides in the material conditions of our living. In their assessment as to what is fundamental to our being, surely these strategies are correct: cut us and we bleed; deny us the fruits of our labor and we rebel. In addition to being both biological creatures and economic beings, however, we are, in the same fundamental manner, storytellers.

There is a story told in anthropological circles about Gregory Bateson, who supposedly said:[1]

> There is a story which I have used before and shall use again: A man wanted to know about mind, not in nature, but in his private large computer. He asked it (no doubt in his best Fortran), "Do you compute that you will ever think like a human being?" The machine then

> set to work to analyze its own computational
> habits. Finally, the machine printed its answer
> on a piece of paper, as such machines do.
> The man ran to get the answer and found,
> neatly typed, the words:
> THAT REMINDS ME OF A STORY[2]

Storytelling is a fundamental quality of our everyday life. This tempts us to say that to be in a story is to be human or even in a more resounding paradox, that to be human is to be in a story. As compelling as these equations are, we recognize, however, that story is narrative and that everyday life is behavior. Consequently, the task is to search for the qualities that narrative and behavior have in common. How does narrative resemble behavior and how does behaving have attributes of narration?

The Narrative Act

Until recently, literary criticism, inspired by the formalist methods of New Criticism or of structuralism, approached the text as a constrained artifact, a thing in itself, detached from both author and reader. Narrative was art, and art was coolly cerebral. In her exploration of point of view in prose fiction, Susan Sniader Lanser has challenged this perspective of narrative as refined cognition. She writes:

> Because writing of literature is verbal activity, an inquiry into point of view at the level of the literary act might well begin by situating fictional writing within the framework of all language use. Though the writing of fiction is, of course, a particular type of linguistic act, it shares with all verbal production a conventional structure which is realized in a particular context. This means the literary communication is basically similar, rather than opposed, to other modes of verbal behavior. (Lanser 1981: 64)

If we intentionally blur the distinction between literature and the everyday, then the literary text becomes simply another way of speaking. The text becomes an act, a speech act in which point of view becomes an important determinant in the shaping of the text.

Two of the various components Lanser discusses as composing points of view are especially appropriate to the task of relating narrative to behavior, and story to everyday life. These are the privilege or knowledge the narrator has of the textual world and the representation or position of the narrator in the text. Let us continue to follow Lanser and treat these components as continuous variables. Knowledge the narrator has of the events she is recounting ranges from near total ignorance to God-like omniscience. The position of the narrator in the text moves from the point in which the narrator is the principal participant, or the protagonist of her story, toward the point in which she is an objective observer who stands at the margins of the world she is relating.

To these two continuous dimensions I wish to add a third component—a constant. Either as a participant or as an observer, as one who possesses limited or complete knowledge, the narrator cares. Even though she may know all and observe from the extreme edge of the text, the narrator remains focused on the textual world and is concerned about the outcome of the events occurring there.

A graphic display of the continuous dimensions of textual knowledge and position in the text and of the constant care, yields four separate narrative selves whose speech articulates four distinct narratives (see figure 9.1).

Quadrant I is the intersection of limited knowledge and engaged participation. The narrator has only a circumscribed amount of information and is engaged in the text. The text is a diary and the narrator the presumed diarist, who writes, "Today, I ventured forth..."

FIGURE 9.1
THE NARRATIVE SELF AND TYPES OF NARRATIVES

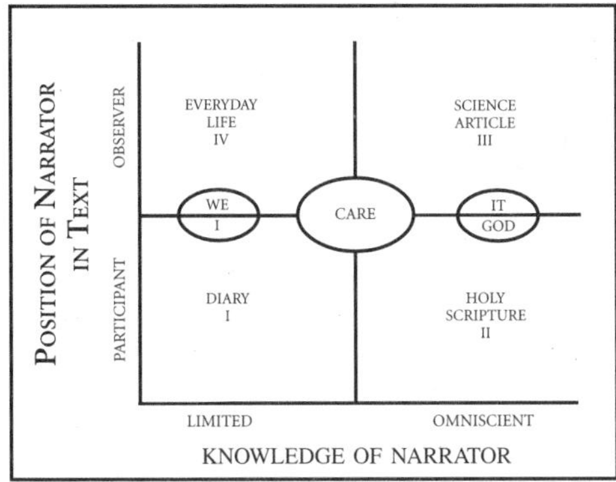

Quadrant II is the intersection of omniscience and participation. The narrator knows all, but is engaged in the text. The narrator appears as a character in the text, yet the narrator, at least according to the text, is the author of the text. The text is, of course, The Holy Scripture and the narrator is God—he or she, but third person—as in "And God said, 'Let there be light…'"

Quadrant III is the intersection of omniscience and detached observation. The narrator knows all and stands at the margins of the textual world. The text produced is that of a science article. The narrator is the scientist-author who has complete knowledge of what is appearing in the article—or if she does not, the referees will reject it because the text was unclear or worse, ambiguous. As an omniscient figure, the narrator is in complete control of the textual world. Yet, nowhere in the text is the narrator clearly positioned. She is at the margins of the text and has the role of observer, as in the frequently occurring phase in such a text, "It has been observed…"

Quadrant IV is a textual world seen from the view of a narrating observer who has only a limited comprehension of the story she is telling. Given the constant, care, such a combination forms a strange and marvelous world; the world that you and me, male and female together, tell, the world of everyday life.

The Behavioral Narrative

If a story is like life, then is not life like a story? If a narrative is an act, is not then behavior a narrative? How do the dimensions of Quadrant IV constitute the narrative of everyday life? How does an observer who is participating in a world of which he has limited knowledge become the narrative self of everyday life? Where is the narrative text of everyday life?

Let's begin by repeating with Lanser, and for that matter with Ricoeur (1979), that text is discourse. Discourse is speaking, and speaking is what we are doing now. The text of everyday life is composed of my speaking silently. We, together in our speaking, are constituting the text of everyday life. Where is the text of everyday life? As we speak, it is here, right here, among us.

As circumscribed in Quadrant IV, the world of everyday, a seemingly uniform text spoken in the bland verbs of conventionality, is in fact diversified, even bewildering. At the extreme of near complete detachment and of severely limited comprehension, the narrator of the everyday is alienated from his discourse. His text is either a scathing indictment of the insanity of the world or a passionate prayer for knowledge. At the lesser extreme of more engagement, our knowledge of what we speak remains limited. In comparison with the information possessed by omniscient narrators of the Holy Scripture and of Science, we are ignorant. We know not the outcome of everyday life; it is open-ended, and stochastic, and its "ultimate meaning [is] subject only to probability laws" (Perinbanayagam 1985:12). Ignorant though we may be, nonetheless, we—you and I—speak. We care.

As we participate in our speaking, we also observe what we do. We are not only observers when we say to one another (or to our selves, which is the same conversation), "Let's look." We are observers even as we participate without that heightened sense of observation. We are observers because we speak.

When we speak, we act; and when we act, as George Herbert Mead (1964) writes, we take the position of the Other and act back towards ourselves. From the Other's point of view, we become an object to ourselves. When I address you, I also address myself. As I observe you, I also observe myself. In this observational act, the inside of each of us, our subjective I's, become the outside of us, our objective Me's. As I am a Me to you, I become a Me to myself. When I as a subject speak to you, I also speak to me as an object. As I distinguish you, I distinguish myself. In the same manner that the author and the reader come to be in the text, so you and I take shape in the dialogue of the everyday.

In Meadian terms, the relationship between you and me is linguistic. Language itself is a vocal gesture that arouses in me the attitude it arouses in you. When a vocal gesture evokes the same response in a speaker that it evokes in the person spoken to, the gesture becomes a significant symbol. In other words, it becomes a name. In everyday life, we name one another. As those who bestow names, we are creating observers even as we participate in the behavior of the everyday, and in our naming we—you and I—create our textual world.

"What does an ethnographer do?" Clifford Geertz rhetorically asks (1973a: 19). We echo the reply, "He writes." The task of the ethnographer is the inscription of everyday discourse, the extraction of "the said from the saying" of those who speak to him (1973a: 19–20). As a participating observer who stands within the text he writes, the ethnographer differs from the rest of us only in that he is more observant. Consequently, in his writing he heightens the composed intersubjectivity of everyday being. He extracts the everyday from its matrix of ho-hum facticity and depicts its utter frailty. With Ernest Becker (1962: 109), he leads us to understand that the world we take for granted is "fundamentally fictitious." He searches among the fictitious text of everyday for themes, plots, and characters. In this search, he tells the human story.

What kind of story is the human story? Is it a Western—a gun-totin', cattle-rustlin', hell-for-leather Western, where the good guys face the bad guys at high noon on the dusty streets of life? Is it a Gothic novel—a creaking-door, musty-odored, pale-figures-on-a-dark-moor Gothic novel, where the heroine discovers an unspeakable horror in her basement? Or is it Science Fiction—an alien-threatened, mutant-riddled, green-oozing Science Fiction, where the technician of special effects puts the finishing touches to the nuclear holocaust as the last survivors lift off to the next universe?

Our story has elements of all of these, the Western, the Gothic, the Science Fiction extravaganza, but at times, it supersedes these genres; it is more bizarre. As the smoke clears away from the Dallas street, it is the good guy who lies crumpled under the sun; the horrors behind the door of the basement at Auschwitz are truly unspeakable; and the neutron bomb, the bomb that kills people but protects property, has won congressional approval. Life *is* stranger than fiction.

Our story has these elements, but much more. It has the sweep, the grandeur, the heroism, and the tragedy of an epic—the epic of Gilgamesh.[3]

Gilgamesh, the Inscriber

We know Gilgamesh, you and I, we know him by his name. From the day of his birth, he was called Gilgamesh; Gilgamesh the place builder. Look at Uruk, Gilgamesh's city. Climb upon its wall and examine well its masonry. Is it not of burnt brick, and did not seven sages lay its foundation? We know Gilgamesh, you and I, we know him by his name. From the day of his birth, he was called Gilgamesh, Gilgamesh the secret-bringer. He went on a long journey, crossed the waters of death, and brought back a story of the days before the flood.

Even for those days, when men had hair like a lion's mane and pride like a stallion's eyes, Gilgamesh was extraordinary. He was two-thirds god and one-third man. He was restless, strong, and full of lust, leaving no virgin to her lover. He wanted to see everything, learn everything, and understand everything. He was two-thirds god and one-third man and none could withstand him.

Then Gilgamesh, the great king, came to know death. In the agony of his knowledge, he cried out. "Oh Ninsun, Oh my mother, what is it to die?"

And Ninsun, his mother, made answer:

"It is to go into the abode out of which none ever return; it is to go to the dark abyss of the dread Goddess, Irkalla. They who dwell there are without light; the beings that live there eat of the dust and feed on the mud."

And Gilgamesh, the great king, groaned loudly, terribly, and tears flowed down his cheeks; no word that was said might comfort him. He groaned, he wept, even though he recalled his shout, reverberating still in the halls of the temple,

> *"Who is splendid among men?*
> *Who is glorious among heroes?"*

And heard his own boastful reply return to him,

> *"Gilgamesh is splendid among men.*
> *Gilgamesh is glorious among heroes."*

Gilgamesh, with the agony that comes from being two-thirds god and one-third man, set forth to find the secret of life. In his journey, Gilgamesh encountered one difficulty after another. Some wore away at his great strength; others sought to confuse his purpose, as did the woman of the wine.

"Gilgamesh, where are you hurrying to? You will never find that life for which you are looking. So fill your belly with good things, dance and be merry, feast and rejoice. Make your wife happy in your embrace, and cherish the little child who holds your hand; for this too is the lot of man." But Gilgamesh's agony, the agony of a man who is two-thirds god, would not let him rest.

At jouney's end Gilgamesh reached the waters of death. At the bottom of the waters of death grew the plant that granted eternal youth. In a feat that only he could achieve, he plucked the plant from the depths. Full of hope now that he had the secret of youth, Gilgamesh returned to Uruk. On the road back, he paused for a moment beside a spring of cool water. While he rested, a snake came out of the spring, snatched the plant, and ate it.

Gilgamesh wept, "Was it for this I toiled with my hands; was it for this I have wrung out my heart's blood? For myself I have gained nothing, but the beast of the earth has the joy of it now. I found a sign, and now I have lost it."

In his despair, Gilgamesh resumed the road that led to his city. As the city, his labor, his work, his acts, his text came into view, his despair lifted and he announced, "Climb up on the wall of Uruk, inspect its foundation, and examine well the brickwork; see if it is not of burnt brick, and did not seven wise men lay these foundations."

This too was the work of Gilgamesh, the king, who traveled the countries of the world. He was wise, he saw mysteries, and he knew secret things. He went on a long journey, was weary, worn out, but returning, engraved on a stone the whole story.

To be human is to be in a story, that is, to speak is to act, to act is to observe, to observe is to inscribe, and to inscribe is to tell a story. We ethnographers, anthropologists you and I, participant observers with limited comprehension, what we seek is to tell the human story, the story of Gilgamesh, the story of one who was two-thirds god and one-third human. Because of the god part that was upon him, Gilgamesh wanted to do everything, learn everything, *understand* everything; but because he was one-third human, he was doomed to fail. It was his lot that he questioned; it was his lot that he received no answer.

Because we speak, because we symbolize, we conjure up worlds where hurts are healed, the hungry are fed, and people do not die; yet because we remain brother to the chimpanzee, cousin to the gorilla, we fail: wounds fester, the hungry starve, and people surely die. As with the Gilgamesh story, however, the human story is not a story of despair; it is a story of achievement. Three million years ago, we walked across the African savanna with a rock in our hand, a dream in our eye, and a word on our lips. Today, we have planted our flag on the moon. Who among nature's creatures can match our record? Where is the one who can best our deeds?

Our task, our lot, as it was that of Gilgamesh, is to speak the text, to inscribe it through our acts, the acts of everyday life, so that those who come after us may read and marvel that here once we strode, authors of our own story.

❋ ❋ ❋

NOTES

1. For example, by Gregory Reck (1986).
2. See Bateson (1979: 3).
3. This account of the acts of Gilgamesh draws upon Richardson (1972), which in turn is based on Sandars (1960) and Gardner and Maier (1984). For a detailed tracing of the coming to be of the Gilgamesh story see Tigay (1983).

❋ ❋ ❋

Thomas Van Nortwick
"The Wild Man: The *Epic of Gilgamesh*"

Thomas Van Nortwick's chapter on Gilgamesh in a 1992 book, *Somewhere I Have Never Travelled,* the first of six chapters, is a comparatist's study of the "second self" in the poem. The other chapters are devoted to *The Iliad* and *The Aeneid.* Like the others, though, Van Nortwick finds in the heroic journey of Gilgamesh "a metaphor for the process of growing up." Key to Van Nortwick's reading of the poem is that Enkidu is "wild," but not "savage." The view of the "double" as a dark force—like Mr. Hyde—is a Victorian view he rejects in favor of the mainly positive features of Enkidu, whose qualities are not identical to the hero's, but complementary.

Like others, Van Nortwick sees Gilgamesh growing up spiritually, seeing himself as part of a larger whole. He likens Gilgamesh's problem to a "mid-life crisis."

For Van Nortwick, Enkidu provides qualities that are not identical to but complementary to the hero. After following the story closely, Van Nortwick emphasizes that Gilgamesh's journey away from the city is quite unlike the travels of Odysseus and Aeneas. Those heroes travel to find a way home; but Gilgamesh returns, changed, accepting the meaning of the city in his life. Where Enkidu had separated Gilgamesh from his citizens, the hero's return to the city involves a reintegration of the second self, the wild man as part of himself.

In Van Nortwick's view, the wilderness and the underworld—"elemental forces outside the reach of culture"—constitute the unconscious, and it is Gilgamesh's task to "grow up" spiritually, to see himself as part of a larger whole. (Ed.)

> Since it has been said that you are my twin and true companion, examine yourself so that you may understand who you are… I am the knowledge of the truth. So while you accompany me, although you do not understand (it), you already have come to know, and you will be called "the one who knows himself." For whoever has not known himself has known nothing, but whoever has known himself has simultaneously achieved knowledge about the depth of all things.
>
> *Book of Thomas the Contender* 138

Robert Bly makes a useful distinction between the *savage* man and the *wild* man:

> We could distinguish between the wild man and the savage man by looking at several details: the wild man's possession of spontaneity, the presence of the female side in him, and his embodiment of positive male sexuality. None of this implies violence toward or domination of other... (in old European initiation rituals). The older males would teach the younger males how to deal with the shadow material in such a way that it doesn't overwhelm the ego or the personality. They taught the encounter more as a kind of play than as a fight. (Bly 1988.53)

Enkidu, dropped to earth as the gods' pinch of clay, is such a man as Bly describes: wild but not savage, spontaneous, at one with the rhythm of nature, exuding raw sexuality that seems to draw, especially in his opposition to Gilgamesh, on a reservoir of femininity. The *Epic of Gilgamesh* is driven by two interconnected polarities, nature/culture and mortal/immortal, and the pivot for the entire structure is the relationship between Gilgamesh and Enkidu. The wild man crosses, hand-in-hand with a harlot, the boundary from nature into culture, then crosses again, this time alone as we all must, beyond the pale of life itself. In each journey he travels as and for both himself and his friend Gilgamesh; at each crossing he draws illumination, like a lightning rod, to the opposing territories. As Gilgamesh follows, he must learn not to walk in the same footprints but to absorb his second self and make his own way, to make one man, new and yet familiar, from two. Looking on lets us think about some knotty and abiding problems: how can we live at peace with what is, letting go of what we wish would be; how can we learn to accept death as part of life; how exactly do we know when we are "grown-up"? This is the first realization we have of the second self in western literature, and it is an impressive debut. □

Gilgamesh as Hero

The presence of the second self would seem to indicate, as I have said, a potential problem, something that might be explored. More specifically, there is something the hero has lost track of or does not yet know and therefore cannot accept about himself—his spiritual development as a man is incomplete in some significant way. The Gilgamesh story has barely begun when problems arise. It seems that Gilgamesh is endowed with extraordinary energy, and his exercise of it is causing distress to his fellow citizens:

> He runs wild with the young lords of Uruk
> through the holy places.
>
> Gilgamesh does not allow the son to go with his father;
> day and night he oppresses the weak—
> Gilgamesh, who is shepherd of Uruk of the Sheepfold.
> Is this our shepherd, strong, shining, full of thought?
> Gilgamesh does not let the young woman go to her mother,
> the girl to the warrior, the bride to the young groom.
> SB I.ii.11–17

The exact nature of Gilgamesh's misbehavior here is slightly obscure, though it seems to be at least partly sexual in nature. As king, he might be demanding the "privilege of the first night" with all the brides; he might also be performing his part in a sacred marriage rite, playing the role of the king who insures the fertility of the crops by sleeping with a surrogate for the goddess Ishtar; then again, it may be that he is simply winning all the potential brides by defeating his male rivals in wrestling matches. For our purposes, it suffices to say that he is overpowering the city in some way that is harmful.

The root cause of this appears in the opening lines of the narrative:

> Two-thirds of him is divine, one-third human.
> The image of his body the Great Goddess designed.
> SB I.ii.1–2

Gilgamesh is the first in a long line of western heroes who straddle the boundary between human and divine. Such creatures are by nature problematical, to themselves and those around them. They might exhibit all the strengths and weaknesses of deities, exerting their enormous power for good or evil, depending on where their appetites drive them; they sometimes transcend the reach of human morality, because they are simply too powerful. All of this sounds very appealing for the hero, if not for his fellows, but a mixed lineage is also a mixed blessing. Being akin to the gods clearly raises large expectations; being human may impair their fulfillment. Too powerful to have real peers among mortals, not strong enough to mix with the gods, the hero may be an isolated, lonely man. Most pressing of all is the problem of mortality: will the hero escape death? The answer, in all but a very few cases, has been no, and learning to accept that verdict is certainly one of Gilgamesh's greatest challenges.

Viewed from the author's perspective, the hero of mixed lineage affords the opportunity to explore one of life's most significant turning points. All of us, if we live long enough, come to a moment when we accept the fact that our life is finite, that we will die. In the aftermath, nothing is quite the same. Life had looked like a collection of possible futures, some realized, some only waiting for our attention. Suddenly those roads not taken appear to be definitely *behind* us; instead of standing at the beginning of an open vista, we are in *the middle* of something finite, with a past stretching in one direction, and a future that looks somehow narrower. At the end of the journey now stands a boundary we had not seen before, and it changes the way we see everything on this side of it.

Such a realization need not be entirely depressing. If death will take away the world, its prospect also clarifies what it is that we most treasure, removes false issues, adds perspective. If life's finitude seems to restrict our possibilities, it also relieves us of the burden of unlimited potential—we are what we are, we do what we can, and we can more easily learn to love ourselves and others as flawed but game mortals than as unfulfilled deities. All of this means that the acceptance of one's own maturity, painful though it may be, is one prerequisite for emotional maturity, because without it we cannot really know ourselves for what we are.

It should not surprise us to find the second self as part of the exploration of life's finitude. If the fact of mortality can bring us to be easier on ourselves, then one aspect of this would be the acceptance of parts of ourselves that our former godlike perspective would not accommodate. In the Gilgamesh epic, the two elements are firmly linked: Enkidu is created as a solution to the problems brought on by Gilgamesh's extraordinary nature. Let us note immediately two things: the overtly therapeutic function of Enkidu within the framework of the story—he is sent on a mission from the gods, who want things to get better in Uruk—and the lack of mystery about Enkidu's origins. We are a fair distance from the dark, haunting stranger who appears as from nowhere in nineteenth-century fiction to torment the unsuspecting hero. The gods' expectation within the story is that this new creature will bring relief to the citizens of Uruk; looking from without as readers familiar with the motif of the second self, we are curious about how the wild man fits into the dynamic spiritual growth in the hero.

Exploring this distinction will help us keep our bearings. Though the gods' explicit intervention and intent may appear to make the therapeutic role of the second self that we are discussing *a part of the fabric of the story*, as it is not in, say, *Doctor Jekyll and Mr. Hyde*, this is not so. This drive toward spiritual growth in the logic of our story is a dynamic imposed from *outside* the frame of the narrative by its author, not from within by fictional transcendent powers. Though the gods of ancient epic, Mesopotamian, Greek, or Roman, may intervene in the life of the mortals to good effect, they do so to please themselves, not to forward the progress of mortals toward spiritual wholeness as a worthy goal in itself. If they save a city, it is because they feel a personal sense of ownership, and they might just as well destroy a city for equally private reasons. Just so, they may have favorite mortals or ones they hate—the *Odyssey* is driven by the counterbalancing love of Athena and hatred of Poseidon for its hero. In this sense, the fact that Enkidu is sent by the gods is coincidental to his role as a second self. Likewise, though Gilgamesh has his divine protectors, principally his mother, as a group the gods are indifferent to his spiritual state, except as it forwards or impedes their personal aims. They will give Gilgamesh a companion if being less lonely will divert him from wearing out the citizens, not because they feel sorry for him in his isolation, and they certainly have no interest in what is our present preoccupation as readers outside the story, his need to integrate the second self. □

The Return of Enkidu

Utnapishtim's sobering questions begin a profound thematic synthesis that integrates various strands of the story. At the center stands the figure of the second self, "man-as-he-was-at-the-beginning." Though he comes from the wild into the city, Enkidu's effect on Gilgamesh has been to separate him from the rest of the citizens. Before the wild man's appearance, the king's energy is a problem, but he is at least fully immersed in the life of the city. Meeting his "second image" stirs up in him the desire for adventure, in particular that kind of glory-seeking which has the goal of distinguishing the two heroes from the rest of the citizens, raising them to some higher plane by virtue of their extraordinary skill and strength. The apogee of this movement comes in Gilgamesh's speech to the citizens after the killing of the Bull of Heaven.

The death of Enkidu provides a check to heroic self-assertion, but not to the separation of Gilgamesh from his fellows. Now driven by fear of death rather than defiance of it, the king travels yet further beyond the pale of human culture, to the poem's version of the dark Underworld. There has been some gain realized already, in that Enkidu's destruction has made death real for Gilgamesh, in a way that his former heroic perspective prevented. But as I have said, knowing something and accepting it are not the same—denial must have its day, and this latter form proves no less strong than the heroic brand.

Gilgamesh's journey into darkness, an outward representation of an inward process, brings him to a new source of truth, deeper and more profound than anything he has yet experienced. Utnapishtim, who corresponds on some level to the nonrational, inner part of Gilgamesh's self, delivers the bad news that Gilgamesh cannot escape the mortal part of his nature. The particular way he puts the point, noting the identical fate awaiting both Gilgamesh and Enkidu, effects an abrupt and significant shift in the role Enkidu plays in the evolution of Gilgamesh toward maturity. Suddenly, Gilgamesh's intense identification with his second self becomes not a force isolating him from the rest of humanity, but rather the ultimate example of his essential kinship with all other mortals. To put it another way, Enkidu becomes a goad to humility, not hubris.

The motif of the second self has been closely integrated throughout the story with the polarities nature/culture and mortal/immortal. Enkidu's transition from the wilderness to Uruk provided Sîn with a vehicle for exploring the former, his death, the latter. As a result, the two antitheses have been woven together in ways that illuminate both. The heroic perspective dominating the earlier adventures was a reflection of the cultural preoccupation with renown as a hedge against oblivion, and led to an easy defiance of the reality of death. So it is, we have observed, that Gilgamesh can contemplate a reprieve for Humbaba, since the monster's begging would provide sufficient proof of the two heroes' prowess—the reality of death is less important than glory. In the world of nature, survival is a genuine issue, death is a real possibility, and so Enkidu, still in touch with these necessities, insists on killing the monster.

Once death intrudes into the artificial world of culture, it destroys the illusion of invulnerability that man's creativity can provide. At the same time, it reminds us that we, as mortal creatures, participate in the world of nature, of death and renewal—culture cannot insulate us from the destiny that we share with wild animals. In this sense, Enkidu's journey into Uruk at first suggests a misleading dichotomy between humans and animals, between creatures of the wild and those of the city. His death and Gilgamesh's reactions to it then offer a corrective to the original view, displacing our attention from the boundary between nature and culture, or animals and humans, which turns out to be less absolute than we thought, toward the definitive boundary between mortals and immortals.

This new focus reinforces, as I have said, the need for Gilgamesh to let go of the perspective that emphasized the ways in which the extraordinary part of his nature set him apart from other humans, and to embrace instead those parts of himself that he shares with all other creatures who must die. At the same time, manipulating the polarities allows Sîn to explore the original "problem" of Gilgamesh, his domination and the hubris that it at least implied, from a wider perspective, as the "problem" inherent in the human illusion of culture as a way of denying the reality of death. In this sense, Gilgamesh plays the typical role of hero in any culture, representing an outsized version of every human, testing the limits of human life as a way of refining our understanding of them.

I have said that grieving raises critical issues for the spiritual evolution of Gilgamesh. Though Enkidu is not explicitly mentioned when Gilgamesh makes his final return to Uruk, one has the sense that Gilgamesh's period of grieving for his dead friend is at an end. The suffering that Enkidu's passing brought for Gilgamesh is tied closely in the story to the king's quest for a way to escape his own death. Both were a form of denial, specifically culture's denial of the reality of the wilderness, and in accepting the inevitability of his own mortality, Gilgamesh by implication accepts the wild man as a part of himself: he reintegrates the second self. In this sense, when Utnapishtim orders that Gilgamesh wash off the dirt of the journey, put aside the animal skins, and dress again in the clothes of the city, he signals an end to the period of grieving. But the shedding of clothing from the wilderness need not anymore signal a break with the reality of the wild, because Gilgamesh has now accepted, on a deeper level, the presence of the wilderness inside himself. The loss of Enkidu has, then, made a difference in the way Gilgamesh sees the world: death, once something to be defied, then to be denied, has become a part of life; Enkidu, lost forever, is at the same time found again.

Conclusion: Life from Death

The synthesis, satisfying though it may be, leaves the troublesome question with which we began. Why does the wild man have to die in order that Gilgamesh be able to accept him as alive *within himself*? Why must one kind of gain be preceded by another kind of loss? The answer, such as it is, lies in the nature and function of the second self as metaphor within the story.

Enkidu's creation ties him to the wilderness as opposed to the culture of Uruk, and marks him as complementary in some sense to Gilgamesh. We might suppose then that the embrace that brings their initial confrontation to an end might also mean that Gilgamesh has accepted the complementary qualities that the wild man embodies. But the story does not go this way. Rather, the appearance of Enkidu seems to drive Gilgamesh further into the heroic perspective to which the wild man stands in opposition. This might seem puzzling, but not if we consider how a confrontation like the one before the bridal chamber in the poem often works in "real life." Faced with parts of ourselves that we do not recognize, would like perhaps not to recognize, we deny the kinship, and often lean away from the new and into the old, accentuating the familiar qualities that complement the strange new ones. So it is when Gilgamesh faces a specter of the unacknowledged "wilderness" inside himself, a complex of attitudes and feelings opposed to the heroic view of life and death that is on display in the first half of the story. Instead of becoming more "wild," he launches an adventure that is driven by a more intense version of the same way of seeing the world that seems to have informed his behavior when he was overwhelming the city: everything he does presupposes the importance of marking the *difference*, in strength, determination, birthright, between the king and his subjects. The events that follow, the killing of Humbaba and the bull, the proposition of Ishtar, seem to lead him further along the same trajectory toward the extreme position reflected in his boasting speech after the death of the bull.

The death of Enkidu is seen within the story as retribution for killing the bull. It also suggests by its placement some kind of punishment for the hubristic excess of the two heroes. From where we stand, on the other hand, the death looks like the final act of denial, of pushing away from the strange qualities of the wild man—Gilgamesh "kills" Enkidu by running away from what he represents.

We note here that the flow of interior events that we see as students of the second self seems to run counter to the surface logic of the story; Sîn tells us that Gilgamesh is thrilled to have a friend, someone to end his isolation, to share the adventures that now suddenly open up. To see his behavior as a *denial* of what his new friend represents seems perverse, somehow flying in the face of what the story says. But again, is it so unusual to discover that what felt good at the time turns out to have been harmful, or "good" in some way we could not foresee, that what seemed a token of our superiority was actually a sign of vulnerability, *if only we could have seen it for what it really was*? The motif of the second self has the effect, then, of opening up for our consideration the gap between what we see in the sometimes narrow vision of conscious life and the different vista afforded by including truths from the darkness inside us.

With this in mind, consider again the implications of Enkidu's death. From inside the story, Enkidu's passing looks entirely negative: Gilgamesh has lost his friend, and worse yet, he himself must be held partly responsible, since he seems to have initiated the adventures. We too hold Gilgamesh "responsible," but see the affair in a different context, one that supplies a level of motivation not evident on the surface of the story and makes the king's complicity less ironic. But still, why death as a prelude to self-realization?

The insistent question drives us back to metaphor. I have said that in response to Enkidu's death Gilgamesh appears to return, first within himself and then without in the search for Utnapishtim, to a state that is represented by two symbols within the poem: the wilderness and the underworld. Both imply the presence of elemental forces outside the reach of culture, and a corresponding diminishment of human control. The analogous state in the metaphor of psychology is of course the unconscious, and the notion that the journey to the underworld is a symbol of the confrontation of the unconscious is not a new idea.

So Enkidu's death drives Gilgamesh into a dark place where his heroic mastery avails him nothing. He emerges from that state a changed man, different in ways that suggest the influence of just those qualities that characterized the wild man: a respect for the limits of human control over nature, a sense of kinship with his fellow creatures enforced by the universality of death. The second self returns, not as a separate being, but as part of the hero, and we may say that from our perspective this is appropriate: the second self appears when there is a "problem" in the hero, particularly something he has not realized about himself that is leading him to act badly; by objectifying what is unacknowledged, the second self allows the hero to react to his deficiency, by denying it, pushing away from it, finally killing it; the act of killing the second self pushes the hero out of the world he has created to serve his denial, and into the darkness, variously characterized; this darkness forces the hero to face and accept the reality he has been trying to escape, and he can then welcome the stranger back. The second self as a separate being is no longer necessary, because his mission is complete, and he can return to where he always was, inside the hero.

As it happens, Jung's metaphors are particularly apt to this configuration. In this perspective, Enkidu represents the Shadow, the unacknowledged parts of the self present in the personal unconscious. For the conscious mind to come to terms with these parts of the self is the first step, in this model, toward psychic wholeness. But often the Shadow is initially frightening, repugnant, to the conscious mind, not fitting the persona—an arbitrary conflation by each person of elements from the collective unconscious with his or her own characteristics—we want to show the world. Denial follows fear, but the repressed always returns, because the self, the totality formed by the conscious mind (ego), the personal unconscious and the collective unconscious, regulates the flow of energy within the psyche. If the conscious mind (Gilgamesh) refuses to admit the Shadow (Enkidu), then the qualities the Shadow embodies become more active in the unconscious, eventually causing trouble again on the conscious level.

How does Gilgamesh's story reflect as art what we call life? What can we learn about ourselves by reading the poem? Large questions, but suitable for a work of art as deep and comprehensive as this. There is certainly much to be learned here about the interrelations between maturity, humility, and acceptance—lessons, indeed, that seem to contradict some of the common connotations of the word "heroic." The word conjures up other words: young, powerful, defiant (Odysseus is something of an exception here). Certainly Gilgamesh is all of these, and yet the poem, taken as a whole, offers an implicit critique of the association of these qualities with the fully realized male. To grow up in the fullest sense, what I have called spiritually, the poem suggests that Gilgamesh must learn to see himself not as preeminent among men, but as part of a larger whole, ruled by forces often beyond his ability to control. Rather than challenge his limitations, he must learn to accept them and live within them: maturity requires humility, which requires acceptance—not defiance, not denial.

Ideas like this are not very often associated with young men. Rather, the kind of realignment of perspective Gilgamesh seems to achieve is usually part of what we now call the "mid-life crisis," when the first rush of self-assertion has played itself out for most men, often leaving them puzzled and lost, less in control of their lives and the world than they once thought. This is also the time when parents begin to die, then perhaps a friend or two as well, and the realization that Ereshkigal or her surrogate looks at "me, *me*" begins to come over us, with the attendant feeling of options closed off, roads not taken receding out of reach.

Gilgamesh, then, traverses while still obviously a young man the territory now covered by most men in the years from twenty to forty (picking round numbers). While perhaps straining the bounds of naturalism, this is appropriate in another sense, in that heroes in western literature often function, as I have said, as boundary testers, traveling conspicuously through some stretch of life and lighting it up for the rest of us. It may surprise us that his journey leaves us with a "middle-aged" view of the world, but we will see that this perspective is in fact common to all the poems we explore here.

As a second self, Enkidu leads the king around a "jolly corner," to face the truths he has been denying. In this sense, the wild man is for Gilgamesh what Gilgamesh is for us, one who leads into undiscovered country, testing and redefining the meaning of life. The story of the second self may then be a kind of hero story within a hero story, with one part of the self showing the way for another until a final reintegration is possible. This last thought suggests another: that the world as we see it, particularly in the challenges and obstacles it throws up before us, is more about us and our ways of seeing and less about the others we share it with than we may think; the key to growing up may be in taking ownership of what was always ours:

> … and when the light surrounded me
> I was born again: I was the owner of my own darkness.
> Pablo Neruda, *100 Love Sonnets*

❋ ❋ ❋

NOTES

The standard scholarly text for the Gilgamesh epic in English is by Speiser in Pritchard 1969, with extensive commentary on the state of the various texts and on the historical and religious background for the poem. This book is also a good source for studying the place of the Gilgamesh epic in the context of other Near Eastern literature. Jacobsen 1976 is an excellent general study of Near Eastern literature, with a helpful survey of the religious background and extensive bibliography. See also Kramer 1961, Kramer 1969, and Kramer 1979. Maier's notes to the translation in Gardner and Maier 1984 are unfailingly illuminating to the nonspecialist.

On the Gilgamesh epic as myth, stressing the nature-culture polarity, see Kirk 1970.132–152. Tigay 1982 gives a thorough analysis of the evolution of the story through its various versions, and has extensive bibliography on all aspects of the poem. For more of the latter, see also Gardner and Maier 1984.vii–viii.

Keppler 1972.14–26 has an argument for the origins of the second self motif in ancient stories about twins. While I am not convinced that the motif began this way, Keppler's discussion of the poem is good. On the poem as a story of the double, see also Gardner and Maier 1984.15–16, 42.

Halperin 1989 is a thorough and convincing discussion of the erotic context for the friendship between Gilgamesh and Enkidu.

❋ ❋ ❋

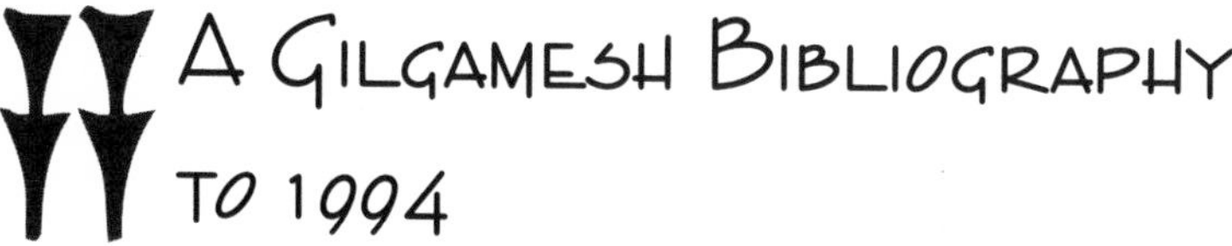
A Gilgamesh Bibliography
to 1994

ABBREVIATIONS

AASOR	Annual of the American Schools of Oriental Research
AB	Assyriologische Bibliothek
Ac. Or.	Acta Orientalia
Act. Ant.	Acta Antiqua Academiae Scientiarum Hungaricae
AEPHEH	Annuaire. École Pratique des Hautes Études... Sciences historiques et philologiques
AfO	Archiv für Orientforschung
AHw	Von Soden, Akkadisches Handwörterbuch
AJA	American Journal of Archaeology
AJP	American Journal of Philology
AJSL	American Journal of Semitic Languages and Literatures
AKA	King and Budge, Annals of the Kings of Assyria
AM	Oppenheim, Ancient Mesopotamia
ANEH	Hallo and Simpson, The Ancient Near East: A History
ANET	Pritchard, ed., Ancient Near Eastern Texts Relating to the Old Testament
An. Or.	Analecta Orientalia
An. St.	Anatolian Studies
AO	Der Alte Orient
AOAT	Alter Orient und Altes Testament
APNM	Huffmon, Amorite Personal Names in the Mari Texts
AR	Ungnad, Assyrische Rechtsurkunden
ARAB	Luckenbill, Ancient Records of Assyria and Babylonia
ARM	Archives Royales de Mari
Ar. Or.	Archiv Orientální
AS	Assyriological Studies
AV	Anniversary Volume (used for Festschriften)
BA	Beiträge zur Assyriologie und semitischen Sprachwissenschaft
BAL	Borger, Babylonisch-Assyrische Lesestücke
BASOR	Bulletin of the American Schools of Oriental Research
BE	The Babylonian Expedition of the University of Pennsylvania, series A: Cuneiform Texts
Bi. Or.	Bibliotheca Orientalis
BJRL	Bulletin of the John Rylands Library
BM	Tablets in the collections of the British Museum
BMQ	British Museum Quarterly
BSOS	Bulletin of the School of Oriental and African Studies
BWL	Lambert, Babylonian Wisdom Literature

CAD	Gelb et al., The Assyrian Dictionary of the Oriental Institute of the University of Chicago (each volume is cited by the letter[s] of the alphabet it covers; thus CAD B, CAD M2, etc.)
CAH	Cambridge Ancient History
CBQ	Catholic Biblical Quarterly
CBS	Tablets in the collections of the University Museum, University of Pennsylvania
CRRAI	Compte rendu de la Rencontre Assyriologique Internationale
CT	Cuneiform Texts from Babylonian Tablets in the British Museum
EI	Eretz-Israel
Falkenstein AV	Edzard, ed., Heidelberger Studien…
GAG	Von Soden, Grundriss der akkadischen Grammatik
GETh.	Thompson, The Epic of GILGAMESH: Text, Transliteration, and Notes
Gressmann and Ungnad	Das Gilgamesch-Epos
GSL	Garelli, ed., Gilgameš et sa légende
HBS	Kramer, History Begins at Sumer
Hecker	Hecker, Untersuchungen zur akkadischen Epik
Heidel	Heidel, The Gilgamesh Epic and Old Testament Parallels
Heth. Wb.	Friedrich, Hethitisches Wörterbuch
HKL	Borger, Handbuch der Keilschriftliteratur
HUCA	Hebrew Union College Annual
ICC	International Critical Commentary
IEJ	Israel Exploration Journal
Ist. Mit.	Istanbuler Mitteilungen
Jacobsen AV	S. J. Lieberman, ed., Sumerological Studies … Jacobsen
JANES	Journal of the Ancient Near Eastern Society of Columbia University
JAOS	Journal of the American Oriental Society
JBL	Journal of Biblical Literature
JCS	Journal of Cuneiform Studies
JEOL	Jaarbericht van het Vooraziatisch-Egyptisch Genootschap "Ex Oriente Lux"
JKF	Jahrbuch fur Kleinasiatische Forschung
JNES	Journal of Near Eastern Studies
JQR	Jewish Quarterly Review
JRAS	Journal of the Royal Asiatic Society of Great Britain and Ireland
JSOR	Journal of the Society of Oriental Research
JSS	Journal of Semitic Studies
K	Tablets from the Kuyunjik collection, British Museum

KAR	Keilschrifttexte aus Assur religiösen Inhalts
KAV	Schrader, Keilinschriften und Das Alte Testament
KAR	Keilschrifttexte aus Assur verschiedenen Inhalts
KB	Keilinschriftliche Bibliothek
Kbo	Keilschrifttexte aus Boghazkoï
KNELL	Kindlers Neues Literatur Lexikon
Kramer, AV	Eichler, ed., Kramer Anniversary Volume
KUB	Keilschrifturkunden aus Boghazkoï
Lambert and Millard	Atra-ḫasīs
Landsberger AV	Güterbock and Jacobsen, eds., Studies... Landsberger
LCL	Loeb Classical Library
LKU	Falkenstein, Literarische Keilschrifttexte aus Uruk
LSS	Leipziger semitistische Studien, Neue Folge
MAOG	Mitteilungen der Altorientalischen Gesellschaft
MDOG	Mitteilungen der Deutschen-Orientgesellschaft
MI	S. Thompson, Motif-Index of Folk Literature
MIO	Mitteilungen des Instituts für Orientforschung
MVAG	Mitteilungen der Vorderasiatischen Gesellschaft
MVEOL	Mededelingen en verhandelingen van het Vooraziatisch Egyptisch Gezelschap/Gerootschop "Ex Oriente Lux"
NABU	Nouvelles Assyriologiques Brèves et Utilitaires
N.F.	Neue Folge
N.S.	New Series
OBS	Speiser, Oriental and Biblical Studies
OECT	Oxford Editions of Cuneiform Texts
OIP	Oriental Institute Publications
OLZ	Orientalistische Literaturzeitung
Or.	Orientalia (all references to New Series)
Or. Ant.	Oriens Antiquus
Or. Suec.	Orientalia Suecana
PAPhS	Proceedings of the American Philosophical Society
PBS	Publications of the Babylonian Section, University Museum, University of Pennsylvania
PRT	Klauber, Politisch-religiöse Texte aus der Sargonidenzeit
PRU	Nougayrol et al., Le Palais royal d'Ugarit
PSBA	Proceedings of the Society of Biblical Archaeology
RA	Revue d'assyriologie et d'archéologie orientale
RAcc	Thureau-Dangin, Rituels Accadiens
RAI	Recontre assyriologique internationale
RAr	Revue archeologique
RB	Revue biblique
RBA	Jastrow, The Religion of Babylonia and Assyria
RBPH	Revue belge de philologie et d'histoire
RE	Realencylopedie der Klassischen Altertumswissenschaften (ed. Pauly-Wissowa)

RÉS	Revue d'études sémitiques
RHA	Revue hittite et asianique
RHR	Revue de l'histoire des religions
RLA	Ebeling and Meissner et al., Reallexikon der Assyriologie
SAHG	Falkenstein and von Soden, Sumerische und akkadische Hymnen und Gebete
SAKI	Thureau-Dangin, Die sumerischen und akkadischen Königsinschriften
SBH	Reisner, Sumerisch-babylonische Hymnen nach Thontafeln griechischer Zeit
SKIZ	Römer, Sumerische "Königshymnen" der Isin-Zeit
SKLJ	Jacobsen, ed., The Sumerian King List
SLTNi	Kramer, Sumerian Literary Texts from Nippur...
SMEA	Studi Micenei ed Egeo-Anatolici (Rome)
SP	Gordon, Sumerian Proverbs...
SRT	Chiera, Sumerian Religious Texts
SSA	Van Dijk, La Sagesse suméro-acadienne
StOr	Studia Orientalia Edidit Societas Orientalis Fennica
STC	King, The Seven Tablets of Creation
STT	Gurney and Finkelstein, The Sultantepe Tablets
SVT	Supplements to Vetus Testamentum
TCL	Textes cunéiformes du Louvre
TCS	Texts from Cuneiform Sources
TIM	Texts in the Iraq Museum
TLB	Tabulae Cuneiformae a F.M. Th. de Liagre Bohl Collectae
TLZ	Theologische Literaturzeitung
TSBA	Transactions of the Society of Biblical Archaelogy
TuL	Ebeling, Tod und Leben...
UET	Ur Excavations, Texts
UM	Tablets in the collections of the University Museum, University of Pennsylvania
UVB	Vorläufiger Bericht über die von dem Deutschen Archäeologischen Institut und der deutschen Orient-Gesellschaft aus Mitteln der deutschen Forschungsgemeinschaft unternommenen Ausgrabungen in Uruk-Warka
VAB	Vorderasiatische Bibliothek
VAS	Vorderasiatische Schriftdenkmäler der königlichen Museen zu Berlin
WbM	Haussig, Wörterbuch der Mythologie
WO	Die Welt des Orients
WVDOG	Wissenschaftliche Veröffentlichungen der Deutschen Orient-Gesellschaft
WZJ	Wissenschaftliche Zeitschrift der Friedrich-Schiller-Universität Jena, Gesellschafts-und-Sprachwissenschaftliche Reihe

WZKM	Wiener Zeitschrift für die Kunde des Morgenlandes
YBC	Tablets in the Yale Babylonian Collection
YNER	Yale Near Eastern Researches
YOR	Yale Oriental Series, Researches
YOS	Yale Oriental Series, Texts
ZA	Zeitschrift für Assyriologie; volumes cited according to consecutive numeration from ZA 1 (1886), without shifting to New Series (Neue Folge) numbers employed since ZA 35 (= ZA N.F. 1)
ZDMG	Zeitschrift der deutschen Morgenländischen Gesellschaft

❋ ❋ ❋

A GILGAMESH BIBLIOGRAPHY TO 1994

The bibliography includes works cited in the articles plus the major bibliographies that have dealt with *Gilgamesh*: Leon de Meyer (1960), Lubor Matouš (1964), Rykle Borger (1967–75), Louis L. Orlin (1969), Wayne J. Buchanan (1979), Jeffrey H. Tigay (1982), Jelena O. Krstović and Zoran Minderović (1989), *FirstSearch* WorldCat and the annual bibliography of *Orientalia*.

Abou-Assaf, Ali, Pierre Bordreuil, and Alan R. Millard. *La statue de Tell Fekherye et son inscription bilingue assyro-araméenne.* Paris: Éditions Recherche sur les civilisations, 1982.

Abrahams, Roger D. "Personal Power and Social Restraint in the Definition of Folklore." *Towards New Perspectives in Folklore.* Ed. Americo Paredes and Richard Bauman. Austin: U of Texas P, 1972. 16–30.

Abrahams, Roger D., and George Foss. *Anglo-American Folksong Style.* Englewood Cliffs: Prentice Hall, 1968.

Abusch, Tzvi. "Gilgamesh's Request and Siduri's Denial" (Part I). *The Tablet and the Scroll: Near Eastern Studies in Honor of W. W. Hallo.* Ed. M. E. Cohen, et al. Bethesda, MD: CDL, 1993. 1–14.

Abusch, Tzvi. "Gilgamesh's Request and Siduri's Denial. Part II: An Analysis and Interpretation of an Old Babylonian Fragment about Mourning and Celebration." *JANES* 22 (1993): 3–17.

Abusch, Tzvi. "Ishtar's Proposal and Gilgamesh's Refusal: An Interpretation of The Gilgamesh Epic, Tablet 6, Lines 1–79." *History of Religions* 26 (1986): 143–87; selections rpt. Krstović. 365–74.

Abusch, Tzvi. "Mesopotamian Anti-Witchcraft Literature: Texts and Studies. Pt. 1: The Nature of *Maqlû:* Its Character, Divisions, and Calendrical Setting." *JNES* 33 (1974): 251–62.

Abusch, Tzvi. "Mourning the Death of a Friend: Some Assyriological Notes." *Frank Talmage Memorial Volume.* Vol. I. Ed. Barry Warfish. Haifa: Haifa UP and UP of New England, with Brandeis UP, 1993. 53–62.

Abusch, Tzvi. "The Demonic Image of the Witch in Standard Babylonian Literature: The Reworking of Popular Conceptions by Learned Exorcists." *Religion, Science, and Magic: In Concert and in Conflict.* Ed. Jacob Neusner, et al. NY/Oxford: Oxford UP, 1989. 27–58.

Abusch, Tzvi, John Huehnergard, and Piotr Steinkeller, ed. *Lingering Over Words: Studies in Ancient Near Eastern Literature in Honor of William L. Moran.* Atlanta: Scholars Press, 1990.

Adler, C. "The Legends of Semiramis and the Nimrod Epic." *Johns Hopkins University Circular* 55 (1887).

Adrados, Francisco Rodriguez. "Ibico 61 y el influjo del *Gilgameš* en Grecia." *Aula Orientalis* 5 (1987): 5–9.

Aelian. *On the Characteristics of Animals.* Tr. A. F. Scholfield. 3 Vols. Cambridge, MA: Harvard UP, 1958–59. London: Heinemann, 1958–59.

Afanasyeva, Veronika Konstantinovna. "Gilgamesh and Enkidu in Glyptic Art and in the Epic." *Klio* 53 (1971): 59–75.

Afanasyeva, Veronika Konstantinovna. *Gilgamesh i Enkidu.* Moscow: Nauka, 1979.

Agyagtablak uzenete. Budapest: Magyar Helikon, 1963.

Ahmad, Muhammad Khalifah. *Al-Usturah wa-al-Tarikh fi al-Turath al-Sharqi al-Qadim.* Baghdad: Dar al-Shu'un al-Thaqafiyah al-Ammah, 1988.

Ahmad, Sami Sa'id. *Kilkāmish.* Baghdad: Wizarat al-Thaqafah wa-al Ilam, 1990.

Albright, William Foxwell. "The Anatolian Goddess Kubaba." *AfO* 5 (1929): 229–31.

Albright, William Foxwell. *From the Stone Age to Christianity.* 2nd. Ed. Garden City, NY: Doubleday, 1957.

Albright, William Foxwell. "Gilgamesh and Engidu, Mesopotamian Genii of Fecundity." *JAOS* 40 (1920): 307–35.

Albright, William Foxwell. "The Goddess of Life and Wisdom." *AJSL* 36 (1919–20): 258–94.

Albright, William Foxwell. "The Mouth of the Rivers." *AJSL* 35 (1919): 161–95.

Albright, William Foxwell. "The Name and Nature of the Sumerian God Uttu." *JAOS* 42 (1922): 197–200.

Aldrich, Joan Marie. *The Quest for Immortality in the Gilgamesh Epic.* Thesis, U of Virginia, 1990.

Alexander, Hartley Burr. *Latin American Mythology.* Vol. 11 *Mythology of All Races.* Boston: Marshall Jones Co., 1920.

Alexander, Hartley Burr. *North American Mythology.* Vol. 10 *Mythology of All Races.* Cambridge, MA: Archaeological Institute of America, 1916.

Alexander, Michael, tr. *Beowulf, a Verse Translation.* Harmondsworth, England: Penguin, 1973.

Ali, Fahil Abdulwahid. *Sumerian Letters: Two Collections from the Old Babylonia Schools.* Ann Arbor, MI: University Microfilms, 1964.

Al-Jadir, Walid. "The World's Oldest Library: *Gilgamesh.*" *A Journal of Modern Iraqi Arts* 3 (1987): 55–57.

Allen, T. W., W. R. Halliday, and E. E. Sikes. *The Homeric Hymns.* 2nd. Ed. Oxford: Clarendon P, 1936.

Allotte, François-Maurice de la Fuÿe. "Voyage à la recherche d'Utanaptištim." *RA* 25 (1928): 18–19.

Al-Sawwa'h, Firas. *Kun'uz al-Amaq.* [*Treasures from the Depths: A Reading of the Epic of Gilgamesh*]. Damascus: Al-'Arabi lil 'Tib'a'ah wa-al Nashr wa al-Tawz'i, 1987.

Al-Sawwa'h, Firas. *Malhamat Jiljamish.* Beirut: Dar al-Kalamat al-Zashur, 1983.

Alster, Bendt. "An Aspect of 'Enmerkar and the Lord of Aratta.'" *RA* 67 (1973): 101–109.

Alster, Bendt. "Court Ceremonial and Marriage in the Sumerian Epic 'Gilgamesh and Huwawa.'" *BASOR* 55 (1992): 1–18.

Alster, Bendt, ed. *Death in Mesopotamia.* Copenhagen: Akademisk Forlag, 1980.

Alster, Bendt. "Dilmun, Bahrain, and the Alleged Paradise in Sumerian Myth and Literature." *Dilmun: New Studies in the Archaeology and Early History of Bahrain.* Ed. Daniel T. Potts. Berlin: Dietrich Reimer Verlag, 1983. 39–74.

Alster, Bendt. *Dumuzi's Dream.* Copenhagen: Akademisk Forlag, 1972.

Alster, Bendt. "Enki and Ninḫursag" *Ugarit Forschung* 10 (1978): 15–27.

Alster, Bendt. "The Enmerkar-Lugalbanda Cycle: Tales from Ancient Sumer." Sasson. *Civilizations of the Ancient Near East* 2315–2326.

Alster, Bendt. "Lugalbanda and the Early Epic Tradition in Mesopotamia." Abusch. *Lingering Over Words.* 59–72.

Alster, Bendt. "The Paradigmatic Character of Mesopotamian Heroes." *RA* 68 (1974): 49–60.

Alster, Bendt. *Studies in Sumerian Proverbs.* Copenhagen: Akademisk Forlag, 1975.

Alster, Bendt, and Herman Vanstiphout. "Laḫar and Ashnan: Presentation and Analysis of a Sumerian Disputation." *Acta Sumerologica* 9 (1987): 1–43.

Alter, Robert. *The Art of Biblical Narrative.* NY: Basic Books, 1981.

Alzuguren, Juan Errandonea. *Eden y paradiso.* Madrid: Ediciones Marova, 1966.

Amiet, Pierre. *Bas-reliefs imaginaires de l'Ancien Orient.* Paris: Hôtel de la Monnaie, 1973.

Amiet, Pierre. *La glyptique mésopotamienne archaïque.* 2nd. Ed. Paris: Éditions du Centre national de la recherche scientifique, 1980.

Amiet, Pierre. "L'homme oiseau dans l'art mésopotamien." *Or.* 21 (1952): 149–67.

Amiet, Pierre. "Le problème de la représentation de Gilgameš dans l'art." *GSL.* 169–73.

Amiet, Pierre. "Review of *The Mark of Ancient Man.*" *JAOS* 100 (1980): 185–86.

Ammons, A. R. *Sumerian Vistas: Poems.* NY: Norton, 1987.

Anastaplo, G. "An Introduction to Mesopotamian Thought: The Epic of Gilgamesh." *The Great Ideas Today.* Chicago: Encyclopaedia Britannica, 1986.

Anderson, Andrew Runni. *Alexander's Gate, Gog and Magog, and the Inclosed Nations.* Cambridge, MA: Mediaevel Academy, 1932.

Anderson, Brian. "Gilgamesh." *Cleopatra.* Normandale Community College 11/14/77. [Videorecording].

Anderson, F. I., and D. N. Freedman. *Hosea.* Garden City, NY: Doubleday, 1980.

Anderson, G. A. *A Time to Mourn, A Time to Dance: The Expression of Grief and Joy in Israelite Religion.* University Park, PA: Pennsylvania State UP, 1991.

Andersen, O. *Die Diomedesgestalt in der Ilias.* Oslo: Some & Co., 1978.

Anderson, Walter. *Ueber P. Jensens Methode der vergleichenden Sagenforschung.* Dorpat: K. Matthiesens Buchdruckeri, 1930.

Anonymous. "The Epic of Gilgamesh." *Ur* (1982): 1–2.

Ardolino, Frank R. "The Americanization of the Gods: Onomastics, Myth, and History in Roth's *The Great American Novel.*" *Arete* 3 (1985): 37–60.

Aries, Philippe. *Centuries of Childhood.* NY: Vintage, 1965.

Armen, Jean-Claude. *Gazelle-Boy: Beautiful, Astonishing and True. A Wild Boy's Life in the Sahara.* London: Pan Books, 1976.

Arnaud, M. "La Bibliothèque d'un devin syrien à Meskéné-Emar (Syrie)." *Comptes rendus des séances de l'Academie des inscriptions et belles-lettres.* Paris: Klincksieck, 1980. 375–88.

Arnaud, M. *Recherches au pays d'Astata, Emar VI/14.* Paris: Éditions Recherche sur les civilisations, 1985–87.

Asena, Orhan. *Les dieux et les hommes; ou, Gilgamesh.* Ankara: Ayyildiz Matbaasi, 1961.

Asher-Greve, J. M. *Frauen in altsumerischer Zeit.* Malibu: Undena, 1985.

Assmann, E. "Titaia, Titanen und der Tartaros." *Babyloniaca* 6 (1912): 236–39.

Assmann, J. "Der schöne Tag—Sinnlichkeit und Vergänglichkeit im altagyptischen Fest." *Das Fest.* Ed. W. Haug and R. Warning. Munich: Fink, 1989. 23–25.

Astour, Michael C. *Hellenosemitica. An Ethnic and Cultural Study in West Semitic Impact on Mycenaean Greece.* Leiden: E. J. Brill, 1965, 1967.

Astour, Michael C. "Tamar the Hierodule." *JBL* 85 (1966): 185–96.

Athearn, Hope Green. *Gilgamesh, A Novel.* San Francisco: San Francisco State College, 1970.

Attinger, P. "Enki et Ninḫursaga." *ZA* 74 (1984): 1–52.

Attridge, H. W., and R. Oden. *De Dea Syria.* Chico, CA: Undena, 1976.

Auffarth, Christoph. *Der drohende Untergang: "Schöpfung" in Mythos und Ritual im Alten Orient und in Griechenland am Beispiel der Odyssee und des Ezechielbuches.* Berlin: de Gruyter, 1991.

Azrie, Abed, tr. *L'Épopée de Gilgamesh.* Tr. from Arabic. Paris: Berg International, 1979; Moulins: Impomee, 1986.

Babcock, Barbara A., ed. *The Reversible World: Symbolic Inversion in Art and Society.* Ithaca: Cornell UP, 1978.

Bachelard, Gaston. *The Psychoanalysis of Fire.* Boston: Beacon, 1964.

Bailey, John A. "Initiation and the Primal Woman in *Gilgamesh* and Genesis 23." *JBL* 89 (1970): 137–50.

Bailkey, Nels M., ed. *Readings in Ancient History: Thought and Experience from Gilgamesh to St. Augustine.* 4th. Ed. Lexington, MA: D. C. Heath, 1992.

Bain, F. W. *A Digit of the Moon.* NY: G. P. Putnam's Sons, 1910.

Baker, Charles. *Gilgamesh: A Musical Presentation.* 1251 Green Street, San Franciso, CA 94109. [Lyric paraphrase and score].

Bakir, Guven. *Sophilos: Ein Beitrag zu seinem Stil.* Mainz am Rhein: Philipp von Zabern, 1981.

Baltrusaitis, Jurgis. *Gilgamesh.* N.P.: Revue d'art et d'esthétique, 1935.

Bannister, Jo. *Gilgamesh.* NY: Doubleday, 1989.

Banton, Michael B., ed. *The Social Anthropology of Complex Societies.* London: Tavistock, 1966.

Baqir, Taha. "Comments on Ancient Mesopotamian Mythology" (in Arabic). *Sumer* 7 (1951): 20–52.

Baqir, Taha. *Malḫamat Kilkāmish.* Baghdad: Manshurat Wizarat al-Ilam, 1970.

Baqir, Taha, and Francis Bashir. "Gilgamesh Epic" (in Arabic). *Sumer* 6 (1950): 42–80.

Barnatan, Marcos Ricardo, and Nuria Salvatella. *Gilgamesh.* Barcelona: Lumen, 1986.

Baron, Samuel, ed. and tr. *The Travels of Olearius in Seventeenth-Century Russia.* Stanford: UP, 1967.

Barr, J. *Comparative Philology and the Text of the Old Testament.* Oxford: Clarendon Press, 1968.

Barrelet, Marie Therèse. *Figurines et reliefs en terre cuite de la Mésopotamie antique.* Paris: Librairie orientaliste P. Geuthner, 1968.

Barth, Frederik. *Ritual and Knowledge Among the Baktaman of New Guinea.* New Haven: Yale UP, 1975.

Barton, George Aaron. *A Critical and Exegetical Commentary on the Book of Ecclesiastes.* Edinburg: T & T Clark, 1908.

Barton, George Aaron. "A New Babylonian Parallel to a Part of Genesis 3." *JAOS* 39 (1919): 287.

Bartra, Agusti. *La epopeya de Gilgamesh.* Mexico: Consejo Nacional para la Cultura y las Artes, 1993.

Bateson, Gregory. *Mind and Nature.* NY: Dutton, 1979.

Bathrick, David. "Cultural Studies." *Introduction to Scholarship in Modern Languages and Literatures.* 2nd. Ed. Joseph Gibaldi. NY: The Modern Language Association of America, 1992. 320–40.

Batto, Bernard F. "The Covenant of Peace: A Neglected Ancient Near Eastern Motif." *CBQ* 49 (1987): 187–211.

Batto, Bernard F. "Paradise Reexamined." *The Biblical Canon in Comparative Perspective.* Ed. K. Lawson Younger, Jr., William W. Hallo, and Bernard F. Batto. Lewiston: Edwin Mellen, 1991. 33–66.

Batto, Bernard F. *Slaying the Dragon: Mythmaking in the Biblical Tradition.* Louisville: Westminster/John Knox, 1992.

Batto, Bernard F. "The Sleeping God: An Ancient Near Eastern Motif of Divine Sovereignty." *Biblica* 68 (1987): 153–77.

Batto, Bernard F. *Studies on Women at Mari.* Baltimore: Johns Hopkins UP, 1974.

Batto, Bernard F. "The Yahwist's Primeval Myth." *Slaying the Dragon.* 41–71.

Bauer, J. "Leben in der Urzeit Mesopotamiens." *AfO* 19 (1982): 377–83.

Bauer, Theo. *Akkadische Lesestücke.* I. Rome: Pontifical Biblical Institute, 1953. 38–45.

Bauer, Theo. "Bemerkungen zur VI. Tafel des Gilgamesch-Epos." *OLZ* 24 (1921): 72–74.

Bauer, Theo. *Das Inschriftenwerk Assurbanipals vervollständigt und neu bearbeitet.* Leipzig: Hinrichs, 1933.

Bauer, Theo. "Ein viertes altbabylonisches Fragment des Gilgameš-Epos." *JNES* 16 (1957): 254–62.

Baumann, Hermann. *Das doppelte Geschlecht: Ethnologische Studien zur Bisexualität in Ritus und Mythos.* 2nd. Ed. Berlin: D. Reimer, 1980.

Baumgartner, Walter. "Herodots Babylonische und Assyrische Nachrichten." *Ar. Or.* 18 (1950): 69–106.

Becker, Ernest. *The Birth and Death of Meaning.* NY: Free Press, 1962.

Beckman, Diane Susan. *The Wild Man: Images of Liminality: Prolegomena to a Study of Gilgamesh and Montaigne's Des Cannibales.* Thesis, University of North Carolina, 1993.

Begg, Ian, Douglas Upfold, and Terrance D. Wilton. "Imagery in Verbal Communication." *Journal of Mental Imagery* 2 (1978): 165–86.

Belden, George. *Gilgamesh: For Contralto, Piano, Percussion, Tape.* North Texas State University, 1976. [Musical Score].

Belden, George. *Gilgamesh.* NY: Society of Composers, Inc., 1989. [Musical Score].

Belden, George. "Gilgamesh." *America Sings!* Brooklyn: Capstone Records, 1992. [Audio Recording].

Bell, Robert R. *Worlds of Friendship.* Beverly Hills: Sage, 1981.

Bellows, Henry Adams, tr. *Poetic Edda.* NY: American-Scandinavian Foundation, 1923.

Benito, Carlos Alfredo. *"Enki and Ninmaḫ"* and *"Enki and the World Order."* Ph.D. diss., U of Pennsylvania, 1969.

Ben-Zion. *Alilat Gilgamesh: 36 Tahritim.* Tel-Aviv: Eked, 1980.

Beran, Thomas. "Assyrische Glyptik des 14. Jahrhunderts." *ZA* 52 (1957): 141–215.

Berezowsky, Nicolai. *Gilgamesh: A Cantata for Narrator, Solo Voices, Mixed Chorus and Orchestra.* NY: Weaver-Levant, 1947. [Musical Score].

Berlin, Adele. *Enmerkar and Enšuḫkešdanna: A Sumerian Narrative Poem.* Philadelphia: U Museum, 1979.

Bernal, Martin. *Black Athena: The Afroasiatic Roots of Classical Civilization.* I: *The Fabrication of Ancient Greece, 1785–1985.* London/New Brunswick, NJ: Free Association Books/Rutgers UP, 1987; II: *The Archaeological and Documentary Evidence.* London/New Brunswick, NJ: Free Association Books/Rutgers UP, 1991.

Bernhardt, Inez, and Samuel Noah Kramer. "'Enki und die Weltordnung,' ein sumerischer Keilschrift-Text über die 'Lehre von der Welt' in der Hilprecht Sammlung und im University Museum of Pennsylvania." *WZJ* 9 (1959–60): 231–56.

Bernhardt, Inez, and Samuel Noah Kramer. "Götter-Hymnen und Kult-Gesänge der Sumerer auf zwei Keilschrift 'Katalogen' in der Hilprecht-Sammlung." *WZJ* 6 (1956–57): 389–95.

Bersani, Leo, and Ulysse Dutoit. *The Forms of Violence.* NY: Schocken, 1985.

Bertholet, Alfred. *Van Goor's Encyclopedisch Woordenboek der Godsdiensten.* 'S-Gravenhage: Van Goor, 1970.

Bethe, Erich. *Homer: Dichtung und Sage.* Leipzig: Teubner, 1927.

Beye, Charles R. "The Epic of Gilgamesh, the Bible, and Homer. Some Narrative Parallels." *Mnemai. Classical Studies in Memory of Karl K. Hulley.* Ed. Harold D. Evjen. Chico: Scholars Press, 1984. 7–20.

Bezold, Carl/Karl. *Babylonisch-Assyrisches Glossar.* Heidelberg: Carl Winter's Universitätsbuchhandlung, 1926.

Bezold, Carol, August Kopff, and Franz Boll. "Zenit- und Aequatorialgestirne am babylonischen Fixsternhimmel." *Sitzungsberichte der Bayerischen Akademie des Wissenschaften* 11 (1913): 11.

Bickerman, E. J. *Four Strange Books of the Bible.* NY: Schocken, 1967.

Biggs, Robert D. "The Abū-Ṣalābīkh Tablets." *JCS* 20 (1966): 73–88.

Biggs, Robert D., tr. "Akkadian Didactic and Wisdom Literature." *ANET.* 592–607.

Biggs, Robert D. "The Ebla Tablets. An Interim Perspective." *Biblical Archaeologist* 43 (1980): 76–87.

Biggs, Robert D. *Inscriptions from Tell Abū-Ṣalābīkh*. Chicago and London: U of Chicago P, 1974.

Biggs, Robert D. *ŠÀ.ZI.GA: Ancient Mesopotamian Potency Incantations.* Locust Valley, NY: Augustin, 1967.

Binder, G. *Die Aussetzung des Königskindes: Kyros und Romulus.* Meisenheim am Glan: A. Hain, 1964.

Bing, J. D. "Gilgamesh and Lugalbanda in the Fara Period." *JANES* 9 (1977): 1–4.

Bing, J. D. "On the Sumerian Epic of Gilgamesh." *JANES* 7 (1975): 1–10.

Binyamin, Danel David Davit. *Gilgamesh: megala sefraya Aturaya.* El Sobrante, CA: Youel A. Baaba Library, 1992.

Black, Jeremy A., and W. J. Tait. "Archives and Libraries in the Ancient Near East." Sasson. *Civilizations of the Ancient Near East.* Vol. 4. 2197–210.

Black, M. *The Book of Enoch.* Leiden: E. J. Brill, 1985.

Blair, Walter, and Hamlin Hill. "The Great American Novel." *Critical Essays on Philip Roth.* Ed. Sanford Pinsker. Boston: G. K. Hall, 1982. 217–28.

Blanc, Yannick. *Enquête sur la mort de Gilgamesh.* Paris: Editions du Felin, 1991.

Blasting, Ralph, and Mahmood Karimi-Hakak. *Gilgamesh Conquest.* [Drama performed March 8, 1991, Towson State University, Towson, New Jersey].

Blenkinsopp, Joseph. "The Search for the Prickly Plant: Structure and Function in the Gilgamesh Epic." *Structuralism.* Nashville: Vanderbilt University, 1975.

Blixen, Hyalmar. *El cantar del Guilgamesh.* Montevideo: Universidad del la Republica, 1980.

Bloch, Augustyn. *Dialogi; Gilgamesz.* Poland: Muza, 1980. [Audio Recording].

Bloch, Augustyn. *Gilgamesz: Ballet Music in the Concert Version.* Krakow: Polski Wydawn, 1970. [Musical Score].

Bloedow, Edmund F. "The Trojan War and Late Helladic III C." *Praehistorische Zeitschrift* 63 (1988): 23–52.

Bloom, Harold. *The Book of J*. NY: Grove Weidenfeld, 1990.

Bloom, Harold. *The Western Canon*. NY: Harcourt Brace, 1994.

Bly, Robert. *A Little Book on the Human Shadow*. NY: 1988.

Boas, Franz. *Indianische Sagen von der Nord-Pacifischen Küste Americkas*. Bonn: Holos Verlag, 1895.

Boehmer, Rainer Michael. *Die Entwicklung der Glyptik während der Akkad-Zeit*. Berlin: de Gruyter, 1965.

Bohannan, Paul. "Artist and Critic in an African Society." *The Artist in the Tribal World*. Ed. Marian W. Smith. Glencoe, IL: Free Press, 1961. 85–94.

Böhl, Franz Marius Theodor de Liagre. *Akkadian Chrestomathy*. I. Leyden: Nederlandsch Archaeologisch-Philologisch Instituut voor het Nabije Oosten, 1947.

Böhl, Franz Marius Theodor de Liagre. "Zum babylonischen Ursprung des Labyrinths." *An. Or.* 12 (1935): 6–23; rpt. *Opera Minora*. 324–38.

Böhl, Franz Marius Theodor de Liagre Bohl. "Einleitende Bemerkungen der 'Erläuterungen' zum 'Gilgamesch-Epos.'" *National Heldendicht van Babylonie*. Amsterdam: H. J. Paris, 1958. 111–19; Tr. Heinz Wolters, rpt. Oberhuber. *Das Gilgamesch-Epos*. 312–24.

Böhl, Franz Marius Theodor de Liagre. "Die Fahrt nach dem Lebenskraut." *Ar. Or.* 18 (1950): 107–22.

Böhl, Franz Marius Theodor de Liagre. "Gilgameš. B. Nach akkadischen Texten." *RLA* 3: 364–72.

Böhl, Franz Marius Theodor de Liagre. "Gilgamesch und Adapa als Beispiele einer Historisierung des Mythos." *Proceedings of the 7th Congress for the History of Religions*. Amsterdam: 1951, 100–102.

Böhl, Franz Marius Theodor de Liagre. "Das Gilgamesch-Epos bei den Alten Sumerern." *MVEOL* 7 (1947): 145–77.

Böhl, Franz Marius Theodor de Liagre. *Het Gilgamesj-Epos. Nationaal Heldendicht van Babylonië*. Amsterdam: H. J. Paris, 1941; 2nd. Ed., 1952; 3rd. Ed., 1958.

Böhl, Franz Marius Theodor de Liagre. "Mythos und Geschichte in der Altbabylonischen Dichtung." *Opera Minora*. 223–31.

Böhl, Franz Marius Theodor de Liagre. *Opera Minora.* Groningen Jakarta: J. B. Wolters, 1953.

Böhl, Franz Marius Theodor de Liagre. "Het problem van eeuwig leven in de cyclus en het Epos van Gilgamesj." *Jaargang* 9 (1948): 1–43.

Böhl, Franz Marius Theodor de Liagre. *Het problem van eeuwig leven in de cyclus en het epos van Gilgamesj.* Antwerp: Uitgeversmij. N.V. Standaard-Boekhandel, 1948.

Böhl, Franz Marius Theodor de Liagre "Das Problem Ewigen Lebens im Zyklus und Epos des Gilgamesch." *Opera Minora.* 234–62, 498–502; rpt. Oberhuber. *Das Gilgamesch-Epos.* 237–75.

Böhl, Franz Marius Theodor de Liagre. "Die Religion der Babylonier und Assyrer." *Christus und die Religionen der Erde.* 2nd. Ed. Franz Konig. Vienna: Verlag Herder, 1956. 443–98.

Böhl, Franz Marius Theodor de Liagre, J. H. Hospers, and Jaap Kruyff. *Gilgamesj: De Elfde Zang.* Utrecht: De Roos, 1985.

Boissier, Alfred. "Fragment de la légende de Atram-ḫasis." *RA* 28 (1931): 91–97.

Boll, Franz. "Antike Beobachtung farbiger Sterne, mit einem Beitrage von Carl Bezold." *Abhandlungen der Bayerischen Akademie der Wissenschaften* 30 (1916): 102–25.

Boll, Franz. *Aus der Offenbarung Johannis: Hellenistische Studien zum Weltbild der Apokalypse.* Leipzig-Berlin: B. G. Teubner, 1914.

Boll, Franz. *Sphaera: Neue Griechische Texte und Untersuchungen zur Geschichte der Sternbilder.* Leipzig: B. G. Teubner, 1903.

Bomer, Franz, ed. *P. Ovidius Naso, Metamorphoses, Books 8–9.* Heidelberg: C. Winter, 1977.

Bonner, Campbell. "*Kestos Imas* and the Saltire of Aphrodite." *American Journal of Philology* 70 (1949): 1–6.

Borger, Rykle (Riekele). *Akkadische Zeichenliste.* Neukirchen-Vluyn: Verlag Butzon and Bercher Kevelaer, 1971.

Borger, Rykle. *Babylonisch-Assyrische Lesestücke.* 3 Vols. Rome: Pontifical Biblical Institute, 1963.

Borger, Rykle. "Die Beschwörungsserie *bīt meseri* und die Himmelfahrt Henochs." *JNES* 33 (1974): 183–96.

Borger, Rykle. "Critical Studies by Tablet." *HKL* 1 (1967): 555–57; *HKL* 2 (1975): 292–94.

Borger, Rykle. "Gilgamos: Der kleine Pauly." *Lexikon der Antike.* 2 (1967): 800–801.

Borger, Rykle. "Gott Marduk und Gott-König Sulgi als Propheten." *Bi. Or.* 28 (1971): 22–23.

Borger, Rykle. *Handbuch der Keilschriftliteratur.* Vol. 1. Berlin: de Gruyter, 1967; Vol. 2, 1975.

Borger, Rykle. *Die Inschriften Asarhaddons, Königs von Assyrien.* Graz: E. Weidner, 1956.

Borger, Rykle. "*niṣirti bārûti*, Geheimlehre der Haruspizin." *Bi. Or.* 14 (1957): 190–95.

Borger, Rykle. "Review of CAD A." *Bi. Or.* 20 (1969): 74–75.

Borger, Rykle. "Tonmännchen und Puppen." *Bi. Or.* 30 (1973): 176–83.

Borger, Rykle. "Die Weihe eines Enlil-Priesters." *Bi. Or.* 30 (1973): 163–76.

Borowski, Elie. "Le cycle de Gilgameš, à propos de la collection de cylindres orientaux du Musée d'Art et d'Histoire." *Genava* 22 (1944): 1–20.

Boscawen, W. St. Chad. *From Under the Dust of Ages.* London: The Temple Co., 1886.

Boscawen, W. St. Chad. "Notes on Assyrian Religion and Mythology." *TSBA* 6 (1878): 535–42.

Boscawen, W. St. Chad. "Notes on the Religion and Mythology of the Assyrians." *TSBA* 4 (1876): 267–301.

Boscawen, W. St. Chad. "The Twelfth Izdubar Legend." *Records of the Past* 9 (1877): 129–30.

Bossert, Helmuth Theodor. *Altsyrien Kunst und Handwerk.* Tübingen: E. Wasmuth, 1951.

Botta, Paul Emile, and M. E. Flandin. *Monument de Ninive.* Paris: 1849; rpt. Osnabruck: Biblio Verlag, 1972.

Bottéro, Jean. "Akkadian Literature: An Overview." Sasson. *Civilizations of the Ancient Near East.* Vol. 4. 2293–2304.

Bottéro, Jean. *L'Epopée de Gilgameš: Le grand homme qui ne voulait pas mourir*. Paris: Gallimard, 1992.

Bottéro, Jean. *La femme, l'amour et la guerre en Mésopotamie ancienne.* Paris: Poikilia, 1987.

Bottéro, Jean. "Gilgamesch, der König, der nicht sterben wollte." *UNESCO Kurier* 9 (1989): 30.

Bottéro, Jean. *Mésopotamie: l'écriture, la raison et les dieux.* Paris: Gallimard, 1987; *Mesopotamia: Writing, Reasoning and the Gods.* Tr. Zainab Bahrani and Marc Van de Mieroop. Chicago: U of Chicago P, 1992.

Bottéro, Jean. "La mythologie de la mort en Mesopotamie ancienne." Alster. *Death in Mesopotamia.* 25–52.

Bottéro, Jean. *La religion babylonienne.* Paris: Presses Universitaires de France, 1952.

Bottéro, Jean. "The Substitute King and His Fate." *Mesopotamia: Writing, Reasoning and the Gods.* 138–55.

Bottéro, Jean, and Samuel Noah Kramer. *Lorsque les dieux faisant l'homme: Mythologie mésopotamienne.* Paris: Gallimard, 1989.

Bowlby, John. *Attachment and Loss.* Vol. 2. NY: Basic Books, 1976.

Bowra, Cecil Maurice. *The Greek Experience.* NY: Mentor, 1957.

Bowra, Cecil Maurice. "The Poetry of Action." *Heroic Poetry.* London: Macmillan, 1952. 48–90; selections rpt. Krstović. 3–13.

Boyajian, Zabelle C. *Gilgamesh: A Dream of the Eternal Quest.* London: G. W. Jones, 1924.

Brain, Robert. *Friends and Lovers.* NY: Basic Books, 1976.

Brandon, S. G. F. *Creation Legends of the Ancient Near East.* London: Hodder & Stoughton, 1963.

Brandon, S. G. F. "The Epic of Gilgamesh: A Mesopotamian Philosophy." *History Today* 11 (1961): 18–27; selections rpt. Krstović. 314–15.

Brandon, S. G. F. *The Epic of Gilgamesh, A Mesopotamian Philosophy of Life.* NY, 1969.

Brandon, S. G. F. "Mesopotamia: Resignation to Time's Annihilation." *Time and Mankind.* London: Hutchinson and Co., 1951. 44–55.

Braswell, B. K. "Mythological Invention in the Iliad." *Classical Quarterly* 21 (1971): 1–8.

Brenk, Frederick E. "Aphrodite's Girdle: No Way to Treat a Lady." *Classical Bulletin* 54 (1977): 17–20.

Bridson, D. Geoffrey. *The Quest of Gilgamesh.* Cambridge: Rampant Lions Press, 1972.

Brillante, C. "Le leggende Tebane e l'archeologia." *SMEA* 21 (1980): 309–40.

Brillante, C., M. Cantilena, and C. O. Pavese, eds. *I Poemi epici rapsodici non omerici e la tradizione orale.* Padua: Antenore, 1981. 29–48.

Brockhoff, Victoria, and Hermann Lauboech. *Als die Götter noch mit den Menschen sprachen. Gilgamesch und Enkidu.* Freiburg im Breisgau: Herder, 1981.

Brown, Peter. *The Body and Society: Men, Women and Sexual Renunciation in Early Christianity.* NY: Faber, 1988.

Brückner, M. "Jesus und Gilgamesch." *Die Christl. Welt* 9 (1907): 193–203.

Bruner, Edward M. "Ethnography as Narrative." *The Anthropology of Experience.* Ed. Victor W. Turner and Edward M. Bruner. Urbana: U of Illinois P, 1986. 139–55.

Bruner, Edward M., ed. *Text, Play, and Story: The Construction and Reconstruction of Self and Society.* Washington, D.C.: American Ethnological Society, 1984.

Brünnow, Rudolph Ernst. "Assyrian Hymns, 2." *ZA* 4 (1889): 225–58.

Bryson, Bernarda. *Gilgamesh, Man's First Story.* NY: Holt, Rinehart, 1967.

Buccellati, Giorgio. *The Amorites of the UR III Period.* Naples: Istituto Orientale di Napoli, 1966.

Buccellati, Giorgio. "On Poetry—Theirs and Ours." Abusch. *Lingering Over Words.* 105–34.

Buccellati, Giorgio. "Tre saggi sapienza Mesopotamica, 1." *Or. Ant.* 11 (1972): 1–36.

Buccellati, Giorgio. "Wisdom and Not: The Case of Mesopotamia." *JAOS* 101 (1981): 35–48.

Buchanan, Wayne J. *Gilgamesh, A Bibliography*. Philadelphia: U of Pennsylvania, 1979.

Bucher, Karl. *Industrial Evolution*. NY: Henry Holt, 1901.

Buck, Carl D. *A Dictionary of Selected Synonyms in the Principal Indo-European Languages*. Chicago: U of Chicago P, 1949.

Buck, Robert J. *A History of Boeotia*. Edmonton: U of Alberta P, 1979.

Budge, Sir Ernest Alfred Wallis. *The Babylonian Story of the Deluge and the Epic of Gilgamesh, with an Account of the Royal Libraries of Nineveh*. London: British Museum, 1920; Ed. C. J. Gadd, 1930.

Budge, E. A. Wallis. *The Babylonian Story of the Deluge as Told by Assyrian Tablets from Nineveh*. London: British Museum, 1920.

Budge, E. A. Wallis. *The History of Alexander the Great*. London: C. J. Clay, 1896.

Burckhardt, Georg E. *Gilgamesch. Eine Erzählung aus dem alten Orient*. Leipzig: Insel-Verlag, 1916; 2nd. Ed., 1920; 3rd. Ed. Wiesbaden: Insel-Verlag, 1958.

Burckhardt, Georg E., and Joseph Hegenbarth. *Das Gilgamesch-Epos: Eine Dichtung aus dem alten Orient*. Berlin: Rutten & Loening, 1991.

Buren, Elizabeth Douglas van. "The Rain-Goddess as Represented in Early Mesopotamia." *Analecta Biblica* 12 (1959): 343–55.

Buren, Elizabeth Douglas van. "The Sacred Marriage in Early Times in Mesopotamia." *Or.* 13 (1944): 1–72.

Buren, Elizabeth Douglas van. "The *ṣalme* in Mesopotamian Art and Religion." *Or.* 10 (1942): 65–92.

Buren, Elizabeth Douglas van. "The Scorpion in Mesopotamian Art and Religion." *AfO* 12 (1937): 1–28.

Burkert, Walter. "Buzyge und Palladion." *Zeitschrift für Religions- und Geistesgeschichte* 22 (1970): 356–68.

Burkert, Walter. *Greek Religion, Archaic and Classical*. Oxford and Cambridge, MA: Oxford UP, 1985.

Burkert, Walter. "Homerstudien und Orient." *Zweihundert Jahre Homer-Forschung: Rückblick und Ausblick*. Ed. J. Latacz. Stuttgart: B. G. Teubner, 1991. 155–81.

Burkert, Walter. *Homo Necans: The Anthropology of Ancient Greek Sacrificial Ritual and Myth.* Berkeley: U of California P, 1983.

Burkert, Walter. "Literarische Texte und funktionaler Mythos. Zu-Ištar und Atrahasis." *Funktionen und Leistungen des Mythos. Drie altorientalische Beispiele.* Ed. J. Assmann, W. Burkert, and F. Stolz. Freiburg/Göttingen: Universitätsverlag, 1982. 63–82.

Burkert, Walter. "'Or Also a Godly Singer,' Akkadian and Early Greek Literature." *The Orientalizing Revolution.* 88–127.

Burkert, Walter. *Die orientalisierende Epoche in der griechischen Religion und Literatur.* Heidelberg: Carl Winter Universitätsverlag, 1984; Tr. Margaret E. Pinder and Walter Burkert, *The Orientalizing Revolution, Near Eastern Influence on Greek Culture in the Early Archaic Age.* Cambridge, MA: Harvard UP, 1992.

Burkert, Walter. *Structure and History in Greek Mythology and Ritual.* Berkeley: U of California P, 1979.

Burney, Charles Fox. "The Mythical Element in the Story of Samson." *The Book of Judges.* London: Rivingtons, 1918. 391–408.

Burrows, Eric. "Review of Chiera, *Sumerian Religious Texts.*" *JRAS* (1926): 318–319.

Burstein, Stanley Mayer. *The "Babyloniaca" of Berossos.* Malibu: Undena, 1978.

Burton, Richard F. *A Plain and Literal Translation of the Arabian Nights' Entertainment.* London: Burton Club, 1900.

Burton, Richard, tr. *The Arabian Nights' Entertainments.* Ed. B. A. Cerf. NY: Random House, 1959.

Butterworth, E. A. S. *The Tree at the Navel of the Earth.* Berlin: de Gruyter, 1970.

Buttrick, G. A., et al., eds. *The Interpreter's Dictionary of the Bible.* 4 Vols. NY and Nashville: Abingdon, 1962.

Cagni, Luigi. *L'epopea di Erra.* Rome: Instituto di Studi del Vicino Oriento, 1969; *The Poem of Erra.* Malibu: Undena, 1977.

Cagni, Luigi, Ugo Bianchi, Giovanni Pettinato, Sergio A. Picchioni, and Mirella Meli, eds. *Gli Assiri.* Rome: De Luca Editore, 1981.

Calmeyer, Peter. "Gilgameš. D. In der Archäologie." *RLA* 3: 372–74.

Calmeyer, Peter. *Reliefbronzen in babylonischem Stil.* München: Verlag de Bayer, 1973.

Calmeyer, Peter. "Ein Neuer Becher der Werkstatt zwischen Zalu AB und dem Gebiet der Kakavand." *Acta Praehistorica et Archaeologica* 1 (1970): 81–86.

Cameron, Alan. "The Last Days of the Academy at Athens." *Proceedings of the Cambridge Philological Society.* N.S. 14 (1968): 7–29.

Camp, Claudia V. "The Wise Women of 2 Samuel: A Role Model for Women in Early Israel?" *CBQ* 43 (1981): 14–29.

Camp, J. McK. "A Drought in the Late Eighth Century B.C." *Hesperia* 48 (1979): 397–411.

Campbell, Joseph. "The Consort of the Bull." *The Masks of God: Occidental Mythology.* NY: Viking, 1964. 42–94; selections rpt. Krstović. 319–21.

Campbell, Joseph. "The Ultimate Boon." *The Hero with a Thousand Faces.* Cleveland: World Publishing, 1956. 172–93.

Campbell Thompson, R. *The Epic of Gilgamesh: Text, Transliteration, and Notes.* Oxford: Clarendon Press, 1930.

Campbell Thompson, R., tr. *The Epic of Gilgamesh, A New Translation... Rendered Literally into English Hexameters.* London: Luzac and Co., 1928.

Camus, Albert. *Notebooks, 1935–1942.* NY: Alfred A. Knopf, 1963.

Caplice, Richard I. *The Akkadian Namburbi Texts: An Introduction.* Malibu: Undena, 1974.

Caplice, Richard I. *The Akkadian Text Genre Namburbi.* Diss., U of Chicago, 1963.

Caplice, Richard I. *Introduction to Akkadian.* 3rd. Ed. Rome: Biblical Institute Press, 1988.

Caplice, Richard I. "Namburbi Texts in the British Museum, 5." *Or.* 40 (1971): 133–83.

Carne-Ross, D. S. "From the Baked Bricks: The Poem of Gilgamesh." *The New Criterion* 11 (1992): 68–74.

Caroline. *Gilgamesh.* London: Caroline, 1975. [Audio Recording].

Carter, Theresa A. "Dilmun: At Sea or Not At Sea." *JCS* 39 (1987): 54–117.

Caspers, Elisabeth C. L. During. "In the Footsteps of Gilgamesh: In Search of the 'Prickly Rose.'" *Persica* 12 (1987): 57–95.

Caspers, Elisabeth C. L. During. "Pearl Fishery in the Arabian Gulf and the 'Prickly Rose' of Gilgamesh." *Bi. Or.* 40 (1983).

Cassirer, Ernst. *The Logic of the Humanities.* New Haven: Yale UP, 1961.

Cassuto, Umberto. *A Commentary on the Books of Genesis.* 2 Vols. Tr. I. Abrahams. Jerusalem: Magnes, 1961, 1964.

Cassuto, Umberto M. D. "Gilgamesh." *Encyclopaedia Biblica Instituti Bialik* 2 (1954): 490–95.

Castellino, Giorgio. "Incantation to Utu." *Or. Ant.* 8 (1969): 1–57.

Castellino, Giorgio. "Les Origines de la civilisation selon les textes bibliques et les textes cunéiformes." *SVT* 4 (1957): 116–37.

Castellino, Giorgio. *Sapienza babylonese.* Turin: Societa Editrice Internationale, 1962.

Castellino, Giorgio. *Testi Sumerici e Accadici.* Turin: Unione tipografico-editrice torinese, 1977.

Castellino, Giorgio. *Two Šulgi Hymns*. Rome: Istituto di Studi del Vicino Oriente, Università di Roma, 1972.

Castellino, Giorgio. "Urnammu. Three Religious Texts." *ZA* 52 (1957): 1–57; 53 (1959): 106–32.

Caws, Mary Ann, and Christopher Prendergast, ed. *The HarperCollins World Reader.* Vol. 1. *Antiquity to the Early Modern World.* NY: HarperCollins, 1994.

Celada, B. "Progresos en historia mesopotamica especialmente en sus redaciones con la Biblia [i. a. Epopeya de Gilgames; El Diluvio]." *Sefarad* 2 (1942): 383–435.

Ceram, C. W. "George Smith: The Story of the Flood." *Gods, Graves, and Scholars.* Tr. E. G. Garside and Sophie Wilkins. Rev. Ed. NY: Vintage, 1986. 301–16.

Chamberlin, Ann. *The Virgin and the Tower.* NY: Pocket Books, 1979.

Chao, Le-sheng. *Chi-erh-chieh-mei-shih.* Shen-yang: Liao-ning jen mmin chu pan she, 1981.

Charpin, Dominique. *Le clergé d'Ur au siècle d'Hammurabi (xix–xvii siècles AV. J.C.).* Geneva: Librairie Droz, 1986.

Chase, Richard. *Quest for Myth.* Baton Rouge: Louisiana State UP, 1949.

Chichetto, James William. *Gilgamesh, Book Two, Chapter One: And Other Poems.* n.p.: Four Zoas Night House, 1983.

Chiera, Edward. *Sumerian Epics and Myths.* Chicago: UP, 1934. N. 21–31.

Chiera, Edward. *Sumerian Religious Texts.* Upland, PA: Crozer Theological, 1924.

Chiera, Edward. *Sumerian Texts of Varied Contents.* Chicago: UP, 1934, 1972. N. 88.

Chikovani, M. Y. "The Theme of a Youth Seeking Immortality in Ancient Folklore and Literature." *Proceedings of the Twenty-Sixth International Congress of Orientalists* 2 (1968): 63–68.

Child, Francis J. *The English and Scottish Popular Ballads.* 5 Vols. Boston: Houghton Mifflin, 1882–98.

Childs, B. S. "The Birth of Moses." *JBL* 84 (1965): 109–22.

Ciecierska-Chtapowa, Teresa. "L'idée de la révolution dans les premiers drames d'Orhan Asena." *Folio Orientalia* 20 (1979): 57–75.

Civil, Miguel (Michel). "The 'Message of Ludingirra to His Mother' and a Group of Akkado-Hittite 'Proverbs.'" *JNES* 23 (1964): 1–11.

Civil, Miguel. "Review of T. Pinches, *CT 44* (1963)." *JNES* 28 (1969): 70–72.

Civil, Miguel. "The Sumerian Flood Story." Lambert and Millard. *Atrahasis.* 138–45, 167–72.

Clark, M. W. "The Flood and the Structure of the Prepatriarch History." *Zeitschrift für die alttestamentliche Wissenschaft* 83 (1971): 184–211.

Clark, Raymond J. *Catabasis: Vergil and the Wisdom-Tradition.* Amsterdam: Gruner, 1979.

Clay, Albert Tobias. *Babylonian Records in the Library of J. Pierpont Morgan.* New Haven: Yale UP, 1920, 1929.

Clay, Albert Tobias. *Miscellaneous Inscriptions in the Yale Babylonian Collection.* New Haven: Yale UP, 1915.

Clermont-Ganneau, C. *L'imagerie Phénicienne et la mythologie iconologique chez les Grecs.* Paris: E. Leroux, 1880.

Clifford, James. *The Predicament of Culture: Twentieth-Century Ethnography, Literature, and Art.* Cambridge, MA: Harvard UP, 1988.

Clifford, Richard J. *Creation Accounts in the Ancient Near East and in the Bible.* Washington, DC: Catholic Biblical Association, 1994.

Cloche, Paul. *Thèbes de Béotie.* Namur: Secrétariat des publications, Facultés universitaires, 1952.

Coates, William. *The Secret of Utnapishtim: For Soprano and Archiphone.* 1989. [Musical Score].

Coe, Charles Norton. *Wordsworth and the Literature of Travel.* NY: Bookman Associates, 1953.

Cogan, M. "A Technical Term for Exposure." *JNES* 27 (1968): 133–35.

Cohen, Mark E. *The Canonical Lamentations of Ancient Mesopotamia.* Potomac, MD: Capital Decisions, 1988.

Cohen, Sol. *Enmerkar and the Lord of Aratta.* Ann Arbor, MI: University Microfilms, 1973.

Cohen, Sol. "Studies in Sumerian Lexicography, 1." Eichler. *Kramer Anniversary Volume.* 97–110.

Cohen, Yehudi A., ed. *Social Structure and Personality.* NY: Holt, Rinehart and Winston, 1961.

Colakis, Marianthe. "Gilgamesh and Philip Roth's Gil Gamesh." [Unpublished Essay].

Coldstream, J. N. "Hero-Cults in the Age of Homer." *Journal of Hellenic Studies* 96 (1976): 8–17.

Cole, Thomas. *Democritus and the Sources of Greek Anthropology.* Cleveland: American Philological Association, 1967.

Coleman, Wim, and Pat Perrin. *Retold World Myths.* Logan, Iowa: Perfection Learning, 1993.

Comte, Hubert. *A Epopeia de Gilgamesh.* Lisbon: Edicoes Antonio Ramos, 1979.

Contenau, Georges. *Les Antiquités Orientales.* Paris: Morance, 1928, 1930.

Contenau, Georges. *La Civilisation d'Assur et de Babylone.* Geneva: Editions Famot, 1975.

Contenau, Georges. *Le Déluge babylonien suivi de Ishtar aux enfers, La Tour de Babel.* 1st. Ed. Paris: Payot, 1941; New Ed., 1952.

Contenau, Georges. *L'épopée de Gilgamesh, poème babylonien.* Paris: L'Artisan du Livre, 1939.

Contenau, Georges. *La Vie Quotidienne à Babylone et en Assyrie.* Paris: Librairie Hachette, 1950, 1964.

Conybeare, F. C., et al. *The Story of Aḥiḳar*. 2nd. Ed. Cambridge: UP, 1913.

Cook, A. B. "The European Sky-God." *FolkLore* 15 (1904): 264–315.

Cook, A. B. *Zeus, A Study in Ancient Religion.* 3 Vols. Cambridge: UP, 1914, 1940.

Cook, Captain James. *Journals.* Vol. 1. Ed. J. C. Beaglehole. London: Hakluyt Society, 1955.

Cook, Charles W. "'The Epic of Gilgamesh' as a Ritual Drama." *Ball State University Forum* 24 (1983): 42–48; selections rpt. Krstović. 352–54.

Cook, Charles W. *Gilgamesh, The World's Oldest Drama.* Colorado Springs, CO: Contemporary Drama Service, 1974.

Cooper, Jerrold S. "Appendix A. The Trophies of Ninurta." *An. Or.* 52 (1978): 141–53.

Cooper, Jerrold S. "Bilinguals from Boghazkoï." *ZA* 61 (1971): 1–22; 62 (1972): 62–81.

Cooper, Jerrold S. "Gilgamesh and Agga: A Review Article." *JCS* 33 (1981): 22–41.

Cooper, Jerrold S. "Gilgamesh Dreams of Enkidu: The Evolution and Dilution of Narrative." Ellis. *Essays… Finkelstein.* 39–44.

Cooper, Jerrold S. "More Heat on the AN.IM.DUGUD Bird." *JCS* 26 (1974): 121.

Cooper, Jerrold S. "A Sumerian ŠU-ÍL-LA from Nimrud with a Prayer for Sin-Šar-Iškun." *Iraq* 32 (1970): 51–67.

Cooper, Jerrold S. "Symmetry and Repetition in Akkadian Narrative." *JAOS* 97 (1977): 508–12.

Coote, Robert B., and David Robert Ord. *The Bible's First History.* Philadelphia: Fortress Press, 1989.

Cornault, Joel. *Éloge de Gilgamesh.* Église-Neuve d'Issack: Federop, 1992.

Cornford, Francis M. "A Ritual Basis for Hesiod's *Theogony.*" *The Unwritten Philosophy.* Cambridge: UP, 1950, 1967. 95–116.

Cornwall, P. B. "On the Location of Dilmun." *BASOR* 103 (1946): 3–11.

Cors i Meya, Jordi. *El viatge al mon dels morts en l'odissea.* Bellaterra: Universitat aut'onoma de Barcelona, 1984.

Coward, Harold G., and Joseph R. Royce. "Toward an Epistemological Basis for Humanistic Psychology." *Humanistic Psychology: Concepts and Criticisms.* Ed. Joseph R. Royce and Leendert P. Mos. NY: Plenum, 1981.

Cowley, A. E. *Gesenius' Hebrew Grammar.* Oxford: Clarendon Press, 1910.

Crane, Gregory. "Circe and the Near East." *Calypso. Backgrounds and Conventions of the Odyssey.* Frankfurt am Main: Athenäum, 1988. 61–85.

Crawley, A. E. *The Mystic Rose: A Study of Primitive Marriage.* Rev. T. Besterman. London: Methuen, 1927.

Crichton, Michael. *Travels.* NY: Alfred A. Knopf, 1988.

Cross, Frank M. *Canaanite Myth and Hebrew Epic.* Cambridge, MA: Harvard UP, 1973.

Culianu, Ioan P. *Out of This World. Other-Worldly Journeys from Gilgamesh to Albert Einstein.* Boston: Shambhala, 1991.

Curtin, Jeremiah. *Myths and Folklore of Ireland.* Boston: Little, Brown, 1890.

Curtiss, Susan. *Genie: A Psycholinguistic Study of a Modern-Day "Wild Child."* NY: Harcourt Brace, 1977.

Curtius, Ernst Robert. "Comic Elements in the Epic" and "Kitchen Humor and Other Ridicula." *European Literature and the Latin Middle Ages.* Tr. Willard R. Trask. London: Routledge and K. Paul, 1953. 429–31, 431–35.

Curtius, Ludwig. *Studien zur Geschichte der Altorientalischen Kunst.* Munich: K.- Bayerischen Akademie der Wissenschaften, 1912.

Le cycle de Gilgamish, à propos de la collection de cylindres orientaux du Musée d'art et d'histoire. Geneva: Musée d'art et d'histoire, 1944.

Czer, L. "Der mythische Lebensbaum und die ficus ruminalis." *Act. Ant.* 10 (1962): 315–35.

Dahood, Mitchell. *Psalms I.* Garden City, NY: Doubleday, 1965.

Daiches, Samuel. "Das Gilgameš-Epos und das Hohelied." *OLZ* 15 (1912): 60–62.

Daise, Michael A. *Death and Perceptions of Reality in Ancient Mediterranean Epic: Gilgamesh, The Iliad and the Aeneid.* Thesis, Drew University, 1993.

Dalley, Stephanie. "Gilgamesh in the Arabian Nights." *JRAS* 3 (1991): 1–17.

Dalley, Stephanie. *Myths from Mesopotamia: Creation, The Flood, Gilgamesh and Others.* NY/Oxford: Oxford UP, 1989.

Damaluji, Summaya, tr. *The Epic of Gilgamesh.* Tr. from the Arabic of Taha Baqer. Baghdad: Dar al-Ma'mun, 1989.

Damrosch, David. "Gilgamesh and Genesis." *The Narrative Covenant: Transformations of Genre in the Growth of Biblical Literature.* Ithaca: Cornell UP, 1987. 88–143.

Däniken, Erich von. "Fiery Chariots from the Heavens." *Chariots of the Gods?* Tr. Michael Heron. NY: Bantam Books, 1970. 45–54.

David, Martin. "Action et histoire (Épopée de Gilgameš)." *Revue philosophique* 148 (1958): 289–312.

David, Martin. "L'épisode des oiseaux dans les récits du Déluge." *Vetus Testamentum* 7 (1957): 189–90.

David, Martin. "De quelques problèmes soulevés par l'épopée de Gilgamesh. Analyse de plusieurs publications récentes." *RES* 5 (1939): 32–48.

David, Martin. "Le Récit du déluge et l'epopée de Gilgameš." *GSL.* 153–59.

Day, John. *God's Conflict with the Dragon and the Sea.* Cambridge: UP, 1985.

De Meyer, Leon. "Introduction bibliographique." *GSL.* 1–30.

Degh, Linda. *Folktales and Society: Storytelling in a Hungarian Peasant Village*. Bloomington: Indiana UP, 1969.

Deimel, Anton. *Die Inschriften von Fara III*. Leipzig: J. C. Hinrichs, 1922.

Deimel, Anton. "Nimrod (Gen. X, 8–12)." *Or.* (series prior) 26 (1927): 76–80.

Delitzsch, Friedrich. *Assyrisches Handwörterbuch*. Leipzig: Hinrichs, 1896.

Delitzsch, Fr. *Assyrische Lesestücke*. 5th. Ed. Leipzig: J. C. Hinrichs, 1912.

Delitzsch, Friedrich. *Babel and Bible. Two Lectures*. Ed. C. H. W. Johns. NY: G. P. Putnam's Sons, London: Williams and Nargate, 1903.

Delougaz, P. P. "Animals Emerging from a Hut." *JNES* 27 (1968): 184–97.

Demakopoulou, Katie, and D. Konsola. *Archaeological Museum of Thebes: Guide*. Athens: General Direction of Antiquities and Restoriation, 1981.

Demsky, Aaron. "The Education of Canaanite Scribes in the Mesopotamian Cuneiform Tradition." *Bar-Ilan Studies in Assyriology Dedicated to Pinhas Artzi*. Ed. Jacob Klein and Aaron Skaist. Ramat Gan: Bar-Ilan U, 1990. 157–90.

Deubner, Ludwig. *Kleine Schriften zur klassischen Altertumskunde*. Konigstein: Hain, 1900, 1982.

Dhorme, Paul/Édouard. *Choix de texte religieux assyro-babyloniens*. Paris: V. Lecoffre, 1907.

Dhorme, Paul/Édouard. "Le Déluge babylonien." *RB* 39 (1930): 481–502; rpt. *Recueil Édouard Dhorme*. 62–74.

Dhorme, Paul/Édouard. *La littérature babylonienne et assyrienne*. Paris: Les Presses Universitaires de France, 1937.

Dhorme, Paul/Édouard. *Recueil Édouard Dhorme*. Paris: Impr. nationale, 1951.

Dhorme, Paul/Édouard. *Les Religions de Babylonie et d'Assyrie*. 2nd. Ed. Paris: Presses Universitaires de France, 1949.

Dhorme, Paul/Édouard. "Review of Langdon, *Sumerian Paradise*." *RB* 30 (1921): 309–13.

Diakonoff, Igor M. "L'énigme de Gilgameš (Sur les relations du mythe et de la poésie épique." *Culture et art du monde antique et de l'Orient.* Vol. 1. Moscow, 1958. 5–26. [in Russian]

Diakonoff, Igor Mikhailovich. *Epos o Gilgameshe: "O vse vidavshem."* Moscow: Izd-vo Akademii nauk SSSR, 1961.

Diakonoff, Igor Mikhailovich. "Die Gestalt des Gilgameš." *Obraz Gilgamesa.* Leningrad/Moscow: Kultura i iskusstvo, 1958. 1–26; tr. Sigrid Richter, rpt. Oberhuber. *Das Gilgamesch-Epos.* 325–60.

Diakonoff, Igor Mikhailovich. "Gosudarstvennyi stroj Drevnejsevo Sumera." *Vestnik drevnei istorii* (1952): 118–25.

Diakonoff, Igor Mikhailovich. "Obraz Gilgameša." *Trudy gosudarstvennova Ermitaža.* Leningrad/Moscow, 1958. 1–26.

Diakonoff, Igor Mikhailovich. "Review of Böhl, *Het Gilgamesj Epos*, and Matouš, *Epos o Gilgamešovi.*" *Bi. Or.* 18 (1961): 61–67.

Diakonoff, Igor Mikhailovich. *Structure of Society and State in Early Dynastic Sumer.* Los Angeles: Undena, 1974.

Diakonoff, Igor Mikhailovich. "Thorns and Roses." *Rocznik orientalistyczny* 41 (1980): 19–24.

Diakonoff, Igor Mikhailovich, and N. B. Jankowska. "An Elamite Gilgameš Text from Argistiḫenele, Urartu (Armavirblur, 8th century B.C.)." *ZA* 80 (1990): 102–24.

Dick, Bernard F. "Ancient Pastoral and the Pathetic Fallacy." *Comparative Literature* 20 (1968): 27–44.

Dickel, Michael J., and Stefan Slak. "Imagery Vividness and Memory for Verbal Material." *Journal of Mental Imagery* 7 (1983): 121–26.

Didion, Joan. *The White Album.* NY: Pocket Books, 1979.

Dieckmann, Chr. *Das Gilgamiš-Epos in seiner Bedeutung für Bibel und Babel.* Leipzig: Christoph Steffen, 1902.

Dihle, Albrecht. *Homer-Probleme.* Opladen: Westdeutscher Verlag, 1970.

Dijk, Jan van. *Vorderasiatische Schriftdenkmäler der Staatlichen Museen zu Berlin.* Berlin: Akademie-Verlag, 1987.

Dijk, Johannes Jacobus Adrianus van. "La 'confusion des langues': Note sur le lexique et sur la morphologie d'Enmerkar, 147–155." *Or.* 39 (1970): 302.

Dijk, Johannes Jacobus Adrianus van. *Cuneiform Texts: Old Babylonian Letters and Related Material.* Wiesbaden: O. Harrassowitz, 1965.

Dijk, Johannes Jacobus Adrianus van. *Cuneiform Texts: Texts of Varying Content.* Leiden: Brill, 1976.

Dijk, Johannes Jacobus Adrianus van. "Le Dénouement de 'Gilgameš au bois de cèdres' selon LB 2116." *GSL.* 69–81.

Dijk, Johannes Jacobus Adrianus van. "Ein ergänzendes Fragment Gilgamesh and the Land of the Living." *Tabulae cuneiformae a F. M. Th. de Liagre Böhl collectae II.* Leiden, 1957. N. 4.

Dijk, Johannes Jacobus Adrianus van. "La Fête du nouvel an dans un texte de Šulgi." *Bi. Or.* 11 (1954): 83–88.

Dijk, Johannes Jacobus Adrianus van. "L'Hymne à Marduk avec intercession pour le roi Abī'ešuḫ." *MIO* 12 (1966): 57–74.

Dijk, Johannes Jacobus Adrianus van. "IM 526 15: Un songe d'Enkidu." *Sumer* 14 (1958): 114–21.

Dijk, Johannes Jacobus Adrianus van. "Incantations accompagnant la naissance de l'homme." *Or.* 44 (1975): 52–79.

Dijk, Johannes Jacobus Adrianus van. "Le Motif cosmique dans la pensée sumérienne." *Ac. Or.* 28 (1964): 1–59.

Dijk, Johannes Jacobus Adrianus van. *La Sagesse suméro-accadienne.* Leiden: Brill, 1953.

Dijk, Johannes Jacobus Adrianus van. *Textes divers.* Leiden: Nederlandisch instituut voor het nabije oosten, 1957.

Dijk, Johannes Jacobus Adrianus van. "Textes divers du Musée de Baghdad, 23." *Sumer* 13 (1957): 65–133; 15 (1959): 5–14.

Dijk, Johannes Jacobus Adrianus van. "Die Tontafeln aus der Grabung in Éanna." *UVB 18* Ed. H. J. Lenzen, et al. Berlin: Gebr. Mann, 1962. 39–62.

Dijk, Johannes Jacobus Adrianus van. "VAT 8382: Ein zweisprachiges Königsritual." Edzard. *Heidelberger Studien.* 233–68.

Dijk, Johannes Jacobus Adrianus van. "Ein weiterest Fragment zur altbab. Version aus Tell Harmal IM 52750." *Sumer* 15 (1959): 8ff., N. 23.

Dirlmeier, F. "Homerisches Epos und Orient." *Rhm* 98 (1955): 18–37.

Doll, Mary. "Hearing Images." *Journal of Mental Imagery* 7 (1983): 135–42.

Dolphin, Jeremy, ed. *The Collected Works of Caravan of Dreams Theater.* Vol. 1. *Gilgamesh.* London: Synergetic Press, 1993.

Donaldson, Ian. *The World Upside-Down: Comedy from Jonson to Fielding.* Oxford: UP, 1970.

Dorr, Hermann Josef. *Die kosmische Gestalt des Gilgamesch.* Düsseldorf-Eller: [Self-publication], 1968.

Dossin, Georges. *Correspondance de Šamsi-Addu et de ses fils.* Paris: Imprimerie Nationale, 1950.

Dossin, Georges. "Les deux songes de Gilgamesh." *Le Muséon* 59 (1946): 63–66.

Dossin, Georges. "Enkidou dans l'épopée de Gilgameš." *Académie Royale de Belgique: Bulletin de la classe des lettres…, series 5* 42 (1956): 580–93.

Dossin, Georges. "L'Inscription de fondation de Iaḫdum-Lim, roi de Mari." *Syria* 32 (1955): 1–28.

Dossin, Georges. *Le Pâleur d'Enkidou.* Louvain: Imprimerie Orientaliste M. Istas, 1931.

Dossin, Georges. "Un Rituel du culte d'Ištar provenant de Mari." *RA* 35 (1938): 1–13.

Dover, Kenneth James. *Greek Homosexuality.* Cambridge: UP; NY: Vintage, 1978.

Drews, Robert. "The Babylonian Chronicles and Berossus." *Iraq* 37 (1975): 39–55.

Driel, G. van, T. J. H. Krispijn, M. Stol, and K. R. Veenhof, ed. *Zikir Shumin: Assyriological Studies Presented to F. R. Kraus on the Occasion of his Seventieth Birthday.* Leiden: E. J. Brill, 1982.

Driver, Godfrey Rolles, and J. C. Miles. *The Babylonian Laws.* 2 Vols. Oxford, Clarendon Press, 1952–55.

Driver, Godfrey Rolles. "Mythical Monsters in the Old Testament." *Studi Orientalistici in onore de Giorgio Levi della Vida* 1 (1956): 234–49.

Driver, S. R. *The Book of Genesis.* 3rd. Ed. New York: Gorham, 1904.

Driver, S. R. *An Introduction to the Literature of the Old Testament.* Cleveland: World/Meridian, 1956.

Duberman, Martin. *Black Mountain, An Experiment in Community.* NY: E. P. Dutton, 1972.

Duchemin, Jacqueline. "Contribution à l'histoire des mythes Grecs, les luttes primordiales dans l'Iliade à la lumière des sources proche-orientales." *Miscellanea di studi classici in onore di Eugenio Manni.* Vol. 3. Rome: G. Bretschneider, 1980. 837–79.

Duchemin, Jacqueline. *Prométhée. Histoire du mythe de ses origines orientales à ses incarnations modernes.* Paris: Belles lettres, 1974.

Duchesne-Guillemin, Marcelle. "*Pukku* and *mekkû*." *Iraq* 45 (1985): 151–56.

Duchesne-Guillemin, Marcelle. "Variations on the Scraper: As Origin...Gilgamesh Epic." *The Mankind Quarterly* 23 (1982): 161–82.

Dumezil, Georges. *Mythe et épopée.* 2nd. Ed. Paris: Gallimard, 1974.

Dumont, Jean-Paul. *The Headman and I: Ambiguity and Ambivalence in the Fieldworking Experience.* Austin: U of Texas P, 1978.

Dunand, Maurice. *Fouillers de Byblos.* Paris: P. Geuthner, 1939.

Dundes, Alan, ed. *The Flood Myth.* Berkeley: U of California P, 1988.

Dundes, Alan, ed. *Sacred Narrative: Readings in the Theory of Myth.* Berkeley: U of California P, 1984.

Dunne, John S. "Preface" and "The Kings of Erech." *The City of the Gods: A Study in Myth and Mortality.* NY: Macmillan, 1965. v–ix, 1–15.

Dux, Günter. *Liebe und Tod im Gilgamesch-Epos: Geschichte als Weg zum Selbstbewusstsein des Menschen.* Vienna: Passagen-Verlag, 1992.

Dybko, Iryna. *Gilgamesh. Poems.* Klifton, NJ: I. Dybko, 1984.

Ebeling, Erich. *Altorientalische Texte zum Alten Testament.* Ed. Hugo Gressmann. 2nd. Ed. Berlin/Leipzig, 1926. 150–98.

Ebeling, Erich. "Aruru." *RLA* 1: 160.

Ebeling, Erich. "Aššur. 3) Hauptgott Assyriens." *RLA* 1: 196–98.

Ebeling, Erich. "Enkimdu." *RLA* 2: 382.

Ebeling, Erich. "Fragments of the VIth. Tablet." *KAR I, 3* (1971): N. 115; *KAR II, 4* (1923): N. 319–20.

Ebeling, Erich. *Keilschrifttexte aus Assur.* I. Leipzig: Hinrichs, 1915–19.

Ebeling, Erich. *Keilschrifttexte aus Assur.* II. Leipzig: Hinrichs, 1920–23.

Ebeling, Erich. "Liebeszauber im Alten Orient." *MAOG* 1 (1925): 195–208.

Ebeling, Erich. "Ein Preislied auf die Kultstadt ArbaIlu aus Neuassyrischer Zeit." *JKF* 2 (1952–53): 274–82.

Ebeling, Erich. *Quellen zur Kenntnis der babylonischen Religion.* Vol. 1. Leipzig: Hinrichs, 1918.

Ebeling, Erich. *Tod und Leben nach den Vorstellungen des Babylonier.* Berlin/Leipzig: de Gruyter, 1931.

Ebeling, Erich, Bruno Meissner, et al., ed. *Reallexikon der Assyriologie.* Berlin/Leipzig: de Gruyter, 1932. = *RLA*

Eddy, Samuel Kennedy. *The King is Dead.* Lincoln, Nebraska: UP, 1961.

Edelkoort, A. H. "De voorstellingen omtrent dood en doodenrijk in het Gilgmaeš-Epos." *Nieuwe Theologische Studien* 8 (1925): 161–68.

Edwards, Ruth B. *Kadmos the Phoenician. A Study in Greek Legends and the Mycenaean Age.* Amsterdam: Adolf M. Hakkert, 1979.

Edwards, Thomas W. "Review of *The Great American Novel.*" *New York Times Book Review* (May 6, 1973): 27.

Edzard, Dietz Otto. "The Early Dynastic Period," "The Third Dynasty of Ur—Its Empire and Its Successor States," and "The Old Babylonian Period." *The Near East: The Early Civilizations.* Ed. Jean Bottéro, Elena Cassin, and J. Vercoutter. New York: Delacorte, 1967. 52–90, 133–231.

Edzard, Dietz Otto. "Enmebaragesi, contemporian de Gilgameš." *GSL.* 57.

Edzard, Dietz Otto. "Enmebaragesi von Kiš." *ZA* 53 (1959): 9–26.

Edzard, Dietz Otto. "Gilgamesh." *Wörterbuch der Mythologie.* Vol. 1 (1963): 165–67.

Edzard, Dietz Otto. "Gilgameš und Huwawa A. I. Teil." *ZA* 80 (1990): 165–203.

Edzard, Dietz Otto. "Gilgameš und Huwawa A. II. Teil." *ZA* 81 (1991): 165–233.

Edzard, Dietz Otto. *"Gilgameš und Huwawa:" Zwei Versionen.* Munich: C. H. Beck, 1993.

Edzard, Dietz Otto. ed. *Heidelberger Studien zum alten Orient, Adam Falkenstein.* Wiesbaden: Harrassowitz, 1967.

Edzard, Dietz Otto. "Kleine Beiträge zum Gilgameš-Epos." *Or.* 54 (1985): 46–55.

Edzard, Dietz Otto. "Mesopotamien. Die Mythologie der Sumerer und Akkader." *Wörterbuch der Mythologie.* Ed. H. W. Haussig. Vol. 1: *Götter und Mythen im Vorderen Orient.* Stuttgart: Ernst Klett, 1965.

Edzard, Dietz Otto. "Selbstgespräch und Monolog in der akkadischen Literatur." Abusch. *Lingering over Words.* 149–62.

Edzard, Dietz Otto. "Sumerische Komposita mit dem Nominalpräfix nu-." *ZA* 55 (1962): 91–112.

Edzard, Dietz Otto. *Die "zweite Zwischenzeit" Babyloniens.* Wiesbaden: Harrassowitz, 1957.

Edzard, Dietz Otto. "Zahlen, Zählen und Messen im Gilgameš Epos." *Text, Methode und Grammatik.* Ed. Walter Gross, Hubert Irsigler, Theodor Seidl. St. Ottilien: EOS Verlag Erzabtei, 1991. 57–66.

Eekhout, J. H. *Gilgamesj. Soemerisch-Babylonisch Epos in Twaalf Tafelen.* Nijkerk: G. F. Callenbach, 1925; 2nd. Ed., 1938.

Effenterre, Henri van. *Les Béotiens: Aux frontières de l'Athènes antiques.* Paris: Errance, 1989.

Ehelolf, Hans. *Mythen und Rituale.* Berlin: Staatliche Museen, 1926.

Ehelolf, Hans. *Texte Verschiedenen Inhalts.* Berlin: Staatliche Museen, 1944. 1–3.

Eichler, Barry L., ed., *Kramer Anniversary Volume. Cuneiform Studies in Honor of Samuel Noah Kramer.* Kevelaer: Butzon & Bercker: NeukirchenVluyn: Neukirchner Verlag, 1976.

Eisenmenger, Johann Andreas. *Entdecktes Judenthum.* 2 Vols. Königsberg: n.p., 1711.

Eisenstadt, Shmuel Noah, and Lius Roniger. *Patrons, Clients and Friends: Interpersonal Relations and the Structure of Trust in Society.* Cambridge: UP, 1984.

Eisler, Robert. *Weltenmantel und Himmelszelt.* München: C. H. Beck, 1910.

Eliade, Mircea. "The Mesopotamian Religions." *A History of Religious Ideas: From the Stone Age to the Eleusinian Mysteries.* Vol. 1. Tr. Willard R. Trask. Chicago: U of Chicago P, 1978. 56–84; selections rpt. Krstović. 341–42.

Eliade, Mircea. *The Myth of the Eternal Return.* Willard R. Trask. Princeton: UP, 1954.

Eliade, Mircea. *The Rites and Symbols of Initiation.* NY: Harper Torchbooks, 1965.

Eliade, Mircea. *The Sacred and the Profane.* Tr. Willard R. Trask. NY: Harvest Books, 1959; Harper and Row, 1961.

Elisseeff, Nikita. *Thèmes et motifs des mille et une nuits.* Beirut: Institut Français de Damas, 1949.

Ellis, Maria de Jong, ed. *Essays on the Ancient Near East in Memory of Jacob Joel Finkelstein.* Hamden, CT: Archon, 1977.

Ellis, Maria de Jong. "Gilgamesh's Approach to Huwawa's Dwelling: A New Text." *AfO* 28 (1981–82): 123–31.

Ellis, Maria de Jong. "*Ṣimdatu* in the Old Babylonian Sources." *JCS* 24 (1971–72): 74–82.

Ellis, Richard S. *Foundation Deposits in Ancient Mesopotamia.* New Haven: Yale UP, 1968.

Engnell, Ivan. *Studies in Divine Kingship in the Ancient Near East.* Uppsala: Almqvist & Wiksells, 1943; 2nd. Ed. Oxford: Blackwell, 1967.

Fadil, 'Abd al-Haqq. *Huwa alladi' ra' a. Malhmat qilqimiš*. Beirut: Dar al-Najlah al-zba'ah wa al-Nasr wa al-Tuzi'a, 1972.

Falkenstein, Adam. "Die Anunna in der sumerischen Überlieferung." *Studies in Honor of Benno Landsberger on his 75th Birthday.* Ed. Hans Gustav Güterbock. Chicago: UP, 1965. 127–40.

Falkenstein, Adam. "Zur Chronologie der sumerischen Literatur." *CRRAI* 2. Paris: Imprimerie Nationale, 1951. 12–27.

Falkenstein, Adam. "Gebet I. Das Gebet in der sumerischen Überlieferung." *RLA* 3: 156–60.

Falkenstein, Adam. "Gilgameš. A. Nach sumerischen Texten." *RLA* 3: 357–63.

Falkenstein, Adam. "Zur Gilgamesh und Agga." *AfO* 21 (1974): 47–50.

Falkenstein, Adam. *Grammatik der Sprache Gudeas von Lagaš*. Vol. 1. Rome: Pontifical Biblical Institute, 1949.

Falkenstein, Adam. *Die Haupttypen der sumerischen Beschwörung; Literarisch Untersucht.* Leipzig: Hinrichs, 1931.

Falkenstein, Adam. "Zu 'Inannas Gang zur Unterwelt.'" *AfO* 14 (1941–44): 113–38.

Falkenstein, Adam. "Zu den Inschriftenfunden der Grabung in Uruk-Warka, 1960–61." *Baghdader Mitteilungen* 2 (1963): 1–82.

Falkenstein, Adam. *Literarische Keilschrifttexte aus Uruk.* Berlin: Staatliche Museen, 1931.

Falkenstein, Adam. "Review of Kramer, *Sumerian Mythology*." *Bi. Or.* 5 (1948): 163–67.

Falkenstein, Adam. *Das Sumerische. Handbuch der Orientalistik.* Pt. 1: *Der nahe und der mittlere Osten*; Vol. 2: *Keilschriftforschung und alte Geschichte Vorderasiens*; Secs. 1–2: "Geschichte der Forschung," "Sprache und Literatur." Leiferung 1. Leiden: Brill, 1959.

Falkenstein, Adam. "Sumerische religiöse Texte, 2. Ein Šulgi-Lied." *ZA* 50 (1952): 61–91.

Falkenstein, Adam. "Der sumerische und der akkadische Mythos von Inannas Gang zur Unterwelt." *Festschrift Werner Caskel.* Ed. E. Graf. Leiden: Brill, 1968. 96–110.

Falkenstein, Adam. "Zum sumerischen Lexikon." *ZA* 58 (1967): 5–15.

Falkenstein, Adam. "Zur Überlieferung des Epos' von Gilgameš und Ḫuwawa." *JNES* 19 (1960): 65–71.

Falkenstein, Adam. "Untersuchungen zur sumerischen Grammatik (Fortsetzung)." *ZA* 48 (1944): 69–118.

Falkenstein, Adam, and Wolfram von Soden. *Sumerische und akkadische Hymnen und Gebete.* Zurich/Stuttgart: Artemis, 1953.

Faraone, C. A. "Aphrodite's *Kestos* and Apples for Atalanta: Aphrodisiacs in Early Greek Myth and Ritual." *Phoenix* 44 (1990): 219–43.

Farber-Flügge, Gertrud. *Der Mythos "Inanna und Enki" unter besonderer Berücksichtigung der Liste der me.* Rome: Biblical Institute, 1973.

Fasold, David. *The Ark of Noah.* NY: Knightsbridge Press, 1988, 1990.

Farnell, Lewis Richard. *The Cults of the Greek City States.* Cleveland: Bell and Howell, 1909, 1969.

Fauth, Wolfgang. "Ištar als Löwengottin and die löwenköpfige Lamaštu." *WO* 12 (1981): 21–36.

Feagles, Anita. *He Who Saw Everything.* NY: Young Scott, 1966.

Feigin, Samuel I. "Ḫum-ḫum." *Miscellanea Orientalia (Festschrift Deimel).* Rome: Pontifical Biblical Institute, 1935. 82–100.

Ferry, David, tr. *Gilgamesh, A New Rendering in English Verse.* NY: Farrar, Straus and Giroux, 1992.

Figulla, Hugo Heinrich. "Zur Erklärung des babylonischen Epen." *OLZ* 15 (1912): 433–41.

Figulla, Hugo Heinrich. *Letters and Documents of the Old Babylonian Period.* London: British Museum; Philadelphia, University Museum, U of Pennsylvania, 1953.

Finet, André. "Citations littéraires dans la correspondance de Mari." *RA* 68 (1947): 35–47.

Finkel, H. J. "The Search for Dilmun." *The Mariner's Mirror* 62 (1976): 211–33.

Finkel, Irving. "Necromancy in Ancient Mesopotamia." *AfO* 29–30 (1983–84): 1–17.

Finkelstein, Jacob J. "ana bīt emim šasū." *RA* 61 (1967): 127–36.

Finkelstein, Jacob J. "The Antediluvian Kings: A University of California Tablet." *JCS* 17 (1963): 39–51.

Finkelstein, Jacob J. "Bible and Babel: A Comparative Study of the Hebrew and Babylonian Religious Spirit." *Commentary* 26 (1958): 431–44.

Finkelstein, Jacob J. "The Genealogy of the Hammurapi Dynasty." *JCS* 20 (1966): 95–118.

Finkelstein, Jacob J. "A Late Old Babylonian Copy of the Laws of Hammurapi." *JCS* 21 (1967): 39–48.

Finkelstein, Jacob J. "Mesopotamian Historiography." *Cuneiform Studies and the History of Civilization*. Philadelphia: American Philosophical Society, 1963.

Finkelstein, Jacob J. *The Ox That Gored*. Philadelphia: American Philosophical Society, 1981. 54.

Finkelstein, Jacob J. "On Some Recent Studies in Cuneiform Law." *JAOS* 90 (1970): 243–56.

Finkelstein, Jacob J. "The So-called 'Old Babylonian Kutha Legend.'" *JCS* 11 (1957): 83–88.

Finnegan, Ruth. *Oral Poetry. Its Nature, Significance, and Social Context*. Bloomington: Indiana UP, 1977.

Finnegan, Ruth. *A World Treasury of Oral Poetry*. Bloomington: Indiana UP, 1978.

Fiore, Silvestro. "Myths and Epics" and "Conclusion." *Voices from the Clay: The Development of Assyro-Babylonian Literature*. Norman, OK: U of Oklahoma P, 1965. 136–219, 229–37; selections rpt. Krstović. 325–28.

Fish, Thomas. "A Rylands Cuneiform Tablet Concerning the Conquest of Kish under Agga, by Gilgamesh." *BJRL* 19 (1935). 362–72.

Fish, Thomas. "The Zû Bird." *BJRL* 31 (1948): 162–71.

Fishbane, Michael. *Text and Texture*. NY: Schocken, 1979.

Fittschen, Klaus. *Untersuchungen zum Beginn der Sagendarstellungen bei den Griechen*. Berlin: Hessling, 1969.

Fitzmyer, J. A. *The Aramaic Inscriptions of Sefire*. Rome: Pontifical Biblical Institute, 1967.

Flugel, J. C. *The Psycho-Analytic Study of the Family*. London: The Hogarth Press, 1931.

Fokkelman, J. P. *Narrative Art in Genesis*. Amsterdam: van Gorcum, 1975.

Foley, Helene P. "Review of Slater, *The Glory of Hera*." *Diacritics* 5 (1975): 31–36.

Foley, John Miles. *Oral-Formulaic Theory and Research. An Introduction and Annotated Bibliography*. NY: Garland, 1985.

Ford, O. J. "Regaining the Primordial (Charles Olson as Teacher)." *Athanor* 1 (1971): 52–7.

Fordyce, Christian James. *Catullus: A Commentary.* Oxford: UP, 1961, 1990.

Forke, Alfred. "Ko Hung, der Philosoph und Alchimist." *Archiv für Geschichte der Philosophie* 41 (1932): 115–26.

Forsyth, Neil. "Huwawa and his Trees: A Narrative and Cultural Analysis." *Acta Sumerologica* 3 (1981): 13–29.

Förtsch, Wilhelm. "Der Vater des Gilgameš." *OLZ* 18 (1915): 367–70.

Fossey, J. M., and J. Morin, eds. *Boeotia Antiqua.* Amsterdam: J. C. Gieben, 1989.

Foster, Benjamin. "Ea and Ṣaltu." Ellis. *Essays.* 79–84.

Foster, Benjamin. "Gilgamesh: Sex, Love and the Ascent of Knowledge." *Love and Death in the Ancient Near East, Essays in Honor of Marvin H. Pope.* Ed. John H. Marks and Robert M. Good. Guilford, CT: Four Quarters, 1987. 21–42.

Foster, Benjamin R. "Humor and Cuneiform Literature." *JANES* 6 (1974): 69–85.

Foster, Benjamin R. "OB Gilgamesh Pa i 22." *RA* 77 (1983): 92.

Foster, Benjamin R. "A Postscript to the 'Letter of Gilgamesh.'" *An. St.* 32 (1982): 43–44.

Foster, Benjamin. "Review of Oberhuber, *Das Gilgamesch-Epos.*" *Bi. Or.* 36 (1979): 185–88.

Foster, Benjamin. "Wisdom and the Gods in Ancient Mesopotamia." *Or.* 43 (1974): 344–54.

Foucault, Michel. *This is Not a Pipe.* Tr. James Harkness. Berkeley: U of California P, 1982.

Fox, Michael V., ed. *Temple in Society.* Winona Lake: Eisenbrauns, 1988.

Fraenkel, Hermann F. *Ovid: A Poet between Two Worlds.* Berkeley: U of California P, 1989.

Frank, Carl. "Zur den Wortspielen *kukku* und *kibâti* in Gilg. Ep. XI." *ZA* 36 (1925): 218.

Frankena, Rintje. "Nouveaux fragments de la sixième tablette de l'épopée de Gilgameš." *GSL.* 113–22.

Frankena, Rintje. "The Vassal Treaties of Esarhaddon and the Dating of Deuteronomy." *Oudtestamentliche Studien* 14 (1965): 122–54.

Frankfort, Henri. *Cylinder Seals: A Documentary Essay on the Art and Religion of the Ancient Near East.* London: Macmillan, 1939.

Frankfort, Henri. *Kingship and the Gods.* Chicago: UP, 1948.

Frankfort, Henri, and H. A. Frankfort, eds. *Before Philosophy.* Baltimore: Penguin, 1959.

Frankfort, Henri, and Thorkild Jacobsen. *Stratified Cylinder Seals from the Diyala Region.* Chicago: Oriental Institute, 1955.

Frazer, Sir James George. *Folklore in the Old Testament.* Abridged Ed. New York: Tudor Press, 1923.

Frazer, Sir James George. *The Golden Bough.* One-Volume Ed. NY: Macmillan, 1922.

Frazer, Sir James George. *Myths of the Origin of Fire.* London: Macmillan, 1930.

Freedman, R. David. "The Dispatch of Reconnaisance Birds in Gilgamesh XI." *JANES* 5 (1973): 123–29.

Frenkian, C. M. "L'Épopée de Gilgamesh et les poèmes homériques." *Studies in Ancient Oriental Civilization* 2 (1959): 89–106.

Frenkian, C. M. "Remarks on the Origin of the Gilgamesh Epic." *Studies in Ancient Oriental Civilization* 4 (1962): 91–94.

Friedlander, Israel. *Die Chadhirlegende und der Alexanderroman.* Berlin /Leipzig: B. G. Teubner, 1913.

Friedman, Albert B., ed. *The Viking Book of Folk Ballads of the English-Speaking World.* NY: Viking, 1956.

Friedman, Richard Elliott. *Who Wrote the Bible?* NY: Summit Books, 1987.

Friedman, Shmuel. *Alilot Gilgamesh, Melekh Erekh.* Tel-Aviv: Sh. Friedman, 1992.

Friedrich, Johannes. "Zur Einordnung hethitischer Gilgamesch-Fragmente." *Or.* 30 (1961): 90–91.

Friedrich, Johannes. "Die hethitischen Bruchstücke des Gilgameš-Epos." *ZA* 39 (1930): 1–82.

Friedrich, Johannes. *Hethitisches Wörterbuch.* Heidelberg: Carl Winter Universitätsverlag, 1952.

Friedrich, Johannes. "Hittite Texts of Gilgamesh." *AfO* 15 (1945–51): 105–13.

Friedrich, Johannes. *Kleinasiatische Sprachdenkmäler.* Berlin: W. de Gruyter, 1932. 32–34.

Friedrich, Paul. *The Meaning of Aphrodite.* Chicago: UP, 1978.

Fries, Karl. *Studien zur Odyssee.* Vol. 1. Leipzig: J. C. Hinrichs, 1910.

Fritz, V. "'Solange die Erde steht: Vom Sinn der jahwistischen Fluterzählung in Gen 68." *Zeitschrift für Alttestamentliche Wissenschaft* 94 (1982): 599–614.

Frobenius, Leo. *The Childhood of Man.* Philadelphia: Lippincott, 1909.

Frost, Honor. "Gilgamesh and the 'Things of Stone.'" *Report of the Department of Antiquities, Cyprus* (1984): 96–100.

Frost, Honor. "Stone Anchors as Clue to Bronze Age Trade Routes." *Thracia Pontica* 1 (1982): 85–107.

Frothingham, A. L. "The Cosmopolitan Religion of Tarsus and the Origin of Mithra." *AJA* 22 (1918): 63.

Frymer-Kensky, Tikva. "The Atrahasis Epic and Its Significance for Our Understanding of Genesis 19." *Biblical Archaeology* 40 (1977): 147–55.

Frymer-Kensky, Tikva. "The Ideology of Gender in the Bible and the Ancient Near East." *DUMU-E_2-DUB-BA-A: Studies in Honor of Åke W. Sjöberg.* Ed. Herman Behrens, et al. Philadelphia: University Museum, 1989. 185–91.

Frymer-Kensky, Tikva. "Inanna—The Quintessential Femme Fatale." *Biblical Archaeology Review* 10 (1985): 62–64.

Frymer-Kensky, Tikva. "The Marginalization of the Goddesses." *In the Wake of the Goddesses: Women, Culture and the Biblical Transformation of Pagan Myth.* NY: Free Press, 1992. 70–80, 241–43.

Fulbeck, Jack. *Gilgamesh.* Los Angeles: Deporte Press, 1955.

Furlani, Guiseppe. "L'Epopea di Gilgames come inno all'amacizia." *Belfagor* 1 (1946): 577–89.

Furlani, Giuseppe. "'Das Gilgamesch-Epos,' Eine Einführung." *Miti Babilonesi e Assiri.* Firenze: G. C. Sansoni, 1958. 111–62. rpt. Oberhuber. *Das Gilgamesch-Epos.* 375–433.

Furlani, Giuseppe. "Das Gilgamesch-Epos als Hymnus auf die Freundschaft." *L'Epopea di Gilgameš come inno all'amicizia*; tr. Rudiger Schmitt, rpt. Oberhuber. *Das Gilgamesch-Epos.* 219–36.

Gadd, Cyril John. "Ebeḫ-il and His Basket Seat." *RA* 63 (1969): 1–10.

Gadd, Cyril John. "The Epic of Gilgamesh, Tablet XII." *RA* 30 (1933): 129–143.

Gadd, Cyril John. "The Gilgamesh Epic in Sumerian." *BMQ* 7 (1933): 79–80.

Gadd, Cyril John. *Ideas of Divine Rule in the Ancient Near East.* London: Oxford UP, 1948.

Gadd, Cyril John. "Some Contributions to the Gilgamesh-Epic." *Iraq* 28 (1966): 105–21.

Gadd, Cyril John. *Teachers and Students in the Oldest Schools.* London: U of London, School of Oriental and African Studies, 1956.

Gadd, Cyril John, and Samuel Noah Kramer. *Literary and Religious Texts.* London: British Museum, 1963.

Gagnon, Alain. *Gilgamesh.* Chicoutimi, Quebec: JCL, 1986.

Galtier, Emile. *Mémoires et fragments inédits, réunis et publiés.* Cairo: Imp. l'Institut Français d'archéologie orientale. 1912.

Gammie, John G., and Leo G. Perdue, eds. *The Sage in Israel and the Ancient Near East.* Winona Lake: Eisenbrauns, 1990.

Garbini, G. "Gilgamesh." *Enciclopedia dell'arte antica classica e orientale.* Ed. R. Bianchi Bandinelli. Rome: Istituto della Enciclopedia italiana, 1958–1960. Vol. 3. 895–97.

Gardiner, Sir Alan H. *Egyptian Letters to the Dead.* London: The Egypt Exploration Society, 1928.

Gardner, John. "The Dialogue of the Dead." *The Sunlight Dialogues.* 507–36; selections rpt. Krstović. 340–41.

Gardner, John. *The Sunlight Dialogues.* NY: Alfred A. Knopf, 1972.

Gardner, John, and John Maier. *Gilgamesh, Translated from the Sîn-leqi-unninnī Version*. NY: Knopf, 1984.

Garelli, Paul. "La conception de la beauté en Assyrie." Abusch. *Lingering Over Words*. 173–78.

Garelli, Paul, ed. *Gilgameš et sa légende*. Paris: Imprimerie Nationale and Librarie C. Klincksieck, 1960. = *GSL*

Garneau, Michel. *Gilgamesh*. Montreal: Agence de distribution populaire, 1976.

Garnica, Ana Maria Jimenez. "El fondo religioso de la tabilla VI (El Toro Cellate) del poema de Gilgamesch." *Sefarad* 43 (1983): 27–40. [With English summary].

Garrison, Daniel. *Gilgamesh and Utnapishtim*. Austin, TX: Steck-Vaughn Co., 1994. [Braille].

Gaster, Theodor H(erzl). "Angel." *The Interpreter's Dictionary of the Bible*. Ed. G. A. Buttrick, et al. Vol.1. NY and Nashville: Abingdon, 1962. 128–34.

Gaster, Theodor H. *The Holy and the Profane: Evolution of Jewish Folkways*. 2nd. Ed. NY: Morrow, 1980.

Gaster, Theodor H. *Myth, Legend, and Custom in the Old Testament*. NY: Harper & Row, 1969.

Gaster, Theodor H. "Myth and Story." *Numen* 1 (1954): 184–212; rpt. Dundes. *Sacred Narrative*. 110–36.

Gaster, Theodor H. *The Oldest Stories in the World*. NY: Viking Press, 1952.

Gaster, Theodor H. "Semitic Mythology." *Funk and Wagnall's Standard Dictionary of Folklore, Mythology and Legend*. Ed. Maria Leach. NY: Funk and Wagnall's, 1949–50.

Gaster, Theodor H. *Thespis: Ritual, Myth and Drama in the Ancient Near East*. Rev. Ed. Garden City, NY: Doubleday, 1961.

Gatewood, John B. "A Short Typology of Ethnographic Genres, or Ways to Write About Other Peoples." *Anthropology and Humanism Quarterly* 9 (1984): 5–10.

Gatto, Ettore Lo. *Histoire de la littérature Russe*. Bruges: Desclee de Brouwer, 1965.

Gatz, Bodo. *Weltalter, goldene Zeit und sinnverwandte Vorstellungen.* Hildesheim: G. Olms, 1967.

Geertz, Clifford. *The Interpretation of Culture.* NY: Basic Books, 1973.

Geertz, Clifford. *Local Knowledge: Further Essays on Interpretive Anthropology.* NY: Basic Books, 1983.

Gehring, U., and H. G. Niemeyer, eds. *Die Phönizier im Zeitalter Homers.* Mainz: Zabern, 1990.

Gelb, Ignace Jay, et al., eds. *The Assyrian Dictionary of the Oriental Institute of the University of Chicago.* Chicago: Oriental Institute; Glückstadt, Germany: Augustin, 1956–.= *CAD*

Gelb, Ignace Jay. *Hurrians and Subarians.* Chicago: U of Chicago P, 1944.

Gelb, Ignace Jay. "Introduction." *CAD* I (A). Part I. Chicago: Oriental Institute, 1964. vii–xiii.

Gelb, Ignace Jay. *A Study of Writing.* Chicago: U of Chicago P, 1963.

Gemser, Berend. "Odysseus-Utanapištim." *AfO* 3 (1926): 183–85.

Gennep, Arnold van. *The Rites of Passage.* Chicago: U of Chicago P, 1972.

Genouillac, Henri de. *Fouilles Françaises d'El-Akhymer: Premières recherches archéologiques à Kish.* I. Paris: E. Champion, 1924. N. 174.

George, A. R. "The Day the Earth Divided: a Geological Aetiology in the Babylonian Gilgameš Epic." *ZA* 80 (1990): 214–19.

Geraldo, Nelson. *A caminho de Gilgamesh: Vertigios para a reconstituicao de um bailado.* 2nd. Ed. Lisbon: Estudios Cor, 1967.

Gerard-Rousseau, Monique. *Les mentions religieuses dans les tablettes mycéniennes.* Rome: Edizioni dell'Ateneo, 1968.

Gerhardt, M. I. *The Art of Storytelling: A Literary Study of the 1001 Nights.* Leiden: Brill, 1963.

Gerhart, M, J. P. Healey, and A. M. Russell. "Sublimation of the Goddess in the Deitic Metaphor of Moses." *Semeia* 61 (1993): 167–82.

Germain, Gabriel. *Genèse de l'Odyssée: Le fantastique et le sacré*. Paris: Presses Universitaires de France, 1954.

Gese, Hartmut. "The Idea of History in the Ancient Near East and the Old Testament." *Journal for Theology and the Church* 1 (1965): 134–42.

Gese, Hartmut. *Die Religionen Altsyriens, Altarabiens und der Mandäer*. Stuttgart: W. Kohlhammer, 1970.

Gessain, Robert. *Un Gilgamesh sibero-eskimo*. Paris: Laboratoire d'Anthropologie du Museum National d'Histoire Naturelle, 1986.

Gianfilippi, Gian Franco. *Gilgamesh, romanzo*. Milan: Gastaldi, 1959.

Gibson, Thomas. "The Sharing of Substances versus the Sharing of Activity Among the Buid." *Man* 20 (1985): 392–98.

Gifford, E. H. *Eusebii Pamphili Evangelicae Praeparationis*. Vol. 3, Pt. 1. Oxford: Typographeo Academico, 1903.

Giles, Herbert Allen. *A Chinese Biographical Dictionary*. New York: Paragon Book Gallery, 1898.

Gilgameš. Agyagtablak uzenete. Budapest: Europa Konyvkiado, 1974.

Gilgameš et sa légende. Ed. Paul Garelli. Paris: Imprimerie Nationale, 1960. =*GSL*

Gill, William Wyatt. *Myths and Songs from the South Pacific*. London: H. S. King, 1876.

Ginsberg, H. L., ed. *The Five Megilloth and Jonah*. Philadelphia: Jewish Publication Society, 1969.

Ginsberg, H. L. "The Quintessence of Koheleth." Biblical and Other Studies. Ed. A. Altmann. Cambridge, MA: Harvard UP, 1963. 47–59.

Ginsberg, H. L., tr. "Ugaritic Myths, Epics and Legends." *ANET* 129–55.

Ginzberg, Louis. *The Legends of the Jews*. Philadelphia: The Jewish Publication Society of America, 1911.

Giovannini, Adalberto. *Étude historique sur les origines du catalogue des vaisseaux*. Berne: Francke, 1969.

Gladstone, William Ewart. *Landmarks of Homeric Study*. London: Macmillan, 1890.

Glassner, M. "Mahlzeit." *RLA* 7 (1988): 263–64.

Goddard, Dwight, tr. *Laotzu's Tao and wu-wei.* Santa Barbara: D. Goddard, 1935.

Goedicke, Hans. "Adam's Rib." *Biblical and Related Studies Presented to Samuel Iwry.* Ed. Ann Kort and Scott Morschauwer. Winona Lake, IN: Eisenbrauns, 1985. 73–76.

Goetze, Albrecht, tr. "Hittite Myths, Epics, and Legends." *ANET.* 120–28.

Goetze, Albrecht. "An Incantation against Diseases." *JCS* 9 (1955): 8–18.

Goetze, Albrecht. "Short or Long a? (Notes on Some Akkadian Words)." *Or.* 16 (1947): 239–50.

Goetze, Albrecht, and Selim J. Levy. "Fragment of the Gilgamesh Epic from Megiddo." *Atiqot* 2 (1959): 121–28.

Gold, Penny Shine. *The Lady and the Virgin: Image, Attitude and Experience in Twelfth-Century France.* Chicago: UP, 1985.

Goldin, J. *The Fathers According to Rabbi Nathan.* New Haven: Yale UP, 1955.

Gordis, R. *Koheleth: The Man and His World.* 3rd Ed. NY: Schocken, 1968.

Gordon, Cyrus H. *The Common Background of Greek and Hebrew Civilizations.* 2nd. Ed. NY: Norton, 1962.

Gordon, Cyrus H. "Homer and the Bible. The Origin and Character of East Mediterranean Literature." *HUCA* 26 (1955): 43–108.

Gordon, Cyrus H. *From Mycenae to Homer.* NY: Norton, 1964.

Gordon, Cyrus H. *Ugaritic Literature.* Rome: Pontifical Biblical Institute, 1949.

Gordon, Edmund I. "Mesilim and Mesannipadda—Are They Identical?" *BASOR* 132 (1953): 27–30.

Gordon, Edmund I. "A New Look at the Wisdom of Sumer and Akkad." *Bi. Or.* 17 (1960): 122–52.

Gordon, Edmund I. "The Sumerian Proverb Collections: A Preliminary Report." *JAOS* 74 (1954): 81–85.

Gordon, Edmund I. "Sumerian Proverbs and Fables." *JCS* 12 (1958): 1–21, 43–75.

Gordon, Edmund I. *Sumerian Proverbs: Glimpses of Everyday Life in Ancient Mesopotamia.* Philadelphia: University Museum, U of Pennsylvania, 1959.

Gossmann, P. F., ed. *Das Era-Epos.* Würzburg: Augustinus Verlag, 1956.

Gottwald, Norman K. *The Tribes of Yahweh: A Sociology of the Religion of Liberated Israel 1250–1050 B.C.*. Maryknoll, NY: Orbis, 1979.

Grace, Terry. *Gilgamesh Epic.* Normandale Community College, 1979. [Audio Recording].

Graf, F. "Review of *Catabasis: Vergil and the Wisdom-Tradition.*" *Gnomon* 35 (1981): 545–48.

Grafman, R. "Bringing Tiamat to Earth." *IEJ* 22 (1972): 47–49.

Grant, Michael. *Roman Myth.* London: Weidenfeld and Nicolson, 1971.

Gray, John. *Near Eastern Mythology.* New Rev. Ed. London: Hamlyn, 1982.

Grayson, A. Kirk, tr. "Akkadian Myths and Epics." *ANET*. 501–18; revisions of Speiser, "Akkadian Myths and Epics." *ANET*. 601–19.

Grayson, A. Kirk, and Wilfred G. "Akkadian Prophecies." *JCS* 18 (1964): 730.

Green, Anthony. "Beneficent Spirits and Malevolent Demons: The Iconography of Good and Evil in Ancient Assyria and Babylonia." *Visible Religion* 3 (1984): 80–105.

Green, Margaret W. *Eridu in Sumerian Literature.* Diss., U of Chicago, 1975.

Green, Peter. *Ovid: The Erotic Poems.* Harmondsworth: Penguin, 1988.

Greenberg, Moshe. *Understanding Exodus.* NY: Behrman House, 1969.

Greene, Thomas. *The Descent from Heaven: A Study in Epic Continuity.* New Haven: Yale UP, 1963.

Greenfield, J. C. "Scripture and Inscription." *Near Eastern Studies in Honor of William Foxwell Albright.* Ed. Hans Goedicke. Baltimore: Johns Hopkins UP, 1971. 253–68.

Greengus, Samuel. "Old Babylonian Marriage Ceremonies and Rites." *JCS* 20 (1966).

Greengus, Samuel. "The Old Babylonian Marriage Contract." *JAOS* 89 (1969): 505–32.

Greengus, Samuel. *Old Babylonian Tablets from Ishchali and Vicinity.* Istanbul: Nederlands Historische-Archaeologisch Instituut in Het Nabije Oosten, 1979.

Gresseth, Gerald K. "The Gilgamesh Epic and Homer." *Classical Journal* 70 (1974–75): 1–18.

Gressmann, Hugo. *Altorientalische Texte zum Alten Testament.* 2nd. ed. Berlin/Leipzig: de Gruyter, 1926.

Gressmann, Hugo, and Arthur Ungnad. *Das Gilgamesch-Epos.* Göttingen: Vandenhoeck & Ruprecht, 1911.

Grice, Ettalene Mears. *Chronology of the Larsa Dynasty.* NY: AMS Press, 1980.

Griffin, Jasper. *The Oxford History of the Classical World.* Ed. J. Boardman et al. Oxford/NY: Oxford UP, 1986.

Griffiths, Bill. *The Epic of Gilgamesh. Episode One, Gilgamesh and Enkidu.* Market Drayton, Shropshire: Tern Press, 1992.

Griffiths, Bill. *The Story of the Flood from Gilgamesh.* London: Pirate Press, 1970.

Grimme, H. "Babel und Koheleth-Jojakin." *OLZ* 8 (1905): 432–38.

Groneberg, Brigitte. "Die sumerisch-akkadische Inanna/Ištar: Hermaphroditos?" *WO* 17 (1986): 25–46.

Groneberg, Brigitte. "TILPĀNU = Bogen." *RA* 81 (1987): 115–24.

Groneberg, Brigitte. *Untersuchungen zum Hymnisch-epischen Dialekt der altbabylonischen literarischen Texte.* Diss., Munster, 1972.

Grottanelli, C. "Horatius, i Curiatii e II Sam. 2, 12–28." *Annali dell'Istituto Orientale di Napoli* 35 (1975): 547–54.

Grube, Wilhelm, and Herbert Mueller, tr. *Feng-Shu-Yen-I. Die Metamorphosen der Götter.* Leiden: E. J. Brill, 1912.

Grunebaum, G. E. von. *Medieval Islam.* 2nd. Ed. Chicago: UP, 1953.

Gruppe, O. *Die griechischen Kulte und Mythen in ihren Beziehungen zu den orientalischen Religionen.* Vol. 1. Leipzig, 1887.

Guillaud, Lauric. *L'aventure mystérieuse de Poe à Merrit ou l'Orphelin de Gilgamesh.* Liège: Ed. du CEFAL, 1993.

Gumilew, N. S. *Gilgamesh, Vavilonskii Epos.* St. Petersburg: Izd. Z. I. Grzhebina, 1919.

Gundel, Wilhelm. *Neue astrologische Texte des Hermes Trismegistos.* Munich: Verlag der Bayerischen Akademie der Wissenschaften, 1936.

Gundel, Wilhelm. *De Stellarum Appellatione et Religione Romana. RE* s.v. Scorpius, p. 602.

Gunderson, Lloyd. "The Human Situation and its Religious Implications." *Discourse* 7 (1964): 357–80.

Gundlach, Susan. "Gilgamesh: The Quest for Immortality." *Calliope: World History for Young People* 3 (1991): 7–12.

Gunkel, Hermann. "Jensens Gilgamesch-Epos in der Weltliteratur." *Deutsche Literaturzeitung* 30 (1909): 90–111; rpt. Oberhuber. *Das Gilgamesch Epos.* 74–84.

Gunkel, Hermann. *Schöpfung und Chaos in Urzeit und Endzeit.* Göttingen: Vandenhoeck & Ruprecht, 1895.

Gunn, James E. *The Road to Science Fiction.* NY: New American Library, 1977.

Gurdjieff, G. I. *Meetings with Remarkable Men.* NY: E. P. Dutton, 1969.

Gurney, Oliver R. "The Assyrian Tablets from Sultantepe." *Proceedings of the British Academy* 41 (1956): 21–41.

Gurney, Oliver R. "Gilgamesh XI 78." *RA* 75 (1981): 189.

Gurney, Oliver. R. *The Hittites.* Baltimore: Penguin, 1966.

Gurney, Oliver R. *Some Aspects of Hittite Religion.* Oxford: UP, 1977.

Gurney, Oliver R. "The Sultantepe Tablets (continued). 4. The Cuthaean Legend of Naram-Sin." *An. St.* 5 (1955): 93–113; 6 (1956): 145–64.

Gurney, Oliver R. "The Sultantepe Tablets (continued). 6. A Letter of Gilgamesh." *An. St.* 7 (1957): 127–35.

Gurney, Oliver R. "Two Fragments of the Epic of Gilgamesh from Sultantepe." *JCS* 8 (1954): 87–95.

Gurney, Oliver R., and Jacob J. Finkelstein, *The Sultantepe Tablets.* Vol. 1. London: British Institute of Archaeology at Ankara, 1957.

Gurney, O. R., and Samuel Noah Kramer. "Two Fragments of Sumerian Laws." *Studies in Honor of B. Landsberger.* Chicago: U of Chicago P, 1965. 14.

Gustavs, A. "Das giku(g) der Diorit-Platte Ur-Ninas." *AfO* 8 (1932): 53–54.

Güterbock, Hans Gustav. "Die historische Tradition und ihre literarische Gestaltung bei Babyloniern und Hethitern bis 1200." *ZA* 42 (1934): 1–91; 44 (1938): 451–49.

Güterbock, Hans Gustav. "Hittite Mythology." Kramer. *Mythologies of the Ancient World.* Garden City, NY: Doubleday, 1961. 139–79.

Güterbock, Hans Gustav. "The Song of Ullikumi. Revised Text of the Hittite Version of a Hurrian Myth." *JCS* 5 (1951): 135–61; 6 (1952): 8–42.

Güterbock, Hans Gustav, and Thorkild Jacobsen, eds. *Studies in Honor of Benno Landsberger.* Chicago: U of Chicago P, 1965.

Guthrie, William Keith Chambers. *A History of Greek Philosophy.* 6 Vols. Cambridge: UP, 1981.

Haas, Volkert. *Hethitische Berggötter und hurritische Steindämonen.* Mainz on Rhein: P. von Zabern, 1982.

Haas, Volkert. *Magie und Mythen in Babylonien.* Gifkendorf: Merlin Verlag, 1986.

Haas, Volkert, and G. Wilhelm. *Hurritische und luwische Riten aus Kizzuwatna.* Kevelaer/Neukirchen-Vluyn: Butzon & Bercker/Neukirchener Verlag, 1974.

Häfker, Hermann. *Gilgamesch. Eine Dichtung aus Babylon.* Munich: G. D. W. Callwey, 1924.

Häfker, Hermann. "Zum Verständnis des Gilgamesch-Epos." *Gilgamesch. Eine Dichtung aus Babylon.* 78–90; rpt. Oberhuber. *Das Gilgamesch-Epos.* 138–45.

Haigh, A. E. *The Attic Theatre.* 3rd. Ed. (revised and in part rewritten by A. W. Pickard-Cambridge). Oxford: Clarendon Press, 1907.

Halbreich, Harry. *Bohuslav Martinu.* Zurich: Atlantis-Verlag, 1968.

Hallo, William W. "Antediluvian Cities." *JCS* 23 (1970–71): 57–67.

Hallo, William W. "On the Antiquity of Sumerian Literature." *JAOS* 83 (1963): 167–76.

Hallo, William W. "Beginning and End of the Sumerian King List in the Nippur Recension." *JCS* 17 (1963): 52–57.

Hallo, William W. "The Coronation of Ur-Nammu." *JCS* 20 (1966): 133–41.

Hallo, William W. "The Cultic Setting of Sumerian Poetry." *Actes de la 17e rencontre assyriologique internationale.* Ham-sur-Heure, Belgium: Comité Belge de Recherches en Mesopotamie, 1970. 116–34.

Hallo, William W. "The Date of the Fara Period: A Case Study in the Historiography of Early Mesopotamia." *Or.* 42 (1973): 228–38.

Hallo, William W. "Toward a History of Sumerian Literature." *AS* 20 (1976): 181–203.

Hallo, William W. "Individual Prayer in Sumerian: The Continuity of a Tradition." *JAOS* 88 (1968): 71–89.

Hallo, William W. "The Lame and the Halt." *EI* 9 (1969): 66–70.

Hallo, William W. "Lugalbanda Excavated." *JAOS* 103 (1983): 165–80.

Hallo, William W. "New Hymns to the Kings of Isin." *Bi. Or.* 23 (1966): 239–47.

Hallo, William W. "New Viewpoints on Cuneiform Literature." *IEJ* 12 (1962): 13–26.

Hallo, William W. "The Royal Inscriptions of Ur: A Typology." *HUCA* 33 (1962): 1–43.

Hallo, William W. "Sumerian Literature: Background to the Bible." *Bible Review* (June, 1988): 28–38.

Hallo, William W. "The Women of Sumer." *The Legacy of Sumer.* Ed. Denise Schmandt-Besserat. Malibu: Undena, 1976. 23–40.

Hallo, William W., and J. J. A. van Dijk. *The Exaltation of Inanna.* New Haven: Yale UP, 1968.

Hallo, William W., and William L. Moran. "The First Tablet of the SB Recension of the Anzu Myth." *JCS* 31 (1969): 65–115.

Hallo, William W., and W. K. Simpson. *The Ancient Near East: A History*. NY: Harcourt Brace Jovanovich, 1971.

Halperin, David M. "Heroes and their Pals." *One Hundred Years of Homosexuality*. NY: Routledge, 1990. 75–87.

Hamburger, Michael, ed. and tr. *Friedrich Hölderlin: Poems and Fragments*. Ann Arbor: U of Michigan P, 1967.

Hamilton, Edith. *Mythology*. NY: Mentor, 1940.

Hamilton, Edith. *The Roman Way*. NY: Norton, 1932.

Hamilton, Leonidas Le Cenci. *Ishtar and Izdubar. The Epic of Babylon*. London/New York: W. H. Allen and Co., 1884; rpt. *Babylonian and Assyrian Literature*. Ed. Epiphanius Wilson. NY: P. F. Collier, 1901. 31–58.

Hammond, Dorothy, and Alta Jablow. "Gilgamesh and the Sundance Kid: The Myth of Male Friendship." *The Making of Masculinities: The New Men's Studies.* Ed. Harry Brod. Boston: Allen and Unwin, 1987. 241–58.

Hampe, Roland. *Frühe griechische Sagenbilder in Böotien*. Athens: Deutsches Archaologisches Institut, 1981.

Handler, Richard, and Daniel Segal. "Narrating Multiple Realities: Some Lessons from Jane Austen for Ethnographers." *Anthropology and Humanism Quarterly* 9 (1984): 15–21.

Hansman, J. "Gilgamesh, Humbaba, and the Land of the Erin-Trees." *Iraq* 38 (1976): 23–35.

Harding, Mitchell. *The Epic of Gilgamesh*. Berkeley: Pacifica Tape Library, 1960. [Audio Recording].

Hardman, Paul D. *Homo-affectionalism: Male Bonding from Gilgamesh to the Present*. San Francisco: GLB Publishers, 1993.

Harper, Edward T. "The Legend of Etan-Gilgamos and His Kindred in Folklore." *The Academy* 995 (1891): 515–16.

Harrell, John. *A Storyteller's Omnibus*. Kensington, CA: York House, 1985.

Harris, Mark. *Bang the Drum Slowly*. NY: Dell, 1973.

Harris, Rivkah. *Ancient Sippar*. Istanbul: Nederlands Historisch-Archaeologisch Instituut te Istanbul, 1975.

Harris, Rivkah. "The Female 'Sage' in Mesopotamian Literature." Gammie. 3–17.

Harris, Rivkah. "Images of Women in the Gilgamesh Epic." Abusch. *Lingering Over Words.* 219–30.

Harris, Stephen L. *The Humanist Tradition in World Literature: An Anthology of Masterpieces from Gilgamesh to The Divine Comedy.* Columbus, OH: Merrill, 1970.

Harrison, Jane Ellen. *Prolegomena to the Study of Greek Religion.* 3rd. Ed. Cambridge: UP, 1922.

Hastings, James, ed. *Encyclopedia of Religion and Ethics.* Vol. 10. NY: Charles Scribners Sons, 1951.

Haupt, Paul. *Das Babylonische Nimrodepos.* Leipzig: Hinrichs, 1884.

Haupt, Paul. "The Beginning of the Babylonian Nimrod Epic." *JAOS* 22 (1901): 1–6.

Haupt, Paul. "Circe and Astarte." *JAOS* 38 (1918): 332.

Haupt, Paul. "Ištar's Azure Necklace." *BA* 10 (1927): 96–106.

Haupt, Paul. "The Partitions of the Ark." *Johns Hopkins University Circular* 325 (1920): 27–29.

Haupt, Paul. "Philological and Linguistic Studies." *American Journal of Philology* 46 (1925): 197–212.

Haupt, Paul. "The Rainbow after the Deluge." *JAOS* 41 (1921): 181.

Haupt, Paul. "Restoration of Line 127 of the Flood-tablet." *JAOS* 46 (1926): 344.

Haupt, Paul. "The Ship of the Babylonian Noach, and other Papers." *BA* 10 (1927): xxii + 281 pp.

Haupt, Paul. "On Two Passages of the Chaldean Flood-Tablet." *Proceedings of the American Oriental Society* (1894): 105–11.

Haupt, Paul. "The Volcano in Engidu's Dream." *JAOS* 38 (1918): 336.

Haupt, Paul. "Die XII. Tafel des babylonischen Nimrod-Epos." *BA* 1 (1890): 48–80, 94.

Hays, H. R. *The Dangerous Sex: The Myth of Feminine Evil.* NY: G. P. Putnam's Sons, 1964.

Hecker, Karl. *Untersuchungen zur akkadischen Epik*. Kevelaer: Butzon & Bercker; Neukirchen-Vluyn: Neukirchener Verlag, 1974.

Hecker, Karl. "Untersuchungen zur akkadischen Metrik." *AOAT* 8 (1974): 113–35.

Heidegger, Martin. *Being and Time*. Tr. John Macquarrie and Edward Robinson. NY: Harper and Row, 1962.

Heidegger, Martin. *Poetry, Language, Thought*. Tr. Albert Hofstadter. NY: Harper and Row, 1971.

Heidel, Alexander. *The Babylonian Genesis*. Chicago: U of Chicago P, 1942; 2nd. Ed., 1965.

Heidel, Alexander. *The Gilgamesh Epic and Old Testament Parallels*. Chicago: UP, 1949; 2nd. ed. 1963.

Heidel, Alexander. "A Neo-Babylonian Gilgamesh Fragment." *JNES* 11 (1952): 140–43.

Heimpel, Wolfgang. "A Note on 'Gilgamesh and Agga.'" *JCS* 33 (1981): 242–43.

Heimpel, Wolfgang. "The Sun at Night and the Doors of Heaven in Babylonian Texts." *JCS* 38 (1986): 127–51.

Heimpel, Wolfgang. *Tierbilder in der sumerischen Literatur*. Rome: Biblical Institute Press, 1968.

Heinimann, Felix. *Nomos und Physis*. Darmstadt: Wissenschaftliche Buchgesellshaft, 1987.

Heintz, J.G. *Figurative Language in the Ancient Near East*. London: Akkadica 37, 1984.

Helck, Wolfgang. *Die Beziehungen Aegyptens und Vorderasiens zur Äegäis: bis ins 7. Jahrhundert vor Chr*. Darmstadt: Wissenschaftliche Buchgesellschaft, 1979.

Held, George F. "Parallels between The Gilgamesh Epic and Plato's Symposium." *JNES* 42 (1983): 133–41.

Held, Moshe. "A Faithful Lover in an Old Babylonian Dialogue." *JCS* 15 (1961): 1–26.

Hendel, R. S. "Of Demigods and the Deluge: Toward an Interpretation of Genesis 6: 14." *JBL* 106 (1987): 13–26.

Henning, W. B. "The Book of the Giants." *BSOAS* 11 (1943): 52–74.

Henning, W. B. "Ein manichäisches Henochbuch." *SOAW* (1934): 1–11.

Henning, W. B. "Soghdische Miszellen." *BSOS* 8 (1935–37): 583.

Henry, Teuira. *Ancient Tahiti: Based on Material Recorded by J. M. Orsmond.* Honolulu/NY: Kraus Reprint, 1971.

Henshaw, Richard A. *Female and Male. The Cultic Personnel. The Bible and the Rest of the Ancient World.* Allison Park, PA: Pickwick Publications, 1994.

Hermann, W. "Das Todesgeschick als Problem in Altisrael." *MIO* 16 (1970): 14–32.

Herodotus. *The Persian Wars.* Tr. George Rawlinson. NY: Random House, 1942.

Hesiod. *Works and Days.* Indianapolis: Hackett, 1993.

Heubeck, Alfred. "Betrachtungen zur Genesis des homerischen Epos." *GSL.* 185–92.

Heubeck, Alfred. *Die Homerische Frage.* Darmstadt: Wissenschaftliche Buchgesellschaft, 1988.

Hilion, G. *Le Déluge dans la Bible et les inscriptions akkadiennes et sumériennes.* Paris: P. Geuthner, 1925.

Hiltebeitel, Alf. "Rāma and Gilgamesh: The Sacrifice of the Water Buffalo and the Bull of Heaven." *History of Religions* 19 (1980): 187–223.

Himmelfarb, Martha. *Tours of Hell. An Apocalyptic Form in Jewish and Christian Literature.* Philadelphia: U of Pennsylvania P, 1983.

Hirsch, Hans. "Die Akkadischen Gilgameš-Überlieferungen." *Kindlers Literatur Lexikon.* Zurich: Kindler, 1992.

Hirsch, Hans. "Akkadische Grammatik—Erörterungen und Fragen." *Or.* 44 (1975): 245–322.

Hirsch, Hans. "Akkadische Streitgespräche." *Kindlers Literatur Lexikon.* Zurich: Kindler, 1974.

Hirsch, Hans. "The Prince and the Pauper." *AfO* 35 (1988): 109–10.

Hoberum, Barry. "George Smith (1840–1876): Pioneer Assyriologist." *Biblical Archaeologist* 46 (1983): 41–42.

Hodges, Elizabeth Jamison. *A Song for Gilgamesh.* NY: Atheneum, 1971.

Hoekstra, A. *Epic Verse before Homer. Three Studies.* Amsterdam: North Holland Publishers, 1981.

Höfer, O. "Seuechoros." *Ausführliches Lexikon der griechischen und römischen Mythologie.* Ed. W. H. Roscher. Leipzig: Teubner, 1909–15; rpt. Hildesheim and NY: Olms, 1977. Vol. 4, col. 789.

Hoffner, Harry A. "The ARZANA House." *Anatolian Studies Presented to Hans Gustav Güterbock.* Ed. K. Bittel, et al. Istanbul: Nederlands Historische-Archaeologisch Instituut in Het Nabije Oosten, 1974. 113–21.

Hoffner, Harry A., Jr. "Enki's Command to Atrahasis." Eichler. *Kramer Anniversary.* 241–45.

Hoffner, Harry A., Jr. "A Hittite Analogue to the David and Goliath Contest of Champions?" *CBQ* 30 (1968): 220–25.

Hoffner, Harry A., Jr. "Remarks on the Hittite Version of the Naram-Sin Legend." *JCS* 23 (1970–71): 17–22.

Hoffner, Harry A. "Symbols for Masculinity and Femininity: Their Use in Ancient Near Eastern Sympathetic Magic Rituals." *JBL* 85 (1966): 326–34.

Holmberg, Uno. *Die religiösen Vorstellungen der altaischen Völker.* Tr. E. Kunze. Helsinki: Folklore Fellows Communications, 1938.

Holscher, U. "Anaximander und der Anfang der Philosophie." *Hermes* 81 (1953): 257–77, 385–418.

Homer. *The Iliad.* Tr. Richard Lattimore. Chicago: U of Chicago P, 1951.

Homer. *The Iliad.* Tr. E. V. Rieu. Harmondsworth: Penguin, 1950.

Homer. *Odyssey.* Tr. Richard Lattimore. NY: Harper and Row, 1975.

Homer. *The Odyssey.* Tr. Walter Schewring. Oxford: UP, 1980.

Hommel, Fritz. *Ethnologie und Geographie des Alten Orients.* Munich: C. H. Beck, 1926.

Hommel, Fritz. "Gish-dubarra, Gibil-gamish, Nimrod." *PSBA* (1893): 291–300.

Hommel, Fritz. *Die Schwur-Göttin Esch-Ghanna und ihr Kreis.* Munich: C. H. Beck, 1912.

Hommel, Fritz. "A Supplementary Note to Gibil-gamish." *PSBA* (1893–94): 13–15.

Honigman, John J. "The Personal Approach in Cultural Anthropological Research." *Current Anthropology* (1976): 243–61.

Hooke, Samuel Henry. *Babylonian and Assyrian Religion.* London: Hutchinson's University Library, 1953.

Hooke, Samuel Henry. *Middle Eastern Mythology.* Baltimore: Penguin, 1963.

Horovitz, Josef. "Buluqja." *ZDMG* 55 (1901): 519–25.

Hoskisson, P. "Emar as an Empirical Model of the Transmission of Canon." *The Bible Canon in Comparative Perspective: Scripture in Context IV.* Ed. K. Lawon Younger, Jr., W. W. Hallo, and B. Batto. Lewiston, NY: Edwin Mellen Press, 1991. 21–32.

Hospers, J. H. *Gilgamesj: de elfde zang: de zondvloed en het levenskruid.* Utrecht: De Roos, 1985.

Howald, Ernst. *Die Sieben gegen Theben. Rektoratsrede.* Zurich: Art. Institut Orel Fussli, 1939.

Hrozný, Bedřich. "Hittite and Hurrian Fragments from Bogazkoi." *KBo* 6 (1921): N. 30–33.

Hrozný, Bedřich. "Le nom et la caractère de Gilgameš." *CRRAI* (1938): 114–18.

Hruška, B. "Acte und neue Streiflichter zur Gestalt 'Gilgameš.'" *Ar. Or.* 50 (1982): 347–50.

Hruška, B. "Das spätbabylonische Lehrgedicht 'Inannas Erhöhung.'" *Or.* 37 (1969): 473–522.

Huffmon, H. B. *Amorite Personal Names in the Mari Texts.* Baltimore: Johns Hopkins UP, 1965.

Humez, Alexander, and Nicholas Humez. *The Life of Bongo Bill.* Cambridge, MA: Titanic, 1976. [Audio Recording].

Hummelauer, Franz von. *Altbabylonische Sagen.* Freiburg im Breisgau: 1876.

Hunger, Hermann. *Babylonische und assyrische Kolophone.* Kevelaer: Verlag Butzon & Bercker; Neukirchen-Vluyn: Neukirchener Verlag, 1968.

Hunger, Hermann. *Spätbabylonische Texte aus Uruk.* Vol. 1. Berlin: Gebr. Mann, 1976.

Hurston, Zora Neale. *Dust Tracks on a Road.* NY: Arno Press and The New York Times, 1969.

Hurwitz, Siegmund. *Lilith, die erste Eva.* Zurich: Daimon Verlag, 1980.

Hymes, Dell. "Ethnopoetics, Oral-Formulaic Theory, and Editing Texts." *Oral Tradition* 9 (1994): 330–70.

Hymes, Dell. *Reinventing Anthropology.* NY: Vintage, 1974.

Indy, Vincent D'. *Istar: Variations symphoniques, op. 42.* Paris: Durand, 1897. [Musical Score].

Ingalls, Jeremy. "The Epic Tradition: I, II, and III." *East-West Review* 1, Nos. 1, 2, 3 (Spring, 1964; Autumn, 1964; Spring, 1965): 42–69; 173–211; 271–305.

Inglott, Peter Serracino. "The Structure of the Gilgamesh Epic." *Melita Theologica* 17 (1965): 1–19; rpt. Valletta, Malta: Royal University Students' Theological Association, 1965.

Ingpen, Robert R., and Barbara Hayes. *Folk Tales and Fables of the Middle East and Africa.* NY: Chelsea House, 1994.

Jackson, Danny P., tr. *The Epic of Gilgamesh.* Wauconda, IL: Bolchazy-Carducci, 1992.

Jackson, W. T. H. *The Hero and the King: An Epic Theme.* NY: Columbia UP, 1982.

Jacobs, J. "Jus Primae Noctis." *The Jewish Encyclopedia.* Ed. I. Singer. NY/London: Funk & Wagnalls, 1904. 7: 395.

Jacobs, Robert G. "Gilgamesh: The Sumerian Epic that Helped Lord Jim to Stand Alone." *Conradiana* 4 (1972): 23–32.

Jacobsen, Thorkild. "Ancient Mesopotamian Religion: The Central Concerns." *Cuneiform Studies and the History of Civilization.* Philadelphia: American Philosophical Society, 1963.

Jacobsen, Thorkild. "The Battle Between Marduk and Tiamat." *JAOS* 88 (1968): 104–108.

Jacobsen, Thorkild. "Death in Ancient Mesopotamia." Alster. *Death in Mesopotamia.* 19–24.

Jacobsen, Thorkild. "Early Political Development in Mesopotamia." *ZA* 52 (1957): 91–140.

Jacobsen, Thorkild. "The Eridu Genesis." *JBL* 100 (1981): 513–29.

Jacobsen, Thorkild. "The Gilgamesh Epic: Tragic and Romantic Vision." Abusch. *Lingering Over Words.* 231–50.

Jacobsen, Thorkild. *The Harab Myth.* Malibu: Undena, 1984.

Jacobsen, Thorkild. *The Harps that Once: Sumerian Poetry in Translation.* New Haven: Yale UP, 1987.

Jacobsen, Thorkild. "How Did Gilgameš Oppress Uruk?" *Ac. Or.* 8 (1930): 62–74.

Jacobsen, Thorkild. "The Inscription of Takil-ili-su of Malgium." *AfO* 12 (1937–39): 363–66.

Jacobsen, Thorkild. "Mesopotamia." *The Intellectual Adventure of Ancient Man.* Ed. H. Frankfort and H. A. Frankfort. Chicago: UP, 1947; rpt. as *Before Philosophy.* Baltimore: Penguin, 1959, 137–234.

Jacobsen, Thorkild. "Mesopotamian Religion: An Overview." *Encyclopedia of Religion.* 9: 447–69.

Jacobsen, Thorkild. "New Sumerian Literary Texts." *BASOR* 102 (1946): 12–17.

Jacobsen, Thorkild. "Notes on Nintur." *Or.* 42 (1973): 274–98.

Jacobsen, Thorkild. "Notes on Selected Sayings," and "Additional Notes (1959)." Gordon. *Sumerian Proverbs.* 447–87, 547–50.

Jacobsen, Thorkild. "Parerga Sumerologica." *JNES* 2 (1943): 117–21.

Jacobsen, Thorkild. "Pictures and Pictorial Language (The Burney Relief)." Mindlin. *Figurative.* 1–11.

Jacobsen, Thorkild. "Primitive Democracy in Ancient Mesopotamia." *JNES* 2 (1943): 165–74.

Jacobsen, Thorkild. "Second Millennium Metaphors. 'And Death the Journey's End': *The Gilgamesh Epic.*" *The Treasures of Darkness.* 195–219.

Jacobsen, Thorkild. "The Stele of the Vultures, Col. IX." Eichler. *Kramer Anniversary Volume.* 247–59.

Jacobsen, Thorkild. *The Sumerian King List.* Chicago: U of Chicago P, 1939.

Jacobsen, Thorkild. "Sumerian Mythology: A Review Article." *JNES* 5 (1946): 128–52.

Jacobsen, Thorkild. *The Treasures of Darkness: A History of Mesopotamian Religion.* New Haven: Yale UP, 1976.

Jacobsen, Thorkild. *Toward the Image of Tammuz and Other Essays.* Ed. W. L. Moran. Cambridge, MA: Harvard UP, 1970.

Jacobsen, Thorkild, and Samuel Noah Kramer. "The Myth of Inanna and Bilulu." *JNES* 12 (1953): 160–88.

Jacoby, F. *Die Fragmente der griechischen Historiker.* Pt. 3C. *Autoren über einzelne Länder.* 2 Vols. Leiden: Brill, 1958.

Jager, Bernd. "The Gilgamesh Epic: A Phenomenological Exploration." *Review of Existential Psychology and Psychiatry.* 12 (1973): 1–43.

Jager, Bernd. "The Three Dreams of Descartes." *Review of Existential Psychology and Psychiatry* 8 (1968).

Jamieson, Donald G., and Myron G. Schimpf. "Self-Generated Images Are More Effective Mnemonics." *Journal of Mental Imagery* 4 (1980): 25–33.

Jankelevitch, Vladimir. *L'aventure, l'ennui, le sérieux.* Paris: Aubier, 1963.

Janko, Richard. *The Iliad: A Commentary.* Vol. 4. Cambridge: UP, 1992.

Jaritz, Kurt. *Babylon und seine Welt.* Bern: Francke, 1964.

Jaritz, Kurt. *Geheimschriftsysteme im Alten Orient.* Graz: Akademische Druck- u. Verlagsanstalt, 1966.

Jaritz, Kurt. *Schamanistisches im Gilgamesh-Epos.* Baden-Baden: Akademische Verlag, 1971.

Jason, Heda, and Dmitri Segal, eds. *Patterns in Oral Literature.* The Hague: Mouton, 1977.

Jastrow, Marcus. *A Dictionary of the Targumim, The Talmud Babli and Yerushalmi, and the Midrashic Literature.* 2 Vols. NY: Pardes, 1950.

Jastrow, Morris. "Adam and Eve in Babylonian Literature." *AJSL* 15 (1899): 193–214.

Jastrow, Morris. "Adraḫasis and Parnapištim." *ZA* 13 (1898): 288–301.

Jastrow, Morris. *Aspects of Religious Belief and Practice in Babylonia and Assyria.* rpt. NY: Benjamin Blom, 1971.

Jastrow, Morris. "On the Composite Character of the Babylonian Creation Story." *Orientalische Studien Theodor Nöldeke.* Ed. C. Bezold. Giezen: Toplemann, 1906. 2: 969–82.

Jastrow, Morris. "Gilgamesh and Enkidu." *JAOS* 38 (1918): 3–32.

Jastrow, Morris. "Introduction." *An Old Babylonian Version of the Gilgamesh Epic.* 9–60; selections rpt. Krstović. 303–309.

Jastrow, Morris. "The New Version of the Babylonian Account of the Deluge." *The Independent* 2567 (1898): 67; 2568 (1898): 78.

Jastrow, Morris. *The Religion of Babylonia and Assyria.* Boston: Ginn, 1898; *Die Religion Babyloniens und Assyriens.* Giessen: J. Ricker, 1905–1912.

Jastrow, Morris. "Sumerian Myths of Beginnings." *AJSL* 33 (1916): 107–120.

Jastrow, Morris, and A. T. Clay. *An Old Babylonian Version of the Gilgamesh Epic.* New Haven: Yale UP, 1920.

Jaynes, Julian. *The Origin of Consciousness in the Breakdown of the Bicameral Mind.* Boston: Houghton Mifflin, 1976.

Jean, Charles-François. "L'Origine des choses d'après la traduction sumérienne de Nippur." *RA* 26 (1929): 33–38.

Jeffery, Lilian Hamilton. *Archaic Greece. The City-states c. 700–500 B.C.* London/Tunbridge: Methuen, 1976.

Jensen, Hans Jørgen Lundager. "Gilgameš-epet: Kosmologie og antropologi." *Religionsvidenskabeligit Tidsskrift* 2 (1983): 57–84.

Jensen, Peter Christian Albrecht. *Assyrisch-Babylonische Mythen und Epen.* Berlin: Reuther & Reichard, 1900–01.

Jensen, Peter Christian Albrecht. "Aussetzungsgeschichten." *RLA* 1: 322–24.

Jensen, Peter Christian Albrecht. "Das babylonische Nationalepos, judäische Nationalsagen, Ilias und Odysse." *Verhandlungen der 55. Versamml. deutscher Philologen und Schulermänner in Erlangen 1925.* Leipzig: Eduard Pfeiffer, 1926. 28–29.

Jensen, Peter Christian Albrecht. "Der babylonische Sintflutheld und seiner Schiff in der israelitischen Gilgamesch-Sage." *Orientalische Studies Th. Nöldeke gewidmet.* Vol. 2. Giessen: J. Ricker, 1906. 983–96.

Jensen, Peter Christian Albrecht. "Entgegnung auf den Artikel *Moses, Jesus und Gilgamesch* von Herrn Pastor Cordes in dieser Zeitung vom 8. April 1909." *Volksblatt für Harburg, Wilhelmsburg und Umgegend* 102 (1909).

Jensen, Peter Christian Albrecht. "Die Entrückung des babylonischen Sintfluthelden zum Götterlande in einem indisch-deutsche Gilgamesch-Märchen vom Himmelreich." *MAOG* 4 (1928–29): 99–107.

Jensen, Peter Christian Albrecht. "Gilgamesch. Ein Beitrag zur Bibelforschung." *Frankfurter Zeitung*. 50 and 51 (February 1920, 1909).

Jensen, Peter Christian Albrecht. *Gilgamesh-Epos, Judäische Nationalsagen, Ilias und Odyssee.* Leipzig: Eduard Pfeiffer, 1924.

Jensen, Peter Christian Albrecht. "Gilgamesch und die geschichtliche Existenz Jesu. Kontroverse von Professor P. Jensen (Marburg i. H.) gegen Professor Schmiedel (Zürich)." *Beilage zum "Schweizerischen Protestantenblatt."* 22 (May 29, 1909).

Jensen, Peter Christian Albrecht. "Das Gilgamiš-Epos und Homer. Vorläufige Mitteilung." *ZA* 16 (1902): 125–34.

Jensen, Peter Christian Albrecht. "Das Gilgamiš-Epos in der israelitischen Legende. Eine vorläufige Mitteilung." *ZA* 16 (1902): 406–12.

Jensen, Peter Christian Albrecht. *Das Gilgamesch-Epos in der Weltliteratur*. I. *Die Urpsrünge der alttestamentlichen Patriarchen, Propheten, und Befrier-Sage in der neutestamentlichen Jesus-Sage.* Strassburg: Verlag von Karl J. Trubner, 1906–28; II. *Die israelitischen Gilgamesch-Sagen in den Sagen der Weltliteratur.* Marburg: A. Ebel, 1929.

Jensen, Peter Christian Albrecht. "Zum 'Gilgamesch-Epos in der Weltliteratur.' Zwei Fragen an Professor V. Christian." *ZA* 39 (1930): 294–97.

Jensen, Peter Christian Albrecht. "Gišgimaš (= Gilgamiš) ein Kossäer?" *ZA* 6 (1891): 340–42.

Jensen, Peter Christian Albrecht. *Hat der Jesus der Evangelien wirklich gelebt? Eine Antwort an Prof. Dr. Julicher.* Frankfurt a. M.: Neuer Frankfurter Verlag, 1910.

Jensen, Peter Christian Albrecht. *Moses, Jesus, Paulus. Drei Sagenvarianten des babylonischen Gott-Menschen Gilgamesch.* 2nd. Ed. Frankfurt a. M.: Neuer Frankfurter Verlag, 1909; 3rd. Ed. Frankfurt a. M.: Neuer Frankfurter Verlag, 1910.

Jensen, Peter Christian Albrecht. "Moses, Jesus, Paulus. Erwiderung auf die Kritik des Herrn Gustav Wörpel." *Kieler Zeitung 25727 and 25729* (February 24–25, 1910).

Jensen, Peter Christian Albrecht. "Nachträge zu meinen Thesen über die griechischen Gilgamiš-Sagen." *ZA* 16 (1902): 413–14.

Jensen, Peter Christian Albrecht. "Noch einmal Moses, Jesus und Gilgamesch." *Arbeiter-Zeitung. Sozialdem. Tagblatt für die Kontone Zürich und Thurgau.* 67 and 70 (March 20 and 24, 1909).

Jensen, Peter Christian Albrecht. "Review of Jastrow and Clay, *An Old Babylonian Version of the Gilgamesh Epic*." *OLZ* 24 (1921): 268–70.

Jensen, Peter Christian Albrecht. "Review of R. C. Thompson, *The Epic of Gilgamesh: A New Translation*." *OLZ* 32 (1929): 643–53.

Jensen, Peter Christian Albrecht. "Im Streit um Gilgamesch." *Frankfurter Zeitung* 215 (August 5, 1909).

Jensen, Peter Christian Albrecht. "Zur Vorgeschichte des Gilgameš-Epos." *Festschrift Eduard Sachau zum 70. Geburtstage.* Ed. Gotthold Weil. Berlin: Vereinigung Wissenschaftlicher Verleger, 1915. 72–86. rpt. Oberhuber. *Das Gilgamesch-Epos.* 85–103.

Jensen, Peter Christian Albrecht. "Wider Herrn Professor Kohler in Nr. 77 der Arbeiter-Zeitung." *Arbeiter-Zeitung* 84 and 86 (April 10 and 14, 1909).

Jeremias, Alfred. *Babylonsiche Dichtungen, Epen und Legenden.* Leipzig: J. C. Hinrichs, 1925.

Jeremias, Alfred. *Handbuch der Altorientalischen Geisteskultur.* Leipzig: J. C. Hinrichs, 1913; 2nd. Ed. Berlin/Leipzig: W. de Gruyter, 1929.

Jeremias, Alfred. *Die Höllenfahrt der Ištar*. Munich: F. Straub, 1886.

Jeremias, Alfred. "Izdubar." *Ausführliches Lexikon der griechischen und römischen Mythologie.* Ed. W. H. Roscher. Leipzig: Teubner, 1890–94; rpt. Hildesheim and NY: Olms, 1978. Vol. 2, cols. 773–823.

Jeremias, Alfred. *Izdubar-Nimrod. Eine altbabylonische Heldensage.* Leipzig: Teubner, 1891.

Jestin, Raymond Riec. "La Conception sumérienne de la vie post mortem." *Syria* 33 (1956): 113–18.

Johnson, Obed Simon. *A Study of Chinese Alchemy.* Shanghai: Commercial Press, 1928.

Joines, Karen Randolph. "Winged Serpents in Isaiah's Inaugural Vision." *JBL* 86 (1967): 410–15.

Jolles, A. "Etana oder Gilgameš?" *OLZ* 14 (1911): 389–90.

Jong, J. W. de. "The Overburdened Earth in India and Greece." *JAOS* 105 (1985): 397–400.

Jordan, Franzis. "Das Gilgamesch-Epos." *In den Tagen des Tammuz. Altbabylonische Mythen.* München: R. Piper & Co. Verlag, 1950. 169–93; rpt. Oberhuber. *Das Gilgamesch-Epos.* 276–91.

Jung, Carl Gustav. *Collected Works.* Tr. R. F. C. Hull. 19 Vols. Princeton: UP, 1902–1958.

Jung, Carl Gustav. "The Dual Mother Role." *Psychology of the Unconscious.* Tr. Beatrice M. Hinkle. NY: Dodd, Mead and Co., 1957. 341–400.

Jung, Carl Gustav. *The Integration of the Personality.* NY/Toronto: Farrar and Rinehart, 1939.

Jung, Carl Gustav, ed. *Man and His Symbols.* NY: Dell, 1968.

Jung, Carl Gustav. *Modern Man in Search of a Soul.* London: K. Paul, 1949.

Kakar, Sudhir. *The Inner World: A Psychoanalytic Study of Childhood and Society in India.* New Delhi: Oxford UP, 1978.

Kakascik, Joan. *The Epic of Gigamesh and Life Stage Development Theory.* Thesis, Boston University, 1975.

Kakosy, L. "L'épopée de Gilgamesh: Babel." *Revue International de la Traduction* 14 (1968): 195–200.

Kakrides, J. Th. *Homeric Researches.* Lund: Gleerup, 1949.

Kammenhuber, A. "Die hethitischen und hurritischen Gilgameš-Überlieferungen." *Kindlers Literatur Lexikon* 18 (1992): 46–7.

Kammenhuber, A. "Die hethitische und hurrische Überlieferung zum 'Gilgameš-Epos.'" *Münchener Studien zur Sprachwissenschaft* 21 (1967): 45–58.

Kamminga, J. C. C. "Einige Bermerkungen zu Gilgameš P, Y und Nin. XI 15." *Akkadica* 36 (1984): 18–20.

Kampers, Franz. *Alexander der Grosse und die Idee des Weltimperiums in Prophetie und Sage.* Freiburg: Herder, 1901.

Kampers, Franz. *Mittelalterliche Sagen vom Paradiese und vom Holze des Kreuzes Christi.* Cologne: J. P. Bachem, 1897.

Kantor, Helene J. "Oriental Institute Museum Notes No. 13: A Bronze Plaque with Relief Decoration from Tell Tainat." *JNES* 21 (1962): 93–117.

Kapelrud, Arvid S. *The Violent Goddess: Anat in the Ras Shamra Texts.* Oslo: Universitetsforlaget, 1969.

Kapp, A. "Ein Lied auf Enlilbani von Isin." *ZA* 51 (1961): 76–87.

Karageorghis, Vassos. *Salamis. Recent Discoveries in Cyprus.* NY: McGraw-Hill, 1969.

Katz, Dina. *Gilgamesh and Akka.* Groningen: Styx Publications, 1993.

Katz, Dina. "Gilgamesh and Akka: Was Uruk Ruled by Two Assemblies?" *RA* 81 (1987): 105–14.

Kellner, Maximilian Lindsay. *The Deluge in the Izdubar Epic and in the Old Testament.* Cambridge: Church Review, 1888.

Kenney, E. J. ed. *P. Ovidi Nasonis Amores, Medicamina faciei femineae, Ars amatoria, Remedia Amoris.* Oxford: Clarendon, 1961.

Keppler, Carl. *The Literature of the Second Self.* Tucson: U of Arizona P, 1972.

Kern, Otto, ed. *Orphicorum Fragmenta.* 2nd. Ed. Berlin: Weidmann, 1963.

Kerouac, Jack. *On the Road.* NY: New American Library, 1957.

Khawam, R. *Les Mille et une Nuits.* Paris: Phebus, 1986.

Kidd, William Thomas. *The Epic of Gilgamesh: An Opera Cycle.* Thesis, Virginia Commonwealth University, 1981. [Musical Score].

Kidder, Tracy. *The Soul of a New Machine.* Boston: Atlantic-Little, Brown, 1981.

Kienast, Burkhart. *"qabal lā maḫār."* *JCS* 29 (177): 73–77.

Kierkegaard, Søren. *Begrebet Angest. Samlede Woerker.* Vol. 4. Copenhagen: Drachman, Herberg, Lange, 1922.

Kikawada, Isaac. "Two Notes on Eve." *JBL* 91 (1972): 33–37.

Kikawada, Isaac M., and Arthur Quinn. *Before Abraham Was.* Nashville: Abingdon Press, 1985.

Kilmer, Anne Draffkorn. "The Mesopotamian Concept of Overpopulation as Reflected in Mythology." *Or.* 41 (1972): 160–77.

Kilmer, Anne Draffkorn. "A Note on an Overlooked Word-Play in the Akkadian Gilgamesh." Driel. 128–32.

Kilmer, Anne Draffkorn. "Notes on Akkadian *uppu.*" *Essays... Finkelstein.* 129–38.

Kilmer, Anne Draffkorn. "The Symbolism of the Flies in the Mesopotamian Flood Myth." *Language, Literature and History.* Ed. Francesca Rochberg-Halton. New Haven: AOS, 1987.

King, Leonard William. *Catalogue of the Cuneiform Tablets in the Kouyanjik Collection of the British Museum, Supplement.* London: British Museum, 1914.

King, Leonard William. *Chronicles Concerning Early Babylonian Kings.* 2 Vols. London: Luzac, 1907.

King, Leonard William. *CT 13.* London: British Museum, 1901.

King, Leonard William. *The Seven Tablets of Creation.* 2 Vols. London: Luzac, 1902.

King, Leonard William, and E. A. Wallis Budge. *Annals of the Kings of Assyria.* Vol. 1. London: British Museum, 1902.

Kirby, Bill. "Gilgamesh in the Outback." *Rebels in Hell.* Ed. Janet Morris and Martin Caidin. NY: Baen Books, 1986.

Kircher, Athanasius. *Mundus Subterraneus.* Amsterdam: Joannem Janssonium, 1665.

Kirk, Geoffrey S. *The Iliad: A Commentary.* Cambridge: UP, 1985.

Kirk, Geoffrey S. "Nature and Culture: Gilgamesh, Centaurs and Cyclopes." *Myth, Its Meaning and Functions in Ancient and Other Cultures.* Berkeley: Cambridge UP and U of California P, 1970. 132–52.

Kirk, Geoffrey S. *The Nature of Greek Myths.* Harmondsworth: Penguin, 1974.

Kirk, Geoffrey S. *The Songs of Homer*. Cambridge: UP, 1962.

Kirk, Geoffrey S., J. E. Raven, and M. Schofield. *The Presocratic Philosophers*. Cambridge: UP, 1983.

Kishtainy, Khalid. "The Epic of Gilgamesh." *Ur* (1979): 32–34.

Klauber, Ernst Georg. *Politisch-religiöse Texte aus der Sargonidenzeit*. Leipzig: Pfeiffer, 1913.

Klein, Jacob. "The 'Bane' of Humanity: A Lifespan of One Hundred Twenty Years." *Acta Sumerologica* 12 (1990): 57–70.

Klein, Jacob. "The Capture of Agga by Gilgameš (GA 81 and 99)." *JAOS* 103 (1983): 201–204.

Klein, Jacob. "A New Nippur Duplicate of the Sumerian Kinglist in the Brockmon Collection, University of Haifa." *Aula Orientalis* 9 (1991): 123–29.

Klein, Jacob. "Review of Wilcke, *Das Lugalbandaepos*." *JAOS* 91 (1971): 295–99.

Klein, Jacob. "Šulgi and Gilgamesh: Two Brother-Peers (Šulgi O)." Eichler. *Kramer Anniverary Volume*. 271–92.

Klein, Melanie. *The Psychoanalysis of Children*. Rev. Ed. NY: Delacorte, 1975.

Kluger, Rivkah Shärf. *The Archetypal Significance of Gilgamesh, A Modern Hero*. Ed. H. Yehezkel Kluger. Einsiedeln, Switzerland: Daimon Verlag, 1991.

Kluger, Rivkah Schärf. "Einige psychologische Aspekte des Gilgamesch-Epos." *Aspekte Analytischer Psychologie* 6 (1975).

Kluger, Rivkah Schärf. *Satan in the Old Testament*. Evanston: Northwestern UP, 1967.

Knight, William Francis Jackson. *Cumaean Gates*. Oxford: B. Blackwell, 1936.

Knudtzon, Jörgen Alexander. *Assyrische Gebete an den Sonnengott*. 2 Vols. Leipzig: Pfeiffer, 1893.

Knudtzon, Jörgen Alexander. *Die El-Amarna-Tafeln*. 2 Vols. Leipzig: Hinrichs, 1915.

Koch, Heidemarie. "Elamisches Gilgmeš-Epos oder doch Verwaltungstäfelchen?" *ZA* 83 (1993): 219–36.

Köcher, Franz. "Der babylonische Göttertypentext." *MIO* 1 (1953): 57–107.

Köcher, Franz. "Ein spätbabylonischer Hymnus auf den Tempel Ezida in Borsippa." *ZA* 19 (1959): 236–40.

Koefoed, Aase. "Gilgameš, Enkidu and the Nether World." *Acta Sumerologica* 5 (1983): 17–23.

Kohler, Josef, and Arthur Ungnad. *Assyriche Rechtsurkunden.* Leipzig: Pfeiffer, 1913.

Kohler, K. "The Eagle of Etan-Gilgamos and His Kindred in Folklore." *The Academy* 985 (1891): 284.

Koklugiller, Ahmet. *Gilgameš*. Tr. from English. Istanbul: Can Yaynlar, 1984.

Komoróczy, Geza. "Akkadian Epic Poetry and Its Sumerian Sources." *Act. Ant.* 23 (1975): 41–63.

Komoróczy, Geza. "Berosos and the Mesopotamian Literature." *Act. Ant.* 21 (1973): 125–52.

Komoróczy, Geza. "Cinq cylindres-sceaux de la Mésopotamie archaïque." *Bulletin du Musée National Hongrois des Beaux-Arts* 19 (1961): 3–9.

Komoróczy, Geza. "A sumer mitological epika." *Ethnographia* 84 (1973): 274–300.

Koopman, Ann Elizabeth. *Structure, Symbol, and The Epic of Gilgamesh.* Honors Paper, Lawrence University, 1977.

Kopp, Sheldon B. *If You Meet the Buddha on the Road, Kill Him!* Ben Lomond, CA: Science and Behavior Books, 1972.

Kopp, Sheldon B. *Guru: Metaphors from a Psychotherapist.* Palo Alto, CA: Science and Behavior Books, 1971.

Korošec, Viktor. "Gilgameš vu sous son aspect juridique." *GSL* 161–66.

Kosay, Hamit Zubeyr. *Ausgrabungen von Alaca Höyük.* Ankara: Im Auftrage der Türkischen Geschichtskommission, 1966.

Koschaker, Paul. "Beiträge zum altbabylonischen Recht." *ZA* 35 (1924): 192–212.

Kovacs, Maureen Gallery, tr. *The Epic of Gilgamesh.* Stanford: UP, 1989.

Kovacs, Maureen Gallery. "The Epics of Gilgamesh." *Asian Art* 5 (1992): 53–69.

Kraeling, Emil G. "Xisouthros, Deucalion and the Flood Traditions." *JAOS* 67 (1947): 177–83.

Kramer, Samuel Noah. "The 'Babel of Tongues': A Sumerian Version." *JAOS* 88 (1968): 108–111.

Kramer, Samuel Noah. "Corrections to The Epic of Gilgameš and its Sumerian Sources." *JAOS* 64 (1944): 83.

Kramer, Samuel Noah. "The Death of Gilgamesh." *BASOR* 94 (1944): 2–12.

Kramer, Samuel Noah. "The Death of Ur-Nammu and His Descent to the Netherworld." *JCS* 21 (1967): 104–22.

Kramer, Samuel Noah. "Dilmun, the Land of the Living." *BASOR* 96 (1944): 18–28.

Kramer, Samuel Noah. "Enki and His Inferiority Complex." *Or.* 39 (1970): 103–10.

Kramer, Samuel Noah. *Enki and Ninḫursag: A Sumerian "Paradise" Myth.* New Haven: American Schools of Oriental Research, 1945.

Kramer, Samuel Noah. *Enmerkar and the Lord of Aratta.* Philadelphia: University Museum, U of Pennsylvania, 1952.

Kramer, Samuel Noah. "The Epic of Gilgameš and Its Sumerian Sources. A Study in Literary Evolution." *JAOS* 64 (1944): 7–23.

Kramer, Samuel Noah. "Gilgameš: Some New Sumerian Data." *GSL.* 54–68.

Kramer, Samuel Noah. "Gilgamesh and Agga. With comments by Thorkild Jacobsen." *AJA* 53 (1949): 1–18.

Kramer, Samuel Noah. *Gilgamesh and the Ḫuluppu-Tree.* Chicago: UP, 1938.

Kramer, Samuel Noah. "Gilgamesh and the Land of the Living." *JCS* 1 (1947): 3–46.

Kramer, Samuel Noah. *History Begins at Sumer.* Garden City: Anchor Doubleday, 1959; *L'Histoire commence à Sumer.* Paris: Librarie Arthaud, 1959; 3rd. Ed. Philadelphia: U of Pennsylvania P, 1981; for first edition, see *From the Tablets of Sumer.*

Kramer, Samuel Noah. "Inanna's Descent to the Nether World Continued and Revised." *JCS* 5 (1951): 1–17.

Kramer, Samuel Noah. "Langdon's Historical and Religious Texts from the Temple Library of Nippur—Additions and Corrections." *JAOS* 60 (1940): 247–48.

Kramer, Samuel Noah, ed. *Mythologies of the Ancient World.* Garden City, NY: Doubleday, 1961.

Kramer, Samuel Noah. "New Literary Catalogue from Ur." *RA* 55 (1961): 169–76.

Kramer, Samuel Noah. "The Oldest Literary Catalogue: A Sumerian List of Literary Compositions Compiled About 2000 B.C." *BASOR* 88 (1942): 10–19.

Kramer, Samuel Noah. *From the Poetry of Sumer.* Berkeley/ Los Angeles: U of California P, 1979.

Kramer, Samuel Noah. "Poets and Psalmists." *The Legacy of Sumer.* Schmandt-Besserat. 3–21.

Kramer, Samuel Noah. "Review of Van Dijk, *LUGAL UD MELAM-bi NIRGAL.*" *JAOS* 105 (1985): 135–39.

Kramer, Samuel Noah. *The Sacred Marriage Rite: Aspects of Faith, Myth, and Ritual in Ancient Sumer.* Bloomington: Indiana UP, 1969; *Le Mariage sacré: à Sumer et à Babylone.* Tr. and adapted Jean Bottéro. Paris: Berg International, 1983.

Kramer, Samuel Noah. "Shulgi of Ur: A Royal Hymn and a Divine Blessing." *The Seventy-Fifth Anniversary Volume of the Jewish Quarterly Review.* Ed. A. A. Neuman and S. Zeitlin. Philadelphia: Jewish Quarterly Review, 1967. 369–80.

Kramer, Samuel Noah. "The Sumerian Deluge Myth." *An. St.* 33 (1983): 115–21.

Kramer, Samuel Noah. "Sumerian Epic Literature." *Atti del convegno internazionale sul tema: La poesia epica e la sua formazione (Roma, 28 marzo 3 aprile 1969).* Roma: Academia Nazionale dei Lincei, 1970. 825–37.

Kramer, Samuel Noah. *Sumerian Literary Texts from Nippur in the Museum of the Ancient Orient at Istanbul.* New Haven: American Schools of Oriental Research, 1944.

Kramer, Samuel Noah. "Sumerian Literature." *PAPhS* 85 (1942): 293–323.

Kramer, Samuel Noah. "Sumerian Literature: A General Survey." *The Bible and the Ancient Near East: Essays in Honor of William Foxwell Albright.* Ed. G. E. Wright. Garden City, NY: Doubleday, 1965. 327–52.

Kramer, Samuel Noah. "Sumerian Literature and the Bible." *Studia Biblica et Orientalia* 3 (1959): 185–204; rpt. Tollers and Maier. *The Bible in its Literary Milieu.* 272–84.

Kramer, Samuel Noah. "Sumerian Literature and the British Museum." *PAPhS* 124 (1980): 299–310.

Kramer, Samuel Noah. *Sumerian Mythology.* Philadelphia: American Philosophical Society, 1944; Rev. Ed. NY: Harper & Brothers, 1961.

Kramer, Samuel Noah, tr. "Sumerian Myths and Epic Tales," "Sumerian Hymns," "Sumerian Lamentation," "Sumerian Sacred Marriage Texts," and "Sumerian Miscellaneous Texts." *ANET.* 37–59, 573–86, 611–19, 637–45, 646–52.

Kramer, Samuel Noah. "Sumerian Similes: A Panoramic View of Some of Man's Oldest Literary Images." *JAOS* 89 (1969): 1–10.

Kramer, Samuel Noah. *The Sumerians: Their History, Culture, and Character.* Chicago: UP, 1963.

Kramer, Samuel Noah. "Sumero-Akkadian Interconnections: Religious Ideas." *Aspects du contact suméro-akkadien. Geneva,* N.S. 8 (1960): 272–83.

Kramer, Samuel Noah. *From the Tablets of Sumer. 25 Firsts of Man's Recorded History.* Indian Hills, CO: Falcon's Wing Press, 1956; for subsequent editions, see *History Begins at Sumer.*

Kramer, Samuel Noah. "Tales of Gilgamesh: The First Case of Literary Borrowing." *History Begins at Sumer.* 3rd. Rev. Ed. Philadelphia: U of Pennsylvania P, 1982. 241–55.

Kramer, Samuel Noah. "The Temple in Sumerian Literature." Fox. 1–16.

Kramer, Samuel Noah. "The Women of Ancient Sumer: Gleanings from Sumerian Literature." *RAI* 33 (1987): 107–112.

Kramer, Samuel Noah, and Inez Bernhardt. *Sumerische Literarische Texts aus Nippur.* Berlin: Akademie-Verlag, 1961. N. 12–14.

Kramer, Samuel Noah, and John Maier. *Myths of Enki, The Crafty God.* NY: Oxford UP, 1989.

Kramer, Samuel Noah, and Diane Wolkstein. *Inanna: Queen of Heaven and Earth: Her Hymns and Stories from Sumer.* NY: Harper and Row, 1983.

Kraus, Fritz Rudolf. "Altmesopotamisches Lebensgefühl." *JNES* 19 (1960): 117–32.

Kraus, Fritz Rudolf. "Der Brief des Gilgameš." *An. St.* 30 (1980): 109–22.

Kraus, Fritz Rudolf, tr. "Einleitung in das Gilgameš-Epos" by B. Landsberger. *GSL.* 31–38.

Kraus, Fritz Rudolf. "Zur Liste der alteren Könige von Babylonien." *ZA* 50 (1952): 29–60.

Kraus, Fritz Rudolf. *Vom mesopotamischen Menschen der altbabylonischen Zeit und seiner Welt.* Amsterdam: North Holland, 1973.

Kraus, Fritz Rudolf. *Nippur und Isin nach altbabylonischen Rechtsurkunden.* New Haven: Archaeological Museum of Istanbul and ASOR, 1951.

Kraus, Fritz Rudolf. "Provinzen des neusumerischen Reiches von Ur." *ZA* 51 (1955): 45–75.

Krauskopf, Ingrid. *Der Thebanische Sagenkreis und andere griechische Sagen in der etruskischen Kunst.* Mainz am Rhein: P. von Zabern, 1954.

Krebernik, Manfred. *Die Beschwörungen aus Fara und Ebla.* Hildesheim/NY: Olms Verlag, 1985.

Kristensen, W. B. "De plaats van het zondvloedverhaal in het Gilgameš-Epos." *Verslagen en Mededeelingen der Koninklijke Akademie van Wetenschappen.* Afd. Letterkunde, 5th reeks, Deel 2 (1915): 54–63.

Krohn, Kaarle. *Magische Ursprungsrunen der Finnen.* Helsinki: Folklore Fellows Communications, 1924.

Krstović, Jelena, and Zoran Minderović, eds. *Classical and Medieval Literature Criticism.* Vol. 3. Detroit: Gale Research, 1989. 301–75.

Krstović, Jelena, and Zoran Minderović. "Epic of Gilgamesh, Circa 1200–1000 B.C." Krstović. 301–303.

Kruiningen, Harry von. *Gilgamesj. De mens in verzet tegen zijn noodlot.* Amsterdam: De Priehoek, 1974.

Kugler, Franz Xaver. *Sternkunde und Sterndienst in Babel.* Münster in Westfalia, 1907.

Kula, John. *The Epic of Gilgamesh as Commissioned by Morgan.* Vancouver: Pulp Press, 1975.

Kullmann, Wolfgang. "Ein vorhomerisches Motiv im Iliasproömium." *Philologus* 99 (1955): 167–92.

Kullmann, Wolfgang. *Das Wirken der Gotter in der Ilias.* Berlin: Akademie Verlag, 1956.

Kunstmann, Walter. G. *Die Babylonische Gebetsbeschwörung.* Leipzig: Hinrichs, 1932.

Kupper, Jean-Robert. "Les Différentes Versions de l'épopée de Gilgameš." *GSL.* 97–102.

Kupper, Jean-Robert. *Les Nomades en Mésopotamie au temps des rois de Mari.* Paris: Bibliothèque de la Faculté de Philosophie et Lettres de L'Université de Liège, 1957.

Kutscher, Raphael, and Claus Wilcke. "Eine Ziegel-Inschrift des Königs Takil-Iliššu von Malgium, gefunden in Isin und Yale." *ZA* 68 (1978): 95–128.

Labat, René. *Le Caractère religieux de la royauté assyro-babylonienne.* Paris: Librarie d'Amérique et d'Orient, 1939.

Labat, René. "Compte rendu des conférences Assyrien." *Annuaire d' Ecole Pratique des Hautes Études* (1971): 67–70.

Labat, René. "L'écriture cunéiforme et la civilisations mésopotamienne." *L'écriture et la psychologie des peuples.* Ed. Marcel Cohen et al. Paris: Librairie Armand Colin, 1963. 73–92.

Labat, René. "Gilgamesh VII–X." *AEPHEH* 103 (1970–71): 73–78.

Labat, René. *Manuel d'épigraphie akkadienne.* Paris: Imprimerie Nationale, 1963.

Labat, René. *Le Poème babylonien de la création.* Paris: Librarie d'Amérique et d'Orient, 1935.

Labat, René, A. Caquot, M. Sznycer, and M. Vieyra, ed. *Les Religions du Proche-Oriente asiatique.* Paris: Fayard/Denoël, 1970.

Laessøe, Jørgen. "The Atraḫasīs Epic: A Babylonian History of Mankind." *Bi. Or.* 13 (1956): 90–102.

Laessøe, Jørgen. "Literary and Oral Tradition in Ancient Mesopotamia." *Studia Orientalia Ioanni Pedersen... Dicata.* Copenhagen: E. Munksgaard, 1953. 205–18.

Lagrange, M. *Étude sur les Religions Sémitiques.* 2nd. Ed. Paris: Victor Lecoffre, 1905.

Lamberg-Karlovsky, C. C. "Dilmun—Gateway to Immortality." *JNES* 41 (1982): 45–50.

Lambert, Maurice, and Jacques R. Tournay. "Enki et Ninḫursag." *RA* 43 (1949): 105–36.

Lambert, Wilfred G. "An Address of Marduk to the Demons." *AfO* 19 (1959–60): 114–17.

Lambert, Wilfred G. "Ancestors, Authors and Canonicity." *JCS* 11 (1957): 1–14, 112.

Lambert, Wilfred G. "Another Trick of Enki?" *Marchands, Diplomates et Empereurs.* Ed. Paul Garelli, Dominique Charpin, and Francis Johānnes. Paris: ÉRC, 1991. 415–19.

Lambert, Wilfred G. *Babylonian Literary Texts.* London: British Museum, 1965.

Lambert, Wilfred G. *Babylonian Wisdom Literature.* Oxford: Clarendon Press, 1960.

Lambert, Wilfred G. "Berossus and Babylonian Eschatology." *Iraq* 38 (1976): 171–73.

Lambert, Wilfred G. "A Catalogue of Texts and Authors." *JCS* 16 (1962): 59–77.

Lambert, Wilfred G. "Devotion: The Languages of Religion and Love." Mindlin. *Figurative.* 25–39.

Lambert, Wilfred G. "Divine Love Lyrics from the Reign of Abi-ešuḫ." *MIO* 12 (1966): 41–56.

Lambert, Wilfred G. *Zum Forschungsstand der sumerisch-babylonischen Literatur-Geschichte.* Wiesbaden: Franz Steiner Verlag, 1977.

Lambert, Wilfred G. "Gilg. I i 41." *RA* 73 (1979): 89.

Lambert, Wilfred G. "Gilgameš in Religious, Historical and Omen Texts and the Historicity of Gilgameš." *GSL.* 39–56.

Lambert, Wilfred G. "Gilgamesh and the Magic Plant." *Biblical Archaeologist* 45 (1982): 69.

Lambert, Wilfred G. "Gilgamesh in Literature and Art: The Second and First Millennia." *Monsters and Demons in the Ancient and Medieval Worlds.* Ed. Ann E. Farkas, et al. Mainz on Rhine: Verlag Philipp von Zabern, 1987. 37–52 and illustrations.

Lambert, Wilfred G. "Goddesses in the Pantheon: A Reflection of Women in Society?" *RAI* 33 (1987): 125–30.

Lambert, Wilfred G. "History and the Gods: A Review Article." *Or.* 39 (1970): 170–77.

Lambert, Wilfred G. "The Hymn to the Queen of Nippur." Driel, 208–16.

Lambert, Wilfred G. "The Interchange of Ideas Between Southern Mesopotamia and Syria-Palestine as Seen in Literature." *Mesopotamien und seine Nachbarn.* Ed. Hans-Jorg Nissen and Johannes Renger. Berlin: Dietrich Reimer, 1982. 311–16.

Lambert, Wilfred G. "Literary Style in First Millennium Mesopotamia." *JAOS* 88 (1968): 123–32.

Lambert, Wilfred G. "A Middle Assyrian Medical Text." *Iraq* 31 (1969): 28–39.

Lambert, Wilfred G. "Morals in Ancient Mesopotamia." *JEOL* 15 (1958): 184–96.

Lambert, Wilfred G. "Myth and Mythmaking in Sumer and Akkad." Sasson. *Civilizations of the Ancient Near East.* 1825–36.

Lambert, Wilfred G. "New Light on the Babylonian Flood." *JSS* 5 (1960): 113–23.

Lambert, Wilfred G. "A New Look at the Babylonian Background of Genesis." *Journal of Theological Studies.* N.S. 16 (1965): 287–300; rpt. Tollers and Maier. *The Bible in its Literary Milieu.* 285–97.

Lambert, Wilfred G. "Niṣir or Nimuš?" *RA* 80 (1986): 185–86.

Lambert, Wilfred G. "Prostitution." *Außenseiter und Randgruppen.* Ed. Volkert Haas. Konstanz: Universitätsverlag Konstanz, 1992. 127–58.

Lambert, Wilfred G. "The Reign of Nebuchadnezzar I: A Turning Point in the History of Ancient Mesopotamian Religion." *The Seed of Wisdom: Essays in Honour of T. J. Meek.* Ed. W. S. McCullough. Toronto: U of Toronto P, 1964. 3–13.

Lambert, Wilfred G. "Review of *AHw* Fascicles 5 and 6." *JSS* 12 (1967): 100–105.

Lambert, Wilfred G. "Review of M. Ellis, *Studies...Finkelstein.*" *JNES* 39 (1980): 172–74.

Lambert, Wilfred G. "The Theology of Death." Alster. *Death in Mesopotamia.* 53–66.

Lambert, Wilfred G. "Three Unpublished Fragments of the Tukulti-Ninurta Epic." *AfO* 18 (1957–58): 38–51.

Lambert, Wilfred G. "Two Texts from the Early Part of the Reign of Ashurbanipal." *AfO* 18 (1957–58): 382–87.

Lambert, Wilfred G., and A. R. Millard. *Atraḫasīs. The Babylonian Story of the Flood, with "The Sumerian Flood Story" by M. Civil.* Oxford: Clarendon P, 1969.

Lambert, Wilfred G., and Simon Parker. *Enuma Eliš: The Babylonian Epic of Creation: The Cuneiform Text.* Oxford: Clarendon Press, 1966.

Landsberger, Benno. "Einige unerkannt gebliebene oder verkannte Nomina des Akkadischen." *WZKM* 56 (1960): 109–29; 57 (1961): 1–23.

Landsberger, Benno. "Einleitung in des Gilgameš-Epos." Tr. F. R. Kraus. *GSL.* 31–36; rpt. Oberhuber. *Das Gilgamesch-Epos.* 171–77.

Landsberger, Benno. "Jungfräulichkeit: Ein Beitrag zum Thema 'Beilager und Eheschliessung.'" *Symbolae Iuridicae et Historicae Martino David Dedicatae.* Ed. J. A. Ankum, R. Feenstra, and W. F. Leemans. Leiden: Brill, 1968. 2: 41–105.

Landsberger, Benno. "Zur vierten und siebenten Tafel des Gilgamesch-Epos." *RA* 62 (1968): 97–135.

Landsberger, Benno, and J. V. Kinnier Wilson. "The Fifth Tablet of Enuma Elish." *JNES* 20 (1961): 154–79.

Lang, Bernhard. "Non-Semitic Deluge Stories and the Book of Genesis. A Bibliographical and Critical Survey." *Anthropos* 80 (1985): 605–616.

Langdon, Stephen Herbert. *The Epic of Gilgamesh.* Philadelphia: University Museum, 1917.

Langdon, Stephen Herbert. "The Epic of Gilgamesh." *The Pennsylvania Museum Journal* 8 (1917): 29–38.

Langdon, Stephen Herbert. *Historical and Religious Texts from the Temple Library of Nippur.* Munich: A. Pries, 1914. N. 31, 35, 55.

Langdon, Stephen Herbert. "Notes on the Philadelphia and the Yale Tablets of the Gilgamesh Epic." *JRAS* (1929): 343–46.

Langdon, Stephen Herbert. "Philological Note on the Epic of Gilgamesh, Book XI, 88." *JRAS* (1925): 718–20.

Langdon, Stephen. *Semitic Mythology.* Boston: Archaeological Institute, 1931.

Langdon, Stephen Herbert. "The Sumerian Epic of Gilgamish." *JRAS* (1932): 91–148.

Langdon, Stephen. *Sumerian Epic of Paradise, the Flood, and the Fall of Man.* Philadelphia: University Museum, 1915; *Le Poème sumérien du paradis, du déluge et de la chute de l'homme.* Tr. C. Virolleaud. Paris: Leroux, 1919.

Langdon, Stephen. *Sumerian Liturgical Texts.* Philadelphia: University Museum, 1917. 124–26.

Langdon, Stephen Herbert. *The Weld-Blundell Collection.* Vol. 2. *Historical Inscriptions* London: Oxford UP, 1923.

Langer, Birgit. *Gott als "Licht" in Israel und Mesopotamien.* Klosterneuburg: Verlag Österreichs Katholisches Bibelwerk, 1989.

Langer, Susanne. *Feeling and Form: A Theory of Art.* NY: Charles Scriber's Sons, 1953.

Lanser, Susan Sniader. *The Narrative Act.* Princeton: UP, 1981.

Lansing, John B., et al. *The Travel Market, 1958, 1959–60, 1961–62.* Lansing, MI: U of Michigan, 1963.

Large, Brian. *Martinu.* London: Duckworth, 1975.

Laroche, Emmanuel. "Catalogue des Textes Hittites." *RHA* 14 (1956): 33–38, 69–116; 15 (1957): 30–89; 16 (1958): 18–64.

Laroche, Emmanuel. *Catalogue des textes hittites.* Paris: Klincksieck, 1971.

Laroche, Emmanuel. "Mythologie d'origine étrangère. 12. Gilgameš." *Textes mythologiques hittites en transcription.* Ed. Emmanuel Laroche. *RHA* 26 (1968): 121–38.

Laroche, Emmanuel. "Premier supplément." *RHA* 30 (1972): 94–133.

LaSor, William Sanford. "Samples of Early Semitic Poetry." *The Bible World. Essays in Honor of Cyrus H. Gordon.* Ed. Gary Rendsburg, et al. NY: KTAV, 1980. 99–212.

Latacz, Joachim. *Homer.* Munich: Artemis, 1989.

Lattimore, Richard, tr. *The Iliad of Homer.* Chicago: UP, 1951.

Lattimore, Richard, tr. *The Odyssey.* NY: Harper Colophon Books, 1965.

Layard, Austen Henry. *Discoveries in the Ruins of Nineveh and Babylon.* London: John Murray, 1853.

Layard, Austen Henry. *Monuments of Nineveh.* London: Murray, 1853.

Leed, Eric J. "Introduction, for a History of Travel," and "Reaching for Abroad: Departures." *The Mind of the Traveler, from Gilgamesh to Global Tourism.* NY: Basic Books, 1991. 17+, 25–31.

Leeming, David Adams. *Mythology: The Voyage of the Hero.* Philadelphia: J. B. Lippincott, 1973.

Leeuwen, Nicholas Dirk van. *Het Bijbelsch-Akkadisch-Schumerisch Zondvloedverhaal.* Amsterdam: H. A. van Bottenburg, 1920.

Leeuwen, Raymond C. Van. "Isa 14:12, ḥôlēš 'algwynu and Gilgamesh, XI, 6." *JBL* 99 (1980): 175–84.

Lehmann-Haupt, C. F. *Babyloniens Kulturmission einst und jetzt.* Leipzig, 1903.

Lehmann-Haupt, C. F. *Paulys Realencyclopadie der classischen Altertumswissenschaft.* Stuttgart, 1894–1980.

Leibovitz, Nahum. *Studies on the Book of Genesis* (in Hebrew). Jerusalem, 1966.

Leichty, Erle V. "The Colophon." *Studies Presented to A. Leo Oppenheim.* Ed. R. D. Biggs and J. A. Brinkman. Chicago: U of Chicago P, 1964. 147–54.

Leichty, Erle V. "Demons and Population Control." *Expedition* 13 (1971): 22–26.

Leichty, Erle V. *The Omen Series Šumma Izbu*. Locust Valley, NY: Augustin, 1970.

Leick, Gwendolyn. "Love and Eros in Akkadian Narrative Literature." *Sex and Eroticism in Mesopotamian Religion.* London: Routledge, 1994. 247–98.

Leonard, William Ellery, tr. *Gilgamesh, Epic of Old Babylonia.* NY: Viking, 1934; rpt. Lunenburg, VT: Limited Editions Club, 1974. Illustrations Irving Amen.

Lerner, Gerda. "The Origin of Prostitution in Ancient Mesopotamia." *Signs: Journal of Women in Culture and Society* 11 (1986): 236–54.

Lesky, Albin. *Die tragische Dichtung der Hellenen.* Göttingen: Vandenhoeck and Ruprecht, 1972.

Levi-Strauss, Claude. *Tristes Tropiques: An Anthropological Study of Primitive Societies in Brazil.* Tr. John Russell. NY: Atheneum, 1961.

Levy, G. R. "Type B: The Quest." *The Sword from the Rock: An Investigation into the Origins of Epic Literature and the Development of the Hero.* London: Faber and Faber, 1953. 120–73; selections rpt. Krstović. 313–14.

Levy, Selim J. "Two Cylinders of Nebuchadnezzar II in the Iraq Museum." *Sumer* 3 (1947): 41–8.

Lewis, Brian. *The Sargon Legend.* New Haven: ASOR, 1980.

Lewis, J. P. *A Study of the Interpretation of Noah and the Flood in Jewish and Christian Literature.* Leiden: Brill, 1968.

Lewis, Sinclair. *Dodsworth.* NY: New American Library, 1967.

Lewis, Theodore J. *Cults of the Dead in Ancient Israel and Ugarit.* Atlanta, GA: Scholars Press, 1989.

Lewy, Hildegard and Julius. "The Origin of the Week and the Oldest Westasiatic Calendar." *HUCA* 17 (1942–43): 1–152.

Leyton, Elliott, ed. *The Compact: Selected Dimensions of Friendship.* Toronto: UP, 1974.

Lichtheim, Miriam. *Ancient Egyptian Literature.* 3 Vols. Berkeley: U of California P, 1973, 1976, 1980.

Lichtheim, Miriam. "The Songs of the Harpers." *JNES* 4 (1945): 178–212.

Lie, A. G. *The Inscriptions of Sargon II, King of Assyria.* Paris: P. Geuthner, 1929.

Lieberman, Saul. *Hellenism in Jewish Palestine.* NY: Jewish Theological Seminary of America, 1962.

Lieberman, Saul. *The Tosefta: According to Codex Vienna… The Order of Nashim.* NY: Jewish Theological Seminary of America, 1967.

Lieberman, Saul. *Tosefta Kifshutah: A Comprehensive Commentary on the Tosefta. Pt. 6, Order Nashim.* NY: Jewish Theological Seminary of America, 1967.

Lieberman, Stephen J., ed. *Sumerological Studies in Honor of Thorkild Jacobsen.* Chicago: U of Chicago P, 1976.

Limet, Henri. *L'anthroponymie sumérienne.* Paris: Les Belles Lettres, 1968.

Limet, Henri. "Les Chants épiques sumériens." *RBPH* 50 (1972): 3–23.

Lindahl, Carl. "The Oral Aesthetic and the Bicameral Mind." *Oral Tradition* 6 (1991): 130–36.

Lindahl, Carl. "Transition Symbolism on Tombstones." *Western Folklore* 45 (1986): 165–85.

Littmann, E. "Alf Layla wa-Layla." *Encyclopedia of Islam.* 2nd. Ed. Leiden: Brill, 1979. 1: 358–64.

Livingston, Alasdair. *Court Poetry and Literary Miscellanea.* Helsinki: UP, 1989. 119–20.

Livingstone, Alasdair. *Mystical and Mythological Explanatory Works of Assyrian and Babylonian Scholars.* Oxford: Clarendon Press, 1986.

Lloyd-Jones, H. "Stasinus and the Cypria." *Stasinos. Syndesmos Hellenon Philologon Kyprou* 4 (1968/72): 115–22.

Loomis, Roger Sherman, ed. *Arthurian Literature in the Middle Ages.* Oxford: Clarendon Press, 1959.

Lord, Albert B. "Gilgamesh and Other Epics." Abusch. *Lingering Over Words.* 371–80.

Lord, Albert B. "Homer and Other Epic Poetry." *A Companion to Homer.* Ed. A. J. B. Wace. NY: Macmillan, 1963. 179–214.

Lord, Albert B. *The Singer of Tales.* Cambridge, MA: Harvard UP, 1960.

Lord, Mary Louise. "Near Eastern Myths and the Classical Relatives." *The Teaching of Classical Mythology*. Amherst, MA: NECN Publications, 1981.

Loretz, Oswald. *Ugarit und die Bibel.* Darmstadt: Wissenschaftliche Buchgesellschaft, 1990.

Lovejoy, Arthur O., and B. Boas. *Primitivism and Related Ideas in Antiquity*. Baltimore: Johns Hopkins, 1935.

Lowth, R. *Lectures on the Sacred Poetry of the Hebrews.* 2 Vols. London: J. Johnson, 1787.

Lucas, F. L., tr. *Gilgamesh, King of Erech.* London: Golden Cockerel, 1948. 12 engravings by Dorothea Braby.

Luckenbill, Daniel David. *Ancient Records of Assyria and Babylonia.* 2 Vols. Chicago: U of Chicago P, 1926–27.

Luckenbill, Daniel David. *The Annals of Sennacherib.* Chicago: U of Chicago P, 1924.

Luckenbill, Daniel David. "Shût-abni, those of stone." *AJSL* 38 (1922): 96–102.

Luis, K. R. R. Gros, et al. *Literary Interpretations of Biblical Narratives.* Nashville: Abingdon, 1974, 1982.

Lukas, Franz. *Die Grundbegriffe in den Kosmogonien der alten Völker.* Leipzig: W. Friedrich, 1893.

Lundberg, Donald E. *The Tourist Business.* NY: Van Nostrand Reinhold, 1990.

Lutz, Henry Frederick. *Early Babylonian Letters from Larsa.* New Haven: Yale UP, 1917.

Lyon, David Gordon. *Keilschrifttexte Sargon's, Königs von Assyrien, 722–725 v. Chr.* Leipzig: Hinrichs, 1883.

Maass, Ernst. *Commentariorum in Aratum Reliquiae.* Berlin: Weidmann, 1898.

Machinist, Peter B. "Literature as Politics: The Tukulti-Ninurta Epic and the Bible." *CBQ* 38 (1976): 455–82.

MacKendrick, Paul Lachlan, tr. *The Roman Mind at Work.* NY: Van Nostrand, 1958.

Mad. David. "L'épisode des oiseaux dans le récit du Déluge." *Vetus Testamentum* 7 (1957): 189–90.

Mad. David. "Gilgamesh et l'histoire de l'argent." *Ar. Or.* 17 (1949): 100–109.

Mad. David. "De quelques problèmes soulevés par l'épopée de Gilgamesh. Analyse de plusieurs publications récentes." *RES* 5 (1939): 32–48.

Maidman, Maynard Paul. "The Tehip-tilla Family of Nuzi: A Genealogical Reconstruction." *JCS* 28 (1976): 127–55.

Maier, John. "The Ancient Near East in Modern Thought." Sasson. *Civilizations of the Ancient Near East.* Vol. 1. 107–22.

Maier, John. "Appendix: Translating *Gilgamesh.*" Gardner and Maier. 275–304.

Maier, John. "Authors and Mouths: The Case of *Gilgamesh.*" *CEA Critic* 47 (1985): 3–12.

Maier, John. "Une catégorie de la littérature mondiale: La littérature archaïque." *Littérature générale/Littérature comparée* 6 (1992): 21–33.

Maier, John. "Charles Olson and the Poetic Uses of Mesopotamian Scholarship," with an Appendix by Jack M. Sasson, "Musical Settings for Cuneiform Literature: A Discography." *JAOS* 103 (1983): 227–35.

Maier, John. "The File on Leonidas Le Cenci Hamilton." *American Literary Realism, 1870–1910* 11 (1978): 25–31.

Maier, John. "Gilgamesh: Anonymous Tradition and Authorial Value." *Neohelicon* 14 (1988): 83–95.

Maier, John. "Gilgamesh—by Gardner." *Aramco World Magazine* 34 (1983): 4–11.

Maier, John. "Introduction: The One Who Saw the Abyss." Gardner and Maier. 1–54; selections rpt. Krstović. 354–65.

Maier, John. "Mesopotamian Names in *The Sunlight Dialogues*; Or, MAMA Makes It To Batavia, New York." *Literary Onomastics Studies* 4 (1977): 33–48.

Maier, John. "The Signature of the *Translateur.*" *Thor's Hammer: Essays on John Gardner.* Ed. Jeff Henderson. Batesville, Arkansas: U of Central Arkansas P, 1985. 89–99.

Maier, John. "Three Voices of Enki: Strategies in the Translation of Archaic Literature." *Comparative Criticism.* Vol. 6. Cambridge: UP, 1984. 101–117.

Maier, John. "Translating Archaic Literature." *Babel* (Budapest) 29 (1983): 76–82.

Maier, John. "Translating *Gilgamesh* XII." *Translation Perspectives.* Ed. Marilyn Gaddis Rose. Binghamton: Translation Research and Instruction Program, 1984. 45–56.

Maier, John. "The 'Truth' of a Most Ancient Work: Interpreting a Poem Addressed to a Holy Place." *Centrum,* N.S. 2 (1982): 27–44.

Maier, John, Paul Ferguson, Sarah Mathiessen, and Frank McConnell. "John Gardner. The Art of Fiction LXIII." *The Paris Review* 21 (1979): 36–74; rpt. *Writers at Work.* Ed. George Plimpton. NY: Viking, 1984. 375–410.

Maier, John, and John Gardner. "*Gilgamesh* XII." *MSS* 2 (1983): 165–72.

Maier, John, and Parvin Ghassemi. "Postmodernity and the Ancient Near East." *Alif, Journal of Comparative Poetics* (Cairo) 4 (1984): 77–98.

Maitland, F. W., and Sir Frederick Pollock. *The History of the English Laws, Before the Time of Edward I.* Vol. 1. Cambridge: UP, 1968.

Makemson, Maud Worcester. *The Morning Star Rises: An Account of Polynesian Astronomy.* New Haven/London: Yale UP/Oxford UP, 1941.

Makkawi, Abd Al-Ghaffar. *Mukhamat Jiljamish.* Cairo: Dar al-Hilal, 1992.

Malamat, Abraham. "Campaigns to the Mediterranean by Iahdunlim and Other Early Mesopotamian Rulers." Güterbock and Jacobsen. *Studies...Benno Landsberger.* 365–73.

Malbran-Labat, Florence. *Gilgamesh.* Estella, Spain: Editorial Verbo Divino, 1983.

Malbran-Labat, Florence. *Gilgamesh.* Paris: de Cerf, 1982.

Malinowski, Bronislaw. *Magic, Science and Religion.* Garden City, NY: Doubleday, 1954.

Mallowan, Max E. L. *Nimrud and its Remains.* II. London: Collins, 1966.

Mallowen, Max E. L. "Noah's Flood Reconsidered." *Iraq* 26 (1964): 62–82.

Mandell, Sara. "Liminality, Altered States, and the Gilgamesh Epic." [Unpublished essay].

Mansfield, Jaap. "Aristotle and Others on Thales, on the Beginnings of Natural Philosophy." *Mnemosyne* 38 (1985): 123–29.

Marcatante, John. "Gilgamesh, The King Who Discovered His Other Self." *Tales from World Epics*. NY: Amsco School Publications, 1990.

Marcel, Jean. *Le chant de Gilgamesh: Récit sumérien*. Montreal-Nord: VLB, 1979.

Mardrus, Joseph C. *The Book of the Thousand Nights and One Night*. Tr. E. Powys Mathers. London: G. Routledge, 1947.

Markoe, Glenn. *Phoenician Bronze and Silver Bowls from Cyprus and the Mediterranean*. Berkeley: U of California P, 1985.

Marszewski, T. "The 'Cedar-Land' Motif in the Sumerian Poem about Gilgamesh. The Problem of Its Origin." *Folia Orientalia* 11 (1969): 201–22.

Martin, Didier. *Un sage universel: l'épopée de Gilgamesh*. Paris: Éditions G. Frères, 1979.

Martinu, Bohuslav. *The Epic of Gilgamesh*. Czech Republic: Supraphon, 1994. [Audio Recording].

Martinu, Bohuslav. *The Epic of Gilgamesh*: For Soloists, Mixed Chorus, and Orchestra. Vienna: Universal Edition, 1958. [Musical Score].

Martinu, Bohuslav. *The Epic of Gilgamesh* (Oratorio). Slovak Philharmonic Choir, Zdenek Kosler. Bratislava, 1989. Marco Polo CD #8.223316.

Martinu, Bohuslav. *Gilgamesh*. N.P.: Marco Polo, 1990. [Audio Recording].

Mason, Eugene, tr. *Aucassin and Nicolette and Other Medieval Romances and Legends*. London: Dent, 1910.

Mason, Herbert, tr. *Gilgamesh, A Verse Narrative*. NY: New American Library, 1970; Boston: Houghton Mifflin, 1972.

Matouš, Lubor. "Die Entstehung des Gilgamesch-Epos." *Das Altertum* 4 (1958): 195–208; rpt. Oberhuber. *Das Gilgamesch-Epos*. 360–74.

Matouš, Lubor. *Epos o Gilgamesovi.* Prague, 1958.

Matouš, Lubor. "Zur neueren epischen Literatur im alten Mesopotamien." *Ar. Or.* 35 (1967): 1–25.

Matouš, Lubor. "Zur neueren Literatur über das Gilgameš-Epos." *Bi. Or.* 21 (1964): 3–10.

Matouš, Lubor. "Zu neueren Übersetzungen des Gilgameš-Epos." *Ar. Or.* 44 (1976): 63–67.

Matouš, Lubor. "Les Rapports entre la version sumérienne et la version akkadienne de l'épopée de Gilgameš." *GSL.* 83–94.

Matouš, Lubor. "Review of Garelli, *Gilgameš et sa Légende*." *Bi. Or.* 21 (1964): 3–10.

Matsushima, Eiko. "Le Rituel Hiérogamique de Nabu." *Acta Sumerologica* 9 (1987): 131–71.

Matsushima, Eiko. "Les Rituels du Mariage Divin dans les Documents Accadiens." *Acta Sumerologica* 10 (1988): 95–128.

May, Rollo, ed. *Existence.* NY: Simon and Schuster, 1958.

Mayer, Maximilian. *Die Giganten und Titanen in der antiken Sage und Kunst.* Berlin: Weidmann, 1887.

Mayer, W. R. "Ein Mythos von der Erschaffung des Menschen und des Königs." *Or.* 56 (1987): 55–68.

Mayer, W. R. *Untersuchungen zur Formensprache der babylonischen "Gebetsbeschwörungen."* Rome: Biblical Institute, 1976.

McBride, S. Dean, Jr. *The Deuteronomic Name Theology.* Diss., Harvard University, 1969.

McCall, Henrietta. *Mesopotamian Myths.* London: British Museum, 1990.

McCartney, E. S. "Notes on Reading and Praying Audibly." *Classical Philology* 43 (1948): 184–87.

McCown, Donald E., and R. C. Haines. *Nippur I: Temple of Enlil, Scribal Quarter and Soundings.* Chicago: U of Chicago P, 1967.

McNeill, William H., and Jean W. Sedlar, eds. *The Origins of Civilization.* NY: Oxford UP, 1968.

McWalter, E. G. "Hitting the Road." *New York Times Magazine*. 27 May 1984. 46.

Mead, George Herbert. *George Herbert Mead on Social Psychology*. Ed. Anselm Strauss. Chicago: UP, 1964.

Meade, C. Wade. *Road to Babylon*. Leiden: E. J. Brill, 1974.

Meek, Theophile James, tr. "The Code of Hammurabi." *ANET*. 163–80.

Meid, Wolfgang, and Helga Trenkwalder, eds. *Im Bannkreis des Alten Orients*. Innsbruck: Innsbrucker Beiträge zur Kulturwissenschaft, 1986.

Meier, Gerhard. "Ein Kommentar zu einer Selbstpradikation des Marduk aus Assur." *ZA* 47 (1942): 241–46.

Meier, Gerhard. "Die zweite Tafel der Serie bīt mēseri." *AfO* 14 (1941–44): 139–52.

Meier, Samuel A. "Women and Communication in the Ancient Near East." *JAOS* 111 (1991): 540–47.

Meissner, Bruno. *Alexander und Gilgamos*. Leipzig: Eduard Pfeiffer, 1894.

Meissner, Bruno. *Ein altbabylonisches Fragment des Gilgamosepos*. Berlin: Peiser, 1902.

Meissner, Bruno. *Babylonien und Assyrien*. 2 Vols. Heidelberg: Carl Winter Universitätsverlag. 1920–25.

Meissner, Bruno. *Beiträge zum assyrischen Wörterbuch*. Vol 2. Chicago: U of Chicago P, 1932.

Mendelsohn, Isaac, ed. *The Religions of the Ancient Near East: Sumero-Akkadian Religious Texts and Ugaritic Epics*. Indianapolis: Bobbs-Merrill, 1955.

Merkelbach, Reinhold. *Mithras*. Königstein: Hain, 1984.

Metzger, Bruce M. *The Text of the New Testament: Its Transmission, Corruption, and Restoration*. 2nd. Ed. NY: Oxford UP, 1968.

Meyer, Leon de. "Introduction bibliographique." *GSL*. 1–30.

Michalowski, Piotr. "Royal Women of the Ur III Period." *JCS* 31 (1979): 171–76.

Michalowski, Piotr. "Sumerian Literature: An Overview." Sasson. *Civilizations of the Ancient Near East.* Vol. 4. 2279–292.

Mielke, Thomas R. P. *Gilgamesh, König von Uruk.* Reinbek bei Hamburg: Rowohlt, 1990.

Milik, J. T. *The Books of Enoch.* Oxford: Clarendon Press, 1976.

Millard, A. R. "The Etymology of Eden." *Vetus Testamentum* 34 (1984): 103–106.

Millard, A. R. "Gilgamesh X: A New Fragment." *Iraq* 26 (1964): 99–105.

Millard, A. R. "A New Babylonian 'Genesis' Story." *Tyndale Bulletin* 18 (1967): 3–18.

Millard, A. R. "The Sign of the Flood." *Iraq* 49 (1987): 63–69.

Miller, Gary D., and P. Wheeler. "Mother Goddess and Consort as Literary Motif Sequence in the Gilgamesh Epic." *Act. Ant.* 29 (1981): 81–108.

Miller, Patrick D., Jr. *Genesis 1–11: Studies in Structure and Theme.* Sheffield: U of Sheffield P, 1978.

Mills, P. L. "The Journey of Gilgamesh to the Isles of the Blest." *JAOS* 48 (1928): 3–42.

Mindlin, Murray. "The Word in the Beginning: The Figurative Language in the Ancient Near East." *Lettre Arch.* 7 (1984): 108–110.

Mindlin, Murray, et al., eds. *Figurative Language in the Ancient Near East.* London: School of Oriental and African Studies, 1987.

Mitchell, W. J. T., ed. *On Narrative.* Chicago: U of Chicago P, 1981.

Moore, C. A. *Esther.* Vol. 7B. The Anchor Bible. Ed. W. F. Albright and D. N. Freedman. Garden City, NY: Doubleday, 1971.

Moore, Fl. de. *La geste de Gilgameš confrontée avec la Bible et avec les documents historiques indigènes*. Louvain, 1898.

Moortgat, Anton. *Vorderasiatische Rollsiegel.* Berlin: Gebr. Mann, 1940.

Moran, William L., tr. "Akkadian Letters." *ANET.* 623–32.

Moran, William L. "Atrahasis: The Babylonian Story of the Flood." *Biblica* 52 (1971): 51–61.

Moran, William L. "The Epic of Gilgamesh: A Document of Ancient Humanism." *Bulletin of the Canadian Society for Mesopotamian Studies* 22 (1991): 15–22.

Moran, William L. "The Gilgamesh Epic: A Masterpiece from Ancient Mesopotamia." Sasson. *Civilizations of the Ancient Near East.* Vol. 4. 2327–336.

Moran, William L. "Gilg. I i 41." *RA* 71 (1977): 190–91.

Moran, William L. "New Evidence from Mari on the History of Prophecy." *Biblica* 50 (1969): 15–56.

Moran, William L. "Ovid's *Blanda Voluptas* and the Humanization of Enkidu." *JNES* 90 (1991): 121–27.

Moran, William L. "Review of Röllig, *Altorientalische Literaturen.*" *JAOS* 100 (1980): 189–90.

Moran, William L. "Rilke and the Gilgamesh Epic." *JCS* 32 (1980): 208–10.

Morgenstern, Julian. "On Gilgamesh Epic XI, 274–320: A Contribution to the study of the role of the serpent in Semitic mythology." *ZA* 4 (1929): 284–300.

Morris, Greg. "A Babylonian in Batavia: Mesopotamian Literature and Lore in *The Sunlight Dialogues.*" *John Gardner: Critical Perspectives.* Ed. Robert A. Morace and Kathryn VanSpanckeren. Carbondale, IL: Southern Illinois UP, 1982. 28–45, 157–58.

Morris, Ian. *Burial and Ancient Society: The Rise of the Greek City-state.* Cambridge: UP, 1987.

Morris, Peter E., and Peter J. Hampson. *Imagery and Consciousness.* London: Academic Press, 1983.

Moscati, Sabatino. *Ancient Semitic Civilizations.* London: Elek Books, 1957.

Mosshammer, A. A. *Georgius Syncellus, Ecloga Chronographica.* Leipzig: Teubner, 1984.

Mourad, Khireddine. *Le chant d'Adapa.* Paris: Agence de Cooperations Culturelle et Technique, 1989.

Mowinckel, Sigmund. "Einige Bemerkungen zur Einreihung der Gilgamešfragmente." *ZA* 30 (1916): 243–76.

Mowinckel, Sigmund. "Zur Göttlichkeit des Gilgameš und zur Entstehungszeit des Gilgameš-Epos." *Ac. Or.* 16 (1938): 244–50.

Mowinckel, Sigmund. "Noch einmal die Gilgameš-Fragmente." *ZA* 32 (1918): 78–91.

Mowinckel, Sigmund. "Zur siebenten Tafel des Gilgameš-Epos." *Ac. Or.* 15 (1937): 160–65.

Mowinckel, Sigmund. "Wer War Gilgameš?" *Ac. Or.* 15 (1937): 141–60; rpt. Oberhuber. *Das Gilgamesch-Epos.* 153–70.

Muhll, Peter Von der. *Kritisches Hypomnema zur Ilias.* Basel: F. Reinhardt, 1952.

Mullen, E. Theodore. *The Assembly of the Gods: The Divine Council in Canaanite and Early Hebrew Literature.* Atlanta, GA: Scholars Press, 1980.

Müller, Hans-Peter. "Gilgameschs Trauergesang um Enkidu und die Gattung der Totenklage." *ZA* 68 (1978): 233–50.

Müller, Hans-Peter. "Das Motif für die Sintflut. Die hermeneutische Funktion das Mythos und seiner Analyse." *Zeitschrift für die alttestamentliche Wissenschaft* 97 (1985): 295–316.

Munn, Nancy. *The Fame of Gawa.* NY: Penguin, 1975.

Murray, Gilbert. *Five Stages of Greek Religion.* Oxford: Clarendon, 1925.

Murray, Gilbert. *The Rise of the Greek Epic.* NY: Oxford UP, 1960.

Muss-Arnolt, William. *Assyrian and Babylonian Literature.* Ed. Robert Francis Harper. 2nd. Ed. NY: D. Appleton and Co., 1904.

Muss-Arnolt, William. *A Concise Dictionary of the Assyrian Language.* Berlin: Reuther & Reichard; NY: Lemcke & Buchner, 1905.

Muss-Arnold, William. "The Gilgamesh Narrative." *Assyrian and Babylonian Literature.* 324–69.

Myerhoff, Barbara, and Jay Ruby. "Introduction." Ruby. *A Crack in the Mirror.* 2–35.

Myhre, Øyvind. *Magiske verdener: Fantasilitteraturen fra Gilgamesj til Richard Adams.* Trondheim: J. W. Cappelens Forlag, 1979.

Nadel, Siegfried F. *The Foundations of Social Anthropology.* London: Cohen and West, 1951.

Nadel, Siegfried F. *The Theory of Social Structure.* London: Cohen and West, 1957.

Nagler, Michael N. *Spontaneity and Tradition: A Study in the Oral Art of Homer*. Berkeley: U of California P, 1974.

Nashef, Kh. "The Deities of Dilmun." *Akkadica* 38 (1984): 1–33.

Naster, Paul. "*ṣullulu* dans Gilgamesh XI, 31." *Symbolae biblicae mesopotamicae*. 295–98.

Nestyev, Israel V. *Prokofiev*. Stanford: UP, 1960.

Neynes, Gregorio. *O Caminho de Gilgamesh*. Rio de Janeiro, 1937.

Nikolic, Nikola. *Gilgameš i druge legende starog Babilona*. Zagreb: Tisk. Stunkovisc i Poljak, 1936.

Nikolov, Vesselin. "Gilgamesh." *Jazz and Something More—*. N.P.: Balkanton, 1987. [Audio Recording].

Njozi, Hamza M. "The Flood Narrative in the Gilgamesh Epic, The Bible and the Qur'an: The Problem of Kinship and Historicity." *Islamic Studies* 29 (1990): 303–309.

Noegel, Scott B. "A Janus Parallelism in the Gilgamesh Flood Story." *Acta Sumerologica* 13 (1991): 419–21.

Nola, Alfonso M. di. "Gilgamesh." *Enciclopedia della Religioni*. Florence: Vallecchi Editore, 1971. 3: Cols. 195–205.

Norden, E. P. *Vergilius Maro: Aeneis, Buch VI*. Leipzig/Berlin, 1934.

Nørgård, Per. "Gilgamesh." *Dansk Musik Antologi, 3*. Denmark: DMA, 1975. [Audio Recording].

Nørgård, Per. *Gilgamesh; Voyage into the Golden Screen*. N.P.: Dacapo, 1990. [Audio Recording].

Nørgård, Per. "Gilgamesch—en 500-arig aktualitet." *Nutida musik* 17 (1973–74): 5ff.

Norris, H. T. *The Cambridge History of Arabic Literature*. Vol. 1. Cambridge: UP, 1983.

North, Robert. "Status of the Warka Expedition." *Or.* 26 (1957): 185–256.

Norton, Charles Eliot, tr. *The Divine Comedy of Dante Alighieri*. Boston/NY: Houghton Mifflin, 1902.

Nortwick, Thomas Van. "The Wild Man: The *Epic of Gilgamesh*." *Somewhere I Have Never Travelled: The Second Self and the Hero's Journey in Ancient Epic*. NY: Oxford UP, 1992. 8–38, 186, 190.

Notscher, F. "Die Gilgamesch-Dichtung." *Augustinianum* 1 (1961): 120–23.

Nougayrol, Jean. "L'Épopée babylonienne." *Atti del convegno internazionale sul tema: La poesia epica e la sua formazione (Roma, 28 marzo 3 aprile 1969).* Roma: Accademia Nazionale dei Lincei, 1970. 839–58.

Nougayrol, Jean. "Une nouvelle 'mise à mort' de Ḫumbaba." *RA* 47 (1953): 3–4.

Nougayrol, Jean, et al. *Le Palais royal d'Ugarit III.* Paris: Imprimerie Nationale and Librarie C. Klincksieck, 1955.

Nougayrol, Jean. "*Sirrimu* (non **purîmu*) 'âne sauvage.'" *JCS* 2 (1948): 203–208.

Nougayrol, Jean. *Ugaritica V.* Paris: Imprimerie Nationale and Librarie Orientaliste Paul Geuthner, 1968.

Noveck, M. *The Mark of Ancient Man. Ancient Near Eastern Stamp Seals and Cylinder Seals. The Gorelick Collection.* Brooklyn: Brooklyn Museum, 1975.

O'Flaherty, Wendy Doninger. *Androgynes and Other Mythical Beasts.* Chicago: UP, 1980.

O'Flaherty, Wendy Doniger, and Mircea Eliade. "Androgynes." *The Encyclopedia of Religion.* NY: Macmillan, 1987. 1: 276–81.

Oberhuber, Karl. "Gilgamesch." Oberhuber. *Das Gilgamesch-Epos.* 1–22.

Oberhuber, Karl, ed. *Das Gilgamesch-Epos.* Darmstadt: Wissenschaftliche Buchgesellschaft, 1977.

Oberhuber, Karl. *Der Numinose Begriff "ME" im Sumerischen.* Innsbruck: Innsbrucker Beiträge zur Kulturwissenschaft, 1963.

Oberhuber, Karl. "Odysseus-Utis in altorientalischer Sicht." *Festschrift Leonhard C. Franz.* Ed. O. Menghin and H. M. Ölberg. Innsbruck: Sprachwissenschaftliches Institut der Leopold-Franzens-Universität, 1965. 307–12.

Oberhuber, Karl. "Wege der Gilgamesch-Forschung, Ein Vorwort." Oberhuber. *Das Gilgamesch-Epos.* xiii–xxvi.

Ochshorn, Judith. "Ishtar and Her Cult." *The Book of the Goddess.* Ed. Carl Olson. NY: Crossroad Publishing, 1983. 16–28.

Oden, Robert A. "Divine Aspirations in Atrahasis and in Genesis 1 11." *Zeitschrift für alttestamentliche Wissenschaft* 93 (1981): 214–15.

Oden, Robert A. *God and Mankind: Comparative Religion.* Kearneysville, WV: The Teaching Company, 1991. [Audio Recording].

Oden, Robert A. "Grace or Status? Yahweh's Clothing of the First Humans." *The Bible Without Theology: The Theological Tradition and Alternatives to It.* NY: Harper & Row, 1987. 92–105.

Oden, Robert A. *Religious Heroes. Gilgamesh and the Dawn of History.* Arlington, VA: The Teaching Company, 1990. [Audio Recording].

Oelsner, J. "Ein Beitrag zu keilschriftlichen Königstitulaturen in hellenistischer Zeit." *ZA* 56 (1964): 262–74.

Offner, G. "Jeux corporels en Sumer." *RA* 56 (1962): 31–38.

Olson, Charles. *Additional Prose.* Ed. George F. Butterick. Bolinas: Four Seasons, 1974.

Olson, Charles. *Archaeologist of Morning.* London: Cape Goliard Press, 1970.

Olson, Charles. *Call Me Ishmael.* NY: Harcourt, Brace, 1947.

Olson, Charles. *Causal Mythology.* San Francisco: Four Seasons Foundation, 1969.

Olson, Charles. "Dogtown the Dog Bitch." *Olson* 9 (1978): 46.

Olson, Charles. "The four quarters." *Olson* 9 (1978): 38.

Olson, Charles. *Human Universe and Other Essays.* Ed. Donald Allen. NY: Grove Press, 1967.

Olson, Charles. *Letters for Origin, 1950–1956.* Ed. Albert Glover. NY: Grossman, 1970.

Olson, Charles. "like two spiders." *Olson* 9 (1978): 39.

Olson, Charles. *The Maximus Poems.* NY: Jargon/Corinth Books, 1960; Vol. 3. Ed. Charles Boer and George F. Butterick. NY: Grossman, 1975.

Olson, Charles. "A Norm for my love in her NOMOS, or..." *Olson* 9 (1978): 37.

Olson, Charles. "Notes for the Proposition: Man is Prospective." *boundary 2* 2 (1973/1974): 1–6.

Olson, Charles. *Selected Writings.* Ed. Robert Creeley. NY: New Directions, 1966.

Olson, Charles. "she is the sea..." *Olson* 9 (1978): 19.

Olson, Charles. *The Special View of History.* Ed. Ann Charters. Berkeley: Oyez, 1970.

Olson, Charles. "Transpositions." *Alcheringa* 5 (1973): 5–11.

Ong, Walter J. *Orality and Literacy.* NY: Methuen, 1982.

Opificius, Ruth. *Das altbabylonische Terrakottarelief.* Berlin, 1961.

Opificius, Ruth. "Gilgamesch und Enkidu in der bildenden Kunst." *Hundert Jahre Berliner Gesellschaft für Anthropologie, Ethnologie und Urgeschichte* 2 (1970): 286–92.

Opitz, D. *Propylaen Kunstgeschichte 14.* Berlin: Propylaen Verlag, 1977.

Opitz, D. "Der Tod des Ḫumbaba." *AfO* 5 (1929): 207–13.

Oppenheim, A(dolf) Leo. *Ancient Mesopotamia: Portrait of a Dead Civilization, with an appendix, "Mesopotamian Chronology of the Historical Period," by J. A. Brinkman.* Chicago: U of Chicago P, 1964.

Oppenheim, A. Leo, tr. "Babylonian and Assyrian Historical Texts." *ANET.* 265–317, 556–67.

Oppenheim, A. Leo. "Das Gilgamesch-Epos." *Ancient Mesopotamia.* 255–63; tr. Karl Nicolai rpt. Oberhuber. *Das Gilgamesch-Epos.* 434–45.

Oppenheim, A. Leo. *The Interpretation of Dreams in the Ancient Near East.* Philadelphia: American Philosophical Society, 1956.

Oppenheim, A. Leo. "Laterculis Coctilibus." *Mesopotamia.* 228–87; selections rpt. Krstović. 321–23.

Oppenheim, A. Leo. "Mesopotamian Mythology, 1–3." *Or.* 16 (1947): 207–38; 17 (1948): 17–58; 19 (1950): 129–58.

Oppenheim, A. Leo. "A New Prayer to the Gods of the Night." *Analecta Biblica* 12 (1959): 282–301.

Oppenheim, A. Leo. "The Seafaring Merchants of Ur." *JAOS* 74 (1954): 6–17.

Oppenheim, Max von. *Tell Halaf III: Die Bildwerke.* Ed. Anton Moortgat. Berlin: de Gruyter, 1955.

Oppert, Jules. *Le poèm chaldéen du déluge.* Paris: J. Kugelmann, 1885.

Ordover, Andrew C. *Gilgamesh.* Ohio Theatre, NY. [Drama performed March–April, 1995].

Orlin, Louis L. *Ancient Near Eastern Literature: A Bibliography of One Thousand Items on the Cuneiform Literatures of the Ancient World.* Ann Arbor, MI: Campus Publishers, 1969.

Ortega, Jose Ortega. *Khol, Gilgamesh y la muerte.* Murcia: Editora Regional de Murcia, 1990.

Ortner, Sherry. "Is Female to Male as Nature Is to Culture?" *Women, Culture, and Society.* Ed. Michelle Z. Rosaldo and Louise Lamphere. Stanford: UP, 1974. 67–87.

Osten, H. H. von der. "Medalhavsmuseet." *Bulletin* 1 (1961): 2–7.

Østrup, F. L. *Genfremstilling af det gamle babyloniske Gilgamesh-epos om Venneparet Gilgamesh og Engidu.* Copenhagen: Nyt Nordisk Forlag, 1940.

Osze, Andrew. *Gilgamesh.* St. Louis, MO: American Hungarian Review, 1980.

Otten, Heinrich. "Eine Beschwörung der Unterirdischen aus Bogazkoy." *ZA* 54 (1961): 114–57.

Otten, Heinrich. "Die erste Tafel des hethitischen Gilgamesch-Epos." *Ist. Mit.* 8 (1958): 93–125.

Otten, Heinrich. "Gilgameš. C. Nach hethitischen Texten." *RLA* 3 (1968): 372.

Otten, Heinrich. *Keilschrifttexte aus Boghazkoi.* Berlin: Mann, 1955.

Otten, Heinrich. "Zur Überlieferung des Gilgameš-Epos nach den Boğazköy-Texten." *GSL.* 139–43.

Otten, Heinrich, and Jana Siegelová. "Die hetitischen Gula-Gottheiten und die Erschaffung der Menschen." *AfO* 23 (1970): 32–38.

Ottinger, N. "Die 'dunkle Erde' im Hethitischen und Griechischen." *WO* 20–21 (1989–90): 83–98.

Ovid. *Metamorphoses.* Tr. M. A. Innes. Harmondsworth, England: Penguin, 1955.

Owen, David I. "The World's Great Epics III. Gilgamesh." *Horizon* 15 (1973): 112–16.

Oyens, Tera de Marez. *Gilgamesh Quartet: For Four Trombones.* Amsterdam: Donemus, 1988. [Musical Score].

Paine, Robert. "In Search of Friendship: An Exploratory Analysis in 'Middle-Class' Culture." Man 4 (1969): 505–24.

Palacios, Miguel Asin. *La Escatalogia musulmana en la Divina Comedia.* Madrid: Imp. de E. Maestre, 1919.

Pallis, Marco. *Peaks and Lamas.* 4th. Ed. London: Cassell and Co., 1946.

Pallis, Svend Aage. *The Babylonian Akitu Festival.* Copenhagen: Bianco Lunos Bogtrykkeri, 1926.

Palmer, George Herbert, tr. *The Odyssey.* Boston: Houghton Mifflin, 1921.

Pannwitz, Rudolf. *Gilgamesch-Sokrates, Titanentum und Humanismus.* Stuttgart: Klett, 1966.

Panofsky, Erwin. "Et in Arcadia ego: Poussin and the Elegiac Tradition." *Meaning in the Visual Arts.* Garden City: Doubleday, 1955.

Papke, Werner. "Die Geburt Enkidu's und Gilgameš's erster Traum." *RAI* 28 (1981): 289–94.

Papke, Werner. *Die Sterne von Babylon. Die geheime Botschaft des Gilgamesh—nach 4000 Jahren entschlüsselt.* Bergish Gladbach: Gustav Luebbe Verlag, 1989.

Parlee, M. B., et al. "The Friendship Bond." *Psychology Today* 13 (1979): 42–54, 113.

Parrot, André. *Déluge et arche de Noé.* Neuchatal: Delachaux et Niestle, 1952.

Parrot, André. *Mission archéologique de Mari II. Le Palais.* Paris: P. Geuthner, 1959.

Parrot, André. "Scenes de guerre à Larsa." *Iraq* 31 (1969): 64–67.

Parpola, Simo. "The Assyrian Tree of Life: Tracing the Origins of Jewish Monotheism and Greek Philosophy." *JNES* 52 (1993): 161–208.

Parry, Milman. *The Making of Homeric Verse.* NY/Oxford: Oxford UP, 1971.

Paul, Shalom M. "The Cognate Semitic Terms for Mating and Copulation." *Vetus Testamentum* 32 (1982): 492–94.

Paul, Shalom M. "Heavenly Tablets and the Book of Life." *JANES* 5 (1973): 345–53.

Paul, Shalom M. "Psalm 72:5—A Traditional Blessing for the Long Life of the King." *JNES* 31 (1972): 351–55.

Paul, Shalom M. *Studies in the Book of the Covenant in the Light of the Cuneiform and Biblical Law.* Leiden: Brill, 1970.

Paul, Sherman. *Olson's Push.* Baton Rouge, Louisiana UP, 1978.

Paulys Realencyclopadie der classischen Altertumswissenschaft. Stuttgart/Munich: Alfred Druckenmuller Verlag, 1894–1980. = *RE*

Pausanias. *Description of Greece.* Tr. W. H. S. Jones and H. A. Ormerod. Vol. 2. London: Heinemann, 1926.

Pearce, Laurie E. "The Scribes and Scholars of Ancient Mesopotamia." Sasson. *Civilizations of the Ancient Near East.* Vol. 4. 2265–278.

Peinado, Federico Lara. *Poema de Gilgamesh.* Madrid: Editora Nacional, 1980.

Perinbanayagam, R. S. *Signifying Acts.* Carbondale: Southern Illinois UP, 1985.

Pettinato, Giovanni. *Das altorientalische Menschenbild und die sumerischen und akkadischen Schöpfungsmythen.* Heidelberg: Carl Winter Universitätsverlag, 1971.

Pettinato, Giovanni. *Catalogo dei testi cuneiformi di Tell Mardikh-Ebla.* Naples: Istituto Univerario Orientali di Napoli, 1979.

Pettinato, Giovanni. *Ebla: Un impero inciso nell'argilla.* Milan: Arnoldo Mondadori Editore, 1979.

Pettinato, Giovanni. *Old Canaanite Cuneiform Texts of the Third Millennium.* Tr. Matthew L. Jaffe. Malibu: Undena, 1979.

Pettinato, Giovanni. "The Royal Archive of Tel-Mardikh-Ebla." *Biblical Archaeologist* 39 (1976): 50.

Pettinato, Giovanni. *Le saga di Gilgamesh.* Milan: Rusconi, 1992.

Pfeiffer, Robert Henry, tr. "Akkadian Observations on Life and the World Order." *ANET*. 434–40.

Pfeiffer, Robert Henry. *State Letters of Assyria and Babylonia.* New Haven: American Oriental Society, 1935.

Picard, Barbara Leonie. *Three Ancient Kings: Gilgamesh, Hrolf Kraki, Conary.* London: Kaye and Ward, NY: F. Warne, 1972.

Pierce, Frederick. *Dreams and Personality.* NY: D. Appleton, 1931.

Pilard, Virginia Ferrell. *Gilgamesh Epic Tapestry.* 8010 Dutch Oak Circle, Spring, TX 77379. [8' x 5' Quilt.]

Pinches, Theophilus Goldridge. "Gilgameš and the Hero of the Flood." *PSBA* (1903): 113–22, 195–201. Plates after p. 122.

Pio, J. R. *L'épopée de Gilgamesh.* Paris: EDIFRA, 1989.

Pitt-Rivers, Julian Alfred. *The People of the Sierra.* NY: Criterion, 1954.

Plant, W. Gunther, et al. *The Torah: A Modern Commentary.* NY: Union of American Hebrew Congregations, 1981.

Pliny. *Natural History.* Vol. 2. Tr. H. Ruckhum. Cambridge: Harvard UP, 1947.

Poebel, Arno. *Historical Texts.* Philadelphia: University Museum, University of Pennsylvania, 1914.

Poebel, Arno. *Historical and Grammatical Texts.* Philadelphia: University Museum, University of Pennsylvania, 1914.

Poebel, Arno. "Der Name der Mutter des Gilgameš." *OLZ* 17 (1914): 4–6.

Pohl, Frederik. "Gilgamesh in the Outback." *The New Hugo Winners.* Ed. Isaac Asimov. Vol. 2. Riverdale, NY: Baen Books, 1992.

Polin, Claire C. J. *Scenes from Gilgamesh.* NY: Seesaw Music Corp., 1974. [Musical Score].

Pope, Marvin H. *Job.* Vol. 15. The Anchor Bible. Ed. W. F Albright and D. N. Freedman. 2nd. Ed. Garden City, NY: Doubleday, 1973.

Pope, Marvin H. *Song of Songs.* Vol. 7C. The Anchor Bible. Ed. W. F. Albright and D. N. Freedman. Garden City, NY: Doubleday, 1977.

Pope, Marvin H., and Jeffrey H. Tigay. "A Description of Baal." *Ugarit-Forschungen* 3 (1971): 117–30.

Poplicha, Joseph. "A Sun Myth in the Babylonian Deluge Story." *JAOS* 47 (1927): 289–301.

Porada, Edith. *The Art of Ancient Iran. Pre-Islamic Cultures.* London: Crown Publishers, 1965.

Porada, Edith. *Corpus of Ancient Near Eastern Seals in North American Collections I. The Collections of the Pierpont Morgan Library.* NY: Pantheon, 1948.

Porada, Edith. "Seal Impressions of Nuzi." *AASOR* 24 (1947): 3–138, + 54 plates.

Potts, Daniel T., ed. *Dilmun: New Studies in the Archaeology and Early History of Bahrain.* Berlin: Dietrich Reimer Verlag, 1983.

Poulet, Georges. *Exploding Poetry: Baudelaire/Rimbaud.* Tr. Françoise Meltzer. Chicago: U of Chicago P, 1984.

Pratt, Mary Louise. "Fieldwork in Common Places." *Writing Culture: The Poetics and Politics of Ethnography.* Ed. James Clifford and George E. Marcus. Berkeley: U of California P, 1986. 27–50.

Pratt, Mary Louise. *Toward a Speech Act Theory of Literary Discourse.* Bloomington: Indiana UP, 1977.

Prévot, Dominique. "L'Épopée de Gilgamesh: un scénario imitiatiquo?" *Les rites d'initiation.* Louvain-la-Neune: Centre d'Histoire des religions, 1986.

Prince, John Dyneley. "Note sur le nom Gilgameš." *Babyloniaca* 2 (1907): 62–64.

Printz, W. "Gilgamesch und Alexander." *ZDMG* 85 (1931): 196–206.

Pritchard, James B., ed. *Ancient Near Eastern Texts Relating to the Old Testament.* 3rd Ed. Princeton: Princeton UP, 1969. = *ANET*

Proosdij, B. A. van. "Fragment van het Gilgamesj Epos ontdekt." *Poenix* 1 (1955): 16.

Proosdij, B. A. van. "Gilgamesj." *JEOL* 8 (1942): 6–81.

Proosdij, B. A. van. "Voor-Aziatische Philologie, inzonderheid het Gilgameš-Epos." *JEOL* 2 (1934): 32–35.

Proosdij, B. A. van. "Het Zondvloedverhall in het Gilgamesjepos." *Kernmomenten der antieke beschaving en haar moderne beleving.* Leiden: E. J. Brill, 1947. 15–18.

Pruyser, Paul W., and J. Tracy Luke. "The Epic of Gilgamesh." *American Imago* 39 (1982): 73–93; selections rpt. Krstović. 343–49.

Przyluski, J. "Kubaba et Kombabos." *RHA* 5 (1940): 205–209.

Purvis, J. D. *The Samaritan Pentateuch and the Origin of the Samaritan Sect.* Cambridge, MA: Harvard UP, 1968.

Quay, Timothy, and Stephen Quay. *Epic of Gilgamesh.* NY: First Run Icarus Films, 1985. [Audiovisual Recording].

Raab, Irmgard. *Zu den Darstellungen des Parisurteils in der griechischen Kunst.* Frankfurt: Lang, 1972.

Rabinovic, E. G. "The Story of Gilgamesh and the Symbolism of Initiation." *VDI* 131 (1975): 780–86. [Russian, with English summary]

Rad, Gerhard von. "The Form-Critical Problem of the Hexateuch." *The Problem of the Hextateuch and Other Essays.* NY: McGraw-Hill, 1966. 1–78.

Rad, Gerhard von. "Typological Interpretation of the Old Testament." *Essays on Old Testament Hermeneutics.* Ed. Claus Westermann. Tr. James Luther Mays. 2nd. Ed. Richmond: John Knox, 1964. 17–39.

Radau, Hugo. *The Babylonian Expedition of the University of Pennsylvania. Series A: Cuneiform Texts.* Philadelphia: U Museum, 1911.

Radau, Hugo. *Hilprecht Anniversary Volume.* Leipzig: J. C. Hinrichs, 1909. N. 11–12.

Radau, Hugo. *Sumerian Hymns and Prayers to God "Nin-ib" from the Temple Library of Nippur.* Philadelphia: Department of Archaeology, University of Pennsylvania, 1911.

Raglan, FitzRoy Richard Somerset, Baron. *The Hero.* London: Methuen, 1936.

Rainey, Anson F. *El Amarna Tablets 359–379.* Kevelaer: Butzon and Bercker; Neukirchen-Vluyn: Neukirchner Verlag, 1970.

Ramsoy, Odd. "Friendship." *International Encyclopedia of the Social Sciences.* Ed. David L. Sills. NY: Crowell Collier and Macmillan, 1968. 6: 12–17.

Rank, Otto. *The Myth of the Birth of the Hero and Other Writings.* Ed. Philip Freund. NY: Vintage, 1959.

Ranke, Hermann. *Gilgamesch. Das altbabylonische Gilgamesch-Epos.* Hamburg: L. Friederichsen, 1924.

Ranke, Hermann. "Zur Vorgeschichte des Gilgamesch-Epos." *ZA* 49 (1950): 45–49.

Ranoszek, R. "Review of Schott, *Das Gilgamesch-Epos.*" *ZDMG* 88 (1934): 209–11.

Rappaport, Izaak. *The Biblical Flood Story is Not Linked to Any Babylonian Prototype.* London: [Author's Self-Publication], 1981.

Rappaport, Izaak. "The Flood Story in Bible and Cuneiform Literature." *Dor Le Dor* 12 (1982–84): 95–103.

Rappaport, Izaak. *Tablet XI of the Gilgamesh Epic and the Biblical Flood Story.* Tel-Aviv: Tel-Aviv University, 1981.

Rassam, Hormuzd. *Asshur and the Land of Nimrod.* NY: Easton and Mains, 1897; rpt. London: Gregg International Pub., 1971.

Ravn, Otto Emil. *Babylonske religiøse Tekster.* Copenhagen: Gydlendalske Boghandel, 1953.

Ravn, Otto Emil. *De gamle babyloneres zyn pa liv og dod.* Copenhagen: V. Pios, 1919.

Ravn, Otto Emil. "Notes on Selected Passages in *Enuma Eliš* and *Gilgameš.*" *Or.* 22 (1955): 28–54.

Ravn, Otto Emil. "The Passage on Gilgamesh and the Wives of Uruk." *Bi. Or.* (1953): 12–13.

Rawlinson, Henry and George Smith. *The Cuneiform Inscriptions of Western Asia* 4 (1875): 48–49, 50–51; 2nd. Ed. with T. G. Pinches, 1891.

Raymond J. Clark, "Origins: New Light on Eschatology in Gilgamesh's Mortuary Journey." [Unpublished Essay].

Razamanoglu, Muzaffer. *Gilgameš destani.* Istanbul: Maarif Matbaasi, 1944.

Reallexikon der Assyriologie. Vol. 4. Berlin/NY: de Gruyter, 1972–75. = *RLA*

Reck, Gregory G. "Introduction: Fiction's Niche in Anthropology." *Lament and Exodus.* Ed. Bruce T. Grindal and Gregory G. Reck Washington, D.C.: Society for Humanistic Anthropology, 1988.

Reck, Gregory G. "Narrative Anthropology." *Anthropology and Humanism Quarterly* 8 (1983): 8–12.

Reck, Gregory G. "Narrative Anthropology." Paper presented at the American Anthropological Association meeting, Philadelphia, 1986.

Redfield, R. *The Primitive World and its Transformations.* Ithaca: Cornell UP, 1953.

Redford, D. B. "The Literary Motif of the Exposed Child (Cf. Ex.ii, 110)." *Numen* 14 (1967): 209–28.

Reeves, John C. "Utnapishtim in the Book of Giants?" *JBL* 112 (1993): 110–15.

Reiff, Tana. "Gilgamesh, Who Wanted to Live Forever." *Adventures.* Syracuse, NY: New Readers Press, 1993. [Audio Recording].

Reimer, P. J. *Zeven tegen Thebe.* Diss., Amsterdam, 1953.

Reiner, Erica, tr. "Akkadian Treaties from Syria and Assyria." *ANET.* 531–41.

Reiner, Erica. "Die akkadische Literatur." *Altorientalische Literaturen: Neues Handbuch der Literaturwissenschaft.* Ed. W. Röllig. Vol. 1. Wiesbaden: Akademische Verlagsgesellschaft Athenaion, 1978. 151–210.

Reiner, Erica. "City Bread and Bread Baked in Ashes." *Languages and Areas: Studies Presented to George V. Bobrinskoy.* Chicago: U of Chicago P, 1967. 116–20.

Reiner, Erica. "The Etiological Myth of the 'Seven Sages.'" *Or.* 30 (1961): 1–11.

Reiner, Erica. "Fortune-telling in Mesopotamia." *JNES* 19 (1960): 23–35.

Reiner, Erica. *A Linguistic Analysis of Akkadian.* The Hague: Mouton, 1966.

Reiner, Erica. "Plague Amulets and House Blessings." *JNES* 19 (1960): 148–55.

Reiner, Erica. *Šurpu: A Collection of Sumerian and Akkadian Incantations.* Graz: E. Weidner, 1958.

Reiner, Erica. *Your Thwarts in Pieces, Your Mooring Rope Cut.* Ann Arbor: U of Michigan P, 1985.

Reiner, Erica, and Hans G. Güterbock. "The Great Prayer to Ishtar and Its Two Versions from Boğazköy." *JCS* 21 (1969): 255–66.

Reinhardt, Karl. *Das Parisurteil.* Frankfurt am Main: V. Klostermann, 1938.

Reisman, Daniel. "Iddin-Dagan's Sacred Marriage Hymn." *JCS* 25 (1973): 185–202.

Reisner, Gerge Andrew. *Sumerisch-babylonische Hymnen nach Thontafeln griechischer Zeit.* Berlin: Spemann, 1896.

Rendsburg, Gary A. "Note on Genesis XXXV." *Vetus Testamentum* 34 (1984): 361–66.

Rendsburg, Gary A. *The Redaction of Genesis.* Winona Lake, Indiana: Eisenbrauns, 1986.

Rendzov, Mihail. *Gilgameš.* Skopje: Makedonska Kniga, 1977.

Renger, Johannes. "Zur fünften Tafel des Gilgamesch-Epos." Rochberg-Halton. 317–26.

Renger, Johannes. "Gilg. P ii 32 [PBS 10/3]." *RA* 66 (1972): 190.

Renger, Johannes. "Heilige Hochzeit. A. Philologisch." *RLA* 4: 251–59.

Renger, Johannes. "Mesopotamian Epic Literature." *Heroic Epic and Saga: An Introduction to the World's Great Folk Epics.* Ed. F. J. Oinas. Bloomington, Indiana: Indiana UP, 1978. 27–48.

Renger, Johannes. "Untersuchungen zum Priestertum der altbabylonischen Zeit, 2." *ZA* 59 (1969): 104–230.

Rexroth, Kenneth. "The Epic of Gilgamesh." *Classics Revisited.* NY: New Directions, 1965, 1986. 1–4; selections rpt. Krstović. 323–24.

Reynolds, William H. "Per Nørgard." *The New Grove Dictionary of Music and Musicians.* Ed. Stanley Sadie. NY: Macmillan, 1980. 13: 278–80.

Rice, Roberta Wyatt. *The Development of the Gilgamesh Epic in Art.* Thesis, Virginia Commonwealth University, 1972.

Richardson, Miles. "Anthropologist—the Myth Teller." *American Ethnologist* 2 (1975): 517–33.

Richardson, Miles. "Gilgamesh and Christ: Two Contradictory Images of Man in Search of a Better World." *Aspects of Cultural Change.* Ed. Joseph Aceves. Athens, GA: U of Georgia P, 1972. 7–20.

Richardson, Miles. "Point of View in Anthropological Discourse: The Ethnographer as Gilgamesh." *Anthropological Poetics.* Ed. Ivan Brady. London: Rowman and Littlefield, 1991. 207–14.

Ricoeur, Paul. "The Model of the Text: Meaningful Action Considered as a Text." *Interpretive Social Science.* Ed. Paul Rabinow and William M. Sullivan. Berkeley: U of California P, 1979. 73–102.

Ricoeur, Paul. *The Rule of Metaphor.* Tr. Robert Czerny. Toronto: U of Toronto P, 1977.

Ricoeur, Paul. *The Symbolism of Evil.* Tr. Emerson Buchanan. Boston: Beacon Press, 1969. 171–74, 175–91.

Riessler, P. "Zur Lage des Göttesgartens bei den Alten." *Theologische Quartalschrift* 98 (1916): 273–313.

Riordan, James, and Brenda Ralph Lewis. "Gilgamesh the Mighty Warrior." *An Illustrated Treasury of Myths and Legends.* NY: Peter Bedrick, 1988. 32–37. Illustrations Victor Ambrus.

Rittig, D. *Assyrisch-Babylonische Kleinplastik magischer Bedeutung vom 13. bis 6. Jh. v. Chr.* Diss., Munich, 1977.

Rivers, William Halse R., ed. *Essays on the Depopulation of Melanesia.* Cambridge: UP, 1922; rpt. NY: AMS, 1972.

Roberts, J. J. M. *The Earliest Semitic Pantheon.* Baltimore: Johns Hopkins UP, 1972.

Rodgers, Bernard J., Jr. *Philip Roth.* Boston: Twayne Publishers, 1978.

Rogers, Robert William. *Cuneiform Parallels to the Old Testament.* NY: Eaton and Mains, 1912. 80–102.

Roggia, Gian Battista. "Einleitung zu Das Gilgamesch-Epos." *"L'epopea di Gilgamesch" con introduzione di G. B. Roggia.* Milan: Fratelli Bocca, 1944; tr. Felizitas Kiechl, 1977, Oberhuber. *Das Gilgamesch-Epos.* 178–218.

Roheim, Geza. *The Eternal Ones of the Dream.* NY: International Universities P, 1945.

Roheim, Geza. *The Origin and Function of Culture.* NY: Nervous and Mental Disease Monographs, 1943.

Roheim, Geza. *War, Crime, and the Covenant.* Monticello, NY: Journal of Clinical Psychopathology, 1945.

Romano, James V. "Heroism in the Gilgamesh Epic." *Eight Essays in Classical Humanities.* Ed. G. S. Schwartz. Millburn, NJ: R. F. Publishing, 1975. 1–8.

Römer, William Henrik Philibert. "The Religion of Ancient Mesopotamia." *Historia Religionum: Handbook for the History of Religions.* Vol. 1. *Religions of the Past.* Ed. C. J. Bleeker and G. Widengren. Leiden: Brill, 1969. 115–94.

Römer, William Henrik Philibert. "Review of Diakonoff, *Structure of Society and State.*" *Bi. Or.* 32 (1975): 380–82.

Römer, William Henrik Philibert. "Studien zu altbabylonisch epischen Texten, 1." Edzard. *Heidelberger Studien.* 185–99.

Römer, William Henrik Philibert. *Sumerische "Königshymnen" der Isin-Zeit.* Leiden: Brill, 1965.

Römer, William Henrik Philibert. *Das Sumerische Kurzepos "Bilgameš und Akka."* Neukirchen-Vluyn: Kevelaer, 1980.

Rooth, Anna Birgitta. *The Raven and the Cross: An Investigation of a Motif in the Deluge Myth in Europe, Asia and North America.* Helsinki: Suomalainen Tiedeakatemia Academia Scientiarum Fennica, 1962.

Roppen, George, and Richard Sommer. *Strangers and Pilgrims. An Essay on the Metaphor of the Journey.* Oslo: Norwegian UP, 1964.

Roscher, W. H. *Omphalos.* Leipzig: Abhandlung Sachs, 1913.

Rosenfield, Claire. "The Shadow Within: The Conscious and Unconscious Use of the Double." *Stories of the Double.* Ed. Albert J. Guerard. Philadelphia: Lippincott, 1967.

Rosengarten, Yvonne. *Trois aspects de la pensée religieuse sumérienne.* Paris: Boccard, 1971.

Rosenthal, Franz, tr. "Canaanite and Aramaic Inscriptions." *ANET.* 653–62.

Roth, Philip. *The Great American Novel.* NY: Farrar, Straus, and Giroux, 1973.

Roth, Philip. "On *The Great American Novel.*" *Reading Myself and Others.* NY: Farrar, Straus, and Giroux, 1975. 89–90.

Roux, Georges. *Ancient Iraq.* Harmondsworth, England: Pelican,1966.

Rowton, Michael B. "The Date of the Sumerian King List." *JNES* 19 (1960): 156–62.

Rowton, Michael B. "The Woodlands of Ancient Western Asia." *JNES* 26 (1967): 261–77.

Ruby, Jay, ed. *A Crack in the Mirror: Reflexive Perspectives in Anthropology.* Philadelphia: U of Pennsylvania P, 1982.

Ruby, Jay. "Exposing Yourself: Reflexivity, Anthropology, and Film." *Semiotica* 30 (1980): 153–80.

Russell, Margaret. *A Dig for the Devil.* Thesis, San Diego State College, 1969.

Sachs, Abraham Joseph, tr. "Akkadian Rituals." *ANET.* 331–45.

Sachs, Arieh. *Mivhar ha-shirah ha-erotit: me-alilot Gilgamesh ad Leonard Kohen.* Jerusalem: Keter, 1989.

Safavi, Hasan. *Pahlavan-namah-'i Gil Gamish.* Tehran: Amir Kabir, 1977.

Saggs, H. W. F. *The Greatness That Was Babylon.* NY: New American Library, 1962.

Sahagun, Bernardino de. *Florentine Codex: General History of the Things of New Spain.* Tr. Anderson and Dibble. 2nd. Ed. Santa Fe, New Mexico: School of American Research, 1970.

Salihi, Wathiq al-. "Hercules-Nergal at Hatra." *Iraq* 33 (1971): 113–15.

Salihi, Wathiq al-. "Hercules-Nergal at Hatra (II)." *Iraq* 35 (1973): 65–9.

Sallis, John, ed. *Heidegger and the Path of Thinking.* Pittsburgh: Duquesne UP, 1970.

Salonen, Armas. *Gilgamesh-Eepos.* Porvoo: W. Soderstrom, 1943.

Salonen, Armas. *Nautica Babyloniaca.* Helsinki: Societas Orientalis Fennica, 1942.

Sandars, N(ancy) K., tr. *The Epic of Gilgamesh.* Baltimore, MD: Penguin, 1960; Rev. Ed. 1972; Rev. Ed. 1975; Rev. Ed.,1988.

Sandars, N. K. *L'epopea di Gilgamiš.* Tr. Alessandro Passi. Milano: Adelphi Edizioni, 1986.

Sandars, N. K. *A Epopeia de Gilgamesh.* Lisbon: Edicoes Antonio Ramos, 1979.

Sandars, N. K. *Gilgamesh.* Lisbon: Vega, 1989.

Sandars, N. K. *Gilgamiš*. Istanbul: Can Yayinlari, 1984.

Santillana, Giorgio de, and Hertha von Dechend. *Hamlet's Mill: An Essay on Myth and the Frame of Time.* Boston: Gambit, 1969. 288–316, 317–25.

Saporetti, Claudio. "Gilgameš e Minosse." *Mesopotamia* 21 (1986): 237–47.

Sarignac, J. de. "La Saggessic du Qoheleth et L'épopée de Gilgamesh." *Vetus Testamentum* 8 (1978): 318–23.

Sarna, Nahum M. *Understanding Genesis: The Heritage of Biblical Israel.* NY: Jewish Theological Seminary and McGraw-Hill, 1966; NY: Schocken Books, 1970.

Sarsowsky, Abraham. "Sachliche und sprachliche Aufschlüsse zum Gilgameš-Epos." *Haḳedem* 1 (1907): 131–38.

Sarsowsky, Abraham. "Sachliche und sprachliche Aufschlüsse zum Gilgameš-Epos." *Haḳedem* 2 (1908): 1–10.

Sartre, Jean-Paul. *Being and Nothingness.* Tr. Hazel E. Barnes. NY: Philosophical Library, 1968.

Sasson, Jack M. "Canaanite Maritime Involvement in the Second Millennium B.C." *JAOS* 86 (1966): 126–38.

Sasson, Jack M., ed. *Civilizations of the Ancient Near East.* 4 Vols. NY: Charles Scribner's Sons, 1995.

Sasson, Jack M. "Instances of Mobility Among the Mari Artisans." *BASOR* 190 (1968): 46–54.

Sasson, Jack M. "Some Literary Motifs in the Composition of the Gilgamesh Epic." *Studies in Philology* 69 (1972): 259–79; selections rpt. Krstović. 336–40.

Sasson, Jack M. "The 'Tower of Babel' as a Clue to the Redactional Structuring of the Primeval History [Gen. 11:9]." *The Bible World: Essays in Honor of Cyrus H. Gordon.* Ed. G. Rendsburg, et al. NY: KTAV, 1980. 211–19.

Sasson, Jack M. "The Worship of the Golden Calf." *Orient and Occident: Essays Presented to Cyrus H. Gordon.* Ed. H. A. Hoffner, Jr. Kevelaer: Verlag Butzon & Bercher; Neukirchen-Vluyn: Neukirchener Verlag, 1973. 151–59.

Sauveplane, E. "Une épopée babylonienne—*Is-ṭu-Bar*—Gilgamés." *RHR* (1892–93).

Sawwa'h, Firas. *Kunuz al-Amaq*. Damascus: al-Arabi lil-Tiba'ah wa al-Nashr wa al-Tawzi, 1987.

Sayce, Archibald Henry. *Babylonian Literature.* London: Samuel Bagster and Sons, 1877.

Sayce, Archibald Henry. "Gilgameš." *PSBA* (1903): 266.

Sayce, Archibald Henry. "The Hittite Version of the Epic of Gilgameš." *JRAS* (1923): 559–71.

Sayce, Archibald Henry. *Lectures Upon the Assyrian Language and Syllabary.* London: Samuel Bagster, 1877.

Sayce, Archibald Henry. *Lectures on the Origin and Growth of Religion as Illustrated by the Religion of the Ancient Babylonians.* 2nd. Ed. London: Williams and Norgate, 1888.

Sayce, Archibald Henry. "Nimrod in the Assyrian Inscriptions." *The Academy* 1054 (1892): 53.

Sayce, Archibald Henry. *Reminiscenses.* London: Macmillan, 1923.

Sayers, Dorothy L., tr. *The Song of Roland.* Baltimore: Penguin, 1957.

Schachter, A. "The Theban Wars." *Phoenix* 21 (1967): 1–10.

Schefold, Karl. *Frühgriechische Sagenbilder.* Munich: Hirmer Verlag, 1964.

Schefold, Karl. *Myth and Legend in Early Greek Art.* London: Thames & Hudson, 1966.

Scheil, Vincent. "Notules LIX. Sur les deux songes de Gilgameš." *RA* 16 (1919): 114–15.

Schlesinger, Walter. "Lord and Follower in German Institutional History." *Lordship and Community in Medieval Europe: Selected Readings.* Ed. Frederic L. Cheyette. NY: Holt, Rinehart and Winston, 1968.

Schliephacke, Bruno P. *Gilgamesch sucht die Unsterblichkeit.* Munich: Deri Eichen Verlag, 1948–49.

Schmandt-Besserat, Denise, ed. *The Legacy of Sumer.* Malibu: Undena, 1976.

Schmidt, Brian. "Flood Narratives of Ancient Western Asia." Sasson. *Civilizations of the Ancient Near East.* Vol. 4. 2337–352.

Schmidt, E. G. "Himmel-Erde-Meer im frühgriechischen Epos und im alten Orient." *Philologus* 125 (1981): 1–24.

Schmidt, H. "Das Gilgamesch-Epos und die Bibel." *Theol. Rundschau* (1907): 189–208, 229–36.

Schmidt, Nancy J. "Ethnographic Fiction: Anthropology's Hidden Literary Style." *Anthropology and Humanism Quarterly* 9 (1984): 11–14.

Schmidtke, Friedrich von. "Gilgameschs Sterben nach Erlösung vom Tode." *Morgenland* 28 (1936): 7–23.

Schmitt, Rudiger. *Dichtung und Dichtersprache in indogermanischer Zeit.* Wiesbaden: Harrassowitz, 1967.

Schmökel, Hartmut, tr. *Das Gilgamesch-Epos.* Stuttgart: Kohlhammer, 1966; 2nd. Ed., 1971; 3rd. Ed., 1985.

Schneider, Hermann. "Die Entwicklung des Gilgameschepos" (Auszug). *Zwei Aufsätze zur Religionsgeschichte Vorderasiens.* 60–84; rpt. Oberhuber. *Das Gilgamesch-Epos.* 48–73.

Schneider, Hermann. *Zwei Aufsätze zur Religionsgeschichte Vorderasiens.* Leipzig: J. C. Hinrichs, 1909; rpt. NY: Johnson Reprint, 1968.

Schneider, Marius. "*Pukku* und *mikku.* Ein Beitrag zum Aufbau und zum System des Gilgamesch-Epos." *Antaios* 9 (1967–68): 262–83.

Schneider, Vera. *Gilgamesh.* Zurich: Origo-Verlag, 1967.

Schneider, Vera. "Gilgamesch und die drei Gerechten der Bibel." *Antaios* 6 (1964): 355–72.

Schollmeyer, Anastasius Franz. *Sumerische-babylonische Hymnen und Gebete an Šamaš: Studien zur Geschichte und Kultur des Altertums.* Vol. 1. *Ergänzungsband.* Paderborn: Schöningh, 1912.

Schoneveld, Jacobus H. *De oorpsong van het Bijbels Zondvloedverhall.* Groningen, 1938.

Schott, Albert, tr. *Das Gilgamesch-Epos neu übersetzt und mit Anmerkungen versehen.* Leipzig: Reclam, 1934; 2nd. Ed., revised and enlarged by W. von Soden. Stuttgart: Reclam, 1958; 3rd. Ed., 1970; 4th. Ed., 1977.

Schott, Albert. "Die inschriftlichen Quellen zur Geschichte Éannas." *UVB 1.* Ed. Julius Jordan. Berlin: Gebr. Mann, 1930.

Schott, Albert. "Zu meiner Übersetzung des Gilgameš-Epos." *ZA* 42 (1934): 921–43.

Schott, Albert. "Review of Dossin, *La Pâleur D'Enkidou.*" *OLZ* 36 (1933): 519–22.

Schott, Albert. *Die Vergleiche in den akkadischen Königsinschriften.* Leipzig: Hinrichs, 1926.

Schott, Albert. "Wann entstand das Gilgamesch-Epos?" *Festschirft Kahle.* Leiden: E. J. Brill, 1935. 1–14.

Schott, Albert. *Vorarbeiten zur Geschichte der Keilschriftliteratur.* Stuttgart: W. Kohlhammer, 1935.

Schoultz, Curt A. *Gilgamesh and the Gods.* Manitoba: Pierian Press and Cone Mune Visigraph, 1978.

Schrader, Eberhard. *Die Keilinschriften und Das Alte Testament.* Ed. H. Zimmern and H. Winchler. 3rd. Ed. Berlin: Reuther & Reichard, 1903.

Schrader, Eberhard. *Sammlung von Assyrischen und Babylonischen Texten in Umschrift und Übersetzung.* Berlin: H. Reuther & Reichard, 1889.

Schramm, W. "Zu Gilgameš Tf. VII, III, Z. 9 (Thompson, EG S. 45)." *RA* 64 (1970): 94.

Schroeder, Otto. *Keilschifttexte aus Assur verschiedenen Inhalts.* Leipzig: Hinrichs, 1920.

Schuler, Einar von. "Gilgameš-Epos in Kleinasien." *Wörterbuch der Mythologie.* 1 (1963): 165–67.

Schurer, Emil. *The History of the Jewish People in the Age of Jesus Christ.* Rev. Ed. Edinburgh: Clark, 1986.

Schurr, V. "Das Gilgamesch-Epos." *Theologie der Gegenwart in Auswahl* 5 (1962): 173–75.

Schurtz, H. *Altersklasse und Männerbunde.* Berlin, 1902.

Schwartz, Elliott. *Electronic Music: A Listener's Guide.* Rev. Ed. NY: Da Capo Press, 1973.

Schwarzbaum, H. "The Overcrowded Earth." *Numen* 4 (1957): 59–74.

Schweizer-Vüllers, Andreas. *Gilgamesch: Von der Bewußtwerdung des Mannes; Eine Religionspsychologische Deutung.* Zürich: Theologischer Verlag, 1991.

Schwenn, Friedrich. *Die Menschenopfer bei den Griechen und Römern.* Gießen: A. Topelmann, 1915.

Schwerner, Armand. "The Archaeology of the Self: The Poetry of Armand Schwerner: The Tablets I–XXIV." *Dialectical Anthropology* 11 (1986): 335–80.

Schwerner, Armand. *The Tablets I–XXVI.* London: Atlas, 1989.

Schwerner, Armand. *The Tablets XVI–XVIII.* Boston: Heron Press, 1976.

Schwerner, Armand. *The Tablets I–XVIII.* Dusseldorf/Munich: S. Press Tonbandverlag, 1975. [Recording]

Schwyzer, Eduard. *Griechische Grammatik, Auf der Grundlage.* 3 Vols. Munich: C. H. Beck, 1939.

Scurlock, JoAnn. "Death and the Afterlife in Ancient Mesopotamian Thought." Sasson. *Civilizations of the Ancient Near East.* Vol. 3. 1883–894.

Sede, Gerard de. *Les Templiers sont parmi nous.* Paris: R.Julliard, 1962.

Segal, Charles. "Ancient Texts and Modern Literary Criticism." *Arethusa* 1 (1968): 1–25.

Segal, J. B. "Additional Note on Hercules-Nergal." *Iraq* 35 (1973): 68–69.

Seler, Eduard. *Gesammelte Abhandlungen zur Amerikanischen Sprach- und Altertumskunde.* 5 Vols. Graz: Akademische Druck- u. Verlagsanstalt, 1960–61.

Seters, John Van. *Abraham in History and Tradition.* New Haven: Yale UP, 1975.

Seux, M.J. *Épithètes royales akkadiennes et sumériennes.* Paris: Letouzey et Ané, 1967.

Seyersted, Per. *Gilgamesj: han som sa alt.* Oslo: Cappelen, Nikolai Olsens tr., 1979.

Shabandar, Sumaya. *The Epic of Gilgamesh.* Berkshire, England: Garnet, 1994.

Shaffer, Aaron. "Gilgamesh, The Cedar Forest and Mesopotamian History." *JAOS* 103 (1983): 307–313.

Shaffer, Aaron. "The Mesopotamian Background of Eccl. 4: 9–12." *EI* 8 (1967): 247–50 (Hebrew; English summary, 75*).

Shaffer, Aaron. "New Light on the 'Three-Ply Cord.'" *EI* 9 (1969): 159–60 (Hebrew; English summary, English section, 138–39).

Shaffer, Aaron. *The Sumerian Sources of Tablet XII of the Epic of Gilgameš*. Diss., U of Pennsylvania, 1963.

Sharvananda, Swami, tr. *Kena Upanishad.* Madras: Mylapore, 1932.

Siegel, Bernard. J. "Slavery During the Third Dynasty of Ur." *American Anthropologist* 49 (1947): [41].

Siegel, Ben. "The Myths of Summer: Philip Roth's *The Great American Novel.*" *Contemporary Literature* 17 (1976): 171–90.

Siegelová, Jana. *Appu-Märchen und Ḫedammu-Mythus*. Wiesbaden: O. Harassowitz, 1971.

Silverberg, Robert. *Gilgamesh the King.* NY: Arbor House, 1984.

Silverberg, Robert. *Gilgamesh ha-melekh.* Tr. Aryeh Ha-shavyah. Tel Aviv: Am Oved, 1990.

Silverberg, Robert. "Gilgamesh in the Outback." *Rebels in Hell.* NY: Baen Books, 1986.

Silverstein, T. "Dante and the Legend of the Mi'raj." *JNES* 11 (1952): 89–110, 187–97.

Simeon, Remi. *Dictionnaire de la Langue Nahuatl o Mexicana.* 2nd. Ed. Graz: Mexico: Siglo Veintiuno, 1981.

Simmel, G. *Philosophische Kultur.* Leipzig: W. Klinkhardt, 1911.

Simon, Ted. *Jupiter's Travels.* Garden City, NY: Doubleday, 1980.

Simpson, W. K., ed. *The Literature of Ancient Egypt: An Anthology of Stories, Instructions, and Poetry.* New Ed. New Haven: Yale UP, 1973.

Sjöberg, Åke W. "Die göttliche Abstammung der sumerisch-babylonischen Herrscher." *Or. Suec.* 21 (1972): 87–112.

Sjöberg, Åke W. "Miscellaneous Sumerian Texts. 1." *Or. Suec.* 23–24 (1974–75): 159–81.

Sjöberg, Åke W. *Der Mondgott Nanna-Suen in der sumerischen Überlieferung.* Pt. 1. *Texte.* Stockholm: Almqvist and Wiksell, 1960.

Sjöberg, Åke W. "The Old Babylonian Eduba." S. J. Lieberman. *Sumerological Studies.* 159–79.

Sjöberg, Åke W. "Ein Selbstpreis des Königs Ḫammurapi von Babylon." *ZA* 54 (1961): 51–70.

Sjöberg, Åke W. "'Trials of Strength': Athletics in Mesopotamia." *Expedition* 27 (1985): 7–9.

Sjöberg, Åke W., and Eugen Bergmann. *The Collection of the Sumerian Temple Hymns*, and G. G. Gragg, *The Keš Temple Hymn*. Locust Valley, NY: Augustin, 1969.

Skeel, Caroline. *Travel in the First Century after Christ*. Cambridge: UP, 1901.

Smith, Barbara Herrnstein. *Poetic Closure: A Study of How Poems End*. Chicago: UP, 1968.

Smith, C. C. "Knowledge from before the Flood." *Encounter* 31 (1970): 31–44.

Smith, George. *Assyrian Discoveries*. NY: Scribner, Armstrong and Co., 1876. 165–223.

Smith, George. "The Chaldean Account of the Deluge." *Lecture to the Society of Biblical Archaeology*, Dec. 3, 1872.

Smith, George. "The Chaldean Account of the Deluge." *TSBA* 2 (1873): 213–34.

Smith, George. *The Chaldean Account of Genesis*. NY: Scribner, Armstrong, 1876; rpt. Minneapolis: Wizards Bookshelf, 1977; New Ed. A. H. Sayce, NY: Scribner, Armstrong and Co., 1880.

Smith, George. *Chaldäische Genesis*. Tr. Friedrich Delitzsch. Leipzig: Hinrich, 1876.

Smith, George. "Eleventh Tablet of the Izdubar Legends." *Records of the Past* 7 (1877): 129–30.

Smith, George. "The Eleventh Tablet of the Izdubar Legends. The Chaldean Account of the Deluge." *TSBA* 3 (1874): 588–96.

Smith, Sidney. "*b/pukk/qqu* and *mekku*." *RA* 30 (1933): 153–69.

Smith, Sidney. "The Face of Humbaba." *Annals of Archaeology and Anthropology* (Liverpool) 11 (1924): 107–14.

Smith, Sidney. "The Face of Humbaba." *JRAS* (1926): 440–42.

Soden, Wolfram von. "Zum akkadischen Wörterbuch, 81–87." *Or.* 25 (1956): 241–50.

Soden, Wolfram von. *Akkadisches Handwörterbuch*. 2nd. Ed. 3 Vols. Wiesbaden: Harrassowitz, 1985. = *AHw*

Soden, Wolfram von. "Als die Götter (auch noch) Mensch waren. Einige Grundgedanken des altbabylonischen Atramḫasīs-Mythus." *Or.* 38 (1969): 415–532.

Soden, Wolfram von. "Beiträge zum Verständnis des babylonischen Gilgameš-Epos." *ZA* 53 (1959): 209–35.

Soden, Wolfram von. "Bemerkungen zu den von Ebeling in 'Tod und Leben' Band I bearbeiten Texten." *ZA* 43 (1936): 268.

Soden, Wolfram von. *Einführung in die Altorientalistik.* Darmstadt: Wissenschaftliche Buchgesellschaft, 1985; *The Ancient Orient: An Introduction to the Study of the Ancient Near East.* Tr. Donald G. Schley. Grand Rapids: Eerdmans, 1994. 215–19.

Soden, Wolfram von. *Ergänzungsheft zum Grundriß der akkadischen Grammatik.* Rome: Pontifical Biblical Institute, 1969.

Soden, Wolfram von. "Die erste Tafel des altbabylonischen Atramḫasīs-Mythus. 'Haupttext' und Parallelversionen." *ZA* 68 (1978): 50–94.

Soden, Wolfram von. *Grundriss der akkadischen Grammatik.* Rome: Pontifical Biblical Institute, 1952.

Soden, Wolfram von. "Die Hebamme in Babylonien und Assyrien." *AfO* 18 (1957–58): 119–21.

Soden, Wolfram von. "Der hymnisch-epische Dialekt des Akkadischen." *ZA* 40 (1931): 163–227; 41 (1933): 90–183.

Soden, Wolfram von. "Kleine Beiträge zu Text und Erklärung babylonischer Epen." *ZA* 58 (1967): 189–95.

Soden, Wolfram von. "Das Problem der zeitlichen Einordnung akkadischer Literaturwerke." *MDOG* 85 (1953): 14–26.

Soden, Wolfram von. "Review of Böhl, *Het Gilgamesj-Epos*, 2d ed." *OLZ* 50 (1955): 513–16.

Soden, Wolfram von. "Review of *Essays on the Ancient Near East in Memory of J. J. Finkelstein.*" *ZA* 69 (1979): 155–57.

Soden, Wolfram von. "Status Rectus-Formen vor dem Genitiv im Akkadischen und die sogenannte uneigentliche Annexion im Arabischen." *JNES* 19 (1960): 163–71.

Soden, Wolfram von. "Sumer, Babylon, und Hethiter bis zur Mitte des zweiten Jahrtausends v. Chr." *Propylaen Weltgeschichte.* Ed. G. Mann and A. Heuss. Berlin: Propylaen, 1961. 1: 523–609.

Soden, Wolfram von. "Die Unterweltsvision eines assyrischen Kronprinzen." *ZA* 43 (1936): 1–31.

Sollberger, Edmond. *The Babylonian Legend of the Flood.* London: British Museum, 1962; 3rd. Ed., 1971.

Sollberger, Edmond. "Une lecture du signe GÍN." *AfO* 16 (1953): 2–30.

Sollberger, Edmond. *Royal Inscriptions. Pt. 2. UET 8.* London: British Museum and University of Pennsylvania, 1965.

Sollberger, Edmond. "The Rulers of Lagash." *JCS* 21 (1967): 279–91.

Sollberger, Edmond. "The Tummal Inscription." *JCS* 16 (1962): 40–47.

Solmsen, F. "The Two Near Eastern Sources of Hesiod." *Hermes* 117 (1989): 413–22.

Sonneck, F. "Die Einführung der direkten Rede in den epischen Texten." *ZA* 46 (1940): 225–35.

Sordi, M. "Mitologia e propaganda nella Beocia arcaica." *Atene e Roma,* N.S. 2 (1966): 15–24.

Speirs, John. *Medieval English Poetry: The Non-Chaucerian Tradition.* London: Faber and Faber, 1971.

Speiser, E(phraim). A(vigdor). tr., "Akkadian Myths and Epics." Rev. A. K. Grayson. *ANET.* 601–19.

Speiser, E. A. "'Eḍ in the Story of Creation." *BASOR* 140 (1955): 9–11.

Speiser, E. A. "The Epic of Gilgamesh." *The Ancient Near East, An Anthology of Texts and Pictures.* Princeton: UP, 1955. 2: 72–99.

Speiser, E. A. *Genesis.* Vol. 1. The Anchor Bible. Ed. W. F. Albright and D. N. Freeman. Garden City, NY: Doubleday, 1964.

Speiser, E. A. "Gilgamesh VI 40." *JCS* 12 (1958): 41–42.

Speiser, E. A. "The Idea of History in the Ancient Near East." *Oriental and Biblical Studies.* 270–312.

Speiser, E. A. "Mesopotamia: Evolution of an Integrated Civilization." *At the Dawn of Civilization: The World History of the Jewish People.* First Series: *Ancient Times.* Ed. E. A. Speiser. New Brunswick, NJ: Rutgers UP, 1964. 1: 173–266, 366–72.

Speiser, E. A. *Oriental and Biblical Studies.* Ed. J. J. Finkelstein and M. Greenberg. Philadelphia: U of Pennsylvania P, 1967. 270–312.

Speiser, E. A. "PĀLIL and Congeners: A Sampling of Apotropaic Symbols." Güterbock and Jacobsen. *Studies… Benno Landsberger.* 389–93.

Speiser, E. A. "The Rivers of Paradise." *Festschrift Johannes Friedrich.* Heidelberg: Carl Winter Universitätsverlag, 1959. 473–85; rpt. *Oriental and Biblical Studies.* 23–34.

Speiser, E. A. "TWTPT." *JQR* 48 (1957–58): 208–17.

Speleers, L. *Catalogue des intailles et empreintes orientales des Musées Royaux d'Art et d'Histoire.* Brussels: Vromant, 1943.

Spence, L. *Myths and Legends of Babylonia and Assyria.* London: George G. Harrap, 1916.

Sperling, S. David. "Genesis 41:40: A New Interpretatioan." *JANES* 10 (1978): 113–19.

Sproule, Anna, and Peter Bailey. *Les guerriers.* Paris: Études Vivantes, 1981.

Stamm, Johann Jakob. *Die akkadische Namengebung.* Leipzig: Hinrichs, 1939.

Stamm, Johann Jakob. "Das Gilgamesch-Epos und seine Vorgeschichte." *Asiatische Studien* 6 (1952): 9–29; rpt. Oberhuber. *Das Gilgmesch-Epos.* 292–311.

Stark, Carolyn Jean. *A Comparative Study of Two Epics, Gilgamesh and Beowulf.* Thesis, Texas Technological College, 1966.

Stark, Freya. *The Journey's Echo.* NY: Ecco Press, 1963.

Starlin, Jim. *Gilgamesh II.* Vol. 1. *A Mad New World.* NY: DC Comics, 1989.

Starlin, Jim. *Gilgamesh II.* Vol. 2. *Land of the Nightshadow.* NY: DC Comics, 1989.

Starlin, Jim. *Gilgamesh II.* Vol. 3. *Twilight Blood.* NY: DC Comics, 1989.

Starlin, Jim. *Gilgamesh II.* Vol. 4. *Much To Do About Nothing.* NY: DC Comics, 1989.

Starobabilonska, Powiesc. *Gilgamesz.* Warsaw: Panstwowy Instytut Wydawniczy, 1986.

Stefanini, Ruggiero. "Enkidu's Dream in the Hittite 'Gilgamesh.'" *JNES* 28 (1969): 40–47.

Stefanini, Ruggiero. "Da Gilgamesh a Petronio." *Paideia* 22 (1967): 293–95.

Stefanini, Ruggiero. "Il Poema di Ghilgames." *Ausonia. Rivista di lettere e arti* 25 (Siena, Italy, 1970): 7–39.

Steinkeller, Piotr. "More on the Ur III Royal Wives." *Acta Sumerologica* 3 (1981): 77–92.

Stella, Luigia Achillea. *Il poema di Ulisse.* Florence: Nuova Italia, 1955.

Stella, Luigia Achillea. *Tradizione Micenea e poesia dell'Iliade.* Rome: Edizioni dell/Anteneo & Bizzarri, 1978.

Stephens, Ferris J. "A Reexamination of the Old Babylonian Gilgamesh Tablet at Yale." *Or.* 25 (1956): 273.

Stephens, Ferris J., tr. "Sumero-Akkadian Hymns and Prayers." *ANET.* 383–92.

Stewart, John O. *Curving Road.* Urbana: U of Illinois P, 1975.

Stewart, John O. *Drinkers, Drummers, and Decent Folk: Ethnographic Narratives of Village Trinidad.* Albany: SUNY P, 1989.

Stiller, Robert. *Gilgamesz.* Warsaw: Panstwowy Instytut Wydawniczy, 1967.

Stimson, J. F. *The Legends of Maui and Tahaki.* Honolulu: Bernice P. Bishop Museum, 1934.

Stokes, M. C. "Hesiodic and Milesian Cosmologies." *Phronesis* 7 (1962): 19–21.

Stol, M. "Die boodschap van het Gilgamesj epos." *Akkadica* 23 (1981): 1–22.

Stol, M. "Gilgamesh Epic XI, 54." *AfO* 35 (1988): 78.

Stout, Janis P. "The Misogyny of Roth's *The Great American Novel.*" *Ball State University Forum* 27 (1986): 72–75.

Straus, E. *On Obsession.* NY: Johnson Reprint, 1968.

Streck, Maximilian. *Assurbanipal und die letzten Assyrischen Könige bis zum Untergang Nineveh's.* Leipzig: Hinrichs, 1916.

Strika, Fiorella Ippolitoni. "Prehistoric Roots: Continuity in the Images and Rituals of the Great Goddess Cult in the Near East." *Revista degli studi orientali* 57 (1983): 1–41.

Strommenger, Eva, and Max Hirmer. *The Art of Mesopotamia.* London: Thames and Hudson, 1964.

Strong, Sandford Arthur. "On Some Oracles to Esarhaddon and Ašurbanipal." *BA* 2 (1894): 627–45.

Sullivan, Harry Stack. *The Interpersonal Theory of Psychiatry.* NY: Norton, 1953.

Svankmajer, Jan. "Epic of Gilgamesh." *The Brothers Quay.* NY: Voyager Company, 1994. [Audiovisual Recording].

Sweet, Ronald F. G. "The Sage in Akkadian Literature: A Philological Study" and "The Sage in Mesopotamian Palaces and Royal Courts." Gammie. 45–65, 99–107.

Syme, Ronald. *History in Ovid.* Oxford: Clarendon, 1978.

Symeonoglou, Sarantis. *The Topography of Thebes from the Bronze Age to Modern Times.* Princeton: UP, 1985.

Symeonoglou, Sarantis. *Kadmeia.* Goteborg: P. Astrom, 1973.

Szarzyńska, Krystyńa. "Some Remarks on the So-Called 'Steingebäude' in Archaic Uruk-Warka." *Akkadica* 23 (1981): 45–49.

Śzekeley, János. "Enkidu mítosza." *A Mítosz értelme: Esszek.* Bukarest: Kriterion, 1985.

Szemerenyi, O. "The Origins of the Greek Lexicon. Ex oriente lux." *Journal of Hellenic Studies* 94 (1974): 114–57.

Talbot, H. Fox. "Addenda to Paper on the 'Descent of Ishtar.'" *TSBA* 3 (1874): 357–60.

Talbot, H. Fox. "Ishtar and Izdubar." *TSBA* 5 (1877): 97–121.

Talbot, H. Fox. "Ishtar and Izdubar: Being the Sixth Tablet of the Izdubar Series." *Records of the Past* 9 (1877): 119–24.

Talbot, H. Fox. "Note on the Religious Belief of the Assyrians." *TSBA* 1 (1872): 106–15.

Talbot, H. Fox. "Revised Translation of the Descent of Ishtar, with a Further Commentary." *TSBA* 3 (1874): 118–35.

Tallqvist, Knut Leonard. *Akkadische Götterepitheta.* Helsinki: Societas Orientalis Fennica, 1938.

Tallqvist, Knut. *Assyrian Personal Names.* Helsinki: Societas Orientalis Fennica, 1914.

Tallqvist, Knut. *Gilgameš-Eposet översatt och fölklarat*. Helsinki: Societas Orientalis Fennica, 1945.

Tallqvist, Knut Leonard. *Sumerisch-Akkadische Namen der Totenwelt.* Helsinki: Societas Orientalis Fennica, 1934.

Talmon, Shemaryahu, and Michael Fishbane. "Aspects of the Literary Structure of the Book of Ezekiel." *Tarbiz* 42 (1972–73): 27–41 (Hebrew with English Summary).

Tamen, Pedro. *Gilgamesh.* Tr. from English. Lisbon: Vega, 1989.

Tanakh. A New Translation of The Holy Scriptures According to the Traditional Hebrew Text. Philadelphia: Jewish Publication Society, 1985.

Teatro Gioco Vita. Gilgamesh Maj Diego. 9 Via Maddalena, Piacenza 29100, Italy. [Puppet company presentation]

Temple, Robert K. G. *Conversations with Eternity: Ancient Man's Attempts to Know the Future.* London: Rider, 1984.

Temple, Robert K. G. *Götter, Orakel und Visionen.* Frankfurt: Umschau Verlag, 1982.

Temple, Robert, tr. *He Who Saw Everything, A Verse Translation of The Epic of Gilgamesh.* London: Rider, 1991.

Temple, Robert. "Introduction." *He Who Saw Everything.* vii–xxix.

Thackeray, H. St. J. *Josephus.* Vol. 4. *Jewish Antiquities, Bks. 1–4.* Cambridge, MA: Harvard UP, 1967.

Theiler, Willy. *Untersuchungen zur antiken Literatur.* Berlin: de Gruyter, 1970.

Thomas, D. Winton, ed. *Documents from Old Testament Times.* London: Thomas Nelson, 1958.

Thompson, Reginald Campbell. *A Century of Exploration at Nineveh.* London: Luzac, 1900.

Thompson, Reginald Campbell. *CT 18.* London: British Museum, 1904.

Thompson, Reginald. Campbell. *The Devils and the Evil Spirits of Babylonia.* 2 Vols. London: Luzac, 1903–1904.

Thompson, Reginald Campbell, tr. *The Epic of Gilgamesh: A New Translation.* London: Luzac, 1928.

Thompson, Reginald Campbell. *The Epic of Gilgamesh: Text, Transliteration, and Notes.* Oxford: Clarendon Press, 1930.

Thompson, Stith. *Motif-Index of Folk Literature.* Bloomington, Indiana: Indiana UP, 1955–58.

Thompson, William Irwin. *The Time Falling Bodies Take to Light.* NY: St. Martin's Press, 1981.

Thørbjørnsrud, Berit. "What Can the Gilgamesh Myth Tell Us about Religion and the View of Humanity in Mesopotamia?" *Temenos* 19 (1983): 112–37.

Thucydides. *History of the Peloponnesian War.* Tr. Rex Warner. NY: Penguin, 1986.

Thureau-Dangin, François. "La Fin de la domination gutienne." *RA* 9 (1912): 111–20.

Thureau-Dangin, François. "Ḫumbaba." *RA* 22 (1925): 23–26.

Thureau-Dangin, François. "Notes assyriologiques. 23. Un double de l'inscription d'Utu-Hegal." *RA* 10 (1913): 98–100.

Thureau-Dangin, François. "Rituel et amulettes contre Labartu." *RA* 18 (1921): 161–98.

Thureau-Dangin, François. *Rituels Accadiens.* Paris: E. Leroux, 1921.

Thureau-Dangin, François. *Die sumerischen und akkadischen Königsinschriften.* Leipzig: Hinrichs, 1907.

Tigay, Jeffrey. H. "An Empirical Basis for the Documentary Hypothesis." *JBL* 94 (1975): 329–42.

Tigay, Jeffrey H. ed. *Empirical Models for Biblical Criticism.* Philadelphia: U of Pennsylvania P, 1985.

Tigay, Jeffrey H. *The Evolution of the Gilgamesh Epic.* Philadelphia: U of Pennsylvania P, 1982; selections rpt. Krstović. 349–51.

Tigay, Jeffrey H. "The Image of God and the Flood: Some New Developments." *Studies in Jewish Education.* Ed. A. Shapiro and B. Cohen. NY: Ktav Publishing House, 1984.

Tigay, Jeffrey H. *Literary-Critical Studies in the Gilgamesh Epic: An Assyriological Contribution to Biblical Scholarship.* Diss. Yale U, 1971.

Tigay, Jeffrey. H. "Paradise." *Encyclopaedia Judaica.* Ed. C. Roth. Jerusalem: Keter, 1971. Vol. 13, cols. 77–82.

Tigay, Jeffrey. H. "On Some Aspects of Prayer in the Bible." *Association for Jewish Studies Review* 1 (1976): 363–79.

Tigay, Jeffrey. H. "The Stylistic Criteria of Source Criticism in the Light of Ancient Near Eastern Literature." *Isac Leo Seeligmann Anniversary Volume.* Ed. A. Rofé and Y. Zakovitch. Jerusalem: Hotsaat Elhanan Rubinshayn, 1982.

Tigay, Jeffrey H. "Summary: The Evolution of The Gilgamesh Epic" and "Excursus: The Afterlife of the Epic." *The Evolution of the Gilgamesh Epic.* 241–55.

Tigay, Jeffrey. H. "Was There an Integrated Gilgamesh Epic in the Old Babylonian Period?" Ellis. *Essays...Finkelstein.* 215–18.

Tiger, Lionel. *Men in Groups.* NY: Random House, 1969.

Tollers, Vincent L., and John Maier, ed. *The Bible in its Literary Milieu: Contemporary Essays.* Grand Rapids: Eerdmans, 1979.

Tollers, Vincent L., and John Maier, ed. *Mappings of the Biblical Terrain: The Bible as Text.* Lewisburg, PA: Bucknell UP, 1990.

Tournay, Raymond Jacques. *L'Épopée de Gilgamesh.* Paris: Éditions du Cerf, 1994.

Tournay, Raymond Jacques. "Inscription d'Anam, roi d'Uruk et successeur de Gilgamesh." *Near Eastern Studies in Honor of William Foxwell Albright.* Ed. Hans Goedicke. Baltimore: Johns Hopkins UP, 1971. 453–57.

Trible, Phyllis. *God and the Rhetoric of Sexuality.* Philadelphia: Fortress Press, 1978.

Tromp, Nicolas J. *Primitive Conceptions of Death and the Nether World in the Old Testament.* Rome: Pontifical Biblical Institute, 1969.

Tropper, Josef. "'Beschwörung' des Enkidu? Anmerkungen zur Interpretation von 'Gilgamesh, Enkidu und die Unterwelt' 240–43." *WO* 17 (1986): 19–24.

Tseretheli, Michael von. *Gilgamešiani. Babilonusi eposi.* Istanbul, 1924.

Tsevat, Matitiahu. "Common Sense and Hypothesis in Old Testament Study." *HUCA* 47 (1976): 217–30.

Turner, Edith. *The Spirit and the Drum: A Memoir of Africa.* Tucson: U of Arizona P, 1987.

Turner, Victor. "Betwixt and Between: The Liminal Period in Rites of Passage." *Betwixt and Between.* Ed. Louise Mahdi, Stephen Foster, and Meredith Little. La Salle, IL: Open Court, 1987.

Turok, Paul. *Evocations: Four Songs on Ancient Texts.* NY: Independent Music Publishers, 1955. [Musical Score].

Tylor, Edward. B. *Primitive Culture.* 2 Vols. NY: Henry Holt, 1883; rpt. NY: Harper, 1958.

Uehlinger, C. *Weltreich und "eine Rede": Eine neue Deutung der sogenannten Turmbauerzählung (Gen. 11,19).* Fribourg: Editions-Univérsitaires, 1990.

Unger, Eckhard. "Gilgamesch und Engidu." *Reallexikon der Vorgeschichte* 4 (1926): 337.

Ungnad, Arthur. *Gilgamesch-Epos und Odyssee.* Breslau: Arthur Ungnad Selbstverlag, 1923. 3–32; rpt. Oberhuber. *Das Gilgamesch-Epos.* 104–37.

Ungnad, Arthur. "Das hurritische Fragment des Gilgamesch-Epos." *ZA* 35 (1924): 133–40.

Ungnad, Arthur. *Die Religion der Babylonier und Assyrer.* Jena: E. Diederich, 1921.

Ungnad, Arthur, and Hugo Gressmann. *Das Gilgamesch-Epos. Neu übersetzt.* Gottingen: Vandenhoeck and Ruprecht, 1911.

Ungnad, Arthur, and Lubor Matouš. *Grammatik des Akkadischen.* Munich: Verlag C. H. Beck, 1969.

Urbach, E. E. "Mishnah." *Encyclopaedia Judaica.* Ed. C. Roth. Jerusalem: Keter, 1971. Vol. 7, cols. 93–108.

Vallas, Leon. *Vincent D'Indy.* 2 Vols. I: *La Jeunesse (1851–1886)*; II: *La Maturité; la viellesse (1886–1931).* Paris: Albin Michel, 1950.

VanderKam, James C. *Enoch and the Growth of an Apocalyptic Tradition.* Washington, DC: Catholic Biblical Association, 1984.

VanderKam, James C. "The Righteousness of Noah." *Ideal Figures in Ancient Judaism: Profiles and Paradigms.* Chico, CA: SBL/Scholars Press, 1980. 13–32.

Vanstiphout, Herman L. J. "The Craftsmanship of Sîn-leqi-unninnī." *Orientalia Lovaniensia Periodica* 21 (1990): 45–79.

Vanstiphout, Herman L. J. "Gilgameš and Agga, Fragment X (N 1250)." *NABU* 3 (1989): 73–74. N. 99.

Vanstiphout, Herman L. J. "Inanna/Ishtar as a Figure of Controversy." *Struggles of the Words.* Ed. H. G. Kippenberg, et al. Berlin: de Gruyter, 1984. 224–38.

Vanstiphout, Herman L. J. "A Note on the Series 'Travel in the Desert.'" *JCS* 29 (1977): 52–56.

Vanstiphout, Herman L. J. "Some Remarks on Cuneiform *écritures.*" Vanstiphout. *Scripta Signa Vocis.* 217–34.

Vanstiphout, Herman J. L. "Towards a Reading of 'Gilgamesh and Agga.'" *Aula Orientalis* 5 (1987): 129–41.

Vanstiphout, Herman L. J. "Towards a Reading of 'Gilgamesh and Agga,' Part II: Construction." *Orientalia Lovaniensia Periodica* 17 (1986): 33–50.

Vanstiphout, Herman L. J., et al., eds. *Scripta Signa Vocis.* Groningen: Egbert Forsten, 1986.

Vaux, Roland de. "Les Combats singuliers dans l'Ancien Testament." *Biblica* 40 (1959): 495–508.

Veenker, Ronald A. "Forbidden Fruit: Ancient Near Eastern Sexual Metaphors." [Unpublished essay].

Veenker, Ronald A. "Gilgamesh and the Magic Plant." *Biblical Archaeologist* 44 (1981): 199–205.

Veenker, Ronald A. "Noah, Herald of Righteousness." *Proceedings: Eastern Great Lakes and Midwest Biblical Societies* 6 (1986): 204–18.

Veenker, Ronald A. "A Response to W. G. Lambert." *Biblical Archaeologist* 45 (1982): 69.

Vermes, Geza. *The Dead Sea Scrolls in English.* London: Penguin, 1977.

Vidal-Naquet, Pierre. "The Black Hunter and the Origin of the Athenian Ephebeia." *Proceedings of the Cambridge Philological Society* N.S. 14 (1968): 49–64.

Vikentiev, Vladimir. "Bouloukuja-Gilgamesh-Naufragé. Rapports folkloriques arabes, babyloniens et égyptiens." *Bulletin of the Faculty of Arts (Fouad I University)* 10 (1948): 1–54.

Vikentiev, Vladimir. "Le conte égyptien des Deux Frères et quelques histoires apparentées [e. a. l'épopée de Gilgamesh]." *Bulletin of the Faculty of Arts (Fouad I University)* 11 (1949): 63–114.

Vikentiev, Vladimir. *L'énigme d'un papyrus*. Cairo: Hachette, 1940.

Virgil. *The Aeneid*. Tr. C. Day Lewis. Garden City, NY: Doubleday, 1952.

Virolleaud, Charles. "Le Dieu Shamash dans L'Ancienne Mésopotamie." *Eranos Jahrbuch*. Vol. 10. Zurich: Rhein-Verlag, 1944. 57–79.

Virolleaud, Charles. "La Montagne des Cèdres dans les traditions de l'ancient Orient." *RHR* 101 (1930): 16–26.

Virolleaud, Charles. "De quelques survivances de la légende babylonienne concernant la plante de vie." *Journal asiatique* 239 (1951): 127–32.

Virolleaud, Charles. "Le Voyage de Gilgamesh au Paradis." *RHR* 101 (1930): 202–215.

Visic, Marko. *Knjizevnost drevnog Bliskog istoka*. Zaghreb: Naprijed, 1993.

Vogelzang, Marianna E. "Patterns Introducing Direct Speech in Akkadian Literary Texts." *JCS* 42 (1990): 50–70.

Vogelzang, Marianna E., and W. J. Van Bekkum. "Meaning and Symbolism of Clothing in Ancient Near Eastern Texts." Vanstiphout. *Scripta*. 61–70.

Vulpe, Nicola. "*Gilgamesh* and the Specific Nature of Poetry." *Contacts between Cultures*. Ed. A. Harrah. Vol. 1. Lewiston, NY/Queenston, Ontario: Cultural Press, 1992. 152–59.

Vulpe, Nicola. "Irony and the Unity of the *Gilgamesh* Epic." *JNES* 53 (1994): 275–83.

Vyalniev, I. *Bilgamys dastany*. Baku: Gyanjlik, 1985.

Wace, A. J. B., and F. H. Stubbings. *A Companion to Homer*. London: Macmillan, 1967.

Waddell, Laurence Austine. *The Aryan Origin of the Alphabet*. London: Luzac & Co., 1927.

Waddell, Laurence Austine. *The Indo-Sumerian Seals Deciphered*. Hawthorne, CA: Omni Publications, 1925.

Waerden, B. L. van der. "The Thirty-Six Stars." *JNES* 8 (1949): 6–26.

Wagenvoort, W. "The Journey of the Souls of the Dead to the Isles of the Blessed." *Mnemosyne* 24 (1971): 1–13.

Wakeman, Mary. "Ancient Sumer and the Women's Movement." *Journal of Feminist Studies in Religion* 1 (1985): 7–27.

Wakeman, Mary K. *God's Battle with the Monster.* Leiden: E. J. Brill, 1973.

Wakeman, Mary K. "Sacred Marriage." *Journal of the Study of the Old Testament* 22 (1982): 21–31.

Walcott, P. *Hesiod and the Near East.* Cardiff: U of Wales P, 1966.

Walde, Alois. *Vergleichendes Wörterbuch der Indogermanischen Sprachen.* Vol. 2. Berlin/Leipzig: de Gruyter, 1927.

Waldman, Nahum. "A Biblical Echo of Mesopotamian Royal Rhetoric." *Essays on the Occasion of the Seventieth Anniversary of the Dropsie University.* Ed. A. I. Katsch and L. Nemoy. Philadelphia: Dropsie University, 1979. 449–55.

Waldman, Nahum M. "The Imagery of Clothing, Covering, and Overpowering." *JANES* 19 (1989): 161–70.

Waldman, Nahum M. "The Wealth of Mountain and Sea: The Background of a Biblical Image." *JQR* 71 (1981): 176–80.

Ward, William Hayes. *The Seal Cylinders of Western Asia.* Washington, DC: Carnegie Institute, 1910.

Ward, William A. "A Sumerian Motif on a Phoenician Seal." *Archéologie au Levant.* Ed. R. Saidah. Lyon/Paris: Maison de l'Orient/Diffusion de Boccard, 1982. 221–24.

Warren, Henry Clarke. *Buddhism in Translations.* Cambridge, MA: Harvard UP, 1896.

Watson, Wilfred. G. E. *Classical Hebrew Poetry: A Guide to its Techniques.* Sheffield, England: JSOT Press, 1984.

Webb, Henry Law. *The Everlasting Quest.* London: Macmillan, 1917.

Weber, Markus. *Die mythologische Erzählung in Ovids Liebeskunst: Verankerung, Struktur und Funktion.* Frankfurt am Main/Bern: P. Lang, 1983.

Weber, Otto. *Altorientalische Siegelbilder.* Leipzig: J. C. Hinrichs, 1920.

Weber, Otto. "Das Gilgamesch-Epos." *Die Literatur der Babylonier und Assyrer, Ein Überblick.* Leipzig: J. C. Hinrich'sche Buchhandlung, 1907. 90–92; rpt. Oberhuber. *Das Gilgamesch-Epos.* 44–47.

Webster, Thomas B. L. *From Mycenae to Homer*. 2nd. Ed. London: Methuen, 1964.

Weidner, Ernst F. "Das Gilgameš-Epos bei den Hethitern." *Oostersch Genootschap in Nederland.* Leiden: Brill, 1925. 18–19.

Weidner, Ernst F. "Zu Gilgamesch-Epos, Tafel l, I, 12." *AfO* 16 (1952–53): 80.

Weidner, Ernst F. *Handbuch der babylonischen Astronomie.* Vol. 1. Leipzig: Hinrichs, 1915.

Weidner, Ernst F. *KUB 4.* Berlin: Staatliche Museen, 1922.

Weidner, Ernest F. "Ein neues Bruchstück der XII. Tafel des Gilgameš-Epos." *AfO* 10 (1936): 363–65.

Weidner, Ernest F. "Recueil de tour des fragments (hittites & hurrites)." *KUB* 8 (1923): N. 48–62.

Weiher, Egbert von. "Ein Fragment des Gilgameš-Epos aus Uruk." *ZA* 62 (1972): 222–29.

Weiher, Egbert von. "Ein Fragment der 5. Tafel des Gilgameš-Epos aus Uruk." *Baghdader Mitteilungen* 11 (1980): 90–105.

Weiher, Egbert von. "Gilgameš und Enkidu. Die Idee einer Freundschaft." *Baghdader Mitteliungen* 11 (1980): 106–19.

Weiher, Egbert von. *Spätbabylonische Texts aus Uruk.* 4 Vols. Berlin: P. von Zabern, 1976–93.

Weinfeld, M. "The Common Heritage of Convenantal Traditions in the Ancient World." *I trattati nel mondo antico.* Ed. L. Canfora, M. Liverani, and C. Zaccagnini. Rome: "L'Erma" di Bretschneider, 1990. 175–91.

Weiss, Harvey. "Kish, Akkad, and Agade." *JAOS* 95 (1975): 434–53.

Weiss, Johannes. *Jesus von Nazareth: Mythus oder Geschichte? Eine Auseinandersetzung mit Kalthoff, Drews, Jensen.* Tübingen: J. C. B. Mohr, 1910.

Weissbach, Franz Heinrich. *Die Keilinschriften der Achämeniden.* Leipzig: Hinrichs, 1911.

Wellek, René, and Austin Warren. *Theory of Literature.* 3rd. Ed. NY: Harcourt, Brace & World, 1956.

Wells, David Arthur. *The Wild Man from the "Epic of Gilgamesh" to Hartmann Von Aue's "Iwein."* Belfast: The Queen's University, 1975.

Welsh, Andrew. *Roots of Lyric: Primitive Poetics and Modern Poetry*. Princeton: UP, 1978.

Wendlandt, W. *Gilgamesch. Der Kampf mit dem Tode. Ein Lebenslied.* Berlin, 1927.

Wente, E. F. "Egyptian 'Make Merry' Songs Reconsidered." *JNES* 21 (1962): 118–28.

West, George. "Almeda Riddle: Now Let's Talk About Singing." 3/4 in. Video. Talking Traditions.

West, Martin Litchfield. "Ancient Near Eastern Myths in Classical Greek Religious Thought." Sasson. *Civlizations of the Ancient Near East.* Vol. 1. 33–42.

West, Martin Litchfield. "Near Eastern Material in Hellenistic and Roman Literature." *Harvard Studies in Classical Philology* 73 (1969): 113–34.

West, Martin Litchfield. *Early Greek Philosophy and the Orient.* Oxford: Clarendon, 1971.

West, Martin Litchfield, ed. *Hesiod: Theogony*. Oxford: UP, 1966.

West, Martin Litchfield. "Hesiodea." *Classical Quarterly* N.S. 11 (1961): 130–45.

West, Martin Litchfield, ed. *Hesiod: Works and Days.* Oxford: UP, 1978.

West, Martin Litchfield. "The Rise of the Greek Epic." *Journal of Hellenic Studies* 108 (1988): 151–72.

West, S., A. Heubeck, and J. B. Hainsworth, ed. *A Commentary on Homer's Odyssey*. 2 Vols. Oxford: Clarendon, 1988–89.

Westbrook, Raymond. "The Enforcement of Morals in Mesopotamian Law." *JAOS* 104 (1984): 753–56.

Westenholz, Joan Goodnick. "Metaphorical Language in the Poetry of Love in the Ancient Near East." *RAI* 38 (1992): 381–87.

Westenholz, Joan Goodnick. "Towards a New Conceptualization of the Female Role in Mesopotamian Society." *JAOS* 110 (1990): 510–21.

Westermann, Claus, ed. *Essays on Old Testament Hermeneutics.* Tr. James Luther Mays. 2nd. Ed. Richmond: John Knox, 1964.

Westermann, Claus, ed. *Genesis 1–11: A Commentary*. Tr. John Scullion. Minneapolis: Augsburg, 1984.

Westermarck, Edward. *The History of Human Marriage.* 5th. Ed. 3 Vols. London: Macmillan, 1921.

Westwood, Jennifer. *Gilgamesh and Other Babylonian Tales.* NY: Coward-McKann, 1970.

Weverbergh, Louis Julien. *Gilgamesj herschrijven.* The Hague: A. Manteau, 1968.

Wheatley, Paul. *The Pivot of the Four Quarters. A Preliminary Enquiry into the Origins and Character of the Ancient Chinese City.* Chicago: Aldine Publishing Company, 1971.

Whitney, William Dwight, tr. *Atharva Veda Sanhita.* 2 Vols. Cambridge, MA: Harvard UP, 1905; rpt. Delhi: Nag, 1987.

Wiggermann, F. A. M. *Babylonian Prophylactic Figures: The Ritual Texts.* Diss., Amsterdam, 1986; 2nd. Ed. *Mesopotamian Protective Spirits: The Ritual Texts.* Groningen: Styxx & PP, 1992.

Wiggermann, F. A. M. "Exit Talim!" *JEOL* 27 (1981–82): 90–105.

Wilamowitz-Moellendorff, Ulrich von. *Der Glaube der Hellenen.* 2 Vols. Berlin: Weidmann, 1931–32.

Wilamowitz-Moellendorff, Ulrich von. "Die sieben Tore Thebens." *Hermes* 26 (1891): 191–242.

Wilamowitz-Moellendorff, Ulrich von. *Kleine Schriften.* 5 Vols. Berlin: Akademie Verlag, 1962–71.

Wilcke, Claus. "Die Anfänge der akkadischen Epen." *ZA* 67 (1977): 153–216.

Wilcke, Claus. "Familiengründung im Alten Babylonien." *Geschlechtsreife und Legitimation zur Zeugung.* Ed. E. W. Müller. Freiburg/München: Albert, 1985. 295–98.

Wilcke, Claus. "Formale Gesichtspunkte in der sumerischen Literatur." S. J. Lieberman. *Sumerological Studies.* 205–316.

Wilcke, Claus. "Ḫuwawa/Ḫumbaba." *RLA* 3: 530–35.

Wilcke, Claus. "Zum Königreich in der Ur III Zeit." *CRRAI* (1971): 177–232.

Wilcke, Claus. "ku-li." *ZA* 59 (1969): 65–99.

Wilcke, Claus. *Das Lugalbandaepos.* Wiesbaden: Harrassowitz, 1969.

Wilcke, Claus. "Politische Opposition nach sumerischen Quellen: der Konflict zwischen Königtum und Ratsversammlung. Literaturwerke als politische Tendenzschriften." *La Voix de l'opposition en Mésopotamie.* Brussels: Institut des Hautes Études de Belgique, 1975. 37–65.

Wilcke, Claus. "Eine Schicksalsentscheidung für den Toten Urnammu." *Actes de la 17e rencontre assyriologique internationale.* Ham-sur-Heure, Belgium: Comité de Recherches en Mesopotamie, 1970. 81–92.

Wilcke, Claus. "Sumerische Lehrgedichte." *Kindler's Literatur Lexikon.* Zurich: Kindler, 1965. Vol. 6. cols. 2135–42.

Wilcke, Claus. "Ein weiteres Gilgameš-Fragment aus Emar?" *NABU* 3 (1989): 5 N. 5.

Wilhelm, Gernot. "Neue akkadische Gilgameš-Fragmente aus Ḫattusa." *ZA* 78 (1988): 99–121.

Williams, Charles Allyn. *Oriental Affinities of the Legend of the Hairy Anchorite.* 2 Vols. Urbana: U of Illinois P, 1925–26.

Williams, Dyfri. *Greek Vases in the J. Paul Getty Museum.* Malibu, CA: The Museum, 1983.

Williams, R. J. "Scribal Training in Ancient Egypt." *JAOS* 92 (1972): 214–21.

Williamson, Robert W. *Religious and Cosmic Beliefs of Central Polynesia.* 2 Vols. Cambridge: UP, 1933.

Wilson, James V. Kinnier. "On the Fourth and Fifth Tablets of the Epic of Gilgameš." *GSL.* 103–11.

Wilson, J. V. Kinnier. "Hebrew and Akkadian Philological Notes." *JSS* 7 (1962): 173–83.

Wilson, J. V. Kinnier. *The Legend of Etana.* Warminster, England: Aris & Phillips, 1985.

Wilson, J. V. Kinnier. "Lugal ud melambi nirgal: New Texts and Fragments." *ZA* 54 (1961): 71–89.

Wilson, J. V. Kinnier. "Some Contributions to the Legend of Etana." *Iraq* 31 (1969): 8–17.

Wilson, J. V. Kinnier. "The Story of the Flood." Thomas. *Documents from Old Testament Times.* 17–26.

Wilson, John A., tr. "Egyptian Myths, Tales, and Mortuary Texts," "Egyptian Didactic Tales," "Egyptian Observations," and "Egyptian Secular Songs and Poems." *ANET*. 3–36, 405–10, 431–34, 467–71.

Wilson, John R. "The Gilgamesh Epic and the Iliad." *Échos du monde classique/Classical Views* 30 (1986): 25–41.

Wilson, Robert, and David Byrne. *The Forest.* Brooklyn Academy of Music. December 210, 1988. [Musical Drama].

Winter, Irene J. *A Decorated Breastplate from Hasanlu, Iran.* Philadelphia: U Museum, 1980.

Winter, Urs. *Frau und Göttin.* Freiburg: Universitätsverlag, 1983.

Wirth, Hermann. *Homer und Babylon.* Freiburg in Breisgau: Herder & Co., 1921.

Wiseman, Donald J. "Additional Neo-Babylonian Gilgamesh Fragments." *GSL*. 123–35.

Wiseman, Donald J. "A Gilgamesh Epic Fragment from Nimrud." *Iraq* 37 (1975): 157–63.

Wiseman, Donald J. "The Laws of Hammurabi Again." *JSS* 7 (1962): 161–72.

Wiseman, P. J. *Ancient Records and the Structure of Genesis: A Case for Literary Unity.* Nashville: Thomas Nelson, 1985.

Wittfogel, Karl A. *Oriental Despotism: A Comparative Study of Total Power.* New Haven: Yale UP, 1957.

Wittgenstein, Ludwig. *Tractatus Logico-Philosophicus.* London: Routledge & K. Paul, 1922.

Wittlin, Josef, and Marek Zulawski. *Gilgamesz: powiesc starobabilonska.* Warsaw: Panstwowy Instytut Wydaniczy, 1986.

Witzel, Maurus P. "Die Diorit-Platte Ur-Ninas (und das Rohrhaus im Gilgameš-Epos)." *AfO* 7 (1931): 33–36.

Witzel, Maurus P. "Gilgamesh erobert Kisch und bereitet dessen Dynastie (unter Agga) ein Ende." *Or.* 5 (1936): 331–46.

Witzel, Maurus P. "Noch einmal die sumerische Himmelstier-Episode." *Keilschriftliche Miscellanea.* Rome: Pontifical Biblical Institute, 1933. 44–88.

Wohlstein, Herman. *The Sky-God An-Anu.* Jericho, NY: Paul A. Stroock, 1976.

Wolf, Margery. "Chinese Women: Old Skills in a New Context." *Woman, Culture, and Society.* Ed. Michelle Z. Rosaldo and Louise Lamphere. Stanford: UP, 1974. 157–72.

Wolf, Tom. *The Right Stuff.* NY: Farrar, Straus and Giroux, 1979.

Wolff, Hans Walter. "The Kerygma of the Yahwist." *The Vitality of the Old Testament Traditions.* Ed. W. Brueggemann and H. W. Wolff. 2nd. Ed. Atlanta: John Knox, 1982. 41–62.

Wolff, Hope Nash. "Gilgamesh, Enkidu, and the Heroic Life." *JAOS* 89 (1969): 392–98.

Wolff, Hope Nash. *A Study in the Narrative Structure of Three Epic Poems: "Gilgamesh," the "Odyssey," "Beowulf."* NY: Garland Pub. Co., 1987.

Woodroffe, Sir John (Arthur Avalon), ed. *Tantric Texts.* Delhi: Motilal Benarsidass, 1913.

Woolley, C. Leonard. "Babylonian Prophylactic Figures." *JRAS* Series 3 (1926): 689–713.

Wordsworth, William. *Poetical Works.* Vol. 3. Oxford: Clarendon Press, 1968.

Wright, David. *The Disposal of Impurity: Elimination Rites in the Bible and in Hittite and Mesopotamian Literature.* Atlanta: Scholars Press, 1987.

Wünsche, August. *Die Sagen von Lebensbaum und Lebenswasser, altorientalischen Mythen.* Leipzig: E. Pfeiffer, 1905.

Yadin, Yigeal. "A Note on the Scenes Depicted on the 'Ain-Samiya Cup." *IEJ* 21 (1971): 82–85.

York, H. "Heiliger Baum." *RLA* 4: 269–82.

Young, Gordon Douglas. "Utu and Justice: A New Sumerian Proverb." *JCS* 24 (1972): 132–34.

Younger, K. Lawson Jr., William W. Hallo, and Bernard F. Batto, eds. *The Biblical Canon in Comparative Perspective.* Lewiston, NY: Edwin Mellen, 1991.

Yusuf, Sherif. "Ishtar, The Mother Goddess of The Sumerians, Babylonians and Assyrians." *Ur* (1982): 68–69.

Zamarovsky, Voojtiech. *Gilgameis.* 2nd. Ed. Prague: Albatros, 1983.

Zeman, Ludmila. *Gilgamesh the King, Retold and Illustrated.* Montreal: Tundra, 1992. [Children's Version]

Zeman, Ludmila. *Gilgamesh le roi.* Montreal: Livres Toundra, 1992.

Zeman, Ludmila. *Girugameshuo monogatari.* Tr. Matsuno Masako. Tokyo: Iwanami Shoten, 1993.

Zeman, Ludmila. *The Revenge of Ishtar.* Montreal: Tundra Books, 1993.

Zeman, Ludmila. *La Revanche d'Ishtar.* Montreal: Livres Toundra, 1993.

Zeman, Ludmila. *Journey to the Underworld.* Montreal: Tundra, 1994.

Zeman, Ludmila. *Voyage au pays souterrain.* Montreal: Livres Toundra, 1994.

Zimmer, Heinrich. *Myths and Symbols in Indian Art and Civilization.* Princeton: UP, 1946.

Zimmern, Heinrich. "Zum babylonischen Neujahrsfest." *Berichte über die Verhandlungen der Sächsischen Gesellschaft der Wissenschaften* (Leipzig) 58 (1906): 126–56; 70 (1918): pt. 3, 52 pp.

Zimmern, Heinrich. *Beiträge zur Kenntnis der babylonischen Religion.* Leipzig: J. C. Hinrichs, 1901.

Zimmern, Heinrich. *Belti.* Baltimore: Johns Hopkins, 1926.

Zimmern, Heinrich. "Besprechung von: P. Jensen, *Das Gilgamesch-Epos in der Weltliteratur.*" *ZDMG* 83 (1929): 171–77; rpt. Oberhuber. *Das Gilgamesch-Epos.* 146–52.

Zimmern, Heinrich. "Darstellung des Gilgamesch-Epos." *Die Keilinschriften und das Alte Testament.* Ed. Eberhard Schrader. 3rd. Ed. Berlin: Reuther & Reichard, 1903. 566–82; rpt. Oberhuber. *Das Gilgamesch-Epos.* 23–43.

Zimmern, Heinrich. "Deluge." *Encyclopedia Biblica* 1 (1899): 1055–66.

Zimmern, Heinrich. "Die sieben Weisen Babyloniens." *ZA* 35 (1923): 151–54.

Zimmern, Heinrich. *Zum Streit um die "Christusmythe." Das*

babylonsiche Material in seinen Hauptpunkten dargestellt. Berlin: Reuther & Richard, 1910.

Zimmern, Heinrich. *Sumerische Kultlieder aus altbabylonischer Zeit.* Leipzig: Hinrichs, 1913.

Zimmern, Heinrich. "Zur Totenklage des Gilgameš um Enkidu." *ZA* 35 (1924): 154–56.

Zimmern, Heinrich. "Ein Zyklus altsumerischer Lieder auf die Haupttempel Babyloniens." *ZA* 39 (1930): 245–76.

Zug, Charles G., III. "From Sumer to Babylon: The Evolution of the Gilgamesh Epic." *Genre* 5 (1972): 217–34.

Zwettler, Michael J. *The Oral Tradition of Classical Arabic poetry. Its Character and Implications.* Columbus, OH: Ohio State UP, 1978.

* * *

The Epic of
Gilgamesh

The second edition features

- Expanded Introduction by Robert D. Biggs
- Essay: "*Gilgamesh:* An Appreciation" by James G. Keenan
- Revised Verse Rendition and Prefatory Remarks by Danny P. Jackson

and includes, from the first edition

- 15 Original Woodcut Illustrations by Thom Kapheim
- 18 Photographs of Ancient Artifacts

Second Student Edition, 1997 (paper, black and white illustrations)
ISBN 0-86516-352-9

Also still available:
First Library Edition (cloth, 4-color illustrations)
ISBN 0-86516-251-4
First Deluxe Edition (paper, 4-color illustrations)
ISBN 0-86516-252-2

Bolchazy-Carducci Publishers
www.bolchazy.com